WEB PROGRAMMING AND INTERNET TECHNOLOGIES

An E-Commerce Approach

SECOND EDITION

Porter Scobey, PhD

Saint Mary's University

Pawan Lingras, PhD

Saint Mary's University

JONES & BARTLETT
LEARNING

World Headquarters
Jones & Bartlett Learning
5 Wall Street
Burlington, MA 01803
978-443-5000
info@jblearning.com
www.jblearning.com

Jones & Bartlett Learning books and products are available through most bookstores and online booksellers. To contact Jones & Bartlett Learning directly, call 800-832-0034, fax 978-443-8000, or visit our website, www.jblearning.com.

Substantial discounts on bulk quantities of Jones & Bartlett Learning publications are available to corporations, professional associations, and other qualified organizations. For details and specific discount information, contact the special sales department at Jones & Bartlett Learning via the above contact information or send an email to specialsales@jblearning.com.

07885-5

Production Credits

VP, Executive Publisher: David D. Cella
Acquisitions Editor: Laura Pagluica
Editorial Assistant: Taylor Ferracane
Director of Vendor Management: Amy Rose
Director of Marketing: Andrea DeFronzo
Marketing Manager: Amy Langlais
VP, Manufacturing and Inventory Control: Therese Connell

Composition and Project Management: S4Carlisle Publishing Services
Cover Design: Kristin E. Parker
Rights & Media Specialist: Merideth Tumasz
Media Development Editor: Shannon Sheehan
Cover Image: © Godruma/Shutterstock
Printing and Binding: RR Donnelley
Cover Printing: RR Donnelley

Library of Congress Cataloging-in-Publication Data
Names: Scobey, Porter, author. | Lingras, Pawan, author.
Title: Web programming and Internet technologies : an E-commerce approach /
    Porter Scobey, PhD, Pawan Lingras, PhD, both of Saint Mary's University.
Description: Second edition. | Burlington, Massachusetts : Jones & Bartlett
    Learning, [2017] | Includes bibliographical references and index.
Identifiers: LCCN 2016028087 | ISBN 9781284070682
Subjects: LCSH: Web site development. | Business enterprises—Data processing.
Classification: LCC TK5105.888 .S388 2017 | DDC 006.7—dc23 LC record available at https://lccn.loc.gov/2016028087

6048

Printed in the United States of America
20 19 18 17 16   10 9 8 7 6 5 4 3 2 1

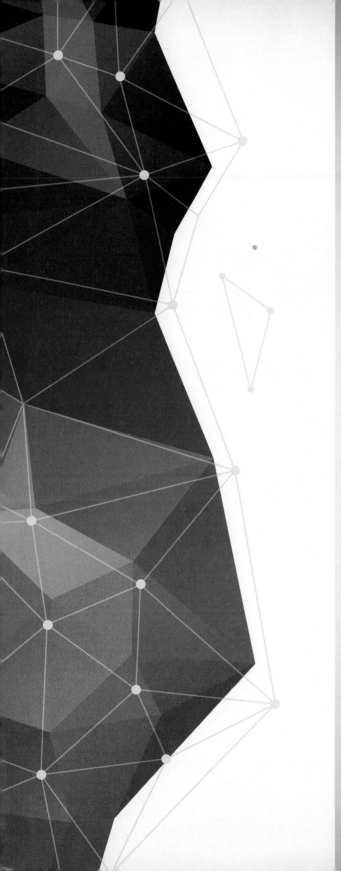

DEDICATION

To the memory of my mother and father, who likely would not have read it, but would have liked a copy for their coffee table; and to Patricia, who might even read it, but would insist that its sojourn on our coffee table be short-lived.
—PORTER SCOBEY

To my family, who may have a similar vague and equally short-lived sense of joy and pride.
—PAWAN LINGRAS

TABLE OF CONTENTS

6   JavaScript for Client-Side Computation and Form Data Validation   193

PREFACE

This second edition of *Web Programming and Internet Technologies: An E-Commerce Approach*, like the first, is designed to be used as a textbook for first- or second-year Computer Science or Information Technology courses. It can also be used for independent study by anyone interested in getting a broad introduction to a useful subset of the many technologies commonly used to develop commercial and recreational websites. The text has undergone a major revision, which is described in detail in **What's New in the Second Edition**.

It is once again the authors' hope (and belief) that if a student exercises due diligence by working through all of the questions, exercises, and other activities that the book provides, he or she will be well on the way to becoming a competent web developer. Because such a diverse set of technologies is required to create anything beyond a trivial website, it is not possible for any book to provide in-depth discussion of every topic without overwhelming the reader with the sheer volume of information. Therefore, this cannot be a full text on any of the technologies described. However, each chapter has a section at the end entitled **What Else You Might Want or Need to Know**. This section contains material that, if pursued, can take the reader well beyond the text material. There is also a **References** section, which contains annotated links pointing the way to further professional development. A developer must always try to be aware of alternative technologies, but our main focus here is to develop a single cohesive example that illustrates a particular collection of open source and widely used technologies. However, our focus in this text is still on the basics, and our goal is to supply key knowledge that will continue to be useful for web development long after whatever currently fashionable libraries or frameworks have disappeared or been replaced.

Chapter-by-Chapter Overview

Chapter 1, **Setting the Scene**, is the first of two foundational chapters. It provides an introduction to the Internet and the World Wide Web and the relationship they share. A discussion of web servers and browsers helps readers understand the nature of communication on the World Wide Web. The chapter also discusses some essential Internet concepts, including the *Internet Protocol (IP)*, *IP addresses*, *domains*, and *domain name servers*. Knowledge of these basic Internet terms and concepts will help readers understand how to establish a presence on the web. At the end of this chapter readers get a feel for where we are going by looking at a real-world commercial website and identifying the features that we will explore at some length in subsequent chapters.

Chapter 2, **Establishing a Web Presence**, provides readers with the first of many "hands-on" experiences to come. We begin with a discussion of *Internet Service Providers* and some of the tools readers can use to begin web page development. Then we discuss the creation of a very simple web page and how to "put it up on the web", using the occasion to introduce the notion of a *MIME type*. Our goal in this chapter is to get a first web page "up and running" in the simplest possible way, while introducing a selection of the minimal tools needed to do so. We also discuss file permissions as a first step toward making a website secure.

Chapter 3, HTML for Content Structure, begins the development of an e-commerce website that will expand in functionality with each succeeding chapter of the text. This is a unique feature of our approach: a strict policy of applying each new topic discussed to a single, extended example. This example will show the development of a website for a real commercial enterprise, and will run throughout the text. The initial version seen in this chapter is a very simple website that uses only some very basic features of the *HyperText Markup Language* (*HTML*). A very important point that we emphasize here is that HTML is concerned *only* with the *structure* of the content, or information, contained in our web pages, and *not* with the presentation or behavior of the content on those pages. In addition to many of the "legacy" HTML elements, such as headings, paragraphs, lists, tables, links, images and entities, we introduce several of the new HTML5 *semantic elements*. HTML tags attributes are introduced as necessary for the HTML elements we discuss. The chapter also introduces *Server-Side Includes* (*SSI*) as one mechanism for including common markup in many different web pages.

Chapter 4, CSS for Content Presentation, immediately addresses one of the problems we ignored in the previous chapter, that of the *presentation* of our web page content. We continue to emphasize how important it is to keep structure and presentation separate as we think about and build our web pages. This will be particularly important as our site becomes more complicated and populated with a larger number of pages. We want our users to experience the same "look and feel" as they "surf" from one of our pages to the next, and we need a mechanism to provide this consistency. The use of *Cascading Style Sheets* (*CSS*) allows us to define a presentation style that can be applied consistently to all the web pages on our site and also permits us to easily change any aspect of the presentation that we wish to modify. We discuss selectors and a number of property/value pairs for color, fonts, and other presentation aspects of web pages, as well as the use of a *CSS reset* and an overview of the CSS *cascade* and *inheritance*. We also discuss the very important CSS *box model*, and show how CSS combined with some of the new HTML5 semantic elements can give much more "meaning" to the various parts of your web pages. We introduce some new CSS3 features and give a simple example of *responsive web design*. The final version of our **Nature's Source** website in this chapter also introduces the new HTML5 video element to replace the static home page image in earlier versions.

Chapter 5, HTML Forms for Data Collection, extends the HTML of Chapter 3 to provide the forms and associated "widgets" (form controls) that allow users to enter data on a web page. Generally that data is then submitted across the web by the browser to a server, where it may be stored in a database or processed in some other way. The submission process and server-side processing will be discussed in more detail in later chapters. Here we are focused on just the forms themselves. We present the `form` element itself, as well as form controls for single and multiple lines of text input, radio buttons and checkboxes, dropdown list boxes, and the buttons for the (eventual) submission of form data, and for resetting the form during submission if necessary. We also discuss form organization with fieldsets and legends, and enhanced accessibility via the `label` element. At the end of this chapter we begin our discussion of how some of the new HTML5 form controls will allow us to perform data validation that used to require JavaScript, which provides a convenient segue into the next chapter.

Chapter 6, JavaScript for Client-Side Computation and Form Data Validation, introduces the JavaScript programming language, which we use here to perform some simple arithmetic calculations and to check the data entered by our users into our forms for validity. The language is relatively easy to learn and use, even for nonprogrammers, and we discuss data types, variables, expressions, functions (built-in and programmer-defined), and simple decision making. We also learn about the *Document Object Model* (*DOM*), an *Application Programming Interface* (*API*) that provides a programmer with access, via JavaScript in our case, to various parts of a web page for examination and manipulation. Validation of form data can be performed using JavaScript and regular expressions, and we illustrate both this approach to validation, as well as the more recent approach in which HTML5 form controls can perform their own validation, without any assistance from JavaScript. Because this kind of HTML5 support is not universally supported by browsers, we also introduce the **Modernizr** tool, which permits a web developer to check for the availability of a particular form control in a particular browser. These features are part of what we need to know if our business is to carry on a successful and secure two-way communication with our users.

Chapter 7, JavaScript for Client-Side Content Behavior, discusses additional capabilities of JavaScript and the DOM. There are many ways in which JavaScript can be used to add some "dynamic" activity to our web pages, which have been quite "static" up to now. In particular, readers learn how to place a rotating sequence of business-related images on the home page, and how to implement a simple dropdown menu. Implementing these features permits us to introduce more JavaScript language features (loops and decision making with switch), as well as JavaScript events, HTML event attributes, and the idea of using a JavaScript global function for controlling image rotation.

Chapter 8, PHP for Server-Side Preprocessing, introduces another programming language, PHP. Unlike JavaScript, which works on the client side, PHP is a server-side technology. Our web pages up to this point have essentially been served from the server to the user's browser in the form they were created. This chapter changes all that. PHP is a programming language in which programs[1] can be used to create or modify web pages "on the fly". This means that the user receives an HTML document that has been created using instructions from the PHP program, possibly based on input that has previously been received from the user on the client side. A single PHP program can potentially be used to create an arbitrary number of different HTML pages. We begin the chapter by demonstrating how an existing web page can easily be enhanced with the addition of a simple PHP script (embedded within the HTML) that displays a Welcome message including the date and time. This gives us an excellent opportunity to introduce AJAX and show how we can combine JavaScript and PHP to update the Welcome message periodically to keep the date and time current. Next we discuss the GET and POST methods, and when to use each. Then we move on to perform more sophisticated actions like sending our form data to the server

---

[1]The "programs" written in both PHP and JavaScript are also frequently called scripts.

for processing and providing email feedback to users after they have submitted their form data, while simultaneously recording the form data on the server for later analysis by our "business", if desired. Throughout the chapter we discuss the necessary features of PHP as a programming language, highlighting as we go the similarities and differences when comparing it with JavaScript.

Chapter 9, **MySQL for Server-Side Data Storage**, introduces MySQL,[2] one of the most widely used (and open source) database systems on the web. Any business will sooner or later need to make use of a database of some sort to keep track of inventory and customer contact information, as well as customer preferences and similar kinds of information. Furthermore, the information stored may be represented in various formats. Users browsing the website of a business will often need access to this database in order to see information on a product or service, to provide personal information to the business, and to conduct transactions such as placing online orders and paying for them. This chapter discusses some of the most fundamental database concepts in the context of the **MySQL** database management system. Database design goals and what makes a "good" database are the first order of business, including a brief introduction to database normalization. We discuss the design of our **Nature's Source** database and how to work with it (or any MySQL database) using both **phpMyAdmin** (as a "front end" to MySQL) and the command-line interface.

Chapter 10, **PHP and MySQL for Client-Server Database Interaction**, once again proves the old maxim that sometimes the whole is greater than the sum of its parts. The real power of PHP programs to generate dynamically an unlimited number of pages that change over time without the web developer changing the program can be exploited with the help of web databases. These databases can be continuously updated through automatic or human-assisted data collection programs. For example, the website **amazon.com** makes suggestions such as, "Those who purchased this item also purchased the following items." Such purchase-inducing suggestions can be generated using information retrieved from a database consisting of all purchase records. Or, we can have a store manager enter new products and information about them, such as their descriptions, prices, and pictures of the items. A PHP program can then read the information from a database and dynamically create an online catalog, prepare an invoice for a user's purchase order, accept payment from the user and provide the user with a comforting confirmation of payment, and then (finally) send the order information to the warehouse for processing. An introduction to the interaction of PHP and a MySQL database is covered in this chapter by showing how various PHP `mysqli_xx()` functions can be used to communicate with a MySQL database. The features discussed and implemented include registration of new users in the database of a business, logging in and logging out with a typical username/password combination, displaying to the user product information from the database, and simulated online purchasing of products, with corresponding database inventory updates.

---

[2]Sun Microsystems acquired MySQL in 2008, after which Sun itself was acquired by Oracle, in 2010. Given that Oracle is the vendor of one of the world's most successful enterprise database systems, some concerns have been raised about the long-term viability of MySQL, which began life as an upstart, open source alternative to Oracle's product. In the way these things happen on the Internet and the World Wide Web, MySQL is likely to survive in some form, with a dedicated group of support volunteers, even if an attempt is made to kill it off.

Chapter 11, **XML (eXtensible Markup Language) for Data Description**, introduces XML, the high-level, data-driven markup language that, for many different applications, is a kind of "lingua franca" for the World Wide Web. One of the difficulties in web communication is the wide variety of formats that have been (and still are) used to represent the many kinds of data that appear all over the Internet. XML represents the best attempt yet to provide all web users with a standardized way of representing most, if not all, forms of data. For example, HTML was "rewritten" as an XML "application" and became XHTML. This illustrates how XML may be regarded as a *metalanguage* for describing a wide variety of other languages. Business applications can use those languages to communicate and exchange data on the Web. We could also use it in a similar way to describe the kind of data we deal with in our online business. In this chapter readers will again study just some of the basics of this powerful technology and we will suggest how you may wish to employ it to describe your own business data. We discuss the (relatively few) rules of XML, draw the distinction between *well-formed* XML documents and *valid* XML documents, with reference to both the *Document Type Definition* (*DTD*) and the *XML schema*. We also show how to use CSS to style an XML document when it is displayed in a browser.

Chapter 12, **Collecting, Analyzing, and Using Visitor Data**, discusses some techniques, such as the collection of web logs for collecting information about the browsing and buying habits of your customers. That information can be put to use in various ways, from enhancing the experience of users when they visit your website, to encouraging your customers to explore other parts of your website and perhaps make additional purchases.

The text is designed to be most useful for students who enjoy a hands-on learning experience, with a need-to-know approach to the introduction of new topics. This is consistent with our view that the bulk of what we discuss should be directly applicable to the development of the website for our simple sample business that proceeds throughout the text.

How to Use This Text

With the book organized into 12 chapters, a very intense 3-month course could cover the entire text at the rate of approximately one chapter per week. The first couple of chapters could easily be covered more quickly, depending on the background and maturity of the audience, and individual instructors may want (or need) to spend more than a week on one or more of the later chapters.

In any case, a course delivered at this pace would necessarily need to omit much of the material in the **What Else You May Want or Need to Know** sections. However, if most or all of this material is used to supplement the core material, and a more leisurely pace is followed, there is enough material in the text for two courses that would span two semesters, with the split occurring at the end of either Chapter 6 or Chapter 7. If an instructor desires to cover fewer topics in greater detail in a single course, Chapters 11 and 12 could be omitted, and this is an option that has worked well for one of the authors during class testing of the text material. In fact, in a 12-week course that includes some of Chapter 11 on XML, it has been difficult to complete all parts of Chapter 10.

Information technology courses could use the same sequences, but focus on the e-commerce design and perhaps leave some of the programming-based activities to their more technically oriented compatriots.

What's New in the Second Edition

First, users of the first edition should be aware that what hasn't changed is our overall goal and approach, which is to use the continual development of a single online health-products business example to introduce and make use of the fundamental techniques of website development. This is a text about the basics, about producing a reasonably full-featured website "from scratch", and not about any of the many (and rapidly changing) libraries and frameworks that are available. We start from scratch and take the student or reader through one path to the end product of an online store with simulated purchases via web browser communication with a database of products and customers. Along the way, the student learns enough HTML5, CSS3, JavaScript, PHP, and MySQL to construct his or her own online business website that "parallels" the one we develop in the text. The first 10 chapters of the text cover this development. The last two chapters are not essential to this unified flow, but give brief introductions to XML for data description and some techniques for analyzing website visitor data.

Updates to the second edition include:

▶ The first 10 chapters have been completely revised to bring them up to date with HTML5 and CSS3. All files have been revised accordingly and will validate according to the W3C HTML5 and CSS3 standards (using the W3C validation sites). The new HTML5 markup from Chapter 4 onward incorporates many of the new HTML5 "semantic" tags for better page structure and some new CSS3 features for improved styling. All the figures in the text for these chapters have also been updated to reflect these changes.

▶ Our discussion of CSS now includes an introduction to the idea of "responsive" design, in which we make use of a "media query" to invoke a different CSS layout for our website pages when a tablet-size viewport is detected.

▶ Our website structure makes improved use of the HTML base tag and SSI (Server-Side Includes) to include common parts of multiple pages from one location, thereby avoiding the "maintenance nightmare" of having to keep multiple copies of the same information up to date as the website is updated and/or modified. When we get to our discussion of PHP, the SSI facility is replaced by PHP includes.

▶ Although we still use JavaScript for some form data validation tasks, we also show how the new HTML5 form controls can perform validation on their own, without resorting to JavaScript. Because so much on the web is a moving target and because cross-browser implementation of these new form controls is not uniform, we also show how to use the Modernizr tool to determine which new HTML5 and CSS3 features have actually been implemented in your browser.

▶ We introduce AJAX and put it to work in a simple use case on our website: refreshing the date and time in our Welcome message.

▶ All `mysql_xx()` function calls have been upgraded to use the improved `mysqli_xx()` versions. We still feel that the procedural approach in this context is preferable (and easier) for students coming to these ideas for the first time. In other words, if you don't already have an object-oriented mind-set, this may not be the best place to develop one.

▶ We now include more "utility scripts" to illustrate some concepts in a very simple context before incorporating them into our live website (AJAX, GET vs. POST, and sessions, for example).

▶ We also include some utility scripts for command-line monitoring of MySQL database tables when developing and testing the PHP interface between a website and a database.

▶ Each directory of our website corresponding to a text chapter now has one or more "readme" files containing useful information about the files in that directory, such as brief descriptions of file content, the order in which they should be studied, or how a given file relates to others in the same location.

▶ Student exercises on the "parallel project" now contain more detail on how to proceed with emulating the text example. This should be particularly helpful by the time the student gets to Chapter 10, which is a long chapter in which "everything comes together".

▶ In addition to updating our HTML, CSS, and code files, we have also done a lot of "refactoring". That is, we have tried to improve the names of variables, the names of files, and formatting of markup and code, in order to enhance file readability, as well as to clarify file grouping and organization.

▶ We now include some discussion of some very useful tools for helping web developers deal with all the things that can go wrong when developing websites, such as the Web Developer toolbar and Firebug for the Firefox browser, and analogous tools for other browsers.

▶ We have better business-related images for the "rotating image" feature of our home page. They have better resolution and are uniformly sized so that they better fill the allotted space. Also, the product images for our online store are now simply different-colored "placeholder" images, rather than the fuzzy images of products that often did not correspond to the product descriptions (in the first edition of the text).

▶ The index has been expanded and improved, and we hope it will prove more useful.

▶ Users of the text will be able to download and install their own complete copy of the **Nature's Source** website used as the sample website in the text, including the product and customer database necessary for the final e-store version of the site as described in Chapter 10 of the text. For access to the webpages and programs, as well as details on how to install, please visit go.jblearning.com/Scobey2e.

End-of-Chapter Exercises and Resources

Each chapter of the text has five important end-matter sections:

1. **Quick Questions to Test Your Basic Knowledge** is a group of questions that have short answers that can be found in, or deduced from, the current chapter material. Instructors may download the answers to these questions from go.jblearning.com/Scobey2e.

2. **Short Exercises to Improve Your Basic Understanding** are short activities that usually involve some hands-on effort and are based on the material in the current chapter. These are the kinds of exercises that don't necessarily have "answers", because some of them simply direct students to perform certain actions to gain familiarity with a particular topic, or just to see the result.

3. **Exercises on the Parallel Project** are activities involving the project each student will have chosen to run in parallel with the one in the text, and in which he or she

implements, in that chosen project, the same (or similar) features seen in the sample project of the text. These exercises are designed to be open-ended in the sense that they do not have specific answers, nor will each student or team of students (as the case may be) come up with the same "answer". Indeed, these exercises are posed in such a way that different solutions are practically mandated.

4. **What Else You May Want or Need to Know** contains material that should help students consolidate and extend their knowledge and understanding of the current chapter. This material, combined with links from the References, can serve as a springboard for the instructor or student who wishes to go beyond what is presented in the text. An instructor may wish to use something from this section for an additional short class presentation or as the basis for additional assignments or projects for students.

5. **References** will contain, for the most part, links to websites that give further details or explanations of the topics covered in the current chapter.

Instructor and Student Resources

Additional instructor and student resources are available via Jones & Bartlett Learning's catalog page go.jblearning.com/Scobey2e. These include:

▶ Slides in PowerPoint format.
▶ Answers to end-of-chapter Quick Questions.
▶ Test Bank.
▶ Suggestions for how to use the text.
▶ A zip file containing the complete **Nature's Source** website for local installation. All of the web pages and programs available in the zip file have been tested. Some of these require certain facilities on an actual web server, and instructions have been provided in the accompanying document "How to Install Your Own Copy of Our Nature's Source Website".

Constructive criticism of any kind is always welcomed by the authors. In particular, specific suggestions for clarification in the wording, changes in the order of topics, or the inclusion or exclusion of any particular items that would contribute to the overall goals of the text are appreciated. An errata page for the textbook is available at go.jblearning.com/Scobey2e.

Porter Scobey and Pawan Lingras
Department of Mathematics and Computing Science
Saint Mary's University
Halifax, Nova Scotia
Canada B3H 3C3

Porter Scobey   E-mail: porter.scobey@smu.ca
Pawan Lingras   E-mail: pawan.lingras@gmail.com

Acknowledgments

The authors would like to thank the many colleagues, family, and friends who have supported and encouraged them during the writing of this text and the preparation of this second edition. In particular, we thank the students who helped us class test the text and provided helpful feedback. Special thanks are due to Sanjiv Jagota and Nature's Source for the images and data that were helpful in modeling the e-commerce website. Thank you also to the following reviewers who provided valuable feedback on this text: Stephen Brinton, Gordon College; Lixin Tao, Pace University; David Tucker, Edinboro University; Venkat N. Gudivada, Marshall University; Tom Gutnick, Northern Virginia Community College; John M. Hunt, Covenant College; Kevin Brewer, Olivet Nazarene University; Kenneth Kleiner, Fayetteville Technical Community College; Susan L. Miertschin, University of Houston; Roberta A. Jolly, Washburn University; Diane R. Murphy, Marty Suydam, Marymount University; John P. Russo, Wentworth Institute of Technology; Petersen W. Gross, Leeward Community College; Michael Geraci, Pacific University. Thank you to our editorial and production teams including Laura Pagluica, Taylor Ferracane, Amy Rose, and Bharathi Sanjeev. We extend our gratitude for their patient help and understanding during the preparation of the book.

TYPOGRAPHIC AND OTHER CONVENTIONS

This section contains a summary of the typographic styles we use throughout the text to identify various entities, including a list of our file extension conventions.

1. An italic font *like this* is used for technical terms (and possibly variations thereof) that are appearing either for the first time, or later in a different context, or perhaps to call your attention to the term again for some reason, as well as for emphasizing ordinary words like *this*. The reader should have no difficulty in telling from the context which usage is in effect.

2. **A bold font like this is used from time to time for a longer passage that is of particular importance, either in context, or for the longer term.** It may also be used to emphasize the name of a software program, like **HTML-Kit**, or the name of an organization or company, like **W3C** or **Microsoft**, and help it to stand out from the surrounding text in a particular context, if required. This font is also used to refer to other sections of the text, such as **References**.

3. A `typewriter-like monospaced font like this` is used for all code, for showing input to and output from programs, for links, for keystroke shortcuts, and for showing contents of text files.

4. A bold sans-serif font **like this** is used for top-level menu choices and submenu choices.

5. Each figure in the text that shows either the full or partial contents of a file, the display of a file as it would appear in a browser window, or a diagram, is accompanied by two pieces of information:

   ▶ The full pathname of the relevant file (including the files that are display images)
   ▶ A caption detailing the (possibly partial) contents of the file (or what the display image is showing you)

   All of these files are available from the book's website.

6. Table 1 shows the file extension conventions that we will follow in this text to refer to its associated files. Most markup and source code files will have the name of the file in a comment line at or near the beginning of the file. This first file-naming comment line may be accompanied by a second comment on one or more lines, indicating briefly the nature or purpose of the file content. Exceptions to this convention are those very simple files we use to begin the discussion of some topics.

TABLE 1 FILE CONTENT TYPES AND THEIR CORRESPONDING FILE EXTENSIONS.	
File Contents	**File Extension**
Ordinary text	.txt
HTML markup	.html
Cascading Style Sheets	.css
`JavaScript code`	`.js`
PHP code	.php
XML markup	.xml
A textfile containing comma-separated values	.csv
A textfile containing SQL commands	.sql
An image file, usually a screen capture	.jpg
A zip file	.zip

CHAPTER ONE

Setting the Scene

CHAPTER CONTENTS

Overview and Objectives

While the *Internet* has been around for more than four decades, its usage has exploded since the advent of the *World Wide Web* in the early 1990s. From a web developer's point of view, the web technologies of that time were very simple, mostly consisting of *HyperText Markup Language* (*HTML*) in its most basic form. Almost everything that one needed to know could be explained in a book of modest size. The technologies have since proliferated beyond anyone's expectations, and it is now impossible for any individual to be an expert in everything that is used in website development around the world.

In this book we will make an attempt to capture the essential features of several technologies one can use to launch a career as a web developer. The aim is to provide sufficient information about web development without overwhelming the reader. We will use the example of an e-commerce business and demonstrate that the core knowledge contained in this book can indeed be used to develop credible websites.

At the end of this chapter, we list the various technologies that will be covered in this book, and also mention a few alternate competing technologies that we will not discuss, just to give you a sense of what is "out there". There are many libraries, frameworks, and other tools that a web developer can use to help build or enhance a website, but that we will have neither the time nor the space to consider. This is a text about developing a reasonable website "from scratch", and giving you, our reader, the background skills necessary to understand, tweak, and even extend those other more sophisticated tools if and when you decide to use them.

Beginning with this one, each chapter of this text ends with a collection of activities to be performed, and other follow-up material. The first of these sections contains "short-answer questions to test your basic knowledge" (of the material directly covered in the current chapter). Next comes a section of "short exercises to improve your basic understanding" (of the procedures discussed in the current chapter). These exercises will be mostly of the hands-on variety.

Then there is the key section covering "exercises on the parallel project". This will be an ongoing project throughout the text, which will allow you to develop a website whose content will be of your own choosing, but whose functionality will parallel that of the major **Nature's Source** online business example that we introduce in the text and continue to develop and enhance with new capabilities from chapter to chapter.

There is also a section on "what else you may want or need to know". This section provides additional material, however brief, on some topics that were not covered, or perhaps merely mentioned, in the chapter itself, and either directly supplements that material or suggests follow-up action that you might take to extend and consolidate your knowledge. Pursuing these additional resources can help you to achieve a higher level of sophistication in the use of those technologies described in the chapter, or to explore some of the alternate competing technologies. Time constraints may not permit you to complete all of the suggested activities in this "what else" group, but we hope to provide sufficient direction so that the book will not only help you ramp up to the information superhighway, but also give you pointers on going the distance if you wish to do so.

A final section on references will contain annotated links to websites of interest, where you are most likely to find the most up-to-date information on any particular topic. Keep in mind that links may change or disappear completely, but if you enter relevant key words into a search engine like Google, you will likely be able to find where the link went, or discover a suitable alternative site.

Our goals in this chapter are the following:

▶ To distinguish between the Internet and the World Wide Web

▶ To explain client-server architectures, as illustrated by web browsers and web servers

▶ To discuss how web browsers and web servers communicate

▶ To take a brief look at a real-world e-commerce website

▶ To outline the technologies we will discuss in this text, and mention a few of the competing technologies and other tools that we will not discuss

1.1 What Is the Internet?

The *Internet* is a worldwide collection of computers and other devices connected by various means such as copper wire, fiber optics, and wireless communications of various kinds. Businesses, governments, organizations, schools and universities, private homes, and "people on the go" are all "connected to the Internet", or "wired".

The Internet came into existence at the end of the 1960s, driven by a cold war desire of the U.S. military to have a secure means of communication in the event of nuclear war. Initial development was under the auspices of the Advanced Research Projects Agency (ARPA) in the United States, and what eventually became "The Internet" was at first called ARPANET. The first developments were performed by a small number of research institutions funded by ARPA, but by the late 1970s and early 1980s several other networks had been developed. With the growing interest of businesses and private individuals, over one million computers had been connected by 1992. The Internet has continued to expand at rates that are difficult to measure, but it has clearly become ubiquitous, in much of the "developed" world at least.

1.2 What Is the World Wide Web?

The *World Wide Web* (generally abbreviated as *WWW* or *W3*) is a "software infrastructure" consisting of many different communication standards for gaining access to, and exchanging information over, the Internet. Many different kinds of computer software applications that run on computers connected to the Internet use those communication standards to provide that access and/or make those exchanges. The presence of a *web browser* is the most familiar sign that access to the World Wide Web, or just "the web", is available.

The development of what eventually became the World Wide Web was started in the late 1980s by Tim Berners-Lee and others at CERN (the French acronym for the European Laboratory for Nuclear Research). The idea was to use the notion of *hypertext* so that scientific documents could be made available over the Internet to anyone who had a connected computer. The term *hypertext* refers to the "linking" of documents to one another in such a way that one can easily go from viewing one document to viewing another related document via a "link" to that other document that appears in the first document. *HTML* was developed for the purpose of describing the structure of documents containing such links that would be made available, and "browsers" with simple text-based interfaces (Lynx being one of the better known ones) were used to retrieve and display these documents. It was not until Mosaic, the first widely used browser with a *Graphical User Interface* (*GUI*), was developed that the World Wide Web really took off. The rest, as everyone now knows, is history.

1.3 What Is Meant by a Client-Server Architecture?

The *client-server architecture* is one approach to communication between two software applications that usually (but not always) reside on physically distinct machines. In typical client-server communication a *client machine* first sends a request to a *server machine*. The server then either honors the request by returning to the client whatever was requested, or returns an error that indicates why the request could not be honored. At least this is the ideal response, and when an error is returned it is up to the software (and perhaps a user) on the client side to decide what happens next.

1.4 How Do Web Browsers and Web Servers Fit the Client-Server Model?

In the client-server context of the web, a "web browser" is a "client program" that a user employs to contact, over the Internet, other computers that are running "server software" and are therefore capable of responding to requests sent by a browser for information to be displayed in the browser window. At the time of this writing (2015) Google's Chrome web browser appears to hold the dominant market share, with Firefox a strong second. The number of Microsoft

Internet Explorer users has fallen rapidly in recent years, at least partly because of its failure to implement many web standards properly, but at the moment it is still in third place. Opera is an excellent browser, but still has a relatively small number of users, and Safari is often the browser of choice among Apple aficionados. This browser scene is likely to exhibit even more volatility as time goes on, particularly if Microsoft puts a significant effort into regaining lost user share.

The term *web server* is potentially confusing because sometimes it refers to a software program, and sometimes it refers to the computer on which that program runs. Just knowing this should help you to tell from the context which one is being referenced in any given situation. In either case, the "web server" is the server side of the client-server architecture in the context of the web, and it is the program (or the machine) that responds to requests from browsers. At the time of this writing the most popular web server is the open-source Apache, but Microsoft's IIS (Internet Information Server) is widely used by those in the Microsoft camp.

1.5 How Do Web Browsers and Web Servers Communicate?

In this section, we will look at a number of concepts that are necessary to understand if we are to get a sense of how web browsers and web servers communicate with each other.

1.5.1 Web Protocols and Layered Communication Architectures

Communication protocol

A *communication protocol* is simply an agreement by two or more parties about what rules will be followed when communications between or among the parties take place. Humans use (mostly informal) protocols all the time when communicating. Think, for example, of making a simple telephone call: A caller dials the number, the phone at the other end rings, a person picks up the receiver and says, "Hello", the caller identifies himself or herself and states the purpose of the call, the recipient responds, there are perhaps more exchanges, after which the caller says, "Thank you. Goodbye." Finally, the caller hangs up, and the recipient then hangs up as well. That's a communication protocol in action.

Web protocol

A *web protocol* is, similarly, an agreed-upon set of rules and data formats to be used when two or more computers or other devices, or application programs running on those machines, wish to communicate across the Internet, usually but not always on behalf of human users. In any given communication it is likely that there will be several different protocols involved.

Common web protocols

There are many protocols in use on the web. Here is a very short list of some of the more common ones:

▶   *TCP/IP* (*Transmission Control Protocol/Internet Protocol*), a two-part protocol that underlies pretty much everything that travels over the web. This is the low-level "lingua franca" of the World Wide Web. If TCP/IP went away tomorrow, the web would cease to exist. One of the reasons it is so widely used is that it guarantees delivery of the information that was sent.

▶   *UDP* (*User Datagram Protocol*), another protocol that can also be used as the underlying transport protocol for information, and though it may be faster to use if you are moving large multimedia files (for example), it does not guarantee that all of the information will arrive safely. This may not be an important consideration if you do not care that your final photograph is missing a pixel or two.

▶   *HTTP* (*HyperText Transfer Protocol*), the protocol that browsers use to send requests for information to servers and that a server uses to send the requested information back to a browser.

▶   *FTP* (*File Transfer Protocol*), the protocol used to transfer files from one computer to another across the Internet.

▶   *TELNET* (*TELephone NETwork*) and *SSH* (*Secure SHell*) are both protocols that can provide "terminal emulation" when used to connect, over the Internet, to a remote computer and log in to an account on that computer. TELNET has been around for many years, but its use is discouraged these days because of security concerns, in favor of SSH, which is a more secure protocol for the transfer of information.

Layered communication architectures

One difficulty with trying to understand how things happen on the web is that there are so many of these web protocols, and often it is not clear which ones are in play. A second difficulty arises from the fact that all these protocols are just parts of a much "bigger picture".

In a nutshell, any communication over the Internet between two computers can be viewed in the following way: Data starts in an application on the first computer, "trickling down" to the actual hardware on that machine, passing over the Internet to the hardware of the second computer, then "bubbling up" to the application running on that second machine that is expecting it. If the second application replies, the process is reversed. On each machine, the data passes through several communication "layers".

There are different models of these layers, including the seven-layer *Open Systems Interconnect Model* and the four-layer *Internet Model*. Much more could be said about these models, and the many protocols that are found at the various layers within them, but it would take us too far afield. The average web developer does not need to know any more about them than you now know. (But we do suggest you seek out more information on these concepts in the **What Else** section at the end of this chapter.)

1.5.2 Web Addresses and Address Resolution via DNS

Just as a letter being sent by regular mail needs to have the address of its destination affixed if it is not to go astray, so does a request for information sent from a browser out on the Internet need to supply the "address" of the recipient to which the request is being sent.

IP addresses

Every computer attached to the Internet has a unique *IP address*, which has the form a.b.c.d, where each of the values a, b, c, and d is a positive integer in the range 0..255, and the intervening periods are a required part of the syntax. This allows for just over four billion different 32-bit addresses. So, if we are not to exhaust our available supply of addresses, another scheme must eventually be implemented. This is the IPv6 scheme (our current four-part address scheme is called IPv4), which is currently under development and implementation, and which will provide more Internet addresses than we are ever likely to need. Blocks of IP addresses are issued to organizations, businesses, educational institutions, governments, and even countries, which then redistribute them "internally" to subgroups and individuals.

Fully qualified domain names

So, though a computer will find it very convenient to work with a numerical "address" like 123.234.235.236, humans prefer names to numbers since they are usually easier to remember. Thus a computer with the preceding address may also have a name, or, more accurately and completely, a *Fully Qualified Domain Name (FQDN)*, which could be something of the form

```
myhost.mycompany.myregion.com
```

if it's a commercial website, or

```
someschool.downyonder.edu
```

if it's an educational site.

Host machines and domains

The characters following the last period of an FQDN indicate the largest "domain" to which that name belongs, and can be a country code, such as ca for Canada, or one of a small number of specific designations, such as .edu for an educational institution, .com for a commercial enterprise, .gov for a government, or .org for an organization (essentially noncommercial) of some kind. The name at the left of the domain name (i.e., to the left of the first period) is generally the name of the host machine, and as one proceeds from left to right through the domain name, the succeeding names represent larger and larger domains to which that host machine belongs.

The domain name system and domain name servers

Because humans tend to use FQDNs and computers will use the actual numerical IP address when communicating with one another, there has to be a system to convert addresses from one form to the other. This is the *Domain Name System* (*DNS*), and the machines connected to the Internet that perform the service of "resolving" any FQDN to its corresponding IP address are called *Domain Name Servers* (for which the acronym is also *DNS*), or simply "name servers". Although it is possible to use IP addresses directly when "surfing the Web", few humans would do so, so this process of "address resolution" is a very important part of what goes on as part of the traffic over the web.

1.5.3 URLs, URNs, and URIs

The most frequently encountered of these three acronyms is (probably) URL, then URI, and finally (and much less frequently, if at all) URN, though this may be changing.

Uniform Resource Locator (URL)

A URL is, as its name suggests, a *uniform* (or "standard") way of referring to the *location* of a web document (or, more generally, to the location of a web *resource* of whatever kind, not necessarily what we would normally think of as a "document"). Naturally, therefore, the fully qualified domain name of the host machine on which the resource is located forms an integral part of the URL for that resource. However, it is not enough to know *where* the resource is located. One must also know, and be able to specify, *how* the resource will be accessed (i.e., the method, or *protocol*, that will be used to access the resource). After all, not every web "resource" is just a page to be displayed. So, a URL quite often has the form

```
scheme:address_of_resource
```

in which `scheme` is, more often than not, the familiar `http` (though it could very well be something else, such as `ftp`), and `address_of_resource` itself has the following form:

```
//FQDN/path_from_document_root/name_of_resource
```

Thus if you enter something very typical, like

```
http://cs.smu.ca/jobs/2015/current.html
```

into your browser's "address window" and click on Go or press Enter, you are saying you want to retrieve the document current.html using the http protocol scheme, from the server whose fully qualified domain name is cs.smu.ca. The forward slash (/) immediately following cs.smu.ca refers to the directory on that host, which is the host's *document root* (the main directory where the web server stores files that it can serve to requesting browsers). This directory may, of course, also have lots of subdirectories that also contain "servable" files, and which help to keep the website organized. The rest of the path (starting from the document root, wherever it might be located, which is something we cannot determine from the URL) is jobs/2015/, and the final item is the name of the actual desired resource, current.html. Sometimes you will see a URL that looks like

```
http://cs.smu.ca/~porter/courses/index.html
```

in which the *tilde* symbol (~) indicates that the name porter is the name of a user on the host system and that cs.smu.ca/~porter/ is the home directory (or personal document root) for this particular user on this server.

Uniform Resource Name (URN)

A URN is a name that has the same form as a URL, but may not identify an actual location on the Internet. So, a URN can be used to talk about something without implying its existence or indicating how to retrieve a particular resource referenced by the name.

Uniform Resource Identifier (URI)

A URI is a more general concept than either a URL or a URN. According to Wikipedia,[1] the "contemporary" viewpoint is that URLs and URNs are both "context-dependent aspects of a URI and rarely need to be distinguished". In fact, it is suggested in the same Wikipedia article that the term URL may be falling into disuse, since it is "rarely necessary to distinguish between URIs and URLs", and the more "user-friendly" term *web address* is now more frequent in any case.

1.6 A Real-World E-Commerce Website

The bold prediction from the 1990s that "If your business is not on the World Wide Web, you will soon not be in business" still contains a certain ring of truth today. It is true that the lack of a web presence may not drive a small business with a loyal clientele and ongoing word-of-mouth advertising out of business. However, many such businesses have established, and continue to establish, a web presence to communicate information to their existing clients and attract new customers. This book will discuss technologies that can be used to add increasing levels of sophistication to the web presence of a business.

Let us look at the well-developed e-commerce website of Jones & Bartlett Learning, the publisher of this book, to understand some typical aspects of an e-commerce website.

FIGURE 1.1 shows a partial view of the home page of Jones & Bartlett Learning. The top-left corner has the logo of the company and at the top-right is a "search window" that allows the user to search for items of interest on the website.

---

[1] See http://en.wikipedia.org/wiki/Uniform_Resource_Identifier.

FIGURE 1.1 `graphics/ch01/jbHome.jpg`
The home page of Jones & Bartlett Learning (publisher of this text) at `http://www.jblearning.com/`.

A menu of various options appears on the toolbar below the logo, and an additional menu of subject areas appears down the left side. These types of menu options are typical of most commercial websites, though they may appear in many different forms. In general they allow you to get more information about a company, contact the company, shop for its products, and obtain help, as they do in this case. Here the rest of the page includes information about the products and links to obtain more information about them.

The structure of such a web page is specified using the HTML, and its layout and styling with Cascading Style Sheets (CSS). We will be studying the essential features of HTML in Chapter 3, and CSS in Chapter 4.

If you choose different menu options, you will notice that the basic layout of the site remains consistent as you move from one part of the website to another. Such a consistent presentation is also best achieved by the use of CSS. If you hover your mouse over any one of the subject-area menu options at the left, you can access a sequence of "popup" submenu items that will permit you to "drill down" deeper into the website to get to more and more specific information. Such

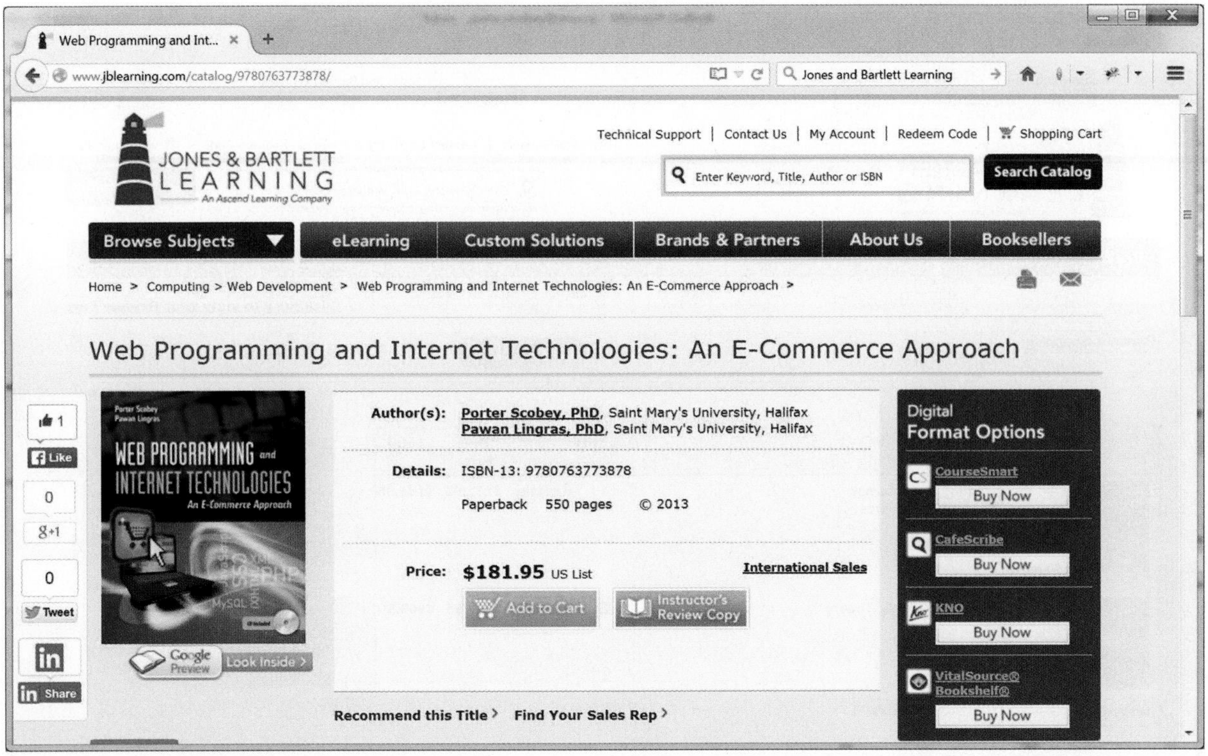

FIGURE 1.2 `graphics/ch01/jbBook.jpg`
A web page display showing one of many book titles from Jones & Bartlett Learning.

dynamic behavior is often achieved with JavaScript, the topic of Chapters 6 and 7. JavaScript will also allow us to provide simple animations rotating business-related images on our home page. This provides an effect that is similar to, though simpler than, that of the alternating display shown on the Jones & Bartlett home page.

If we click on any one of the subject-matter category options and choose a book title, we will be entering the realm of e-commerce, as shown in **FIGURE 1.2**, where we see the first edition of this text as an example. Not only can we get detailed information about the book, we can also add it to our "shopping cart".

If we decided to buy multiple titles, our "order form" would appear similar to that shown in **FIGURE 1.3**, where we have decided to purchase one copy of the first edition of this book and two copies of another book (also coauthored by one of the authors of this text). This web page is essentially an online "order form", which allows us to enter the desired quantity of each book. We introduce HTML forms in Chapter 5 and discuss the validation and processing of form data in Chapters 6, 7, and 10. A "shopping cart" order form like this is dynamically generated using web programming with languages such as Personal Home Page (PHP). Note that the information used to create this dynamic form comes both from the user and from a database that is internal to the

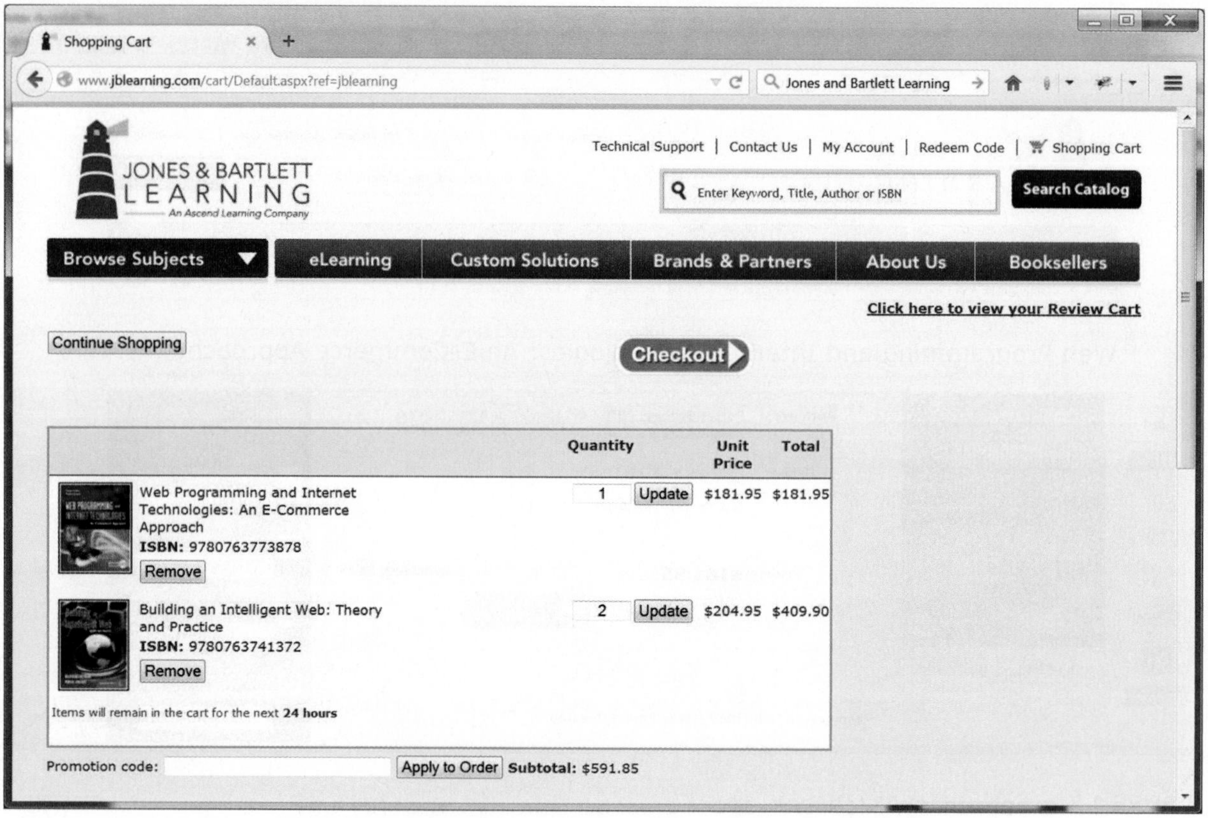

FIGURE 1.3 `graphics/ch01/jbCheckout.jpg`
An order form page from the Jones & Bartlett Learning site showing the purchase of two titles.

Jones & Bartlett Learning website. We will see how PHP and a popular database package called MySQL can be used to handle such shopping cart activity for our fictional business in Chapters 9 and 10.

1.7 The Technologies We Will Discuss

Our goal in this text is to familiarize you with most of the basic principles underlying website development. At the same time, you need to be aware that the implementation of those principles on an actual website can be performed in various ways, and we will have the time and space to introduce only some of the implementation technologies.

Our approach is to take the *open-source* route, which means that we shall have the distinct advantage of being able to use a lot of "production quality" free software applications and utilities. This kind of software should never be regarded as inferior for the simple reason that it is free. In fact, software often tends to be one of the great counterexamples to the old saying, "You get what you pay for." With open-source software, history shows that you often get much more than you pay for. And the hard truth is that you may get bad software no matter how much you pay for it. As always, the safest rule to follow is: Buyer beware! This applies, of course, whether or not you have actually "bought" anything.[2]

After our brief introduction to the World Wide Web in this chapter, and once we have dealt with the nitty-gritty of actually "getting onto the web" in the next chapter, we will start our discussion of the following web technologies, in the order listed:

- ▶ *HTML* will provide us with a way to describe the *structure* of each document we wish to place on our website.
- ▶ *CSS* will allow us to give each of our web documents the layout and presentational style we wish it to have.
- ▶ We will also use CSS to give a brief introduction to *responsive design*, which is the idea that a well-designed website should be able to recognize the kind of device, and the size of the viewport, upon which it is being displayed, and adjust itself accordingly.
- ▶ Web forms give our website visitors a chance to enter data that we can use in conducting business transactions with those visitors.
- ▶ *JavaScript* is a "client-side" programming language for performing computations and input data validation, as well as user interactivity, in the browser context. (See the next two items as well.)
- ▶ *DOM* (*Document Object Model*) provides a tree-like structural model of a web document, and an API (*Application Programming Interface*) that allows languages like JavaScript to access and modify parts of a web page during and after its display, often under user control.
- ▶ *DHTML* (stands for *Dynamic HTML*, which is what the combined usage of HTML, CSS, JavaScript, and the DOM is generally called) is another acronym you will often encounter in the context of producing interactivity for the browser user, but it is not really a separate technology.
- ▶ *PHP* (*PHP: Hypertext Preprocessor*, originally *Personal Home Page*) is a server-side programming language that permits the creation, on the server, by running a PHP program (or *script*), web pages whose content can vary each time that page is created.
- ▶ *AJAX* (*Asynchronous JavaScript And XML*) is not a separate technology, but rather a combination of several preexisting technologies that we can use to refresh only part of a web page, thus avoiding the need to refresh a complete page when only a small part of it needs to change.
- ▶ *MySQL* is the implementation of a relational database system, which can be used to store virtually any kind of business data, and that we can access and use on our websites.
- ▶ Web access to a MySQL database on a server can be performed by a PHP program on that server and controlled from our website.

---

[2] Software that is actually free should not be confused with shareware, which is software that (usually) you may use without restriction for a while, but you are required to pay for it eventually if you continue to use it. This requirement is often based on the honor system, and whether the developer gets paid is thus dependent on the integrity of the user.

▸ *XML (eXtensible Markup Language)* provides a text-based and very flexible way of describing data of any kind and, together with some associated technologies, permits such data to be easily transferred between all manner of applications, on and off the web.

▸ *DTD (Document Type Definition)* is a frequently used method for validation of XML documents.

▸ *XSLT (eXtensible Stylesheet Language Transformations)* is a language for transforming an XML file in various ways, including into HTML for display in a browser.

▸ Collection and analysis of website visitor data on the server via such techniques as web logs and cookies.

All of the technologies we will discuss are freely available, either automatically simply because you have installed a web browser, or by downloading the appropriate software from the Internet. There are many additional options we will not discuss that are also freely available. However, there is an equally large number of proprietary solutions available from companies like **Microsoft** (*Active Server Pages*, or *ASP*) and **Adobe** (*Flash*). Flash was formerly a Macromedia product, but Adobe has acquired Macromedia.

1.8 Some Alternative Technologies and Additional Tools

Some of the technologies mentioned previously that we will cover in later chapters are absolutely essential for any web developer to know. At a bare minimum, these include HTML, CSS, and JavaScript. In fact, on the client side of the browser-server relationship, each of these is basically "the only game in town" for its particular purpose. However, on the sever side, our choice of the combination of PHP and MySQL is only one of many different alternatives among competing technologies. These range from *Perl*, which is a much older, but very powerful and flexible, programming language that uses something called the *Common Gateway Interface* (*CGI*) for performing the same kinds of actions for which we will use PHP, all the way up to *Node.js*, which is a relatively recent server-side technology that has allowed JavaScript to become a powerful tool on the server as well as in the browser.

Keep in mind that this is a text about fundamentals, the nitty-gritty of web design. Learning what we have to show you here will stand you in good stead for years to come. Although there will certainly be changes and extensions to HTML, CSS, and JavaScript, the essentials will remain the same. And even if you choose not to use PHP and/or MySQL, what we cover when we discuss those technologies will still be useful if you choose one of the alternatives.

You will also likely have heard about many fabulous CSS and JavaScript libraries and frameworks, and even complete solutions to the problem of setting up a website and getting it online with almost no effort. In this context the names and acronyms you are likely to encounter include Bootstrap, Foundation, HTML5 Boilerplate, AngularJS, Backbone.js, Ember, Knockout, jQuery, Prototype, script.aculo.us, MooTools, Dojo, the Yahoo! UI Library, WordPress, Django, Joomla! . . . and the list goes on and on.

Each one of these tools, and many more like them that are available now and will appear in the future, may well have a place in the web developer's toolbox. Whether any one of them should become resident in your toolbox is a choice you should wait to make, until you have a reasonable grasp of the fundamentals and can properly evaluate a particular tool for whatever web development activity you plan to undertake. You should definitely be aware that these tools exist, and some of them are very, very useful and widely used. jQuery is a prime example of one in this category, for example. Do not think we are discouraging their use; it's simply that our focus is elsewhere. We have to walk before we can run, let alone soar . . .

Summary

In this chapter, we looked at some of the key concepts of interest to those approaching web development. These included the Internet, the World Wide Web itself, web browsers, and web servers. We also gained some insight into communication on the web and discussed some of the major protocols, such as TCP/IP and HTTP. We also learned about IP addresses, Fully Qualified Domain Names, and how DNS are used to convert one to the other. We also distinguished between URLs, URNs, and URIs. Finally, we got a glimpse of an actual e-commerce website. We closed the chapter by briefly describing the technologies that will be used to develop various features of our own website and that are commonly encountered in many e-commerce websites, including HTML, CSS, JavaScript, AJAX, PHP, and MySQL.

 # Quick Questions to Test Your Basic Knowledge

In this section of each chapter you will find questions that invite short answers, and you should be able to find those answers directly in, or at least be able to infer those answers directly from, the material in the current chapter.

1. What are three different ways computers can be "connected" to one another? The fact that "connected" is enclosed in quotes is a hint to one of the ways.
2. What is the difference between the Internet and the World Wide Web?
3. What does the acronym ARPANET stand for, and what is its relation to the Internet?
4. If each decade is divided into two "periods", an "early half" and a "late half" (early 1990s and late 1990s, for example), in what period was the Internet "invented", and in what period was the World Wide Web "invented"?
5. What would you give as a single sentence to describe the relationship between CERN, HTML, and Tim Berners-Lee?

6. What is the term that refers to the "linking together" of documents so that one can move easily from viewing one document to viewing another document to which it is linked?

7. What was the name of the first widely used text-based browser, and the name of the first widely used GUI-based browser?

8. What is the term used to describe the "architecture" illustrated by the relationship between a web browser and a web server?

9. What are the two (potentially confusing) meanings of the term *web server*?

10. What are the two web browsers that currently have the most users? Note that the answer to this question may well depend on when it is being asked?

11. What is a "communication protocol"?

12. What is the acronym for the underlying web protocol that is used nearly universally these days to move information across the Internet, and what does that acronym stand for?

13. When and why might you find it useful to use the UDP web protocol?

14. If a friend tells you she has just used ftp, what has she probably done?

15. What are the names of two different models that describe the "layered architecture" used when a program on one computer communicates over the Internet with a program on another computer?

16. What form does an IP address have?

17. Can you give an example of a valid IP address and an invalid IP address and state why the first is valid and the second is not?

18. What is IPv6, and what problem will it solve?

19. What is an FQDN, and how does it relate to an IP address?

20. What are the two possible meanings of the acronym DNS?

21. What are the names and brief descriptions of each part of the URL shown below?

```
http://cs.smu.ca/~pawan/opinions/comments.txt
```

22. What is the difference between a URL, a URN, and a URI?

Short Exercises to Improve Your Basic Understanding

In this section of each chapter you will find short, mostly hands-on, exercises that ask you to perform activities based on the material of the current chapter.

1. Find a computer connected to the Internet with at least two web browsers installed on it. Choose several different websites (the home pages of Microsoft, Google, Adobe, and You-Tube, for example). Use each browser to visit each of those pages and note any differences between the appearance of each page from one browser to the next. This is a good way to convince yourself that the "web experience" is not yet as consistent as we might like it

to be. It is also a good way to convince you at the outset that we must always be vigilant in constructing our web pages to be as certain as we can be that we have minimized any differences that will be seen by visitors to our web pages who happen to be using different web browsers.

2. On the basis of the preceding exercise, formulate a *best practice* that you (and *all* web developers) should follow consistently.

3. Locate a real-world e-commerce website (other than the Jones & Bartlett Learning site used in this chapter) that actually sells products online. Browse the site as though you were going to be an actual customer, choosing items and placing them in the site's "shopping cart", perhaps deleting some items along the way, and then proceeding to check out before canceling the transaction. This will give you a sense of where we are heading in our discussions in the rest of this book.

4. In this chapter we made the statement that IPv6 would provide "more Internet addresses than we are ever likely to need". Do a search to find out how many addresses it will actually provide, and decide whether you agree with that statement.

5. The problem of running out of IP addresses is not quite as dire as we might have suggested, because of something called *Network Address Translation* (*NAT*, yet another acronym). This technology permits one unique address on the Internet to "map" into many other addresses that are "hidden" behind that one that appears on the Internet, thus expanding the effective number of available IP addresses. Do a search for more information on NAT if this idea intrigues you. In fact, you may already be using NAT in your home network.

Exercises on the Parallel Project

Since this is the first chapter, and the first group of exercises of this type, we need to say a few words about what we mean by our idea of a "parallel project".

Beginning in Chapter 2 we will be using the example of a business called **Nature's Source** that sells health products online to illustrate all of the topics for web development that we discuss. This example will extend throughout the text, and we want you to develop your own "parallel business" and its corresponding "parallel website" by implementing the same functionality for your business and website that you see in our text example.

Your task for this first parallel project exercise is to produce and submit a single textfile, as described in the specifications given in what follows.

So let's get started. The first thing you need to do is to think about what kind of "business" you would like to run, and for which you would like to develop a website. Our only restrictions[3] are that it cannot be an online store for health products, which is our own main example. It is

---

[3] The institutional environment in which you are working may have other restrictive criteria of which we cannot possibly be aware, but of which you should be aware. Decency, for example, or political correctness.

worth giving some thought to this choice, since you will be committed to it for the rest of your work with this text, unless you want to make major and time-consuming changes midstream. If you know of an actual existing business that does not have a website and would like one, that too is a possibility to consider.

The main thing to keep in mind is that for the time being you are to think mainly about website **content** related to your business, because you will be producing only a single textfile. In other words, there is no place for any styling or other enhancements at the moment. Nevertheless, it will be helpful to begin thinking about the **structure** of your content, because the next step (in the next "parallel project" exercise) will be to describe that structure using HTML element tags (i.e., to create a "real" web page). And that page and subsequent pages will be based on the text **content** you create for this exercise, as well as any content you add later.

This does not mean that you won't be able to make changes later. It's just that it's always a good idea to minimize the need for later revisions as much as possible. So, it will save you time later if you choose carefully now the wording of any paragraphs that you eventually want to go on your "home page", as well as on other "pages" of the website for your business. The advantage of making such decisions now is that you will have to worry about it less in later submissions when you are turning your plain text into HTML elements, and splitting your content into several logical parts to put into several separate files to create several new website pages. And remember . . . even though it's "only" text you are preparing, it should at least be formatted in such a way that the logical grouping of the various parts of the text makes sense to a reader.

Keep in mind as you work that you are in fact preparing web page content for a business, so do not put anything on in that you would not want a visitor to your site to see, or that does not make sense in that context. For example, there should be no indication that this is an assignment in a course! The bottom line here is that you must have the proper "website mind-set" as you prepare your content.

Since your website must be developed in such a way that it "parallels" the sample **Nature's Source** website developed in the text, it will be very helpful to look ahead at the various versions of the text website as they appear in the upcoming chapters. As you do this, note that all but one of the links on our home page are "generic" in the sense that they could apply to any online business. The one exception is the **Your Health** menu option, which is specific to the kind of business conducted by **Nature's Source**.

Having chosen the type of your business, you now need to "flesh it out" by making some additional choices, and here is a description of the (minimal amount of) content you must have in the textfile for this exercise:

1. Begin with a title that contains the name of your business.
2. Next, include several lines giving location and contact information for your business.
3. Follow this with two or three paragraphs providing some relevant information that serves to introduce your visitors to your business. This is information that will serve as the main

content of your home page as your website develops. It should be whatever you would want your visitors to see and read about your business when they first come to the business's website. Your mind-set must be that you do have a business, and you want to grab the attention of your website's visitors and get them interested in buying your products and/or employing your services.

4. Next comes a list of your products and/or services. These must appear in several categories (at least four) and each category must contain several products or services (at least six). The details will, of course, depend on the nature of your business, but if you cannot come up with at least this many offerings, perhaps you should consider going with another business. This is information that will eventually be moved to other pages on your website and, much later, into a database for your "e-store".

5. Add a paragraph or two giving a brief history of your company and how it developed (make this up if you don't have an actual business). Think of it as something that might eventually go under an **About Us** link.

6. Add a paragraph or two giving a brief "vision and mission statement" summarizing your company's approach to its business (again, make this up if you don't have an actual business). This too could be another sub-item of **About Us**.

7. Now choose an aspect of your business that is special with respect to your business (analogous to the **Your Health** category of **Nature's Source**), and add a couple of paragraphs about that part of your business.

8. Finally, add a copyright notice to establish "ownership" of your website and its content. This would be a good place to put your name and might perhaps be the only place where your name should appear.

Once you have made these choices, enter them into a textfile called my_business.txt. Make sure that the file content is well organized from a conceptual point of view, and pay particular attention to spelling and grammar. You can never assume that your viewers (and potential customers) will not be put off by bad spelling and poor grammar. Also, be prepared to submit this file for approval in some way that will be described by your instructor if you are required to do so.

 # What Else You May Want or Need to Know

This section of each chapter will contain items that may simply extend or enhance material in the chapter in some way, questions for which you may need to search elsewhere for the answers, or further exercises to help you consolidate and extend your knowledge and understanding of the chapter material and possibly how it relates to the material of one or more other chapters. A Google search may often be useful.

1. There are probably more web browsers than you thought there were. Try to name 10 different web browsers and the platform(s) on which they run (since some browsers are available on more than one platform).

2. During the early days of the web, many people used things that had names like Gopher, Veronica, Archie, and Jughead. What were these "technologies" and why are we no longer using them today?

3. What does the acronym W3C stand for?

4. What is the IETF and what does it do?

5. In the context of the Internet, what does the acronym RFC stand for, and what role does an RFC play in the ongoing development of the Internet?

6. The two HTTP *request methods* that are most often used in communication between web browsers and web servers are GET and POST. Describe briefly the main difference between them. We will come back to these much later in the text, but you may wish to explore them now for a sneak preview.

7. What are some of the other, less frequently used, HTTP request methods and for what purpose is each one used?

8. When an HTTP request is made by a browser to a server, a *status code* is returned by the server to the browser. Often the user does not see, and may not even be aware of, these status codes. But . . . what is (probably) the most commonly encountered HTTP status code that an average user will actually see?

9. Name the seven layers of the *Open Systems Interconnect Model*, as well as the four layers of the *Internet Model*, and indicate where the two models "match up".

10. We mentioned that the part of a URL to the right of the rightmost period in the URL is the "largest domain" in that URL and is generally either a two-letter *country code*, like ca for Canada or au for Australia, or a three-or-more-letter designation like gov for a government department, com for a commercial enterprise, or edu for an educational institution. Newer designations in this last category are gradually being accepted, such as mobi for mobile-compatible sites and travel for travel and tourist industry-related sites. Do a search to see if you can find an up-to-date list of Internet top-level domains.

11. The full syntax of a URL is actually somewhat more complicated than we showed in this chapter. In all its glory it can look something like this:

    ```
    scheme://username:password@domain:port/
    path?query_string#anchor
    ```

    Here the username:password will be required if the resource is password protected, though the more usual approach is to have the user fill in a *login form* that requires a username and corresponding password. The :port part of the URL may be required to indicate the *port number* on which the server is "listening" for requests to access a particular resource. By default, web servers generally listen on port number 80, and other standard services have their own assigned port numbers, so whether this part of the URL is required depends on the situation. The query_string that is separated from the path portion of the URL by a question mark (?) represents some information that is being sent to the server from the browser, and will likely be "processed" by the destination resource on the server. This information might be data from a web page form, for example. We will come back to this later in the text as well. And finally, the #anchor represents a special marker on a web page that tells the browser to go to that part of the page and start its display from there rather than from the beginning of the page. If you keep an eye on your browser's address window as you surf the web, you may see some or all of these features in the URLs that you observe.

12.   As you browse the Internet you will of course be using the http protocol scheme (or its secure counterpart, https) as you visit various sites. But sometimes you wish to open, in your browser, a document or some other "resource" that is located on your own computer. In this case, the corresponding file is not being "served" by a web server; instead it is simply being opened in the browser in much the same way it would be opened by any other program running on your computer. However, there is another protocol scheme that the browser uses to deal with files in this situation, the file protocol. For example, if you have the file test.html on your Windows PC in the location

```
C:\MyWork\web\test.html
```

and you open this file in your browser and then check your browser's address window you will likely see this:

```
file:///C:/MyWork/web/test.html
```

Here, file:// corresponds to http:// in the sense that the general syntax of a URI requires that it start with the name of the protocol scheme, followed by a colon (:) and two forward slashes (//). The third forward slash may be interpreted as the "top-level directory" of your computer, and the rest is just the path down to the file. Note that even though Windows uses backslashes (\) to separate portions of a path, these have become forward slashes, which is the Linux/Unix way of doing things, and is also the generic format for paths in this context. You may also type a file URI directly into your browser address window if you know the local path to the file.

 # References

Most of our references are links to Internet sites, including many to Wikipedia. Keep in mind, though, that the web is a very dynamic place, and sites come and go, or change their URLs. Thus some of the links we provide may have changed or even disappeared when you try them. If this turns out to be the case, you can probably find the new location of the site or a different but comparable site by going to Google and providing a few appropriate search terms. Such is the wonderfully convenient nature of today's World Wide Web. As for Wikipedia itself, we have found it to be a reasonably reliable source of useful and up-to-date information. It is, of course, always a good policy, which we try to follow ourselves and which we recommend to you, to verify the accuracy of any information you get from the Internet or any other source, by comparing what several different sources say about it.

1. You can read about the history of the World Wide Web at this location:

    ```
    http://en.wikipedia.org/wiki/History_of_the_World_Wide_Web
    ```

2. "The World Wide Web Consortium (W3C) is an international community that develops standards to ensure the long-term growth of the web." This is a quote from their website, which you can find at:

    ```
    http://www.w3.org/
    ```

    From here you can follow links to read about all the web-related standards the Consortium has approved or has under development.

3. You can find a great deal of information that allows you to compare many different browsers in various ways at the following site:

    ```
    http://en.wikipedia.org/wiki/Comparison_of_web_browsers
    ```

4. The Web Standards Project has prepared some "Acid Tests" browser users can employ if they wish to see how well their browser of choice does in handling web standards. If you're interested, check out this link:

    ```
    http://www.acidtests.org/
    ```

5. The acronym *gTLD* stands for *generic Top Level Domain*. Why is it a small g? Who knows? But you can find a list of country codes for top-level domains that are countries, and a list of the other top-level domains as well, at this location:

    ```
    http://en.wikipedia.org/wiki/
    List_of_Internet_top-level_domains
    ```

    This should remain a relatively dynamic site, as newer top-level domains get added to the growing pool.

6. For further information on the URL/URN/URI question, check out the following site:

    ```
    http://en.wikipedia.org/wiki/Uniform_Resource_Locator
    ```

7. You can probably find more details on URL syntax than you will ever need to know at this site:

   ```
   http://www.w3.org/Addressing/URL/5_BNF.html
   ```

8. For more information on the file scheme for accessing files on your computer with your browser, see:

   ```
   http://en.wikipedia.org/wiki/File_URI_scheme
   ```

9. Here are URLs for some of the useful tools we mentioned, but will not discuss:

   ```
   http://getbootstrap.com/
   ```

   ```
   http://foundation.zurb.com/
   ```

   ```
   https://html5boilerplate.com/
   ```

   ```
   https://angularjs.org/
   ```

   ```
   http://backbonejs.org/
   ```

   ```
   http://emberjs.com/
   ```

   ```
   http://knockoutjs.com/
   ```

   ```
   https://jquery.com/
   ```

   ```
   http://prototypejs.org/
   ```

   ```
   https://script.aculo.us/
   ```

   ```
   http://mootools.net/
   ```

   ```
   https://dojotoolkit.org/
   ```

   ```
   http://yuilibrary.com/
   ```

   ```
   https://wordpress.com/
   ```

   ```
   https://www.djangoproject.com/
   ```

   ```
   http://www.joomla.org/
   ```

CHAPTER **TWO**

Establishing a Web Presence

CHAPTER CONTENTS

Overview and Objectives

In order to create a professional website, you will have to learn some basic facts about many of the technologies listed in the previous chapter, and this will take time. However, most computing types like to get their feet wet by getting a crude product "out there", and then systematically learning how to make it better. That is, in fact, our approach in this text . . . start simple and enhance your site with new features as you learn about them. In this chapter, you will get a quick start by creating a website containing only a simple text document. The focus of the chapter is to learn some of the basic steps involved in getting a website "up and running" for the whole world to see, but in the simplest possible way. The following two chapters will focus on content organization (first, in Chapter 3), and then on presentation details (second, in Chapter 4).

So, in this chapter you will learn the following:

▶ What an Internet Service Provider is, and what services you can normally expect from one

▶ What web development tools you need to get started

▶ How to create a simple, text-only web page

▶ How to display and test a web page before "going live" (putting your web page on the web)

▶ What's involved in putting your web page online

▶ A little bit about *MIME* types and how browsers use them to determine the kind of document they are asked to process

2.1 What Is an Internet Service Provider (ISP)?

An Internet Service Provider (ISP) is a business or an organization that provides Internet connections for its customers or members by enabling data transmission between computers in workplaces or homes and other computers on the Internet. In most populated areas, these data transmissions take place through physical cables or wires. On the other hand, customers who reside or work in remote locations, or who are "on the road" a lot, may be served using wireless data transmission. In fact, as time goes on there is an increasing and accelerating trend toward wireless technologies. Particularly in developing countries, the quickest and easiest way to get more people connected to the rest of the world is to "go wireless".

It can be very confusing to read about the various technologies that may be used just to connect to the Internet. It is a world of mysterious acronyms and other arcane terms. Though we will not discuss any of these technologies in detail, and you do not need to know anything about them to become a web developer, you might find it useful to be able to put at least some of them into context if you encounter the terms. We therefore include a sampling of some of the acronyms you might encounter, with brief descriptions of the technologies for which they stand.

Wired Internet service provided by an ISP may come in a variety of technological forms, including:

▶ Simple dial-up through ordinary phone lines via a modem, which these days is essentially a "legacy" technology, at least in the developed world

▶ Cable modem service, often provided by the same company that supplies your TV signal

▶ *Integrated Services Digital Network* (*ISDN*), a set of communication standards that are used for simultaneous digital transmission of voice, video, data, and other network services over the traditional circuits of the public switched telephone network and which has been around since the late 1980s

▶ *Asymmetric Digital Subscriber Line* (*ADSL*), a data communications technology that utilizes frequencies that are not used by a voice telephone call and which enables data transmission over copper telephone lines faster than a conventional voiceband modem can provide

▶ *Fiber-To-The-Premises* (*FTTP*), a generic term that may be used as a generalization of several possible configurations that use optical fiber deployment instead of metal wire for a broadband network architecture to homes or small businesses

Wireless communications for both voice and data are evolving on a continuous basis, and access choices of this form include:

▶ *Wi-Fi*, a wireless technology about which people still argue whether it is an abbreviation, an acronym, or a trademark, but which is generally used by PCs or other appropriately enabled devices to access the Internet in homes and offices, or at "Wi-Fi hotspots" in public places, without the need for a wired connection, provided a wireless network connected to the Internet is within range

▶ *Code Division Multiple Access* (*CDMA*), a technology that allows several users to share bandwidth of different frequencies (a concept called *multiplexing*)

▶ *Global System for Mobile* communications (*GSM*), the most popular standard for mobile telephone systems in the world and, as of 2014, the default global standard for mobile communications

▶ *Worldwide interoperability for Microwave Access* (*WiMAX*), a telecommunications protocol that provides both fixed and fully mobile Internet access

These options vary greatly in terms of *bandwidth* (rate of data transmission), accessibility, and cost.

As well as providing data transmission, most ISPs provide additional services, which may include email, network data storage, and the opportunity to create a website and "put it up on the web" so that people around the world may view it if they wish. This ability to create a website is provided by giving you an exclusive URL and a file repository for your web documents. If you are working in a school, college, or university environment, your system administrator can also provide you with a similar ability to create your own website. You will need to consult your ISP, or system administrator, or instructor, or knowledgeable friends for more information on your particular local situation.

2.2 What Tools Will You Need to Begin Your Web Development?

Beginners may be surprised at how little you need to get started with web development. All you really need is a simple text editor and a web browser. And a computer, of course, but you don't even have to be connected to the Internet to get under way.

Many novices who start to work with simple web pages tend to use *What-You-See-Is-What-You-Get* editors. You may have seen their acronym (*WYSIWYG*) in print, or overheard the term in conversation (pronounced "whizzy-wig"). These editors allow you to use a graphical user interface to type in the content and press buttons to specify the formatting. The formatted document is saved in a form that is called *HyperText Markup Language (HTML)*. HTML was the original specification for creating web pages, and has undergone many changes since its inception. We will discuss some of its history in Chapter 3.

The HTML markup created by WYSIWYG editors can often be very complicated, which makes it difficult to modify and enhance such documents "behind the scenes" at the source level. Therefore, you will be using (and we recommend using) tools that enable you to directly type in both the content and the formatting markup for any given page. One can use any basic text editor, such as **Notepad**, **Notepad++**, or **EditPad Lite** on Windows, and **Vim** or **Emacs**, or even **pico** on Linux or UNIX systems.

However, there are other text editors that cater to the HTML document family, such as **Sublime Text** or **Brackets**, which are cross-platform (which these days means available for UNIX-like systems—including Linux—Windows, and Mac), and **HTML-Kit**,[1] which is only available for Windows. In addition to helping you create your HTML documents, a text editor will also help you write web programs in different programming languages such as JavaScript and PHP, and may provide assistance for doing so as well.

While we will not be explicitly discussing the creation of multimedia documents, we will discuss how to embed them in our website. There are many easy-to-use programs for creating image, animation, audio, and video files, and a lot of them are freely available as well. Since new and better ones are appearing all the time, if you need such a program the best thing to do is search the web using Google or some other search engine to determine what is currently available and recommended.

---

[1] One of the authors has used the justly renowned "Build 292" of this program extensively and found it very useful. In fact, HTML-Kit was used to format most of the HTML files you see in this text. We have chosen how we wish to format our HTML markup, and then had this program do it for us as we compose and test our files. The program is freely available for individual academic use, so students may want to try it.

```
 1                    Welcome to the Website
 2                            of
 3                      Nature's Source
 4
 5      This is our first foray onto the World Wide Web.
 6      We are a small company dedicated to the health
 7      of our customers through natural remedies.
 8
 9      We have a wide range of products that include:
10
11        - books, and multimedia documents that help you get
12          healthy and stay healthy
13        - herbal medicines
14        - equipment for injury free body toning exercises
```

FIGURE 2.1 `ch02/first.txt`
The textfile that will be used as the first web page for **Nature's Source**.

2.3 How Do You Create a Simple, Static Web Page?

Throughout this text we will be using a running example involving a vastly simplified version of an actual business named **Nature's Source**[2] that serves customers who seek a naturally healthy lifestyle. Our goal will be to present just the essential features of the development of such a website, but you may wish to compare our simplified development with "the real thing" as we proceed.

A typical website consists of a number of documents of various kinds. It is very important to make sure that they are properly organized in a logical directory structure. For example, on our sample website, web documents discussed in this chapter will be in a directory[3] called `ch02`.

We start our web development exercise with a document containing simple text only, which we can produce with any text editor. This first document will be called `first.txt` and its contents are shown in **FIGURE 2.1**. The line numbers shown in Figure 2.1 are not part of the actual file. They are provided when a file is displayed in the text to make it easier for us to refer to various parts of that file.

As simple as this file of plain text is, it still conveys the basic information we want our potential customers to see. All we have to do now is "put it up on the web". You will see how to do this shortly. We should point out, however, that this file will not provide very exciting viewing. In fact, it will simply be displayed in the browser window looking just as we typed it into our editor. Also, it will not provide any interaction with the user. For this reason, it is called a *static web page*, as opposed to a *dynamic web page*, which *does* provide interaction with the user, by allowing user

---

[2] See http://www.natures-source.com/.
[3] We will use the words *directory* and *folder* synonymously.

input or by retrieving and displaying data from a database, for example. We will discuss dynamic web pages in later chapters.

So, our next task it to make sure we *can* display this file in a browser, which we do in the following section.

2.4 How Do You Test a Web Page "Offline" before "Going Online"?

It is always a good idea to test a web page "offline" or "locally" on the computer where you created it, before actually putting it on your website, which is often referred to as "going online", or "going live". This can easily be done with most simple documents by viewing them in a browser directly from your hard disk, provided such documents do not require any computation or other input from a web server. If you launch your favorite web browser and click on the `File` menu, you will see an option for opening a file. If you choose that option, a "file open dialog box" will appear. Navigate through your directory structure and choose the file `first.txt` from the `ch02` subdirectory. We are assuming here that you have made a copy of the directory structure and files associated with this text. These are available from the book's website, and we will continue to make references like this throughout the text.

Note that we have explicitly said here that you should open your browser first, then navigate to the file and open it from within the browser. In particular, you should *not* double-click on the file to open it. This will almost certainly cause a program other than your browser to open the file (perhaps even the editor you used to create the file). This is because the file has a `.txt` extension, and most operating systems will try to open such a file with an editor, not a browser, when the file is double-clicked.

File extensions like `.txt` (note that it usually doesn't matter whether or not we think of the period as being part of the file extension) are often used to indicate the *Multipurpose Internet Mail Extensions (MIME) type* of a file. *MIME* is a protocol that was used in the early days of the Internet to help distinguish the various extensions that users wanted to attach to their emails. It has since grown to include designations for all of the many kinds of files that appear on the web and that have to be handled by browsers themselves, or by browser add-ons or extensions, and other web programs. An explicit MIME type is often sent as part of the communication between browsers and servers and is unseen by users, except for the fact that the kind of file involved in a transaction can often be inferred by looking at the extension (`.txt` for a textfile, `.html` for an HTML file, or `.mp3` for an audio file containing a song, for example).

FIGURE 2.2 shows how `first.txt` will look in a web browser. The textfile we have created looks the same as it did in the editor in which it was created, and there is a good reason for this. The file has a `.txt` extension, and the browser knows that a file with this extension should be displayed "as is". That is why we formatted the file reasonably well when creating it in the editor.

But even our best formatting efforts applied to a plain textfile will leave much to be desired on our web page. For example, we might like to have the header appear in a large bold font at the top of the page. Including an image related to our business would be a nice touch, and having

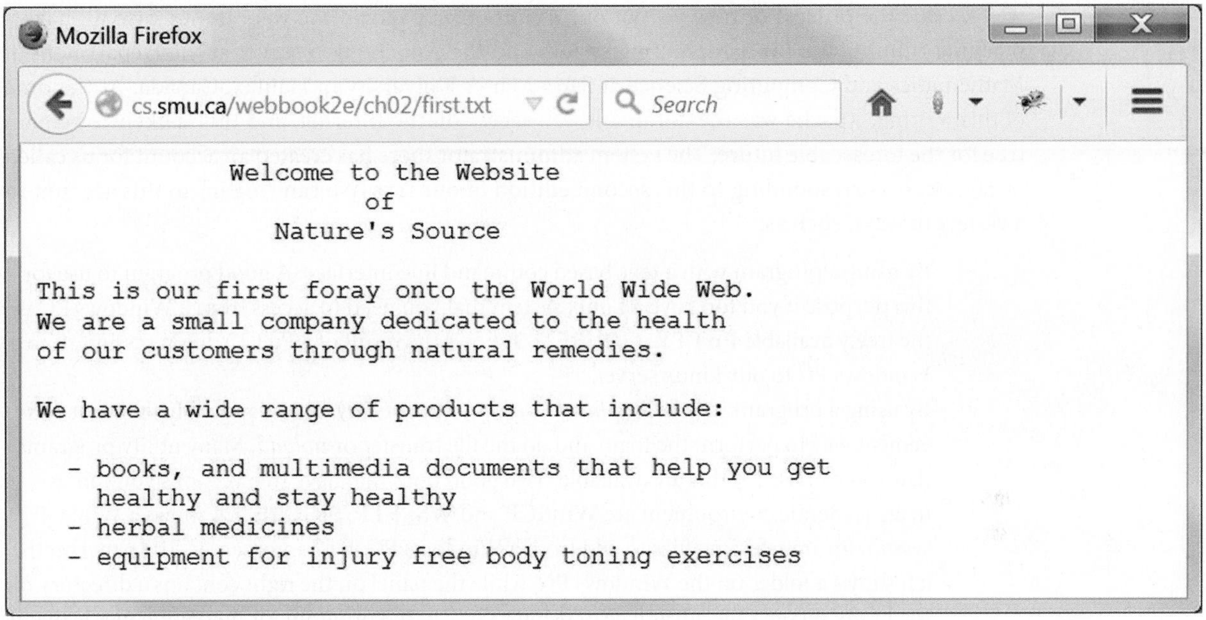

FIGURE 2.2 `graphics/ch02/displayFirstTxt.jpg`
A display of `ch02/first.txt` in the Firefox browser.

hyperlinks to other documents would make it seem more like a "real" web page. None of this is possible with simple text, but we will look at all of these interesting possibilities, and more, in the next two chapters. For now, let us focus on the mechanics of getting our simple textfile to appear as a web page on the World Wide Web.

2.5 How Do You "Go Live" on the Web Once You're Ready?

In order to place our simple textfile on the World Wide Web as a "web page", we will obviously need Internet access. This may be obtained through a private *ISP* or your academic institution. Both the ISP and the institution will have web servers that provide space for users to store their pages and have them "served" to the web and viewed by anyone who browses to the appropriate URL. You should contact your ISP or institutional system administrator to obtain the answers to two key questions:

1. How do I access the web space that is available for me to place my documents and allow me to "go live" on the web?
2. What is the URL for the web space that is available to me?

Because there are so many possible answers to each of these questions, all we can do here is provide an example from our own experience to give you an idea of what is involved. Thus we describe the process of how we put our `first.txt` page on the web. In our case we have a machine running the **Linux** operating system and the **Apache** web server at the Department of Mathematics and Computing Science at Saint Mary's University in Halifax, Canada. At the time of this writing, Apache was the dominant web server on the Internet, and this is likely to remain true for the foreseeable future. The system administrator there has created an account for us called `webbook2e`, corresponding to this second edition of our text. We can "log in" to this account in a variety of ways, such as:

▶ By using a program with a text-based command line interface. A good program to use for this purpose if you too have a Linux system that you need to access from a Windows PC is the freely available **PuTTY**. **FIGURE 2.3** shows the result of a PuTTY login session from a Windows PC to our Linux server.

▶ By using a program with a *Graphical User Interface (GUI)*. This is probably the most convenient way to perform the login and do the file transfer or *upload*. Many utility programs that you can use for this are available. Two good ones that have free versions you can use in an academic environment are **WinSCP** and **WS_FTP**. **FIGURE 2.4** shows a WinSCP session for transferring files to and from a Windows PC to a Linux server. The panel on the left shows a folder on the Windows PC, while the panel on the right contains a directory on the Linux server. One advantage of using a GUI-based program for uploading files is that it will let you "drag and drop" your files from your PC to the server. This, in turn, allows you to ignore most of the potentially confusing and trouble-causing details of the file transfer

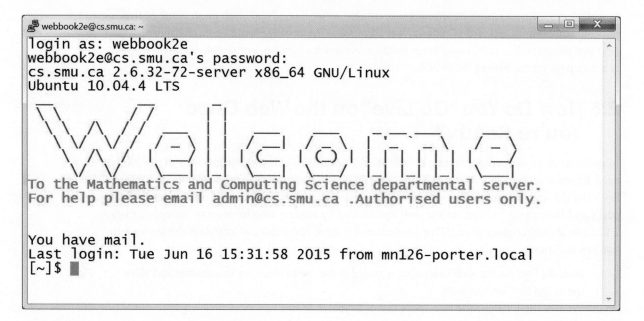

FIGURE 2.3 `graphics/ch02/putty.jpg`
A display of the command-line interface using PuTTY software.

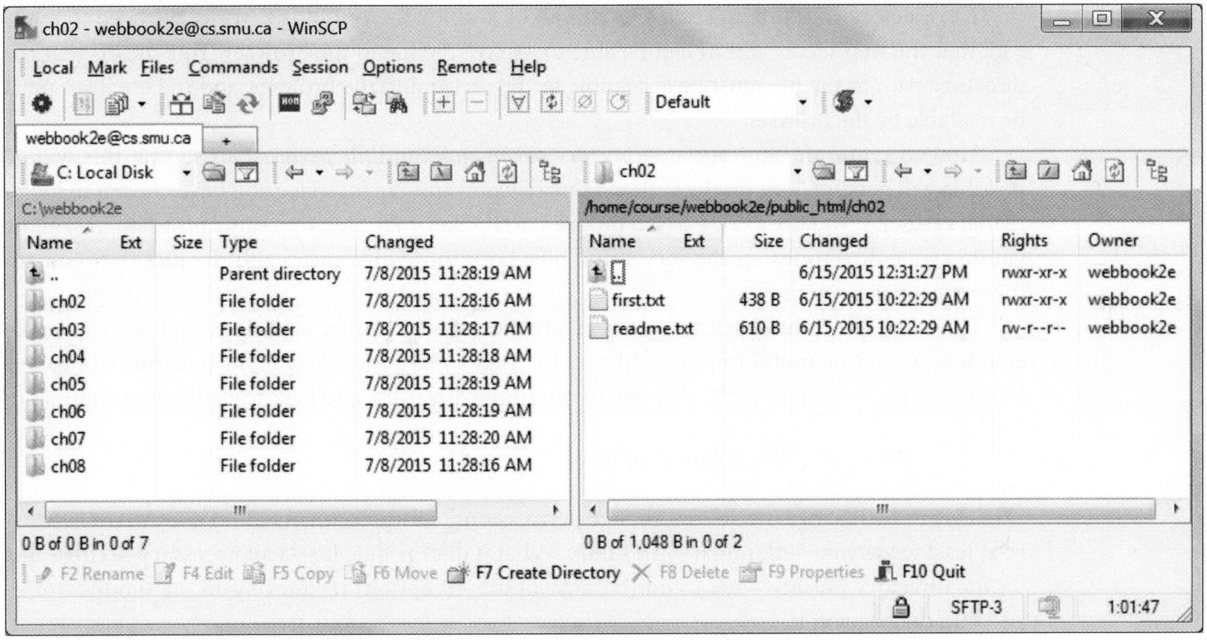

FIGURE 2.4 `graphics/ch02/winscp.jpg`
A display of the graphical user interface using WinSCP software for file transfer.

settings and procedure. In either case, once we have logged in we then use (either explicitly or implicitly) a file transfer protocol or program such as **ftp** or **scp** to do the actual file transfer. We need to log in to the account and gain direct access to it for the purpose of *uploading* files from our PC to the server, and hence to our "website".

Once logged in, we have to find or create the directory that will be searched by the web server for our files. On our Linux system running Apache, the standard location for storing web documents is a directory called `public_html`, which is located in a user's home directory. If such a directory does not exist, we must first create it, and then place a copy of our `first.txt` file in it. A directory like this is called the *document root* of a website, because it is the top-level directory of the directory hierarchy in which all files for the website are stored. The name public_html is very typical for a website document root, but it is not required and other names are both possible and actually used.

Actually, in order to keep our website well organized, we will first create, within `public_html`, a subdirectory called `ch02` (corresponding to Chapter 2), and copy our file `first.txt` into that subdirectory. For simplicity and consistency (two goals we are always striving to achieve), it is a good idea to now begin constructing a directory structure that parallels that of the text. This will allow you to easily keep track of your own versions of the files you are working on that are text-related.

Next, before checking to see if the file can be seen by the rest of the world, we need to make sure that the web server will in fact be able to "serve" the file to the browser. This means that the directory path to the file must be accessible to the server and the browser, and the file itself must be readable by the browser.

How to set up the appropriate *directory permissions* and *file permissions* so that this will be possible will depend both on the system you are using and the interface you have chosen to log in to that system. If you use a GUI-based program to upload your files, that same program may allow you to create directories on the server and give both those directories and the files they contain the correct permissions.

However, let's come back to our own situation. Since similar situations will be reasonably common, it may be useful to point out that we used a text-based command-line interface to our Linux system (PuTTY, in fact), changed to our home directory, and gave the following command:

```
chmod -R 755 public_html
```

This is the "change mode", or "change permissions" Linux command, and a mysterious one it is, at least for anyone unfamiliar with Linux. What it does is this: It sets all necessary permissions for the directory `public_html` and (because of the -R option) recursively all the subdirectories and files underneath it.

The mysterious number 755 in the above command is an *octal number*[4] that specifies the nature of the permissions to be set. The first digit specifies the permissions for the user (owner) of the file or directory, the second digit specifies permissions for the group of users to which the user (owner) belongs, and the last of the three digits specifies permissions for all other users. The value 7 means "anything goes". That is, the user (the owner) has all possible permissions for the given file or directory (read, write, and execute). On the other hand, a 5 means "readable and executable, but not writable/modifiable", which is generally the kind of access a file owner wants the world at large to have for his or her website files. Thus we are allowing general users to read and execute our files, but not to write to (modify) them.[5] There is more to this that we have said here; in particular, a given permission (executable, for example) may mean something different for a directory than it does for a file, but our needs do not require us to go into this kind of detail.

In fact, this is way too much information if this is not your situation, but it gives you some idea of what is involved in making your website and its files accessible to the world at large. Moreover, equivalent permission settings will have to be made, whatever your situation might be.

Once our document is in the right place, and appropriate access permissions are set for the directories and the document, here's the next question: How do we (or how does anyone, for that matter) view the document? As you will recall from the URL discussion in Chapter 1, we need

---

[4] An octal number is a base-8 number that may only contain digits from the range 0..7. By way of comparison, decimal numbers, as you know, are base-10 numbers that use digits from the range 0..9.

[5] This is an oversimplification, of course, but will do for now. We have glossed over some details and subtleties that may puzzle you as well. For example, if a directory on a Unix-like system is "executable" you can read (display a list of) what's in it.

the correct URL for the file, so that we can enter it into the address box of our browser. Here is the correct URL to use for access to this first file on the website for this book:

```
http://cs.smu.ca/webbook2e/ch02/first.txt
```

If you type this URL into your web browser, or a web browser on any computer anywhere on the Internet, you should see a display of the file contents that looks like what you see in Figure 2.2. The file will be sent from the Saint Mary's University web server to your computer via the Internet. However, keep in mind that even a simple document like this one may look different from what you see in Figure 2.2. For one thing, we have reduced the size of the actual display to get a figure that would fit nicely into the text as Figure 2.2, and you may be using a different browser.

Summary

In this chapter we extended the Internet and World Wide Web concepts from the previous chapter by discussing some implementation-level details. The discussion started with ISPs. We then identified a decent editor and a web browser as the two basic tools a web developer needs to get started. We showed an example of the simplest kind of web document—a file of text—and saw how to view it through a web browser.

We introduced the idea of the MIME type of a file, and pointed out that browsers use this information about a file to deduce how they should handle the file. We also showed the relationship between the MIME type and the file extension.

Finally, we showed you various issues involved in actually putting a web document on the web for the entire world to see. Depending on local conditions, the actual steps may vary widely, so we illustrated the procedure in the context of uploading a file from a Windows PC to an account on a Linux machine, from where it will be served by an Apache web server. This is likely to be a fairly common scenario. In this context, a web developer needs to remember that directory and file permissions on a website are extremely important to get right.

Now that these basic "infrastructure" details are out of the way, you are ready to study the HTML markup code that will allow you to provide more exciting web documents that include enhancements such as *hyperlinks* and images.

 ## Quick Questions to Test Your Basic Knowledge

1. What is an ISP, and what are the main services you would expect an ISP to provide?
2. What is the major difference between ISDN and WiMAX, based on the little we have said about these things in this chapter?

3. What is the acronym for the default global standard for mobile communications, and what is the full name of that technology?

4. What is the currently dominant web server on the Internet? Note that this is another of those questions whose answer may depend on when it is asked.

5. What are the two most basic tools you need to start your web development career, and what are specific examples of such tools on your particular *platform*? (This use of the term *platform* simply means some combination of computer, monitor, operating system, and perhaps other features.)

6. What does the acronym WYSIWYG stand for, and why do we recommend that you do *not* use a WYSIWYG tool for creating your web pages?

7. What is the difference between a static web page and a dynamic web page?

8. You should always "test" a web page before "putting it up on the web". What does this mean, and how should you go about testing a web page "offline"?

9. What does the acronym MIME stand for, and where were MIME types originally used?

10. How is a file extension used by a browser?

11. What is meant by *uploading* a file, and, though we have not used the term until now, what do you suppose is meant by *downloading* a file?

12. What is a "document root", and what is a very common name for one?

13. Why is it important to have the correct permissions set on the files and directories of your website?

Short Exercises to Improve Your Basic Understanding

1. Most computing environments, even most home computers, will have a choice of editors. Explore your particular situation and make a list of all the editors you have to choose from. However, be careful not to confuse any word processor you might have with an editor. A word processor will put characters into your file that you cannot see and that will cause you no end of trouble when you are preparing a simple textfile, or a file of HTML markup. You want an editor, not a word processor. On Windows, for example, **Notepad** is an editor, while **WordPad** is a (very simple) word processor. So, you should not use WordPad for writing HTML, and though you could use Notepad, there are much better alternatives.

2. Do a little "research" to determine which of the editors you discovered in the previous exercise might be the best choice for creating web pages. You need to look for editor facilities that deal explicitly with HTML. Make sure that you have full control of the code you enter into a file. It can be very frustrating if the software tries to be too "helpful". If none of your available local choices seem adequate, the Internet is your resource to find something better, and you should find one of the options mentioned earlier to your liking.

3. Now explore your system and make a list of all the programs you might be able to use to upload files or copy files to your website. Once again check out the capabilities of each in your particular context, and try to decide which will be the best choice. And if you come up dry locally, it's back to the Internet.

4. We mentioned that on a Linux server the numerical permission 755 for web pages is fairly common. So is 644. See if you can find out the difference between the two, and then decide which one is actually the more appropriate for the file in this chapter.

Exercises on the Parallel Project

In the Exercises on the Parallel Project section from Chapter 1 you created a simple textfile called `my_business.txt` containing some basic facts about your chosen business. That file should contain the name of your business, some location and contact information, some information about your business to pique customers' interest, a list of your products and services, a brief history, your mission statement, a description of some unique aspect of your business, and copyright information. Now is your chance to revisit this first pass, add or subtract material if required, reformat if necessary, correct any spelling and grammar mistakes, and (finally) "put it up on the web". Here are the steps you need to follow:

1. First, make sure that your ISP is in place, and that you know what the URL of your website will be, as well as the name of the location where you must place your file and how to gain access to that location.

2. Second, make sure you have decided what software you will be using (editor, browser, and a program to upload files to your website), and that you are reasonably comfortable using all of them.

3. Compare the content and formatting of your `my_business.txt` with the content and formatting of our file `first.txt` of Figure 2.1. Your file will contain considerably more information than is in `first.txt`, but you can use `first.txt` and its display in Figure 2.2 to get an idea of the overall impression the first web page for your business should create in the viewer's mind. Revise your `my_business.txt` file accordingly.

4. Upload your `my_business.txt` file to the appropriate location on your server.

5. Browse to your `my_business.txt` file on your website using at least two different browsers, and note any differences in the display from one browser to the next. There should not be any significant differences.

6. Sometimes things "show up" when a web page is viewed in a browser that were not easy to see, or were overlooked when the content was viewed in an editor. If that happens to you with your first web page, it's back to the drawing board. Revise your page as necessary using your editor, upload it again (overwriting the older version), and take another look in your browser(s). Repeat this sequence until you are happy with the result.

What Else You May Want or Need to Know

1. Although any editor will do for creating web pages, before long a typical web developer grows tired of typing in all of those HTML tags over and over again. That's when the desire for something better grows too strong to resist. Every platform will have "something better", something that will let you enter HTML tags with the press of a key or the click of a mouse, for example, so you need to be prepared to check out the current state of affairs when the mood hits you. See the **References** in the next section for links to some choices.

2. Whether you use a simple editor or a high-powered IDE for web development, there is one problem you should be aware of, since it may rear its ugly head at any time. Or, you may never encounter it in a lifetime of web development. Life is like that.

   It's the so-called *end-of-line problem*, and it's caused by the fact that computing platforms do not agree on what character or characters should be used to mark the end of a line in a file of text. For example, Microsoft Windows uses a two-character combination, the carriage return and line feed (CRLF), while Linux and Unix use a single line feed (LF) character, and before its operating system became Unix-based, the Macintosh used a single carriage return (CR).

   The upshot of this disparity is that when textfiles are moved from one platform to a different platform, the transfer may take place in such a way that the end-of-file characters are not handled properly and as a result the file may not display properly on the destination platform.

   The reason that you may never encounter this problem is that nowadays many, if not most, programs are "smart" (at least smarter than they used to be) when it comes to dealing with this problem. A program used to transfer files may be smart enough to convert the end-of-line marker(s) on the source platform to the appropriate, and different, end-of-line marker(s) on the destination platform. A program used to display or edit a file at the destination may be smart enough to display the file properly even if the end-of-line character(s) are not the correct ones for that platform.

   One scenario in which you might see this problem is this: Suppose you have a file containing only text on your website, which is located on a Linux system, and suppose that file has proper line endings (the LF character). Suppose you need to make a change in the file and you download it to your PC with a program that does not convert the line endings. If you then open the file in a simple editor like Notepad on Windows, you will find that all the text in the file shows up as a single long line, because Notepad is not smart enough to handle the file properly.

   So, now you know. Keep this in mind if you should encounter a problem that might be related to what we have discussed here. If you can (i.e., if you have two different platforms available), try your own file-transfer program and editor to see if they behave properly in this regard, or to see if you can produce the problem we have described.

3. Earlier in the chapter we made the (unsupported) statement that, "At the time of this writing, Apache was the dominant web server on the Internet, and this is likely to remain true for the foreseeable future." You should always take such statements with a grain of salt, at least until you have attempted to verify them independently. To confirm statements like this, you can do a web search for relevant information. And although much information on the web is also to be taken with more than a grain of salt, you can get some idea of what the truth may be by looking at the same data or information on various sites. See the following **References** for some relevant links.

4. In this chapter we discussed some of the details that would be involved if you were setting up your website on a Linux server. You can, of course, also set up a web server on your Windows machine, provided you are connected to the Internet. You do not have to be connected to test your web pages, but to "go live" you need to be connected to the Internet via an ISP. As for the web server itself, you can set up **Apache** on your Windows machine, or use Microsoft's **IIS (Internet Information Server)**. The following **References** contain links to further information if you wish to try either of these options.

References

1. Here are Wikipedia links to pages that provide more information on the various wired and wireless technologies used to connect to the Internet that we mentioned in this chapter, as well as a couple of wireless ones—*Long Term Evolution* (*LTE*) and *Wireless Mesh Networking* (*WMN*)—that we did not mention earlier:

```
ISDN: http://en.wikipedia.org/wiki/Integrated_Services_
      Digital _Network

ADSL: http://en.wikipedia.org/wiki/Asymmetric_Digital
      _Subscriber_Line

FTTP: http://en.wikipedia.org/wiki/Fiber_to_the_x

Wi-Fi: http://en.wikipedia.org/wiki/Wi-Fi

CDMA: http://en.wikipedia.org/wiki/
      Code_division_multiple_access

GSM: http://en.wikipedia.org/wiki/GSM
```

```
WiMAX: http://en.wikipedia.org/wiki/WiMAX

LTE: http://en.wikipedia.org/wiki/3GPP_Long_Term_Evolution

WMN: http://en.wikipedia.org/wiki/Wireless_mesh_network
```

2. Here are links to the software tools we mentioned for establishing cross-platform connections and transferring files:

```
PuTTY: http://www.putty.org/

WS_FTP: http://www.ipswitch.com/

WinSCP: http://winscp.net/eng/index.php
```

3. It is always a risk to recommend a particular piece of software, but if you are creating your web pages on Windows and are permitted to install software on your system, you should check out a program like **HTML-Kit** or any similar software you can find that provides an IDE and will therefore allow you to easily create (and modify) HTML markup. Build 292 of HTML-Kit (the free version) is available from the following website:

```
http://htmlkit.com/download/
```

Excellent cross-platform programs, which are more than just editors, but somewhat less than a full-blown IDE, are **Sublime Text** and **Brackets** (but note that at the time of this writing neither of these program allowed you, by default, to print a copy of the file you are editing, a bit of a disadvantage if you like to study hard copy):

```
http://www.sublimetext.com/

http://brackets.io/
```

Two very powerful and flexible IDEs are **Eclipse** and **NetBeans**. Both are also free, but the downside is that each one has a fairly steep learning curve. Here are the relevant links:

```
http://www.eclipse.org/

http://netbeans.org/
```

4. The following are "just" editors, but saying that belies their usefulness, since they all have (or can be given) features that go far beyond those provided by a simple editor like Notepad for Windows. They are all available for the Windows platform, though Vim and Emacs "grew up" in the Unix environment and can be found on virtually any Unix or Linux system in some form. In fact, Unix and Linux users generally split into two

categories—Vim (or vi, the original program) users and Emacs users—and sometimes you have to leave town in a hurry if you choose the wrong place and time to claim that one of these programs is better than the other.

```
Vim: http://www.vim.org/

Emacs: http://www.gnu.org/software/emacs/

EditPad Lite: http://www.editpadpro.com/editpadlite.html

Notepad++: https://notepad-plus-plus.org/
```

5. Here are a couple of sites to check for browser usage statistics:

```
http://www.w3schools.com/browsers/browsers_stats.asp

http://news.netcraft.com/archives/web_server_survey.html
```

6. The site

```
http://www.whatbrowser.org
```

will tell you what browser and what version of that browser you are using. It can also provide a few potentially useful tweaks for your browser of choice, as well as some informational links and some helpful links should you wish to try an alternate browser.

7. If you wish to use Microsoft Windows as your underlying platform, you may want to start here

```
http://www.microsoft.com/web/downloads/platform.aspx
```

for Microsoft's version of what you should have, or if you wish to have a nice Apache setup that includes the MySQL database software and the PHP server-side programming language (both of which you will be studying later), try one of these sites (the first is cross-platform, the second is specifically for Windows, and the third specifically for Mac users):

```
http://www.apachefriends.org/en/xampp-windows.html

http://www.wampserver.com/en/

https://www.mamp.info/en/
```

CHAPTER **THREE**

HTML for Content Structure

CHAPTER CONTENTS

Overview and Objectives

The time has now come to learn the essentials of the latest widely used incarnation of the *HyperText Markup Language, HTML5*. This language will not only help you create the look of most of the web pages you see every day, but it will also provide the foundation for many of the technologies you will be using later on in this book. Our immediate goal will be to extend our simple website by incorporating some commonly used HTML markup, adding more pages, and introducing the notion of web page *validation*. Then we will show how to extract the common parts of our web pages and place them in one location, from there to be included everywhere they are needed, thus allowing us to make changes in one place that will "show up everywhere".

So, in this chapter we will discuss the following topics:

▶ A brief history of HTML

▶ The importance of maintaining both a conceptual and physical separation of the structure and presentation of our web page content

▶ HTML tags and elements

▶ The basic structure of every web page

▶ The DOCTYPE declaration and web page validity

▶ Some basic HTML markup, including the head, title, and body of a page, as well as headings, paragraphs, line breaks, tables, images, comments, tag attributes, and HTML entities

▶ Multipage websites and hyperlinks connecting the various pages

▶ A mechanism for inclusion of common material in several different website documents

▶ The new HTML5 semantic elements and how they got their names

3.1 The Long Road to HTML5, the New Norm

It has been a long and tortuous journey getting to HTML5, the current standard for web page markup, and the journey is not yet over. The first documents on the World Wide Web were created using the original, and very primitive, version of the *HyperText Markup Language (HTML)*. The history of HTML goes back to 1980, when Tim Berners-Lee, a physicist, began to create a system for sharing documents among fellow physicists. The first specification for HTML was eventually published in 1991 by Berners-Lee, and HTML subsequently evolved through several standards, until its development was essentially "frozen" at version 4.01. Then along came XHTML,

TABLE 3.1 Some major milestones in the "tortured" history of HTML.

Date	Version	Notes
1991	original	Tim Berners-Lee first publicly describes HTML.
1995	HTML 2.0	First standard.
1996	—	W3C assumes control of HTML specs.
January 1997	HTML 3.2	First version developed and standardized by W3C.
December 1997	HTML 4.0	
December 1999	HTML 4.01	HTML "frozen" at this version; everyone supposed to start using XHTML.
January 2000	XHTML 1.0	This was HTML rewritten as an XML (more strict) application.
May 2001	XHTML 1.1	Included some relatively minor changes to XHTML 1.0.
January 2008	HTML5	HTML5 published as a "Working Draft" by the W3C.
2009	XHTML 2	Work discontinued on XHTML.
May 2011	HTML5	W3C establishes clear milestones for HTML5.
October 2014	HTML5	W3C declares HTML5 standard complete (which does not mean that every browser, or even any browser, has implemented all features).

which was essentially HTML rewritten to comply with the much stricter standards of XML (see Chapter 11), and for a while this became a commonly accepted standard for use by all web browsers and developers. XHTML is very similar to HTML, and many people regarded it as an improvement over HTML because it required developers to be more careful and consistent when writing markup code. Unfortunately, as time went on the web community decided it wanted less strict standards, rather than more, so further development of the XHTML standard stalled, and work on XHTML 2 was eventually halted altogether, in late 2009. See TABLE 3.1 for a brief summary of HTML and XHTML history.

Although XHTML is no longer the standard that you should follow, it had many "rules" that you can still use as "guidelines" when you write your HTML markup, and doing so will result in much "better" web pages. We will provide more details on this approach later, and we recommend that all new web page markup code (including yours) be written using the guidelines we will present. And if, by chance, you have already written some XHTML markup using its much stricter rules, there is virtually nothing you will have to "unlearn".

3.2 A Very Important Distinction: Structure vs. Presentation

The purpose of HTML is to describe the *structure* of a web page. That is, HTML is used to indicate which parts of the page content should be treated as headers, which should be ordinary paragraphs of text, and what should be placed in the rows and columns of a table, for example. Note that this notion of structure does *not* include any mention of such things as what fonts should be used for the various items of text, nor in what color that text should appear. These are aspects of the *presentation* of the page content, and you will find it convenient to keep these two aspects of each web page separate in your mind, as well as in the actual documents that make up your web pages. For one thing, doing so will make it much easier for you to change the "look and feel" of your page design, should you decide to do so.

Unfortunately, during the early days of web development, browser developers got impatient and "jumped the gun" by inventing HTML tags such as <font> to deal with presentational aspects of their web pages. This was not always done consistently from browser to browser, which was one problem, and it was eventually recognized as a bad idea in any case. The solution was to describe the presentational aspects of a web page using *Cascading Style Sheets* (*CSS*), which we will discuss in the next chapter.

3.3 HTML Tags and Elements

An HTML document, such as the one shown in **FIGURE 3.1**, contains nothing but text. In fact, it will contain "ordinary text" that you want to display on your web page, as well as *markup* (i.e., "formatting commands" or "structure-indicating commands") that describe the *structure* of your document. This markup is specified using *HTML tags*. An HTML tag is a single letter or "keyword" enclosed in angled brackets < >, as in <html> or <p>. This "keyword" may or may not be an actual "word". More often than not it is just some mnemonic sequence of one or more alphanumeric characters. When referring to an HTML tag, we may or may not include the angle brackets, depending on context. For example, we may refer to "the <p> tag", or simply "the p tag".

Usually, but not always, HTML tags come in pairs. Each pair encloses the content to which that pair applies, and the tag pair together with its content is called an *HTML element*. Thus we can also refer to a "p element" and mean some particular <p>...</p> tag pair and its content.

Often it is convenient to think of the opening and closing tags of the element as indicating the beginning and end of a formatting instruction for the enclosed text. Both tags in the pair use the same keyword. However, the tag that indicates the end of the element has a forward slash (/) before its keyword.

```
 1   <html>
 2   <head>
 3   <title>Nature's Source</title>
 4   </head>
 5   <body>
 6   <h1>
 7   Welcome to the Website of Nature's Source
 8   </h1>
 9   <p>
10   This is our first foray onto the World Wide Web.
11   We are a small company dedicated to the health
12   of our customers through natural remedies.
13   We have a wide range of products that include:
14
15     - books, and multimedia documents that help you get
16       healthy and stay healthy
17     - herbal medicines
18     - equipment for injury free body toning exercises
19   </p>
20   </body>
21   </html>
```

FIGURE 3.1 `ch03/first.html`
The HTML markup for the first version of a single-file website for **Nature's Source**.

For example, we have a tag `<html>` that indicates the beginning of an HTML document. It is paired with the tag `</html>` that indicates the end of the HTML document. Everything included in this pair is the HTML document, or, looked at another way, the entire HTML document is an `html` element. Similarly, a `<p>` tag indicates the beginning of a paragraph, the next `</p>` tag indicates the end of that paragraph, and the two tags, together with the actual text of the paragraph between them, comprise a p element.

> **HTML is not case-sensitive, so any HTML tag may contain all lowercase letters, all uppercase letters, or a mixture of both, but we (and most developers) recommend using all lowercase. This is one example of an XHTML rule that we recommend as an HTML guideline.**

An HTML document file will typically have an extension of either `.html` or `.htm`. Thus our first HTML document file (shown in Figure 3.1) is called `first.html`. Note that the content of `first.html` is just the content of `first.txt` from Chapter 2 with the addition of some HTML tags. Note as well that we have for the moment deliberately left the text formatted as it was in `first.txt`, and have placed all HTML tags at the left margin, except for the closing `</title>` tag.

With our next example we shall begin paying more attention to formatting to make our HTML more readable (to human readers).

3.4 The Basic Structure of Every Web Page

Figure 3.1 gives us some idea of what goes into the making of an HTML document. Although it is not strictly necessary, it is a very good idea (what we might call a "best practice") to make sure that every HTML document has the following general form:

```
<html>
  <head>
    <title> ... </title>
  </head>
  <body>
    ...
  </body>
</html>
```

Here the outermost `<html>...</html>` tag pair indicates the nature of the entire document. In this "skeletal" code we show as well, for the first time, the indentation level (two spaces) we will use to help make our code more readable.

Note that each HTML document should be separated into a `head` element and a `body` element by the `<head>...</head>` and `<body>...</body>` tag pairs. The information enclosed in the `<head>...</head>` tag pair is general information *about* the web page that *is not shown* in the display area of the browser window, while the information enclosed in the `<body>...</body>` tag pair is the actual page content and *is shown* in the display area of the browser window.

Before continuing the discussion, let's take a moment to look at **FIGURE 3.2**, which shows how `first.html` will look in a web browser.

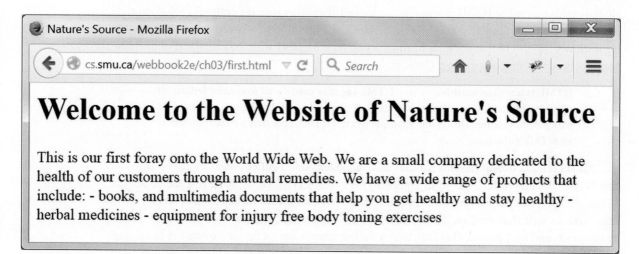

FIGURE 3.2 `graphics/ch03/displayFirstHtml.jpg`
A display of `ch03/first.html` in the Firefox browser.

Notice that the top bar (the "title bar") of the browser window shows the name of the browser itself, and, depending on your browser and settings, it may show the "title" of the web page. This title is the one specified using the tag pair `<title>...</title>` that appears inside the `<head>...</head>` tag pair (in other words, it's the content of the `title` element).

Although the `<body>...</body>` tag pair contains the content that is displayed in the browser window, note that all the "formatting" we were so careful to insert in our textfile `first.txt` (see Figure 2.1) has disappeared. That formatting was also preserved when the file was displayed in the browser as a simple textfile, as shown in Figure 2.2. But all that formatting has been lost, now that the file is being viewed by the browser as an HTML file. The reason for this is that there is a different MIME type at play here (`text/html` rather than `text/plain`, because of the `.html` file extension), and the browser has its own ideas about how the content of such a file, containing ordinary text along with some markup, should be formatted. We can now see that this is different from how it thinks plain text, in a file with a `.txt` extension, should be formatted.

This is why we need to tell the browser how it should view the "structure" of our file, which we do using appropriate tags. In fact, we look at how to structure the content in the body of `first.html` in the next section.

3.5 Some Basic Markup: Headings, Paragraphs, Line Breaks, and Lists

The body of our first HTML document, shown in Figure 3.1, contains just two HTML elements.

The first tag pair, `<h1>...</h1>`, is used to specify a first-level heading element. The number `1` that follows `h` indicates the heading level. An `h1` heading provides the largest display of its content, while `h2` provides the second largest display of its content, and so on, down to `h6`.

The second tag pair in our first HTML document is `<p>...</p>`. The `<p>` opening tag indicates the beginning of a paragraph and the `</p>` closing tag marks the end of that paragraph. Even though we have typed the contents of the paragraph in the file `first.html` in Figure 3.1 with a format that seems reasonable, its display shown in Figure 3.2 completely ignores the formatting specified using our manually inserted line breaks and indentations. The paragraph appears as "running text". If we want to break lines and provide an indented and itemized list, we will have to insert additional tags to indicate the desired structure.

In the `ch03` subdirectory of the book's website files you will find a version of the file modified in just this way. It is called `second.html` and contains the required additional formatting tags. The file itself is shown in **FIGURE 3.3**. Its display in a web browser appears in **FIGURE 3.4**.

The first thing to note about Figure 3.3 is the first line, which illustrates an HTML comment. Comments in HTML have the following syntax:

```
<!-- Text of the comment goes here. -->
```

Such comments can be single-line, multi-line, or end-of-line, but cannot be nested. In other words, one comment cannot be placed inside another.

```
1   <!-- second.html -->
2   <html>
3    <head>
4     <title>Nature's Source</title>
5    </head>
6    <body>
7     <h1>Welcome to the Website of Nature's Source!</h1>
8     <p>This is our first foray onto the World Wide Web. We are a small
9     company dedicated to the health of our customers through natural
10    remedies.
11    <br>
12    We have a wide range of products that include:</p>
13    <ul>
14     <li>books, and multimedia documents that help you get healthy and
15     stay healthy</li>
16     <li>herbal medicines</li>
17     <li>equipment for injury free body toning exercises</li>
18    </ul>
19   </body>
20  </html>
```

FIGURE 3.3 `ch03/second.html`
The HTML markup for the second version of a single-file website for **Nature's Source**.

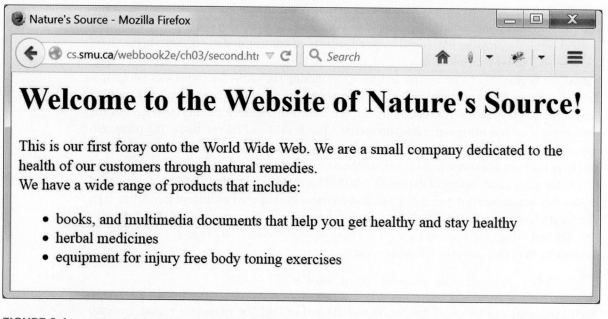

FIGURE 3.4 `graphics/ch03/displaySecondHtml.jpg`
A display of `ch03/second.html` in the Firefox browser.

The second thing to note about the file is that it has been formatted using our particular formatting choices, which we will attempt to keep consistent throughout the text. There are many different formatting styles you could use for HTML "source code" (a term you quite often hear, but since it's not really "code" in the usual sense, a much better term is HTML *markup*). Ours is, of course, just one of those styles. It is a reasonable one, however, and you could do worse than imitate it. The main features of our formatting style include an indentation level of two spaces, and the fact that when one element is nested inside another, the inner element is indented a further level with respect to the outer. Most decent editors and IDEs can be configured to perform this sort of formatting automatically, but no matter what software you use you often need to do a little format-tweaking after the fact to get things just the way you want them. Whatever style you use, or are required to use, be sure to use it consistently.

You also see three new HTML tags in `second.html`. The first of these new tags is `br` (line 11), which is used to insert a line break into the text. This `<br>` element is different from previous elements you have seen. It does not come with a tag pair, and has no closing tag. Elements like this are also called *empty elements*, since they have no content.

The second new tag is `ul`. The `<ul>...</ul>` pair (lines 13 and 18) lets us create an *unordered list* by enclosing all the items in our list. Such a list is one in which the list items are not numbered; instead, each list item is preceded by the same symbol, which is often a "bullet" by default. Every item in the list is, in turn, enclosed within a `<li>...</li>` tag pair, which illustrates `li`, the third new tag.

As you can see in Figure 3.4, the use of `<h1>`, `<p>`, `<br>`, `<ul>`, and `<li>` makes it possible for us to create a reasonably formatted web page, which is already much improved over the display of plain text.

But there is more to a web page than well-formatted text. We will soon introduce more HTML tags by adding to our web page a table with rows and columns, as well as images. But before doing that we need to discuss a very important aspect of web development: how to ensure that our web pages are *valid*, and why we should do so.

3.6 What Does It Mean for a Web Page to Be Valid?

So far we have been creating web pages more or less "on the fly", trying as we go to show you some useful HTML features in context. You may have begun to wonder if we know what we're talking about. Our pages do show up in browser windows and have a reasonable appearance, but how confident does that make you feel?

Historically, browsers have been written to be very "forgiving" when displaying web pages. In other words, even if web designers were not very careful when designing their web pages, and didn't follow all the rules, a browser would often still be able to do a reasonable job of displaying such pages. That is one reason why the web contains so many very badly constructed web pages: Folks could be sloppy and get away with it; they were and they did.

In any case, you have a right to expect that a browser will be able to display any one of your web pages, so long as it is a *valid web page*. But what exactly does this mean? Simply put, it means that if you are using HTML to mark up your web pages, then you should "do the right thing" when creating those pages. Thus a web developer should know what the rules and guidelines are, and should try to follow them.

This is not as bad or onerous as it may seem at first. As we have already mentioned, HTML5 is much less strict than XHTML, but we think it is still worthwhile to follow some XHTML rules, even if they are not, strictly speaking, "rules" in HTML5. We will not provide all the rules we eventually want to use at this point, just a short but useful subset to get us started:

1. Use lowercase for all tag names (required for XHTML, recommended for HTML5).
2. Use both opening and closing tags for all elements with content (required for XHTML, recommended for HTML5).
3. Make sure tag pairs are properly nested (required for XHTML, and just a really good idea in any case).

These are three guidelines that we recommend you follow when writing your HTML markup. There are many ways in which you could not follow these guidelines, and still have a web page that displays fine and even validates as HTML5, but adherence to the guidelines will make your markup much more readable, modifiable, and thus maintainable.

The last of the above guidelines, the "proper nesting of tags", is one we have in fact followed, but not mentioned explicitly. It's easiest to show what this means by giving an example where tags are *not* properly nested. Suppose we had created a file in which the tag order was like this:

```
<head>
<title>
...
</head>
</title>
```

Then we would be violating this rule because the `title` element must be *completely* contained within the `head` element. In general, if the opening tag `<tag2>` *follows* the opening tag `<tag1>`, then the closing tag `</tag2>` must *precede* the closing tag `</tag1>`. This applies whether the elements in question are contained in either the `head` element or the `body` element of the page.

We will say more about HTML rules and guidelines as time goes on, but for now you will be safe (and your pages will be valid) if you simply emulate the practices you observe in our sample files.

3.7 How Can We Determine if a Web Page Is Valid?

It is one thing to feel confident that you have followed all the necessary rules for inserting HTML markup code into your web page files, but is there a way you can be certain you have done so?

The answer, fortunately, is *yes*. You can submit your file to an **online validator**, of which there are several. To do this you browse to the online validator site, enter the URL of the web page you wish to validate into the validator, and click a button that starts the validation process. The

```
1    <!DOCTYPE html>
2    <!-- third.html -->
3    <html lang="en">
4      <head>
5        <meta charset="utf-8">
6        <title>Nature's Source</title>
7      </head>
8      <body>
9        <h1>Welcome to the Website of Nature's Source!</h1>
10       <p>This is our first foray onto the World Wide Web. We are a small
11       company dedicated to the health of our customers through natural
12       remedies.
13       <br>
14       We have a wide range of products that include:</p>
15       <ul>
16         <li>books, and multimedia documents that help you get healthy and
17         stay healthy</li>
18         <li>herbal medicines</li>
19         <li>equipment for injury free body toning exercises</li>
20       </ul>
21     </body>
22   </html>
```

FIGURE 3.5 ch03/third.html
The HTML markup for the third version of a single-file website for **Nature's Source**. Same content as second.html, but new or modified lines 1, 3, and 5 now contain information that a validator will use during the validation process.

validator will then provide a feedback report telling you either that your page is fine, or that you have violated one or more of the rules.

Since online validators are usually capable of validating not only HTML5 web pages, but also very early and more recent versions of HTML, as well as XHTML, it is necessary to tell a validator what version of HTML (or XHTML) has been used in the construction of the web page you are validating, as well as some information about the *encoding scheme* (character set) you are using. To do this you need to add some informational lines at the beginning of your file. In particular, although not everything we list here may be strictly necessary, we recommend that you do each of the following:

1. Add a DOCTYPE declaration to indicate the version of the markup language being used. This is actually very important, since it tells the validator what markup version you're using, information it will need to perform a validation. (See the first line of **FIGURE 3.5**, which shows the DOCTYPE for HTML5.)
2. Modify the opening html tag by giving it a lang *attribute* that indicates what (natural) language the web page is using. (See line 3 of Figure 3.5, which indicates that the language of our web page is English. Tag attributes will be discussed later.)

3. Place a `meta` element within the document `head` element to indicate the encoding scheme being used. (See line 5 of Figure 3.5, which indicates that we are using the utf-8 character set, a very commonly used web page standard.)

This may sound a little scary, but all of this is much simpler now with HTML5 than it used to be with XHTML, and fortunately you can easily turn it into a ritual, then stop thinking about it. The file `third.html` is a copy of `second.html` modified to contain this information for the validator. Figure 3.5 shows this file, which now contains all of the information mentioned above.

Having to do this for each file that you wish to have validated is the bad news. The good news is that you can treat the lines containing all of this additional information as "boilerplate" markup that you simply copy and insert into any new file you are creating. Then, as long as you "follow the guidelines" in the rest of the document (for the kind of document you said it would be, in our case HTML5), that document should validate without any problem

Now, once you have prepared your document and inserted the validation information, how do you actually validate it? There are a number of validation sites on the Internet, including this one:

```
http://validator.w3.org
```

This site is maintained by the World Wide Web Consortium itself and is very easy to use. At the time of this writing this site seemed to be in transition, so you might find a recommendation to go elsewhere if you use this site. Not to worry. You will always be able to find a site or a tool to validate your web pages, and you should always do so.

To use the above site for validating one of your web pages, first go to the site and enter the URL of the web page you wish to have validated into the window provided for that purpose. Then click on the button marked `Check`. You will then either be told that your page is valid, or be given an itemized report on the ways it violates the specifications of the document type (`DOCTYPE`) against which it was validated.

For example, **FIGURE 3.6** shows a (partial) validator display just as the file `third.html` is about to be validated, and in **FIGURE 3.7** we see a display (again partial) of the validator showing a successful validation of that file.

3.8 Validating with the Firefox Web Developer Add-on

As you have just seen, it is possible to perform web page validation just by entering the URL of the page to be validated into the validator. However, given the frequency with which you should be validating your pages during the development process, this is a lot of effort that you do not want to repeat as often as would be necessary.

To our rescue comes the **Web Developer** add-on tool for Firefox. Notice we say it comes to "our" rescue, and it can come to your rescue as well, if you are using Firefox as your browser of choice. However, all browsers have either built-in features, or available add-ons, that can be very

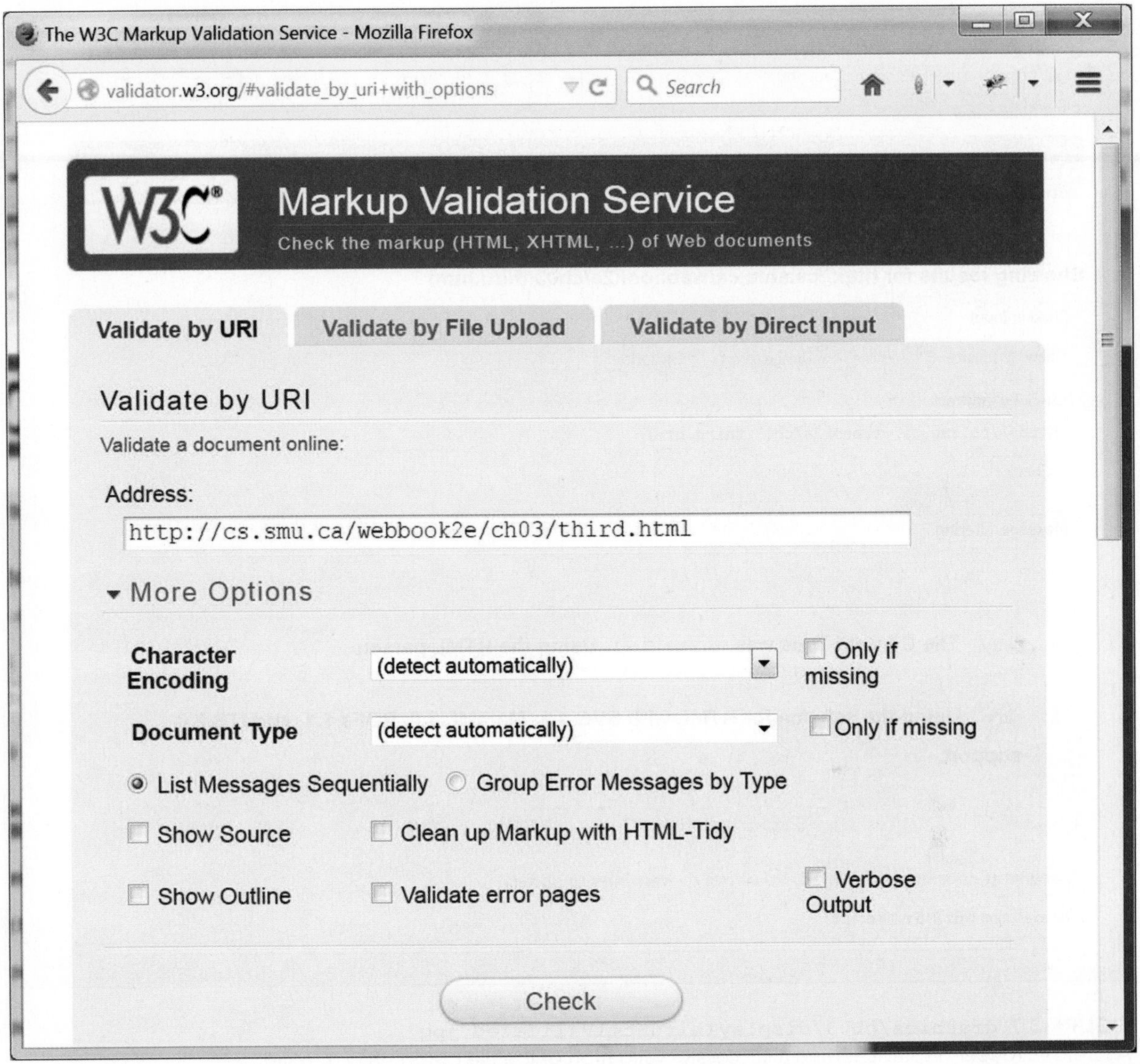

FIGURE 3.6 `graphics/ch03/displayThirdHtmlToValidate.jpg`
A Firefox browser display just before clicking the Check button to validate the file `ch03/third.html`.

helpful to web developers. We will describe how we use the Firefox Web Developer add-on to help us quickly validate web pages, but the tool can be used for many other things as well, and you should explore the possibilities if you install it.

First, you do need to install it, and we should say here we are referring to the Web Developer Firefox add-on available from `chrispedrick.com`. This add-on is also available for the Chrome and Opera browsers, but in our judgement it is more convenient to use in Firefox. Once

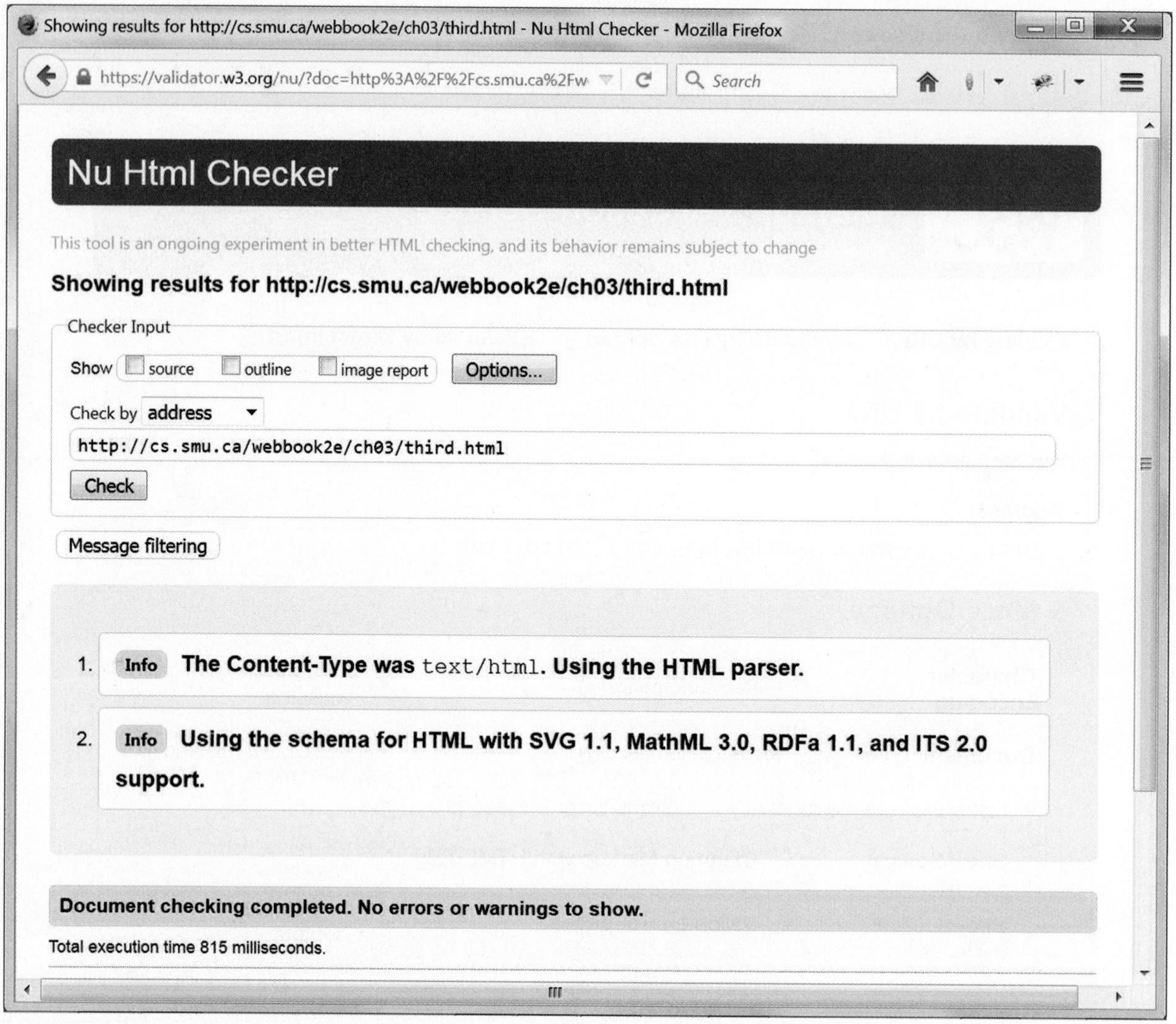

FIGURE 3.7 `graphics/ch03/displayThirdHtmlValidated.jpg`
A Firefox browser display showing a successful validation of the file `ch03/third.html`.

you have it installed and activated you have an extensive toolbar extending across your browser window underneath your address bar. One of the menu items is **Tools**, and clicking on it reveals a dropdown list of choices, one of which is **Validate HTML**. Clicking on that submenu option will cause the current page to be validated at the W3C site discussed earlier. Note that there is also a keystroke shortcut for this operation, namely `Ctrl+Shift+V`. The Web Developer add-on about to perform a validation is illustrated in **FIGURE 3.8**.

By the way, the keystroke combination `Ctrl+Shift+V` is not built-in, but it (or another keystroke combination) can be set under the Web Developer's **Options** menu, if there is no built-in keystroke combination for this action by the time you install the add-on. Click first on

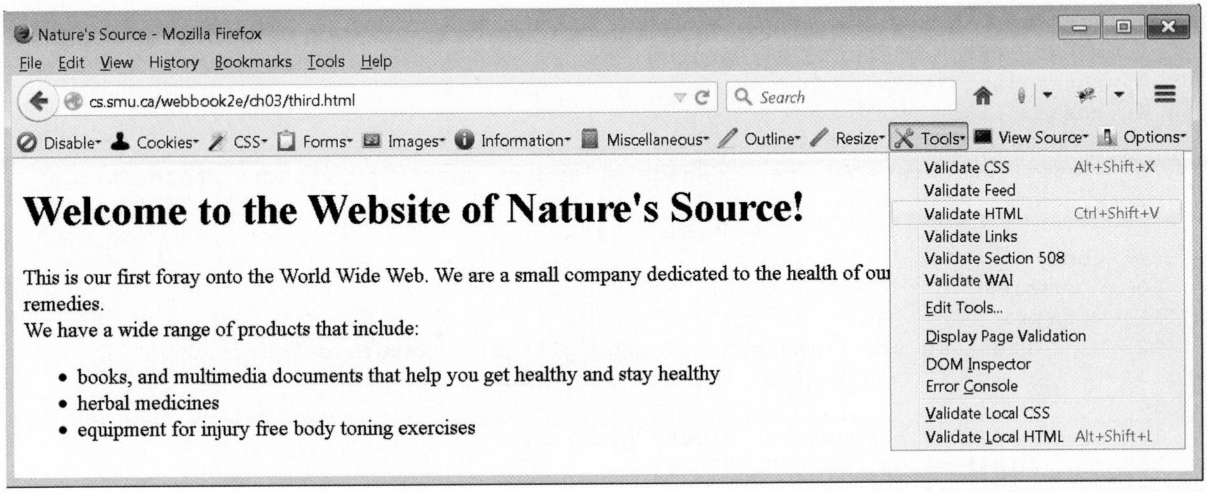

FIGURE 3.8 `graphics/ch03/WebDeveloper.jpg`
A Firefox browser display showing the activated Web Developer toolbar and the Options dropdown menu about to validate the file ch03/`third.html`.

Options, then **Options** . . ., finally **Tools**, where you can click on the Validate option you want to edit. In addition to editing (or setting) the keystroke shortcut, you can also choose the site you want to use for validating, if you wish. Try to choose a keystroke combination that is not used for anything else in your local context.

Also, do not confuse the **Validate HTML** option with the **Validate Local HTML** option. The former is for validation of a page that has been loaded into your browser from a web server, while the latter (but not the former) can be used if you have simply opened the web page file from a directory on your personal computer.

3.9 Tables, Images, and Tag Attributes

The images and other multimedia files that appear on web pages are in fact stored in separate files and embedded into the appropriate web pages during the display process. When dealing with several such files, it is important to set up certain conventions for file organization. We have created a subdirectory called `nature1` under the directory `ch03` of our website files, which contains the web page and related files used in this section. If you look in that directory, you will notice that there are two items in the directory, a file called `index.html` and a subdirectory called `images`. The filename `index.html` has a special meaning. We are telling the web server that users should access the contents of the directory `nature1` through the file `index.html`. Let us find out what happens when we try to access the directory `nature1` on our website with this URL:

```
http://cs.smu.ca/webbook2e/ch03/nature1/
```

If you enter the above URL into your web browser, the web server will display the web page produced by the file `index.html` from the directory `ch03/nature1`. This file is shown in **FIGURE 3.9**.

```
1   <!DOCTYPE html>
2   <!-- index.html for ch03/nature1 -->
3   <html lang="en">
4   <head>
5     <meta charset="utf-8">
6     <title>Nature's Source - Canada's largest specialty vitamin store</title>
7   </head>
8
9   <body>
10    <table>
11      <tr>
12        <td><img src="images/naturelogo.gif" alt="Nature's Source Logo"
13                 width="608" height="90"></td>
14
15        <td>5029 Hurontario Street Unit 2<br>
16        Mississauga, ON L4Z 3X7<br>
17        Tel: 905.502.6789<br>
18        Fax: 905.890.8305</td>
19      </tr>
20
21      <tr>
22        <td>
23          <h3>Welcome to Nature's Source - Protecting your health
24          naturally!</h3>
25
26          <p>Founded in 1998, Nature's Source was created to serve those who
27          use alternative healing methods. Offering only the highest quality
28          vitamins, minerals, supplements &amp; herbal remedies, Nature's
29          Source takes great pride in helping people live healthier, happier
30          lives.</p>
31
32          <p>Many companies that talk about customer service fail to deliver.
33          Nature's Source exists to truly serve all the needs of their
34          customers. Each location features dedicated on-site therapists
35          along with knowledgeable staff who ensure that every customer
36          receives the best quality information available. Continuing
37          education seminars are a regular event at Nature's Source.</p>
38        </td>
39
40        <td><img src="images/outdoor4.jpg" alt="Get healthy and stay healthy"
41                 width="256" height="256"></td>
42      </tr>
43    </table>
44  </body>
45  </html>
46
```

FIGURE 3.9 `ch03/nature1/index.html`
The HTML markup for the home page of this chapter's first version of a multi-file website for **Nature's Source**, using a simple (and temporary) table layout, and containing links to two image files.

FIGURE 3.10 `graphics/ch03/nature1/displayIndexHtml.jpg`
A display of `ch03/nature1/index.html` in the Firefox browser. Photo: © AlexBrylov/iStockphoto

Note that we do not have to specify the filename `index.html`, although we could do so. This is because the Apache web server looks for a file with this name "by default" when you browse to a directory. In fact, most any browser can be configured to look for a specific file (or for several different specific files) when the user browses to a directory, and though often the name of such a file is specified to be `index.html`, it may therefore be something else, such as `home.htm`, or even `default.asp`.

The actual browser display of this file is shown in **FIGURE 3.10**. You can also load this file by opening the file `nature1/index.html` in the `ch03` folder, if you have copied the textbook files to your computer.

Let's examine Figure 3.9 a little more closely to see what's new in `nature1/index.html`. The display of this file in the web browser, as shown in Figure 3.10, shows that the contents of the web page are arranged in a table format. This table contains a total of four cells. The top-left cell contains the logo of our company. In the top-right cell, we have the address and other contact information for the company. General information about the company is in the bottom-left cell. Finally, an image that may convey what the company is all about is embedded in the bottom-right cell. For example, in our case, this (subliminal) message might be, "Use our products to get fit and enjoy the great outdoors!"

There are four new tags in the HTML markup of the file `nature1/index.html`, shown in Figure 3.9. Three of them are related to the table used to create the table of cells on our web page:

1. The `table` element itself is specified by the `<table>...</table>` tag pair and the complete contents of the table (its rows and columns) are the content of this element.
2. Each row of the table is specified by a `<tr>...</tr>` tag pair. Since this particular table has two rows, it has two `tr` elements.
3. Similarly, each column of the table is specified by a `<td>...</td>` tag pair, and you can think of `td` as standing for "table data". In this table each row contains two columns, so each row has two `td` elements "nested" within it.

This is also the first of our HTML documents to display an image on its web page. This is done using an `<img>` element. This is another empty element, like the `<br>` element. Of course, if we are going to display an image that is contained in a file, we have to specify the name of the image file, and possibly the full path to that file, if it is not in the same directory as the page that uses it. We have placed the two images in a subdirectory called `images`. One of these images is our **Nature's Source** logo, and the other is the fourth of a group of six business-related images we will use in a later chapter when we implement a "rotating image" feature on our website. It is common practice to put all the images to be used in a given context in a single directory. While the directory name can be anything, `images` seems like an appropriate name and is a popular convention among web developers.

Now, if the `<img>` tag is not a pair, obviously we can't make the path to the file the content of the pair. So, what do we do? Well, now we get to see another aspect of HTML tags, the *tag attribute*. Study the `img` tag from lines 12 and 13 in the `index.html` file of Figure 3.9:

```
<img src="images/naturelogo.gif" alt="Nature's Source Logo"
width="608" height="90">
```

This line shows four *attributes* of the `img` tag. These are `src`, `alt`, `width`, and `height`. Note the syntax: First, attributes always follow the tag name inside the opening tag (although in this case there is *only* an opening tag), and second, each attribute is followed by an equals sign (=) and then by its *attribute value*, which is enclosed in quotes.

> Not every HTML tag attribute needs to have a value. But if an attribute does have a value, you may choose to enclose that value in quotes, or not, unless the value has a space in it, in which case the quotes are necessary. However, it's just simpler and safer to quote attribute values always. Both single quotes and double quotes are permitted, but be consistent. We also recommend using all lowercase for tag attribute names, just as we did for tag names. This is another XHTML rule that we recommend following as an HTML5 guideline.

The value of the `src` attribute of this `img` tag is the path to the file that contains the logo image we want to appear in the first column of the first row of our table, namely `images/naturelogo.gif`. In other words, this image is the content of the first `td` element in that row (lines 12–13). In a similar way, the image in the file `images/outdoor4.jpg` is made to appear in the second column of the second row (lines 40–41). Thus the `src` attribute of the `<img>` tag is mandatory: the browser has to know where the image file is located: It's in the `images` subdirectory, which itself is in the same location as the `index.html` file.

Another mandatory attribute for the `img` tag is `alt`, whose value specifies the text to be displayed in case the image itself cannot be displayed for any reason. An image might not be displayed for any number of reasons. For example, the image file may be inaccessible, the browser may not support graphics, or a user with a visual disability may have the graphical display turned off. The text from the `alt` attribute value may also appear in a popup text box when your mouse hovers over the image (or may not appear, depending on the browser).

By "mandatory" in this context, we mean that a web page containing an `<img>` tag will not validate as HTML5 if either attribute is omitted. The web page will still display if the `alt` attribute is omitted; it just won't validate as HTML5. Of course, the image won't display, nor will the page validate, if the `src` attribute is omitted.

The `width` and `height` attributes of the `img` tag give the dimensions of the image as we want it to appear on our page. The values of these two attributes are in *pixels*, a unit of "screen real estate" about which we will say more in the next chapter on CSS. For now just think of a pixel as a single point in an on-screen image. The word *pixel* is short for "picture element", and its actual size depends on your screen resolution. This is generally the default unit in HTML whenever you do not specify the unit to be used for some measurement. The abbreviation for pixel is `px`, but the unit should be omitted in this context, as it is the assumed default and, in fact, *must* be omitted if the page is to validate. This is also new in HTML5.

The `width` and `height` attributes are not mandatory, but without them the browser will display the image using its actual size, which may not be what we want. The ideal situation is that an image is the exact size you want to display, so the browser does not have to do any extra work to "scale" the image to meet your requested dimensions. You should still tell the browser what those dimensions are, however, since this allows the browser to "set aside" exactly the right amount of screen space for the image, even before downloading it. If an image is not the size you want it to be for display on your web page, it is better to use an image editing program to crop or scale the image to the exact size (or something close to the exact size) you want, to improve the loading speed of your page.

Actually, most HTML tags have attributes, including the attributes we have just discussed for the `img` tag. The reason we haven't discussed attributes before is that, unlike two of the four we have seen for the `img` tag, most tag attributes are optional. All tags have "default behavior", and attributes can be used to supply necessary or helpful information for the tag, or to alter tag behavior in some useful way.

Let's pause a moment for a key observation. In Figures 3.9 and 3.10 we have done something that you may still see quite often on the Web—for the very good reason that at one time things *had* to be done this way—and which we will continue to do in this chapter, simply because we have not yet discussed the tools that will allow us to avoid it, but which you should see less and less frequently on the web as time goes on, and which you should try to avoid in new markup, once you have CSS at your disposal.

What is it that we have done? Well, we have used the HTML `table` element *for page layout purposes*, and this is now regarded as a design no-no. HTML tables should only be used to display tabular data, like that shown in Table 3.1 or Table 3.2. To avoid having to use tables in this way, however, we need *CSS*, which we cover in the next chapter. There we will show you how to achieve the same layout effect you see in Figures 3.9 and 3.10, but using CSS layout instead of HTML table layout.

Browser support for CSS features has been improving rapidly in recent times, even among the laggards, of which Internet Explorer was one of the worst, even when it was the dominant web browser.

3.10 HTML Entities

Another new HTML feature we see in `nature1/index.html` is the use of the special character code `&amp;` (see line 28 of Figure 3.9), which produces the ampersand character (`&`) when the web page is displayed.

Some characters have special meanings in HTML (the angle brackets enclosing tags, for example) and so if you simply want to display one of these characters you cannot just enter it into your file because it will be interpreted as having its special meaning rather than just appear as itself, thus causing the browser no end of confusion. Such *special characters* are often called *metacharacters* in general, and *HTML entities* in our current context.

You need a special code to tell the browser to display such a character. Each such code starts with an ampersand (`&`), ends with a semicolon (`;`), and in between has a word or character string indicating the character in question. The fact that the ampersand is used in this way is what makes the ampersand itself a metacharacter. A short list of commonly used HTML entities (metacharacters) is shown in **TABLE 3.2**.

3.11 Adding More Web Pages to Our Site and Connecting Them with Hyperlinks

A fundamental characteristic of the World Wide Web is the ease with which you can navigate from one web page to another page, either on the same site or on another site anywhere in the world, just by clicking on a *link* to a second page that appears in the first page. We are now ready

TABLE 3.2 HTML entities, also called "special characters" or "metacharacters".		
HTML Entity	**Meaning**	**Actual Symbol**
&amp;	ampersand	&
&gt;	greater than	>
&lt;	less than	<
&divide;	divide	÷
&plusmn;	plus/minus	±
&cent;	cent	¢
&euro;	euro	€
&pound;	British pound sterling	£
&yen;	Japanese yen	¥
&copy;	copyright	©
&reg;	registered	®
&trade;	trademark	TM

to develop a more elaborate website consisting of multiple pages, with links (or, more formally, *hyperlinks*) connecting them.

We have placed the files for this version of our website in a subdirectory called ch03/nature2. Once again the index.html file constitutes the "home page" of this simple website. The HTML markup for this version of our index.html file is shown in **FIGURE 3.11**, and the browser display of the file appears in **FIGURE 3.12**. The browser display is not fancy, but it shows a typical website *structure* for a company, with the company logo at the top, followed by a row of menu links, then the main content area, and finally a footer, which in this case contains two additional menu links.

In this new version of our index.html file we continue to use a table for layout, this time a table with four rows and five columns. Note that the first row (the logo row) and third row (the main content display area) contain the same content as the previous version of our index.html file, except that the contact information that appeared to the right of the logo has been removed and now appears on the page available under the Locations link, which you can reach, in turn, by clicking the **Contact Us** menu item on our "home page".

```
1   <!DOCTYPE html>
2   <!-- index.html for ch03/nature2-->
3   <html lang="en">
4     <head>
5       <meta charset="utf-8">
6       <title>Nature's Source - Canada's largest specialty vitamin store</title>
7     </head>
8     <body>
9       <table>
10        <tr>
11          <td colspan="5">
12          <img src="images/naturelogo.gif" alt="Nature's Source"
13              width="608" height="90">
14          </td>
15        </tr>
16        <tr>
17          <td><a href="index.html">Home</a></td>
18          <td><a href="pages/estore.html">e-store</a></td>
19          <td><a href="pages/products.html">Products+Services</a></td>
20          <td><a href="pages/yourhealth.html">Your Health</a></td>
21          <td><a href="pages/about.html">About Us</a></td>
22        </tr>
23        <tr>
24          <td colspan="3">
25          <h3>Welcome to Nature's Source:
26          Protecting your health naturally!</h3>
27          <p>Founded in 1998, Nature's Source was created to serve those who
28          use alternative healing methods. Offering only the highest quality
29          vitamins, minerals, supplements &amp; herbal remedies, Nature's
30          Source takes great pride in helping people live healthier, happier
31          lives.</p>
32          <p>Many companies that talk about customer service fail to deliver.
33          Nature's Source exists to truly serve all the needs of their
34          customers. Each location features dedicated on-site therapists
35          along with knowledgeable staff who ensure that every customer
36          receives the best quality information available. Continuing
37          education seminars are a regular event at Nature's Source.</p>
38          </td>
39          <td colspan="2">
40          <img src="images/outdoor4.jpg" alt="Get healthy and stay healthy"
41          width="256" height="256">
42          </td>
43        </tr>
```

FIGURE 3.11 `ch03/nature2/index.html`
The HTML markup for the home page of this chapter's second version of a multi-file website for **Nature's Source**, to which a main menu row and a footer row have been added.

```
44       <tr>
45         <td colspan="3">Nature's Source &copy; 2015 Porter Scobey and Pawan
46         Lingras</td>
47         <td><a href="pages/contact.html">Contact Us</a></td>
48         <td><a href="pages/sitemap.html">Site Map</a></td>
49       </tr>
50     </table>
51   </body>
52 </html>
```

FIGURE 3.11 `ch03/nature2/index.html` (*continued*)

FIGURE 3.12 `graphics/ch03/nature2/displayIndexHtml.jpg`
A display of `ch03/nature2/index.html` in the Firefox browser. Photo: © AlexBrylov/iStockphoto

3.11.1 A Menu of Hyperlinks

Row two (the main menu) and row four (the footer, with two additional menu items) are new to this version of our home page. The menu items we have chosen and placed in row two, and which will appear on *each* of the pages in this version of our website, include the following:

▶ **Home**, which will always return the user to the home page, and therefore links to the `index.html` file, so that clicking it will again display the view shown in Figure 3.12. (Of course, if you are already at the home page of the website and click this link, you will see no change. If you are looking at any other page and click this link, you will be returned to the home page.)

▶ **e-store**, which will eventually link to our complete e-commerce setup

▶ **Products+Services**, which will take the user to information about the products and services provided by our business

▶ **Your Health**, a business-specific link (Since the business we have chosen is related to health, it is only natural to have more information on that topic available via a link like this one.)

▶ **About Us**, which takes the user to a page giving information about the company

The footer, which will also now appear on each of the pages of our site, contains some typical copyright information and two additional links that might be of interest to a site visitor: **Contact Us** and **Site Map**.

Begin your examination of the HTML markup in Figure 3.11 by looking first at the second row of the table (the second `tr` element), in lines 16 to 22. This second row is the only row that has all five columns (five `td` elements). Each of these columns contains one of our "links", which is the usual shorter term used for the more formal term *hyperlink* like those in our menu.

Links are specified using the `<a>...</a>` tag pair. Each a tag, often called an *anchor tag*, has an `href` attribute, which is a required attribute for an opening a tag. The value of the `href` attribute specifies which URL to open when a user clicks on the link. In our case, all menu item links are to files that reside in a subdirectory called `pages` that is located in the same directory as `index.html`. Note that the **Home** link refers to `index.html` itself, but each of the other links has the form `pages/filename.html`, which reflects the fact that each of the other files is in the subdirectory `pages`. We can have more elaborate values for `href` such as `http://mypyramid.gov/` if we wish to link to some external site. The text between `<a>` and `</a>` is what is displayed in the browser. For example, with the HTML code

```
<a href="pages/estore.html">e-store</a>
```

the browser displays the text `e-store` as a link, and clicking on that **e-store** link takes us to the file `pages/estore.html`, which will then be displayed in the browser window, replacing the display of `index.html`.

Now take a look at the first row of the table (the first `tr` element), in lines 10 to 15. Even though the table has five columns, we only specify one column in this first row. This column actually "spans" all five columns that appear in the second row. This is accomplished by using the attribute `colspan` with a value of `"5"` for the `td` tag of this column, which specifies how many columns of the table this particular column (`td` element) is to span (or "extend over").

In the third row (lines 23–43) we have only two `td` elements, the first of which spans three of the five table columns and the second of which spans the remaining two columns. In the fourth and final row (lines 44–49) we have three `td` elements, with the first one spanning the first three columns of that row, and the remaining two occupying one column each.

As you might guess, the `td` tag also has a `rowspan` attribute (which is not needed or illustrated here), in case we need to have a table cell span more than one row.

3.11.2 Our Site Now Has Many Pages

There are quite a few other page files that belong to our `nature2` website, and you will find them all in the `pages` subdirectory of `ch03/nature2`. In fact, there is a different page corresponding to each link on our home page, so all of the links on our home page are "live". These pages, and others reachable by clicking on new links that appear on these other pages, form a kind of "skeleton" of the website we plan to develop. The links that appear on additional pages will appear in the first column of the main content area row, under the **Home** link of the main menu, and will lead to pages related in some way to that content area.

We will not examine all pages of this site in detail here, but we will look at two additional page documents that we can use to further our discussion. You should, however, take time to visit each of the pages of this version of our website, and note how the "look and feel" is maintained from one page to the next. Keep in mind that for the moment we are not concerned with the presentational style of our pages, but only their structure and (abbreviated) content as we try to get a feel for what our site will eventually provide for our users.

If you click on the **About Us** link on the home page, you will be taken to the page `about.html`, a display of which is shown in **FIGURE 3.13**. This is one of the pages with additional links of the kind mentioned above, which are seen to the left of the main content. These additional links provide, in effect, a submenu for the menu item **About Us**. In a later chapter of the text we will use JavaScript to create dropdown menus as a better alternative to this kind of submenu. All the HTML markup we have used in the file `about.html` is based on the concepts we have already discussed, and you should study the file to confirm this.

The final page document from this group that you will look at now is `sitemap.html`, which comes up if you click on the **Site Map** link at the bottom-right corner of any page on the site. Every website should have a *site map*, since users may not know how to find their way through a labyrinth of menus and submenus to find what they are looking for. A site map should give them a good, concise high-level view of the structure and content of the site.

The browser display of the file `sitemap.html` is shown in **FIGURE 3.14**, and we can see that this page can be viewed as having four "rows", and that the top two rows of the web page, as well as the footer, are the same as all the other page displays on the site.

However, the third row of the markup, which you see in **FIGURE 3.15**, is different in that it contains a *numbered list*, in which some of the list items contain a "nested" *unordered list*, in which each list item is marked by a small empty circle, rather than the solid bullet character that is used as an item marker when an unordered list is not nested. These are browser defaults in action.

FIGURE 3.13 `graphics/ch03/nature2/displayAboutHtml.jpg`
A display of `ch03/nature2/pages/about.html` in the Firefox browser.

The ordered list is specified with the tag pair `<ol>...</ol>`. Each item in the ordered list is specified, in turn, with the tag pair `<li>...</li>`, just as we did previously for unordered lists. We nest an unordered list under four of the seven ordered list items using the `<ul>...</ul>` tag pair we discussed before.

Note that the row of the table containing the ordered list is in two columns (two `td` elements), with items 1 to 4 in the first column (the first `td` element) and items 5 to 7 in the second column (the second `td` element). This is actually achieved by having two ordered lists, with the second one having a `start` attribute with value "5" on its opening `ol` tag.

3.11.3 Beware the "Legacy Fix"!

You can also see another browser default in action on this sitemap page. Note that items 5 to 7 of the ordered list have some extra space above them. This is caused by the fact that whatever content is in

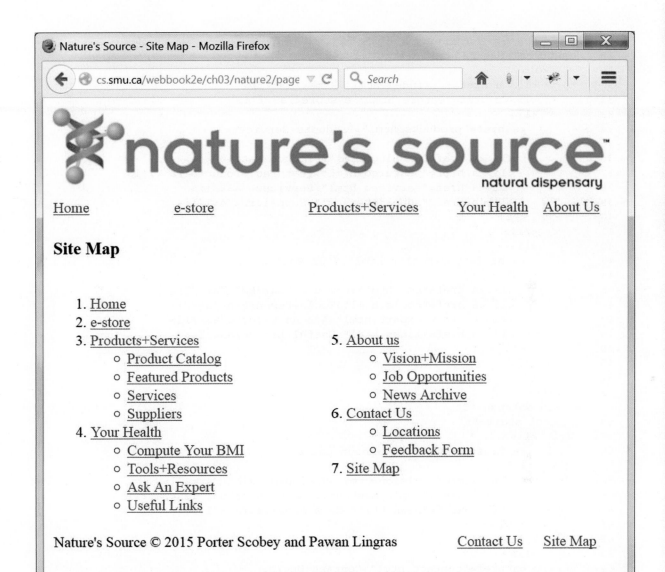

FIGURE 3.14 `graphics/ch03/nature2/displaySitemapHtml.jpg`
A display of `ch03/nature2/pages/sitemap.html` in the Firefox browser.

a `td` element is, by default, vertically centered within that element. Hence the fact that items 5 to 7 of the ordered list in the second column of that row occupy less space than items 1 to 4 in the first column gives the observed effect. We could fix this with the `td align` attribute, but this would cause our page to fail HTML5 validation, so once again we choose to wait till we have a CSS solution. You will encounter this kind of situation often as you develop web pages. Many of the "legacy solutions" to this sort of "problem" will still work if you choose to use them, but they will not validate. Because we always want to have valid pages, the advice is obvious: Avoid this kind of "legacy fix"!

```
28    <tr>
29     <td colspan="2">
30       <ol>
31         <li><a href="../index.html">Home</a></li>
32         <li><a href="estore.html">e-store</a></li>
33         <li>
34           <a href="products.html">Products+Services</a>
35           <ul>
36             <li><a href="catalog.html">Product Catalog</a></li>
37             <li><a href="featured.html">Featured Products</a></li>
38             <li><a href="services.html">Services</a></li>
39             <li><a href="suppliers.html">Suppliers</a></li>
40           </ul>
41         </li>
42         <li>
43           <a href="yourhealth.html">Your Health</a>
44           <ul>
45             <li><a href="bmi.html">Compute Your BMI</a></li>
46             <li><a href="tools.html">Tools+Resources</a></li>
47             <li><a href="expert.html">Ask An Expert</a></li>
48             <li><a href="links.html">Useful Links</a></li>
49           </ul>
50         </li>
51       </ol>
52     </td>
53     <td colspan="3">
54       <ol start="5">
55         <li>
56           <a href="about.html">About us</a>
57           <ul>
58             <li><a href="vision.html">Vision+Mission</a></li>
59             <li><a href="employment.html">Job Opportunities</a></li>
60             <li><a href="news.html">News Archive</a></li>
61           </ul>
62         </li>
63         <li>
64           <a href="contact.html">Contact Us</a>
65           <ul>
66             <li><a href="locations.html">Locations</a></li>
67             <li><a href="feedback.html">Feedback Form</a></li>
68           </ul>
69         </li>
70         <li><a href="sitemap.html">Site Map</a></li>
71       </ol>
72     </td>
73    </tr>
```

FIGURE 3.15 `ch03/nature2/pages/sitemap.html` **(partial)**
The fourth row of the table element in this file. Note the two `td` elements with different `colspan` values, and the nested lists.

3.12 Using Server-Side Includes (SSI) to Make Common Markup Available to Multiple Documents

Note that the version of our Nature's Source website discussed in this section will not display properly unless it is being "served" by an SSI-aware web server. In particular, it will not display properly if you have just copied the files to your computer and try to view the website from there.

This section discusses a very important principle to keep in mind when you are developing your website, and one that we can illustrate quite nicely by taking a closer look at our website in `ch03/nature2`, and how we transform it into the next version of our website, given in `ch03/nature3`.

3.12.1 The "Maintenance Nightmare" Problem

First, note that our `ch03/nature2` website now contains 19 page files in our `pages` subdirectory, and they all contain quite a bit of information that is the same in each file. That is, every one of those page files of this version of the website, as well as the index file, contains four "rows" of information (the logo row, the menu row, the main content row, and the footer row), and only the main content row differs from page to page. Of course, the markup for all four rows appears in each file, even though that markup is exactly the same for the first, second, and fourth rows in each case.

If we carry on like this, we are potentially leaving ourselves wide open to a very serious problem down the road. Suppose that at some point we want to change the wording of a menu option or add a new menu item, or change one of the names in the footer. What does this mean? It means that every single one of those 20 files will have to be edited and modified. And what are the chances that all the changes that have to be made will be made correctly and consistently across all affected files? And then, if another change is required, we will have to do it all over again. If this happens, and it almost certainly will, you will have what is often called a *maintenance nightmare* on your hands, and it should be clear why it has this name.

3.12.2 Identifying and Extracting Common Markup

So, what to do? The central idea is that you want to eliminate, as far as possible, duplicate markup, so that if changes are necessary you only have to make them in one place. To solve this problem we are going to employ a very useful technology called *Server-Side Includes (SSI)*, and also introduce a new HTML tag, the `base` tag. As part of this process, we also restructure the content of the `nature2` version of our website to look like this for the `nature3` version:

```
nature3
  index.html
  /images
    naturelogo.gif
    outdoor4.jpg
  /common
    document_head.html
    logo_row.html
    mainmenu_row.html
    footer_row.html
  /pages
    about.html
    sitemap.html
    (... and the other seventeen page files)
```

The most obvious, and major, difference between the directory structure of ch03/nature2 and that of ch03/nature3 is the appearance of a new subdirectory called common in ch03/nature3. This subdirectory contains these four files: document_head.html, logo_row.html, mainmenu_row.html, and footer_row.html. Each of these files contains markup that is common to the file index.html, as well to the 19 other files in the pages subdirectory. The actual contents of each of these files is shown in **FIGURES 3.17**, **3.18**, **3.19**, and **3.20**. With the common markup removed from all the files where it occurs and placed in these four files, the next question is this: How do we get that common markup into any file where it is needed before the file is sent to the browser for display?

3.12.3 Using SSI to Include Common Markup Where Needed

To answer this question, look at **FIGURE 3.16**, which shows the third version of our index.html file for this chapter. Note that lines 1, 5, 6, and 28 have a similar syntax. For example, here is line 1:

```
<!--#include virtual="common/document_head.html"-->
```

This line, whose syntax must be exactly as shown (and note that there is only a single blank space) causes the Apache server to include the contents of the file document_head.html into this latest version of our index.html file, in place of this line, before index.html is sent to the browser for display. This action of the server software, namely the "including" of the text of an external file on the server before sending it to the browser, is the reason for the terminology used to describe the process: *SSI*. Of course, each file in the pages subdirectory will also have its common markup sections replaced by the same four "virtual include" lines that we see in index.html.

The contents of the file document_head.html are shown in Figure 3.17, and as you can see from that figure, the file contains the initial lines of markup needed by index.html, as well as by each of the other pages in our pages subdirectory. This common piece of markup includes

```
 1   <!--#include virtual="common/document_head.html"-->
 2   <!-- index.html for ch03/nature3 -->
 3     <body>
 4       <table>
 5         <!--#include virtual="common/logo_row.html"-->
 6         <!--#include virtual="common/mainmenu_row.html"-->
 7         <tr>
 8           <td colspan="3">
 9             <h3>Welcome to Nature's Source:
10             Protecting your health naturally!</h3>
11             <p>Founded in 1998, Nature's Source was created to serve those who
12             use alternative healing methods. Offering only the highest quality
13             vitamins, minerals, supplements &amp; herbal remedies, Nature's
14             Source takes great pride in helping people live healthier, happier
15             lives.</p>
16             <p>Many companies that talk about customer service fail to deliver.
17             Nature's Source exists to truly serve all the needs of their
18             customers. Each location features dedicated on-site therapists
19             along with knowledgeable staff who ensure that every customer
20             receives the best quality information available. Continuing
21             education seminars are a regular event at Nature's Source.</p>
22           </td>
23           <td colspan="2">
24             <img src="images/outdoor4.jpg" alt="Get healthy and stay healthy"
25             width="256" height="256">
26           </td>
27         </tr>
28         <!--#include virtual="common/footer_row.html"-->
29       </table>
30     </body>
31   </html>
```

FIGURE 3.16 `ch03/nature3/index.html`
The HTML markup for the home page of this chapter's third version of a multi-file website for **Nature's Source**, which now contains the "virtual include" directives that cause the markup common to all pages in this version of the site to be included from external files.

```
 1   <!DOCTYPE html>
 2   <!-- document_head.html -->
 3   <html lang="en">
 4     <head>
 5       <meta charset="utf-8">
 6       <title>Nature's Source</title>
 7       <base href="http://cs.smu.ca/webbook2e/ch03/nature3/">
 8     </head>
```

FIGURE 3.17 `ch03/nature3/common/document_head.html`
The file containing the initial HTML page markup, which is included in the file `ch03/nature3/index.html`, as well as in each file in the `ch03/nature3/pages` subdirectory.

```
1    <!-- logo_row.html -->
2      <tr>
3        <td colspan="5">
4          <img src="images/naturelogo.gif"
5               alt="Nature's Source"
6               width="608"
7               height="90">
8        </td>
9      </tr>
```

FIGURE 3.18 `ch03/nature3/common/logo_row.html`
The file containing the company logo, which is included in the file `ch03/nature3/common/index.html`, as well as in each file in the `ch03/nature3/pages` subdirectory.

```
1    <!-- mainmenu_row.html -->
2        <tr>
3          <td><a href="index.html">Home</a></td>
4          <td><a href="pages/estore.html">e-store</a></td>
5          <td><a href="pages/products.html">Products+Services</a></td>
6          <td><a href="pages/yourhealth.html">Your Health</a></td>
7          <td><a href="pages/about.html">About Us</a></td>
8        </tr>
```

FIGURE 3.19 `ch03/nature3/common/mainmenu_row.html`
The file containing the main menu, which is included in the file `ch03/nature3/common/index.html`, as well as in each file in the `ch03/nature3/pages` subdirectory.

```
1    <!-- footer_row.html -->
2        <tr>
3          <td colspan="3">Nature's Source &copy; 2015
4          Porter Scobey and Pawan Lingras</td>
5          <td><a href="pages/contact.html">Contact Us</a></td>
6          <td><a href="pages/sitemap.html">Site Map</a></td>
7        </tr>
```

FIGURE 3.20 `ch03/nature3/common/footer_row.html`
The file containing the footer information, which is included in the file `ch03/nature3/index.html`, as well as in each file in the `ch03/nature3/pages` subdirectory.

everything from the DOCTYPE declaration down to the end of the head element. It also includes the promised new HTML base element, which we will explain shortly.

In a similar way, the contents of the logo row, the main menu row, and the footer row of our previous index.html file (from ch03/nature2) are "included" (by SSI) into our ch03/nature3/index.html file by lines 5, 6, and 28 of that file.

By placing common content in four separate files in a subdirectory called `common`, and including their content in `index.html` at the appropriate places, we have accomplished what we set out to do. There is one possible "gotcha", however, which we now point out. While in our `index.html` file the line that includes the `document_header.html` file is

```
<!--#include virtual="common/document_head.html"-->
```

the corresponding line in each of the files in the `pages` subdirectory is different:

```
<!--#include virtual="../common/document_head.html"-->
```

In the above line we need the `../` in front of `common` because the value of `virtual` must be the path to the file to be included, which in this case is the relative path from the `pages` subdirectory to the `common` subdirectory (we go up one level from `pages` to its parent, and then down into `common`).

Now each page document on our site can include all necessary markup from the four files in the `common` subdirectory, and if any changes need to be made to anything in any one of these four files, the changes need only be made in the files in that subdirectory, and those changes will appear in each page of the site the next time the page is displayed. The remaining content of each page document file on our website (the files in `pages`) is specific to that file.

3.12.4 One Thing Leads to Another: A Second Problem

However, we are not quite finished. When we solved this one problem by extracting all the common markup and localizing it in the `common` subdirectory, we have inadvertently created another problem. The problem arises because by default when the `href` value of a link contains a relative path, that path is relative to the directory where the file containing the link is located. We can see what this problem is by looking at `mainmenu_row.html` in Figure 3.19, which contains the markup for our main menu. When that file is included in `index.html`, all the menu links will work fine, because all the menu links are relative to the `nature3` directory, the same directory where `index.html` is located. But when that same file is included in any one of the files in the `pages` subdirectory of `nature3`, none of the menu links will work, because none of the menu links is relative to the `pages` subdirectory.

3.12.5 The `base` Tag Solves Our Second Problem

This is where we introduce the HTML `base` tag, which gets us out of this conundrum. Take a look at line 7 in the file `document_head.html` in Figure 3.17:

```
<base href="http://cs.smu.ca/~webbook2e/ch03/nature3/">
```

This line defines the `href` attribute for the `base` element of the website for our text. Once we have done this, every relative path in the links on our site will be appended to the value of the `href` attribute in our `base` tag before being used. This means (for example) that it doesn't matter whether the file `mainmenu_row.html` has been included in `index.html` or in `pages/about.html`, when we click on the **e-store** menu link, we are activating the following link:

`http://cs.smu.ca/~webbook2e/ch03/nature3/pages/estore.html`

Note that all of the submenu links that appear on any of the page files in the `pages` subdirectory have to be modified in the same way as the main menu links that appear on all pages.

And remember this: If you have installed our textbook files on your own server, you will need to change the value of the `href` attribute of the `base` tag in this file (and in the corresponding file in later chapters) to the appropriate value for your local situation.

3.12.6 Our Revised Site Looks and Behaves Exactly Like the Previous Version

To summarize, our `ch03/nature3` website is a revision of our `ch03/nature2` website, in which each page on the site has been revised to include the markup common to each from four separate files. This, of course, is a "behind the scenes" effect, and if you start by displaying the `index.html` file for this version and then view any or all pages of the site you should see exactly what you saw in the previous version. We sometimes describe this kind of scenario as something that is "transparent to the user".

3.13 The New HTML5 Semantic Elements

In this chapter we have introduced, discussed, and used a sufficient number of HTML elements and some of their attributes to allow us to create some simple but functional web pages. The HTML elements we have chosen to study so far could be described as "legacy" elements, in that they have always been available in HTML.

However, with HTML5 we have access to many new elements of various kinds. We will want to use some of these elements in the next chapter when we begin to discuss CSS, so we mention here some of the more useful ones. Before doing that, however, we need to say a bit more about some "legacy" HTML features and elements, which will help us to understand how some of these new HTML5 elements came to be.

3.13.1 Block-level Elements and Inline-level Elements

An important distinction to be aware of when you are placing HTML elements into your web documents is the difference between *block-level elements* and *inline-level elements*.

Block-level elements occupy their own "vertical space" on the page, and generally cause the browser to place extra space both before and after the element (how much space depends on the element and the browser). Examples of block-level elements that we have seen include the heading elements (`h1`, etc.) and the paragraph element `p`.

Inline elements, such as the `img` element, do *not* cause any additional space to appear either before or after them.

Another aspect of nesting in HTML is that some (but not all) block-level elements permit other block-level elements to be nested inside them, but you cannot nest a block-level element inside an inline element.

This idea of a distinction between block-level elements and inline-level elements remains a useful one, but it has been greatly expanded in HTML5 into a much more complex *content model*, the details of which need not concern you here, and a discussion of which would take us too far afield.

3.13.2 Semantic Elements and Non-Semantic Elements

Another useful distinction to make among HTML elements is that of a *semantic element* vs. a *non-semantic element*. We can also refer, equivalently to *semantic tags* and *non-semantic tags*.

A *semantic element* is an "element whose tag name has meaning". Examples that we have seen are `table` and `img`, since each of these tag names indicates what kind of information is associated with the corresponding element.

A *non-semantic element* is one whose tag name suggests nothing about its content. Two of the most important such elements are the ones we introduce next.

3.13.3 Two More Legacy Elements: `div` and `span`

If you look "behind the scenes" at almost any web page on the Internet, you are likely to see a lot of `div` elements, many of them with an `id` attribute, especially if that page has been there for a while.

The `div` element has been an HTML "workhorse" for many years. It is a block-level element that allows a developer to group any number of other block-level and inline elements together and treat them as a single unit, for styling with CSS or for applying some action via JavaScript, for example. The `id` attribute of a `div` element is used to identify the element for styling or some other purpose.

The `span` element has a similar purpose, except that it is an inline-level element and so must be used to group or enclose only inline elements or information. Words or phrases within a paragraph often appear as content in a `span` element, for example.

Note that both `div` and `span` are non-semantic elements, and that leads directly into the following discussion of some new HTML5 elements.

3.13.4 New Semantic Elements in HTML5

HTML5 has quite a large number of new semantic elements, and here is an alphabetical listing of their tags: `article`, `aside`, `details`, `figcaption`, `figure`, `footer`, `header`, `main`, `mark`, `nav`, `section`, `summary`, `time`. This list contains more new elements than we will need, but there are some here that we will use in our development (`main`, `header`, `nav`, `article`, `footer`), but we will not discuss them in detail until the following chapter when we will combine their use with CSS.

However, if you have read what we said above about what semantic elements are, you should agree that these are, in fact, *semantic elements*. That is, each one of these tags has a name that suggests what kind of information is likely to be associated with its element. For some the distinction might be a bit fuzzy; what's the difference between an "article" and a "section", for example? This is the kind of thing that is treated at length by the new HTML5 content model mentioned earlier, but a full discussion is beyond your needs.

It's important to note that an element like the `header` element, for example, does nothing "extra" for you, in other words nothing that a `div` element with `id="header"` did not do, except greatly improve the conceptual structure of your HTML pages by specifically identifying those parts of your pages that are headers with an "official" semantic tag designed for just that purpose. Browsers will generally treat the `header` element as a block-level element, just as they do a `div` element, but even that is not guaranteed, and if that's what you want you should say so using CSS, as you shall see.

The "back story" of how the names of these semantic tags were chosen is quite interesting. A lot of web pages were examined, and it was found that, for example, many thousands of them had a `div` element with an `id="header"` attribute. Even if some other attribute value, such as `"head"` or `"heading"` was used, the intent of such a `div` was clear. Since for many purposes on the web, it is much easier to deal with tags than with tag attributes, this analysis suggested that a new tag named `header`, whose content would be "header information" for a web page, was warranted, and so one was created. Similar analysis led to the addition to HTML5 of the other tags in the above list.

Summary

In this chapter you first learned that HTML was the first widely used markup language on the web, how it eventually was rewritten as XHTML, which did not "catch on", and then returned to its roots in a new incarnation, HTML5.

We stressed the importance of maintaining a distinction between the structure of the content on a web page and its presentation. HTML should deal only with structure. We distinguished between HTML tags and HTML elements (tag pairs and their content).

Even though the XHTML standard is now behind us, many of its "rules" are still valuable and we recommended they continue to be used as "guidelines" when writing your HTML5 markup:

1. Use only lowercase letters for both tag names and attribute names.
2. Ensure elements with content have both an opening tag and a closing tag.
3. Ensure that tag pairs are properly nested.
4. Enclose attribute values in quotes.

You learned that the basic structure of any HTML document should include at least the following four elements: `html`, `head`, `title`, and `body`.

You saw how to apply some simple markup to the content in the body of an HTML document so that a browser can identify the structural divisions of the web page content and display them accordingly. HTML elements allow you to mark such things as headings, paragraphs, and lists. An element can also be empty (have no content), like the tag for a line break, and element tags can have attributes that can be used to alter the display of the element content or the effect of the element.

Some characters, such as the tag delimiters < and >, cannot appear in an HTML document except in their tag-delimiter context, so if you wish to have such a character in your document you have to use an HTML entity, such as < for <.

You saw how the table element can be used for page layout, even though it should no longer be so used, but with CSS not yet at your disposal you had little choice. Fortunately, you also saw a bona fide use of a table (on our site map page).

You saw how to add images to your web pages, and how to link one web page to another when your site has multiple pages. Furthermore, when multiple pages have content in common, you saw how SSI can be used to avoid the maintenance nightmare of trying to keep duplicate code consistent when updating takes place.

We distinguished between block-level HTML elements and inline-level elements, as well as semantic and non-semantic elements, and pointed out how the new HTML5 semantic elements such as main, header, and footer allow you to create "better" web pages than you could using the traditional approach with div elements.

Finally, you now know what a valid web page is, and how to determine if a given web page is in fact valid.

Quick Questions to Test Your Basic Knowledge

1. Who was Tim Berners-Lee and what part did he play in the origin of the World Wide Web?
2. What is the relationship between HTML and XHTML?
3. What was the last version of HTML before the (temporary) shift to XHTML?
4. HTML was designed to describe web page structure. Some browser vendors tried to make it do more, but they should not have done so. Can you explain what we mean by these two statements?
5. What is the difference between an HTML tag and an HTML element, and how are they related?
6. What is an empty HTML element, and what is its general syntax? Give an example.
7. What is, in your opinion, the best reason for keeping web page "structure" and web page "presentation" separate?
8. What should the high-level structure of every HTML web page document look like?
9. What would you give for a short description of what it means for HTML tags to be "properly nested"?

10. Why do we recommend retaining some XHTML "rules" for our HTML "guidelines"?
11. What is the purpose of a DOCTYPE declaration?
12. For what did we use a meta element?
13. What attribute should the opening html tag of any web page have?
14. What does it mean for a web page (an HTML document) to be valid?
15. How do you determine if an HTML document is valid?
16. What have tables been used for in HTML that they should no longer be used for?
17. What are the HTML comment delimiters?
18. What is a pixel, and what is the abbreviation for it?
19. Why do we need HTML entities?
20. What is the syntax of an HTML entity? Give an example.
21. What are the two required attributes of the img tag?
22. What are two recommended attributes for the img tag?
23. What tag is used for hyperlinks, and what is its only required attribute?
24. We think it's always a good idea to put attribute values in quotes, but when **must** you do so?
25. Why should every nontrivial website have a *site map*?
26. What is the term we used to refer to the problems that almost always arise when you have the same markup in many different pages on your website and have to change something in that markup?
27. What does the acronym SSI stand for, and for what is this technology used?
28. How many files did we use to hold the common markup in our nature3 website files, and what did each contain?
29. What is the syntax of the "virtual include" directive that we used?
30. The path of the file in a "virtual include" directive must be relative to what?
31. For what purpose did we use an HTML base element?
32. What is the difference between an HTML block-level element and an inline-level element? Give an example of each.
33. What is meant by a "semantic element" in HTML? Give a "legacy example" (one from HTML prior to HTML5) and another example that is new in HTML5.

 # Short Exercises to Improve Your Basic Understanding

In these and subsequent exercises, we may sometimes explicitly ask you to make a copy of a file from the text and modify it in some way. However, it is worth pointing out that even in those cases when we do not explicitly ask you to make copies, whenever we ask you to make a change to a file from the text, it should be understood that we really mean for you to first make your own copy of that file and then do whatever is asked to the copy. That way, you can always go back to the original for a fresh copy if necessary.

1. Load the file `first.html` from Figure 3.1 into your browser. It will probably not look exactly like the display we have shown in Figure 3.2. Try changing the size of the browser window to see if you can make it look more like that display. The main thing to note as you do this is how the text in both the heading and the following single paragraph "flows" to conform to the size of the display window.

2. Make a copy of the file `first.txt` from Chapter 2 and call it `first.html`. Note that this `first.html` file will not be the same as the `first.html` file from the beginning of this chapter, since there will be no markup in it. In this case make no changes to your copy other than the file extension. Load both `first.txt` and this new `first.html` into your browser and take careful note of what should be some considerable difference between how the two files are displayed. Explain any differences you see in terms of MIME types. Repeat the exercise with one or more additional browsers to confirm that they all exhibit similar behavior, as should be the case.

3. In the file `second.html` of Figure 3.3 make the line following the line break a separate paragraph, and to the `p` tag of that paragraph add the `align` attribute with a value of `"center"`. Load the revised file into your browser and note how the new paragraph is centered above the list. Then repeat the exercise, this time giving the `align` attribute the value `"right"`. Be aware that although doing this "works", and you will often see it done this way on the web, it is not the way you should accomplish these tasks. It's the kind of "legacy fix" we warned you about, and you should use instead techniques provided by CSS, the topic of the next chapter.

4. In the file `second.html` of Figure 3.3 change the `ul` tag to `ol`, so that you get a numbered list instead of a bulleted list. Note that by default your list items are numbered 1, 2, 3, ... and so on, just as the unnumbered list had a bullet marker as the default. This default style can be changed by setting the value of the `type` attribute. Do a little "research" to find out what the alternatives are. This begs an obvious question: Can you change the default bullet marker for an unordered list in the same way? Find the answer to this question as well.

5. Browse to the file `third.html` of Figure 3.5. Make a copy of its URL; then open up another window in your browser and go to `http://validator.w3.org`, paste in the URL, and click on the `Check` button. You should get a response highlighted in green saying the file validates. Make some changes in the file that will cause it *not* to validate.

6. In the file of Figure 3.9 change the name of both image files so that the browser cannot find them, and then reload the page. In each case you should see the text of the `alt` attribute value in the place where the image would otherwise appear. Try this in more than one browser as well.

7. Go to the **W3Schools** website (`www.w3schools.com`) and study the HTML `table` element, its associated `th`, `tr`, `td`, and `caption` elements and any relevant attributes

(particularly `colspan` and `rowspan`). We have used the `table` element temporarily, of necessity, for page layout (not a good idea for the long term, as we have repeatedly pointed out), but tables are very useful for displaying data that is "tabular" in nature, and that is what they should be used for. Experiment with the table element and note in particular the defaults that are used for displaying text within a `th` element and a `td` element.

8. Create a web page whose content is a table containing the data in Table 3.1.
9. Create a web page whose content is a table containing the data in Table 3.2.

Exercises on the Parallel Project

In these exercises we ask you to replicate, for your previously chosen business, the kinds of web pages we have discussed in the text for our own sample health product business. Since the layout required is a table with two rows and two columns, you may use, as we have done in this chapter, the HTML `table` tag for your page layout, but only because we do not yet have an alternate approach.

1. Before you begin, make sure you have thoroughly explored each of the three versions of our sample website: the single-file version (`nature1`), the version in which each page document has the duplicate markup embedded within it (`nature2`), and the final version in which the common markup has been extracted into the four separate files (`nature3`).
2. Your first task is to produce a single-page website for your business that looks like the web page for **Nature's Source** as shown in the markup of `ch03/nature1/index.html` and the browser display of Figure 3.10, according to the following specifications for the content of each table cell:
    a. The logo for your business goes in the top-left corner of the page. If you have a paint program, and are artistically inclined, you can produce your own logo for this purpose. Even a simple program like the standard Paint program on Windows can be used. Otherwise, at least for the moment, you can either search for a suitable logo on the Internet (googling "free logos" should turn up something) and hope you can find a suitable one to use, or simply place text in this cell for the time being. In any case, the name of your business must appear here.
    b. Your business address and other contact information goes in the top-right corner.
    c. Some general information about your business must appear in the bottom-left "content" part of the page. This should be appropriate reading for someone coming to your site for the first time and should therefore be designed to catch the attention of visitors and make them want to explore the rest of your site as it develops.

d.   Finally, a photographic image relevant to your business must go into the bottom-right corner of your page. You can take such a photo yourself and upload it, or download one from the Internet, provided you do not violate any copyright laws in so doing.

3.   Your second task is to revise and extend the single-page website you created in the previous exercise. The goal is to have it "parallel" either our `nature2` website or our `nature3` website. Recall that `nature3` made use of SSI, while `nature2` did not. You should make sure that SSI is enabled on your sever; otherwise, you run the risk of getting into the kind of "maintenance nightmare" situation we described earlier in this chapter.

> **If this exercise is being assigned in a course, your instructor may ask you to produce a website that is "parallel" to either `nature2`, or to `nature3`, or better yet, produce two different websites, one that "parallels" each of `nature2` and `nature3`. It is a very useful exercise to produce two different websites that look and behave exactly the same, but are constructed quite differently behind the scenes, and that is what you would be doing. Your instructor may or may not insist that your pages validate as HTML5 for this exercise, but you should try to make sure they do.**

So, in any case, your home page should have an appearance analogous to the display in Figure 3.12. Recall that this display would be the same for both versions of our multi-file site (i.e., for both `nature2/index.html` and `nature3/index.html`). The same is true of any other two files having the same name in the subdirectories `nature2/pages` and `nature3/pages`. For simplicity and consistency, make your menu links the same as the (generic) ones we have used (at least for the time being), except that our link called **Your Health** clearly must be replaced with a link more specific to, and appropriate for, your own business.

All links on your home page must be active, that is, each one must link to an actual page and not be a "broken link", and some of those pages must also have their own "submenu" links to other pages in a column at the left, in the manner of our sample site. One thing to note in this context is that if you click on one of these submenu links you get another page in the general context of the main menu link. For example, if you click on the **Your Health** menu option, there are four submenu links at the left of the resulting page. If you then click on **Ask An Expert**, you get that page, but the submenu links at the left now include only the other three that were there before. This behavior should be consistent throughout our site, and your site should emulate this behavior as well.

You need not have exactly the same number of files as our sample site, and of course the content of these additional pages will depend on the nature of your chosen business. Many of these pages can contain a short "coming soon" message, similar to that found on many of the pages of our sample site. But that message should be at least a short paragraph of one or two sentences saying something about just what is "coming soon".

What Else You May Want or Need to Know

1. In keeping with our need-to-know approach in learning new material, in this chapter we have introduced you to only a very small selection of the HTML tags that are available to you when you are constructing the HTML document for one of your web pages. You are likely already curious to see what else is available, and to begin experimenting with various other tags and their attributes. There is no better place to do this than at the **W3 Schools** site, several links to which are given in the **References** section that follows. This is a wonderful site to explore. You will find both reference material and tutorials, as well as examples that you can modify and experiment with right there on the site. However, here, we give a summary list of some tags that includes all those we have discussed, as well as some that are closely related to those we discussed, and some new ones. You should explore further as many of these as you can find time for on your own by going to the website mentioned above, because you will find them useful for constructing your own web pages.

   `html`, `head`, `title`, `body` The "infrastructure" elements used to set up any website.

   `link` The (empty) tag to place in the `head` element of your document if it needs to link to an external document (such as a CSS style sheet, discussed in the next chapter).

   `meta` The (empty) tag to place in the `head` element of your document if your document needs to make available to some external processing agent some high-level information about itself.

   `base` The tag that allows us to set the value of a "base" URL to use for our website, and to which any other relative `href` value on our site will be appended before that `href` value is used as a link destination.

   `h1`, `h2`, `h3`, `h4`, `h5`, `h6` The heading tags that give progressively smaller text.

   `p` The ubiquitous paragraph tag, one of the most frequently used.

   `ul`, `ol`, `li` The tags for bulleted (unnumbered) or numbered generic lists (which can be nested), and their items.

   `dl`, `dt`, `dd` The tags for a special kind of list—a *definition list*—which is convenient when you are defining or explaining a sequence of terms.

   `table`, `tr`, `td`, `th`, `caption` The tags for tables, with rows and columns. The `th` is a new tag (for us) that is often used for the first table cell of a row or the top table cell of a column if the content of that cell is to be used as the label for the rest of the corresponding row or column. Use `th` instead of `td` if you want the text content to appear in bold and centered within the table cell. The `caption` element, which we did not use, allows us to provide a caption for any of our tables.

br The (empty) line-break tag that moves the text following it in a paragraph to the next line, without adding any vertical space.

hr The (empty) horizontal-line tag that creates a horizontal line on a web page, often used for separation purposes.

img The (empty) image tag that permits you to place images on your web pages.

strong, em Tags that emphasize text by making it (usually) bold or italic, respectively. There are also b and i tags for bold and italic, but strong and em are preferred instead, since they provide "logical emphasis", which can let a browser decide how they should be rendered, as opposed to the "physical emphasis" of b and i, which insist on bold and italic.

small A tag used to make text "smaller" (than the surrounding text). There used to be a big tag as well, but for subtle reasons we need not try to explain here it is no longer supported in HTML5, while small does continue to be supported.

pre The tag to use if you want your text to retain the format you used when you typed it into your web page document.

blockquote, q The tags for two kinds of quotations: blockquote if you want your text to have extra space before and after it, and indented margins, and q if you just want quotation marks around it.

address, dfn, var, cite Tags to designate an address, a definition, a variable, and a citation, generally rendered in italics.

code, samp, kbd Tags to designate computer code, sample code or data, and keyboard input, generally rendered in monospace.

div, span Tags for designating parts of a page for processing of some kind (such as CSS styling or responding to JavaScript events).

article, aside, details, figcaption, figure, footer, header, main, mark, nav, section, summary, time Semantic tags new to HTML5, which of course contains many other kinds of new tags. For example, there is a new video tag, which you will see in the next chapter.

applet, basefont, big, center, dir, font, frame, frameset, isindex, menu, s, strike, u, xmp Tags that are *deprecated* (should no longer be used in new web pages), but are nevertheless still supported by many browsers.

2. As you have seen, HTML tags can have attributes. These attributes fall into several categories:

   a. Some attributes are *required*, such as the src attribute and the alt attribute for the img tag, for example.

   b. Some attributes are *optional*, such as the width attribute and the height attribute for the img tag, for example. Note that sometimes, as in the case of these two, even though an attribute is optional it may not be a good idea to omit it.

c. Some attributes are called *core attributes* (or *standard attributes*) because they can be used with virtually any HTML tag. These tags are also optional. These include the `id` and `class` attributes that you will meet in the next chapter in the context of CSS, as well as the `title` and `style` attributes.

d. Some attributes are called *event attributes*, because they can be used to fire up a JavaScript script under certain conditions (when certain "events" happen). For example, the `onclick` attribute might have as its value a JavaScript script that would run when the element with that attribute was clicked on by the user. We will look at event attributes in a later chapter on JavaScript. These attributes are also optional.

3. One of the reasons we often do not provide attributes for our tags when they are optional is because optional tags have default values that tend to be what we want most of the time. It is helpful to become familiar with the default values of commonly used tag attributes.

   For example, the `p` tag has an attribute called `align`, which may take any of the values `"left"`, `"right"`, `"center"`, or `"justify"`. Fortunately, the default value is `left`, since we want our paragraphs to be left-justified most of the time. Furthermore, this attribute is actually deprecated, so you should use CSS to get any alignment effect other than left that you would like to achieve, rather than get it by using this attribute.

4. You know that clicking on a link will usually take you to the beginning of the page at the end of that link, but sometimes the `href` value of a link will look like

   ```
   http://mysite.com/mypage.html#markedspot
   ```

   and in this case clicking on the corresponding link will take you, as usual, to `mypage.html` on `mysite.com`, but rather than displaying that page from the beginning, the browser will start its display of the page at the place on the page identified by an `a` tag having an `id` attribute with a value of `"markedspot"`. Such a location "somewhere down the page" is often called a *bookmark*. For example, if you wanted to go to a certain `h1` heading on the page `mypage.html` by clicking on the above link, you could identify that `h1` heading like this:

   ```
   <h1><a id="markedspot">This is the certain heading</a></h1>
   ```

5. HTML5 became an accepted standard in 2014, but you should not think that's the end of anything. The World Wide Web and all of its "standards" are all moving targets, and you should try to keep your finger on the pulse of developments that are taking place.

6. We mentioned briefly in this chapter the new HTML5 *content model*, when we introduced the older notion of block-level and inline-level elements. Studying the details of this model would be overkill in our context, but it is something you should be aware of and something that you might find useful as time goes on. Check out the link on this subject in the following **References** section, and come back to it from time to time until you get a "feel" for what it's all about. You will probably design and write better web pages as a result.

7. When you want to validate one of your web pages, one of the things you need to ensure is that it contains a `meta` element like the following:

```
<meta charset="utf-8">
```

There are many *character sets* available for use on the web and elsewhere, but as of the time of this writing `utf-8` was the dominant one in use on the web by a very wide margin. UTF is an acronym for *Unicode Transformation Format*, and this particular character encoding is so useful because it is capable of representing pretty much any character you might want to use, in virtually any natural language. We provide a link in the **References** section if you wish to read more about it.

 # References

1. Many of our references here and in the rest of the text will refer you to particular pages on the W3 Schools site, since the site is very useful from both a tutorial and reference perspective, but you may want to start at the home page and explore, so here it is:

```
http://www.w3schools.com/
```

2. Another tutorial site that you may find useful now and later is this one:

```
http://www.tizag.com/
```

3. For further information on HTML and XHTML, including their history and the relationship between them, check the following Wikipedia links (the HTML page has a nice picture of Tim Berners-Lee):

```
http://en.wikipedia.org/wiki/HTML
http://en.wikipedia.org/wiki/XHTML
```

4. You will find lists of available HTML entities here:

```
http://www.w3schools.com/html/html_entities.asp
https://dev.w3.org/html5/html-author/charref
```

5. Anytime you look up an HTML tag on the W3 Schools site, you will also find information on its attributes and their values, but for a general overview of tag attributes see the following links:

```
http://www.w3schools.com/tags/ref_standardattributes.asp
http://www.w3schools.com/tags/ref_eventattributes.asp
```

6. For further information on the differences between HTML and XHTML, see the following link:

    ```
    http://www.w3schools.com/html/html_xhtml.asp
    ```

7. For further information on which elements can be nested inside other elements, see:

    ```
    http://www.cs.tut.fi/~jkorpela/html/nesting.html
    ```

8. To keep an eye on what's happening with HTML5, you can check out the actual specification at

    ```
    http://www.w3.org/TR/html5/
    ```

    and a more web-author-friendly version of the specification here

    ```
    http://dev.w3.org/html5/spec-author-view/
    ```

    as well as a useful page summarizing all markup tags (with a clear indication of which tags are new and which have altered semantics) at this location:

    ```
    http://dev.w3.org/html5/markup/
    ```

    The W3C itself seems to be in a bit of a promotional mood with respect to HTML5, and you too can get on board at this site:

    ```
    http://www.w3.org/html/logo/
    ```

    To read about the differences between HTML5 and HTML4 look here:

    ```
    http://www.w3.org/TR/html5-diff/
    ```

    The *Web Hypertext Application Technology Working Group* (*WHATWG*, pronounced "What-Wig") is a community of folks interested in the "practical" evolution of the web. It was this group whose work eventually convinced the W3C that continued development of the XHTML standard would not be a good idea. Both the W3C and the WHATWG are now fully behind the HTML5 effort, though they remain separate entities. For more information, go to this site and check out the FAQ (Frequently Asked Questions) section in particular:

    ```
    http://www.whatwg.org/
    ```

9. For further information on the HTML5 content model, check this link:

   ```
   http://www.w3.org/TR/2011/WD-html5-20110525/content
   -models.html
   ```

10. Here's a link to the Wikipedia article on UTF-8:

    ```
    https://en.wikipedia.org/wiki/UTF-8
    ```

11. An interesting history of some web developments, including some perhaps-not-so-well-known details, and featuring a number of fascinating photos, can be found here:

    ```
    http://www.w3.org/People/Raggett/book4/ch02.html
    ```

CHAPTER FOUR

CSS for Content Presentation

CHAPTER CONTENTS

Overview and Objectives

In the previous chapter we introduced HTML as the markup language for describing the *structure* of a web page. Thus we use HTML tags to mark the parts of our pages that are headings, paragraphs, list items, and so on.

Every browser will have its own default way of displaying each of these structures, and often these defaults are perfectly adequate for our purposes. On the other hand, there are also many times when we wish to take control of how our pages look, and where on those pages our information is to be displayed. For example, we may want a different font size or text color, or we may want two columns of text rather than one, and that is where *Cascading Style Sheets* (*CSS*) come into play.

In this chapter we will discuss the following:

▶ Why CSS came into existence, and the problem they help to solve

▶ The syntax of a CSS style rule

▶ The placement of style sheets (or style rules) relative to the document (or element) being styled

▶ Some typical examples of style rules

▶ Some common types of CSS property values and their formats

▶ Structuring, commenting, and formatting CSS style sheets

▶ Using the CSS `class` and `id` selectors with the non-semantic HTML `div` and `span` elements, and also with the new HTML5 semantic elements

▶ Inheritance of styles and the "cascading" of styles

▶ The CSS box model

▶ Simple CSS page layout with "floating" `div`s and floating HTML5 semantic elements

▶ CSS reset as a "best practice"

▶ Some new CSS3 features

▶ Styling four different versions of our Nature's Source website with CSS, including one that illustrates "responsive design" and one that contains a video element

▶ Validating our CSS style sheets

4.1 The Rationale for CSS, and a Brief History

In the early days of the web there existed something of a Wild West mind-set, when browser developers were all doing their own thing. Before long there began to appear new HTML tags like the `font` tag, which allowed a developer to specify the font size and color of paragraph text,

TABLE 4.1 A very brief summary of the history of CSS. The term *monolithic* refers to a standard that was "all or nothing", with everything lumped together. By contrast, CSS3 is "modular", allowing conceptually distinct parts to be developed and approved separately.

Date	Version	Notes
1996	CSS 1 (monolithic)	initial specification
1998	CSS 2 (monolithic)	first upgrade to the initial standard
2004	CSS 2.1 (monolithic)	first attempt
2007	CSS 2.1 (monolithic)	second attempt
2011	CSS 2.1 (monolithic)	finally approved
current	CSS3 (modular)	ongoing, with individual modules being separately approved

for example. In other words, HTML was suddenly being used to describe certain presentational aspects of web pages, something that it was never designed to do. To make matters worse, because there were no standards for this sort of thing, different browsers did not always implement their rendering of these HTML "enhancements" in the same way.

By the mid-1990s it was recognized that this was not a good idea, and the font tag, among others, was deprecated, though it is still widely supported. Meanwhile, CSS were being developed—largely based on the work of Bert Bos and Håkon Wium Lie—to separate the description of how a page should look (its "presentation") from the description of the structural content of the page, which is the job of HTML. Though they did not "catch on" immediately, CSS represented such a powerful, versatile, and useful technology that it was really just a matter of time. Certainly nowadays all web developers recognize CSS as an invaluable and indispensable tool that must be in every developer's toolbox.

We introduce some of the main features of CSS in this chapter, but first take a look at TABLE 4.1 to get a sense of the development history of CSS.

4.2 Simple CSS Style Rules and Their Syntax

A CSS *style rule* is a rule that tells a browser how some part of a web page is to be displayed. For example, here are two simple style rules:

```
body {background-color: yellow;}
h1 {color: blue;}
```

These style rules can be used to tell a browser that the entire body of a web page is to have a background color of yellow, and the text of every h1 element on that page is to be displayed in blue.

A collection of style rules is called a *style sheet*, so the two rules above could comprise a very simple style sheet for a web document, as prepared by a web developer. Everything else in this document would be displayed according to browser defaults, possibly modified by the user adjusting browser settings.

The syntax of these two style rules is typical of any simple style rule. In this case, body and h1 are *selectors*. Think of a *selector* as the name of an HTML element tag that has been "selected" to have elements of that kind styled in a certain way.

The other part of a rule, the part appearing within the braces, consists of one or more *declarations*. In this case, each rule has a single declaration. Multiple declarations are separated by semicolons (;), and even if there is only a single declaration, placing a semicolon after it is permitted and in fact may be regarded as a "best practice". The braces and the declaration(s) contained therein are together referred to as a *declaration block*. A declaration block determines just how its corresponding selector element is to be styled.

Thus background-color: yellow is a declaration, and so is color: blue. A declaration contains a *property* (such as background-color or color), followed by the *value* of that property (yellow or blue in this case), and separated from it by a colon (:). We have also placed a space after the colon. This is optional, but it enhances declaration readability.

The sharp-eyed among you will have noticed, by now, an annoying inconsistency in these two style rules. Why is it just "color"? Why not "text-color", or, more generally, "foreground-color"? You might well ask, and the answer is simply that CSS, like everything else, is not perfect. It might have been more helpful, and consistent, if the CSS folks had named the color property text-color or foreground-color, but they didn't, and there's nothing we can do about it now.

4.3 The Placement of CSS Style Rules

Once you have some style rules, the next question is this: How do you arrange to have them applied to one (or more) of your web pages? You have several options, and each one corresponds to a different style sheet "level", a concept we will explore further later on when we discuss the "cascading" aspect of CSS. Meanwhile, in terms of the actual physical location of styles, we have the following options:

1. The *external level*, which permits you to place all of your styles in a separate file (which will normally have a .css extension) and link that file to any and all HTML documents to which you wish to have those styles applied. This is the recommended option and the one we will use.

2. The *document level*, which permits you to group all your styles, place them within an HTML style element, and then place this style element and its contents within the head element of your document. These styles will be applied only to the document in which they appear, and are sometimes called an *embedded style sheet*.

3. The *inline level*, which permits you to apply a given style directly to a single HTML element by making the style rule the value of the style attribute of that HTML element. Do not confuse the *style element* mentioned in the previous item with the *style attribute* mentioned here.

It's very important to remember that embedded styles (at the document level) apply only to the document in which they appear, and a style at the inline level applies only to the HTML element to which it is attached. These options do permit fine-tuning of very specific presentational requirements, either for a single HTML document or a single HTML element, but our preferred first option permits the same collection of styles to be applied to as many documents as we like, and to whatever elements we choose within those documents. Among other things, this means that we could potentially change some aspect of the presentation of our entire website just by making one small change in one location (the style file). The advantages of this approach for site maintenance should be obvious.

We will explore the second and third options above in the exercises, but for now let's take a look at a simple example illustrating our preferred approach.

4.4 A Simple Example

To illustrate the application of CSS style rules stored in an external file, we link the file `simple.css` shown in **FIGURE 4.1** to the HTML file `simple.html` shown in **FIGURE 4.2**. The CSS style sheet of Figure 4.1 contains (as its first line) a CSS-style comment giving the name of the file, followed by the two style rules discussed in section 4.3 above. The HTML file `simple.html` of Figure 4.2 is the same one given as `second.html` in Figure 3.3 of the previous chapter, except that the `head` element now contains the additional line

```
<link rel="stylesheet" type="text/css" href="css/simple.css">
```

shown as line 7, which serves to connect the file of CSS rules to the HTML file where those rules are to be applied. Note that this line introduces the HTML `link` tag (another empty HTML tag that does not come in a tag pair), and three of its attributes:

▶ `rel`, which has the value `stylesheet` to indicate the "relationship" to the current file, of the file named in the `href` attribute

▶ `type`, which has the value `text/css` to indicate that this is a "text file containing CSS rules" (as opposed to some other kind of style file) (When you "view source" and look at the markup of many pages on the Internet, you will often see this `type` attribute and its value, as shown here, in one or more `link` elements on those pages. It used to be required, but in HTML5 the `type` attribute of the `link` element is redundant if we are linking to a CSS file, so from now on we will omit it.)

```
1  /* simple.css for simple.html */
2  body { background-color: yellow; }
3  h1 { color: blue; }
```

FIGURE 4.1 `ch04/css/simple.css`
A very simple CSS style sheet file, containing a CSS comment indicating the name of the file, and two style rules.

```
1   <!DOCTYPE html>
2   <!-- simple.html -->
3   <html lang="en">
4     <head>
5       <meta charset="utf-8">
6       <title>Nature's Source</title>
7       <link rel="stylesheet" type="text/css" href="css/simple.css">
8     </head>
9     <body>
10      <h1>Welcome to the Website of Nature's Source!</h1>
11      <p>This is our first foray onto the World Wide Web. We are a small
12      company dedicated to the health of our customers through natural
13      remedies.
14      <br>
15      We have a wide range of products that include:</p>
16      <ul>
17        <li>books, and multimedia documents that help you get healthy and
18        stay healthy</li>
19        <li>herbal medicines</li>
20        <li>equipment for injury free body toning exercises</li>
21      </ul>
22    </body>
23  </html>
```

FIGURE 4.2 `ch04/simple.html`
An HTML document file having the same content as `ch03/second.html` from Figure 3.3 of Chapter 3, but now linked to `simple.css`.

> ▶ `href`, whose value is the name of the file containing the style rules for this HTML file (and can also be the full path to a file, as in this case, if the style file is not in the same directory as the HTML file to which it is linked) (Note that our CSS file is in a subdirectory called `css`, a common convention that we will follow.)

The result of displaying the HTML file shown in Figure 4.2, with the styles shown in the CSS file of Figure 4.1 applied to it, is shown in **FIGURE 4.3**. Our CSS rules for this web page affect only the color of two HTML elements, `body` and `h1`, but already you can probably get a sense of the possibilities. Not only the color of the text, and the page background color, but many other properties such as font size, font family, and other text properties, as well as higher-level features such as margin widths and page layout, may be controlled by CSS styles.

In this particular HTML file, there was only one `h1` element, but in the absence of any further instructions, *every* `h1` element in this document would have been displayed in blue text, if there had been more. And, of course, the web page has only a single body, and its background is displayed in yellow. You may find these colors not to your taste. The point to be made here, however, is this: If you have, in one place, all of the style rules for all of the `h1` elements on this

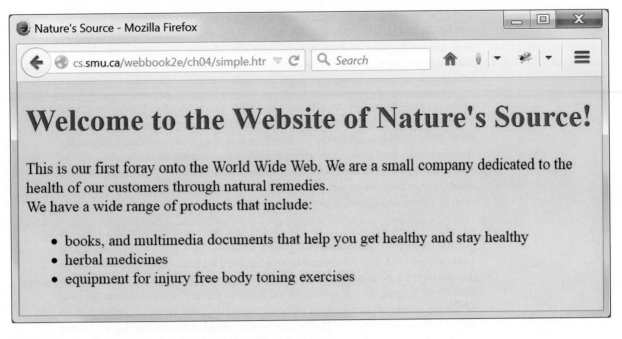

FIGURE 4.3 `graphics/ch04/displaySimpleHtml.jpg`
A Firefox browser display of `ch04/simple.html` from Figure 4.2, styled by the CSS in `ch04/css/simple.css` from Figure 4.1.

page (and possibly on many other pages, if those other pages are also linked to this CSS style document), you can change the color of *all* of those h1 elements by making one small change to the appropriate style rule in the linked CSS document.

4.5 Some Basic CSS Markup: More on Selectors, Declarations, Properties, and Property Values

In the previous section you saw how a (simple) CSS style rule is comprised of a selector, followed by a declaration block, and how a single declaration is in turn comprised of a property and its value, separated by a colon (:). In this section we will give a few examples of some more complex style rules involving multiple selectors and multiple declarations (property-value pairs). These typical examples will give you a good head start in creating style rules to fulfill your own needs, but they do not come close to showing you the full range of possibilities:

   h1, h2, h3 `{color: blue;}` This syntax, containing multiple, comma-separated selectors, means that *all three* header elements corresponding to those three selectors are to be displayed in blue text.

   p `{color: red; font-size: large;}` This syntax, with its two property-value pairs separated by a semicolon (;), means that *both* property-value pairs are to be applied to elements with the p tag (paragraphs). Clearly, a style like this one (large and red) would have the effect of catching your customers' attention and probably annoying them beyond the point of doing business with you.[1] As you might guess, you can have both multiple selectors, as in the preceding example, and multiple property-value pairs, as in the current example, within a single style rule.

`body {font-family: Verdana, Arial, sans-serif;}` This syntax, with a comma-separated list of property values for the `font-family` property, means that the browser should search for the Verdana font first, then Arial, and then whatever the system provides for a generic *sans-serif font* (that's a font *without* the little curlicues at the ends of its letters). If all these searches fail, the browser will simply use its default font, which may or may not be sans-serif. If a font-family name contains spaces, the name must be enclosed in quotes, as in `"Courier New"`, for example.

`ul li {font-style: italic;}` The first thing to note about this syntax is that the list of (two) selectors is *not* comma-separated. This rule says that the text of a list element (`li`), when it appears in an unordered list (`ul`), should be italicized. In this situation `li` is called a *descendant selector*, or sometimes a *contextual selector* (an older term), because the rule only applies to list items that are "descended from" (appear within the context of) an *unordered* list (a `ul` list with bulleted items, say, rather than an `ol` list with numbered items). Thus if a list item appeared within the tags for an ordered list (`ol`), its text would *not* be italicized in that context (at least it wouldn't be because of *this* rule).

The point of these examples is to show you

▶ How several HTML elements may be given the same style.
▶ How a single style may contain specifications for more than one property of an HTML element.
▶ How an HTML element may be given a certain style only if it is found in a particular context.

In the **Short Exercises** section at the end of this chapter you will have an opportunity to experiment with these style variations.

However, we have only shown a very limited number of properties that HTML elements may have, as well as a limited number of their corresponding property values. **TABLE 4.2** shows a few more property categories, in addition to the ones we've seen, along with just some of the properties in each category. There are many more of each, and no values are given for any of the properties in the table. In the next section we provide some additional detail on how CSS specifies font size, lengths of various kinds, and color. See also the **References** section at the end of this chapter for links to further information.

---

[1] The authors are more concerned with the technical aspects of web page development and do not consider themselves design experts. However, you may from time to time encounter a helpful reminder like this one.

TABLE 4.2 Some CSS property categories and some properties from each category.

Some Property Categories	Names of Some Properties in Each Category
background	`background-color, background-image, background-position`
font	`font-size, font-style, font-weight, font-family`
text	`text-align, text-decoration, color`
border	`border-width, border-style, border-color`
margin	`margin-left, margin-right`
padding	`padding-top, padding-bottom`

4.6 Some Common Types of CSS Property Values and Their Formats

One of the best ways to learn CSS is to study some CSS style rules and try to reconcile their content with the display of whatever HTML document employs those rules. However, when you begin to do this there is great potential for confusion, since the values of many CSS properties can be written in so many different ways. Thus if you look at CSS rules written by different authors it is quite likely you will notice inconsistencies that will raise some unsettling questions in your mind until you are able to recognize the equivalence of the various formats.

For example, if you look at **TABLE 4.3** you will see how much variety is possible just with units of measurement (for a property like `font-size`) or color (for a property like `background-color`, or `color` itself). And again, this is just part of the story. For links to more information, see the **References** section at the end of this chapter.

4.6.1 Specifying Measurement Property Values

The information shown in Table 4.3 requires some comment. The first line of information in this table shows that a number of common units like inches (`in`), centimeters (`cm`), and millimeters (`mm`) can be used to specify a measurement property like `font-size`. The point (`pt`) and pica (`pc`) units have been more commonly used by typesetters over the years, but find less use on the web. These units allow the user to choose "absolute" sizes, in contrast to the "relative" units of the next line in the table (`px`, `em`, and `ex`). Relative units are generally preferred to absolute units on the web because they "scale" up and down in size when the user adjusts the size of the browser window in a way that absolute units do not.

TABLE 4.3 Different formats for two kinds of CSS property values.

Property Value Category	Representations for Values in That Category
measurement (absolute units)	in, cm, mm, pt (point) (72pt = 1in), pc (pica) (1pc = 12pt)
measurement (relative units)	px (pixel), em (width of M), ex (height of x), % (percentage)
measurement (absolute keywords)	xx-small, x-small, small, medium, large, x-large, xx-large
measurement (relative keywords)	larger, smaller
color (hex)	#0000FF, #008000, #708090
color (hex short)	#00F, N/A, N/A
color (rgb absolute)	rgb(0,0,255), rgb(0,128,0), rgb(70,80,90)
color (rgb relative)	rgb(0%,0%,100%), rgb(0%,50%,0%), rgb(27%,31%,35%)
color (keywords)	blue, green, slategrey

The first of the relative units is *pixel* (px), whose size depends on screen resolution. The size of the other units is relative to the current font size. An em is the width of a capital M in the current font, an ex is the height of a lowercase x in the current font, and you may also specify a percentage of the current font-size value.

Sizes may also be specified using keywords (xx-large, x-large, and so on). These keywords provide "absolute" measurements only in the sense that you can (usually) expect that xx-large will be the same size as the font-size of the HTML h1 element, x-large the same as that used for the HTML h2 element, and so on, with xx-small "something smaller than h6", since there is no HTML h7 element. The "relative keywords" smaller and larger can also be used to specify a size smaller or larger than the current font size. A factor of 1.2 is generally used when scaling font sizes up or down. For example, the size of h2 text (x-large) is 1.2 times the size of h3 text (large), and so on.

Any of the following values may be regarded, most of the time, as representing the default font size in a browser: 12pt, 16px, 1em, 100%, medium. That fact alone should be enough to convince you to be wary of, and pay careful attention to, all the different variations of CSS property values that you will encounter.

4.6.2 Specifying Color Property Values

The remaining lines of Table 4.2 show the many ways you can specify colors on your web page. One common scheme is to use a "hex value" of six hexadecimal digits, preceded by a hash symbol (#),[2] you can choose any one of 16,777,216 colors. The 16 hexadecimal digits of the base-16 number system are 0 to 9 and A to F (or lowercase a to f). Your monitor may not be able to display all of these colors accurately, so you may be better off going with a color scheme that uses some of the more "standard" colors.

Note that if each group of two digits in a hexadecimal value contains two of the same digit, the value may be written in a shorthand form containing each digit once only. For example, `#22AA99` may be written as `#2A9`.

All colors are composed of various amounts of the three "primary" colors: red, green, and blue. In a six-digit hexadecimal value for color, the first two digits represent the amount of red, the next two the amount of green, and the last two the amount of blue. Thus any one of these colors can have a "hex value" in the range 00 to FF. This corresponds to the range 0 to 255 using decimal notation, or 0% to 100% if percentages are employed, either of which may be used if the user decides to go with the "rgb format" shown in the table.

Keywords like `blue` and `green` can also be used for common colors, as well as some less common ones like `slategrey`, but even here you need to be careful. For example, the color `blue` might be what you actually want when you choose that color, since it has the hex value `#0000FF` (the full amount of blue, and no red or green). But if you choose the keyword `green` for your color, you will get the color with hex value `#008000`, and not (as you might have expected) the color with hex value `#00FF00`. To get the latter color you must choose the keyword `lime`, but surely this is one of those things that is true only "for historical reasons".

Since CSS is case-insensitive, at least in this context, you can also write keyword colors `blue` and `slategrey` as `Blue` and `SlateGrey`. Using capital letters in this way enhances readability for multi-word names. You should decide which convention you wish to follow and stick with it. In other words, do not "mix and match". For reasons that we will discuss later, and just as a good general practice, it is always a good idea, and sometimes a critical requirement, for you to be completely consistent with the capitalization of names you use on your web pages.

The universal browser default color for text is `black` (`#000`), which contains no amount of either red, green, or blue, with a default background color of `white` (`#FFF`), which contains the full amount of all three primary colors.

Color Groupings

There are several "color groupings" you should be aware of as well. We will discuss this aspect of color very briefly here, explore the matter further in the exercises, and give you leads to further information in the end-of-chapter **References**.

The first and smallest of these color groupings consists of the 16 standard CSS colors. They all have keyword names, and here they are: `aqua`, `blue`, `black`, `fuchsia`, `gray`, `green`, `lime`,

---

[2] The symbol # has various names. Its technical name is *octothorpe*, believe it or not, but it is more commonly called the "number sign", or, as we have done, the "hash symbol". You may even see it referred to, somewhat confusingly, as the "pound symbol".

maroon, navy, olive, purple, red, silver, teal, white, yellow. You can expect to see each of them displayed properly in all browsers on all color monitors, regardless of age or computing platform being used.

The next group consists of the 216 colors in the so-called *web palette* of *web-safe colors*, also called the *web-safe palette*.[3] These colors are web-safe in the sense that they will probably display consistently across any platform capable of displaying up to 256 colors. Any color in the web-safe palette must have a hex value composed by choosing three values, with repetition allowed, from the following: 00, 33, 66, 99, CC, and FF. For example, #3366CC (or #36C) and #99FF00 (or #9F0) are web-safe colors. This was an important concept in the early days of the web, when color monitors were much less capable than they are now, but it can still serve as a useful guideline.

Another group of colors consists of all those colors that have recognized names, like the standard names blue and yellow that we have seen already, but many others we have not seen as well. Although many browsers recognize well over a hundred of these additional color names nowadays, there is still not as much conformity as we might like from one browser to another, so using a hex or rgb value for your desired color is usually a "safer" choice, and the one recommended. This is something that is likely to improve, stabilize, and perhaps even become a part of the CSS standard as time goes on.

4.6.3 The Important Takeaway from This Section

The thing to take away from this section is the desirability of choosing some conventions of your own to follow when you need to make use of a unit of measurement or a color or some other property whose values may be expressed in more than one way. Just as your web pages themselves should always have a consistent "look and feel", so should your behind-the-scenes HTML and CSS markup. You can achieve this by always using the same type of representation for a given kind of data. At the same time, become familiar enough with the alternate representations to be able to read the source code of web pages written by other developers when you want to do so.

4.7 CSS Style Sheet Structure, Comments, and Formatting

Because a CSS style sheet file is just a textfile having (normally) a .css extension, it can be created with any text editor. Good practice once again dictates that the file should have a comment containing at least the name of the file, and a brief description of the file's contents if required.

You should also give some thought to the organization of the rules within a style file. One way that lets you find the style of a particular element quickly is simply to order the HTML element selectors alphabetically, but this may only be practical for a short and simple CSS style sheet. Once you have a header, footer, and content sections in your HTML document, you will likely want

---

[3] This color grouping was developed by Lynda Weinman. If you're interested in online training, check out http://lynda.com, an online training company founded by Weinman and acquired in 2015 by LinkedIn.

```
1    /* mystyles.css for mystyles.html
2    A few styles to illustrate the structure and formatting of a
3    CSS style file
4    */
5
6    /* Styles that apply to every element in the body, unless overridden */
7    body {
8      font-family: Verdana, Arial, Helvetica, sans-serif;
9      font-size: large;
10     color: #000;
11     background-color: #FF0; /* yellow */
12   }
13
14   h1 { color: #00F; } /* Overrides body font color style above */
15
16   /* Styles any list item in an unordered list */
17   ul li {
18     font-size: medium; /* Overrides body text font size above */
19     font-style: italic; /* Adds italic style to text of list items */
20   }
```

FIGURE 4.4 `ch04/css/mystyles.css`
A CSS style sheet illustrating CSS comments and style rule formatting.

to group your CSS styles according to these and perhaps other divisions. A preceding comment describing each grouping is always a good idea.

FIGURE 4.4 shows the contents of the file `mystyles.css`. First of all, the file again shows a CSS comment that begins with a forward slash and asterisk as the opening delimiter (`/*`), and ends with an asterisk and forward slash as the closing delimiter (`*/`), as you have already seen in an earlier example. This kind of comment can be used for either single-line comments, multi-line comments, or end-of-line comments, all of which are illustrated in this file. The style of comment used by CSS goes all the way back to the C programming language, and is also used in programming languages of more recent vintage, including C++, Java, and JavaScript.

We find it convenient to format our CSS style files as shown in this example, though you will certainly see other formatting used if you look at other such files. Note that if there is a single declaration, we put everything on one line. Otherwise, we place each declaration on a line of its own, indented two spaces. In virtually every other context, we, who are big fans of readability, are inclined to use vertical alignment of braces as part of our formatting style. However, we find that with CSS, largely because there is no nesting of brace-enclosed blocks, the style illustrated here conserves some vertical space and is actually quite readable, as long as each rule is separated from the next by a blank line.

We apply the styles in this style file (or "style sheet") to an HTML file called `mystyles.html`. We do not show this file because its contents are exactly the same as those of the file `simple.html` of Figure 4.2, except that `mystyles.html` is, of course, now linked to the new CSS style file `mystyles.css`. The resulting display is shown in **FIGURE 4.5**.

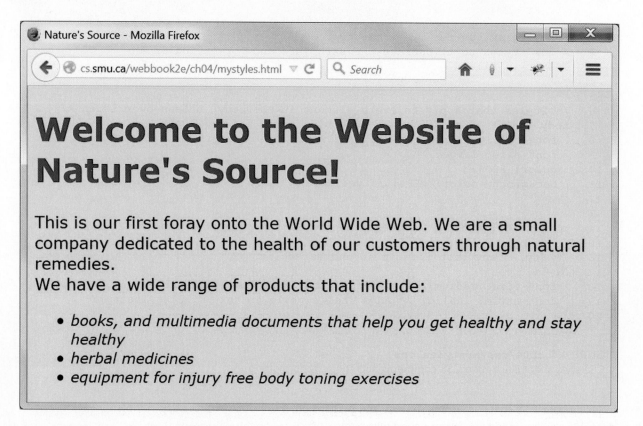

FIGURE 4.5 `graphics/ch04/displayMystylesHtml.jpg`
A Firefox browser display of `ch04/mystyles.html`, styled by the CSS in `ch04/css/mystyles.css` from Figure 4.4. The markup in `ch04/mystyles.html` is exactly the same as that in `ch04/simple.html` from Figure 4.2, except for the link to a different CSS style file.

The style of the `body` tag for the web page shown in Figure 4.5 requires a background color of yellow, with black text in a large Verdana font, if available, unless some other style "overrides" these properties (lines 7–12 of Figure 4.4). The first override takes place with the style of an `h1` element, which sets those elements to be displayed in blue (line 14 of Figure 4.4). The `h1` element also has a much larger font than the regular text, since this is part of the `h1` element's (default, browser-determined) specification, which we have not altered. Finally, an italic style is added to any elements that appear in an unordered list, and in addition, those same list elements have a font of size `medium`, which is just the default size, and which overrides the size `large` we specified earlier, and is used for the paragraph before the list (lines 17–20 of Figure 4.4).

See section 4.9 for more on how this "overriding" is handled in CSS by *inheritance* and *the cascade*.

4.8 The HTML `class` and `id` Attributes and the Non-Semantic HTML `div` and `span` Elements

Whenever we have defined a CSS style, up to this point, that style was applied to one or more HTML elements on a web page because we attached the style directly to one or more HTML tags in the style rule definition. In the context of CSS, each such *HTML element* became a *CSS selector*, and the given CSS style would apply to *each instance* of the HTML element found in the styled document.

As we continue to develop our website, we will also find it convenient to do one or more of the following, which we cannot do with the kinds of style rules we have seen so far:

▶ Apply a given style to some, but not to all, of the HTML elements of a particular type in a web page (to some of the paragraphs, but not to all of them, for example)

▶ Apply a given style to one or more HTML elements of different types at different places in a web page, while at the same time defining the style in only one place (giving this paragraph and that paragraph and those list items the same style, for example, and using just one style definition to do it)

▶ Apply a given style or set of styles to an entire section of a web page (to a contiguous sequence of paragraphs, lists, and other elements, for example, but not to the whole page)

▶ Apply a given style to some part of a page that is not a complete HTML element or group of elements (a single word or phrase within a paragraph, for example)

There are various ways we may accomplish some of these tasks, but the simplest approach to all of them involves the use of one or both of the two HTML attributes `class` and `id`, and the two HTML elements `div` and `span` that we mentioned in the previous chapter as examples of non-semantic elements.

4.8.1 The HTML `class` and `id` Attributes (CSS `class` and `id` Selectors)

Let's begin by stating two important facts:

1. Virtually every HTML element may be given a `class` attribute, or an `id` attribute, or both.
2. Just as any HTML element can become a CSS selector, so can either the `class` attribute or the `id` attribute, so we often refer to the CSS `class` selector or the CSS `id` selector.

Because of these two facts, we are able to use, in addition to element selectors, the `class` and `id` attribute selectors to help us style our web pages in the way that we shall now describe.

We first discuss the CSS class selector, with the help of the following example:

```
.BoldItalic {
  font-weight: bold;
  font-style: italic;
}
```

Here we have what we refer to as a CSS *class selector definition*, or just a *class definition* for short. We have chosen the name for our class to be `BoldItalic`, and we follow the name with the style declarations enclosed within braces, just as we would do for an element selector. Note, however, the period immediately preceding the class name. It is this period that identifies `BoldItalic` as the name of a class whose definition is contained within the following braces. The styles in the definition follow the declaration syntax with which we are already familiar.

Thus a CSS *class definition* is really just a mechanism for giving a name to a group of style declarations. The user-chosen name `BoldItalic` should, of course, be descriptive of the style(s) involved in a useful way. Certainly the name `BoldItalic` is very descriptive, but there is another very good reason why this is not a good name. Try to think of what this reason might be, and we will ask you for the answer in our end-of-chapter **Quick Questions** section.

Note how we capitalize our CSS class names, which is not required, but can serve to enhance readability and help distinguish class names from other entities in your file. This particular kind of CSS class definition is often called a "generic" class, since it can be applied to *any* HTML element, as you will see.

On the other hand, if we knew that we only wanted to apply the styles in the class called `Standout` to certain paragraph elements, we could make this clear, and restrict the use of the class to paragraph elements, by defining the class like this:

```
p.Standout {
   color: #FF0000; /* red */
   background-color: #D3D3D3; /* lightgrey */
}
```

The next question is: Once we have defined a class, how do we use it to achieve the styling it was designed to accomplish? In the case of `p.Standout` we would do this:

```
<p class="Standout">
This paragraph will really stand out on your page ...
</p>
```

Note how we use the `class` attribute of the HTML p tag and give it a value of `Standout` to indicate that this particular paragraph is to be displayed using the `Standout` style, and we could do this for however many paragraphs we wished to display in this way.[4] Other paragraphs, which have no `class` attribute, or whose `class` attributes do not have this value, are unaffected by the styles of the `Standout` class.

On the other hand, if we want to display a paragraph using our `BoldItalic` class, we simply do this:

```
<p class="BoldItalic">
This paragraph will appear in bold italic ...
</p>
```

---

[4] A valid question at this point is: "How does this differ from using the `style` attribute, which is discouraged?" The answer is that if you were to use the `style` attribute in the same way, and wanted to change its style, you would have to change the value of that `style` attribute in every element that had been styled in that way. If you use the `class` attribute, you need only change the definition of that class.

The usage syntax here is exactly the same as it was when we invoked the `p.Standout` class. But here's the difference. If we have a list element that we want to display using `BoldItalic`, we can do it in a precisely analogous way:

```
<li class="BoldItalic">
This list item will appear in bold italic ...
</li>
```

This is okay, since the `BoldItalic` class is "generic" and hence can be used with *any* HTML element tag that has a `class` attribute (virtually all of them do). However, we *cannot* use the `Standout` class here with the list element because it has been restricted to paragraph elements by its definition (recall that we defined it as `p.Standout`).

We could also use both classes for a paragraph, in which case the syntax is this:

```
<p class="BoldItalic Standout">
This paragraph will be styled by both CSS classes ...
</p>
```

The `id` selector is very much like the `class` selector, with respect to the way it is defined and used, but there are two major differences:

1. An `id` selector with a given value *must be unique within a web document*, unlike a `class` selector with a given value, which can appear many times in the same document.
2. The definition of an `id` selector is marked by an initial hash symbol (#), rather than the initial period (.) used in the definition of a `class` selector.

The uniqueness requirement allows an element with a particular `id` value to be distinguished from all other elements on the page. This will be very useful when we wish to access an element from within a JavaScript script, as we will do in later chapters. In our current context, it can be useful simply to identify uniquely a particular part of a web page document for styling.

There is no need to discuss the `id` selector further here, because of its similarity to the `class` selector. However, note that you will see it employed when we use CSS to style our skeleton website for Nature's Source, and you will note as well that we use the same *camel notation*[5] for capitalizing `id` selector names that we use for `class` selectors, except that we begin with a lowercase letter.

4.8.2 The HTML `div` and `span` Elements

Next, we introduce the HTML `div` and `span` elements. Neither of these elements has any default layout of its own. However, since the `span` element is an inline-level element, we can use a `span` tag pair to enclose an "inline" portion of some element on our web page (a word or phrase in a

---

[5] The term *camel notation* as used here means that in multi-word names, the second and subsequent words begin with a capital letter (forming the camel's "humps", so to speak). The first word of the name may or may not be capitalized, depending on convention. For us, for example, class selector names are capitalized, while id selector names are not.

paragraph, for example). Analogously, because the `div` element is a block-level element, we can use a `div` tag pair to enclose some "block-level" portion of our web page (several contiguous paragraph elements, for example).

Since both the `span` tag and the `div` tag may be given a `class` attribute, we can apply any generic `class` or `id` selector to a `span` or `div` element with the same usage syntax we have seen above. For example, if there is a section of the web page in which we wish the text to be displayed using a bold, italic style, we could enclose that part of the web page like this:

```
<div class="BoldItalic">
The part of the web page to have the BoldItalic style goes here ...
</div>
```

Or, if we want a single word within an otherwise "normal" paragraph to have the `BoldItalic` style, we could do this:

```
<p>
Your users might think you a <span class="BoldItalic">nutcase</span>
if you did a great deal of this, but it really is quite handy at times.
</p>
```

Of course, for this particular style you could also achieve the same effect just by using (properly nested) HTML tags, as in `<strong><em>nutcase</em></strong>`, but the CSS approach is much preferred, if only for the ease with which it allows you to change the style: Make one change to the style itself, and see the effect of that change everywhere the style is used!

4.8.3 Using Our Class Definitions

Let's put at least some of this to work. To illustrate our class definitions in action, we add them to the file `mystyles.css` from Figure 4.4 and call the new file `myclasses.css`, which is shown in **FIGURE 4.6**. Note that we have also added a new style, `BlackOnWhiteSerif`, which will provide us with a black serif font on a white background.

The HTML file to which we apply the styles in `myclasses.css` is `myclasses.html`, which is shown in **FIGURE 4.7**. This file contains essentially the same content as the file `simple.html` from Figure 4.2 and `mystyles.html`, which was not shown in the text because it was the same as `simple.html`, except for the link. This version is sufficiently different that we show it again, so that you can see how the markup in the HTML file accesses the CSS classes from the style file. The resulting display can be seen in **FIGURE 4.8**.

If we examine the HTML markup in Figure 4.7, we see that everything in the body of the page *except* the `h1` heading is now enclosed in a `div` element, and that `div` element has the `BlackOnWhiteSerif` generic class style applied to it.

```
1    /* myclasses.css for myclasses.html */
2
3    /* Styles that apply to every element in the body, unless overridden */
4    body {
5      font-family: Verdana, Arial, Helvetica, sans-serif;
6      font-size: large;
7      color: #000;
8      background-color: #FF0; /* yellow */
9    }
10
11   h1 { color: #00F; } /* Overrides body font color style above */
12
13   /* Styles any list item in an unordered list */
14   ul li {
15     font-size: medium; /* Overrides body font size above */
16     font-style: italic; /* Adds italic style to text of list items */
17   }
18
19   /* A "generic" class whose styles can be applied to any element */
20   .BoldItalic {
21     font-weight: bold;
22     font-style: italic;
23   }
24
25   /* A "generic" class whose styles can be applied to any element */
26   .BlackOnWhiteSerif {
27     padding: 30px; /* on all four sides of any element with this style */
28     font-family: Georgia, "Times New Roman", Times, serif;
29     color: #000;
30     background-color: #FFF;
31   }
32
33   /* A class that can only be applied to paragraph elements */
34   p.Standout {
35     padding: 15px; /* on all four sides of any paragraph with this style */
36     color: #F00; /* red */
37     background-color: #D3D3D3; /* lightgrey */
38   }
39
```

FIGURE 4.6 `ch04/css/myclasses.css`

A CSS style file containing the same styles as `ch04/css/mystyles.css` of Figure 4.4, plus two generic classes and one class that applies only to paragraphs.

```
1   <!DOCTYPE html>
2   <!-- myclasses.html -->
3   <html lang="en">
4     <head>
5       <meta charset="utf-8">
6       <title>Nature's Source</title>
7       <link rel="stylesheet" href="css/myclasses.css">
8     </head>
9     <body>
10      <h1>Welcome to the Website of Nature's Source!</h1>
11      <div class="BlackOnWhiteSerif">
12        <p>This is our first foray onto the World Wide Web. We are a small
13        company dedicated to the health of our customers through natural
14        remedies.</p>
15        <p class="Standout">We have a wide range of products that include:</p>
16        <ul>
17          <li>books, and multimedia documents that help you get healthy and
18          stay healthy</li>
19          <li class="BoldItalic">herbal medicines</li>
20          <li>equipment for injury free body toning exercises</li>
21        </ul>
22      </div>
23    </body>
24  </html>
25
```

FIGURE 4.7 `ch04/myclasses.html`
Another HTML document having the same content as `ch04/simple.html` from Figure 4.2, but now styled by the CSS in `ch04/css/myclasses.css`, which also requires adding CSS classes to the HTML markup.

To see how all of this comes together, and before continuing our discussion of this example, we need to say something about how a browser actually decides what style(s) to apply to a particular HTML element as a web page is rendered on the screen, which we do in the following section.

4.9 Inheritance and the Cascade

We are well into a chapter on CSS, but so far we have barely mentioned anything about the "Cascading" part of the title, so you may be starting to wonder why. The simple answer is that much of the time it is not something you need to worry too much about, since it often "takes care of itself". In fact, that is the general idea—it *should* take care of itself. This may well be all you ever need to know about such matters, but we also mention briefly in passing some of the details you may need to pursue if you have a mysterious problem of some kind and you need to track down its source, or you simply want to go beyond the basics.

As with many web technologies, the basic principles are quite straightforward, but the details can be quite complex. In this section we will just provide a brief overview of *inheritance* and the

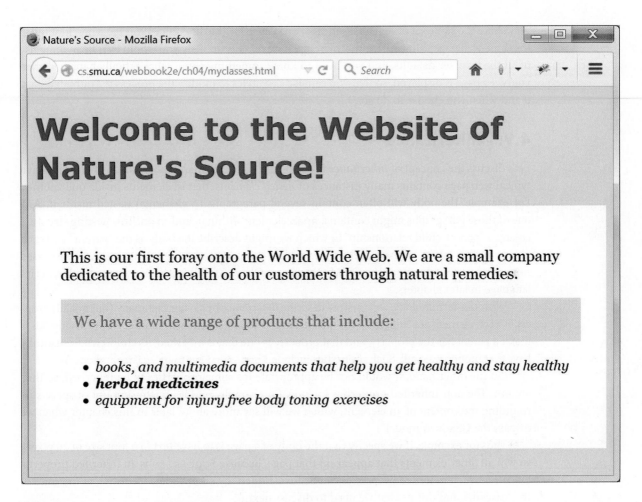

FIGURE 4.8 `graphics/ch04/displayMyclassesHtml.jpg`
A Firefox browser display of `ch04/myclasses.html` from Figure 4.7, styled by the CSS in `ch04/css/mystyles.css` from Figure 4.6.

cascade, which control in a crucial and (normally) unobtrusive way how things are displayed on our web pages. If you have some prior experience with programming (which may be useful for what comes later in this text, but should not be necessary), you will be familiar with the notion of *operator precedence*. This is what determines the order of operations in an arithmetic expression like 2 + 3 * 5 (the multiplication happens first, even though it appears second). Analogous ideas apply in the determination of how CSS styles are applied during the rendering and display of a web page by a browser. Simply put, some styles "take precedence" over others, and we need to know at least a little bit about how this happens.

First of all, when you do not explicitly say how you, want something on one of your web pages to be displayed, each browser has a set of defaults that it will use for that item. Not all browsers may share the same set of defaults, so this is one cause for the differences you see when looking at the same web page using different browsers. However, it is unlikely you would ever be making use of all the browser defaults, and you need to know something about what actually happens when your web page is displayed, so that you can use CSS styles to modify the process to your advantage if and when you choose to do so.

4.9.1 Inheritance

Let's discuss the concept of *inheritance* first. To help you understand inheritance, first recall that a typical web page contains many instances of *nested elements*, that is, elements inside one another. For example, the body will often contain several paragraphs (p elements) nested inside it. Any one of those paragraphs might contain a span element within it, and so on. This nesting structure creates a "parent-child relationship" in which we might describe the body as the "parent" and each paragraph as a "child" of that parent, for example. This parent-child relationship will be discussed further when we talk about the *DOM* (*Document Object Model*) in the context of the JavaScript language in later chapters.

With this terminology, we can now describe *inheritance* by saying that many (but not all) properties of an element are "inherited" by default from the parent element. Another way of saying this is that if a parent has the property, and that property is one that is inherited, its children automatically have that property as well. Such properties include font-family, font-size, and color.

On the other hand, it would not be appropriate for some properties to be inherited, so they are not. The non-inherited properties include, for example, padding (the amount of space surrounding the content of an element, which we will say more about later in this chapter when we discuss the CSS "box model").

Thus for example, if we specify that the body of a page is to have text in a font size of 20 pixels, so will all other elements that appear on that page, because font-size is an inherited property. Of course, such inherited properties can be "overridden" by other styles, according to the rules of the "cascade", and this is what we need to discuss next.

4.9.2 The "Cascade" and Resolution of Style Conflicts

You can easily imagine how a conflict might arise among styles. To take an extreme example, suppose for a given web page you gave a style rule in an external CSS style file that said all paragraph text should be blue. Then, in a document-level style sheet you gave another style rule that said all paragraph text should be green. Furthermore, for the third paragraph on the page, you specified in a style attribute for that p element that its text should be yellow.

This situation represents a "cascading" of styles (three of them, in this case), all applying (potentially, at least) to that third paragraph. What color text do you suppose that third paragraph would actually have?

Well, you could argue that what happens makes intuitive sense, and that's what we meant when we said earlier that most of the time you don't need to concern yourself with "the cascade" and how such conflicts are resolved.

The general rule is that the "most specific" style applies. The full set of rules used to determine the *specificity*[6] of an element and how the cascade will unfold in any given scenario is actually quite complicated, but in this case it simply means that the third paragraph will have yellow text because the attribute style is the "most specific" style that applies to this particular paragraph. In the absence of any other relevant styles, other paragraphs on this web page would have blue or green text depending on which came first in the `head` element of the document, the `style` element containing the embedded rule that says the text should be green or the link to the external document, which contains the rule saying the text should be blue.

The operative rule here is that, *all other things being equal*, whichever style rule is the last one seen by the browser is the one that is applied. Thus in our example, if the link follows the `style` element, the text will be blue, otherwise it will be green.

Because of this operative rule, you should follow these three steps when preparing styles for your website:

1. Begin by putting all your styles in an external style sheet, and linking that file to each of your pages. With luck you will be able to keep all your styles there, and if you can do this (which should be your initial design goal, at least) that's the end of the process.
2. If the styles in a particular document are modifications of the styles in the general document, you may wish to place the modifying styles in a `style` element in the `head` element of that document. If you do this, make sure that the `style` element comes after the `link` element that references the external style sheet, since both will appear in the same document `head` element.
3. As a last resort, if the style of a particular element needs to be tweaked, place the style in the value of the `style` attribute for the element itself. Try to avoid doing this if at all possible, since the practice is currently strongly discouraged, and may eventually be deprecated.

4.9.3 Applying the Theory to Our Example

Now let's go back to our example and explain why you see what you see in Figure 4.8. If you study the HTML markup (Figure 4.7) and its CSS styles (Figure 4.6), you will see that the body is given a background color of yellow and you can see this behind the `h1` welcome header at the top and at the sides and bottom of the display window.

Everything in the `body` element except for the `h1` element is enclosed within a `div` element, to which the class `BlackOnWhiteSerif` has been applied. The white background defined in this class gives a white background to the `div` element. Otherwise, the `div` element would have the

---

[6] The specificity of an element is a numerical quantity that allows elements to be compared to see which has the greater value, a value that can be used to help decide how a certain style is to be applied. If you will permit a moment's editorializing, let us say this: If you find yourself needing to calculate specificity on a regular basis, it is probably time to reevaluate your web development strategy.

default value of `transparent` for its `background-color` property and the yellow background of the `body` element would then "show through". The second paragraph within the `div` has the `lightgrey` background for that paragraph mandated by its `Standout` class.

As for the fonts and font colors, note first of all that a large, black Verdana font is specified as the font for the `body` element, but this font never actually shows up as specified because:

▶ The `h1` header text is blue (according to our styling of that element) and much larger (according to the browser default font size for `h1`, which we have not altered). Note as well that, in terms of specificity, an `h1` within a `body` element is "more specific" than a `body` element alone.

▶ The two paragraphs (`p` elements) in the `body` element are both within the `div` element that is styled by the `class` selector named `BlackOnWhiteSerif`, so they both have the Georgia serif font, again because a `p` element within a `body` element is more specific than a `body` element alone. Moreover, the second paragraph has the `Standout` style applied to it, which is still more specific (to that paragraph), so it has the red text and light grey background of the `Standout` class, in addition to the Georgia serif font.

▶ In the unordered list within the `div` element, the text is also italic, because all unordered list items have been styled italic, and the font size is `medium` (in effect, set back to the browser default). The `middle list` element is given the specific style `BoldItalic`, which of course renders its text bold, but the italic part of that style is redundant, since the overall style of the list is already italic.

Note that both the `BlackOnWhiteSerif` class and the `p.Standout` class also have a `padding` property. The amount of "padding" applied to an element is the amount of space surrounding the content of that element. For example, if a normal paragraph has some padding applied to it, there will be extra space around all four sides of the text in that paragraph. We will discuss more about padding (and margins) later, in the context of the CSS "box model".

The cumulative effect of all these styles results in the rather garish page you see in Figure 4.8. The colors and the spacing are not particularly pleasing, and of course you would probably not want a page to look like this. Nevertheless, from the striking color contrasts and other features of this example you should be able to get a feel for how styles can be used to alter the presentation of your web pages and how potential conflicts among styles are resolved, at least in simple cases.

4.10 Validating Our CSS Style Sheets

In the previous chapter we discussed what is meant for an HTML file to be *valid*. For the same reasons we want our HTML files to be valid (so they may be displayed correctly and consistently, we hope, by all browsers), we also want each of our HTML pages to use a *valid CSS style sheet*. The first requirement, then, is that we must follow all the CSS syntax rules when composing styles for our style sheets. Thus once again, a web developer needs to have at least some familiarity with what these rules are, and be able to follow them. For the most part this simply means following the syntax style for CSS style rules as we have discussed and illustrated them.

Also, as for HTML pages, we can employ a *CSS validator* to check the validity of our CSS style sheets. Here is a link to the CSS validator on the W3C site:

```
http://jigsaw.w3.org/css-validator/
```

To use the validator, first browse to this site, enter the URL of the CSS file you wish to validate, click on **More Options** and make sure the **Profile:** box shows the version of CSS against which you wish to validate your style sheet. Probably the best choice is CSS3, even if you are not actually using any new CSS3 features at the moment, since valid older CSS will still validate as CSS3 without difficulty. We usually refer to this sort of behavior as *backward compatibility*. Finally, click on the **Check** button to activate the validation.

For example, **FIGURE 4.9** shows a partial view of the validator page just as it is about to validate myclasses.css, and **FIGURE 4.10** shows the top part of the resulting browser display after the CSS file has been successfully validated as CSS3.

When validating a CSS style sheet, you actually have a choice: you can enter the URL of the CSS style sheet itself into the validator, or you can enter the URL of an HTML document that uses the style sheet you wish to evaluate. The latter choice will evaluate all the styles used by the HTML document, which may not be what you want if you are using more than a single style sheet source.

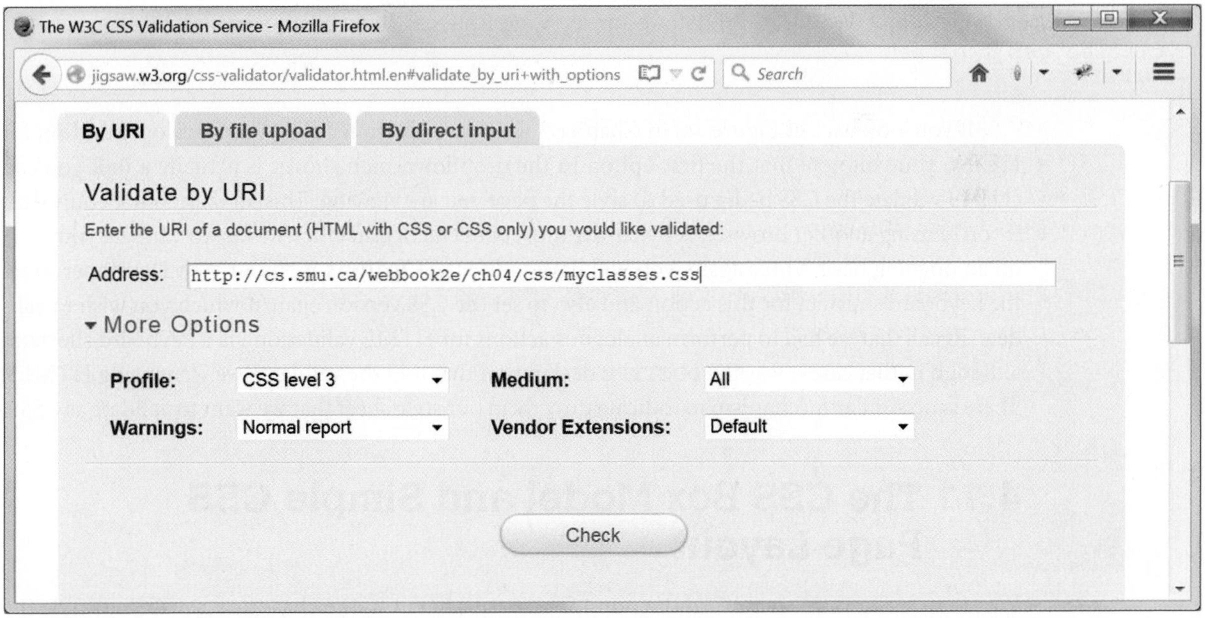

FIGURE 4.9 `graphics/ch04/displayMyclassesCssToValidate.jpg`
A Firefox browser display of the W3C CSS validator page just before clicking the Check button to validate the myclasses.css style sheet.

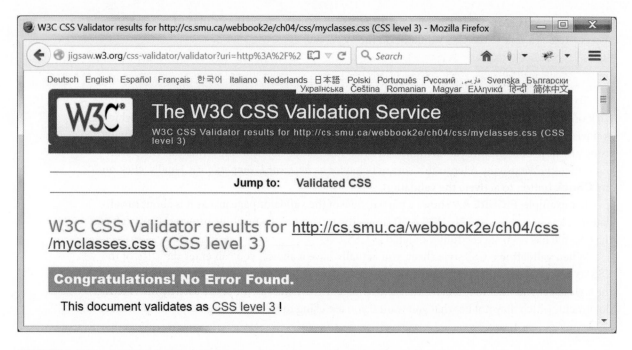

FIGURE 4.10 `graphics/ch04/displayMyclassesCssValidated.jpg`
A Firefox browser display of the W3C CSS validator page showing a successful validation of the `myclasses.css` style sheet.

If you look back at Figure 3.8 in Chapter 3 where we illustrated the Web Developer add-on for Firefox, you will note that the first option in the dropdown men shown is actually a link you can click to validate the CSS being used to style the page you are viewing. This, or something equivalent if you're using another browser, is by far the most convenient and efficient way to validate your CSS on an ongoing basis. Once again, you will have to use the **Options** menu in Web Developer to set the keyboard shortcut for this action and also to set the CSS version against which you wish to validate. Recall that we had to perform analogous actions for HTML validation via a keyboard shortcut, although in that case it was the `DOCTYPE` declaration that told the validator we were using HTML5. There is no similar mechanism to indicate directly in our style sheet that we want to validate as CSS3.

4.11 The CSS Box Model and Simple CSS Page Layout

We are working our way toward the point where we can cut to the chase and use CSS to style the website we have set up for our **Nature's Source** business. But before we do that we need to discuss the following additional concepts: the *CSS box model, CSS float positioning for simple page layout*, and *CSS reset*. It should help your understanding of these ideas to see each of them in isolation before encountering them in practice in the context of our sample website.

4.11.1 The CSS Box Model: A Conceptual View

The CSS box model is important because it underlies everything you see on a web page. Every element, whether it's an inline element, or a block element, or considered as something else within the new HTML5 content model, is treated as a "box", which has a content area at its center. This content area may (or may not) be surrounded by some "padding", which is often just whitespace around the content. This padding, in turn, may (or may not) be enclosed by a "border", and finally, the whole thing may (or may not) be surrounded by a "margin", which again is often just whitespace. These are often properties that you don't need to worry about because for many elements they may be absent altogether, or a browser may have default values for some of them if you do not specify them yourself. This can also be a source of the differences you see in displays of the same page in different browsers, since once again not all browsers will be using the same default values for these properties.

To make matters even more complicated, all three of these content-enclosing entities—padding, border, and margin—may appear on all four sides of the content box, or on just some of the sides. For a high-level, conceptual view of the CSS box model see **FIGURE 4.11**.

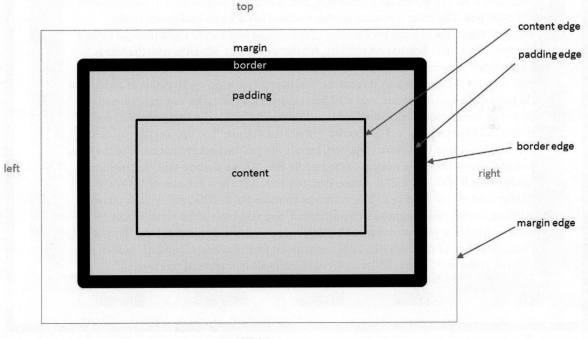

FIGURE 4.11 `graphics/ch04/BoxModel.jpg`
A conceptual view of the four key parts of the CSS box model "from the inside out": content, padding, border, and margin.

4.11.2 The CSS Box Model: A Detailed Example

Next, take a look at **FIGURE 4.12**, for which the corresponding HTML is given in **FIGURE 4.13** and the CSS is shown in **FIGURE 4.14**. This is once again a web page designed not to please the eye, but to illustrate some key points about the CSS box model. Begin by reading the text in Figure 4.12, which explains what you are seeing and encapsulates the essential features of the box model. Although you may be able to read it here in the text, we recommend that you display it in your browser of choice and read it there. It should look the same in any current browser.

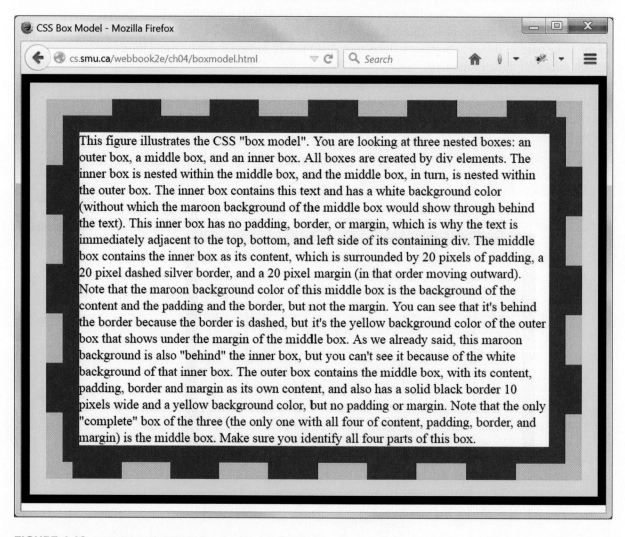

FIGURE 4.12 `graphics/ch04/displayBoxmodelHtml.jpg`
A Firefox browser display of `ch04/boxmodel.html`, illustrating the CSS box model. Be sure to read the content while studying the display.

```
1   <!DOCTYPE html>
2   <!-- boxmodel.html -->
3   <html lang="en">
4     <head>
5       <meta charset="utf-8">
6       <title>CSS Box Model</title>
7       <link rel="stylesheet" href="css/boxmodel.css">
8     </head>
9     <body>
10      <div id='outerBox'>
11        <div id='middleBox'>
12          <div id='innerBox'>
13            This figure illustrates the CSS "box model". You are looking at
14            three nested boxes: an outer box, a middle box, and an inner box.
15            All boxes are created by div elements. The inner box is nested
16            within the middle box, and the middle box, in turn, is nested
17            within the outer box. The inner box contains this text and has a
18            white background color (without which the maroon background of the
19            middle box would show through behind the text). This inner box has
20            no padding, border, or margin, which is why the text is immediately
21            adjacent to the top, bottom, and left side of its containing div.
22            The middle box contains the inner box as its content, which is
23            surrounded by 20 pixels of padding, a 20 pixel dashed silver
24            border, and a 20 pixel margin (in that order moving outward).
25            Note that the maroon background color of this middle box is the
26            background of the content and the padding and the border, but not
27            the margin. You can see that it's behind the border because the
28            border is dashed, but it's the yellow background color of the outer
29            box that shows under the margin of the middle box. As we already
30            said, this maroon background is also "behind" the inner box, but
31            you can't see it because of the white background of that inner box.
32            The outer box contains the middle box, with its content, padding,
33            border and margin as its own content, and also has a solid black
34            border 10 pixels wide and a yellow background color, but no padding
35            or margin. Note that the only "complete" box of the three (the only
36            one with all four of content, padding, border, and margin) is the
37            middle box. Make sure you identify all four parts of this box.
38          </div>
39        </div>
40      </div>
41    </body>
42  </html>
```

FIGURE 4.13 `ch04/boxmodel.html`
The HTML document that produced the CSS box model display of Figure 4.12.

```
1    /* boxmodel.css for boxmodel.html */
2
3    body {
4      padding: 0;
5      margin: 0;
6    }
7
8    div#outerBox {
9      border: 10px solid black; /* Shorthand for styling a border */
10     background-color: yellow;
11   }
12
13   div#middleBox {
14     padding: 20px;
15     border: 20px dashed silver;
16     margin: 20px;
17     background-color: maroon;
18   }
19
20   div#innerBox { background-color: #fff; }
```

FIGURE 4.14 `ch04/css/boxmodel.css`
The CSS style sheet used to style the HTML document in the `ch04/boxmodel.html` file of Figure 4.13 and produce the CSS box model display of Figure 4.12.

If you resize the page in your browser several times while viewing this file, you will experience in real time some essential-to-know default behavior of the box model. In particular, you will note how the various "boxes" on this particular page always expand horizontally to fill the browser window, whatever its width. That is the default behavior when no width is specified for the page body or for an outer box in a page layout.

Just as critical to observe is the fact that the behavior in the vertical direction is quite different. In this direction, only enough "expansion" takes place to accommodate the content, whatever the size of the browser window. Once again, this is best seen and appreciated by adjusting the size of your browser window while displaying the page, but even in Figure 4.12 you can see a white strip along the bottom, which confirms that the boxes have not expanded downward to fill the browser window. Note that throughout any resizing of the browser window, the 20px and 10px widths specified in the CSS style sheet of Figure 4.14 are retained.

Study this example carefully. We do not pretend that it shows you everything there is to know about the CSS box model. However, you can learn a great deal about that model by experimenting with this example, and in particular by changing the property values in the style sheet shown in Figure 4.14.

One final item of interest in this example is the "shorthand" form of the border style shown in Figure 4.14. This works as follows. Line 9 of the file, which is the single style rule

```
border: 10px solid black;
```

is actually a shorthand form for the following three style rules:

```
border-width: 10px;
border-style: solid;
border-color: black;
```

It should be clear that shorthand forms for CSS styles can be handy for reducing the size of your style sheets, and you should become familiar with them. For further information see the **References** section at the end of the chapter.

4.11.3 Simple CSS Page Layout with `float` and `clear` via the "Legacy" Approach with `div` Elements

We already know how the inline and block elements found on a web page are rendered by a browser and displayed on a user's screen. Often, especially with very simple web pages, it may be perfectly okay for a web developer to "go with the flow" and let some or all of the web pages on a site be displayed in the default manner.

On the other hand, users generally expect to see something a little more interesting, especially on a site's home page, with a menu of options leading to other parts of the site, and perhaps some animation or at least an image or two for some color. And nowadays users fully expect to encounter pages capable of user interaction, for feedback, for payment for goods, and so on, especially on the sites of companies that expect to do business with their visitors.

The design of such sites very quickly leads to the desire by developers to exercise control over where things appear on their web pages, and hence to the question of how one can control element positioning via CSS. This too is a complicated subject, so we will give only a brief introduction here, and once again refer you to the **References** section at the end of the chapter for further information.

Another simple example will be useful for illustrating what we want to say here about CSS positioning, and you will also need to study the redesign of our **Nature's Source** website, which we discuss in the following sections.

For our purposes, we only need to understand the use of the CSS `float` and `clear` properties, which are illustrated by the page shown in **FIGURE 4.15**, whose HTML markup and CSS styles are given in **FIGURE 4.16** and **FIGURE 4.17**, respectively. These three figures together comprise the "legacy" version of this example, which makes extensive use of the non-semantic `div` element. In the next section, we "update" this example to a more modern approach, replacing each non-semantic `div` with a new HTML5 semantic element.

Note that the HTML markup in Figure 4.16 consists of four `div` elements nested inside a fifth "outer" `div` element, with each `div` element having an `id` attribute whose value is defined as an `id` selector in the CSS style sheet shown in Figure 4.17. Without the use of the CSS

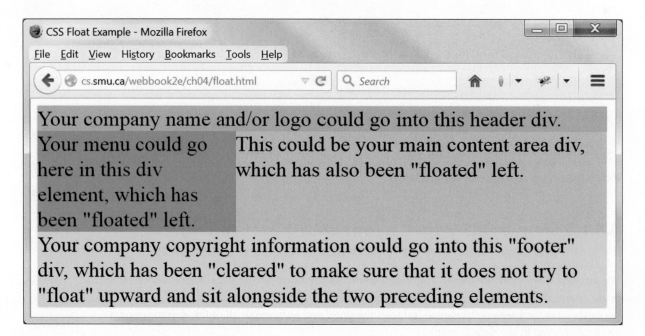

FIGURE 4.15 `graphics/ch04/displayFloatHtml.jpg`
A Firefox browser display of ch04/`float.html`, styled by the CSS in ch04/css/`float.css` and illustrating CSS positioning of `div` elements using floats.

`float` property, all four of the inner `div` elements would display one after the other in a vertical sequence. The `div` identified as `menu`, however, has a `float` property with a value of `left`, which causes that `div` element to "float" up and to the left, with subsequent elements wrapping around it on the right if there is room for them to do so. Similarly, the same property and value for the `div` identified as `content` causes that `div` element also to float up and to the left and position itself to the right of the `div` with value `menu`.

Elements that are "floated" like this must have their widths specified, and the width of the containing element must be adequate to hold the two inner `div` elements side by side if that is how we wish them to appear. The "containing element" in this case is the `div` identified as `page`. Since the `menu` `div` is 35% (of the enclosing `page` `div`) and the `content` `div` is 65% (of the enclosing `page` `div`), this criterion is satisfied. A warning here is in order, however. If you use percentage widths in this way, browser rounding of calculated values may cause the total width of the enclosed elements to exceed the width of their container, leading to problems. For that reason, pixel widths might be safer.

The `clear` property, with its value of `left`, will ensure that the `div` element identified as `footer` does *not* float up and to the left, even if there is room for it.

Elements can also be floated to the right, with a value of `right` for the `float` property, in which case a following element will float upward and wrap itself around the right-floated element on the left, if there is room. But, just for the record, elements cannot be floated to the center.

```
1   <!DOCTYPE html>
2   <!-- float.html -->
3   <html lang="en">
4     <head>
5       <meta charset="utf-8">
6       <title>CSS Float Example</title>
7       <link rel="stylesheet" href="css/float.css">
8     </head>
9     <body>
10      <div id="page">
11        <div id="header">
12          Your company name and/or logo could go into this header div.
13        </div>
14        <div id="menu">
15          Your menu could go here in this div element, which has been
16          "floated" left.
17        </div>
18        <div id="content">
19          This could be your main content area div, which has also been
20          "floated" left.
21        </div>
22        <div id="footer">
23          Your company copyright information could go into this "footer" div,
24          which has been "cleared" to make sure that it does not try to
25          "float" upward and sit alongside the two preceding elements.
26        </div>
27      </div>
28    </body>
29  </html>
30
```

FIGURE 4.16 `ch04/float.html`
The HTML document that produced the display of Figure 4.15. Take particular note of all the `div` elements and their `id` attributes.

4.11.4 Simple CSS Page Layout with `float` and `clear` via the "Modern" Approach with HTML5 Semantic Elements

In this section we redo the example of the previous section, and you should make sure you understand why we bother to do so. The reason is this: We think that seeing how something used to be done, and then how it should be done now, in two side-by-side examples, will give you a much better appreciation for the new way of doing that thing.[7]

---

[7] This is sometimes a very useful approach to learning, and actually has a name: *Ontogeny recapitulates phylogeny*, or *recapitulation theory*. We say no more, except that you might want to google it.

```
1    /* float.css for float.html */
2
3    body { font-size: 1.5em; }
4
5    div#page {
6      width: 650px;
7      background-color: silver;
8    }
9
10   div#header {
11     width: 100%;
12     background-color: aqua;
13   }
14
15   div#menu {
16     float: left;
17     width: 35%;
18     background-color: lime;
19   }
20
21   div#content {
22     float: left;
23     width: 65%;
24   }
25
26   div#footer {
27     clear: left;
28     width: 100%;
29     background-color: yellow;
30   }
```

FIGURE 4.17 `ch04/css/float.css`
The CSS style sheet used to style the HTML document in `ch04/float.html` of Figure 4.16 and produce the display of Figure 4.15.

So, first compare **FIGURE 4.18** with Figure 4.15. They look exactly the same, except in the first the text talks about the `div` elements used to produce it, while in the second the text talks about the new HTML5 semantic elements `header`, `nav`, `article`, and `footer`. Next, compare the HTML document in **FIGURE 4.19** with the one in Figure 4.16, and note how the `div` elements in the first have been replaced by the HTML5 semantic elements in the second. Note too how the value of the `id` attribute of a `div` element relates to the choice of the HTML5 semantic element. This illustrates what we said earlier about how the names of the new HTML5 semantic elements were chosen. Finally, compare **FIGURE 4.20** with Figure 4.17, and note how exactly the same styles are being used, in the first case for styling the `div` elements, and in the second case for styling the semantic elements.

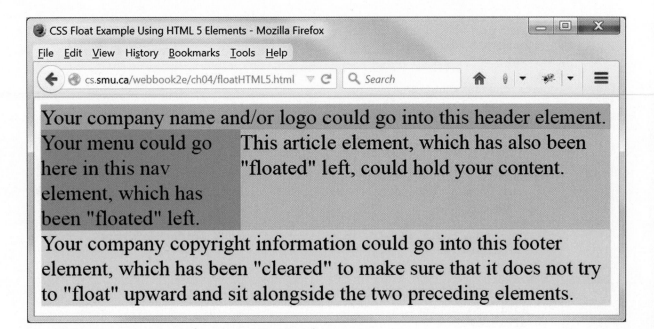

FIGURE 4.18 `graphics/ch04/displayFloatHTML5Html.jpg`
A Firefox browser display of `ch04/floatHTML5.html`, styled by the CSS in `ch04/css/floatHTML5.css` and illustrating CSS positioning of HTML5 semantic elements using floats.

This should not be interpreted to mean that the `div` element is obsolete. Far from it. There will still be lots of occasions when you simply want to group some block-level elements together and those elements have no obvious "natural" group name that suggests itself, and hence no corresponding HTML5 semantic element that you can use.

4.12 CSS Reset: A "Best Practice"

We should mention one other very useful concept that you may wish to explore before proceeding too far with the development of your website: the *CSS reset*. This notion relates to the fact that all browsers work with a number of default values for things like padding, margins, font size, and so on, but these defaults are not consistent across the various browsers.

Thus it makes sense for a web developer to reset certain values to a "baseline level", after which whatever values are desired can be set by the developer, using rules that are seen by the browser later than those that performed the CSS reset.

Some web developers have spent considerable time thinking about this and have recommendations of what to reset and how. Needless to say, they don't all agree. See the **References** section at the end of the chapter for further information.

```
1    <!DOCTYPE html>
2    <!-- floatHTML5.html -->
3    <html lang="en">
4      <head>
5        <meta charset="utf-8">
6        <title>CSS Float Example Using HTML5 Elements</title>
7        <link rel="stylesheet" href="css/floatHTML5.css">
8      </head>
9      <body>
10       <main>
11         <header>
12           Your company name and/or logo could go into this header element.
13         </header>
14         <nav>
15           Your menu could go here in this nav element, which has been
16           "floated" left.
17         </nav>
18         <article>
19           This article element, which has also been "floated" left, could
20           hold your content.
21         </article>
22         <footer>
23           Your company copyright information could go into this footer
24           element, which has been "cleared" to make sure that it does
25           not try to "float" upward and sit alongside the two preceding
26           elements.
27         </footer>
28       </main>
29     </body>
30   </html>
31
```

FIGURE 4.19 `ch04/floatHTML5.html`
The HTML document that produced the display of Figure 4.18. Compare the markup in this figure with that in Figure 4.16 and note how a new HTML5 semantic element has replaced each of the div elements in the previous markup.

For a very simple example, you might want to have the following rule as the very first one in your CSS style sheet:

```
* {
    padding: 0;
    margin: 0;
}
```

This rule uses the *universal selector* (*) to remove any browser-imposed margin and padding from *every* element on your web page, giving you free rein to establish your own margin and

```
1    /* floatHTML5.css for floatHTML5.html */
2
3    body { font-size: 1.5em; }
4
5    main {
6      width: 650px;
7      background-color: silver;
8    }
9
10   header {
11     width: 100%;
12     background-color: aqua;
13   }
14
15   nav {
16     float: left;
17     width: 35%;
18     background-color: lime;
19   }
20
21   article {
22     float: left;
23     width: 65%;
24   }
25
26   footer {
27     clear: left;
28     width: 100%;
29     background-color: yellow;
30   }
```

FIGURE 4.20 `ch04/css/floatHTML5.css`
The CSS style sheet used to style the HTML document of Figure 4.19 and produce the display
of Figure 4.18.

padding for individual elements. Note, however, that this depends on the above rule being properly implemented in the browser, which is unfortunately not guaranteed to be universally true
either. However, we do use this rule ourselves in the restyling of our **Nature's Source** website, as
you will see.

You might find it "safer" to set the `margin` and `padding` properties to zero on all elements
you intend to use individually. For example, note that in the CSS shown in Figure 4.14 we have
used the style rule

```
body {
  padding: 0;
  margin: 0;
}
```

to remove any margin or padding that the browser would otherwise apply to any body element on our site. Because we have done this, we see no whitespace at the top or sides of our box model display in Figure 4.12. It is an interesting experiment to remove this style rule from the CSS file and redisplay `boxmodel.html` in several different browsers to see what (default) spacing shows up in each browser. We have not done this for the CSS used for Figure 4.15 or Figure 4.18, and you can see the surrounding default whitespace inserted by the browser.

4.13 Styling Our Nature's Source Website with CSS (Four Versions, Illustrating CSS3, Simple "Responsive Design", and the New HTML5 video Element)

The implementation of CSS in various browsers has been quite slow and very uneven over the years. Internet Explorer, which for a time was the most widely used browser, was particularly lax in standards compliance. The situation in all major browsers is now much better, and is improving rapidly. In any case, virtually any modern browser can be expected to support the CSS page layout features that permit web developers to move away, finally, from using HTML tables for this purpose.

We will show you in our examples what we believe to be "proper" behavior, given our markup and our styles, and based on current information at the time of this writing. We will also continue to use Firefox as our browser of choice to display our pages the way we think they should look, and the way we hope they will eventually look in all browsers. Your particular browser might not behave in quite the same way, but as time goes on all browsers should converge on the ideal and identical behavior as mandated by the evolving standards. Simply put, in a short text like this one we cannot delve into the intricacies of cross-browser support (making your pages look the same in a number of different browsers), and one hopes that such efforts will be needed less and less in the reasonably near future.[8]

We will discuss in some detail each of the four different versions of our **Nature's Source** website for this chapter, each of which will now be styled with CSS. All of the CSS we have previously discussed in this chapter was available in CSS 2.1, the latest version before the advent of CSS3. In the upcoming discussion we will introduce some additional "legacy" features of CSS, as well as some newer features only available in CSS3. There is much more available from CSS3 than we will have time or space to cover, and you should plan to keep your finger on the pulse of the ongoing development in this area. Once again, see the end-of-chapter **References** section for some useful links.

The four versions of our **Nature's Source** website that we present in this chapter and discuss next are these:

1. Version 1: A Simple Home Page Only (compare its look and feel with `nature1` of Chapter 3)
2. Version 2: A Multipage Site with Menu and Footer (compare its look and feel with `nature2` or `nature3` of Chapter 3)

---

[8] Although we will not discuss the jQuery JavaScript library, this is a good place to mention that one of the nice things it will do for you is this: When using it to perform various tasks on your web pages, you generally don't have to worry about the kind of cross-browser differences we refer to here.

3. Version 3: A Revision of Version 2 Incorporating Some CSS3 and Illustrating Simple "Responsive Design"
4. Version 4: A Copy of Version 3 with the Home Page Image Replaced by a Home Page Video

We will discuss in detail the CSS used to style versions 1 and 2 of this chapter's **Nature's Source** website and present the complete CSS style sheet for each version in the text. For versions 3 and 4 much of the CSS used is the same, so we discuss only the major additions or changes to the previous versions.

4.13.1 Version 1: A Simple Home Page Only

This version of our website is analogous to that of the single-page website in `ch03/nature1`, but the site is now styled with CSS instead of using HTML table layout. Recall that the display in Figure 3.10 of Chapter 3 was produced with HTML table layout by the markup shown in Figure 3.9. In **FIGURE 4.21** we show another version of this display, but this time it is produced by the HTML markup shown in **FIGURE 4.22**, which is linked to the CSS style file shown in **FIGURE 4.23**.

FIGURE 4.21 `graphics/ch04/nature1/displayIndexHtml.jpg`
A Firefox browser display of `ch04/nature1/index.html` from Figure 4.22, the home page of version 1 of our **Nature's Source** website for this chapter, consisting of a single page styled by the CSS in `ch04/nature1/css/default.css` from Figure 4.23. Photo: © AlexBrylov/iStockphoto

```
1    <!DOCTYPE html>
2    <!-- index.html for ch04/nature1 -->
3    <html lang="en">
4      <head>
5        <meta charset="utf-8">
6        <title>Nature's Source - Canada's largest specialty vitamin store</title>
7        <link rel="stylesheet" href="css/default.css">
8      </head>
9      <body>
10       <header>
11         <div id="logo">
12           <img src="images/naturelogo.gif" alt="Nature's Source Logo"
13           width="608" height="90">
14         </div>
15         <div id="address">
16           5029 Hurontario Street Unit 2<br>
17           Mississauga, ON L4Z 3X7<br>
18           Tel: 905.502.6789<br>
19           Fax: 905.890.8305
20         </div>
21       </header>
22       <main>
23        <article>
24          <div id="text">
25            <h4>Welcome to Nature's Source - Protecting your health
26            naturally!</h4>
27            <p>Founded in 1998, Nature's Source was created to serve those who
28            use alternative healing methods. Offering only the highest quality
29            vitamins, minerals, supplements &amp; herbal remedies, Nature's
30            Source takes great pride in helping people live healthier, happier
31            lives.</p>
32            <p>Many companies that talk about customer service fail to
33            deliver. Nature's Source exists to truly serve all the needs of
34            their customers. Each location features dedicated on-site
35            therapists along with knowledgeable staff who ensure that every
36            customer receives the best quality information available.
37            Continuing education seminars are a regular event at Nature's
38            Source.</p>
39          </div>
40          <div id="image">
41            <img src="images/outdoor4.jpg" alt="Get healthy and stay healthy"
42                width="256" height="256">
43          </div>
44        </article>
45       </main>
46      </body>
47    </html>
```

FIGURE 4.22 `ch04/nature1/index.html`
The HTML document that produced the display shown in Figure 4.21. Still using some div elements, but also introducing the HTML5 semantic elements `main`, `header`, and `article`.

```
1    /* default.css for ch04/nature1/index.html */
2
3    * {
4      padding: 0;
5      margin: 0;
6    }
7
8    /* The following line may be redundant, but does no harm. */
9    main, header, article {display: block;}
10
11   body {
12     width: 900px;
13     font-family: Verdana, Arial, Helvetica, sans-serif;
14     font-size: 1em;
15   }
16
17   main, header {
18     margin: 10px;
19     width: 880px;
20   }
21
22   div#logo {
23     float: left;
24     margin: 10px 0;
25   }
26
27   div#address {
28     float: right;
29     margin-top: 20px;
30     text-align: right;
31   }
32
33   div#text {
34     float: left;
35     width: 570px;
36     margin-top: 20px;
37   }
38
39   div#text p {
40     margin: 1em .2em .7em 0;
41   }
42
43   div#image {
44     float: left;
45     width: 310px;
46     margin-top: 20px;
47     text-align: right;
48   }
49
```

FIGURE 4.23 `ch04/nature1/css/default.css`
The CSS style sheet used to style the HTML document `ch03/nature1/index.html` of Figure 4.22 and produce the display in Figure 4.21.

If you look at the HTML markup in Figure 4.22, you see there is no longer any sign of any HTML table element. Instead, we have used a combination of non-semantic HTML `div` elements and their CSS `id` selectors, together with some HTML5 semantic elements, to produce essentially the same display we had in Figure 3.10. This is what we mean by a CSS layout, as opposed to the HTML table layout you saw earlier, and which new markup should avoid.

It is a very simple page layout design that we are using here. You should be prepared to leverage your knowledge of the CSS box model and floats from your study of Figures 4.12 and 4.15 and their associated files to help you understand this version of our **Nature's Source** website.

First, note that at the highest level, from the user's point of view, this page contains four items: the company logo (upper left), the company address (upper right), some text (lower left), and an image (lower right). As the HTML markup in Figure 4.22 shows, each of these is contained in its own `div` element. These `div` elements are identified as `logo`, `address`, `text`, and `image`. Furthermore, the `logo` and `address` divs are enclosed in a higher-level HTML5 semantic `header` element, and the `text` and `image` divs are enclosed in a higher-level HTML5 semantic `article` element. Finally, the article element is contained within a `main` element, only because in this case the `article` element is the only content we have for the "main" part of our web page.

We will now discuss the CSS in Figure 4.23. We make the following observations:

▶ The first style (lines 3–6) is a "CSS mini-reset" that removes padding and margins from all elements by styling the universal selector (`*`) accordingly, and was discussed earlier.

▶ We ensure that each of the HTML5 semantic elements `main`, `header`, and `article` will be treated as a block-level element by setting its display property to a value of `block` (line 9). Browsers will probably treat these elements like this by default, but this is exactly the kind of thing about which you cannot be too careful.

▶ We choose our own default font family and font size for the `body` element (recall that these will be inherited) (lines 11–15). We also do something else here for the first time: We choose a width for the body of 900 pixels. There is nothing special about the value 900; in fact, it might be a little high if you were expecting to have a lot of visitors using monitors with the 800 by 600 screen resolution, but it should not be a problem for most visitors these days.

▶ Note that our chosen width for the `header` and `main` elements, together with their margin widths on the left and right, add up to the width of the `body` element, within which they are contained (lines 17–20).

▶ We do not provide any styles for the `article` element, since by default its width will be the same as its parent, the `main` element, and it needs no other styles. Thus you could easily argue that it was unnecessary even to use an `article` element at all, but you could also just as easily argue that doing so helps us to understand the structure of the HTML markup in Figure 4.22.

▶ The `logo` div and the `address` div (lines 22–31), which form the content of the `header` element, are not given specific widths either. This is because the logo image has an intrinsic width of 608 pixels (see Figure 4.22, line 13), and the remaining horizontal space on the right is more than sufficient to hold the text of the company address. Furthermore, by floating the `logo` `div` left and the `address` `div` right, we ensure that any "leftover whitespace" will be in between the logo and the address.

▶ This style sheet provides a good opportunity to see some CSS "shorthand" style rules in action. Note that in the style for the `header` and `main` elements we have given the `margin` property a single value of `10px`. This means there will be a 10-pixel margin on all four sides of the `header` element as well as the main element. However, let's note here a very important fact that you should not forget:

> **Adjacent margins in the vertical direction "collapse" to the value of the larger of the two adjacent margins. But . . . adjacent margins in the horizontal direction do not collapse. And, by the way, padding does not collapse in any direction.**

In this context that means that the margin at the bottom of the `header` element and the margin at the top of the `main` element, each of which is 10 pixels, will "collapse" to a single 10-pixel value since both values are the same. The `div#logo` style gives the `padding` property a value of `10px 0`. This means that the top and bottom of the `logo` `div` will have 10 pixels of padding, but there will be no padding on either side. Finally, the `div#address` style gives the `padding` property the value `20px 0 0 0`, which puts 20 pixels of padding at the top of this `div`, and no padding on either the left, right, or bottom. Note that when four explicit values are given, the order must be for the top, right, bottom, and left sides. Note too that in this case, when a single nonzero value is required, and it applies to the top only, the entire rule could be replaced by the rule `padding-top: 20px`, and similar options apply to the other three sides if required.

▶ The `text` `div` and the `image` `div` (lines 33–48) are both contained within the `article` element and both are also floated left. To make them sit next to each other and take up the appropriate amount of horizontal space in each case, we give them specific widths that sum to the required total of 900 pixels.

▶ The `div#image` style also includes 20 pixels of margin at the top to push the image down a bit, and a `text-align` property with a value of `right`. This may seem a bit odd, since the `image` `div` contains no text. However, recall that the HTML `img` element is an *inline* element that will show up in the middle of text just like a word, so the `text-align` property has the same effect on an image as it would have on some paragraph text.

▶ Since our "CSS mini-reset" at the beginning of our style sheet removed all margins and padding, we have to restore either or both, even for paragraphs, if we want to have one or the other. Thus we restore just the margins we want for `p` elements within the `text` `div` with the `div#text p` style.

You should take some time to make sure you understand how each of the styles you see in this style sheet affects the relevant markup in the HTML file. Experiment by changing some of the values to see the resulting effect on the page display.

And one final note: If you compare again the browser displays in Figures 3.10 and 4.21, there is really only one obvious difference to a viewer, despite the major "behind-the-scenes" differences. In Figure 3.10 the address text is left-justified, which is the default and we had no (valid) way to change it without CSS. In Figure 4.21 the same text is right-justified, which we think looks a little better, and now, with CSS, we can achieve that effect (see line 30 of Figure 4.23).

4.13.2 Version 2: A Multipage Site with Menu and Footer

This version of our website is analogous to that of either ch03/nature2 or ch03/nature3 (recall that both of those sites looked the same to a viewer), but as with version 1 the site is now styled with CSS instead of using HTML table layout. This is the extended version of our **Nature's Source** website, which has multiple pages in addition to the home page. A main menu appears on each page, as does a footer, which includes two additional menu links. And, as before, some of the additional pages also contain submenu links.

Recall that the display in Figure 3.12 of Chapter 3 was produced with HTML table layout by the markup shown in Figure 3.11. In **FIGURE 4.24** we show the current version of this home page display, this time produced by the HTML markup of ch04/nature2/index.html shown in **FIGURE 4.25** and styled by the CSS of ch04/css/default.css shown in **FIGURES 4.26**, **4.27**, and **4.28**. Note that the markup shown in Figure 4.25 incorporates external HTML markup files accessed via SSI, so for that reason it is, at least "behind the scenes", more like ch03/nature3 than like ch03/nature2.

The first thing you should do is conduct your own "tour" of this version of the website. Make sure that you click on all links to confirm that the pages look the same as they did in Chapter 3. Here in the text we show only the HTML markup for the home page (Figure 4.25), but you should examine the markup files for the other pages on this site as well since we are now employing HTML5 semantic elements in many places where the div element had been used previously, in addition to the use of CSS for layout and styling. We make the following observations and suggestions for your examination of the style sheet for this site (Figures 4.26 to 4.28):

▶ The style sheet has some brief comments describing each of its sections, which you should read to get an overview before looking more closely at the file.

▶ This one style sheet contains all of the CSS for the site. But because not all pages have the same layout, not all styles are used on every page. What is common to each page file is the "document header" information, the logo, the main menu under the logo, and the copyright information and a couple of additional links (a mini-menu, if you like) in the footer. The markup for these common items comes from four external files via SSI, just as it did previously, but that markup is now styled by CSS.

▶ The "content" area of the site pages, the part between the main menu and the footer, has three variations. The home page has some text at the left and an image on the right. It is the only page like this. Most other pages have some text at the right, and a permanently dropped-down menu at the left. Finally, some pages have only text in the content area.

FIGURE 4.24 `graphics/ch04/nature2/displayIndexHtml.jpg`
A Firefox browser display of `ch04/nature2/index.html` from Figure 4.25, the home page of version 2 of our Nature's Source website for this chapter, styled by the CSS in `ch04/nature2/css/default.css` from Figures 4.26, 4.27, and 4.28, and containing menu links to other pages and a footer. Photo: © AlexBrylov/iStockphoto

▶ We do not discuss margins, padding, fonts, text alignment, and the like again, since we hope these have been adequately covered in previous discussions, at least to the point where you should be able to figure out how those things work in the current context. It is worth noting here that when looking at someone else's style sheet you will see numerical values for things like margins, padding, and font size, and you may wonder where these came from. The answer is almost always "by applying a little blood, sweat, and tears"; in other words, by trial and error. You often have to keep experimenting and adjusting such values until you get the right "mix" of values for your particular situation. For example, look at the styling of the nav elements in lines 37 to 51 of Figure 4.26.

▶ The first new feature that we do need to address is the menus, and how they are constructed. Our menus are actually lists, but lists that have had their usual properties radically altered for the current purpose in the following ways:

1. All the menus are *unordered* lists whose items have no list markers (bullets) because they all have been given property `list-style-type: none`. See line 55 in Figure 4.27.

```
1    <!--#include virtual="common/document_head.html"-->
2    <!-- index.html for ch04/nature2 -->
3      <body>
4        <header>
5          <!--#include virtual="common/logo.html"-->
6          <!--#include virtual="common/mainmenu.html"-->
7        </header>
8        <main>
9          <article id="textLeft">
10           <h3>Welcome to Nature's Source:<br>
11             Protecting your health naturally!</h3>
12           <p>Founded in 1998, Nature's Source was created to serve those who
13           use alternative healing methods. Offering only the highest quality
14           vitamins, minerals, supplements and herbal remedies, Nature's
15           Source takes great pride in helping people live healthier, happier
16           lives.</p>
17           <p>Many companies that talk about customer service fail to deliver.
18           Nature's Source exists to truly serve all the needs of their
19           customers. Each location features dedicated on-site therapists
20           along with knowledgeable staff who ensure that every customer
21           receives the best quality information available. Continuing
22           education seminars are a regular event at Nature's Source.</p>
23         </article>
24         <div id="image">
25           <img src="images/outdoor4.jpg" alt="Get healthy and stay healthy"
26                width="256" height="256">
27         </div>
28       </main>
29       <footer>
30         <!--#include virtual="common/footer_content.html"-->
31       </footer>
32     </body>
33   </html>
```

FIGURE 4.25 `ch04/nature2/index.html`
The HTML document that produced the display shown in Figure 4.24. Illustrates use of the HTML5 semantic elements header, main, article, and footer.

```
1    /* default.css for ch04/nature2 */
2
3    /*************************************************************
4    global settings to remove any default padding and margins */
5    * {
6      padding: 0;
7      margin: 0;
8    }
9
```

FIGURE 4.26 `ch04/nature2/css/default.css` (part 1 of 3)
The first lines of the CSS style sheet used to style the HTML document of Figure 4.25 and produce the display of Figure 4.24. These styles are also applicable to every other page on this chapter's version 2 of the **Nature's Source** website.

```
10    /**********************************************************
11    The following line may be redundant, but does no harm. */
12    main, header, footer, nav, article { display: block; }
13
14    /**********************************************************
15    width and margin properties set here apply only to body;
16    font properties set here will be inherited throughout */
17    body {
18      width: 900px;
19      margin-top: 10px;
20      margin-left: 10px;
21      font-family: Verdana, Arial, Helvetica, sans-serif;
22      font-size: 1em;
23    }
24
25    /*******************************************************
26    individual element margins set by trial and error */
27    h3 { margin: .5em 0 .2em; }
28    p { margin: 0 .2em .7em 0; }
29
30    /*******************************************************
31    company logo appears at the top of each page */
32    div#logo { padding: 10px 0; }
33
34    /*******************************************************
35    three kinds of menus: main, footer, and sub */
36
37    nav#mainMenu { /* appears below logo on every page */
38      width: 100%;
39      height: 20px;
40    }
41
42    nav#subMenu { /* appears at left in content area on some pages */
43      float: left;
44      width: 180px;
45    }
46
47    nav#footerMenu { /* appears in the footer of each page */
48      float: left;
49      width: 360px;
50      height: 20px;
51    }
52
```

FIGURE 4.26 `ch04/nature2/css/default.css` (part 1 of 3) (*continued*)

```
53    /*************************************************************
54    three groups of menu links: main, footer and sub */
55    nav ul { list-style: none; }
56
57    nav ul li {
58      float: left;
59      width: 179px;
60      height: 25px;
61      border-right: 1px solid #FFF;
62      background-color: #093;
63      text-align: center;
64    }
65
66    nav ul li a {
67      color: #FFF;
68      text-decoration: none;
69      font-weight: bold;
70      font-size: .7em;
71    }
72
73    nav ul li a:hover {
74      padding: 2px 1px;
75      background-color: #3F3;
76      color: #000;
77    }
78
79    /* vertical (sub)menu items need these revisions */
80    nav#subMenu ul li {
81      border-top: 1px solid #FFF;
82      background-color: #0B3;
83    }
84
85    /*************************************************************
86    only home page has text at left and image at right in content area */
87    article#textLeft {
88      float: left;
89      width: 65%;
90    }
91
92    div#image {
93      float: left;
94      width: 35%;
95      margin-top: 20px;
96      text-align: center;
97    }
98
```

FIGURE 4.27 `ch04/nature2/css/default.css` **(part 2 of 3)**
The middle lines of the CSS style sheet used to style the HTML document of Figure 4.25 and produce the display of Figure 4.24. These styles are also applicable to every other page on this chapter's version 2 of the **Nature's Source** website.

```
 99    /*********************************************************
100    pages with submenus at the left have text at the right */
101    article#textRight {
102      float: left;
103      width: 715px;
104      margin-left: 5px;
105    }
106
107    /*************************************************************
108    list structure must be restored for the site map page, since all
109    padding and margins have been removed by the global settings */
110    article#siteMap ol,
111    article#siteMap ul {
112      margin: 0 30px 10px;
113    }
114
115    /*********************************************************
116    footer contains both a copyright notice and a two-item menu */
117    footer {
118      clear: left;
119      width: 100%;
120      height: 20px;
121    }
122
123    div#copyright {
124      float: left;
125      width: 539px;
126      height: 25px;
127      line-height: 25px;
128      border-right: 1px solid #FFF;
129      background-color: #093;
130      color: #DDD;
131      text-align: center;
132      font-weight: bold;
133      font-size: .9em;
134    }
```

FIGURE 4.28 `ch04/nature2/css/default.css (part 3 of 3)`
The last lines of the CSS style sheet used to style the HTML document of Figure 4.25 and produce the display of Figure 4.24. These styles are also applicable to every other page on this chapter's version 2 of the **Nature's Source** website.

2. Note that the menu options in the main menu and in the footer menu are side by side, not one under the other as they are in the submenu that appears at the left on many of the pages. This side-by-side arrangement is achieved by giving the `float` property of the list items a value of `left`, so that each list item floats upward to the left and settles on the right of its predecessor. See line 58 of Figure 4.27.

3. Because list items are block-level, we can give them a specific width. See line 59 of Figure 4.27.

4. Our menu links are not underlined in the usual way, because we have said that for links we want `text-decoration: none`. See line 68 of Figure 4.27.

▶ A second new feature we need to mention is the use of a CSS *pseudo-class*. You can see one of these in action as you browse the `nature2` site, since every time your mouse hovers over a link, that link is highlighted by a change in the color of the link text as well as the background color of that text. There are four pseudo-classes that can be used with links, though we only use the `:hover` pseudo-class in our style sheet. Here is the syntax and how it works: A style like `a:hover {color: red;}` will cause the text of a link to turn red when the mouse hovers over it, and to turn back to its "normal" color (whatever that might be) when the mouse moves away. Note the colon between the a tag and the actual name (`hover`) of the pseudo-class. Make sure there is no space on either side of this colon. See the style given in lines 73 to 77 of Figure 4.27 for our use of the `hover` pseudo-class.

These are the highlights of the style sheet for the `nature2` version of our website in this chapter. Make sure you study the complete CSS file and reconcile the various styles with what is displayed in your browser.

4.13.3 Version 3: A Revision of Version 2 Incorporating Some CSS3 and Illustrating Simple "Responsive Design"

This version of our **Nature's Source** website gives us an opportunity to introduce the notion of *responsive design*, as well as some new CSS3 features. Since responsive design is itself a large topic, we only scratch the surface. However, you should be aware of the concept and plan to incorporate its ideas into your websites if you continue as a web developer. As for what *responsive design* means, here's a high-level description: Because there are so many different devices of so many different sizes used nowadays to view websites, a well-designed website should be able to "respond" appropriately to the size of the device on which it is being viewed, and to do so such a website must have been constructed with the principles of "responsive design" in mind.

For our simple illustration of responsive design, we show two "views" of the home page of this version 3 of our website: the "desktop view" seen in **FIGURE 4.29** and the "tablet view" seen in **FIGURE 4.32**. To experience the "responsive design effect", you can browse to the page shown in Figure 4.29 on a "desktop computer" and gradually reduce the size of your browser window. This will eventually cause the display to switch to the "tablet view" seen in Figure 4.32, in which the home page image has disappeared and the main menu has gone from one row to two in order to accommodate all the menu options within the reduced width. Note that responsive design is not a new feature of CSS3, but we do use some CSS3 when styling our pages for both "views" of our website pages, as we shall see.

It's important to realize that if you continue reducing the size of your browser window (to "smartphone" size, for example), things will start to come off the rails, simply because our "responsive design" is not capable of handling that scenario. We are just trying to give you the

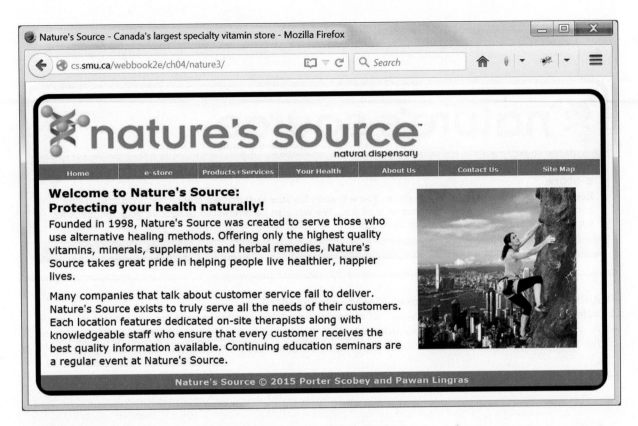

FIGURE 4.29 `graphics/ch04/nature3/desktopIndexHtml.jpg`
A Firefox browser display, in "desktop view", of `ch04/nature3/index.html`, the home page of version 3 of our **Nature's Source** website for this chapter, styled by the CSS in `ch04/nature3/css/desktop.css`. Note that the two menu links formerly in the footer have been moved to the main menu, and the footer now contains only copyright information. Also note the rounded corners produced by CSS3. Photo: © AlexBrylov/iStockphoto

general idea, not the full meal deal. There are many JavaScript libraries that will save you a lot of work in providing this kind of capability to your websites. Here we are using only CSS, no Java-Script. See the end-of-chapter **References** section for links to further information.

By the way, the above discussion described the effect of reducing the browser display from "typical desktop size" to "typical tablet size". We need to make two observations. First, if you are at "tablet view", and then gradually (or quickly) increase the size of your browser window, you will eventually (or suddenly) switch back to "desktop view". Second, if you browse directly to the home page of this version 3 using a tablet device (an iPad, for example), you will see immediately the tablet view of the home page, without any need to adjust the size of your viewport.

As usual, this version of the website contains many more pages that we can reach via the menu links on the home page and elsewhere. For example, the following two pages will contain much more interesting information as time goes on, but for now they simply show that our new

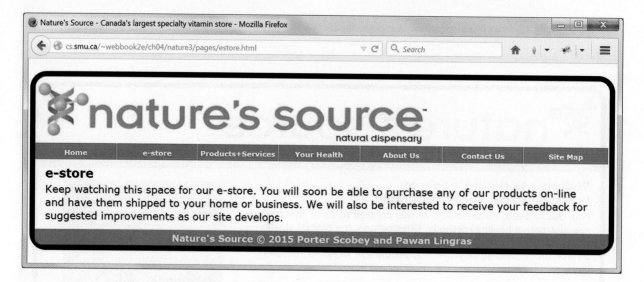

FIGURE 4.30 `graphics/ch04/nature3/desktopEstoreHtml.jpg`
A Firefox browser display, in "desktop view", of `ch04/nature3/pages/estore.html`, our eventual e-store entry-point page, with styles from `ch04/nature3/css/desktop.css`. This is one of the pages from version 3 of this chapter's **Nature's Source** website, reached by clicking on the **e-store** option of the main menu.

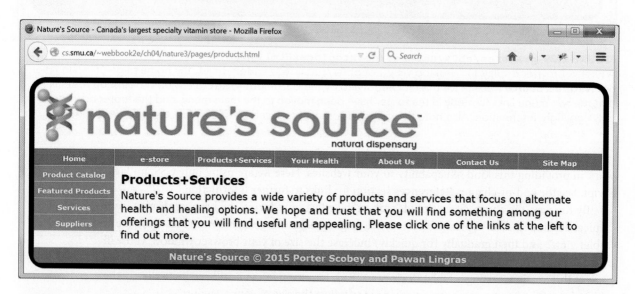

FIGURE 4.31 `graphics/ch04/nature3/desktopProductsHtml.jpg`
A Firefox browser display, in "desktop view", of `ch04/nature3/pages/products.html`, our eventual products database connection page, with styles from `ch04/nature3/css/desktop.css`. This is one of the pages from version 3 of this chapter's **Nature's Source** website, reached by clicking on the **Products+Services** option of the main menu.

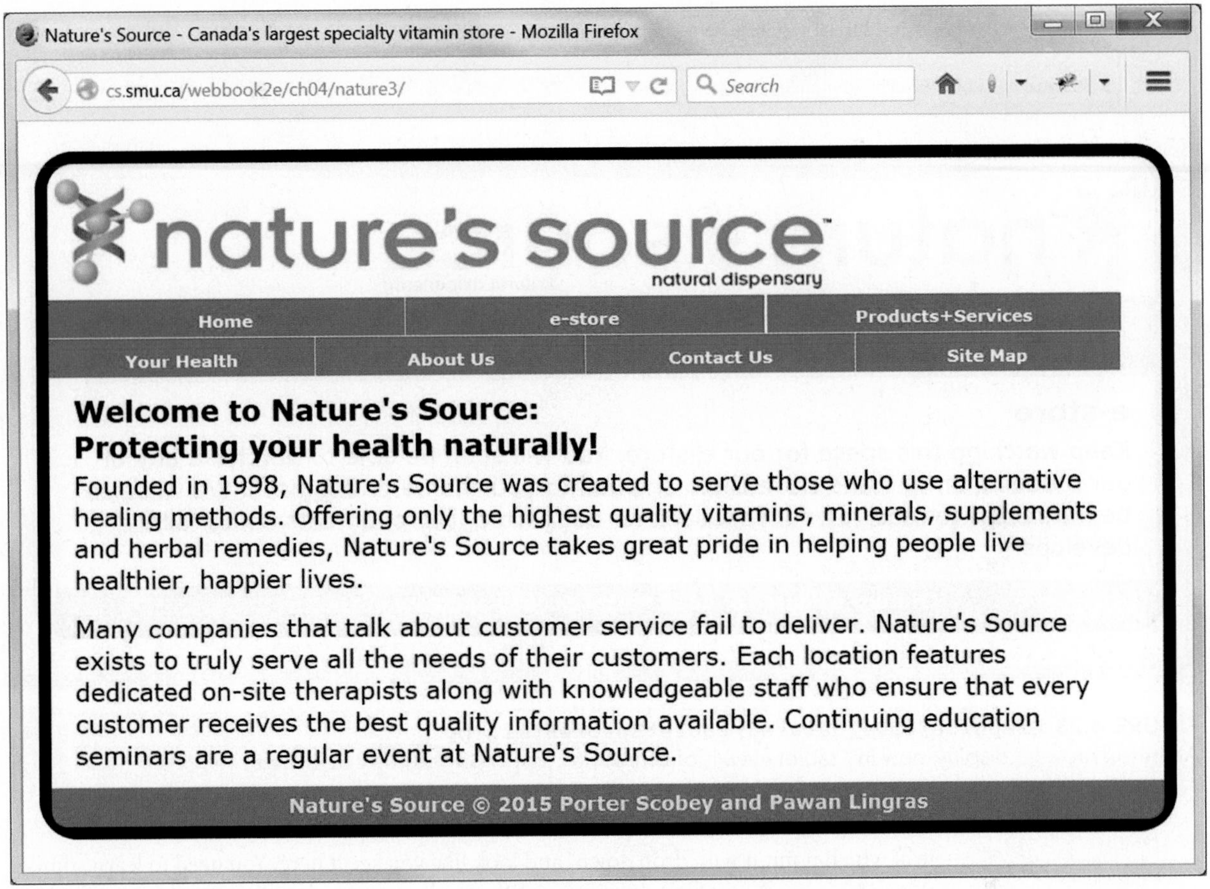

FIGURE 4.32 `graphics/ch04/nature3/tabletIndexHtml.jpg`
A Firefox browser display in "tablet view" of `ch04/nature3/index.html`, the home page of version 3 of our **Nature's Source** website for this chapter, with additional styles from `ch04/nature3/css/tablet.css`. Note the two-level menu and the absence of the home page image.

"look and feel" is maintained as we browse from page to page on our site, whether we are in "desktop view" or "tablet view":

- The page obtained by clicking on the **e-store** menu option, and shown in both Figure 4.30 (desktop view) and **FIGURE 4.33** (tablet view), which at the moment contains only a simple paragraph of text promising things to come.

- The page obtained by clicking on the **Products+Services** menu option, and shown in Figure 4.31 (desktop view) and **FIGURE 4.34** (tablet view), which contains what looks like a dropdown menu at the left. At the moment this menu is in a "permanently dropped-down" state, and you will see a similar thing on most other pages of the site in the current version. Later, you will see how to make this menu hidden until you place the mouse over

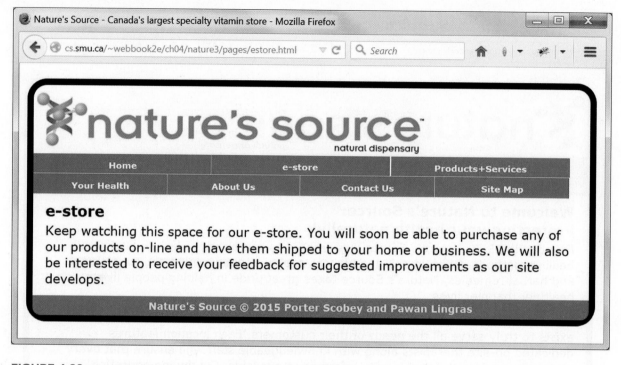

FIGURE 4.33 `Graphics/ch04/nature3/tabletEstoreHtml.jpg`
A Firefox browser display, now in "tablet view", of `ch04/nature3/pages/estore.html`.

it, at which point it will "drop down" and look like you see it here. You need to learn something about JavaScript before you can do this.[9]

Before continuing with the discussion of how we accomplish our simple responsive design effect, let's take a moment to emphasize what has changed in the "look and feel" of this version of our website. If you examine the "desktop view" of our `nature3` home page shown in Figure 4.29 and compare it with the `nature2` home page shown in Figure 4.24, you will note three major differences:

1. The main menu now contains seven menu items, two more than the previous five.
2. The footer now contains only the copyright information, since the two menu items it previously contained have been relocated to the end of the main menu.
3. The entire display is now surrounded by a black border with rounded corners and is centered horizontally on the screen.

These changes in "look and feel" as we go from `nature2` to `nature3` in this chapter have required appropriate adjustments in both HTML markup and CSS styles, but for the most part

---

[9] We should mention in passing that although our particular approach will use JavaScript to produce drop-down menus, it is also possible to do so using only CSS. So much to learn, so little time . . .

FIGURE 4.34 `graphics/ch04/nature3/tabletProductsHtml.jpg`
A Firefox browser display, now in "tablet view", of `ch04/nature3/pages/products.html`.

those changes do not involve anything we have not already discussed, except for the use of the `auto` value for `margin-left` and `margin-right` in our CSS for the `body` element to place it in the center.

There is one feature, however, that is not possible unless we use CSS3, and that is the border with the rounded corners. This is a feature that web developers have long desired, and previously was usually achieved by creating an image with rounded corners and importing that image into the page. With CSS3 you can achieve this border effect very simply with the following two style rules in the style for our `body` element, which are found in lines 20 and 21 of the file `ch04/nature3/css/desktop.css`:

```
border: 8px solid black;
border-radius: 25px;
```

The first of the above style rules is, of course, not new. But the second is new in CSS3. The `border-radius` property value (`25px` in this case) determines the amount of "curvature" in the rounded corner of the border, and it's one of those things for which you have to use trial and error to get the value that you want.

Now let's return to the more interesting discussion of how we achieved our simple responsive design effect. This requires some new HTML markup, as well as two different CSS style sheets:

desktop.css (which is essentially the same as our previous nature2/css/default.css of this chapter) and a brand new tablet.css, which we show in **FIGURE 4.36**.

The basic idea is this: When the browser is in "desktop view", it is using the styles in desktop.css. When the size of the browser window is reduced to "tablet view", the styles in tablet.css are also applied. Note that we used *also applied*. It is not as though tablet.css replaces desktop.css; instead, there may be new styles from tablet.css to apply, or some styles in tablet.css may override styles in desktop.css because of the cascade.

But how does the browser know when to start applying the styles from tablet.css? Well, this is where the new HTML elements in the revised document_head.html shown in **FIGURE 4.35** come into play.

In line 6 of Figure 4.35 you see the new meta element

```
<meta name="viewport" content="width=device-width">
```

and in lines 9 and 10 of the same figure you see the following new link element:

```
<link rel="stylesheet" href="css/tablet.css"
    media="screen and (max-width: 900px)">
```

The meta element is a simple way of telling the browser to use whatever width is available to it on the current device. The new-to-us media attribute of the second link element generates a *media query* when the page is loaded or the browser viewport is resized, and if the width of the viewport drops below the 900px value shown, that's when the second CSS style sheet in tablet.css "kicks in".

Making the home page image "disappear" in the tablet view is very easy. This is accomplished by the following style rule, which appears in line 40 of Figure 4.36:

```
div#image { display: none; }
```

```
 1   <!DOCTYPE html>
 2   <!-- document_head.html -->
 3   <html lang="en">
 4     <head>
 5       <meta charset="utf-8">
 6       <meta name="viewport" content="width=device-width">
 7       <base href="http://cs.smu.ca/webbook2e/ch04/nature3/">
 8       <link rel="stylesheet" href="css/desktop.css">
 9       <link rel="stylesheet" href="css/tablet.css"
10             media="screen and (max-width: 900px)">
11       <title>Nature's Source - Canada's largest specialty vitamin store</title>
12     </head>
```

FIGURE 4.35 `ch04/nature3/common/document head.html`
The revised document_head.html file, now containing both a new meta element and a new link element, which help us to provide our simple "responsive design".

```
1   /* tablet.css for the responsive version of ch04/nature3 */
2
3   /*********************************************************
4   This style sheet takes effect when the width of the
5   viewport (browser window) is reduced to less than
6   900px, or when, upon first loading the page, the
7   device width is seen as less than 900px. */
8
9   /* gives some whitespace on either side of the display */
10  body { width: 95%; }
11
12  /* visually separates a menu link from the one below it */
13  ul#mainLinks li { border-bottom: 1px solid #FFF; }
14
15  /* move 4th and following menu items to second row */
16  ul#mainLinks li:nth-child(4) { clear: left; }
17
18  /* ensures both rows of menu links have same length*/
19  ul#mainLinks li:nth-child(1) { width: 32%; }
20  ul#mainLinks li:nth-child(2) { width: 32%; }
21  ul#mainLinks li:nth-child(3) { width: 32%; }
22  ul#mainLinks li:nth-child(4) { width: 24%; }
23  ul#mainLinks li:nth-child(5) { width: 24%; }
24  ul#mainLinks li:nth-child(6) { width: 24%; }
25  ul#mainLinks li:nth-child(7) { width: 24%; }
26
27  /*********************************************************
28  makes right edges of first and second menu item rows
29  line up, at the expense of a 2px gap instead of a 1px
30  gap between "e-store" and "Products+Services" */
31  nav ul li:nth-child(2) { border-right: 2px solid #FFF; }
32
33  /* makes logo "scale down" as the width decreases */
34  div#logo img {
35    max-width: 70%;
36    height: auto;
37  }
38
39  /* remove the image from the home page*/
40  div#image { display: none; }
41
42  nav#subMenu { float: left; }
```

FIGURE 4.36 `ch04/nature3/css/tablet.css`
The style sheet for the "tablet view" of the `nature3` web pages, containing some styles that also help us with
our simple "responsive design".

```
43
44   /* container for the textual content of each page*/
45   article {
46     float: left;
47     width: 70%;
48     margin-left: 10px;
49   }
50
51   /* same style for both of these in the tablet configuration */
52   article#textOnly,
53   article#textLeft { width: 95%; }
54
55   article#textRight {
56     float: left;
57     width: 70%;
58     margin-left: 10px;
59   }
60
61   /* reduce size of footer text to prevent it overflowing its space */
62   footer { font-size: 80%; }
```

FIGURE 4.36 `ch04/nature3/css/tablet.css` *(continued)*

To convert the menu from one row to two, thus retaining all the options at a readable size as the width decreases, we make use of a new CSS3 feature that gives us fine-tuned access to our menu items. The relevant part of `tablet.css` is shown in lines 15 to 31 of Figure 4.36. Here we are making very good use of the CSS3 `:nth-child()` selector, which works as follows. If we append `:nth-child(n)` (in which n may be an integer, a keyword, or even an expression) to any HTML element, we are referring to every element of that type that is the nth child of its parent. For example, an expression like `p:nth-child(3)` would refer to every paragraph that happened to be the third child of its parent, whatever the element type of that parent. This is particularly convenient for us in this situation, since we can use this selector to style each of our unordered list elements individually.

4.13.4 Version 4: A Copy of Version 3 with the Home Page Image Replaced by a Home Page Video

This fourth and final version of our website for this chapter (found in `ch04/nature4`) is essentially an exact copy of `ch04/nature3`, except for one major change: We have replaced the home page image with a home page video. We have captured a "still image" of the home page with the video playing in **FIGURE 4.37**, but obviously you will have to browse to the page in question to see the video in action.

In going from `nature3` to `nature4` we have to change HTML markup in `index.html` and add some new CSS to both `desktop.css` and `tablet.css`. We discuss the changes here, but you should study your copies of the three files to see them in context.

FIGURE 4.37 `graphics/ch04/nature4/displayIndexHtml.jpg`
A Firefox browser display of ch04/nature4/index.html, the home page of version 4 of our **Nature's Source** website for this chapter, which is an exact copy of version 3, except that the business-related image on the home page has been replaced by a business-related video, via the HTML5 video element, and there is a line of text under the video. Photo: © Easy_Company/iStock

First, in `ch04/nature4/index.html` the `div` with `id` value `image` has been replaced with a `div` with `id` value `video`. This `div` element contains, in turn, a new HTML5 `video` element, as well as an `h3` element with the text we want to appear below the video, as shown here (see lines 24–31 of the file):

```
<div id="video">
  <video width="358" height="188" autoplay loop>
    <source src="videos/outdoor.mp4" type="video/mp4">
    <source src="videos/outdoor.ogg" type="video/ogg">
    Your browser supports neither the mp4 nor the ogg video format.
  </video>
  <h3>Get healthy and fit with us!</h3>
</div>
```

Our `video` element as shown here has four attributes. The `width` and `height` attribute values are in pixels, and have the obvious meaning. The `autoplay` attribute causes the video to start playing as soon as the page loads, and the `loop` attribute causes the video to start over again when it comes to the end. This is the behavior we want for our particular video, but the `video` element has other attributes for other situations. For example, if we wanted the user to have some control over the video playback, we could supply a `controls` attribute. See the **References** for a relevant link.

The content of the video element consists of two `source` elements followed by some text. There could be more `source` elements, if our video was available in additional formats. We will not discuss video formats, since that is another large topic, but one or the other of the `mp4` or `ogg` formats should make the video available to any modern browser. The browser will display the first video from the sequence of source elements that has a video format that the browser understands. If the browser does not understand any of the video formats, the text in the body of the `video` element will be displayed instead. Note that the video format is indicated by the file extension in the `src` attribute value of the `source` element in the usual way, and that `video/mp4` and `video/ogg` are the corresponding MIME types, given as values of the `source` element's `type` attribute. Note that we also now have a new `videos` subdirectory containing our video files. This is analogous to our `images` subdirectory, and is at the same level in our website directory hierarchy.

Of course we need some CSS to deal with these changes in the HTML markup. First, the home page text configuration when the video replaces the image needs to be adjusted, and the `div` containing the `video` element also needs some styling. We have the following additions to `desktop.css` to take care of the "desktop view" (see lines 147–158):

```
article#textLeftWithVideo {
  float: left;
  width: 53%;
  margin-left: 1em;
}
div#video {
  float: left;
  width: 43%;
  padding-top: 50px;
  text-align: center;
}
```

Similarly, when we move to "tablet view" we need the following additions to `tablet.css` (see lines 66–67):

```
article#textLeftWithVideo { width: 95%; }
div#video { display: none; }
```

Summary

CSS were "invented" to help web developers keep separate the description of the structure of their web pages from the description of how those pages are to be displayed. Thus in this chapter we have learned how to use CSS styles to tell a browser how we wish to have the elements in our HTML documents displayed.

A collection of one or more styles is called a style sheet, and a style sheet may be placed in a separate (external) file, in a `style` element within the `head` element of a document, or in the value of a `style` attribute of an HTML element. The first of these three options is the recommended one, and the last should be avoided if at all possible.

A typical simple style rule consists of a selector and a brace-enclosed property-value pair called a declaration. There are many variations on this simple scheme that include multiple selectors, descendant selectors, and multiple declarations. Some property values such as units of measurement and color may be expressed using different formats, and a web developer needs to choose a consistent representation for the values of such properties. Consistency in formatting and commenting CSS style sheets is equally important.

CSS `class` and `id` selectors, combined with both the older, non-semantic HTML `div` and `span` elements, and the newer HTML5 semantic elements like `main`, `header`, `footer`, and `article`, provide a great deal of flexibility in laying out and formatting our web pages.

CSS uses the rules of inheritance, specificity, and "the cascade" to decide which style actually gets applied when there is a conflict. Fortunately, most of the time styles get applied as you would hope and expect, and you can often get by with placing all your styles in a single external style sheet file, with fine-tuning for any particular document performed by placing modifying styles in a `style` element of that document, or even, in extreme cases, in the `style` attribute of a particular element.

The CSS box model underlies most of what appears on a web page, and it is important for a web developer to have at least a basic understanding of content, padding, border, and margin as they relate to this model.

CSS positioning for page layout is much preferred over the legacy approach that used HTML tables. We discussed only CSS "floats", which were sufficient for our purposes.

The CSS reset is a useful concept that permits a web developer to establish a "baseline" set of values for such things as margins, padding, font size, and so on at the beginning of a style sheet and then reset them later on in the style sheet as required. What makes this so useful is that not all browsers use the same defaults for displaying the same elements, so setting a baseline and modifying it exactly as required gives a developer much more confidence that a page will be displayed in the way desired.

Just as HTML documents can (and should) be validated, so can (and should) CSS style sheets. So, as a best practice, you should always validate your CSS style sheets along with your HTML markup.

We saw how a "media query" and two different style sheets could be used to achieve a simple "responsive design" for our website, as we change from a "typical desktop view" to a "typical tablet view", and back again.

Finally, you saw how we could easily replace our home page image with a video by using the new HTML5 `video` element, with appropriate additions to our CSS style sheets.

Quick Questions to Test Your Basic Knowledge

1. What was the reason for the introduction of CSS?
2. Who was responsible for the initial development of CSS?
3. Prior to CSS3, CSS was a "monolithic" standard. What does this mean, and, by contrast, what is the nature of CSS3?
4. How many "levels" of a CSS style sheet are there, what are their names, and what distinguishes one from the other?
5. Which one of the three style sheet levels of the previous question is the recommended one to use whenever possible, and which one are you advised to avoid if at all possible?
6. Using the generic terms *selector*, *property*, *property-value*, *declaration*, *declaration block*, and *rule*, how would you show the syntax of a simple CSS style rule using a diagram?
7. What are the CSS comment delimiters?
8. When you link an external style sheet to an HTML document, what are the two attributes you need for the `link` element, and what are their values?
9. What is the proper syntax for the selectors if you want several different selectors to be styled by the same style rule(s)?
10. If you have several possible values for a `font-family` property, what is the proper syntax for those values, and what should the last one be?
11. In the list of measurement values shown below, which is the "odd one out"? [Hint: What is the context?]

    `12pt, 20px, 1em, 100%, medium`
12. In this chapter we referred to the pixel as a "relative" measurement, as opposed to an "absolute" measurement. Suppose we decided to change our mind and call the pixel a "hybrid" measurement. Can you explain why this might make sense?
13. What are five different ways that color values can be specified in CSS?
14. We mentioned that if you use a six-digit hex number to specify a color value on your web page, you have a choice of 16,777,216 different colors. How is this number computed?
15. Without looking anything up, how would you describe two colors, and the relationship between them, if the two colors have the hex values `#333333` and `#999999`?
16. What is the short-hex value corresponding to the hex value `#AA33FF`?
17. What is the default value of the `background-color` property?
18. How many colors are in the so-called "web-safe palette"?
19. How would you explain the (good) advice to "name CSS classes according to their meaning (also called *semantic naming*), and not according to their appearance"? Can you find an example from this chapter where that advice was not followed but should have been? Hint: Think about the `BoldItalic` class, and think about what it would mean if you wanted to change characteristics of this particular style (to light grey small caps, for example).

20. What is the only difference between the definition of a CSS class selector and a CSS id selector?

21. What is a CSS style rule that would cause the text in all h3, p, and li elements to be displayed with maroon text?

22. What is a CSS style rule that would cause the body of a web page to have a very dark gray background with very light gray text, and what would you say about such a style?

23. If every time you wanted to emphasize a word or phrase in a paragraph, you wanted its content to be displayed in bold italic red text, how would you achieve this?

24. If you have both a style element and a link to an external style file in the head element of a web page document, in which order (generally speaking) should they appear, and why?

25. Here are the four major components of the CSS box model in alphabetical order: border, content, margin, padding. What is their order going from the inside out?

26. To which parts of the box model does the background color apply?

27. What happens if you give the float property for an HTML element the value center?

28. What would be the purpose of the style float: right for an HTML img element?

29. What is the purpose of the style rule clear: both?

30. What is a CSS reset, and how is it used?

31. What should you make a practice of doing with each of your CSS style sheets that you should also do with each of your HTML documents?

32. What new CSS3 property do you need to use if you want a border element with rounded corners?

33. What new CSS3 selector would you use to style any h2 element that happened to be the fifth child of its parent?

34. What is the purpose of the text that should always be present in the body of an HTML5 video element?

Short Exercises to Improve Your Basic Understanding

Another reminder, probably for the last time: Be sure to work with *copies* of the sample files, so you always have the originals to go back to and start over.

1. It might be interesting to begin these exercises with a high-level "experiment" of sorts. Display the home page of each version of our website (nature1 to nature4) in every browser that you have available. Ideally you will see no differences, but try to explain any that you do see.

2. Validate each of the CSS files in this chapter to get a feel for the process. And validate against both CSS 2.1 and CSS3. Some style sheets will validate in both cases. For those which do not, you will see instances of CSS3 being used that will, of course, not validate as CSS 2.1. This is also an easy way to highlight the new CSS3 features we have used.

3. Add the styles of the four examples at the beginning of section 4.5 to the styles in `simple.css` and then redisplay `simple.html`. Be sure to reconcile what you see in the display with the new and revised styles in the style file. Then make a duplicate copy of the three-item list in `simple.html` and place it after the first list in that same file. Now change the `ul` tags of the duplicate list to `ol` tags and redisplay to confirm our claim in section 4.5 that this list will *not* have the text of its items italicized.

4. Create a sample file called `style_levels.html` that illustrates how CSS recognizes and uses the three "style levels": external, embedded, and inline. Construct your file in such a way that you can illustrate how the CSS cascade works by interchanging, within your `head` element, the order of your `style` element and the `link` element that references your external style file.

5. Make arguments for and against the following statement: "Permitting inline CSS styles defeats the whole purpose of CSS, and this practice should be deprecated".

6. Find and make a list of all the CSS "generic" fonts, and include at least one specific font family in each category.

7. CSS can also use "system fonts". Find what they are on your system, make a list of all the names of these fonts, and explain why you might want to use them.

8. Create a web page called `colors.html` that contains a table with three columns showing the names of all 16 standard CSS colors, their hex values, and the actual colors.

9. Create a small example in a file called `standout.html` that shows you can have two classes with the same name but containing different styles, as long as you make them apply to different HTML elements. For example, you could have both `p.Standout` and `li.Standout`.

10. We mentioned and used the CSS `:hover` pseudo-class. Find the names of the other CSS pseudo-classes that apply to links (i.e., to the HTML `a` element), and explain how they are used. Make sure you "discover" the order in which they must be listed in your style sheet if you wish to use all of them.

11. CSS also has something called *pseudo-elements*. Explain the conceptual difference between a pseudo-class and a pseudo-element, and give at least one example of a pseudo-element. And note, by the way, that *pseudo-classes* and *pseudo-elements* are collectively called *pseudo-selectors*.

12. In our box model example (Figure 4.12 and associated files), remove the body style completely and r-display the page in all browsers at your disposal to see if there are any noticeable differences.

13. In our box model example (Figure 4.12 and associated files), change the various values for `padding`, `border`, `margin`, and `background-color` properties and redisplay in your browser. Make sure you understand what you are seeing.

14. In our examples illustrating the `float` property (Figure 4.15 or Figure 4.18), in the corresponding style files (Figure 4.17 or Figure 4.23), the `float` property appears twice and the `clear` property appears once. Choose either of these examples and experiment by

removing all of these properties at once, then one at a time, then two at a time, and for each scenario explain what you see when the page is displayed after the change(s).

15. This exercise will lead you through one sequence of the steps that will turn an ordinary unordered list into a horizontally arranged menu of options. After each step you may want to view the result in more than one browser to see if you can spot any differences. First, create a test file called `list_to_menu.html` with only the following in its body:

```
<ul>
    <li>Go</li>
    <li>Stop</li>
    <li>Speed Up</li>
    <li>Slow Down</li>
</ul>
```

Also create an initially empty embedded style sheet for the page. Then perform the following actions, in order:

- Add the style `* {padding: 0;}` to the style sheet.
- Remove the preceding style and then add the style `* {margin: 0;}` to the style sheet.
- Remove the previous style and add the style `ul {list-style-type: none;}` as the only style in the file.
- Add the following style rule at the beginning of the style sheet:

```
* {
    padding: 0;
    margin: 0;
}
```

This time, and from now on, just add things; don't remove anything from the style sheet.

- Add the following style rule, but only one line at a time, in the order shown, and redisplay after each entry:

```
ul li {
    float: left;
    width: 99px;
    border-right: 1px solid black;
    background-color: #0F0;
    text-align: center;
    font-family: Verdana;
}
```

- Finally, add the following style rule, and be sure to place the mouse over the various menu options after you redisplay:

```
ul li:hover {background-color: #CCC;}
```

This menu does not contain any links, but you can extend the exercise by adding them and having the links (rather than the list element itself) change color during a "mouseover".

16. Experiment with the `padding` and `margin` values in the file `default.css` of Figure 4.23 to see what the effect is. Begin by commenting out lines 3 to 6 of the file to see what the home page of `ch04/nature1` looks like when the browser defaults for those values are being used; then try some values of your own.

17. Experiment with as many different property values in the file `default.css` of Figures 4.26 to 4.28 to see what the effect is, and in particular to see how changing a value causes the display to "come off the rails", if in fact that is what happens. As always, when doing this kind of experimentation, it's a good idea to change one thing at a time, and to undo the last change before you make the next one.

18. Find out what aspects of the presentation of a web page your browser will allow you (as the end user) to modify and how you accomplish those modifications. For example, how do you change the text size of your browser's display or disable its display of images? The fact that any user has the opportunity to make changes like this is of course a good thing, but also another thorn in the side of any web developer.

19. From a browser on your PC or laptop, go to the home page for this chapter's `nature3` website. Experiment with our simple responsive design feature by changing the size of the browser display up and down to get both the desktop view and the tablet view of the site. Then take an iPad or another tablet device and browse to the same website. This should confirm our claim that the "tablet view" of the website shows up immediately.

20. Change the `video` element in the `index.html` file of your copy of our `nature4` website by adding the `controls` attribute and removing the `autoplay` attribute and the `loop` attribute. Reload the page and experiment with the controls that now appear at the bottom of the `video` element. Note that the video no longer begins to play immediately when the page loads, nor does it automatically repeat when it comes to the end.

Exercises on the Parallel Project

As we have pointed out in this chapter, best practice going forward demands that HTML tables no longer be used for web page layout unless what is being laid out is conceptually an actual table of some kind (data, for example), and you should choose the CSS alternative. Also, for these exercises, you should attempt to choose a different color scheme for your business than the one used for the sample business in the text.

1. From the Exercises on the Parallel Project of the previous chapter you should now have a simple home page for the website of your business that looks something like Figure 3.10. Your task in this exercise is to reproduce another very similar simple home page for your business. This time, however, it must use a CSS style sheet for layout and styling, and look like our own sample business website shown in Figure 4.21. Note in particular the change

in justification in the address text at the upper right. Experiment with padding, margin, and other settings to achieve a look that you feel works well for your site.

2. From the Exercises on the Parallel Project of the previous chapter you should also now have a web page for your business that looks something like Figure 3.12. Your task in this exercise is analogous to that of the previous exercise. It is to produce a "better-looking" page, analogous to that shown in Figure 4.24, for the home page of the multipage website for your business. And once again you must use a CSS style sheet for layout and styling, as well as SSI to load in the parts that will be common to all of your pages. Be sure to maintain the same "look and feel" for all the pages on your website, and make sure all your links are active, which will require your `base` element to be set up properly. Bottom line: This version of your website should have the same functionality as the analogous version from the previous chapter, but the entire site must now be laid out and styled with CSS. Of course now might be a good time to add some content to your pages as well.

3. One final requirement for both of the above website versions: All pages must validate as HTML5 and your CSS must validate as CSS3.

 # What Else You May Want or Need to Know

1. The CSS `@import` mechanism is another way to gain access to an external style sheet. Recall that the HTML `link` element associates an external CSS style sheet with the HTML document in which that `link` element appears. On the other hand, the purpose of the `@import` *directive* (that's what it's called, and it's a part of the CSS language, *not* HTML) is to bring an external style sheet into another style sheet. The receiving style sheet can itself be an external style sheet or an embedded style sheet. In any case, the rules say that the `@import` directive must be the first item (except for comments) in whatever style sheet it is placed, though this requirement seems to be ignored by many browsers. Here is its syntax:

```
@import url('[path_if_necessary]filename.ext')
```

Note that it uses `url` rather than `href`, and quotes around the `url` argument are optional.
   One use for this functionality might be to keep either or both of your CSS reset values and your "global" style values in one or two files and then `@import` those files (you can have more than one `@import` directive) at the beginning of the style sheet for your website.

2. You can apply the styles in multiple CSS classes by using a single `style` attribute. Suppose, for example, you have the four CSS classes C1, C2, C3, and C4. Here is

the syntax for styling a single HTML element with all four of those classes (note the white-space-separated class names):

```
<tagname class="C1 C2 C3 C4">content</tagname>
```

3. If you are surfing the web looking for CSS examples, you will quite often run into text that begins like this: "Lorem ipsum . . .". Such text consists of several, perhaps many, paragraphs of "jumbled" Latin text that starts off with these two words at the beginning of the first paragraph, and is convenient to use as "placeholder text" when testing CSS styles. In any case, it is widely used for that purpose and there are websites that will generate any amount of it for you. See the **References** for some relevant links.

4. CSS is case-insensitive. However, if you read that statement quickly and don't stop to think about it, it can be quite misleading. Problems arise because although CSS itself is case-insensitive, when you are writing your CSS styles, you are often including other items that may or may not be case-insensitive, such as font family names and paths to image files. Further problems can be caused by the kind of DOCTYPE you are using, since HTML is case-insensitive as well, while XHTML is case-sensitive, and whether or not you are using JavaScript, which is also case-sensitive. The bottom line here is that it is a best practice and, for that matter, just common sense, to be consistent with the capitalization you use when choosing and writing names, particularly when it comes to the names of your class and id selectors. You would be amazed to know the number of problems you *won't* have if you follow this simple advice.

5. When designing the CSS for your website, it is worthwhile to take some time to leverage as much as you can the inheritance of styles from the body element. By thinking about it and placing as many inheritable properties as you can in the style for the body element, you can ensure that those properties will be inherited and will therefore not have to be replicated elsewhere for individual elements.

6. Some font families are better than others when it comes to displaying web pages. For example, it is generally agreed that Verdana is an excellent sans-serif font, since it is very legible even at very small sizes. Similarly, Georgia is regarded as an excellent serif font for web design. As backup for the Verdana font if it is not available, you can request Arial (for Windows) and Helvetica (for Macintosh). For Georgia you can request Times New Roman (for Windows) or Times (for Macintosh), one of which should be available on virtually any platform. Note that multi-word font family names must be enclosed in quotes.

7. One advantage of having all your styles in a single external file linked to many documents is that when a visitor browses to one of these documents, the style file is downloaded and used to render the document (of course), but most browsers will also store the style sheet in the *cache* of the user's computer. Think of the cache simply as a storage area on the user's computer where things that might be used later are stored for quick access (memory access is much faster than disk access or download speed,

so a cache is often a memory cache but could be a local file in some cases). Then, if the user browses to other documents that use the same style sheet, the browser can use the locally stored version from the cache and not have to download the style sheet again each time a file using it is displayed. This can help to make your site appear faster to your visitors.

However, this same feature can also be a pain in the wazoo for web developers. Let's say you are testing a web page by altering its associated CSS file and reloading the HTML file. But . . . you are just not seeing the changes you *know* you should be seeing. The problem is that the browser is still using the "old" version of the style sheet from the cache and has not downloaded the new version of the file containing your carefully crafted revisions. Even HTML may be stored in the cache and give rise to the same problem. There are ways to force most browsers to reload all required files from their original locations (and thus not use the cached versions). For example, pressing the `Ctrl` key while clicking the browser's `Reload` button will often do the trick. Other options you can try include `Ctrl+F5` and `Ctrl+Shift+R`. Unfortunately there does not seem to be a universal keystroke shortcut convention for this very useful action.

8. When reading CSS styles containing margin and padding values, you need to be aware of some CSS "shortcut" methods of specifying these values. Fortunately, these shortcuts work the same way for both margins and padding, so we will discuss them in the context of margins alone.

   Consider the following four CSS declarations:

   ```
   margin: 10px;
   margin: 10px 20px;
   margin: 10px 30px 40px;
   margin: 10px 20px 30px 40px;
   ```

   The first of these indicates that there should be a 10-pixel margin on all four sides of the element box. The second declaration, which contains only two values, is interpreted to mean that the margin is to be 10 pixels for both top and bottom margins and 20 pixels for both left and right margins. The third declaration, containing three values, specifies a 10px margin for the top, a 30px margin for the left and right sides, and a 40px margin for the bottom. The last declaration specifies a specific and different value for the margin on each of the four sides, so here order is important, and that order is `top`, `right`, `bottom`, `left`.

9. The `font` shorthand styles

   ```
   font: bold 11px Arial;
   font: 11px Arial;
   ```

   specify the `font-size` (`11px`) and `font-family` (`Arial`), as well as the font-weight (`bold`) if desired. Order is important here too. That is, if you want to specify the `font-weight` (`bold`), its value must come first among these three values.

10. In this chapter we have only used the CSS `float` property to help us position elements on our web pages. CSS provides many more properties that you can use for this purpose, and you will eventually need to become familiar with at least some of them. There are some subtleties involved in their use, so you will need to experiment a bit to get comfortable with their application. Here they are:
    - `static` is the default, the position an element will have in the normal flow.
    - `fixed` allows us to place an element wherever we want it, relative to the browser window.
    - `relative` allows us to place an element in a position relative to its normal position.
    - `absolute` allows us to place an element relative to its "nearest ancestor" that has already been positioned, or relative to the body element if no such positioned ancestor exists.
    - `z-index` allows us to specify a "stacking order" for elements and thus place one element "in front of" or "behind" another element, giving a kind of three-dimensional effect.

 # References

1. For information on the history of CSS, including some of the adoption difficulties, the main features of the various specifications, and some information on browser support, see:

   ```
   http://en.wikipedia.org/wiki/Cascading_Style_Sheets#History
   ```

2. For more detailed information on browser support for CSS, check out these sites:

   ```
   http://www.webdevout.net/browser-support-css
   http://www.caniuse.com
   ```

   The second of these sites also provides information on which of the new HTML5 elements can be used in which browser version as well.

3. As was the case for HTML, an excellent place to explore CSS further is, once again, the W3 Schools site. Both the tutorials and examples, as well as the reference material on properties and their values, color, positioning, and various other CSS topics, will help to consolidate your comfort level with CSS, including CSS3:

   ```
   http://www.w3schools.com/css/default.asp
   http://www.w3schools.com/cssref/default.asp
   ```

4. For further information on the best fonts to use on your website, check out the following link:

   ```
   https://www.google.com/fonts
   ```

5. For further information on the use of absolute measurements vs. relative measurements, see:

    ```
    http://www.w3schools.com/cssref/css_units.asp
    ```

6. To see all the web-safe colors, along with their hex and decimal values, follow this link:

    ```
    http://www.web-source.net/216_color_chart.htm
    ```

7. As CSS is updated, the list of colors recognized by most browsers will undoubtedly expand, but you can see the current list at this site:

    ```
    http://www.w3schools.com/colors/colors_names.asp
    ```

8. For further information on the CSS shorthand way of specifying multiple values of a single property, see:

    ```
    http://www.dustindiaz.com/css-shorthand/
    ```

9. For the definitive discussion of the exact rules governing inheritance and the cascade in CSS and for determining specificity, see:

    ```
    http://www.w3.org/TR/CSS2/cascade.html
    ```

10. For the definitive description of the CSS box model, see:

    ```
    http://www.w3.org/TR/CSS2/box.html
    ```

11. For additional information on the CSS box model, including some that offer user inter-activity, check out these sites:

    ```
    http://www.w3schools.com/css/css_boxmodel.asp
    ```

    ```
    http://css-tricks.com/the-css-box-model/
    ```

    Also, try googling "CSS box model" and looking for a link called "Images for CSS box model". Clicking on this link will take you to a large collection of images from all over the Internet that depict various incarnations of the CSS box model.

12. You may be interested in going beyond the simple floats that we discussed in this chapter for page layout, so here are some sites that discuss both floats and additional CSS positioning techniques that give you some idea of the enormous possibilities open to you as you design your website (and be sure to check out other links provided by these sites):

    ```
    http://css.maxdesign.com.au/floatutorial/
    ```

```
http://www.w3schools.com/css/css_positioning.asp
```

```
http://www.brainjar.com/css/positioning/default.asp
```

```
http://www.barelyfitz.com/screencast/html-training/css/
positioning/
```

```
http://www.elated.com/articles/css-positioning/
```

```
http://www.alistapart.com/articles/flexiblelayouts/
```

```
http://www.vanseodesign.com/css/css-positioning/
```

```
http://www.tizag.com/cssT/position.php
```

13. Here is a site that will give you some ideas for your own CSS reset::

```
http://cssreset.com/
```

14. As you know, you can and should validate your CSS style sheets, but you can also have them formatted and "optimized", which means, among other things, having styles consolidated and redundancies removed. Here are some sites that help you do this:

```
http://www.cleancss.com/
```

```
http://www.codebeautifier.com/
```

```
http://www.nigraphic.com/tidycss/
```

15. Here are two sites from which you may download some "Lorem ipsum . . ." text if you need it:

```
http://generator.lorem-ipsum.info/
```

```
http://meettheipsums.com/
```

16. If you would like to play with the new HTML5 video element, try this link:

```
http://www.w3schools.com/html/html5_video.asp
```

CHAPTER **FIVE**

HTML Forms for Data Collection

CHAPTER CONTENTS

Overview and Objectives

Up to this point we have seen only very limited interactivity between the user and any of our web pages. In fact, all a user could do was type in the URL of a page and press Enter to display that page, or click a link on one page to browse to another page.

That is, there has so far been no way for the user to supply any additional information to a website, through one of its web pages, have the site process the information in some way, and then return some new information to the user based on the data supplied. This kind of two-way communication scenario is extremely useful in a business environment, since it permits a user to make product choices, pay for them online, and supply a shipping address, for example.

This chapter marks the beginning of our discussion of how such two-way communication is accomplished, and the first thing we need to study is how a *web form* can be placed on a web page in preparation for accepting information from the user on the client side. In subsequent chapters you will see how that information can be transmitted to the server and how your website can process, and respond to, the data received from its visitors.

In this chapter we will discuss the following:

▶ The general idea of a *web form*

▶ The `form` element (though we postpone a discussion of the GET and POST values of its `action` attribute, since these indicate how we wish to submit the form's data, and in this chapter we are only creating forms, not submitting their data to a server)

▶ The `input` element

▶ The `select` and `option` elements

▶ The `textarea` element

▶ The `submit` and `reset` button elements

▶ The `fieldset` and `legend` elements

▶ The `label` element and its `for` attribute

▶ Setting up a form that allows a user to compute his or her *Body Mass Index* (*BMI*)

▶ Setting up a form that allows a user to submit feedback to our business

▶ Getting ready to submit form data (but not actually submitting it)

Also in this chapter our examples will focus entirely on form design and we will not return to an update of our full website example until Chapter 7, after we have discussed forms (this chapter), form data validation via JavaScript (Chapter 6), and dropdown menus (also implemented using JavaScript) as an example of interaction with the *DOM* (*Document Object Model*) and interactively changing our document's Cascading Style Sheets (CSS) styles (Chapter 7).

5.1 Web Forms Collect User Input Data in a Browser for Transfer to a Server for Processing

We are all familiar, perhaps too familiar, with the forms we have to fill out in our everyday lives, such as employment applications, medical reports, student loan applications, income tax forms, and so on. Online forms contain the same kinds of blank spaces or "textboxes" to be filled in, checkboxes to be checked, and so on, and we need to learn how to set these things up for data entry on our website. Even though a user can only communicate with a website in two basic ways—by clicking on various parts of a web page using a pointing device such as a mouse, or by typing text using a keyboard—such a *web form* allows the information supplied in this way to be quite sophisticated.

Once a web form is filled out, it "looks and feels" much like its paper counterpart. Submitting a web form, however, is accomplished in a different manner. Usually there is a button, often labeled **Submit**, that the user clicks, and there may also be one labeled **Reset**, to permit the user to start over and reenter form data. It is what happens *after* the user clicks **Submit** that we will discuss in later chapters.

We are going to illustrate simple form design through two examples for our business:

1. The first one will be a web page containing a form that is essentially a tool to help users find out if their weight is reasonable by calculating a quantity known as the *BMI*.
2. The second one will be a page containing a standard user-feedback form of the type used by many websites to gather user opinions on everything from the usability of the site to the overall customer experience if it is an e-commerce site.

5.2 The `form` Element

Placing a *form* on a web page is done using an HyperText Markup Language (HTML) `form` element. This `element` acts like a "container" for the usual kinds of things you see on a form, in the sense that between the `<form>` and `</form>` tags you place the other HTML tags that create the visual "widgets" that allow data entry by the user when the web page is displayed.

Let us begin with a web page that will eventually serve as your BMI calculator. Look at the HTML markup from the file `bmi1.html` shown in **FIGURE 5.1** to see how we introduce a form element into a web document. The relevant HTML code is shown in lines 12 and 13 of that file:

```
<form id="bmiForm">
</form>
```

```
 1   <!DOCTYPE html>
 2   <!-- bmi1.html -->
 3   <html lang="en">
 4     <head>
 5       <meta charset="utf-8">
 6       <title>Body Mass Index Calculator</title>
 7     </head>
 8     <body>
 9       <main>
10         <center><h4>Body Mass Index Calculator</h4></center>
11         <p>Body Mass Index (BMI) is used as an indicator of total body fat.</p>
12         <form id="bmiForm">
13         </form>
14         <p>Total body fat is correlated to the risk of certain diseases
15         which can be potentially fatal. BMI is valid for both men and women.
16         However, it should only be used as a guideline as it has some
17         limitations. It may overestimate the body fat in muscular persons and
18         underestimate the body fat in persons who have lost muscle mass.</p>
19         <p>More information can be found at the
20         <a href="http://www.nhlbisupport.com/bmi/bmicalc.htm">National
21         Institute of Health</a> website. Our calculator is based on the
22         formula obtained from this site.</p>
23       </main>
24     </body>
25   </html>
```

FIGURE 5.1 `ch05/bmi1.html`
The HTML markup for our first web page containing a `form` element, but note that this `form` element has
no content.

The displayed web page itself does not look any different (see **FIGURE 5.2**) from any of the previous web pages you have seen so far. The page has no CSS styling and therefore uses the default browser fonts and font sizes and the page will grow and shrink according to any resizing of the browser window.

Note that the mere introduction of the (empty) `form` element has no effect on the display. However, it helps us study the `<form>` tag without worrying about the rest of the details.

We have identified our `form` element as `bmiForm` by giving this value to its (optional) `id` attribute. This is generally a good idea, since we may have more than one form and in any case it allows us to identify the form for styling or access by JavaScript.

We should also say something about the `action` attribute of the `form` element, which is not shown here. The value of the action attribute is generally the name of the server-side script or other program that will process the data from the form when that data is submitted to the server. Since you are not submitting at the moment, you don't need that attribute. However, this is one of the few differences between XHTML and HTML5 that can lead to some confusion. For XHTML markup to validate, the `action` attribute of the `form` tag had to be present and have a value, but if the form was not being submitted that value could be the empty string. What is potentially confusing

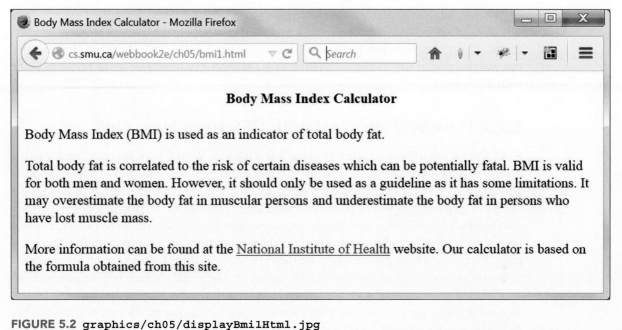

FIGURE 5.2 `graphics/ch05/displayBmi1Html.jpg`
A Firefox browser display of `ch05/bmi1.html`, showing that an empty `form` element produces no visible output.

is that in HTML5 the `action` attribute is optional, but if present the value cannot be the empty string. That is why we simply omit the `action` attribute, but if you are looking at the markup of others you may well see `action=""` as a `form` attribute. In later chapters, when you submit your form data, you will have Personal Home Page (PHP) scripts that run on your server and process that data, and the value of the `action` attribute will then contain the name of one of those scripts.

Obviously, having just an empty `form` element on a web page is not very interesting. The following sections will show you how to put different *form elements* on your BMI calculator page. These other HTML elements that are placed within the form element itself and determine the interactive behavior of the form are also called *form controls*, or, more informally, just "widgets".

5.2.1 A Brief Aside, a Reminder, and Some Good Advice

Just before we move on, let's discuss a brief aside. Note that the HTML file in Figure 5.1 contains an HTML element you have not seen before, a `center` element (see line 10). The effect of this element should be obvious: It centers its content, in this case the `h1` element, and this is certainly a very easy way to achieve that effect.

Unfortunately, the HTML `center` tag is now *deprecated*, which means that even though it still works it should no longer be used in new markup and may eventually not work at all. This begs the question: Why was it deprecated? Well, because "centering" something is a "presentational" aspect of that thing, and therefore rightly should be handled by CSS, which you will do in the next example.

We use the `center` element here to remind you once again that you should try to avoid the easy way out when developing new web pages. One way of staying the course is to make sure you continually validate your web pages. If you attempt to validate the file `bmi1.html`, for example, you will find that in fact it does *not* validate as HTML5, precisely because of the presence of the `center` element.

5.2.2 How Will We Deal with CSS from Now On?

From now on, we will handle our CSS in the following way. We will have, for each chapter, either a single CSS file called `default.css`, (or two files called `desktop.css` and `tablet.css` if we want to make use of responsive design, which we do not in this chapter). Any such files we are using in a given chapter will be placed in a subdirectory called `css`. If we have a `default.css`, it will contain all CSS styles used for the general sample files in that chapter. Not every style will necessarily be used for every sample file in the chapter, but that does not matter. In fact, that is the point. We can put all our styles in one place (one file) and link any HTML document file that needs to use one or more styles in that style file. Of course, for a large and complex website you may well want to have more than one style file, but the point remains. Subsequent files in this chapter will be making use of the version of this file corresponding to this chapter. We will only discuss the `default.css` file if it contains something of particular interest or a new CSS feature of some kind.

If a later chapter also contains an updated version of our complete website, we will put the corresponding files in a subdirectory whose name starts with `nature` and which has its own `css` subdirectory containing its own `default.css` (or `desktop.css` and `tablet.css`, as the case may be). We actually began this convention in the last chapter, where we had four such subdirectories, `nature1` to `nature4`, containing four different versions of our website, but we will not see a `nature` subdirectory again until Chapter 7.

5.3 The `input` Element

One of the most versatile HTML form controls for collecting data from users is the `input` element. It allows you to create *form fields* (places where the user can supply data of some sort) of various types. The kind of data that an `input` form field will accept is determined by the value of its `type` attribute. Here are some possible values for this attribute:

▶ `text` creates a one-line text box whose visible width, in characters, is determined by the value of the `size` attribute, and for which the `maxlength` attribute specifies the maximum number of characters allowed as input.

▶ `radio` creates a "radio button" that usually appears as a small circle in a group of small circles, only one of which may be selected.

▶ `checkbox` creates a small box, generally square, that may be "checked" or "unchecked" and also often appears in a group that (unlike the radio button) permits multiple boxes to be checked.

▶ submit creates a button on which you can place a label (often just the word **Submit**) and, when clicked on with the mouse, causes the data that has been entered in the form to be acted upon.

▶ reset also creates a button on which you can place a label (often just the word **Reset**) and allows the values in the form to be cleared, or set to their default values, thus permitting the user to start over.

So, any desired control is obtained by supplying the appropriate value from the above list as the value of the type attribute of the input tag. For example, in **FIGURE 5.3** you see

```
1   <!DOCTYPE html>
2   <!-- bmi2.html -->
3   <html lang="en">
4     <head>
5       <meta charset="utf-8">
6       <link rel="stylesheet" href="css/default.css">
7       <title>Body Mass Index Calculator</title>
8     </head>
9     <body>
10      <main class="BMI">
11        <h4 class="Centered">Body Mass Index Calculator</h4>
12        <p>Body Mass Index (BMI) is used as an indicator of total body fat. In
13        order to calculate your BMI, please input your height and weight.</p>
14        <form id="bmiForm">
15          <table>
16            <tr>
17              <td>Height:</td>
18              <td><input type="text" name="height" size="7"></td>
19              <td>Units:</td>
20              <td><input type="radio" name="heightUnit" value="in"> inches</td>
21              <td><input type="radio" name="heightUnit" value="cm">
22              centimeters</td>
23            </tr>
24            <tr>
25              <td>Weight:</td>
26              <td><input type="text" name="weight" size="7"></td>
27              <td>Units:</td>
28              <td><input type="radio" name="weightUnit" value="lb">
29                pounds</td>
30              <td><input type="radio" name="weightUnit" value="kg">
31                kilograms</td>
32            </tr>
```

FIGURE 5.3 ch05/bmi2.html
An HTML document containing a form element with input elements of type text, radio, and checkbox.

```
33                <tr>
34                  <td colspan="5">Please check here if you want a detailed
35                    analysis of your BMI:
36                  <input type="checkbox" name="details" value="yes"></td>
37                </tr>
38              </table>
39            </form>
40            <p>Total body fat is correlated to the risk of certain diseases
41            which can be potentially fatal. BMI is valid for both men and women.
42            However, it should only be used as a guideline as it has some
43            limitations. It may overestimate the body fat in muscular persons and
44            underestimate the body fat in persons who have lost muscle mass.</p>
45            <p>More information can be found at the
46            <a href="http://www.nhlbisupport.com/bmi/bmicalc.htm">National
47            Institute of Health</a> website. Our calculator is based on the
48            formula obtained from this site.</p>
49          </main>
50        </body>
51      </html>
```

FIGURE 5.3 `ch05/bmi2.html` (*continued*)

illustrated input controls of type `text` (lines 18 and 26), `radio` (lines 20–21 and 28–31), and `checkbox`. (line 36).

FIGURE 5.4 displays our first "real" form, since it contains some actual "fields", form controls for entering or indicating data input. Each of the controls in the form displayed in Figure 5.4 is created by using an `input` element. These controls include the things that we call "textboxes", "radio buttons", and a "checkbox", and which are produced by the corresponding HTML markup referred to above and seen in the file `bmi2.html` of Figure 5.3.

Note, first of all, as promised in the previous section, that we are no longer using the (deprecated) HTML `center` element for centering our page title, but instead a class called `Centered`, which is defined in this chapter's `default.css`[1] file and used with the `h4` element.

Second, note that for this form we are using a table layout with three rows and four columns to contain the controls used to collect information from the user. We can argue for a table layout here as the appropriate choice, since a table makes sense whether we are *displaying* data, or, as in the current case, *collecting* data. Note that although we are using a table, it is not immediately obvious since we do not display any table borders.

And now for the details . . .

---

[1] As noted previously, unless there is some particular reason to examine the CSS for a particular display, we will not show each and every variation of our `default.css` file as we go from chapter to chapter. You should, however, continue to study the content of these files to answer any questions you may have about any of the displays.

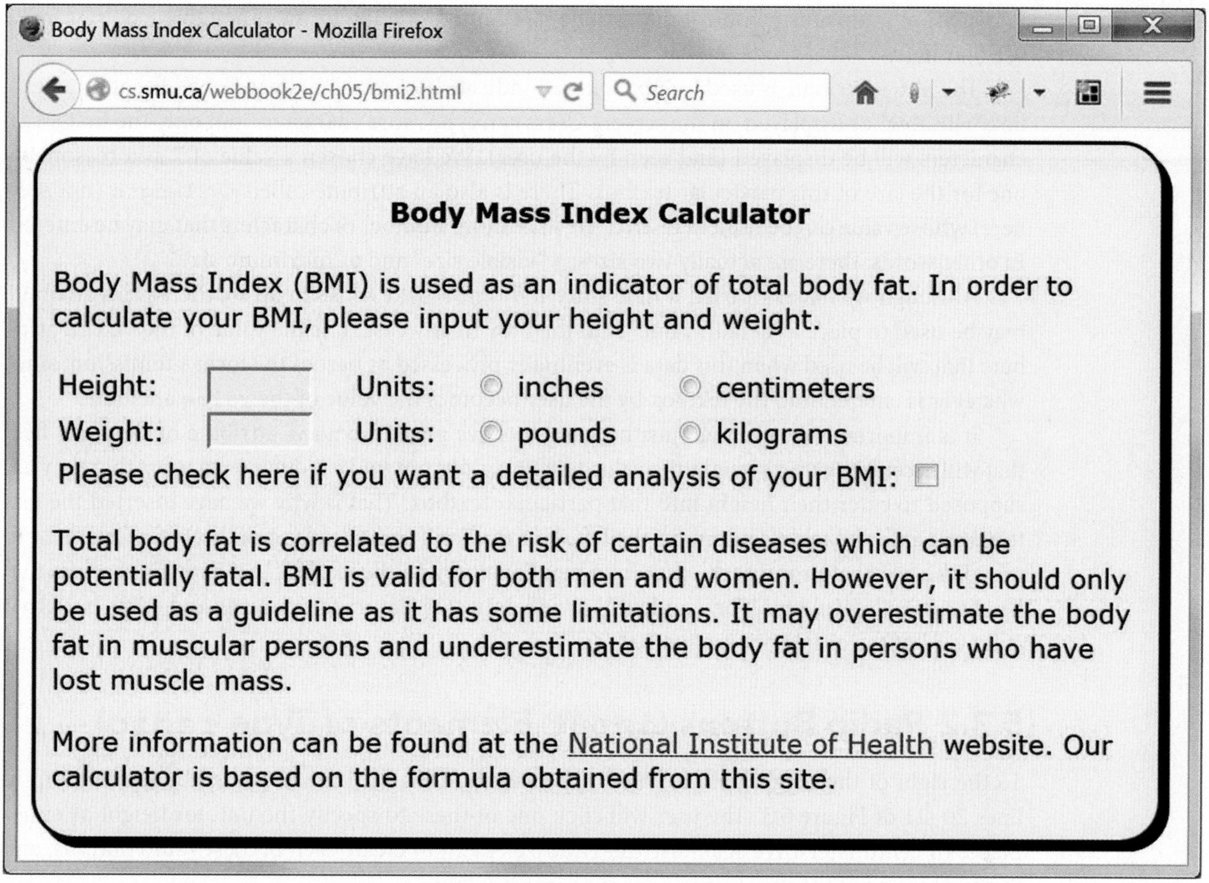

FIGURE 5.4 `graphics/ch05/displayBmi2Html.jpg`
A Firefox browser display of `ch05/bmi2.html`, showing the textboxes, the radio buttons, and the single checkbox.

5.3.1 Textboxes (input **Elements of Type** text)

The empty textbox in the first row of the table (line 18 of Figure 5.3) allows a user to enter his or her height. This is the markup that creates this textbox:

```
<input type="text" name="height" size="7">
```

As you can see, the input element is an empty element, and this one has three attributes. The type attribute tells the web browser what kind of input control this one is (textbox, checkbox, radio button, and so on). In this case, the value text indicates we have a textbox. The name attribute is used to identify this particular HTML element and distinguish it from other elements of the same kind. This will be useful (necessary, in fact) when you write programs to process the information in this form control that will be "submitted" via the form, although we do not make use of it here.

The `size` attribute is used for textboxes to indicate how many characters will fit into the text-box "window" as displayed on the screen. Users can type more characters, but only the first `size` characters will be displayed (and seen by the user). We have chosen a value of 7 as a reasonable one for the size of this particular textbox. There is also an attribute called `maxlength` (not seen here) whose value can be used to restrict the maximum number of characters that may be entered. In other words, there are actually two sizes: a "visible size" and a "maximum size".

Although we have not used it here since it did not make sense to do so, the `value` attribute may be used to place a "default value" into the box. In any case, it is the value of the `value` attri-bute that will be used when this data is eventually processed as part of the form submission, since whatever is entered into the textbox by the user becomes the value of the `value` attribute.

It is important to note that, just because we have given the `name` attribute of the form field that will receive the user's height the value `height`, does not make it obvious to users that they are supposed to enter their height into that particular textbox. That is why we have inserted the text `Height:` into the table column on the left. You can (and should) also use the `label` element to group the text that prompts the user for a height value, and the textbox that actually receives that height, into a logical unit. For simplicity we will omit this feature temporarily and come back to it at the end of the chapter in section 5.9.

5.3.2 Radio Buttons (`input` Elements of Type `radio`)

To the right of the height field we have two radio buttons, which are created by the markup in lines 20–21 of Figure 5.3. The user will click one of these to specify the unit for height as either inches or centimeters. We again use the `input` element to create each of these radio buttons, and this time we need the value `radio` for the `type` attribute.

When used for radio buttons, the behavior of the `input` element is a little more complicated, because radio buttons are normally used in a group. Radio buttons in the same group are identified by having the same value for the `name` attribute. We distinguish them based on the values of their `value` attributes. In our example, the first group of radio buttons contains two buttons and is found to the right of the height field. The common name for this group of radio buttons is `heightUnit`.

The value of the `value` attribute for the first radio button in the group is `in`, corresponding to "inches". The second radio button has the value `cm` for the `value` attribute, corresponding to "centimeters". Using the same name for both radio buttons ensures that only one of them can be selected at a time by the user. You may want to verify this fact by opening the file `bmi2.html` in a browser and clicking on each of these radio buttons in turn. The thing to note is that if one button is "selected", that is, has been clicked and shows a "bullet" in the center of its circle, and then you click the other button, the first one is "deselected" as the second one becomes "selected".

The next row is essentially identical to the previous one in structure and format. It is used to obtain the user's weight and choice of weight unit. Again, we have three `input` elements. The first `input` element, of type `text`, is named `weight`. The next two `input` elements give us radio but-tons grouped under the name `weightUnit`, with values `lb` (for pounds) and `kg` (for kilograms).

5.3.3 Checkboxes (input **Elements of Type** checkbox)

The third type of `input` element lets us create checkboxes. An example of a checkbox also appears in `bmi2.html`, in the table row just below the row for weight input (see line 36 of Figure 5.3). Checkboxes are similar to radio buttons in many ways. Multiple checkboxes can also be grouped together under the same name and distinguished by value just like radio buttons, even though our example only uses a single checkbox. Our checkbox has the name `details` and the value `yes`.

You will note that in the display of Figure 5.4 the checkbox is not checked by default. This is the typical case, and the user is asked to check the textbox if he or she wishes to take the option represented by that particular checkbox. There may, however, be times when you want the checkbox checked by default. To accomplish this, the `input` element also has another attribute with the name `checked`. This attribute need only be present to cause its intended effect. It does not need a value. The point of including the attribute is to have the checkbox checked by default when the page is displayed, should you wish to do that.

The attribute `checked` can also be used (and is, in fact, more often used) for radio buttons, but in that case you should make sure that only one of the radio buttons in the group is checked (the one the user is most likely to choose, presumably).

It should be noted that data from `input` controls of type `radio` or `checkbox` is actually "submitted" by the submit button only if the corresponding `checked` attribute is present.

5.4 The select and option Elements for Dropdown List-boxes

In the previous section we illustrated how radio buttons can be used to allow a user to specify a choice of units for weight and height. Another method for letting the user pick an option is through a dropdown list-box (also called a dropdown menu, but we call this particular version a dropdown list-box to distinguish it from the dropdown menus we introduce in Chapter 7). Dropdown list-boxes are especially useful when the number of options is large, because they use much less display space on a web page.

The web page `bmi3.html` displayed in **FIGURE 5.5** shows a dropdown list-box for units of height and weight. The corresponding `form` element markup is shown in **FIGURE 5.6**. We will only focus on the code between the `<select>...</select>` pairs of tags (the `select` elements) in `bmi3.html` (lines 20–23 and lines 29–32). The rest of the file shows you nothing you have not already seen in `bmi2.html`.

Any `select` element used to create a web page dropdown list-box should be provided with a value for its `name` attribute for the same reasons you would give a name to an `input` element. Each text item corresponding to an option in the dropdown list-box is specified by the text content of an `<option>...</option>` tag pair. By default the option that appears first in the markup will appear in the little window of the dropdown list-box, so you should leave that option empty if you want the box to appear empty.

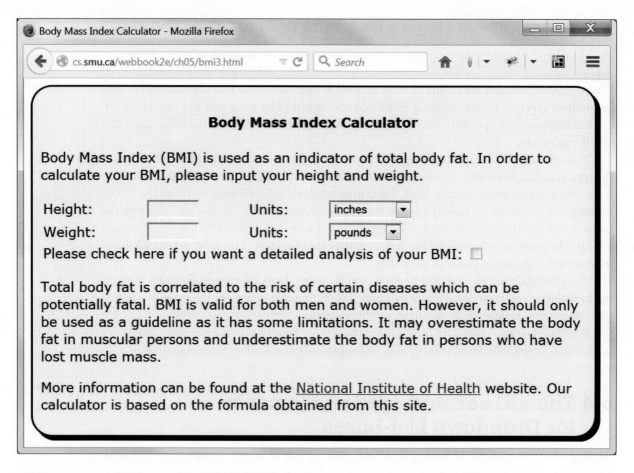

FIGURE 5.5 `graphics/ch05/displayBmi3Html.jpg`
A Firefox browser display of `ch05/bmi3.html`, with dropdown list-boxes replacing the radio buttons shown in Figure 5.4.

In our example, the `select` element for the weight unit has attribute `name="weightUnit"` and the `select` element for the height has attribute unit `name="heightUnit"`. Both of these dropdown list-boxes have only two options.

We have not included `name` attributes for the `option` elements, but when submitting a form you may want to do this as well.

5.5 What Is Missing from the BMI Calculator Web Page?

If you look at the display in Figure 5.5 for a moment, it should be clear that there is something missing. This web page allows the user to enter some information that will be needed to perform a certain kind of calculation, but does not provide any visible way to cause the calculation to take

```
14          <form id="bmiForm">
15            <table>
16              <tr>
17                <td>Height:</td>
18                <td><input type="text" name="height" size="7"></td>
19                <td>Units:</td>
20                <td><select name="heightUnit">
21                  <option>inches</option>
22                  <option>centimeters</option>
23                </select></td>
24              </tr>
25              <tr>
26                <td>Weight:</td>
27                <td><input type="text" name="weight" size="7"></td>
28                <td>Units:</td>
29                <td><select name="weightUnit">
30                  <option>pounds</option>
31                  <option>kilograms</option>
32                </select></td>
33              </tr>
34              <tr>
35                <td colspan="4">Please check here if you want a detailed analysis
36                of your BMI: <input type="checkbox" name="details"
37                value="yes"></td>
38              </tr>
39            </table>
40          </form>
```

FIGURE 5.6 `ch05/bmi3.html` (excerpt)
Partial HTML markup from `ch05/bmi3.html`, showing the two `select` elements that produced the dropdown list-boxes in Figure 5.5.

place. In other words, it is missing a "button" of some kind that the user can click on, and after which the BMI calculation will be performed and the results displayed to the user.

In this chapter we are concerned only with *displaying* the button, not *activating* it. As we have said earlier, we will deal with the calculations in the next chapter. But bear with us for a bit while we also postpone the introduction of buttons onto our BMI calculator page. In the next couple of sections we will start our second example, the feedback form, and use it to introduce both the `textarea` element (for extended text entry) and the `submit` and `reset` buttons for data submission and form reset. Then we will come back to our BMI calculator and extend it with buttons and some other enhancements.

5.6 The `textarea` Element

Providing a mechanism for getting feedback from its visitors should be one of the essential features of any e-commerce website. If the right kind of information is obtained and used properly, the user experience can be enhanced and sales increased.

Our second example illustrates just such a feedback form. The first version of the web page containing this form is in the file `feedback1.html`, shown in **FIGURE 5.7**, and the display of that file is shown in **FIGURE 5.8**.

Almost everything on this web page you have seen before. It has a dropdown list-box to let the user pick a title (or "salutation") such as `Ms.` or `Dr.` This is followed by standard text fields for the user's first name, last name, email address, phone number, and the subject on which the user wishes to provide feedback.

```
1   <!DOCTYPE html>
2   <!-- feedback1.html -->
3   <html lang="en">
4     <head>
5       <meta charset="utf-8">
6       <link rel="stylesheet" href="css/default.css">
7       <title>Contact Us</title>
8     </head>
9     <body>
10      <main class="Feedback">
11        <h4>Feedback Form ... Let Us Know What You Think</h4>
12        <form id="contact">
13          <table>
14            <tr>
15              <td>Salutation:</td>
16              <td><select name="salute">
17                <option> </option>
18                <option>Mrs.</option>
19                <option>Ms.</option>
20                <option>Mr.</option>
21                <option>Dr.</option>
22              </select></td>
23            </tr>
24            <tr>
25              <td>First Name:</td>
26              <td><input type="text" name="firstName" size="40"></td>
27            </tr>
28            <tr>
29              <td>Last Name:</td>
30              <td><input type="text" name="lastName" size="40"></td>
31            </tr>
32            <tr>
33              <td>E-mail Address:</td>
34              <td><input type="text" name="email" size="40"></td>
35            </tr>
```

FIGURE 5.7 `ch05/feedback1.html`
HTML markup for the first version of our feedback form, containing a `textarea` element to receive user comments.

```
36            <tr>
37              <td>Phone Number:</td>
38              <td><input type="text" name="phone" size="40"></td>
39            </tr>
40            <tr>
41              <td>Subject:</td>
42              <td><input type="text" name="subject" size="40"></td>
43            </tr>
44            <tr>
45              <td>Comments:</td>
46              <td><textarea name="message" rows="6" cols="30"></textarea></td>
47            </tr>
48            <tr>
49              <td colspan="2">Please check here if you wish to receive a reply:
50              <input type="checkbox" name="reply" value="yes"></td>
51            </tr>
52          </table>
53        </form>
54      </main>
55    </body>
56  </html>
```

FIGURE 5.7 `ch05/feedback1.html` (*continued*)

It is a good idea to separate the name into two fields, one for the first name and one for the last name. This will help avoid any confusion between first and last names, and also allow you to personalize any response to the user by using his or her first name, or a salutation followed by the last name, depending on the context. The `textarea` element allows you to provide a large text area for the user to enter a message, since you can specify its size by supplying the desired number of rows and columns as values of its `rows` and `cols` attributes.

Some users may just want to have a one-way communication. Others may wish to receive a reply. Therefore, we give the user a choice of receiving a reply using a checkbox at the bottom.

We do need to point out a couple of things about the HTML markup of the form in `feedback1.html` (see Figure 5.7). First, since the salutation is obtained from a dropdown list-box, we have again used a `select` element to contain the options. However, since we did not want to presume any particular salutation, we have left the content of the first `option` element empty (see line 17), causing the dropdown list-box to appear empty in Figure 5.8. Actually, if you look closely you will see that it is not quite empty. Its content is the HTML entity ` `, a useful entity whenever you want to ensure that you have an actual space at some location. In fact it's a "non-breaking" space, so a new line will not be created at that space, which is not a feature you need at this point. Leaving all content out of the option element would work fine as far as displaying the page is concerned, but if you are using an editor to format your code you need to be careful that it does not remove empty elements from your markup. This may be something you want most

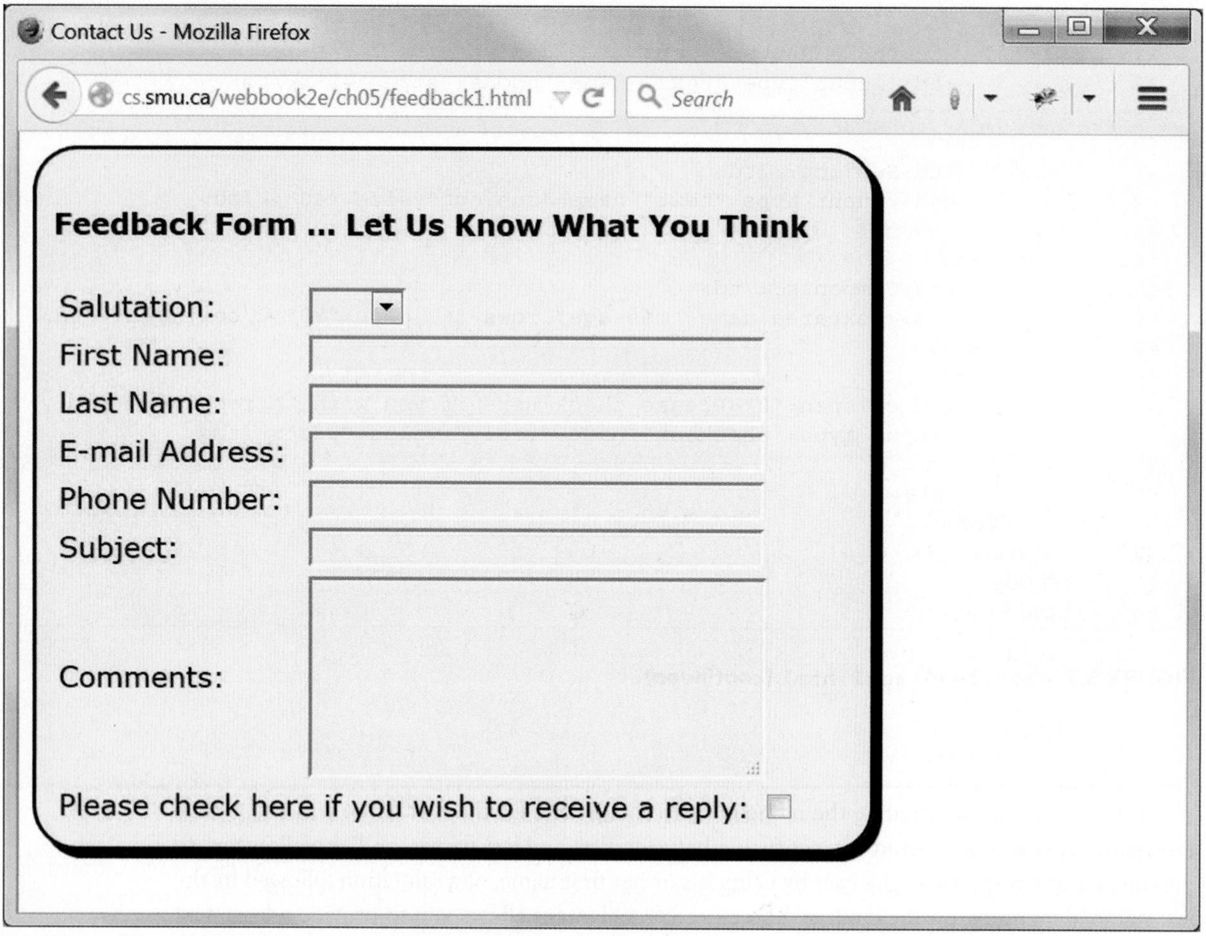

FIGURE 5.8 `graphics/ch05/displayFeedback1Html.jpg`
A Firefox browser display of `ch05/feedback1.html` from Figure 5.7, showing a `textarea` element for user comments.

of the time, but not in this situation, so putting this HTML entity in as the content avoids that problem and has the same effect as an empty `option` element.

There is nothing unusual about the following five fields that are used to collect the first name, last name, email address, phone number, and subject. They are all textboxes created by using `input` elements with their `type` attributes set to `text`.

The second new thing of interest in this form is, of course, the `textarea` element in line 46. This particular `textarea` element has no content between its `<textarea>` and `</textarea>` tag pair, but if you wished to have some default text displayed when the page is rendered, you could supply that text as the element content. Just like other form fields, the `textarea` tag has an attribute called `name`, which we have set to the value `message`. Two additional attributes for the `textarea` tag are `rows` and `cols`, and they allow us to specify the height (number of rows) and width (number of columns, or characters) of the text area, respectively. We have chosen to have 6 lines (rows), each one allowing for 30 characters (columns). By default, a `textarea` element is "scrollable". That means a user can enter more than six lines of text, and the `textarea` control will then show a vertical scroll bar on the right.

The option that determines whether a user receives a reply uses an `input` element with the `type` attribute set to a value of `checkbox`. The name of the field is `reply`. We have set the value to be `yes`, in case the user does check the checkbox and data from this control is submitted. There is no `checked` attribute because we want the checkbox to be unchecked by default when the page displays.

5.7 The `submit` and `reset` Button Elements

In general, every form needs to "submit" the data entered by the user to be processed in some way. This capability is usually provided by a "submit button". Another useful button to have on a form is a "reset button", which can be used to clear any information that may have been entered and give the user a chance to start over.

FIGURE 5.9 shows our complete feedback form that includes buttons for submitting and resetting. Since the rest of the form is exactly the same as the one in `feedback1.html`, we show in **FIGURE 5.10** only the HTML markup that creates these buttons. We use the versatile `input` element to create both the submit and reset buttons.

The `type` attribute must be set to `submit` to get a submit button. The `value` attribute for our submit button is set to **Send Feedback**, which is the text label that appears on the button in the display of the form.

A value of `reset` for the `type` attribute of the `input` element creates a reset button. Its `value` attribute is set to the text **Reset Form**, which appears as the visible label on the reset button when the web page containing the form is displayed. The reset button is immediately active, in the sense that if you enter some data and click on the reset button, the data will disappear from the form. However, we have not yet activated the submit button in the sense of connecting it to a script (program) that will process the data, and will do so only in a later chapter when we have some programming code (a script) to respond when a user clicks on this button and data is submitted.

5.8 Organizing Form Controls with the `fieldset` and `legend` Elements

Usually, the high-level view of a web form consists of several logical parts—required input, optional input, processing buttons, and so on. Each logical part, in turn, consists of a group of fields to collect or deal with in some way a particular category of information, and we now return to our BMI example to discuss how we can emphasize these logical groupings in a web page display.

We have a more refined version of our BMI calculator form shown in the display of `ch05/bmi4.html` in **FIGURE 5.11**. From the figure you can see how the three "logical chunks"

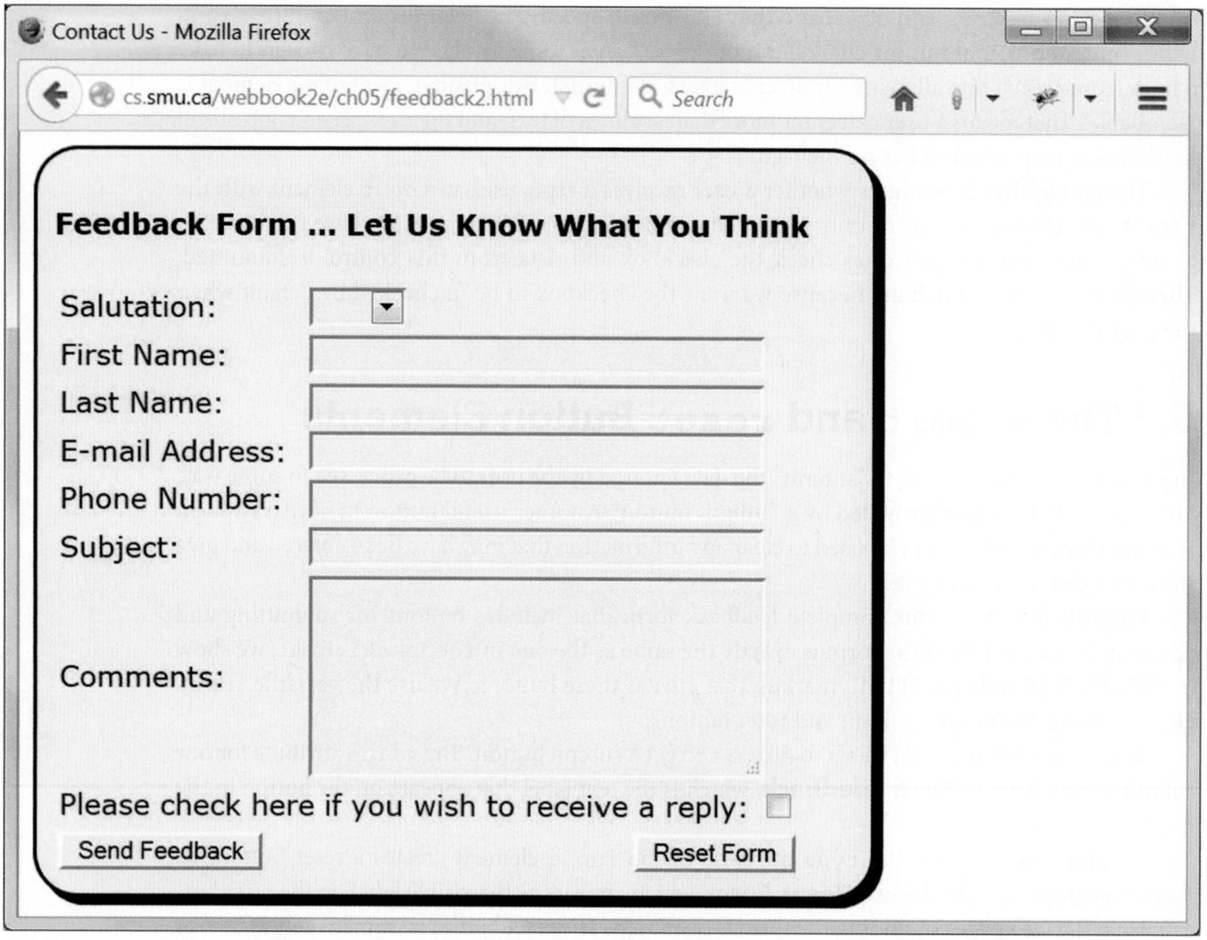

FIGURE 5.9 `graphics/ch05/displayFeedback2Html.jpg`
A Firefox browser display of `ch05/feedback2.html`, now showing the two `input` element buttons for submitting or resetting the form data.

```
52        <tr>
53          <td><input type="submit" value="Send Feedback"></td>
54          <td class="RightAligned"><input type="reset"
55            value="Reset Form"></td>
56        </tr>
```

FIGURE 5.10 `ch05/feedback2.html` **(excerpt)**
Partial HTML markup from `ch05/feedback2.html` showing the `input` elements that produce the submit and reset buttons of Figure 5.9.

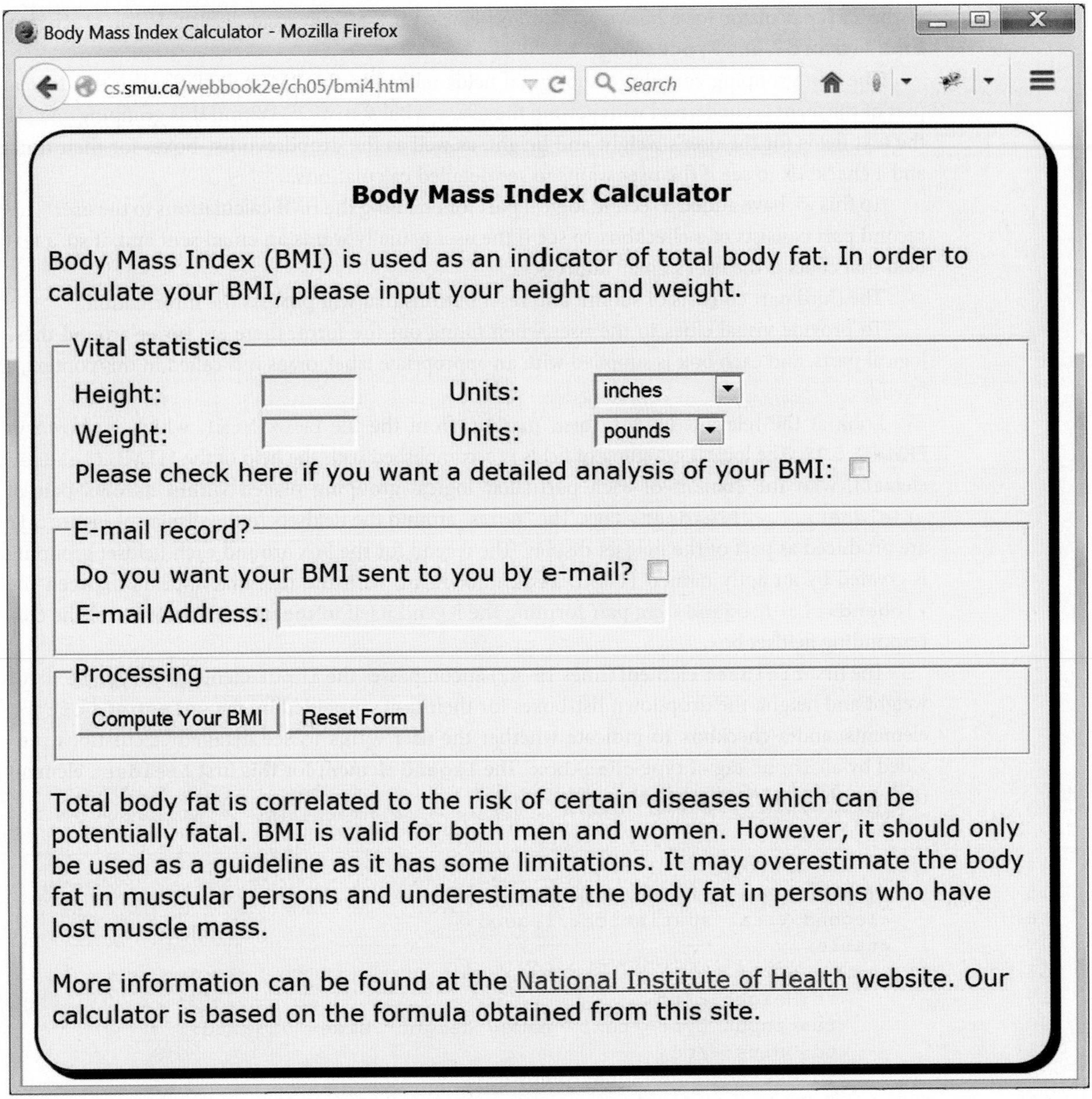

FIGURE 5.11 `graphics/ch05/displayBmi4Html.jpg`
A Firefox browser display of `ch05/bmi4.html`, showing three instances of a `fieldset` grouping with its `legend`.

of the BMI calculator have been grouped and labeled in the web page display: **Vital statistics**, **Email record?**, and **Processing**.

The first grouping contains the original fields related to the BMI calculation, so this logical part of the form is concerned with getting the user's "vital statistics". Within this grouping you see the text fields for the user's weight and height, as well as the dropdown list-boxes for their units and a checkbox to see if the user wants to see detailed calculations.

To this we have added a second logical part for emailing the BMI calculations to the user. This second part consists of a checkbox to see if the user actually wants an email sent and, if so, a text field that collects the user's email address.

The third part consists of submit and reset buttons that will process the information.

To provide visual clues to the user when filling out the form, there are boxes around these logical parts, and each box is supplied with an appropriate label, or, as it is called in this context, a *legend*.

Look at the relevant HTML form markup from the file `bmi4.html`, which is shown in **FIGURE 5.12**. The logical grouping of fields is accomplished with the help of the HTML `fieldset` element, with the content of each particular logical grouping placed within its own pair of `<fieldset>...</fieldset>` tags. The "boxes" around the fieldsets in the display of Figure 5.11 are produced as part of the fieldset display. The legend for the box around each fieldset grouping is created by an aptly named HTML `legend` element, with the text that appears between the `<legend>...</legend>` tag pair forming the legend itself in the upper left corner of the corresponding fieldset box.

The first `fieldset` element (lines 15–42) encompasses the `input` elements of type `text` for weight and height, the dropdown list-boxes for their units provided by the `select` and `option` elements, and a checkbox to indicate whether the user wants to see detailed calculations provided by an `input` tag of type `checkbox`. The `legend` element for this first `fieldset` element contains the text **Vital statistics**.

```
14      <form id="bmiForm">
15        <fieldset>
16          <legend>Vital statistics</legend>
17          <table>
18            <tr>
19              <td>Height:</td>
20              <td><input type="text" name="height" size="7"></td>
21              <td>Units:</td>
22              <td><select name="heightUnit">
23                <option>inches</option>
24                <option>centimeters</option>
25              </select></td>
26            </tr>
```

FIGURE 5.12 `ch05/bmi4.html` **(excerpt)**
Partial HTML markup from `ch05/bmi4.html`, showing the three `fieldset` elements, each with a nested `legend` element.

```
27              <tr>
28                <td>Weight:</td>
29                <td><input type="text" name="weight" size="7"></td>
30                <td>Units:</td>
31                <td><select name="weightUnit">
32                  <option>pounds</option>
33                  <option>kilograms</option>
34                </select></td>
35              </tr>
36              <tr>
37                <td colspan="4">Please check here if you want a detailed
38                analysis of your BMI: <input type="checkbox" name="details"
39                value="yes"></td>
40              </tr>
41            </table>
42          </fieldset>
43          <fieldset>
44            <legend>E-mail record?</legend>
45            <table>
46              <tr>
47                <td colspan="2">Do you want your BMI sent to you by e-mail?
48                <input type="checkbox" name="want_mail" value="yes"></td>
49              </tr>
50              <tr>
51                <td>E-mail Address:</td>
52                <td><input type="text" name="email" size="40"></td>
53              </tr>
54            </table>
55          </fieldset>
56          <fieldset>
57            <legend>Processing</legend>
58            <table>
59              <tr>
60                <td><input type="submit" value="Compute Your BMI"></td>
61                <td><input type="reset" value="Reset Form"></td>
62              </tr>
63            </table>
64          </fieldset>
65        </form>
```

FIGURE 5.12 `ch05/bmi4.html` (excerpt) (*continued*)

The second `fieldset` element (lines 43–55) uses the `legend` text **Email record?**, with the question mark suggesting the user may not wish to provide this information. It consists of two `input` elements. The first `input` element is of type `checkbox` and determines if the user wants to receive the email. The second `input` element is of type `text` and collects the email address of the user, if it is supplied.

The third `fieldset` element (lines 56–64) has the `legend` text `Processing` and two `input` elements, one of type `submit` that gives us the submit button and a second of type `reset` to provide a button for resetting the fields in the form. In the display of this form the two buttons are positioned side-by-side at the left.

Note that the content of each `fieldset` element is now a table. We cannot keep the single-table structure we had in `bmi3.html` and simply add more rows and columns to that table. The reason for this is that for validation a `fieldset` element must be a "child" of the `form` element, and thus cannot be contained within a `table` element with the `table` element being the child of the `form` element.

5.9 Using the `label` Element for Behind-the-Scenes Logical Groupings

In the previous section you saw how the `fieldset` element could be used to group web page elements to provide visual clues to the viewer about the logical grouping of displayed items. It is also a good idea when designing web pages to provide some behind-the-scenes logical grouping as well. For this purpose the `label` element can be used to associate a label with form controls such as `input`, `textarea`, and `select`.

There are a number of good reasons for doing this. First of all, the association enhances the usability of forms. For example, when users of visual web browsers click on a label, the "focus" is automatically set in the associated form element. Thus for users with visual disabilities who are making use of *assistive technologies*, establishing these associations between labels and controls helps clarify the spatial relationships found in forms and makes them easier to navigate.

Earlier in this chapter we mentioned that when designing forms, it is a good idea to group the text that prompts the user for a value with the component that actually receives that value so that they form a logical unit. In this context, a second reason for using a `label` element for logical grouping is that doing so can help to avoid the possibility that text describing a form field will get separated from that field in future changes to the page.

There are two ways to use the `label` element in this way. First, if the text describing an element and the element itself are immediately adjacent to one another, both may simply be included as the content of the `label` element, as in this example:

```
<td>
  <label>
    Height: <input type="text" name="height" size="7">
  </label>
</td>
```

This is referred to as an *implicit label*.

On the other hand, if the text description and the input element are separated (the text appears within one element, and the form control it describes appears within another element), then the `for` attribute of the `label` element may be used to bind the two elements together, as illustrated in the following example:

```
<td>
  <label for="heightValue">Height: </label>
</td>
<td>
  <input id="heightValue" type="text" name="height" size="7">
</td>
```

This is referred to as an *explicit label*, and is preferred to the *implicit label* illustrated above, since it is more likely to be properly interpreted by the current crop of browsers.

Note that the value of the `for` attribute in the `label` element is the same as the value of the `id` attribute in the `input` element, which is what establishes the association between the two.

You might be inclined to try rewriting the above example as

```
<tr>
  <label>
    <td>Height: </td>
    <td><input type="text" name="height" size="7" /></td>
  </label>
</tr>
```

but this will not work. Or, to be more precise, it may work but it won't validate, since a `label` element is not permitted inside a `tr` element in this way because the label and the form control being labeled are in different table cells.

Now take a look at **FIGURE 5.13**, which contains the HTML markup of just the first `fieldset` element from the final version of our BMI calculator form (an excerpt from `ch05/bmi5.html`). You will see that we have revised the HTML `form` markup from Figure 5.12 to include appropriate `label` tags having appropriate `for` attributes. Since Figure 5.13 shows only the first `fieldset` element, you should study the rest of the file, looking for the remaining `label` tags to see where and how they are placed.

Note that placing other elements within a `label` element has absolutely no effect on the display of those other elements. Thus the display of the web page given by `bmi5.html` is identical to that of `bmi4.html` shown in Figure 5.11.

However, adding `label` elements like this is a way of setting up logical groupings that can be used to bind elements together for manipulation purposes and may even serve as documentation during future maintenance of the page. Moreover, from the assistive technology point of view, such groupings can be helpful for visually impaired visitors to your website, for the following reason: The user does not have to click directly on a textbox (for example) to get the focus on that textbox and put the cursor in it for text entry. It is only necessary to click somewhere on the label "for" that textbox, in other words the textbox whose `id` attribute is the same as the `for` attribute of the relevant `label` element.

```
15        <fieldset>
16          <legend>Vital statistics</legend>
17            <table>
18              <tr>
19              <td><label for="height">Height:</label></td>
20              <td><input id="height" type="text" name="height"
21                size="7"></td>
22              <td><label for="heightUnit">Units:</label></td>
23              <td><select id="heightUnit" name="heightUnit">
24                <option>inches</option>
25                <option>centimeters</option>
26              </select></td>
27            </tr>
28            <tr>
29              <td><label for="weight">Weight:</label></td>
30              <td><input id="weight" type="text" name="weight"
31                size="7"></td>
32              <td><label for="weightUnit">Units:</label></td>
33              <td><select id="weightUnit" name="weightUnit">
34                <option>pounds</option>
35                <option>kilograms</option>
36              </select></td>
37            </tr>
38            <tr>
39              <td colspan="4"><label for="details">Please check here if you
40              want a detailed analysis of your BMI:</label>
41              <input id="details" type="checkbox"
42                    name="details" value="yes"></td>
43            </tr>
44          </table>
45        </fieldset>
```

FIGURE 5.13 `ch05/bmi5.html` **(excerpt)**
Partial HTML markup from `ch05/bmi5.html`, showing the first `fieldset` element now revised to contain two `label` elements with `for` attributes that connect them to `input` elements with matching `id` attribute values.

5.10 Getting Ready to Submit Your Form Data

We have gone as far as we can go without any programming. The purpose of the web forms that we have created in this chapter is to allow users to submit data to websites for processing. However, in order to process the data, we need to write computer programs. The kinds of computer programs that we will write are also often called *scripts*, but that is not a distinction that need concern us.

Programming on the web can be broadly placed into two categories: client-side programming and server-side programming. On the client side, the programs run on the user's computer through the web browser. Server-side programming involves the running of programs on the computer that is hosting the web server.

Client-side computing can provide only limited features, as it cannot access any databases, for example. It is also limited by security restrictions on the client's computer. Server-side programming is essential for sophisticated e-commerce-related computing.

We will look at both client-side and server-side computing in the following chapters. We will begin with a study of JavaScript in the next chapter. This will allow you to perform client-side computing that accomplishes the following:

▶ Checking what the user has entered into your forms to make sure it is valid data before you try to do anything with it

▶ Using the data entered into your BMI form to compute and display the user's body mass index value

In subsequent chapters you will use the PHP programming language and the MySQL database management software to do more sophisticated server-side computing.

5.11 HTML5 Form Controls

In this chapter the HTML form controls we introduced have all been available for some time, and you can use a relatively small collection of such controls to create forms for collecting a wide variety of information from your users. However, as you might imagine, HTML5 has added a great deal of new functionality to web forms. Not only are there new form controls, but also new attributes for the preexisting form controls. The problem, at least at the time of this writing, is that the rendering engines in some browsers cannot yet deal with some of these new elements and/or attributes, and even when they do, the way in which they deal with them is not consistent from one browser to the next.

Nevertheless, it is important that you become aware of these new HTML5 form features and try to keep an eye on developments in the area as more browsers begin to provide their capabilities. For example, HTML5 now offers over a dozen new values for the type attribute of the input element. Each new type allows the given input element to receive a specific kind of input data, such as a color, a time, a date, a numerical range, a URL, an email address, or a telephone number (for example). One advantage of these new input elements is that they can be set up to detect whether the data entered into them is of the required type, which avoids having to perform such data checks using JavaScript code separate from the HTML markup. JavaScript is still valuable for this purpose, as you shall see in the next chapter, but some of the work it used to do has now been taken over by HTML5 input elements.

HTML5 has also added more than a dozen new attributes to the input element. One of the most useful of these is the pattern attribute, which you can also use with the "legacy" input elements we have discussed in this chapter. This attribute allows you to describe a "pattern" that the data entered into a particular input element must follow if it is to be accepted, thus allowing you to make your "old-fashioned" input elements behave in much the same way as the newer HTML5 input elements with respect to "validating" the data entered into them.

We will discuss these ideas further in the next chapter, and in the meantime you can find links to further information in the **References** section of this chapter.

Summary

In this chapter we discussed the web form, which is used on our web pages for collecting data input from site visitors. Such a form is created by placing an HTML `form` element in the page document, and then placing within that element a number of *form controls* or "widgets" that are able to receive data from the user in some form.

These controls include various forms of the `input` element (for textboxes, radio buttons, and checkboxes, for example). Radio buttons can be grouped and allow the user to choose only one option from the group. Checkboxes can also be grouped, but allow multiple choices.

Dropdown list-boxes provide a space-saving alternative to a group of radio buttons or checkboxes when the number of choices is large. A dropdown list-box is created by nesting `option` elements inside a `select` element.

If you want more text input than the single line of text allowed by the textbox variant of the input element, you can use a `textarea` element, and choose the number of rows and columns for its initial display, as well as any default text you want it to contain.

For enhanced usability, form controls that belong to the same logical grouping can be physically grouped as the content of a `fieldset` element, with an associated `legend` element. This has the effect of drawing a box around those controls in the display and labeling that box at the upper left with the text that formed the content of the `legend` element.

The `label` element can (and should) be used to provide a logical grouping of an input element and the text used to describe that element. This also has the effect of enhancing usability, since even clicking on the label of a labeled element will shift the focus to that element.

This chapter has taken you as far as we can go without programming, which we begin to discuss in the next chapter.

Quick Questions to Test Your Basic Knowledge

1. What deprecated HTML tag did we introduce in this chapter, just to make a point, and what was the point?
2. What is the purpose of having a form on a web page?
3. If you place an empty `form` element on a web page, what do you see as a result when the page is displayed?
4. What is the purpose of the `action` attribute of a `form` element, and what kind of value does it have?
5. The `action` attribute of the `form` element is optional, but a form element will almost always have one. Nevertheless, none of the forms in this chapter had an `action` attribute. Why not?

6. In HTML5, if a `form` element has an `action` attribute, what is the restriction on the value of that attribute?

7. What are the five different kinds of `input` elements we discussed in detail in this chapter, and what kind of input does each permit?

8. How many lines of text can you put in a textbox created by an `input` element whose `type` attribute has a value of `text`?

9. What is the purpose of the `value` attribute of an `input` element of type `text`?

10. What is determined by the `size` attribute of an `input` element of type `text`?

11. What is determined by the `maxlength` attribute of an `input` element of type `text`?

12. Since all radio buttons in a group are given the same name, how is one distinguished from the others?

13. What is the major behavioral difference between a group of radio buttons and a group of checkboxes?

14. What is the purpose of the attribute `checked` for radio buttons and checkboxes?

15. What should you do if you want the box display of a dropdown list-box to appear empty?

16. What is the purpose of a `fieldset` element, and what other element is generally associated with it?

17. How is a `label` element used to connect an `input` element and the text that labels that `input` element?

18. What role do `label` elements play in assistive technology?

19. What new attribute has HTML5 added to the `input` element that will help even "legacy" `input` element types to check the data they receive?

 # Short Exercises to Improve Your Basic Understanding

1. Try to validate the markup in file `bmi1.html` as HTML5 to confirm that it will *not* validate, and explain *why*.

2. Modify `feedback1.html` so that `Firstname` and `Lastname` show up in the corresponding text boxes when the form is displayed and decide whether you think this is a usability enhancement or simply redundant overkill.

3. Modify `bmi2.html` so that the checkbox indicating that a detailed BMI analysis is desired is automatically checked when the form is displayed.

4. Modify `bmi3.html` so that `inches` and `pounds` do *not* show up in the `Units:` boxes when the form is displayed.

5. Experiment with `bmi4.html` and `bmi5.html` to convince yourself that label tags really do cause the two pages to exhibit the behavioral differences discussed in section 5.9.

6. Can you explain the attribute-value pair `checked="checked"` for radio buttons and checkboxes that you might occasionally see when looking at markup on the web, and also explain why it has this rather unusual form?

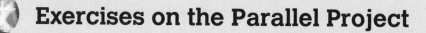

Exercises on the Parallel Project

In these exercises you will create two forms for your own business, so they are "parallel" in the sense that we also discussed two forms. But your forms, though based on the ones we presented, will necessarily be different and more specific to your particular business, as we now describe.

One form that you must create will permit the user to make some choices from among your products or services for later purchase, and the other will ask the user for some feedback on products or services previously purchased.

1. Design and develop a web page containing a form that allows the user to a) Make a single choice from each of two different categories of product or service that your business provides. It should make logical sense that a user would want only at most one of the items in each category. The form must show the price per unit of each item. b) Make multiple choices from a third category of product or service that your business provides. The form must again show the price per unit of each item and in this case also allow the user to enter the quantity required of each item. The tax on products and services must also be indicated (you may assume it is the same for both), and a checkbox provided for users to indicate if they have tax-exempt status. The form must have a button to submit the order and one to reset the form if the user wishes to start over. To complete this web page, provide a suitable title and explanatory text, and format it in such a way that, in your opinion at least, it is pleasing to view.

2. Design and develop a web page containing a form that queries the user on the level of satisfaction with previously purchased products or services from your business. Use the first two categories from your form in exercise 1 above. Within each category have a checkbox for each item to indicate the user has purchased that product or service, and a sequence of radio buttons to indicate the level of satisfaction. For each category, also have a box where the user can enter comments about that category. Provide as well boxes for the user to enter his or her first and last names, and another for email. The form will also need the usual submit and reset buttons. Complete the web page by providing a suitable title and explanatory text, and format it in such a way that it is pleasing to view.

What Else You May Want or Need to Know

1. Forms have long been the major tool in the web developer's toolkit for collecting information from users to be sent to the server for processing. As with many things in life and on the web, simple is probably better, and appropriate variations of the simple web forms we have presented in this chapter may well be adequate for many data collection tasks on your website. Although we have not done so, you can of course use CSS to add all kinds

of styles to your forms, and you will see some very fancy forms as you cruise around the web. However, this is not necessarily a good idea, since many users will be expecting a more or less "standard" form and may not have the time or patience to deal with a form that appears to be too far from the norm. This can impact your business negatively if you are running an e-commerce website. The *KISS principle*[2] is alive and well in web development, and in the use of web forms in particular.

2. The `checked` attribute has only one possible value: `checked="checked"`, which was required in XHTML if you wanted a radio button or checkbox to be checked, but which may be omitted in HTML5. There are other element attributes like this, so you might also see a similar pattern in other contexts. For example, the opening tag of the option element used with the select element has a `selected` attribute that you might similarly see somewhere as `selected="selected"` to indicate that the given option was to be selected. Other attributes in this category include `required`, `multiple`, and `disabled`. And by the way, the action of simply supplying an attribute without a value (when permitted) is called *attribute minimization*.

3. Sometimes the `option` elements within a given `select` element fall into two or more groupings, and you may wish to label the groups for added readability. For example, a dropdown list-box may allow you to choose your favorite pet, and give you the option of choosing from several animals or from several birds. You can group the animals, group the birds, and then label each of these categories with an (empty) `optgroup` element having a `label` attribute whose value is the text you want as your label, as in (for example):

```
<optgroup label="Birds">
```

Do not confuse this `label` *attribute* with the `label` *element* previously discussed.

References

1. This W3C site gives you lots of information and examples of the new HTML5 form features:

    ```
    http://www.w3.org/TR/html5/forms.html
    ```

2. These W3Schools site pages are up to date on HTML5 forms and their elements, and have detailed information and examples involving the new `input` elements and their attributes:

    ```
    http://www.w3schools.com/html/html_forms.asp
    ```

    ```
    http://www.w3schools.com/html/html_form_elements.asp
    ```

---

[2] This is a good principle to google if you've never encountered it before, or even if you have.

```
http://www.w3schools.com/html/html_form_input_types.asp
```

```
http://www.w3schools.com/html/html_form_attributes.asp
```

3. Wikipedia has something to say about almost everything, including web forms:

```
https://en.wikipedia.org/wiki/Form_%28HTML%29
```

4. Here is another site that provides a tutorial on web form building, which you might find helpful if you can ignore the annoying banner that refuses to load properly:

```
http://www.devarticles.com/c/a/Web-Design-Standards/
Web-Forms/
```

5. There are websites that provide ready-to-use forms for various purposes, or even let you "roll your own":

```
http://www.emailmeform.com/
```

```
http://www.123contactform.com/
```

6. Additional sites that you may find helpful (and a Google search will help you find many more):

```
http://www.javascript-coder.com/html-form/html-form-
tutorial-p1.phtml
```

```
http://www.webstandards.org/learn/tutorials/
accessible-forms/beginner/
```

```
https://developer.mozilla.org/en-US/docs/Web/Guide/HTML/
Forms/My_first_HTML_form
```

```
http://www.tutorialspoint.com/html/html_forms.htm
```

CHAPTER **SIX**

JavaScript for Client-Side Computation and Form Data Validation

CHAPTER CONTENTS

Overview and Objectives

We have reached more or less the midpoint of our introduction to website development. From this point on in this text, all the web pages we create will exhibit some kind of dynamic behavior. Some will include two-way, client-server communication, but not until we have studied PHP in later chapters. Sometimes the "look and feel", as well as the content, of a web page may change, based on the current circumstances. The difference in those circumstances may be caused by input from the user, by the date and time of viewing, or by changes in the database of the business. All of this development will be controlled by programming.

We will begin our discussion of web programming with *JavaScript*, one of the most versatile and useful programming languages, yet one of the easiest to learn. In this chapter you will study some of the basic features of the language and use it to perform client-side computations such as the BMI calculations we postponed in the last chapter, and to check the data your users are entering into your web pages to ensure it is the kind of data you are expecting. This is an important aspect of creating a secure website.

So, in this chapter we will discuss the following:

▶ The importance of keeping web page content behavior separate from content structure and content presentation, both conceptually and physically

▶ An overview of JavaScript as a programming language, including a brief history, its limitations, and how you will use it

▶ User notification with JavaScript "popup windows" and writing to a web page with JavaScript

▶ External and embedded JavaScript code

▶ The Document Object Model (DOM) and JavaScript access to it

▶ JavaScript data types and variables, functions (built-in and programmer-defined), expressions, control statements, arrays, and built-in objects

▶ Website security and how JavaScript can help to achieve it

▶ Regular expressions and their use for JavaScript data validation

▶ Updates of our BMI calculator form and feedback form to incorporate validation of user input

This chapter, like the previous one, will not have a `nature` subdirectory containing an updated version of our complete sample website. The sample files of this chapter will focus directly on the chapter topics, namely the use of JavaScript for computation and data validation on the client side. In the next chapter we will present an updated version of our **Nature's Source** website illustrating all features discussed up to that point.

6.1 Another Important Distinction: Structure vs. Presentation vs. Behavior

In Chapter 3 we drew your attention to the important notion of structure vs. presentation of a web page. Now we are about to make our web pages much more interactive by using JavaScript, and that introduces a whole new aspect of web pages: *web page behavior*.

We will follow the same approach we used in separating presentation from content. That is, although there is more than one way to make JavaScript code available to our HTML pages, we will, for the most part, keep our JavaScript code in a separate file, and this is the recommended approach. The goal, then, is to keep the content of each HTML page and its structure separate from the CSS file that determines its presentation style and also separate from the JavaScript code that determines its behavior.

All that having been said, it is nevertheless quite convenient for testing and illustrative purposes to place JavaScript code right in the HTML file where it is to be used, just as it was for CSS.

6.2 What Is JavaScript? (It's *not* Java!)

First, a little bit of history. In the mid-1990s the folks who had developed the Netscape browser began development of a new and appropriately named programming language called LiveScript for adding lively animations to web pages. Brendan Eich is credited with much of the early work. In fact, legend has it that he essentially created the language during what are sometimes referred to as "those famous ten days in May" of 1995. About the same time, Sun Microsystems' Java programming language was fast gaining importance on the Internet, due to its portability across different computing platforms, and its ability to provide users with interactivity on web pages via *Java applets*, small Java programs that could be downloaded from a web page and executed within a browser.

Before long, Netscape and Sun agreed that the name LiveScript would be changed to JavaScript, in an attempt to increase its appeal. Unfortunately, this name change has led to yet more confusion in the web community. Other than similarity in name, there is no obvious relationship between Java and JavaScript. Both languages share similar programming constructs, but the same commonalities are also shared with many other recent languages and can be traced back to the popular C programming language that was developed in the late 1960s.

Nowadays JavaScript is by far the most popular and most widely used programming language on the client side of the client-server architecture, and all web developers need to have a reasonable grasp of this language. See **TABLE 6.1** for a brief historical timeline of JavaScript development.

6.2.1 JavaScript Is Interpreted, Not Compiled

JavaScript is a high-level programming language. Programs in high-level languages need to be translated into machine language prior to execution. There are two types of translators:

> **Compilers** translate an entire program into an executable machine language version that can be executed many times, after this one-time translation.

TABLE 6.1 A very brief summary of the history of JavaScript.

Date	Version	Notes
May 1995	LiveScript	Brenda Eich, working at Netscape, writes the first version of what was first called Mocha, then LiveScript, during the famous "10 days in May".
September 1995	JavaScript	The language name was changed after an agreement with Sun Microsystems, to capitalize on the then current popularity of Java.
1996–1997	JavaScript (ECMA-262)	ECMA (European Computer Manufacturers Association) takes over the standardization process and produces the first standard; so JavaScript becomes one of several implementations of the ECMAScript language standard.
1998	JavaScript 2	ECMAScript 2
1999	JavaScript 3	ECMAScript 3
2000–2004		Microsoft went its own way, and development stalled.
2005		Jesse James Garrett recognizes and points out to the rest of us that a JavaScript-based technique, which he called AJAX, could be used to make web-based applications behave much more like desktop applications, giving rise to a JavaScript renaissance.
December 2009	JavaScript 5	ECMAScript 5 (version 4 never completed)
June 2015	JavaScript 6	ECMAScript 6

Interpreters translate a program one statement at a time to its machine language equivalent, just prior to the execution of that statement, and do this every time the program is run. Interpreted languages are simpler and more portable to different hardware and software platforms, but result in much more translation overhead, since they are translated every time they are executed. This makes them generally less efficient than compiled languages.

JavaScript is an interpreted language that can be used to run programs for web computing on both the client side and the server side. Although server-side web computing using JavaScript was for many years less common, it has recently come into its own with the increasing popularity of libraries like Node.js. This package, which we will not discuss in this text, can be used for retrieving and manipulating data from server-side databases as well as for communicating with other applications running on the server. Traditionally, most server-side computing has been done using other options, including:

▶ Open-source programming languages such as PHP and Python
▶ CGI programming using Perl, also open source

▶ The open-source Java Server Pages (JSP) technology from Sun Microsystems, a company which is now a part of Oracle

▶ A proprietary (*not* open source) alternative such as the Active Server Pages (ASP) technology from Microsoft

We will use the very popular open-source PHP programming language for our server-side computing. Our treatment of JavaScript in this chapter and the next will focus on client-side computing, where it is still most dominant.

6.2.2 Restrictions on What JavaScript Can Do

On the client side, JavaScript code is usually downloaded as part of, or in conjunction with, a web document, and runs in a web browser. By this we mean that the browser has built into it a JavaScript interpreter that is capable of executing any JavaScript code it encounters as the browser is downloading and rendering a web page.

JavaScript is somewhat limited in both its number of features and its general abilities. However, its limited number of features makes it easy to learn, and the restrictions on its abilities are there for a very good reason, since they are based on security concerns. You do not want a JavaScript program from a website to come down to a client's computer and cause deliberate changes to its configuration or inflict other intended or unintended damage. Therefore, the actions that JavaScript can perform on your computer are typically restricted to these:

▶ Computations based on user input

▶ Validation of data entered by the user, before that data is sent to the server for processing

▶ Dynamically adding new HTML elements to a web page, or changing HTML elements already on a web page for some reason

▶ Changing the look and feel of a web page as the user's mouse pointer interacts with the web page

6.2.3 How Will We Use JavaScript?

We will enhance our **Nature's Source** e-commerce website with the use of JavaScript and you learn some essential features of the language as we go, in keeping with our "need-to-know" approach to the learning process. We will be studying JavaScript in two chapters. This chapter describes the use of JavaScript for computation as well as validating data entered by the user (the first two items in the above list). The following chapter uses JavaScript for providing a dynamic look and feel to our web pages (the last two items in the above list).

The treatment of JavaScript provided in these two chapters barely scratches the surface of what is possible using the language. At the end of each chapter, we will again provide pointers to additional resources that you can go to for further information about JavaScript. While previous programming experience will be helpful from now on in this text, we attempt to make this and subsequent chapters self-contained for anyone with a reasonable aptitude for computer programming.

One other thing: Just as we have placed our `.css` files in a subdirectory called `css`, we will place our JavaScript files in a subdirectory called `scripts`. Although our JavaScript files have a file extension of `.js`, we give the directory containing them the more generic name `scripts` (rather than `js`, say), since directories with this name will later contain scripts written in languages other than JavaScript (PHP, for example).

6.3 The Placement of JavaScript Code

In the next section you will see some examples of where you can place your JavaScript code, and which we describe briefly here.

First, you can place JavaScript code directly into your HTML document, either within the `body` element if you want the code to be executed as soon as the browser sees it, or within the `head` element if you wish to define a function or do some setup that you'd like to use later. In either of these cases we say that our JavaScript code is *embedded* in our HTML document, and in such cases the code must form the body of one or more `script` elements.

However, cluttering up an HTML document with JavaScript can make such a document very difficult to understand and maintain, even though it is very convenient in some situations, particularly for performing quick tests. If you do decide to embed some of your JavaScript, you need to keep in mind the sequential nature of the browser's display process, and not place your code at a location where the parts of the page it needs to work with are not yet available.

So, just as we did for external CSS files, we will also recommend as a "best practice" the placing of your JavaScript code into one or more separate files that your HTML markup can access as required. We will place all of our JavaScript code in separate files, except for some short illustrative examples of alternative scenarios. We will use the recommended extension `.js` for these files and keep them in a subdirectory called `scripts`, which will be located off of the main directory where the HTML files that use those scripts reside, or, when we return to our **Nature's Source** websites, in the directory where the `index.html` file for the site is located. In other words, a `scripts` directory will generally be in the same location as the relevant `images` and `css` directories for the given situation.

6.4 A Simple Example in Four Versions

In order to be useful, every computer program must have some kind of output. In web programming, that output will often be some change in a visual or audio effect on a web page. However, the simplest output for most programs in any language is a textual display of some kind, and that is where we will start. We begin with four simple examples, the first three of which produce exactly the same web page display, and the last of which is nearly the same, once it is finished.

6.4.1 Version 1: No JavaScript

FIGURE 6.1 shows the HTML markup for our first example, which is found in the file `ch06/estore.html` and is just an "ordinary" HTML file not involving any JavaScript. Its display is shown in **FIGURE 6.2.** Take a look at the `h3` element in the document in Figure 6.1 (lines 12–15). In this example the content of this element is simply text that we have entered in the usual way.

```
1   <!DOCTYPE html>
2   <!-- estore.html -->
3   <html lang="en">
4     <head>
5       <meta charset="utf-8">
6       <link rel="stylesheet" href="css/default.css">
7       <title>Nature's Source - Canada's largest specialty vitamin store</title>
8     </head>
9     <body>
10      <main class="Narrow">
11        <p><img src="images/naturelogo.gif" alt="Nature's Source"></p>
12        <h3>
13          Watch this space for our e-store.<br>
14          Coming soon ...
15        </h3>
16      </main>
17    </body>
18  </html>
```

FIGURE 6.1 `ch06/estore.html`
This short HTML markup file contains no JavaScript, but serves as version 1 of 4 in our opening sequence of web pages introducing JavaScript.

FIGURE 6.2 `graphics/ch06/displayEstoreHtml.jpg`
A Firefox browser display of `ch06/estore.html` (and `ch06/estoreEmbedded.html` and `ch06/estoreExternal.html` as well, since all three look exactly the same when displayed in the browser).

6.4.2 Version 2: Embedded JavaScript and `document.write()`

Now look at **FIGURE 6.3**, which shows the file `ch06/estoreEmbedded.html`, and in which we see a working example of an "embedded" JavaScript script (lines 13–16). This example shows that you can take an existing HTML document for a web page and insert some JavaScript

```
 1  <!DOCTYPE html>
 2  <!-- estoreEmbedded.html -->
 3  <html lang="en">
 4    <head>
 5      <meta charset="utf-8">
 6      <link rel="stylesheet" href="css/default.css">
 7      <title>Nature's Source - Canada's largest specialty vitamin store</title>
 8    </head>
 9    <body>
10      <main class="Narrow">
11        <p><img src="images/naturelogo.gif" alt="Nature's Source"></p>
12        <h3>
13          <script>
14            document.write("Watch this space for our e-store.<br>");
15            document.write("Coming soon ...");
16          </script>
17        </h3>
18      </main>
19    </body>
20  </html>
```

FIGURE 6.3 `ch06/estoreEmbedded.html`
The HTML markup for version 2 of 4 in our opening sequence of web pages introducing JavaScript. This one contains a simple "embedded" JavaScript script with two output statements.

code directly into that document. The two lines of code in lines 14 and 15 are actual Java-Script "output statements" and form a simple JavaScript program, or *script*. Note that these two statements form the body of a `script` element, which itself is the content of an `h3` element. In other words, instead of typing in the text of the `h3` element body when we create the file, we have arranged for the text to be placed into the `h3` element after the browser downloads the file and executes the script.

A script of any kind that is inserted into an HTML document (or "embedded" in the document, as we also say) will be the content of a `script` element. That is, the script will be placed between a `<script>...</script>` tag pair. Prior to HTML5 you would see the following attribute-value pair on the opening `script` tag: `type="text/javascript"`. This would indicate that the language used in the script body is simple text written in JavaScript (as opposed to some other scripting language). However, just as the `type` attribute is no longer necessary in HTML5 for a `link` element when you are linking to a CSS file, the `type` attribute is no longer necessary in HTML5 for the `script` tag, so long as your scripting language is JavaScript.

The programming language statements between the `<script>...</script>` pair (in other words, the content of the `script` element) is the actual JavaScript program. So, the first JavaScript programming language statement in our first HTML document containing a JavaScript script is this one:

```
document.write("Watch this space for our e-store.<br>");
```

In this statement, it is most convenient to think of `document` as the name of a JavaScript *object* that represents the HTML web page document in which the JavaScript is "embedded" within a `script` element. The *Object-Oriented Programming (OOP)* way of doing things is to use a dot (or period) to connect an object with one of its *methods* for performing a task related to that object. So, even though `document` is actually a "property" of the browser "window object", because it is accessible to JavaScript in the way shown you can think of it as a JavaScript object.

While *method* is the commonly used OOP terminology, programmers who started with the *procedural programming paradigm*, which does not use "objects", sometimes use other terms such as *function* or *procedure* for what we have called a *method*. A JavaScript object generally provides a number of methods that help us achieve our goals with respect to that object. For example, in this case, to display text in a document, JavaScript provides the method called `write()` that "belongs to" the `document` object. When we use the name of a method to refer to that method, we include a set of parentheses following the method name to emphasize that it is in fact a method and not some other kind of JavaScript entity. In JavaScript code, in fact, a method name must always be followed by a set of parentheses, though there may or may not be anything between those parentheses.

We often describe what we are doing here by saying that we are "calling" or "invoking" the `document` object's `write()` method. When we call it, we supply the `write()` method with a string of characters as a *parameter* of the method. The parameter must be enclosed in the pair of parentheses that necessarily follow the method. Some methods don't need any parameters, but a method will quite often require one or more parameters. When there are several parameters, they are given in a comma-separated list between the parentheses. In all cases, whatever parameters are supplied are there to provide the method with information it needs to perform its task.

One type of parameter frequently needed is a string value. A string is a sequence of characters that is generally enclosed in double quotes, though JavaScript allows the use of single quotes to enclose (or *delimit*) a string as well. In the JavaScript statement given above the string is

```
"Watch this space for our e-store.<br>"
```

which we can say, somewhat more formally, is a *literal value* (or actual value) of a JavaScript *data type* named `String`. We will say more about data types and their values later.

This first output statement will output the above string to our document, just as if we had typed the string into the document directly. So what's the point, you might well ask, and why go to all this trouble? The point is just that we are illustrating the `write()` method by getting it to write out a simple string, but we can use it to output lots of other things, such as the result of a calculation, for example.

Note that we have included a bit of HTML code in our string, namely the line break tag `<br>`. This will ensure that any following text will be displayed on the subsequent line by the browser. Note in this context that it is the job of the JavaScript code to put content into our document, but it is the browser's job to display that content.

Note as well that our JavaScript statement ends with a semicolon. JavaScript is more forgiving than conventional languages such as Java and C++ in this regard. It will accept statements that are not terminated by a semicolon. However, it is regarded as good programming practice to use a semicolon to terminate a JavaScript statement.

Our first JavaScript program has another output statement that displays this string:

```
Coming soon ...
```

If you open the file ch06/estoreEmbedded.html in a web browser, you will see the display of these two lines that are output by the JavaScript write() method. The display you saw in Figure 6.2 is exactly the same as the display you will see on this occasion. The only difference is that this time around the text output by this short JavaScript script again shows up in the HTML document as the content of an HTML h3 element, which explains why the display is the same as that of Figure 6.2.

Note that the HTML code <br> in the first output string is not displayed by the web browser. It simply ensures, as usual in HTML markup, that the second string appears on the following line.

6.4.3 Version 3: Linking to an External JavaScript File

Now you will see how we can use in our HTML document some JavaScript code that is kept in a separate file.

FIGURE 6.4 shows the body of the HTML document in ch06/estoreExternal.html. In this case our JavaScript script is in a separate file, namely ch06/scripts/estoreExternal.js.,

```
1   <!DOCTYPE html>
2   <!-- estoreExternal.html -->
3   <html lang="en">
4     <head>
5       <meta charset="utf-8">
6       <link rel="stylesheet" href="css/default.css">
7       <title>Nature's Source - Canada's largest specialty vitamin store</title>
8     </head>
9     <body>
10      <main class="Narrow">
11      <p><img src="images/naturelogo.gif" alt="Nature's Source"></p>
12      <h3>
13        <script src="scripts/estoreExternal.js"></script> 
14        <!-- Without something other than whitespace and the script
15        element in the content of the h3 element, the HTML 5 validator
16        issues an "empty heading" warning. -->
17      </h3>
18      </main>
19    </body>
20  </html>
```

FIGURE 6.4 ch06/estoreExternal.html
The HTML markup for version 3 of 4 in our opening sequence of web pages introducing JavaScript. This one contains a script element that links to the external JavaScript file ch06/scripts/estoreExternal.js.

```
1  //estoreExternal.js
2  document.write("Watch this space for our e-store.<br>");
3  document.write("Coming soon ...");
```

FIGURE 6.5 `ch06/scripts/estoreExternal.js`
The JavaScript file that `ch06/estoreExternal.html` of Figure 6.4 links to and runs when it is being displayed.

which is shown in **FIGURE 6.5.** The file contains only a JavaScript comment with the name of the file, and the two JavaScript statements you have already seen. In JavaScript, if two forward slashes (//) appear on a line, everything following on that line is regarded as a comment, and is ignored by the JavaScript interpreter. JavaScript also allows comments of the form /* comment goes here */, which can extend over multiple lines.

We connect the two files by giving the `src` attribute of the `script` tag in our HTML markup (line 13) with the value `scripts/estoreExternal.js`. Note that the HTML `script` element is like the HTML `img` element in that it has a `src` attribute for access to the required file, and is unlike the `link` element, which has an `href` attribute for that purpose.

A display of `ch06/estoreExternal.html` will again look exactly like the display in Figure 6.2, because once again the final markup being displayed is the same as before. In particular, the executable JavaScript code this time (from the external file `estoreExternal.js`) is no different from the JavaScript code embedded in the HTML of `estoreEmbedded.html` shown in Figure 6.3.

Note that the closing `</script>` tag seen in line 13 of Figure 6.4 is required, even though the `script` element has no content in this case. Furthermore, note the comment in lines 14–16 of Figure 6.4 describing a minor validation problem, which is solved by our old friend, the ` ` HTML entity.

6.4.4 Version 4: Another External Script, the `alert()` Method, and Escape Characters

In our final version of this example we again use an external script, but now introduce a different way of notifying users. This time our user notification appears in a *popup window* produced by the JavaScript `alert()` method. This popup window can contain whatever text message we choose to provide for our users to see.

We use the markup file `ch06/estorePopup.html`, shown in **FIGURE 6.6**, and the external JavaScript file `ch06/scripts/estorePopup.js`, shown in **FIGURE 6.7**, to illustrate the use of the `alert()` method. The body element of `estorePopup.html` is the same as the body element of `estoreExternal.html`, except for the name of the associated JavaScript file. The executable script in this case consists of the statement that calls the `alert()` method, followed by another `document.write()` statement that executes after the user dismisses the popup window produced by `alert()`.

```
1    <!DOCTYPE html>
2    <!-- estorePopup.html -->
3    <html lang="en">
4      <head>
5        <meta charset="utf-8">
6        <link rel="stylesheet" href="css/default.css">
7        <title>Nature's Source - Canada's largest specialty vitamin store</title>
8      </head>
9      <body>
10       <main class="Narrow">
11         <p><img src="images/naturelogo.gif" alt="Nature's Source"></p>
12         <h3>
13           <script src="scripts/estorePopup.js"></script> 
14           <!-- Without something other than whitespace and the script
15           element in the content of the h3 element, the HTML 5 validator
16           issues an "empty heading" warning. -->
17         </h3>
18       </main>
19     </body>
20   </html>
```

FIGURE 6.6 `ch06/estorePopup.html`
The HTML markup for version 4 of 4 in our opening sequence of web pages introducing JavaScript. This one contains a `script` element that links to the external JavaScript file `ch06/scripts/estorePopup.js` containing a call to `alert()`.

```
1    //estorePopup.js
2    alert("Watch this space for our e-store.\n" + "Coming soon ...");
3    document.write("When our e-store arrives, you will have a wide "
4        + "choice of fabulous products!");
```

FIGURE 6.7 `ch06/scripts/estorePopup.js`
The JavaScript file that `ch06/estorePopup.html` of Figure 6.6 links to and runs when it is being displayed.

The `alert()` method, like the `document.write()` method, takes a single parameter of type `String`. This method belongs to `window`, not to `document`, so we could also write `window.alert()`, but this is redundant and unnecessary for methods that belong to the `window` object. Such methods, of which `alert()` is only one, are also called *global* methods.

However, this time the string we are sending to `alert()` is in fact a *concatenation* (a fancy term that means "putting together") of two strings using the plus operator (+). This operator is also used to add numbers in JavaScript, of course, but it is also *overloaded* to be used to "add" two strings as well. The first of these strings illustrates another technique that you have not seen before: the use of the special character \n. Don't be confused by the fact that \n looks like two characters. In fact it really *is* two characters, physically, but in every other way it is treated as, and is considered to be, a single character. The use of a \n in the first string has the effect of starting a new line at the point where it occurs; that is, the following part of the string will appear on the next line, so that the two lines look like this in the popup window:

```
Watch this space for our e-store.
Coming soon ...
```

Don't confuse the use of \n to move to the next line in this context (text in a popup window) with the use of the `<br>` tag to accomplish the same task in an HTML document displayed on a web page. Each works well in its own context, but neither will work in the other context.

There are several other characters like \n, all called *escape characters*. Most modern programming languages that count the C programming language as one of their antecedents use essentially the same set of special characters to specify invisible *control characters*, such as the *newline* character (\n, as discussed above) and the *tab* character (\t), with the help of a backslash (\) character. Since the backslash is used to denote special characters, we also need a special character for the backslash itself (\\). A complete list of special characters in JavaScript and their meanings is shown in **TABLE 6.2**.

FIGURE 6.8 shows the initial result of displaying the `estorePopup.html` file in the browser, and thus running the JavaScript in the file `estorePopup.js`. We first get a popup window that gives us the by-now-familiar message:

```
Watch this space for our e-store.
Coming soon ...
```

The difference this time is that the message will not go away until the user clicks the OK button, thereby "dismissing" the popup window, after which we are left with the normal web page shown

TABLE 6.2 List of special characters available for use in JavaScript strings.

Special Character	Description
\'	single quote
\"	double quote
\&	ampersand
\t	tab
\\	backslash
\b	backspace
\n	new line
\r	carriage return
\f	form feed (page break)

FIGURE 6.8 `graphics/ch06/displayEstorePopupHtml.jpg`
A Firefox browser display of `ch06/estorePopup.html` while the popup window is still active.

FIGURE 6.9 `graphics/ch06/displayEstorePopupHtmlFinal.jpg`
The final Firefox browser display of `ch06/estorePopup.html` after the user has dismissed the popup window shown in Figure 6.8 by clicking OK.

in **FIGURE 6.9**, in which the text has been produced by the call to `document.write()` in lines 3–4 of Figure 6.7.

Depending on what you want your scripts to do, the JavaScript code can become quite involved. For example, it may contain programmer-defined functions that can be called by other parts of the code. If you examine documents found on the web, you will often see such complex code included within the `head` element of a web page. We will be looking at more sophisticated JavaScript in the following sections, and in the next chapter.

6.5 What Is the *Document Object Model* (*DOM*)?

As you know, every HTML document consists of a number of HTML elements that are nested inside one another in whatever arrangement you need to use in order to express the structure of that document. Such a nested structure lends itself quite readily to representation by a tree-like structure like that shown in **FIGURE 6.10** for a very simple HTML document.

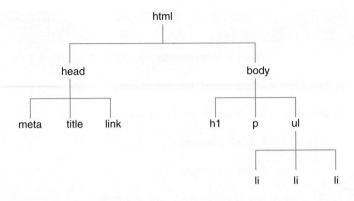

FIGURE 6.10 `graphics/ch06/DOM.jpg`
A view of the corresponding DOM hierarchy of HTML elements for a very simple web page.

A simplified way to view this tree is to think of its "root" (the html element) as being at the top, instead of at the bottom where the root of a tree in the forest would be. Now think of the root as corresponding to the document itself. Immediately below this, at the next level, the first two "branches" are the head element and the body element of the document. At the next level down, in the head element, will be (among other things, perhaps) the meta, title, and link elements, and at this same level, in the body element, will be (probably) some header elements, some p elements for paragraphs, and so on. An HTML document of arbitrary complexity can be represented in a similar manner.

The point of viewing an HTML document in this way is that each of the various elements of the tree is also, in fact, an "object" that can be accessed and manipulated by JavaScript code using the "dot notation" for JavaScript objects that you have already seen and used. When you do this, you are seeing the *DOM* in action. More frequently referred to by its acronym, the *DOM* is a W3C-defined standard that provides an *Application Programming Interface* (*API*) that is in fact language-independent. This means that many different programming languages, only one of which is JavaScript, can access a standard set of objects related to a web document, including the document itself, its tables, the rows and columns in its tables, its images, its headers, its paragraphs, and its various form elements such as textareas and buttons. A list of some of the most common and useful such DOM objects is given in **TABLE 6.3**. See the end-of-chapter **References** for more information.

The DOM also standardizes the ways in which web page elements are accessed and manipulated when HTML documents are being processed. At the highest level, these processes include the modification of HTML elements already on the page, the deletion of such elements, and creation of new HTML elements and adding them to the page. These standards are also programming language and platform independent. In the next chapter you will see how some of these actions can be performed using JavaScript. But they can be carried out using many other programming languages as well.

As you may have guessed by now, we have already encountered the DOM earlier in this chapter when we used, via JavaScript, the write() method of the document property of the window object.

TABLE 6.3 Some HTML DOM objects that may be accessed within an HTML document.

DOM Object	What It Represents
Document	The entire HTML document
DOM objects found within the head element	
Link	A link element
Meta	A meta element
DOM objects found within the body element	
Body	The body element itself
Anchor	An a element
Style	An individual style statement
DOM objects related to images	
Image	An img element
Area	An area element inside an image map
DOM objects related to tables	
Table	A table element
TableCell	A td element
TableRow	A tr element
DOM objects related to forms	
Form	A form element
Event	The state of an event
Button	A button element, or an input element of type button
Checkbox	An input element of type checkbox
FileUpload	An input element of type file
Hidden	An input element of type hidden
Password	An input element of type password

TABLE 6.3 (Continued)	
DOM Object	**What It Represents**
Radio	An input element of type radio
Reset	An input element of type reset
Submit	An input element of type submit
Text	An input element of type text
Select	A select element
Option	An option element
Textarea	A textarea element

6.6 JavaScript and the DOM Interact to Process Our BMI Form

We will use our Body Mass Index (BMI) calculator web page to study JavaScript's interaction with DOM objects (HTML elements), and also, in keeping with our learn-what-we-need-to-know-as-we-go approach, to introduce JavaScript programmer-defined functions, JavaScript variables, and the JavaScript if-else decision-making construct.

The latest version of our BMI calculator is contained in the file ch06/bmiForm.html. The head element of that document is shown in **FIGURE 6.11**. It includes three script elements

```
1    <!DOCTYPE html>
2    <!-- bmiForm.html -->
3    <html lang="en">
4      <head>
5        <meta charset="utf-8">
6        <link rel="stylesheet" href="css/default.css">
7        <script src="scripts/bmiFormProcess.js"></script>
8        <script src="scripts/bmiFormValidate.js"></script>
9        <script src="scripts/bmiCalculate.js"></script>
10       <title>Nature's Source - Canada's largest specialty vitamin store</title>
11     </head>
```

FIGURE 6.11 `ch06/bmiForm.html` **(excerpt)**
The first part of this file shows the head element of the document with its three script elements, each one referencing one of the three different JavaScript scripts we will need to process our BMI form.

(lines 7–9), each of which tells the browser to get the code from one of the following JavaScript code files: `bmiFormProcess.js`, `bmiFormValidate.js`, `bmiCalculate.js`. All of these files are located in the `scripts` subdirectory. Because these `script` elements are in the `head` element and because each of these JavaScript code files contains only JavaScript function definitions, these function definitions are simply loaded in from the files and readied for future use, but no code is actually executed at this point. That is, none of functions is "called" until later.

We will examine each of these script files in detail shortly, but we'll give you an overview of what each contains before moving on. In `bmiFormProcess.js` we have a single function that will "take over" when the user has filled in the BMI form and clicks the button to compute the BMI value. Two things then need to happen. First, the data in the form needs to be checked to see if it's OK, and if it isn't, the user needs to be so notified before proceeding. This is the job of the various functions in `bmiFormValidate.js`. Second, assuming all of the data is OK, the BMI value needs to be computed and the result presented to the user. The functions in `bmiCalculate.js` will handle these tasks.

FIGURE 6.12 shows just the form element from `bmiForm.html`. The opening `form` tag in the first line of Figure 6.12 (line 17 of the file) now has the following new attribute-value pair:

```
onsubmit = "bmiFormProcess()"
```

This is an example of a new kind of tag attribute called an *event attribute*, whose value is a function that is called when the corresponding event occurs. In this case, when the submit button for this form is pressed, the function `bmiFormProcess()` defined in the file `ch06/scripts/bmiForm Process.js`, and previously loaded, will be invoked.

Usually data from a form is sent to the server for processing, but here we are dealing with client-side programming only, so we will not be sending our form data to a server in this chapter. All of our form data processing will be done on the client side using JavaScript. That is why we have omitted the `action` attribute of the `form` tag that we discussed earlier.

6.6.1 A First Programmer-Defined JavaScript Function: Function Syntax

FIGURE 6.13 shows the definition of the function `bmiFormProcess()` from the file `bmiForm-Process.js`. This is our first programmer-defined JavaScript function. The terms *function* and

```
17      <form id="bmiForm" onsubmit="bmiFormProcess()">
18        <fieldset class="SectionBackground">
19          <legend class="LegendBackground">Vital statistics</legend>
20          <table>
21            <tr>
22              <td><label for="height">Your height:</label></td>
23              <td><input id="height" type="text" name="height" size="7"></td>
```

FIGURE 6.12 `ch06/bmiForm.html` (excerpt)
The HTML markup for the `form` element from our BMI form page.

```
24              <td><label for="heightUnit">Choose unit:</label></td>
25              <td><select id="heightUnit" name="heightUnit">
26                <option>inches</option>
27                <option>centimeters</option>
28              </select></td>
29            </tr>
30            <tr>
31              <td><label for="weight">Your weight:</label></td>
32              <td><input id="weight" type="text" name="weight" size="7"></td>
33              <td><label for="weightUnit">Choose unit:</label></td>
34              <td><select id="weightUnit" name="weightUnit">
35                <option>pounds</option>
36                <option>kilograms</option>
37              </select></td>
38            </tr>
39            <tr>
40              <td colspan="4"><label for="details">Please check here if you
41              want a detailed analysis of your BMI:</label>
42              <input id="details" type="checkbox"
43                     name="details" value="yes"></td>
44            </tr>
45          </table>
46        </fieldset>
47        <fieldset class="SectionBackground">
48          <legend class="LegendBackground">E-mail record?</legend>
49          <table>
50            <tr>
51              <td colspan="2"><label for="wantMail">Do you want your BMI sent
52              to you by e-mail?</label> <input id="wantMail" type="checkbox"
53              name="wantMail" value="yes"></td>
54            </tr>
55            <tr>
56              <td><label for="email">E-mail Address:</label></td>
57              <td><input id="email" type="text" name="email" size="40"></td>
58            </tr>
59          </table>
60        </fieldset>
61        <fieldset class="SectionBackground">
62          <legend class="LegendBackground">Processing</legend>
63          <table>
64            <tr>
65              <td><input type="submit" value="Compute your BMI"></td>
66              <td><input type="reset" value="Reset form"></td>
67            </tr>
68          </table>
69        </fieldset>
70      </form>
```

FIGURE 6.12 `ch06/bmiForm.html` **(excerpt)** *(continued)*

```
1   //bmiFormProcess.js
2   //The "driver" function that handles, at the highest level,
3   //the form data validation and display of the the BMI value
4
5   function bmiFormProcess()
6   {
7       var bmiFormObj = document.getElementById("bmiForm");
8       if (bmiFormValidate(bmiFormObj))
9       {
10          var bmi = valueOfBMI(bmiFormObj);
11          if (bmiFormObj.details.checked)
12              displayDetails(bmiFormObj, bmi);
13          else
14              alert("Your BMI: " + valueTo1DecimalPlace(bmi));
15      }
16  }
```

FIGURE 6.13 `ch06/scripts/bmiFormProcess.js`
The JavaScript function `processBMIform()` that handles the high-level duties of calling other functions to validate the form data and compute the BMI value.

method are often used interchangeably. This is generally not a problem, since they are essentially the same thing, though the term *method* is more often used when it belongs to an object, in an object-oriented context, and *function* when it is "stand-alone" and not associated with any object, as in this case.

Let us spend a little time studying the structure of this function. To begin, here is the general format of any function definition:

```
function nameOfFunction(parameter_list)
{
   ... JavaScript code to perform whatever the function does ...
}
```

The first line is the *header* for the function. It begins with the *keyword* `function`, which indicates the beginning of the definition of a function. This is followed by the name of the function, which should be chosen well so that it indicates the purpose of the function. A good rule of thumb to follow when naming functions is this: When the function computes a value, make the name of the function a noun that reflects the kind of value computed, such as `totalCost`. When the function simply performs a task, but does not compute and return a value, give it a name that starts with a verb and indicates the nature of the task performed, such as `displayResults`.[1]

---

[1] But sometimes we let other considerations override this "best practice". For example, here our functions and the file names in which they live all start with `bmi`: `bmiFormProcess`, `bmiFormValidate`, `bmiCalculate`. A convention like this can be a helpful visual aid when trying to locate related files in a directory containing a large number of scripts, for example.

The camel case convention for capitalization mentioned in an earlier chapter should be followed here as well. The function name, in turn, is followed by a comma-separated list of *parameters* the function should receive when it is called, enclosed in parentheses. We call this its *parameter list*, which may be empty if the function does not require any "outside information" to perform its task.

The JavaScript code that actually performs the task of the function is called the *function body* and is enclosed by a pair of braces, { and } (also called *curly brackets*), which immediately follow the function header. Thus the function in Figure 6.13 is `bmiFormProcess()`, and it is one that does not take any parameters. Note that the parentheses are required when the function is called, even if the parameter list is empty. For readability, when referring to functions in the text, we usually use the name of the function and an empty set of parentheses (whether or not the function has any parameters), just to emphasize that we are dealing with a function and not some other entity.

6.6.2 JavaScript Variables

Now we'll examine the JavaScript code in the body of the function `bmiFormProcess()`. The first statement *declares* a *variable* called `bmiFormObj` and *initializes* it with a value obtained by calling another built-in JavaScript function that we will discuss a bit later. Variables are used to store data in our programs. The word *variable* indicates that the stored data in the memory location named by the variable will vary, depending on the circumstances. Because this particular variable will contain a reference to the "object" that represents the `form` element on our web page, we attach the suffix `Obj` to the `id` value of the form element (`bmiForm`) to get our variable name, `bmiFormObj`. This name tells us what kind of value is in the variable, and the suffix provides a visual clue that helps to distinguish this kind of variable from more "ordinary" variables (that do not represent objects) in our code.

In many languages, you need to specify the type of data that will be stored in a given variable. This is not required by JavaScript, which uses a very flexible variable typing convention. In JavaScript the type of a variable is determined by the type of whatever value is assigned to that variable. The same variable can thus hold, at different times, values of different types, including a number, a string, or even a reference to a DOM element. Of course, at any given time it can hold only a single value of one particular type. This kind of typing in a programming language is called *dynamic typing*, since the same variable can be given values of different types "dynamically" as the code containing that variable executes.

However, while this may seem like a handy feature, it can make debugging a real nightmare. Programmers should enforce a strong self-discipline to ensure that their programs are reasonably robust. The best attitude to have toward program bugs is to do your best to avoid them in the first place. As a case in point, although it is not strictly necessary, every variable should be declared by preceding it with the keyword `var`, as shown in the declaration of the variable `bmiFormObj` in the first line of the function body of `bmiFormProcess()` in Figure 6.13, since there may be problems you simply won't have if you make sure to do this.

6.6.3 Accessing a DOM Element via Its `id` Attribute

The first statement in the function `bmiFormProcess()` (line 7 in Figure 6.13) also shows the recommended way, among several ways, of accessing a DOM element in an HTML document via JavaScript. Our variable `bmiFormObj` is assigned the value returned by the `getElementById()` method call in the following statement:

```
bmiFormObj = document.getElementById("bmiForm");
```

This `getElementById()` method call retrieves the DOM element that has the `id` value specified by its parameter (`"bmiForm"` in this case). Line 17 in Figure 6.12 shows the `form` element in the file `bmiForm.html` has an `id` value of `"bmiForm"`, which means that the variable `bmiFormObj` will henceforth represent this form in our JavaScript program.

The value of the `name` attribute of an HTML element can also be used to gain access to that element, as you shall see shortly. So we could have given a `name` attribute to our `form` element and accessed it that way, though for forms this approach is discouraged. In fact, in XHTML the `name` attribute on the `form` element (and several other elements) was actually deprecated.

6.6.4 Making Decisions with the JavaScript `if-else` Statement

Now let's take a look at a fundamental JavaScript control structure. The second line in the body of the function `bmiFormProcess()` (line 8 in Figure 6.13) begins an `if`-statement, which is also called a *conditional statement* because what the statement does is determined by whether the "condition" inside the parentheses is true or false. This particular `if`-statement contains as the second statement in its "body" an example of the most general form of an `if`-statement in JavaScript, which is called an `if-else`-statement, and looks like this:

```
if (condition)
    true-statement; //executed when condition is true
else
    false-statement; //executed when condition is false
```

This works as follows. First, we need to know that `condition` represents a *boolean expression*, which is just an expression whose value may be `true` or `false` (both of which are JavaScript *keywords*), or some other value that may be interpreted as being true or false. There are a number of other such values in each category, some of which we will encounter later.

Now, if the boolean expression we refer to as `condition` has the value `true`, then `true-statement` is executed; otherwise, `false-statement` is executed. The `else` part of this construct is optional, in general, as this function shows.

Note that in this `bmiFormProcess()` function both the `if` part and the `else` part contain only one JavaScript statement. If you want more than one JavaScript statement in either the `if` part or the `else` part, you have to enclose the part that contains two or more statements in braces. If you place even single statements in an `if-else` construct within braces, that makes it very easy to add further statements to either part of the construct at a later time without having to worry about introducing braces at that time. For this reason, doing so is often recommended as a good general programming practice. On the other hand, it could also be argued that not doing so can often make your code somewhat more concise and even enhance readability.

If you look at the first if-statement in the function bmiFormProcess() of Figure 6.13, you will see that the condition, in this case, is actually a call to *another* programmer-defined function named bmiFormValidate(), which has as its input parameter our newly created variable bmiFormObj. This other function is defined in another file, bmiFormValidate.js, and is shown in the partial display of that file in **FIGURE 6.14**. We will examine this second function definition in more detail a little later on.

```
1   //bmiFormValidate.js
2   //Functions to perform data validation on data entered
3   //by the user into the BMI form, and to display appropriate
4   //error messages if problems with the data are discovered
5
6   function bmiFormValidate(bmiFormObj)
7   {
8       var hUnit = bmiFormObj.heightUnit.
9           options[bmiFormObj.heightUnit.selectedIndex].text;
10      var wUnit = bmiFormObj.weightUnit.
11          options[bmiFormObj.weightUnit.selectedIndex].text;
12      var height = bmiFormObj.height.value;
13      var weight = bmiFormObj.weight.value;
14      var email = bmiFormObj.email.value;
15      var heightOK, weightOK, emailOK;
16
17      if (hUnit == "inches")
18          heightOK = inchesValid(height);
19      else
20          heightOK = centimetresValid(height);
21
22      if (wUnit == "pounds")
23          weightOK = poundsValid(weight);
24      else
25          weightOK = kilogramsValid(weight);
26
27      if (bmiFormObj.wantMail.checked)
28      {
29          emailOK = emailValid(email);
30          alert("Warning: The e-mail feature is currently not supported.");
31      }
32      else
33          emailOK = true;
34
35      return heightOK && weightOK && emailOK;
36  }
```

FIGURE 6.14 `ch06/scripts/bmiFormValidate.js` **(excerpt)**
The JavaScript function bmiFormValidate() that handles the high-level validation duties of calling several other lower-level functions to validate each of the individual pieces of form data that have been filled in by the user.

Let us focus on the `if`-statement starting in line 8 of Figure 6.13 for the moment. Since it is the call to the other function, namely `bmiFormValidate(bmiFormObj)` that forms the condition we must test in this case, that function must return either a `true` or a `false` value. Such a function is called a *boolean function*, since (like a boolean expression) it returns one of the two possible boolean values `true` or `false`. If the condition evaluates to `false`, the function `bmiFormProcess()` does nothing, because there is no `else` part. Otherwise, the block of code in lines 9–15 executes (we often refer to any sequence of statements enclosed in braces as a *block of code*). The first statement (line 10) declares a variable called `bmi`. This variable is assigned a value returned by a third programmer-defined function, `valueOfBMI()`, which also receives the variable `bmiFormObj` as a parameter. The function `valueOfBMI()` is also defined in another separate file, `bmiCalculate.js`, which you will see later in **FIGURE 6.18**. We will look at this function definition a little later on as well. In the meantime, let us continue our examination of the `bmiFormProcess()` function.

6.6.5 Accessing a DOM Element via Its `name` Attribute

Once we have calculated the value of the BMI and stored it in our `bmi` variable, the next step is to display that value, which we are going to do in a popup box with a call to the `alert()` function. We had decided earlier that the user should have a choice of receiving either just the BMI value by itself, or a more "detailed" report. The user indicates that choice by checking, on the form, the checkbox whose `name` attribute is `details`, and we need to find out, via our script, whether or not the user has checked that box.

As we mentioned earlier, the `name` attribute can be used directly to access a DOM element without need for a method call. So, look first at lines 42–43 of Figure 6.12 to see that the input element with `type="checkbox"` is the one the user checks if a detailed report is required, and it has both `id="details"` and `name="details"` as attributes. So we could use a call to `getElementById()` as before, but this time we use `bmiFormObj.details`, in which the `details` part is the value of the `name` attribute, not the value of the `id` attribute. When we use `bmiFormObj.details.checked` in line 11 of Figure 6.13 we are referring to the `checked` property of the checkbox, which will have a value of `true` if the user has checked the checkbox named `details` on the form, and `false` if the checkbox has not been checked. If it is checked, we will call another programmer-defined function named `displayDetails()`, with `bmiFormObj` and `bmi` as parameters. This function is also defined in `bmiCalculate.js` and is shown at the end of Figure 6.18. It too will be discussed in detail later on in this chapter.

On the other hand, if the checkbox "named" `details` is not checked, then the value of `bmiFormObj.details.checked` will be `false`, and we will simply call the `alert()` method to display just the computed value of the BMI. The `alert()` method receives a string that is a concatenation of the string `"Your BMI: "` and a string returned by the call to the programmer-defined function `valueTo1DecimalPlace()`. The function `valueTo1DecimalPlace()` takes the variable `bmi` and returns a string equivalent of the numerical value of the BMI with one place after the decimal. And, one more time, this function is also defined in `bmiCalculate.js`, as shown in Figure 6.18, and will be discussed later.

6.7 The Importance of Website Security and How JavaScript Can Help

Every time a user clicks on the submit button of a form, information of some kind that the user has entered into that form will either make its way to the server, for one purpose or another, or be processed on the client side, as you have just seen.

The web is much like the rest of society, in that you will find good folks and bad folks roaming around there, and some of the bad ones might decide to visit your site. If they do, it is difficult to predict what they might attempt to do there. For example, a clever and malicious user might try to slip in some data, through one of your forms, which you were not expecting. That could lead to harmful effects, unless you take steps to prevent this from happening.

Therefore, it is a recommended *best practice* to verify all user-entered input on the client-side before it is sent to the server. This, of course, is only one of the ways you can try to make your website secure from attack, but it is a key one. Note that we say *try*, which is a clue to the sad truth that no matter how much effort you put into making your website secure, hackers will probably always find new ways around your safeguards. Your initial goal, at least, should be to make life as difficult as possible for them.

Even with a web page as simple as the one that computes a BMI, we require the user to enter some data and click on a button to process that data. So, it makes sense that we should be satisfied that the user has entered only the kind of data that we were expecting. Even if a user is not trying to be malicious and simply makes a mistake by entering a letter instead of a number, for example, we don't want our web page to "come off the rails" and perhaps annoy our visitor to the point of leaving our website.

Because JavaScript is the most popular programming language for client-side web computing, and because it can be used to help you make your websites more secure, you need to learn something about how to use it for that purpose. Indeed, you can use JavaScript to verify that all form input from any user is within acceptable ranges before processing it and possibly forwarding it to the web server, and that is one of our main goals in this chapter. Later you shall see how the new `pattern` attribute introduced in HTML5, together with *regular expressions*, can be used to perform some data validation tasks without resorting to JavaScript.

6.8 JavaScript and the DOM Interact to Validate Our BMI Form Data

We illustrate this principle of data validation with the help of JavaScript in the context of our BMI calculator. The `bmiFormValidate()` function, shown in Figure 6.14, is the high-level "driver" function that performs the task of validating all the input entered into the BMI form. The definition of the `bmiFormValidate()` function is a little more involved than that of the `bmiFormProcess()` function. For one thing, this function does take a parameter, `bmiFormObj`, the DOM form object. For another, it calls a number of lower-level functions that we also have to write and all but two of which are shown in **FIGURES 6.15** and **6.16**. The two that are not shown

```
38   function inchesValid(height)
39   {
40       if (height == "" || isNaN(height))
41       {
42           alert("Error: Please input a number for height.");
43           return false;
44       }
45       if (height < 0 || height > 100)
46       {
47           alert("Error: Height must be in the range 0-100 inches.");
48           return false;
49       }
50       return true;
51   }
52
53   function centimetresValid(height)
54   {
55       if (height == "" || isNaN(height))
56       {
57           alert("Error: Please input a number for height.");
58           return false;
59       }
60       if (height < 0 || height > 300)
61       {
62           alert("Error: Height must be in the range 0-300 centimeters.");
63           return false;
64       }
65       return true;
66   }
```

FIGURE 6.15 `ch06/scripts/bmiFormValidate.js` **(excerpt)**
These are the low-level height-validating JavaScript functions from `bmiFormValidate.js`. There are two analogous weight-validating functions that are so similar we do not show them here.

```
98    function emailValid(address)
99    {
100       var p = address.search(/.+@.+/);
101       if (p == 0)
102           return true;
103       else
104       {
105           alert("Error: Invalid e-mail address.");
106           return false;
107       }
108   }
```

FIGURE 6.16 `ch06/scripts/bmiFormValidate.js` **(excerpt)**
This is the last of the low-level data-validating JavaScript functions from `bmiFormValidate.js`. This one performs a very simple regular expression check on the email address entered by the user.

are omitted because of their similarity to the two in Figure 6.15. In this case, we are sending (or passing) to the function the DOM `form` object, called `bmiFormObj`, as that parameter.

The first five JavaScript statements (lines 8–14) in the body of the function `bmiForm-Validate()` shown in Figure 6.14 collect the form input entered by the user for weight and height, along with their corresponding units, as well as the user's email address. Getting the information for the units is a little involved, due to the use of the `select` element. But this gives us a chance to introduce the notion of an *array*, since all the options specified in a `select` element are represented as an array in our JavaScript script.

6.8.1 Simple JavaScript Arrays, and the `options` Array of a `select` Element

An *array* is essentially a list of values, or "components" or "elements", though we try not to use "elements" in this context, to avoid confusion with HTML "elements". Usually, arrays are stored in such a way that each component of the array can be efficiently accessed using a *subscript* (or *index*) that appears in a pair of square brackets following the name of the array.

For example, in JavaScript you can create an array variable `a` to hold five integers, and simultaneously put into that array the first five positive even integers, with this statement:

```
var a = [2, 4, 6, 8, 10];
```

The first index of this array is 0 and the last is 4. Thus `a[2]` refers to the third value, which is 6, and a JavaScript *assignment statement* like `a[3] = 1` would replace the value 8 with the value 1. One major takeaway from this brief discussion of arrays is this: As in other C-based programming languages, the subscripts of arrays in JavaScript start with 0. Since you may be using JavaScript arrays of various sizes, you will need to keep in mind what this means: If a JavaScript array has n elements, the subscripts used to access those elements will go from 0 to n-1 (and *not* from 1 to n).

The array that we have to deal with from our BMI form looks a lot more complicated than it really is. In our BMI form, the DOM element "named" `heightUnit` is the `select` element that allows the user to choose inches or centimeters (see line 25 of Figure 6.12). What this means is that the expression

```
bmiFormObj.heightUnit.options
```

refers to an array of two components, and each component refers to one of the two options in the `select` element.

Let's explain this in a little more detail. Note that the above expression starts with `bmiForm-Obj`, the variable that we are using to refer to the form element shown in Figure 6.12. At the next level down in the DOM hierarchy of this HTML document is the `select` element whose `name` attribute has the value `heightUnit`. Thus in good object-oriented fashion we can refer to this `select` element as `bmiFormObj.heightUnit`. Every select element will, of course, have some `option` elements associated with it that form its content. And, finally, these options are available to us in an array called, not surprisingly, `options`. Note that `bmiFormObj` and `heightUnit` are names that we have made up, but `options` is a built-in name. This kind of expression shows up all the time in JavaScript code, so you should make an effort to become familiar with the syntax. The first time you see it, it can be a little intimidating, but a little usage goes a long way toward understanding.

6.8.2 Getting the Height and Weight Units Chosen by the User

Since there are only two components in this `options` array (two option elements in this `select` element), the first component of the array is given by `bmiFormObj.heightUnit.options[0]` and the second component by `bmiFormObj.heightUnit.options[1]`.

Furthermore, each component of the `options` array refers to one of the `option` elements of the corresponding `select` element, this option element is, of course, a DOM object. It also has a *field* called `text` that gives us the text used to describe that particular option on the web page. (JavaScript objects, and in particular DOM objects, have components just like arrays have components, but in the case of objects we call them *fields*.) So, to continue, in our case,

```
bmiFormObj .heightUnit.options[0].text
```

has a value that is the string `"inches"` and

```
bmiFormObj.heightUnit.options[1].text
```

has the value `"centimeters"`.

Similar expressions, with `heightUnit` replaced by `weightUnit`, will give you `"pounds"` and `"kilograms"` as the text values used to describe the weight unit options.

The question still remains as to which option the user has selected. Just as the DOM object named `heightUnit` had a field containing an array called `options` that we could access, it has another field called `selectedIndex` that provides us with the next piece of information that we need, the index of the value that the user has chosen. If the user has chosen `inches`, then `bmiFormObj.heightUnit.selectedIndex` will be 0 (corresponding to the first component of the `options` array). If the user has chosen `centimeters`, the value of `bmiFormObj.heightUnit.selectedIndex` will be 1 (corresponding to the second component of the `options` array). Therefore, the expression

```
bmiFormObj.heightUnit.options[bmiFormObj.heightUnit.
selectedIndex].text
```

from lines 8–9 of Figure 6.14 will give us the option selected by the user for the height unit, which is then stored in the variable `hUnit`. Similarly, the expression

```
bmiFormObj.weightUnit.options[bmiFormObj.weightUnit.
selectedIndex].text
```

from lines 10–11 of the same figure will give us the option selected by the user for the weight unit, which is then stored in wUnit.

6.8.3 Getting the User's Height and Weight Values, and Email Address

The next two JavaScript statements (lines 12 and 13 of Figure 6.14) retrieve the values of the user's height and weight as entered by the user. Both height and weight are specified using DOM elements of type text we named (not surprisingly) height and weight, and their values are given by a field called value. So bmiFormObj.height.value gives us the string entered by the user into the text field named height and bmiFormObj.weight.value gives us the string entered by the user into the text field named weight. We store them in variables called height and weight, respectively. Similarly, we also store the text entered by the user for the email address into a variable called email. Note here that all user-entered values, whether they are ultimately to be interpreted as numbers or not, are received as text.

6.8.4 Calling Functions to Validate Height, Weight, and Email Values

After retrieving the values entered by the user for height, weight, and email address (lines 12–14 of Figure 6.14), the function declares three variables called heightOK, weightOK, and emailOK (line 15). These variables are expected to hold either a true or a false value, depending on whether the corresponding data entries are in fact OK, or not, and the value for each will be supplied by a call to an appropriate function.

The following three if-else-statements validate the values input by the user for these three quantities: height, weight, and email address. The format and logic of each of the first two if-else-statements are essentially the same. The condition checks to see which unit is used for the height (or weight) and calls an appropriate function for validation. The value "returned" by the function is assigned to heightOK (or weightOK). We will look at these functions more closely shortly, but in the meantime let's just say that the usual way a function "returns" a value is to have a statement like

```
return someValue;
```

as the last statement in its body, which allows the function call to be used like a value of whatever type is being returned by that function.

The conditional if-else-statement for the email address is slightly different. We first check to see if the DOM object bmiFormObj.wantMail is checked. If it is checked then we validate the email address using the function emailValid(). The variable emailOK is set to the value returned by the call emailValid(bmiFormObj), which will be true if the user has clicked the checkbox. If the user has not clicked the checkbox, the function call will return a false value. In this case there will be no email address, so we don't have to check it; we just set the value of the variable emailOK to true. We need this value to be true since it will be part of the overall evaluation of whether "everything is OK", even though no email address has been entered.

Since we are only dealing with client-side computing using JavaScript, we have not implemented the email facility. All that happens is a message using the alert() method will be displayed to announce that email is not yet available. Allowing JavaScript programs to send emails from a client's computer would be a major breach of security since malicious JavaScript code could exploit the ability to send spam from client computers. We will implement the email facility using PHP later when we study server-side computing.

6.8.5 Logical Operators and Compound Boolean Expressions

Once we collect the individual validation flags for the three text fields, namely heightOK, weightOK, and emailOK, we need to check to see if all of them are true (that's why we wanted emailOK to be true even if no email address was entered). If all of them are in fact true, then we should return a true value back from the bmiFormValidate() function. In this case our return statement looks like this (line 35 of Figure 6.14):

```
return heightOK && weightOK && emailOK;
```

All three variables in the above expression—heightOK, weightOK, and emailOK—must be true for the entire expression to have the value true. This is because operator && is the "logical and" operator, and only when all operands connected by the operator && are true does the entire expression have the value true; otherwise, the expression has the value false.

TABLE 6.4 shows the typical logical operators available in JavaScript (and in many other programming languages) for combining simple boolean expressions to express more complex conditions and the results of operations involving these operators. The first two columns list the four possible values for the two logical expressions *expr1* and *expr2*, considered as a pair. The third

TABLE 6.4 The JavaScript logical operators.

expr1	*expr2*	*expr1 && expr2*	*expr1 || expr2*	*!expr1*
true	true	true	true	false
true	false	false	true	false
false	true	false	true	true
false	false	false	false	true

column gives the values for the "logical and" operation *expr1* && *expr2*. The fourth column shows the values of the "logical or" operation *expr1* || *expr2*. The "logical not" operator is represented by the symbol ! and the results of "logical not" applied to *expr1*, that is, !*expr1*, are given in the fifth column.

You should study Table 6.4 carefully. Its content is deceptively simple. Even though the bottom line is that these operators behave in more or less the same way that we English-speaking humans use the words *and, or,* and *not* in everyday language, many programming errors result from the improper use of these operators in code. Note in particular that the "logical or" operator is the so-called "inclusive or", which is true when *either* operand is true or *both* of the operands are true.

Here's a handy rule that summarizes the "and" and "or" columns of Table 6.4:

1. The only way *expr1* && *expr2* can be `true` is if **both** *expr1* and *expr2* are `true`.
2. The only way *expr1* || *expr2* can be `false` is if **both** *expr1* and *expr2* are `false`.

6.8.6 Relational Operators and Functions for Validating Height and Weight Values

Figure 6.15 shows the JavaScript code for validating the height value entered by the user. There are two functions, and both of them use similar logic. The two functions that validate the weight value are not shown because they are completely analogous.

Let's look at the first of the two functions in Figure 6.15, `inchesValid()`, in detail (see lines 38–51). This function is called if the user has indicated that height is specified in inches (the default). It receives the parameter `height`. The function body contains two conditional statements. The first one calls a very handy built-in JavaScript function `isNaN()` (think of this as `isNotANumber()`) with `height` as its parameter. The function call `isNaN(height)` returns a `true` value if `height` is *not* a number (perhaps the user has entered a letter instead of a number, by mistake). In that case, we alert the user with an appropriate message and return the value `false`. Note that after executing the `return` statement, we exit from the function, so the rest of the code will not be relevant in that case. If `isNaN(height)` returns a `false` value, we continue through the rest of the function.

If the `height` value passed to the function `isNaN(height)` is indeed a number, the next conditional statement ensures that the value is reasonable. (For those who are familiar with other programming languages like C++ or Java, this is a scary juncture. We are now about to use an entry as a numerical value that has come in as text, but this is going to be OK because this is JavaScript. All we have done is use `isNaN()` to verify that the entry is "a string that looks like a number", in effect. Those other programmers will be squirming at this point, and rightly so. But that's life on the web.) If the height in inches is less than 0 or if it is greater than 100, we will alert the user that the input for height is invalid and return a `false` value. The condition uses the "logical or" operator || that we saw in Table 6.4. It also uses two *comparison operators*, namely "less than" (<) and "greater than" (>). A complete list of *comparison operators* (also called *relational operators*) that can be used to compare two values in various ways is given in **TABLE 6.5**.

TABLE 6.5 The JavaScript relational (or comparison) operators.

Operator	Description
==	Equal to
!=	Not equal to
<	Less than
<=	Less than or equal to
>	Greater than
>=	Greater than or equal to

If we did not execute the statement `return false;` in either of the two conditionals, we are still in the function `inchesValid()`. That leaves us with the execution of the last statement in the function, that is, `return true;`. That means the function `inchesValid()` will return true if `height` is a number that is greater than or equal to zero and less than or equal to 100 (inches). (We are allowing some very short and some very tall people to use our calculator.) The other function in Figure 6.15 and the two not shown follow similar logic; you should browse through these other three functions to ensure that you understand them as well.

6.8.7 Simple Regular Expressions and a Function for Validating an Email Address

The functions discussed or mentioned in the previous section all validate numerical values. We also need to be able to validate string input, such as email addresses, as well. This is usually done using what are called *regular expressions*. You will study regular expressions in more detail and see more complex examples in an upcoming section when we validate data submitted via our feedback form. Here, we want to make our BMI form functional, so we provide just a sneak preview of regular expressions by using a simple regular expression to validate a very simple email address input.

The function that performs our email address validation is called `emailValid()` and is shown in Figure 6.16. First, note that it accepts a parameter. What is this parameter? If you look back at lines 14 and 29 of Figure 6.14, you can see that when this function is actually called, it is passed as a parameter whatever the user has entered into the email address box of the BMI form, which may or may not be an actual email address. Once the function has that data entry from the user, it uses the built-in JavaScript `search()` function (available to search JavaScript objects of type `String`) to test whether what the user has entered qualifies as a valid email address.

How does the `search()` function know what a valid email address is? It knows because we told it by using a *regular expression*. Since our string is called `address`, our method call will be `address.search()`, and it also needs a parameter. This parameter has to be a "pattern" that we hope to see in the value stored in `address` if it is in fact a valid email address, and this "pattern" is described by a regular expression. A "real" email address would, of course, likely be much more complicated, but in our case we decide to search for a very simple pattern that just consists of one or more arbitrary characters, followed by the specific character @, followed by one or more additional arbitrary characters. We specify this pattern to the `search` method by using a *regular expression* that is enclosed within (or, as we also say, "delimited by") a pair of forward slash characters (/). See line 100 of Figure 6.16.

Regular expressions, which are all about patterns, seem quite mysterious when you first encounter them, but if you stay the course you will find they are very powerful and versatile, and can even be fun to work with.

For example, the pattern that we are interested in here can be specified by the following simple regular expression:

```
.+@.+
```

Note that the two forward slashes in the input to the `search()` method, one at the beginning and one at the end, are delimiters of the regular expression, as we mentioned above, so technically only `.+@.+` comprises the regular expression. In a regular expression, a period (`.`) stands for any character, and a trailing plus sign (+) indicates one or more repetitions of whatever immediately precedes the +. Note that this "repetition" does not mean that the same character has to be repeated, just that there be a "repetition of characters". In other words you *could* have `aaa`, let's say, but you could also have `abcde`, and either would qualify. Thus the two characters `.+` together, as part of a regular expression, simply mean "one or more characters".

So, our pattern will match any string that has one or more characters, followed by a @ character, followed by one or more characters. We are saying, in effect, that as long as we have some characters before and after the @ character, we have an acceptable email address. Clearly, this is not a sufficient validation for an actual email address. But this is just a preview of more sophisticated pattern matching that you will study later on in this chapter.

The `search()` function will return a 0 (zero) if the user entered (only) an email address that matches such a pattern, and –1 if a match is not found. We assign the value returned by the `search()` to a variable p. If p gets the value 0, then the address matches our simple expectations of an email address. Hence, we return a `true` value. Otherwise, we return a `false` value.

So, the user will get a popup message indicating an error if bad input values are entered for height or weight, and also if the user has clicked the checkbox for an email report and then enters a bad email address. The user is also informed that email reports are not yet available. **FIGURE 6.17** shows the error reported when we entered the letter b as the weight value. You should try different valid and invalid values of height, weight, and email address to confirm that our input validation works in all cases.

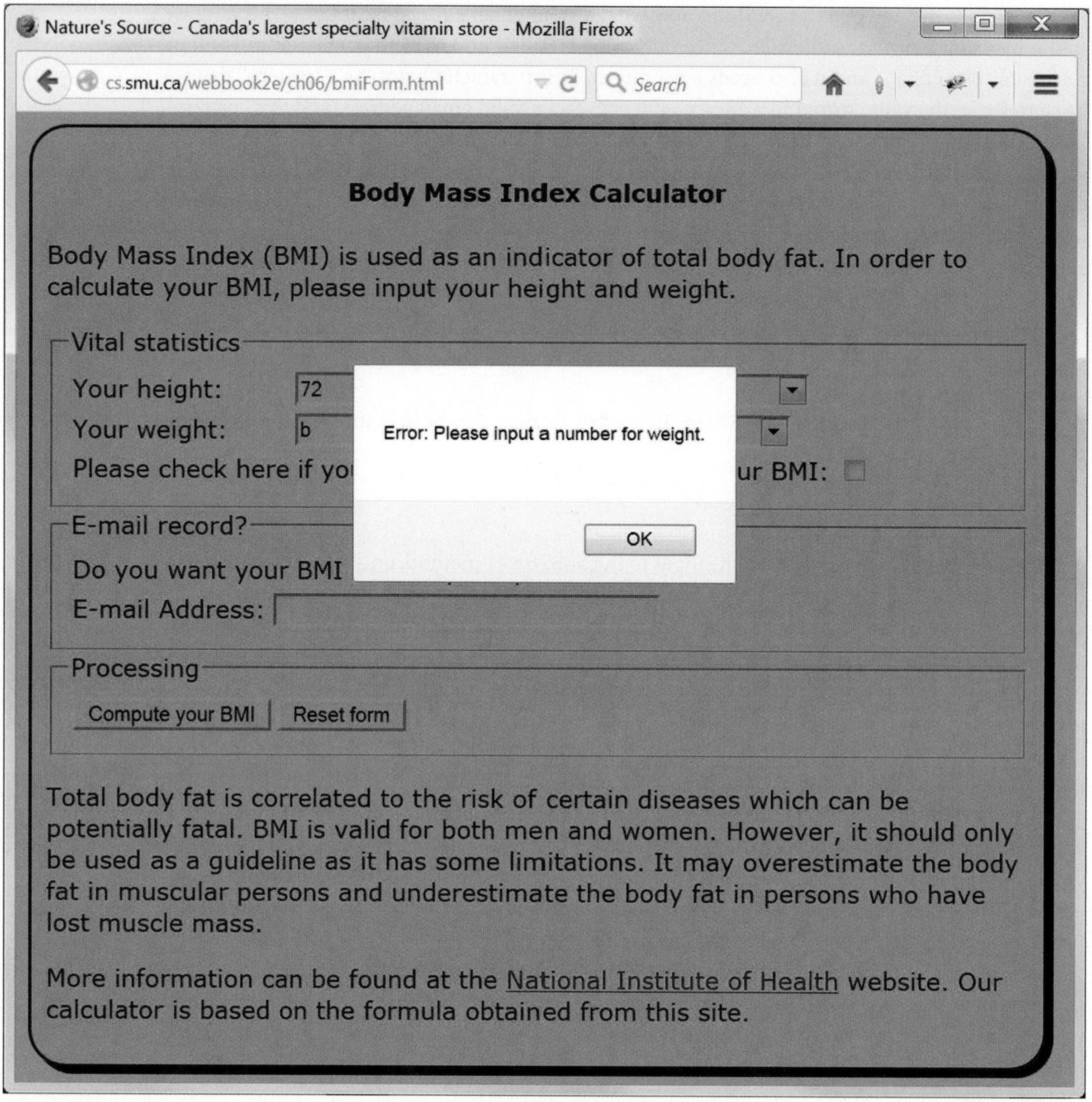

FIGURE 6.17 `graphics/ch06/displayErrorBmiFormHtml.jpg`
The popup error message shown when the BMI form has been given a bad value just for the user's weight.

6.9 JavaScript and the DOM Interact to Compute a BMI Value

Much of JavaScript programming deals with string manipulation. Of course, the language supports numerical computation as well as the testing of numerical values we discussed earlier. In this section, we will use the computation of a BMI value as an example for studying basic numerical computations in JavaScript.

Figure 6.18 shows the file bmiCalculate.js, which contains the four functions we need to perform the required numerical calculations, as well as a function for handling the display of results in the case where the user wants a "detailed" report.

```
1   //bmiCalculate.js
2   //Functions to perform the BMI value calculation,
3   //to one place after the decimal, assuming all data
4   //input by the user has been validated
5
6   function valueOfBMI(bmiFormObj)
7   {
8       var hUnit = bmiFormObj.heightUnit.
9           options[bmiFormObj.heightUnit.selectedIndex].text;
10      var wUnit = bmiFormObj.weightUnit.
11          options[bmiFormObj.weightUnit.selectedIndex].text;
12      var height = bmiFormObj.height.value;
13      var weight = bmiFormObj.weight.value;
14
15      if (hUnit == "inches") height = inchesToCentimetres(height);
16      if (wUnit == "pounds") weight = poundsToKilograms(weight);
17
18      height /= 100.0; //Convert height from centimeters to meters
19      var bmi = weight/(height*height); //kilograms/(meters*meters)
20      return bmi;
21  }
22
23  function inchesToCentimetres(height)
24  {
25      var CENTIMETRES_PER_INCH = 2.54;
26      return height * CENTIMETRES_PER_INCH;
27  }
28
```

FIGURE 6.18 `ch06/scripts/bmiCalculate.js`
The functions that perform the calculation of the BMI value, assuming all input is valid.

```
29   function poundsToKilograms(weight)
30   {
31       var POUNDS_PER_KILOGRAM = 2.20462;
32       return weight / POUNDS_PER_KILOGRAM;
33   }
34
35   function valueTo1DecimalPlace(num)
36   {
37       var intPortion = Math.floor(num);
38       var decimalPortion = Math.round(num*10)%10;
39       var text = intPortion + "." + decimalPortion;
40       return text;
41   }
42
43   function displayDetails(bmiFormObj, bmi)
44   {
45       var hUnit = bmiFormObj.heightUnit.
46           options[bmiFormObj.heightUnit.selectedIndex].text;
47       var wUnit = bmiFormObj.weightUnit.
48           options[bmiFormObj.weightUnit.selectedIndex].text;
49       var height = bmiFormObj.height.value;
50       var weight = bmiFormObj.weight.value;
51       var text = "BMI Report\n" +
52           "Your weight: " + weight + " " + wUnit + "\n" +
53           "Your height: " + height + " " + hUnit + "\n" +
54           "Your BMI: " + valueTo1DecimalPlace(bmi) + "\n";
55       if (bmi < 18.5)
56           text += "Your BMI suggests that you are underweight.\n";
57       else if (bmi < 25)
58           text += "Your BMI suggests that you have a reasonable weight.\n";
59       else if (bmi < 29)
60           text += "Your BMI suggests that you may be overweight.\n";
61       else
62           text += "Your BMI suggests that you may be obese.\n";
63       alert(text);
64   }
```

FIGURE 6.18 `ch06/scripts/bmiCalculate.js` (*continued*)

6.9.1 Numerical Calculations: Three Functions Compute the BMI Value

The function valueOfBMI() is our high-level "driver" function that may call one or both of two lower-level functions if inches and/or pounds need to be converted to metric units, but in any case computes and returns the BMI value. This function is called from the function bmiForm-Process() (see line 10 of Figure 6.13) and receives bmiFormObj as its only parameter. Prior to calling `valueOfBMI()`, the input data values entered by the user have all been validated, so we can assume that the fields `height` and `weight` of `bmiFormObj` contain numbers that lie within appropriate ranges.

The function `valueOfBMI()` (lines 6–21 of Figure 6.18) first extracts the values of `heightUnit, weightUnit, height,` and `weight` from the `bmiFormObj` just as we did in the function `bmiFormValidate()` in Figure 6.14. BMI calculations can be most easily done using all metric quantities. So, if the user has entered height in inches it is converted to centimeters using the function `inchesToCentimetres()` in the first conditional statement. And similarly, if the user has entered weight in pounds, it is converted to kilograms using the function `poundsTo-Kilograms()` in the second conditional statement. The function `valueOfBMI()` then converts the centimeters to meters by dividing height (in centimeters) by 100. Finally, the BMI is then calculated (according to the standard formula for this value) as the ratio of the user's weight to the square of the user's height.

The functions `inchesToCentimetres()` and `poundsToKilograms()` return the centimeter or kilogram equivalents of inches or pounds using appropriate factors. JavaScript does not provide a mechanism for setting programmer-defined constants, which we would find convenient for setting the conversion factors in these two functions (`CENTIMETRES_PER_INCH` and `POUNDS_PER_KILOGRAM`), so we simply make them variables and use for their names an all-caps, word-underscore-separated style that is a typical convention for constants in many languages, such as C++ and Java.

In these functions we also get to see some typical JavaScript arithmetic using the arithmetic operators for multiplication (operator `*`) and division (operator `/`). Of course, JavaScript also provides the addition (`+`) and subtraction (`-`) operators. As usual, multiplication and division have a higher precedence than addition and subtraction. So, for example, the expression `4 - 3 * 8` has the value `-20` because the multiplication takes place before subtraction. This operator-precedence behavior is typical of all programming languages.

JavaScript also provides a remainder (or modulus) operator, as do all the C-based programming languages. This remainder operator is `%` (the percent sign). It returns the remainder resulting from the division of its first operand by its second operand. For example, `47%5` has the value `2`. The remainder operator has the same precedence as the multiplication and division operators. You will see the remainder operator in action a little later on in this section.

6.9.2 Setting the Precision of the BMI Value and Displaying a Detailed Report

Our BMI form gives the user the option of displaying the BMI report in detail, or simply displaying just the value of the BMI. This decision is made in the function `bmiFormProcess()` shown in Figure 6.13. Whether we simply print the BMI using a call to `alert()`, as shown in Figure 6.13, or create a more detailed format using the function `displayDetails()` shown in Figure 6.18, we need to first format the numeric value so that it does not have a variable precision (number of places after the decimal) each time it is shown. That is, we do not want an answer like 20.3896543 one time, and 22.516 the next. We prefer to display it with a single digit after the decimal point

TABLE 6.6 Some constants available in the JavaScript Math object.	
Constants	**Description**
E	Euler's number $e \approx 2.71828$
PI	$\pi \approx 3.14159$
LN2	Natural logarithm of 2
LN10	Natural logarithm of 10
LOG2E	Base-2 logarithm of E
LOG10E	Base-10 logarithm of E
SQRT1_2	$\sqrt{0.5}$
SQRT2	$\sqrt{2}$

every time. Although we could use the JavaScript `toFixed()` function in this context for the job at hand, we write our own short utility function, just to illustrate a common technique that you might find useful here and there.

The function `valueTo1DecimalPlace()` given in lines 35–41 of Figure 6.18 does the requisite formatting and returns the number as its string equivalent with a single digit after the decimal point. This is not necessarily the most elegant way to do it, but it gives us a chance to use two methods that are generally useful and that belong to the built-in JavaScript `Math` object: the `floor()` method and the `round()` method. The `Math` object provides a number of other useful mathematical constants and methods, many of which are shown in **TABLES 6.6** and **6.7**.

Our first task is to isolate the integer portion of the BMI value. The function `floor()` essentially truncates (removes) the digits after the decimal point in a given number. For example, if our BMI calculations resulted in a value `20.589`, then `Math.floor(20.589)` would give the value `20`. We save the value returned by the `floor()` method in a variable called `intPortion`, for obvious reasons, and that gives us the integer part of the BMI value, as desired.

Our second task is to isolate the first digit after the decimal place. In order to do this we employ a bit of clever numeric manipulation that starts with this calculation:

```
Math.round(num*10)
```

Let's explain. We first multiply our number by `10`. In our example, `20.589 * 10` gives us the value `205.89`. We then round off the resulting number to the nearest integer using the `round()` method of the `Math` object, and `Math.round(205.89)` gives us the value `206`. (Note that we want `round()` here, and not `floor()`, which would give us the (incorrect) value `205`.) Now we use the remainder of the division of the resulting number by `10`, that is, `206%10`, which has the value `6`. This gives us `6` as the single digit after the decimal point for the number `20.589`.

TABLE 6.7 Some methods of the JavaScript `Math` object that provide many of the common functions one expects to find in any programming language.

Method	Return Value
`abs(x)`	Absolute value of `x`
`ceil(x)`	Smallest integer greater than or equal to `x`
`floor(x)`	Greatest integer less than or equal to `x`
`round(x)`	Nearest integer to `x`
`max(x,y)`	Maximum of `x` and `y`
`min(x,y)`	Minimum of `x` and `y`
`random()`	Random number greater than or equal to 0 and less than 1
`exp(x)`	`Math.E` to the power `x`
`log(x)`	Natural logarithm (base `Math.E`) of `x`
`pow(x,y)`	x^y
`sqrt(x)`	Square root of `x`

Finally, we concatenate this single digit after the decimal point to the variable `intPortion` and a period to get the string equivalent of the number we want to return, and we have thus converted our original value `20.589` to `20.6`. The details for all of this are a little involved, so if you have not seen calculations like this before you may want to sit back and study the logic for a few minutes.

The function `displayDetails()` shown in lines 43–64 of Figure 6.18 is used to prepare and display a more "detailed" BMI report than just the bare BMI value. As you can see from where it is called (line 12 of Figure 6.13), this function receives two parameters: the `bmiFormObj` itself, as well as the previously computed BMI value now stored in the variable `bmi`. The function first extracts the values of `heightUnit`, `weightUnit`, `height`, and `weight` from `bmiFormObj` in the by-now-familiar way. A variable called `text` is formed by concatenating the values of all these variables, interspersed with appropriate additional text and newline characters (`\n`). Based on the interval within which the value of the BMI falls, a message about whether the BMI is low, high, or reasonable is further appended using a construct that we have not seen before, the "nested" `if-else`-statement. This works as follows: Each condition is tested, in turn, until a `true` condition is found, at which point the statement following that condition is executed and the program continues with the statement following the nested construct. If none of the conditions is `true`, the `else` part of the construct is executed, if there is one; otherwise, the nested construct causes no action. Once again, this is typical of virtually all programming languages. The message thus formed in the variable `text` is displayed to the user using the `alert` method. You can see the display, in a popup window, of results from such BMI form processing that asks for a detailed report in **FIGURE 6.19**.

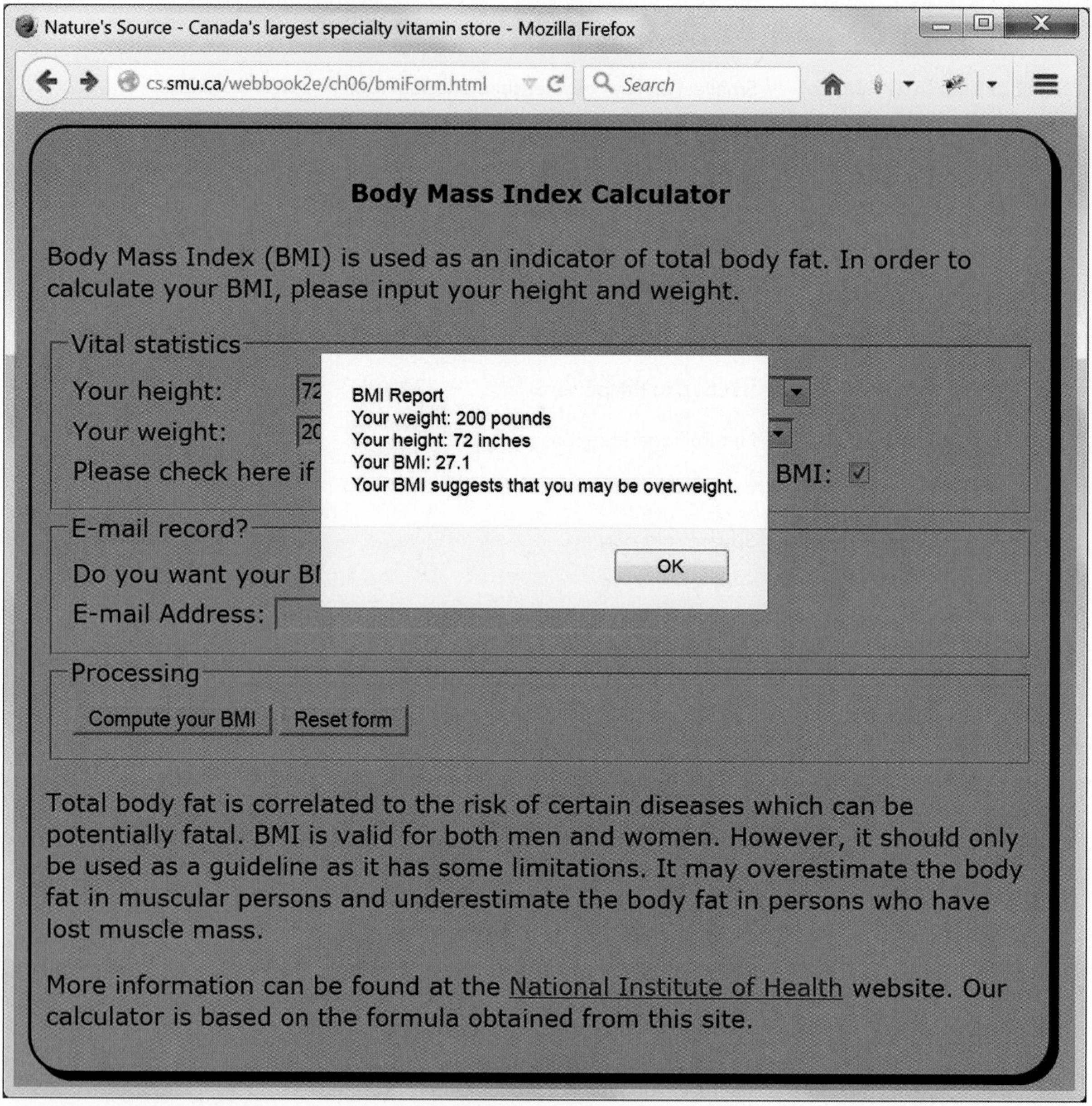

FIGURE 6.19 `graphics/ch06/displayBmiFormHtml.jpg`
The popup message shown when a typical detailed BMI calculation has been successfully performed.

6.10 Regular Expressions in JavaScript and in HTML5

We saw a brief preview of regular expression usage earlier in the chapter when we performed a simple validation of an email address entered into our BMI form. In that situation we used a very short "pattern" described by a regular expression to make sure that the submitted email address contained an @ sign and at least one character before and after that symbol. This scenario, though a trivial one, is very typical of how regular expressions are used.

That is, in a typical situation, you start by creating a regular expression that "describes" what your data should look like, in general. Then you compare your specific data (usually it's an input value from some source, such as a web form) to see if it "lives up to expectations" (matches or contains the data pattern expected). That's a very high-level view, but if you understand the "big picture", that will go a long way toward helping you grasp the details.

Two obvious questions arise:

▶ How do we actually create these "patterns", or regular expressions, that describe our data?
▶ How do we actually compare our data with the regular expression that is supposed to describe it?

Of course we've answered both questions in a simple way by our earlier email example, but now we need to say more about each. Our immediate goal will be to apply our additional regular expression knowledge to the validation of our feedback form input data. In fact, we will use that context for examples as we introduce and discuss new regular expression concepts in general, and provide answers to the above questions. This we will do in the following section. In the meantime we need to make a couple of other points.

The first thing you need to realize is that not only is a regular expression used to describe a pattern in a string, a regular expression is itself a string. And being a string, sometimes it is enclosed in quotes. But not always. For example, our earlier email example regular expression was enclosed in forward slashes when we used it as a parameter in a call to the JavaScript `search()` function. This use of forward slashes to enclose our regular expressions will continue to be the case in this chapter because we will continue to use the `search()` function in our JavaScript validation code.

However, in the next chapter we will make use of the new HTML5 `pattern` attribute, whose value is also a regular expression, but in this case a regular expression enclosed in double quotes. So, just note that the context may determine how you have to delimit a regular expression, but in general the regular expression itself will be the same. In fact, although there are some differences from one programming language to another, virtually all the most commonly used regular expression features in JavaScript are the same as those you will find elsewhere. TABLES 6.8–6.11 list some of the most frequently used (and useful) such features.

A second important high-level notion is this: When we are constructing a regular expression, there are two quite different kinds of characters, "ordinary characters" and "metacharacters"[2]

---

[2] Recall that you have seen these previously in a different context: HTML entities were metacharacters.

TABLE 6.8 Characters denoting positions in JavaScript regular expressions.

Character	Position
^	At the beginning of a string
$	At the end of a string
\b	At a word boundary
\B	Not at a word boundary

TABLE 6.9 Special characters that can be used in JavaScript regular expressions.

Special Character	Description
\0	The null character
\n	The newline character
\f	The form feed (page break) character
\r	The carriage return character
\t	The horizontal tab character
\v	The vertical tab character
\nnn	The character whose ASCII code is octal nnn
\xnn	The character whose ASCII code is hexadecimal nn
\unnnn	The character whose 4-digit Unicode representation is nnnn

(also called "special characters"). An ordinary character is just that character, and represents itself, while a metacharacter, or special character, may be single character or a combination of characters and represents something other than itself.

The best way to illustrate the difference is to recall our earlier simple regular expression example .+@.+ for email validation. Here @ is an ordinary character that represents itself, while both the period (.) and the plus sign (+) are metacharacters. The period represents any character (except the newline character), and the plus character says you want "at least one of" whatever immediately precedes it (in this case the period).

TABLE 6.10 Character classes that can be used in JavaScript regular expressions.

Character Class	Description of what it matches
`[xyz]`	Any single character from the characters enclosed in square brackets
`[^xyz]`	Any single character not among the characters enclosed in square brackets
`.` (period)	Any character except the newline character
`\d`	Any single digit; same as `[0-9]` (A dash denotes a range of values.)
`\D`	Any non-digit character; same as `[^0-9]`
`\w`	Any alphanumeric character, including the underscore; same as `[A-Za-z_0-9]`
`\W`	Any character that is not alphanumeric or an underscore; same as `[^A-Za-z_0-9]`
`\s`	A single whitespace character; same as `[ \r\t\n\f]`
`\S`	A single non-whitespace character; same as `[^ \r\t\n\f]`

TABLE 6.11 Modifiers that can be placed after a pattern (a character or expression) within a JavaScript regular expression to indicate the permissible amount of repetition of that pattern.

Modifier	Description
`{x}`	Exactly x repetitions
`{x,}`	x or more repetitions
`{x,y}`	Minimum x, maximum y repetitions
`?`	No more than 1 repetition (i.e., optional)
`*`	Zero or more repetitions
`+`	One or more repetitions

6.11 JavaScript and the DOM Interact to Validate Our Feedback Form Data

So, in this section we will take a closer look at more complex regular expressions, and use them to perform more sophisticated validation, in the context of our feedback form.

The form fields that we will be validating are those for the first and last name, the telephone number, and the email address. It would be virtually impossible to "validate" whatever the user entered for the subject and comments, so we don't try. However, since the salutation is empty by default, we could check to make sure the user has actually made a choice, but since that would not involve our main focus here on regular expressions, we leave that for an exercise.

This chapter contains the latest version of our feedback form that we developed in the previous chapter. It is located in the file `ch06/feedbackForm.html` and shown in **FIGURE 6.20**. The `head` element of the updated file includes a `script` element (line 7) that tells the browser to get the JavaScript code for validation from the file `feedbackFormValidate.js`, which is located in the `scripts` subdirectory. The opening `form` tag is now modified with a new attribute called `onsubmit`, which has the value `feedbackFormValidate()`. When the submit

```
1    <!DOCTYPE html>
2    <!-- feedbackForm.html -->
3    <html lang="en">
4      <head>
5        <meta charset="utf-8">
6        <link rel="stylesheet" href="css/default.css">
7        <script src="scripts/feedbackFormValidate.js"></script>
8        <title>Nature's Source - Canada's largest specialty vitamin store</title>
9      </head>
10     <body>
11     <main class="Feedback">
12       <h4>Feedback Form ... Let Us Know What You Think</h4>
13       <form id="contactForm" onsubmit="feedbackFormValidate()">
14         <table>
15           <tr>
16             <td>Salutation:</td>
17             <td><select name="salute">
18               <option> </option>
19               <option>Mrs.</option>
20               <option>Ms.</option>
21               <option>Mr.</option>
22               <option>Dr.</option>
23             </select></td>
24           </tr>
```

FIGURE 6.20 `ch06/feedbackForm.html`
The HTML markup for the latest version of our feedback form.

```
25          <tr>
26            <td>First Name:</td>
27            <td><input type="text" name="firstName" size="40"></td>
28          </tr>
29          <tr>
30            <td>Last Name:</td>
31            <td><input type="text" name="lastName" size="40"></td>
32          </tr>
33          <tr>
34            <td>E-mail Address:</td>
35            <td><input type="text" name="email" size="40"></td>
36          </tr>
37          <tr>
38            <td>Phone Number:</td>
39            <td><input type="text" name="phone" size="40"></td>
40          </tr>
41          <tr>
42            <td>Subject:</td>
43            <td><input type="text" name="subject" size="40"></td>
44          </tr>
45          <tr>
46            <td>Comments:</td>
47            <td><textarea name="message" rows="6" cols="30">
48            </textarea></td>
49          </tr>
50          <tr>
51            <td colspan="2">Please check here if you wish to receive a reply:
52            <input type="checkbox" name="reply" value="yes"></td>
53          </tr>
54          <tr>
55            <td><input type="submit" value="Send Feedback"></td>
56            <td><input type="reset" value="Reset Form"></td>
57          </tr>
58        </table>
59      </form>
60    </main>
61    </body>
62  </html>
```

FIGURE 6.20 `ch06/feedbackForm.html` (*continued*)

button for the form is pressed, the function `feedbackFormValidate()` defined in the file `feedbackFormValidate.js` will be invoked. All of this is quite similar to what we did with our BMI form example.

FIGURE 6.21 shows one of the errors we hope to trap through our feedback form data validation. Where this example departs from the previous BMI example is in its enhanced usage of regular expressions for validation purposes.

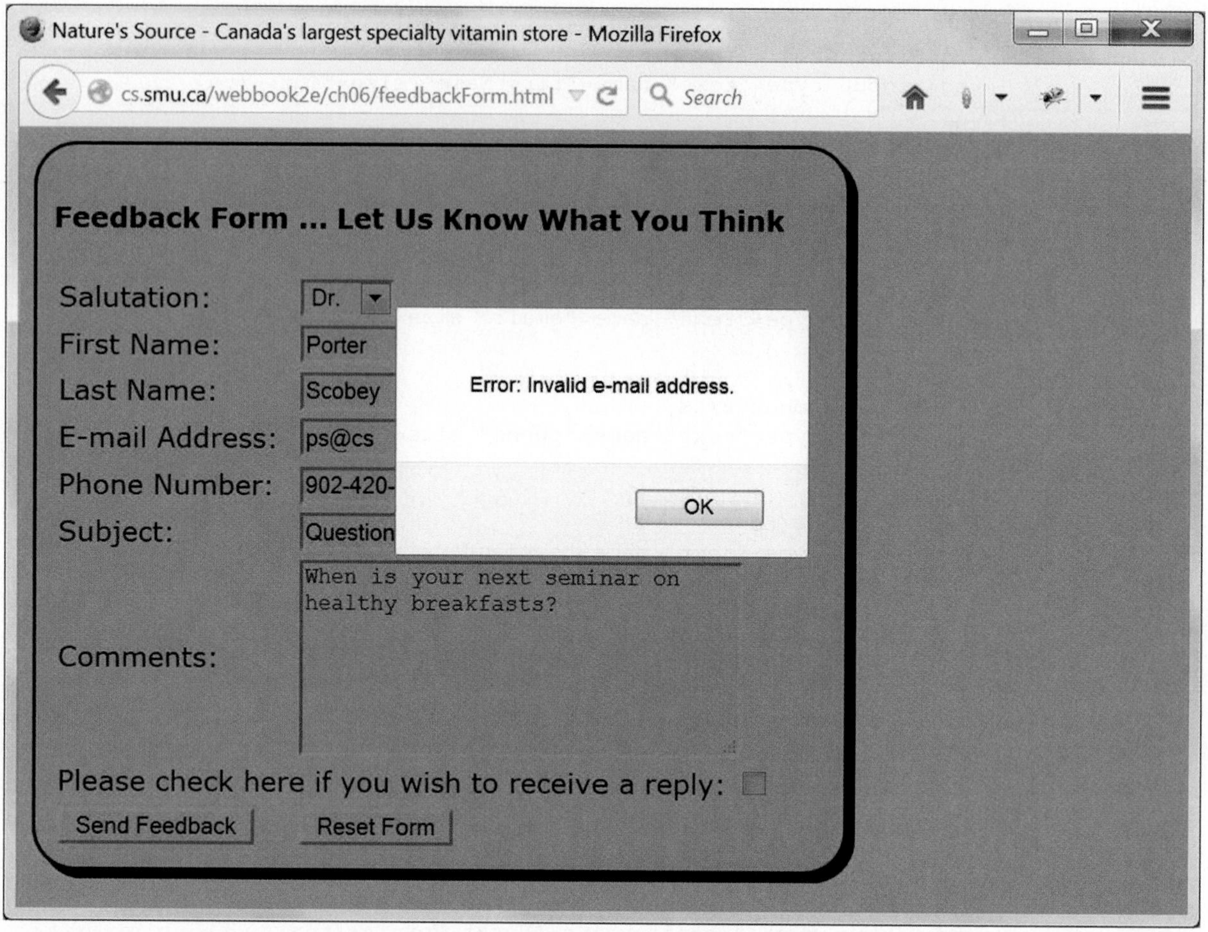

FIGURE 6.21 `graphics/ch06/displayErrorFeedbackFormHtml.jpg`
The popup error message shown when the feedback form has been given a bad value just for the user's email address.

FIGURE 6.22 shows the function `feedbackFormValidate()` from the file `feedback-FormValidate.js`. This high-level "driver" function does not have any new features, but the logic for validation is slightly different from that used in the BMI case. We use the value `contactForm` of the `id` attribute of the form to access the form and get a reference to the form object, which we assign to the variable `contactFormObj`. The values of `firstName`, `lastName`, `phone`, and `email` from the form are validated by appropriate function calls. We begin by taking the "optimistic approach" and assuming by default that all fields are OK and assign a value of `true` to a variable called `everythingOK`. Then, if any one of the fields that we validate has an invalid input value, we set the value of `everythingOK` to be `false` and ultimately return a value

```
 1   //feedbackFormValidate.js
 2   //Functions to perform data validation on data entered by
 3   //the user into the feedback form, and to display appropriate
 4   //error messages if problems with the data are discovered
 5
 6   function feedbackFormValidate()
 7   {
 8       var contactFormObj = document.getElementById("contactForm");
 9       var firstName = contactFormObj.firstName.value;
10       var lastName = contactFormObj.lastName.value;
11       var phone = contactFormObj.phone.value;
12       var email = contactFormObj.email.value;
13       var everythingOK = true;
14
15       if (!validateName(firstName))
16       {
17           alert("Error: Invalid first name.");
18           everythingOK = false;
19       }
20
21       if (!validateName(lastName))
22       {
23           alert("Error: Invalid last name.");
24           everythingOK = false;
25       }
26
27       if (!validatePhone(phone))
28       {
29           alert("Error: Invalid phone number.");
30           everythingOK = false;
31       }
32
33       if (!validateEmail(email))
34       {
35           alert("Error: Invalid e-mail address.");
36           everythingOK = false;
37       }
38
39       if (everythingOK)
40       {
41       if (contactFormObj.reply.checked)
42           alert("Warning: The e-mail feature is currently not supported.");
43       alert("All the information looks good.\nThank you!");
44       return true;
45       }
46       else
47           return false;
48   }
```

FIGURE 6.22 `ch06/scripts/feedbackFormValidate.js` **(Part 1 of 2)**
The "high-level" `feedbackFormValidate()` function from `feedbackFormValidate.js` that calls three other lower-level functions to validate names, telephone numbers, and email addresses.

of `false`. Otherwise, `everythingOK` remains `true`, and in this case we use `alert()` to display the message

```
All the information looks good.
Thank you!
```

and return `true`. Otherwise, we return `false`. In fact, because we are using a sequence of `if`-statements, any and all fields containing invalid data will cause an appropriate error message to be displayed via a call to `alert()`.

Now that the fundamental logical structure of the function `feedbackFormValidate()` is out of the way, we are ready to study the individual functions that actually validate the data. These functions are shown in **FIGURE 6.23**. The basic structure of all of these functions is the same. They search for an acceptable pattern that is specified using a regular expression. If the text conforms to the acceptable pattern, `search()` will return a `0`, as we have seen before.

```
50   function validateName(name)
51   {
52       var p = name.search(/^[-'\w\s]+$/);
53       if (p == 0)
54           return true;
55       else
56           return false;
57   }
58
59   function validatePhone(phone)
60   {
61       var p1 = phone.search(/^\d{3}[-\s]{0,1}\d{3}[-\s]{0,1}\d{4}$/);
62       var p2 = phone.search(/^\d{3}[-\s]{0,1}\d{4}$/);
63       if (p1 == 0 || p2 == 0)
64           return true;
65       else
66           return false;
67   }
68
69   function validateEmail(address)
70   {
71       var p = address.search(/^\w+([\.-]?\w+)*@\w+([\.-]?\w+)*(\.\w{2,3})$/);
72       if (p == 0)
73           return true;
74       else
75           return false;
76   }
```

FIGURE 6.23 `ch06/scripts/feedbackFormValidate.js` **(Part 2 of 2)**
The "lower-level" functions from `feedbackFormValidate.js` that validate names, telephone numbers, and email addresses via JavaScript regular expressions.

If the `search()` function returns 0, our function that is calling `search()` will return a `true` value. Otherwise, it returns a `false` value. The most interesting parts of these functions are the actual regular expressions used in them, so let's take a look at how they are constructed and used.

6.11.1 Validating First and Last Names

Table 6.8 describes some of the commonly used modifiers to indicate the position in a regular expression. A `^` matches the beginning of a string, while a `$` matches the end of the string. These two modifiers appear in the regular expression (line 52)

```
^[-'\w\s]+$
```

from the function `validateName()` in Figure 6.23 (lines 50–57). This regular expression is saying, first of all, that the pattern specified starts at the beginning of a string (`^`) and ends at the end of the string (`$`). No other string can precede or follow the pattern. In fact, we use these two modifiers for every regular expression in the file `feedbackFormValidate.js`. Two other position modifiers that are useful from time to time, but that we do not illustrate here, are `\b`, which matches the beginning or end of a word (i.e., a word boundary), and `\B`, which matches any position that is not the end or beginning of a word (i.e., not a word boundary).

Look at the rest of the regular expression `[-'\w\s]+`. The square brackets enclose a set of characters (often called a *character class*). The character class is matched by any single character from the characters in the character class. And, in this case, we must have one or more of those characters because of the trailing + symbol. Other types of repetition in regular expressions are given in Table 6.11.

Now for the characters in the character set itself. The simplest ones are the hyphen or dash character (`-`), and the single quote or apostrophe character (`'`), which match themselves (i.e., they are "ordinary characters". However, in a square-bracket delimited character set like this you have to be careful of the dash symbol (`-`), since it will only be an "ordinary character" matching itself if it is the first or last character inside the square brackets; otherwise it will denote a range of characters.

The remaining two characters in our set are `\w` and `\s`, and these are actually special characters. They are, in fact, shorthand notations for character classes, so we have in effect two additional character classes within the initial character class. The character class `\w` represents a single alphanumeric character or underscore, while the character class `\s` corresponds to a single whitespace character. A more complete list of character classes is given in Table 6.10. See also Table 6.9 for some additional special characters that can be used in regular expressions. You can always use the ASCII code or Unicode value to specify any of these special characters, as indicated in the table.

After dissecting the regular expression `^[-'\w\s]+$`, you can conclude that it will match a string with one or more repetitions of any combination of alphanumeric, whitespace, hyphen, and single-quote characters. If the string entered for first or last name matches this pattern, then `validateName()` will return a `true` value.

6.11.2 Validating Telephone Numbers

Now look at the `validatePhone()` function in Figure 6.23 (lines 59–67). This function accepts phone numbers with or without an area code. We allow for the use of either a space or a hyphen as separator, but no separator at all is also permissible. Therefore, all of the following variations of a telephone number shown in the block of numbers below are acceptable:

```
902 420 5798     902 420-5798     902 4205798     902420 5798
902420-5798      9024205798       902-420 5798    902-420-5798
902-4205798      420 5798         420-5798        4205798
```

Here is the regular expression that we use to validate a telephone number that has an area code:

```
^\d{3}[-\s]{0,1}\d{3}[-\s]{0,1}\d{4}$
```

As we discussed in the case of regular expressions for first and last names, the use of ^ and $ indicates that no other string is allowed to precede or follow the pattern. Here is our analysis of the pattern:

▶ The initial `\d{3}` means that a telephone number must begin with exactly three digits.
▶ The `[-\s]{0,1}` means that after those three digits the next character may be missing altogether, or it may be a hyphen or a whitespace character. It should be noted that we could have replaced `{0,1}` with `?` to indicate that a hyphen or a space is optional.
▶ We require another three digits, followed again by an optional hyphen or whitespace character. In other words, the first two "sub-patterns" repeat.
▶ The `\d{4}` means that the number must terminate with exactly four digits.

We use this second regular expression to validate a phone number without an area code:

```
^\d{3}[-\s]{0,1}\d{4}$
```

As you can see, it essentially uses the same pieces as the previous regular expression, except for the absence of the area code portion at the beginning.

6.11.3 Validating Email Addresses

Finally, look at the regular expression for validating email, which is more complicated than any we have seen previously:

```
^\w+([\.-]?\w+)*@\w+([\.-]?\w+)*(\.\w{2,3})$
```

Clearly this is the scariest regular expression you've seen yet. But let's not panic, because you know more or less what an email address looks like, and most of what you see here you've already seen in Tables 6.8–6.11. Once we explain a couple of new things, everything should fall into place if you're prepared to study the expression for a few moments.

First, note the use of parentheses (round brackets, if you like). They are used to enclose several entities that we wish to consider as a group, often to be able to apply a repetition factor to the members of the group. Second, note that since the period is a character with a special meaning in regular expressions (i.e., a regular expression *metacharacter*), we have to escape it with a backslash if we want a period to be treated as a real period, as we would want in trying to match an email address.

With these two facts in mind, then, you can see that the subexpression

```
([\.-]?\w+)*
```

which appears twice in the above regular expression means "zero or more instances of an expression that contains at least one alphanumeric character, and these one or more alphanumeric characters may or may not be preceded by a period or a hyphen".

To complete our analysis we note the following:

▶ The regular expression says that the email must have an @ character "somewhere in the middle".

▶ It also says the email address must "start with a word", that is, with one or more alphanumeric characters, which is then followed (prior to the @ character) by any number of the subexpressions discussed above.

▶ Following the @ character, we again have a "word" followed by any number of those same subexpressions. That is, we have the same sort of thing after the @ character that we had before the @ character.

▶ The email address ends with a period followed by a two- or three-character "word". Nowadays, of course, the final part of an email may contain more than three characters, which you could easily accommodate with a minor modification.

▶ You should spend a little time scanning through this regular expression and analyzing its individual parts. While this validation of email is much more refined than what we saw earlier, it is still far from the definitive regular expression for email address validation. The actual validation of an email address may indeed need to be even more involved. A useful exercise might be to look for one or more strings that are invalid email addresses, but that are still acceptable to our JavaScript validation.

▶ **FIGURE 6.24** shows the popup message that appears when all the data in a feedback form has been successfully validated.

6.12 The Modernizr Tool and HTML5 Form Controls

This chapter has concentrated on the use of JavaScript for computation and data validation. Both of these tasks represent traditional use cases for the language, and you may certainly continue to use JavaScript for both of these purposes.

However, HTML5 provides you with some new possibilities for data validation. There are a lot of new form controls available in HTML5 that do not need JavaScript to validate the data

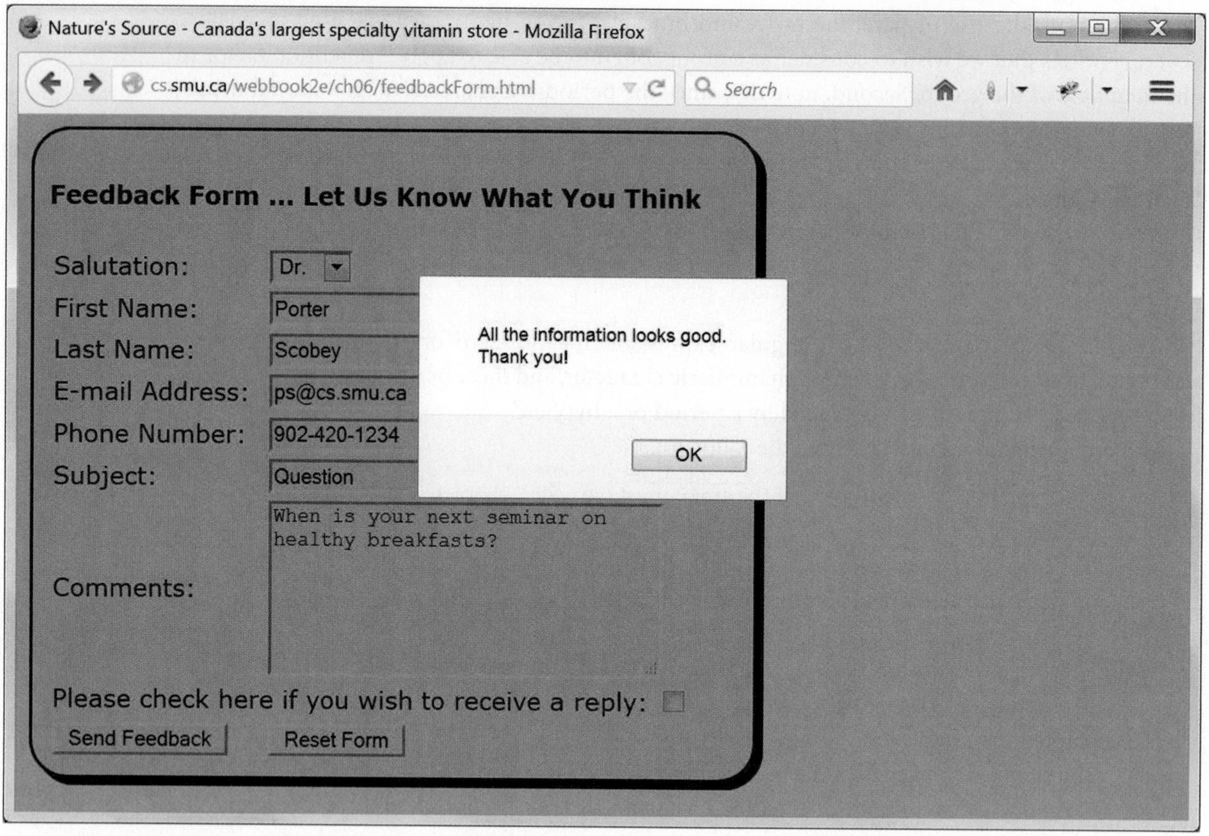

FIGURE 6.24 `graphics/ch06/displayFeedbackFormHtml.jpg`
The popup message shown when the feedback form has been successfully validated.

entered into them. Most of these are variations on the already existing `input` element, obtained by allowing new values for its `type` attribute. Some of these `input` elements allow the user to pick a data value directly, such as a color or a numerical value from a particular range, so there is no need for validation since only valid values can be chosen.

HTML5 has also introduced a new `pattern` attribute that can be used with the "old-fashioned" `input` element with `type="text"`, and also with `input` elements with newer type attribute values like `email`, `password`, `tel`, and `url`. So, for example, rather than write a Java-Script function to validate that a user has entered a valid -email address into an `input` element of attribute type `text`, you simply give that `input` element a `pattern` attribute whose value is the regular expression describing an email address. Then, if the user does not enter a valid email address, the `input` control will not accept it and the form cannot be submitted for processing.

The obvious question here is this: What form controls can I actually use? One way is to go to the excellent site `caniuse.com`, where you will find much more information on what you can use in which version of which browser that you probably want to know. Here we want to mention another

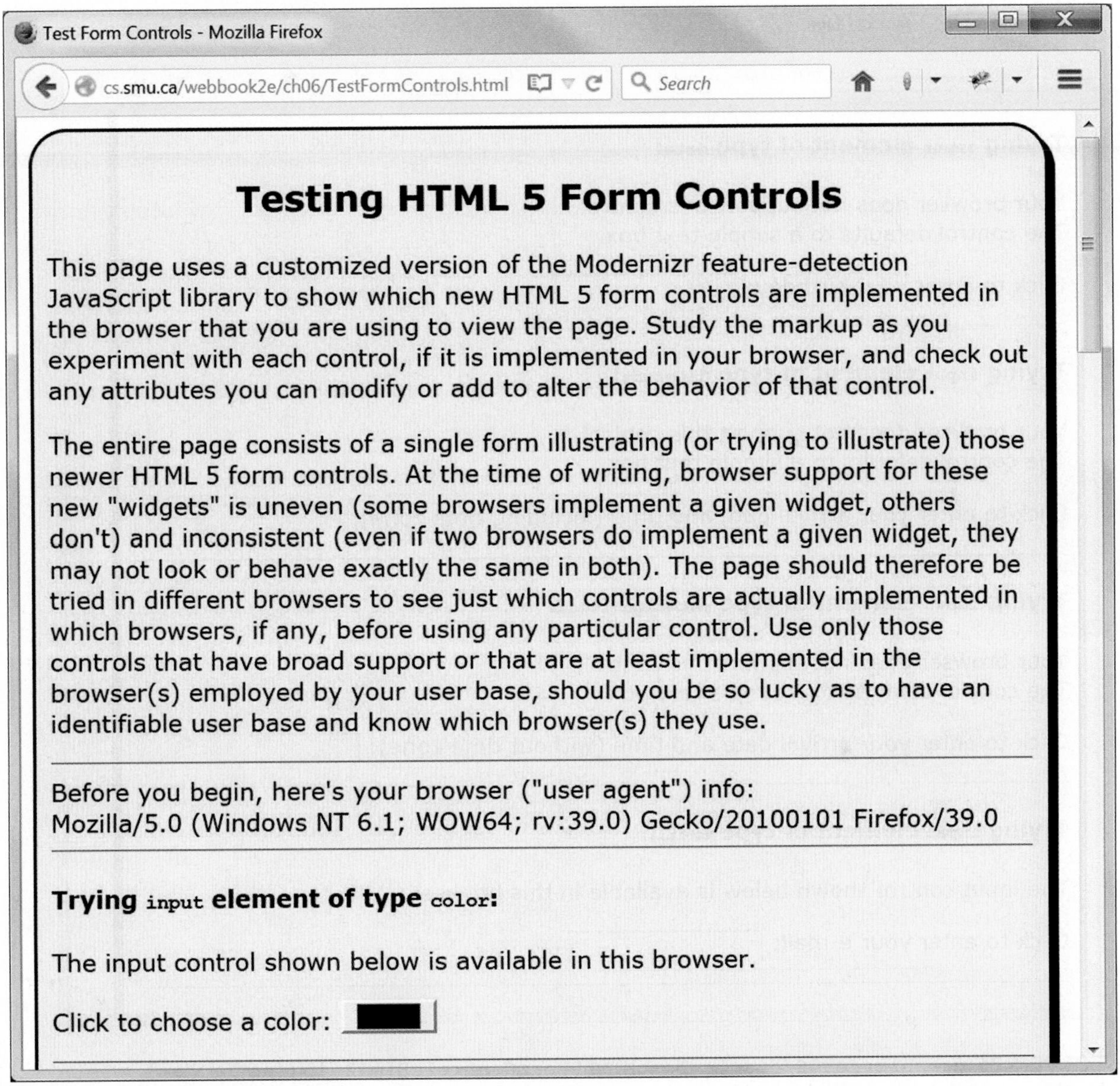
Test Form Controls - Mozilla Firefox
cs.smu.ca/webbook2e/ch06/TestFormControls.html
Search
Testing HTML 5 Form Controls
This page uses a customized version of the Modernizr feature-detection JavaScript library to show which new HTML 5 form controls are implemented in the browser that you are using to view the page. Study the markup as you experiment with each control, if it is implemented in your browser, and check out any attributes you can modify or add to alter the behavior of that control.
The entire page consists of a single form illustrating (or trying to illustrate) those newer HTML 5 form controls. At the time of writing, browser support for these new "widgets" is uneven (some browsers implement a given widget, others don't) and inconsistent (even if two browsers do implement a given widget, they may not look or behave exactly the same in both). The page should therefore be tried in different browsers to see just which controls are actually implemented in which browsers, if any, before using any particular control. Use only those controls that have broad support or that are at least implemented in the browser(s) employed by your user base, should you be so lucky as to have an identifiable user base and know which browser(s) they use.
Before you begin, here's your browser ("user agent") info:
Mozilla/5.0 (Windows NT 6.1; WOW64; rv:39.0) Gecko/20100101 Firefox/39.0
Trying input element of type color:
The input control shown below is available in this browser.
Click to choose a color:

FIGURE 6.25 **`graphics/ch06/displayTestHTML5FormControlsHtml1.jpg` (partial view)**
The top part of the display of the Modernizr example that tests the availability of HTML5 form controls.

excellent site, `modernizr.com`, which allows you to build and download a customized JavaScript library file that will let you detect whether various HTML5 and CSS3 features are available in your current browser. We have created such a JavaScript file, and a corresponding HTML document to make use of it. Two partial displays of that document are shown in **FIGURES 6.25** and **6.26**.

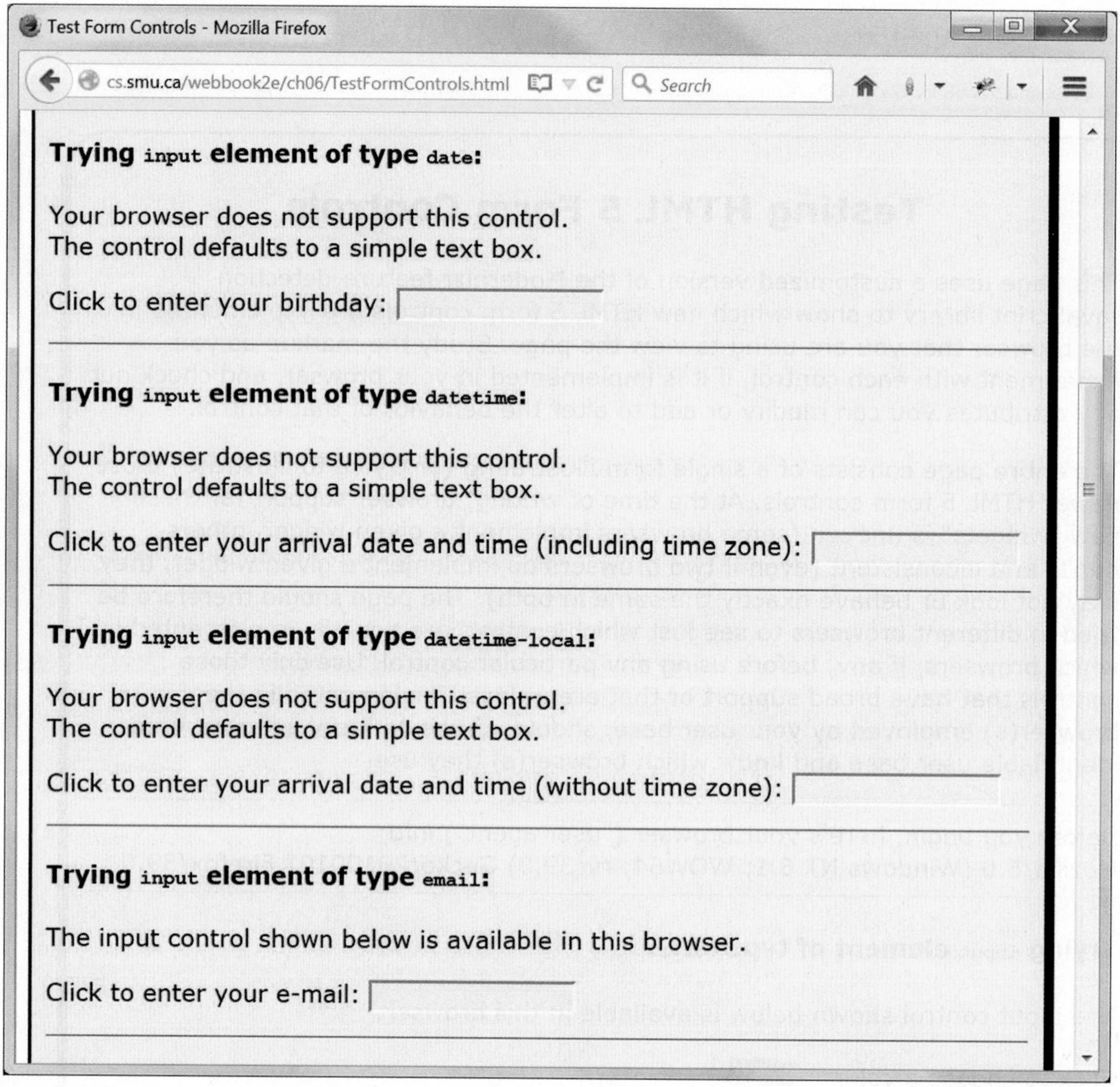

FIGURE 6.26 `graphics/ch06/displayTestHTML5FormControlsHtml2.jpg` **(partial view)**
Another section of the display of the Modernizr example that tests the availability of HTML5 form controls.

In Figure 6.25 you see an explanation of what happens when you load the document. The full details of the browser used are also shown, along with a typical test section that indicates that the `input` element with `type="color"` is available in the browser being used. You need to load this file into your own browser to try this "color picker", if it's available. The next part of the display shown in Figure 6.25 is shown in Figure 6.26, and you can see that some controls are available and are some not.

```
1    <!DOCTYPE html>
2    <!-- TestHTML5FormControls.html -->
3    <html lang="en">
4    <head>
5      <meta charset="utf-8">
6      <link rel="stylesheet" href="css/default.css">
7      <script src="scripts/modernizr_inputtypes.js"></script>
8      <script>
9          function OutputTestResult(inputType)
10         {
11           if (Modernizr.inputtypes[inputType])
12               document.write("The input control shown below is available " +
13                   "in this browser.");
14           else
15               document.write("Your browser does not support this control."
16                   + "<br>The control defaults to a simple text box.");
17         }
18     </script>
19     <title>Test HTML 5 Form Controls</title>
20   </head>
```

FIGURE 6.27 `ch06/TestHTML5FormControls.html` **(excerpt)**
The head element of `ch06/TestHTML5FormControls.html` showing two `script` elements, one that links
to the Modernizr script we have created for form control testing, and one containing a utility function we have
written to interact with the Modernizr script.

```
45         <script>
46             document.write("Before you begin, here's your browser "
47                 + "(\"user agent\") info:" + "<br>" + navigator.userAgent);
48         </script>
49         <hr>
50         <h4>Trying <code>input</code> element of type <code>color</code>:</h4>
51         <script>OutputTestResult("color");</script>
52         <p>Click to choose a color: <input type="color" name="myColor"></p>
53
54         <hr>
55         <h4>Trying <code>input</code> element of type <code>date</code>:</h4>
56         <script>OutputTestResult("date");</script>
57         <p>Click to enter your birthday: <input type="date" name="myBirthday">
```

FIGURE 6.28 `ch06/TestHTML5FormControls.html` **(excerpt)**
Part of the body element of `ch06/TestHTML5FormControls.html` showing a `script` element that
identifies the user's browser, followed by two examples of the use of the script for determining if that browser
supports particular form controls.

FIGURES 6.27 and **6.28** show two excerpts from `TestHTML5FormControls.html`. In
Figure 6.27 you see two things of interest. The first is the `script` element that links to the file
that we built and downloaded at the Modernizr site: `modernizr_inputtypes.js`. This is a

textfile of JavaScript code, but since it has been "minimized" (all unnecessary whitespace has been removed) to increase download speed, it is virtually unreadable.

The second thing of interest in Figure 6.27 is the function `OutputTestResult()` defined in the second `script` element. Each time this function is called, it is passed a value of the `type` attribute of an `input` element. The function then uses the `inputtypes[]` array property of the `Modernizr` object to check whether the current browser supports that particular `input` element and outputs an appropriate message.

In Figure 6.28 you first see a script that uses the browser's `navigator` object and its `user-Agent` property to get the details of the current browser, which is then displayed. Then we created two typical sections in each of which there is some HTML markup and a short `script` showing how we use the `OutputTestResult()` function. Note that if the `input` element of the type being tested is not supported, we simply get an ordinary text box by default in the display.

Summary

JavaScript is the premier programming language used for client-side programming on the web at the present time. It is sufficiently powerful, flexible, and easy to learn that its popularity is justified. On the other hand, because it is not as strict with data typing and other features as some other programming languages, it can be harder to debug programs in the language. Be sure to investigate whatever may be available for your browser of choice to help you with Java-Script debugging.

JavaScript code may be placed directly into an HTML document, in either the `body` element or the `head` element, or it may be placed in a separate file that is associated with the HTML document via the `src` attribute of a `script` tag. Where a particular piece of JavaScript code is placed depends on a number of things, such as whether the code is a function definition, when you want the code to be executed, and whether you are just testing or are in full "production mode". The best practice to follow is this: Like CSS, JavaScript code should generally be kept in a separate file that can be accessed from the HTML document where it is to be used via the `src` attribute of the opening `script` tag of an empty `script` element placed in the `head` of that document. That is, web page behavior should be separated from structure and presentation. However, if you really need some JavaScript code to be executed immediately (as the document is loading), you may find it convenient to insert that code as the content of a `script` element within the `body` element of your HTML document. In this case, make sure that the script is not positioned within the markup in such a way that it attempts to access a part of the page that has not yet loaded.

JavaScript is an interpreted language that is restricted, for security reasons, in the actions it may perform on a user's computer. Its major uses on a client machine include computation, form data validation, and facilitating dynamic web page behavior via access to the DOM a language-independent API that allows JavaScript to perform many actions during and after the time when a web page is loaded.

The JavaScript `alert()` function is a convenient way to inform web page users of input errors when filling out forms.

DOM objects are treated as JavaScript objects, and the methods and fields of these objects can be accessed using the `object.methodName()` or `object.fieldName` syntax of a typical object-oriented environment. The preferred JavaScript way of getting access to the DOM object itself on a web page is to use the `getElementById()` method with an argument that is the value of the `id` attribute for that element (considered as a DOM object). However, the value of the `name` attribute of an element may also be used for access to that element, and this can sometimes be more convenient.

JavaScript data types include numbers (integer and real, with the usual arithmetic operators), strings (which may be concatenated with the + operator), booleans and zero-based arrays, and built-in objects such as the `Math` object. A useful function for determining whether a value is a number is `isNaN()`. Decisions can be made using `if`-statements or `if-else`-statements. All of these can be used to perform client-side calculations as needed.

JavaScript can also be used to verify that data entered into web page forms conforms to the expected input requirements for that form before the data is sent to a server. This is an important security feature that all web designers should take pains to implement. Regular expressions make this goal much easier to accomplish than other methods, so it is worthwhile for any web developer to have at least some knowledge of them.

Much of the work of validating input that has been done with JavaScript in this chapter can be assisted by, or replaced by, some of the latest HTML5 form functionality. The problem is that until all of the most-used browsers have caught up with the standard, the implementation of this functionality will remain incomplete and inconsistent, and hence you must be careful to investigate and test thoroughly before using any new form control. One tool that is useful for doing this is Maximizr.

 # Quick Questions to Test Your Basic Knowledge

1. What happened during those "famous 10 days in May" of 1995?
2. During the development of JavaScript there was a period when not much was happening, but then: Who did what that jump-started a renewal of interest in the language and when did this occur?
3. What are the two major categories of "translation" of high-level programming code to something that an actual machine can run, and into which of these categories does JavaScript fall?
4. Can you think of at least one thing that a JavaScript program running in a web browser would *not* be allowed to do on the client machine?
5. If you want to embed some JavaScript code in your HTML web page, what is the name of the element you use?
6. If you want to place your JavaScript code in an external file, how do you do that?

7. What JavaScript method is used to create a popup window for displaying messages?
8. Even though you are not required to do so, how should you terminate each statement in a JavaScript script if you wish to follow "good programming practice"?
9. How would you describe the difference in the usage of \n and <br> in the context of the current chapter?
10. What is the DOM?
11. What is the recommended way, in a JavaScript script, to get access to a DOM object on a web page?
12. What attribute do you use for an alternate way to get access to a DOM object on a web page?
13. What is the difference between an if-statement and an if-else-statement?
14. If a JavaScript array contains seven elements, what is the range of index (subscript) values you would use to access all the elements of that array?
15. What distinction is sometimes made between the use of the terms *method* and *function*?
16. What is the value of each of the following?
    a) `Math.floor(7.28)`   b) `Math.floor(10.99)`   c) `Math.floor(-3.2)`
17. What is the value of each of the following?
    a) `Math.round(2.34)`   b) `Math.round(5.65)`
    c) `Math.round(8.5)`   d) `Math.round(-3.99)`?
18. What is the value of each of the following?
    a) `Math.ceil(7.28)`   b) `Math.ceil(10.99)`   c) `Math.ceil(-3.2)`?
19. What does it mean to "validate" an item of data entered into one of our forms?
20. Why should we validate the data that a user enters into one of our forms?
21. Why is there no validator that we can use to validate form data entry in the same way that we validate our HTML and CSS?
22. What regular expression would you use if you wanted to validate a license plate number for a jurisdiction in which a valid license plate consists of three capital letters followed by a space and then three digits?
23. What regular expression would you use if you wanted to match a string containing a real number with up to three digits before the decimal point and up to five after it, if in addition the real number may or may not be preceded by a plus or minus sign?
24. What regular expression would you use if you wanted to match either a six-digit or a three-digit hexadecimal color value?
25. What is a verbal description of the kind of string that matches each of the following regular expressions?
    a) `^[A-Z]\w{1,9}$`   b) `^[21]9\d{2}$`   c) `^[^aeiouAEIOU]$`

Short Exercises to Improve Your Basic Understanding

1. An activity that none of us can avoid when we start writing code in any programming language, and JavaScript is no exception, is *debugging*. Hard as we try to avoid them, our code will inevitably contain bugs. If you have prior experience with a programming language like Java or C++, you will have seen some nice (or perhaps not so nice) "compile-time" error messages that are very conveniently provided by the language compiler before you even get to run your program. Since JavaScript is not a compiled language, you are deprived of this "early warning system", and you are generally not aware of any difficulties with your code until you try loading a web page that uses it. When a web page simply refuses to behave as you think it should, you need to be able to take a closer look at things.

   Modern browsers generally contain some built-in capability to help you with JavaScript errors. For example, Firefox has what it calls a "Web Console" and Chrome has the more aptly named "JavaScript Console". Either one is opened up with the key sequence CTRL+Shift+J, and JavaScript problems that occur when you load a web page will show up in that window. Other browsers should have similar functionality.

   So, for this exercise, first take your copy of ch06/bmiForm.html and change the name of the function bmiFormProcess() shown in line 17 of Figure 6.12 so that the function will not be found when required. Now if you try to perform a BMI calculation, things just won't work. Frustrating, right? But now if you open one of the above-mentioned console windows in your browser, clear out any errors that are currently showing, and reload the BMI page to attempt another calculation, an appropriate error message should show up in the console window. This is enough to get you started, but now you should experiment by creating and then "solving" some other problems, with the help of the messages you get in your console window. This kind of experience is invaluable when you are actually involved in the development process. See the **References** for links to some other useful tools.

2. Rewrite the three if-else-statements in the program of Figure 6.14 as six if-statements. Give at least one argument for, and one argument against, this change.

3. Look up the search() method of the JavaScript String object under the JavaScript reference section of the w3schools.com site and determine why it is that we said, earlier in the chapter, that we expected the method to return a value of 0 if it found a match for the regular expression in its argument. When would it return a value other than 0 after a successful search, and what does a nonzero value represent?

4. In Figure 6.17 you see that a user has entered an invalid weight value and your JavaScript script has responded by displaying a popup window with an appropriate message for the user. This is only one of several ways in which the user can go astray when trying to use this form. Your testing regime before "going live" on the Internet should always include as many tests as you can think of to make sure your form is going to behave gracefully in the face of bad data entry by users. In this particular case, you should study the JavaScript code in `bmiFormValidate.js` shown in Figure 6.22 to confirm that you need to test this form to make sure the right message is displayed in each of the following cases:
   - The user enters something other than a number for height.
   - The user enters something other than a number for weight.
   - The user enters a height value that is outside the allowable range. What *is* the allowable range? Is this reasonable?
   - The user enters a weight value that is outside the allowable range. What *is* the allowable range? Is this reasonable?
   - The user asks for an email reply and supplies a valid email address. (The email reply feature is not implemented here.)
   - The user asks for an email reply and supplies an invalid email address.

5. In Figure 6.21 you see an error-message window that is popped up when a user enters an invalid value for the email address in your feedback form, and there would be a similar popup message in the event of an invalid phone number entry. Study the JavaScript code in `feedbackFormValidate.js` shown in Figure 6.22 to confirm that you need, for your own testing of this form, to make sure the right message is displayed in each of the following cases:
   - The user enters an invalid first name.
   - The user enters an invalid last name.
   - The user enters an invalid phone number.
   - The user enters an invalid email address.
   - Be particularly diligent in testing for invalid phone numbers and email addresses.

6. Revise the testing code for our feedback form so that it also tests to make sure that the user has chosen a salutation from the dropdown list, and has not left the salutation box empty.

Exercises on the Parallel Project

Two main goals of this chapter were to show how JavaScript can be used on the client side to perform arithmetic calculations based on data entered into our forms, and to perform validation of that data before performing such calculations. We also introduced regular expressions to help us validate string data.

In this section of the last chapter you developed two forms, one for letting a user choose products or services that your company offers, and one for getting feedback on customer satisfaction. Now you need to make those forms as secure as you can by checking as much of the input as you can to make sure it is nothing other than what you expect it to be. Also, in the case of the "order form", you will need to perform some calculations and display the results to the user. So, complete the following exercises:

1. Write a JavaScript script that validates all user entries for which it makes sense to do so in the form that permits your customers to choose products and/or services. Be sure to inform the user if any data entry is invalid with an appropriate popup message. Once all input has been validated, display to your customer some relevant output related to the data that has been entered. A typical display should include a summary of the items ordered, the quantity of each item, the cost of each item, and the total cost.

2. Write a JavaScript script that validates all user entries for which it makes sense to do so in the form that permits your customers to give you feedback on their experience with your business. Report to the user if a particular entry is invalid, and be sure to tell the user that everything is OK if that is the case.

Some of your data validation and computation can be modeled on what you see in the text examples, but of course some of this will also be peculiar to your particular business.

What Else You May Want or Need to Know

1. When you view JavaScript code that is embedded in an HTML document, especially code that you find out there on the Internet, you may see that code enclosed in a comment block. We could have done this with our embedded code shown in Figure 6.3, and if we had, it would have looked like this:

```
<!--
document.write("Watch this space for our e-store.<br>");
document.write("Coming soon ...");
// -->
```

This arrangement is designed to prevent browsers that cannot, or do not wish to, deal with JavaScript (for whatever reason) from simply displaying the JavaScript code in the browser window. However, since virtually all current browsers support JavaScript, and users do not generally disable JavaScript, this preventive measure is not nearly as necessary as it used to be, and you will be seeing it less and less frequently as time goes on. For simplicity and to conserve space, we opt not to make use of this somewhat outmoded convention.

The idea here is simply that both parties involved (namely, the browser and the Java-Script interpreter) know what they need to know to do the right thing. An older browser, or one ignoring JavaScript, will ignore the tag pair that denotes a `script` element, and the body of this element will be ignored as well, since it is just an HTML comment.

A browser that wants to have the JavaScript code processed will, of course, pass the content of the `script` element to the JavaScript interpreter. JavaScript interpreters have been tweaked to recognize (actually, ignore) the first line, namely

```
<!--
```

and begin processing with the second line of the content (the first line of code). The character sequence used to indicate the end of the JavaScript must be on a new line and must be preceded by two slashes, which are actually the start of a single-line JavaScript comment. This is simply to prevent the JavaScript interpreter from trying to process the closing HTML comment delimiter (`-->`) as JavaScript code.

When code is in an external file, you do not need to enclose the script in an HTML comment in this way, since if JavaScript is not being processed, the `script` tag pair will be ignored, and in this case no JavaScript code actually appears anywhere within the HTML markup.

2. Although we did not discuss JavaScript debugging in detail in this chapter, in the first of our **Short Exercises** we gave some pointers to get you started with this important activity. In addition to the "console windows" we mentioned there that report JavaScript errors, there are other tools you may want to, and probably should, investigate. For example, the Firefox browser also has an add-on called **Firebug** that is also available for other browsers. It is a powerful tool that allows the debugging, editing, and monitoring of any website's CSS, HTML, DOM, and JavaScript, and provides other web development tools as well. This tool, along with the **Web Developer** toolbar for Firefox discussed in an earlier chapter, give you considerable power for analyzing the structure and behavior of your web pages. Though JavaScript is not compiled, tools like **JSLint** or **JSHint** can analyze your code before you run it and report any problems they think you have. See the **References** for the relevant links to these tools.

3. Although you can use JavaScript to check a user's input into your forms, you should not be overly confident that this will prevent a site visitor with evil intent from bypassing your validation code in some malicious way, which a clever hacker may be able to do. The web can be a dangerous place, and when you are browsing it, one of the things you should be aware of is the difference between the `http` and `https` protocols. The first is, of course, the one we have been using all along. The second is a secure version of the HTTP protocol, and the one that should be used by any site that asks you for critical personal information, such as your bank account number and password. There is usually some visual sign that you are visiting a secure site. The `https` and/or a lock icon may appear in the address bar of your browser, for example. However, it is also important that you know you are visiting the site you think you are visiting, since it would defeat the purpose of such security to be visiting a secure but rogue site. One way of avoiding the kind of trap that many web users fall into is to enter the full web address of your intended destination yourself,

rather than click on a link that purports to take you to that site. The implementation of a secure website via `https` and encryption is, however, beyond the scope of this text.

4. In addition to the `alert()` function, JavaScript also has the `confirm()` function and the `prompt()` function, each of which gives you another kind of popup window that may be useful from time to time.

5. We introduced the boolean values `true` and `false` in JavaScript and saw how they could be used to test conditions that would tell you what, if anything, to do next. Unfortunately, things are a little more complicated because values other than these two can often show up in similar situations and be interpreted as either true or false, depending on what the value is. See the **References** for a useful link.

6. In addition to the DOM, there is also (believe it or not) a BOM (Browser Object Model), which provides an API for access to the browser objects. Although it has not been standardized like the DOM, most browsers treat it in a similar manner, and use it to "talk to" the browser via JavaScript. BOM objects include things like the browser window and the browser history. Once again, see the **References** for a link.

7. At this point it might be useful to do two things. First, we should remind you that in this text we concentrate on the basics. As with most basics, if you master them they will serve you well for a very long time. Second, we should point out, of course, that there are many very powerful and useful JavaScript libraries "out there" that you may wish to explore and use if and when you come to develop an actual e-commerce or other similar website. If we were to discuss any of them in detail, that would take us too far afield from our main goal, and we would have to make choices that might become obsolete sooner than we would like. Even one or more or all of HTML, CSS, and JavaScript may eventually go the way of the dodo, but that seems much less likely, at the moment at least. So, we just make the point here again, but also give you at the end of the **References** a few links that you should follow, just to get a feel for what is possible and what you may eventually want to employ in your websites.

 # References

1. You may have been surprised to learn that the organization that counts JavaScript as home is the European Computer Manufacturers Association (ECMA), which at least explains why the formal name for JavaScript is ECMAScript. Or, to be a little more precise, JavaScript is one implementation of the ECMAScript language standard. Here are two links, one to the organization and a second to the latest (at the time of this writing) version of that standard (version 6):

```
http://www.ecma-international.org/

http://www.ecma-international.org/ecma-263/6.0/
```

2. The W3Schools site has both a JavaScript tutorial and a reference on both JavaScript and the DOM and its objects:

   `http://www.w3schools.com/js/default.asp`

   `http://www.w3schools.com/jsref/default.asp`

3. Here are links to two other JavaScript tutorials you may find useful:

   `http://www.tizag.com/javascriptT/`

   `http://www.quackit.com/javascript/tutorial/`

4. Here is a JavaScript language reference that you may find useful:

   `http://javascript-reference.info/`

5. Here is a link to a JavaScript Quick Reference Card that you might want to print and keep handy:

   `http://www.cheat-sheets.org/saved-copy/jsquick.pdf`

6. Here are the links to the Firebug and Web Developer Firefox add-ons, both of which are very helpful for examining a web page in detail and determining what may be wrong with your HTML, your CSS, and/or your JavaScript code:

   `http://getfirebug.com/`

   `https://addons.mozilla.org/en-US/firefox/addon/web-developer/`

7. Here is a link to the W3Schools page that discusses, and provides examples illustrating, those values other than `true` and `false` themselves that may be interpreted as either `true` or `false`:

   `http://www.w3schools.com/js/js_booleans.asp`

8. Here is a link to the W3Schools page that discusses the `Math` object, its constants and functions:

   `http://www.w3schools.com/js/js_math.asp`

9. You will find it extremely edifying to read, study, and experiment with the examples in the section of the W3Schools site entitled "JavaScript HTML DOM". Here is the link to the starting page:

   `http://www.w3schools.com/js/js_htmldom.asp`

10. For some BOM experience, start at the following W3Schools page:

    `http://www.w3schools.com/js/js_window.asp`

11. Here is a partial list of the many exciting websites describing (generally freely available for download) libraries, "front ends", "frameworks", "content management systems", and other web development tools to explore for inspiration:

    `https://jquery.com/` (W3Schools has a tutorial)

    `http://getbootstrap.com/` (W3Schools has a tutorial)

    `https://angularjs.org/http://d3js.org/` (W3Schools has a tutorial)

    `http://foundation.zurb.com/`

    `https://dojotoolkit.org/`

    `http://mootools.net/`

    `http://prototypejs.org/`

    `http://yuilibrary.com/` (no longer being maintained, but still useful)

    `http://d3js.org/`

    `http://backbonejs.org/`

    `http://emberjs.com/`

    `http://d3js.org/`

    `https://wordpress.com/`

    `http://www.joomla.org/`

    `https://www.drupal.org/`

12. Here are the links to JSLint and JSHint:

    `http://jslint.com`

    `http://jshint.com`

CHAPTER SEVEN

JavaScript for Client-Side Content Behavior

CHAPTER CONTENTS

Overview and Objectives

We began our exploration of JavaScript in the previous chapter with a primary focus on client-side computation and data validation. If calculations can be done with JavaScript on the client side (in the browser), and the results presented immediately to the user, this avoids having to send the data to a server and then bring the results back for display. Also, data validation with JavaScript on the client side is one way to help prevent potentially malicious data from being sent to a web server.

In this chapter, we will look at another aspect of JavaScript usage. JavaScript can also help you improve the functionality as well as the appearance of your web pages. In particular, we will enhance our home page by dynamically adjusting its content with a rotating sequence of business-related images, and also with dropdown menu options. In fact, the dropdown menu feature will persist as we navigate to other pages on our website.

In this chapter we will discuss the following:

▶ How to create a rotating sequence of images (often called a "slide show"), along with the associated JavaScript

▶ How to use an `onload` event attribute for the `body` element, whose value will be a JavaScript function that activates our slide show when our home page loads

▶ How to create a JavaScript array of images for our rotating display

▶ How to use the JavaScript `switch`-statement for decision making when we decide what sequence of images to display, based on the day of the week

▶ How to use the JavaScript `for`-loop for repetition when we actually rotate our images

▶ How to create a dynamic dropdown menu, along with the associated CSS and JavaScript

▶ How to use the `onmouseover` and `onmouseout` event attributes, whose values will be JavaScript functions that cause a dropdown menu to appear or disappear

▶ How to use the new HTML5 `pattern` attribute to perform validation of form input data without resorting to JavaScript, and the `required`, attribute to ensure that input that is actually required is not omitted

▶ How to use the `onchange` attribute to provide immediate user notification when a checkbox is clicked

▶ How to provide a Body Mass Index (BMI) report to the user via a new web page that is "persistent", rather than a popup window that has to be "dismissed" before returning to the browser

Recall that in neither of the previous two chapters did we have a complete version of our **Nature's Source** website. However, in this chapter we will again have two versions of this sample site. The first version, found in the `nature1` subdirectory, contains only enough files to display a revised home page and demonstrate both of the new features discussed in this chapter: the "slide show" of rotating images and the dropdown menus. In this version, none of the links on the home page are active.

In the second version, found in the `nature2` subdirectory, the home page is the same as in the first version, except that now *all* links on the home page are active. Most of these just take you to pages with minimal content that you have seen in previous versions of the site. However, we also have two important links that provide the features we discussed in the previous two chapters: one that takes a user to the BMI calculator and a second that goes to our feedback form. In fact, because our menu bar with its dropdown menu options appears on *all* pages in `nature2`, all links are available on all pages.

Recall as well that with `nature3` of Chapter 3, and `nature2`, `nature3`, and `nature4` of Chapter 4, SSI was used for access to the "common" markup for each page of the given website. This will also be true for both `nature1` and `nature2` in this chapter. So, to view either site properly you must either go to the book's website, or set up your own SSI-aware server to serve your own copy of the website. The latter choice is preferable, of course, since that will allow you to experiment and do the exercises more easily.

7.1 Enhancing Our Website with a Home Page "Slide Show" of Rotating Images and Dropdown Menu Options on Every Page

Let's begin with a look at **FIGURE 7.1**, which shows a display of the home page for our sample **Nature's Source** website in this chapter (either the `nature1` version or the `nature2` version).

When compared with the last similar version of our home page (as seen in Figure 4.29, for example), the only visible difference you see (aside from a different image) is the list of dropdown menu[1] options under the **Products+Services** menu item. However, there are actually two major enhancements in this version: in addition to the dropdown menus (also under **Your Health**, **About Us**, and **Contact Us**), the image now shown in the figure is just one of a sequence of six images that continually rotate as long as the page is displayed. In fact, there are two different groups of six images, one that displays during "weekdays" (Monday to Thursday) and shows indoor scenes, and the other that displays during "weekend days" (Friday to Sunday) and shows outdoor scenes. This chapter discusses the new JavaScript and CSS features that enable these enhancements.

---

[1] The dropdown menu we discuss here is based on ideas from the website `http://javascript-array.com/`.

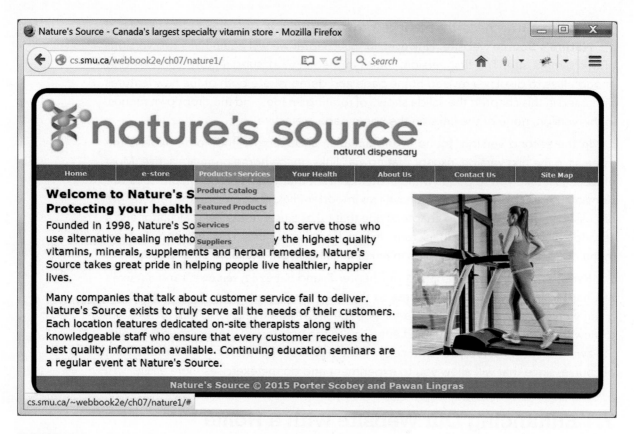

FIGURE 7.1 `graphics/ch07/nature1/displayIndexHtml.jpg`
A Firefox browser display of `ch07/nature1/index.html` (or `ch07/nature2/index.html`), both of which illustrate rotating images and dropdown menus. Photo: © coloroftime/iStockphoto

    The HyperText Markup Language (HTML) file producing the display in **FIGURE 7.1** is `ch07/nature1/index.html`, shown in **FIGURE 7.2**. The only difference between this file and `ch07/nature2/index.html` is the comment in line 2. Note, first of all, the following features of the markup in this file and the files it includes, some of which we will need to discuss at length as we proceed:

1. As another version of our `index.html` document, it continues to make use of four external HTML files included via SSI (lines 1, 5, and 6 and 31 of Figure 7.2).

2. The included file `document_head.html` (shown in **FIGURE 7.3**) now contains two new `script` elements (lines 11 and 12) for access to the `rotate.js` and `menus.js` scripts to handle the image rotation and the dropdown menus. The script in `rotate.js` (**FIGURE 7.5**) will handle the rotating images, and the script in `menus.js` (**FIGURE 7.7**) will handle the dropdown menus. Note that we retain links to both of our CSS files, `desktop.css` and `tablet.css`, so both versions of the website in this chapter can still be viewed in either "desktop view" or "tablet view".

```
1   <!--#include virtual="common/document_head.html"-->
2   <!-- index.html for ch07/nature1 -->
3   <body onload="startRotation()">
4     <header>
5       <!--#include virtual="common/logo.html"-->
6       <!--#include virtual="common/menus.html"-->
7     </header>
8     <main>
9       <article id="textLeft">
10        <h3>Welcome to Nature's Source:<br>
11                    Protecting your health naturally!</h3>
12        <p>Founded in 1998, Nature's Source was created to serve those who
13        use alternative healing methods. Offering only the highest quality
14        vitamins, minerals, supplements and herbal remedies, Nature's
15        Source takes great pride in helping people live healthier, happier
16        lives.</p>
17        <p>Many companies that talk about customer service fail to deliver.
18        Nature's Source exists to truly serve all the needs of their
19        customers. Each location features dedicated on-site therapists
20        along with knowledgeable staff who ensure that every customer
21        receives the best quality information available. Continuing
22        education seminars are a regular event at Nature's Source.</p>
23      </article>
24      <div id="image">
25        <img id="placeholder" src=""
26            alt="Healthy Lifestyle"
27            width="256" height="256">
28      </div>
29    </main>
30    <footer>
31      <!--#include virtual="common/footer_content.html"-->
32    </footer>
33  </body>
34 </html>
```

FIGURE 7.2 `ch07/nature1/index.html`
The index file showing the HTML markup for the home page of our Nature's Source website with rotating images and dropdown menus.

3. The included file `menus.html` (shown in **FIGURE 7.4**) has been revised to accommodate the new dropdown menu feature that we discuss in detail later in this chapter, along with the new menu-related CSS shown in **FIGURE 7.6**.
4. We have introduced the `onload` event attribute (line 3 of Figure 7.2) to start our image rotation once the body of our home page has fully loaded.
5. We have revised the `img` element on our index page (lines 25–27 of Figure 7.2) to handle the sequence of rotating images, rather than a single static image.

```
1   <!DOCTYPE html>
2   <!-- document_head.html -->
3   <html lang="en">
4     <head>
5       <meta charset="utf-8">
6       <meta name="viewport" content="width=device-width">
7       <base href="http://cs.smu.ca/webbook2e/ch07/nature1/">
8       <link rel="stylesheet" href="css/desktop.css">
9       <link rel="stylesheet" href="css/tablet.css"
10          media="screen and (max-width: 900px)">
11      <script src="scripts/rotate.js"></script>
12      <script src="scripts/menus.js"></script>
13      <title>Nature's Source - Canada's largest specialty vitamin store</title>
14    </head>
```

FIGURE 7.3 `ch07/nature1/common/document_head.html`
The common document head file for all pages on the Nature's Source website. The `nature1` website has only one page, but an identical file is used for the complete `nature2` website as well.

7.2 Implementing Our "Slide Show" of Rotating Images

The replacement of a static image on our home page with a "slide show" that consists of a continuous, cyclic display of a sequence of various images related to our business might be regarded in some quarters as somewhat frivolous. On the other hand, it might also help to grab and keep a visitor's attention. It is worth keeping in mind that choosing how much activity to have on your home page (or any page) is both a key design decision and a bit of a balancing act. You can either attract and keep visitors or cause them to quickly abandon your site, depending on how much and what kind of dynamic activity they encounter when they first come to visit.

The general idea of our "slide show" is this. When the script in `rotate.js` of Figure 7.5 is run after the `index.html` page is loaded, the first thing that happens is a determination of the current date. An appropriate collection of images is then assembled, depending on whether it's a weekday or a weekend. Then those images are displayed one after the other, with repetition when the end of the sequence is reached, until the user closes the page or clicks on a link to another page.

For this purpose, we have assembled, in the subdirectory `images` of the `nature1` directory (as well as the `nature2` subdirectory), two sets of images, one set showing indoor exercises and the other showing outdoor exercises. The images of outdoor exercises are named `outdoor1.jpg` to `outdoor6.jpg`. These outdoor images will be displayed on a weekend (Friday to Sunday). On the other hand, the images of indoor exercises will be displayed on weekdays. These image files are named `indoor1.jpg` to `indoor6.jpg`.

```
1    <!-- menus.html -->
2       <nav onmouseout="hide()">
3         <ul class="Links">
4           <li><a href="#" onmouseover="show('m1')">Home</a></li>
5           <li><a href="#" onmouseover="show('m2')">e-store</a></li>
6           <li>
7             <a href="#" onmouseover="show('m3')">Products+Services</a>
8             <div id="m3" onmouseover="show('m3')">
9               <a href="#">Product Catalog</a>
10              <a href="#">Featured Products</a>
11              <a href="#">Services</a>
12              <a href="#">Suppliers</a>
13            </div>
14          </li>
15          <li>
16            <a href="#" onmouseover="show('m4')">Your Health</a>
17            <div id="m4" onmouseover="show('m4')">
18              <a href="#">Compute Your BMI</a>
19              <a href="#">Tools+Resources</a>
20              <a href="#">Ask An Expert</a>
21              <a href="#">Useful Links</a>
22            </div>
23          </li>
24          <li>
25            <a href="#" onmouseover="show('m5')">About Us</a>
26            <div id="m5" onmouseover="show('m5')">
27              <a href="#">Nature's Source</a>
28              <a href="#">Vision+Mission</a>
29              <a href="#">Job Opportunities</a>
30              <a href="#">News Archive</a>
31            </div>
32          </li>
33          <li>
34            <a href="#" onmouseover="show('m6')">Contact Us</a>
35            <div id="m6" onmouseover="show('m6')">
36              <a href="#">Locations</a>
37              <a href="#">Feedback Form</a>
38            </div>
39          </li>
40          <li><a href="#" onmouseover="show('m7')">Site Map</a></li>
41        </ul>
42      </nav>
```

FIGURE 7.4 `ch07/nature1/common/menus.html`
The included HTML file containing the markup for our menu and its dropdown menu items.

```
1   //rotate.js
2   //Handles the image rotation seen on the website's home page
3
4   //Put all of today's information into a JavaScript Date object
5   var today = new Date();
6
7   //Build the appropriate prefix for filenames, depending on whether
8   //today is a weekday (indoor images) or the weekend (outdoor images)
9   var prefix = "images/";
10  switch (today.getDay())
11  {
12      case 0:
13      case 5:
14      case 6:
15          prefix += "outdoor";
16          break;
17      default:
18          prefix += "indoor";
19  }
20
21  //Use that prefix to put the proper sequence of image filenames into an array
22  var imageArray = new Array(6);
23  for (i=0; i<imageArray.length; i++)
24      imageArray[i] = prefix + (i+1) + ".jpg";
25
26  //Perform a "cicular rotation" of the images in the array
27  var imageCounter = 0;
28  function rotate()
29  {
30      var imageObject = document.getElementById('placeholder');
31      imageObject.src = imageArray[imageCounter];
32      ++imageCounter;
33      if (imageCounter == 6) imageCounter = 0;
34  }
35
36  //Called as soon as home page has loaded, to start image rotation
37  function startRotation()
38  {
39      document.getElementById('placeholder').src=imageArray[5];
40      setInterval('rotate()', 2000);
41  }
42
```

FIGURE 7.5 ch07/nature1/scripts/rotate.js
The JavaScript code for handling the rotating images on the home pages of this chapter's nature1 and nature2 websites.

```
37    /********************************************************
38    styles for main menu, dropdown menus, and menu items
39    two groups of links: main menu, and dropdown menus */
40
41    /* for the always-visible main menu options */
42    .Links li {
43      float: left;
44      width: 127px;
45      border-right: 1px solid #FFF;
46      font-weight: bold;
47      font-size: .7em;
48      text-align: center;
49      list-style: none;
50    }
51
52    .Links li:last-child {
53      width: 132px;
54      border-right-width: 0;
55    }
56
57    /* for all links for all menu options */
58    .Links li a {
59      display: block;
60      height: 25px;
61      line-height: 25px;
62      background-color: #048018;
63      color: #FFF;
64      text-decoration: none;
65    }
66
67    .Links li a:hover {
68      background-color: #5FB361;
69      color: #FFF;
70    }
71
72    /* for the dropdown menu options */
73    .Links div {
74      position: absolute;
75      background-color: #048018;
76      visibility: hidden;
77    }
78
79    .Links div a {
80      display: block;
81      width: 124px;
82      margin-top: 2px;
83      padding-left: 3px;
84      background-color: #C5DCC9;
85      color: #048018;
86      text-align: left;
87    }
```

FIGURE 7.6 `ch07/nature1/css/desktop.css` **(excerpt)**
A portion of the "desktop" CSS style file for this chapter, showing the styles for both the always-visible "high-level" main menu headers and the dropdown submenu options.

```
1   //menus.js
2   //Handles the dropdown menus that "drop down"
3   //(really "appear" and "disappear") from the
4   //main menu on each page of the website
5
6   //Flag to indicate if a dropdown menu is visible
7   var isShowing = false;
8
9   //Reference to the current dropdown menu
10  var dropdownMenu = null;
11
12  //Show the drop-down menu with the given id, if it exists, and set flag
13  function show(id)
14  {
15      hide(); /* First hide any previously showing dropdown menu */
16      dropdownMenu = document.getElementById(id);
17      if (dropdownMenu != null)
18      {
19          dropdownMenu.style.visibility = 'visible';
20          isShowing = true;
21      }
22  }
23
24  //Hide the currently visible dropdown menu and set flag
25  function hide()
26  {
27      if (isShowing) dropdownMenu.style.visibility = 'hidden';
28      isShowing = false;
29  }
```

FIGURE 7.7 `ch07/nature1/scripts/menus.js`
The JavaScript `show()` and `hide()` functions for the dropdown menu options in our `nature1` and `nature2` websites.

To understand how the slide show works, you need to examine both the `index.html` file of Figure 7.2, which contains the `onload` attribute and the revised `img` element, and the `rotate.js` script shown in Figure 7.5.

7.2.1 The `onload` Attribute of the `body` Element: Starting the Slide Show after the Home Page Loads

In line 3 of Figure 7.2 we see the following HTML markup for the opening tag of the `body` element:

```
body onload="startRotation()"
```

The `onload` attribute of the `body` tag is another *event attribute* whose value should be whatever action is to be taken once the page with the given body has fully loaded. This action is often, as in this case, simply a function call, but it could also be several JavaScript statements, separated by semicolons. In this case, the JavaScript function being called is `startRotation()`, which has been defined as part of the script in `rotate.js`, and it begins the image rotation that now features prominently on our home page. We will discuss this function shortly.

7.2.2 The Revised `img` Element for the Slide Show

Look a little more closely at the `img` element in the index file of Figure 7.2, which is shown in lines 25–27:

```
<img id="placeholder" src=""
    alt="Healthy Lifestyle"
    width="256px" height="256px">
```

This `img` tag now has an `id` attribute with the value `"placeholder"`, suggesting (correctly) that the `img` element is to "hold the place" for each successive image to be inserted into the image location during the rotation. Also, the value of the `src` attribute starts off as the empty string, but the script will change this value to the name of each successive image file as the rotation proceeds.

The value of the `alt` attribute is `"Healthy Lifestyle"`, a term that may reasonably be applied to all of our images, so it does not have to be changed.

The `width` and `height` attributes have fixed values that are the same, so we have a square image. Recall that for the sake of efficiency all of the images we display should ideally have the same size to eliminate the need for any resizing effort by the browser (or any distortion in the image if the actual dimensions give a different *aspect ratio*). The *aspect ratio* of an image is defined as the ratio of its width to its height.

7.2.3 The `rotate.js` Script

In what follows, we use our discussion of the `rotate.js` script to introduce (or examine further) the following JavaScript topics:

- ▶ The `Date` object
- ▶ The `switch`-statement
- ▶ Creating a new array and "populating" it with values
- ▶ The `for`-loop

The JavaScript Date Object: Getting the Day of the Week

The first of the new JavaScript features we encounter in the `rotate.js` file shown in Figure 7.5 is the JavaScript `Date` data type. The executable part of the script begins in line 5 by creating a new `Date` object (with the `Date()` method call) and storing it in a variable called `today`:

```
var today = new Date();
```

TABLE 7.1 Methods of the `Date` object in JavaScript.	
Method	**Return Value**
`Date()` (the default constructor method has an empty parameter list)	A `Date` object containing all relevant information for today's date and time
`getDate()`	day of the month (1–31)
`getDay()`	day of the week (0–6) (0 is Sunday)
`getFullYear()`	year (a four-digit number)
`getHours()`	hour (0–23)
`getMilliseconds()`	milliseconds (0–999)
`getMinutes()`	minutes (0–59)
`getMonth()`	month (0–11)
`getSeconds()`	seconds (0–59)

A method call of this type is usually referred to as a *constructor method*, or just a *constructor*, since it "constructs" a new object of type `Date`. Those familiar with other languages such as C++ or Java will already be familiar with this terminology and syntax. We gave the variable this name because by default such a `Date` object contains all the information we might need to know that pertains to today's (i.e., the current) date.

There are many pieces of information we might want to know about today, or any other day, and an equal number of methods that we can call on the `Date` object referred to by the `today` variable to get that information. **TABLE 7.1** shows some of those methods. See the **References** section at the end of this chapter for more information.

The particular method we will need is `getDay()`, which returns a value of 5, 6, or 0 if today is Friday, Saturday, or Sunday (respectively), or a value of 1 to 4 if today is a day from Monday to Thursday, inclusive.

The JavaScript `switch`-statement for Decision Making: Choosing Which Group of Images to Rotate

We have already seen how the JavaScript `if..else`-statement can be used to choose between two alternatives, or between two or more alternatives if we choose to use a "nested" `if..else` construct. We could use such a construct in our current situation again, but sometimes it is more convenient to use another kind of statement when we need to choose one alternative from among many (one day from seven possible days of the week in our current context, for example).

The JavaScript `switch`-statement is another form of conditional statement that is found in many other languages as well, including C, C++, and Java, and which allows us to make this kind of choice. Here is the general format of the `switch`-statement:

```
switch (expression)
{
    case value_1:
        statements;
        break;
    case value_2:
        statements;
        break;
        ...
    case value_n:
        statements;
        break;
    default:
        statements;
        break;
}
```

The execution of a `switch`-statement proceeds as follows. First, the `expression` in the parentheses following the keyword `switch` is evaluated. This value is then checked against the value in the first `case` (`value_1` above). If a match is obtained, the statement(s) following this `case` are executed and the `switch`-statement terminates because the `break;` statement at the end of this `case` will cause execution to "break out" of the `switch` and carry on with the statement immediately following the `switch`-statement.

If the value of `expression` does not match the value in the first `case`, the search continues with each of the subsequent `case` values (also called *case labels*) in turn. Any match farther along the way will result in behavior analogous to that we described when we had a match for the first `case`. The values of a case label may be an integer, a character, or even a string, but all case labels should be of the same value type, and `expression` should evaluate to a value of that common type.

Each group of `case` statements in a `switch`-statement is almost always terminated by a `break;` statement to exit the `switch`, once the statements for that `case` have been executed. Sometimes, however, programmers will omit the `break;` in one or more cases to create a "drop through" effect. For example, if you delete the `break;` statement before the second case, and if the value of our `expression` matched `value_1`, the statements in both the first and second case will be executed. In fact, we see one form of this usage in the `switch`-statement in our `rotate.js`.

If no `case` value is matched by the value of `expression`, the statements after `default:` will be executed. While it is not necessary to include the `default:` option as the last part of a `switch` statement, it is a good programming practice to always include it. Also, the `break;` statement at the end of the `default:` option is not strictly necessary, since the `switch`-statement ends at that point in any case.

Now look at how we use the `switch`-statement in `rotate.js` (see lines 9–19 in Figure 7.5). In order to handle the images for our slide show properly, the first thing we need to do is decide which group of images to use, the indoor ones or the outdoor ones. As we know, this depends on the day of the week.

We begin by setting a variable called `prefix` (the prefix to which a number will be added to get an actual file name) to an appropriate initial value. Since every file is located in the subdirectory `images`, we initialize this variable with the string `"images/"` (line 9 of the `rotate.js` script in Figure 7.5):

```
var prefix = "images/";
```

Next, depending on the day of the week, we want to append either `"indoor"` or `"outdoor"` to the value in the variable `prefix`. This is where we use a `switch`-statement in which the expression to be evaluated is `today.getDay()` (lines 10–19 of the `rotate.js` script in Figure 7.5):

```
switch (today.getDay())
{
    case 0:
    case 5:
    case 6:
        prefix += "outdoor";
        break;
    default:
        prefix += "indoor";
}
```

The return value of the method call `today.getDay()` will be an integer in the range from 0 to 6. If it is either 0, 5, or 6 we have a weekend day, since these values correspond to Sunday, Friday, and Saturday, respectively. In these cases we want to append the string `"outdoor"` to our variable `prefix` so that the value of `prefix` becomes the string `"images/outdoor"`. On the other hand, if the value returned is 1, 2, 3, or 4 we have a weekday, and the value of `prefix` becomes `"images/indoor"`.

Note the use of the "special assignment operator" `+=` to add either `"outdoor"` or `"indoor"` to the original value of `prefix`. Most operators in JavaScript can be extended in this way using the assignment operator. In our case, the statement

```
prefix += "outdoor";
```

has exactly the same effect as this statement:

```
prefix = prefix + "outdoor";
```

We have also chosen to not use a `break;` for the first two cases, allowing for the fall-through effect discussed earlier. In fact, those first two cases do not even have statements of their own in this particular `switch`-statement.

In this `switch`-statement we are using our `default:` option to deal with the remaining days of the week, and we will append the string `"indoor"` to our variable `prefix` in that case. Other alternatives to this code will be explored in the end-of-chapter exercises.

Creating Our Own JavaScript Array: Creating Storage for Our Image Filenames

In the previous chapter we had a very brief encounter with a built-in JavaScript array that was useful when accessing certain Document Object Model (DOM) elements. Here our goal is to have an easy way to access a sequence of image files, and the JavaScript array turns out to be the most convenient way to do that, since arrays are generally used to store lists of values of any kind. In our case, therefore, we will store a list of the filenames of the images that will be displayed in our slide show.

Now, however, we have to create our own array. We do this by first declaring a variable called `imageArray` to hold a reference to an array object and then we call the constructor method of the `Array` data type with the operator `new` in much the same way as we did earlier when we created a `Date` object. This statement occurs in line 22 of the `rotate.js` script shown in Figure 7.5:

```
imageArray = new Array(6);
```

The constructor, as always, performs the necessary operations to set up our array. A significant difference this time around is that we provide the value 6 as a parameter to the constructor, which specifies that we want the array to have a size of six (be able to hold six values, i.e., six image filenames). The net effect is as though we now have six variables, named `imageArray[0]`, `imageArray[1]`, `imageArray[2]`, `imageArray[3]`, `imageArray[4]`, and `imageArray[5]`. Note again that arrays in JavaScript (your own as well as any that are built-in) are zero-based; that is, index numbering starts at 0. These are the *components* or *elements* of the array. Thus the array gives us an easy way to handle several, or even a very large number, of variables of the same kind. In fact, we can easily automate the processing of all the array elements with the help of another JavaScript *control statement*, the `for`-loop, which we discuss next.

The JavaScript `for`-loop for Repetition: Storing the Image Filenames in Our Array

A JavaScript script will often require that one or more actions be repeated. For example, to build our array of images, we have to repeat the act of inserting the name of an image file into that array six times. Most C-based programming languages, including JavaScript, have three different kinds of *loop control statements* to handle repetition: the `for`-loop, the `while`-loop, and the `do..while`-loop. Because it is the most convenient choice for our immediate purpose, we examine the `for`-loop more closely here, and discuss the other two in the end-of-chapter exercises.

Here is the general format of a `for`-loop:

```
for (initialization; condition; update)
{
    statements;
}
```

The keyword `for` is followed by a required pair of parentheses containing three semicolon-separated parts: `initialization; condition; update`. The statement(s) in the braces are called the *body* of the `for`-loop. If there is only a single statement in the body, the braces are optional.

This is how we execute a `for`-loop. The `initialization` is performed (once) before the loop begins. Then, if `condition` is true, we execute the body. Next, `update` is performed and `condition` is re-checked. As long as `condition` remains true, we continue to re-execute the loop body and perform `update`, in that order. When a check of `condition` finds it to be false, the loop terminates and script execution continues with the first statement following the `for`-loop.

Of course, most of the time we want the loop to terminate eventually, so we must ensure that `update` eventually causes `condition` to become false.

Once we have set up the "infrastructure" for our image array—the `imageArray` variable itself, and the correct prefix for our image filenames that will go into that array—we can populate the array with the required filenames with a simple `for`-loop (lines 23–24 of `rotate.js` in Figure 7.5):

```
for (i=0; i<imageArray.length; i++)
    imageArray[i] = prefix + (i+1) + ".jpg";
```

The execution of this `for`-loop proceeds as follows:

- The `initialization` sets the variable i to 0.
- The `condition` (`i<imageArray.length`) is then checked. Any JavaScript `Array` object has a `length` property that is accessed using the same dot-notation syntax that is used to access an object method. This condition uses that `length` property, which in this case has the value 6, and since the value of i is currently 0, the `condition` is true.
- Since the `condition` was true, we now execute the (single-statement) body of the `for`-loop. This statement creates the proper filename for the first image and inserts it into the array. The proper filename is created by appending the `prefix` variable with the value of (`i+1`), and then adding the string for the file extension, which is ".jpg". Note that we need i+1 here to avoid the classic "off-by-one" error, because i has started at 0, but the names of the image files start their numbering at 1. If the current day is a weekday (for example), the value of `prefix` to which we are adding this information will be "images/indoor", so that `imageArray[0]` will be assigned the value "images/indoor1.jpg".
- We execute the `update` statement, i++, which increments i to 1.
- We check the variable i to see if it is still less than 6, which it is, so the `condition` is still true.
- We therefore continue by executing the loop body again, which, this time around, assigns the value "images/indoor2.jpg" to `imageArray[1]`.
- This process continues until we have set the final value of our array, `imageArray[5]`, to be "images/indoor6.jpg".
- The following execution of the `update` statement, i++, sets i to 6, which is no longer less than `imageArray.length`.
- At this point the loop terminates, and `imageArray` contains the names of all six image files.

Rotating Our Images: The `rotate()` and `startRotation()` Functions

We have now completed the setup of the array data structure that contains the "slides" (images) for our "slide show", and we are ready to define the functions that actually perform the slide show (the image rotation). It is important to note that the remainder of the script `rotate.js` in Figure 7.5 is in fact just setting up the functions to perform the slide show, but the show does not start as this script executes. It only starts when the page has loaded. This is a difference worth remembering.

To display our images we define two functions, one called `rotate()`, which performs the rotations, and a second one called `startRotation()`, which initializes the first image and then calls `rotate()` to continue with the rotation. Recall that it is the `startRotation()` function that was the value of the `onload` attribute in our `index.html` page. We could have used the `rotate()` function directly as the value of the `onload` attribute, but depending on the speed at which things are happening, a user might see the value of the `alt` attribute in the image location briefly before the rotation got under way. By using the separate function `startRotation()` to initialize the first image directly, and *then* start the rotation, we hope to avoid this possibility.

We should preface our detailed discussion by noting our use of the *global variable* `imageCounter` to keep track of the image we are working with at any given time, and we initialize this variable to 0 (line 27 of Figure 7.5). Global variables are variables declared outside any function, but accessible from within the body of any function. They are very convenient, but also "dangerous" to use, since they can be altered from anywhere in your JavaScript code, and it is therefore easy to alter them inadvertently by mistake, leading to hard-to-find bugs in your code. Use them sparingly and very carefully, if you must use them at all. Our only excuse here is that our script is very short and the variable is only being accessed in one place and we would not want to put it inside our function since then it would be set to 0 each time our function was called, instead of being incremented each time, which is what we need.

The function `rotate()` (lines 28–34 of Figure 7.5) performs the actual image rotation. Each time it is called, it first creates a variable called `imageObject` and assigns it a reference to the DOM `img` element on our home page. Recall from the discussion of `index.html` that the `img` element had an `id` attribute with a value of `'placeholder'`, so we get this reference with a call to the `getElementById()` method. (Note that we are using single quotes here, but only as a not-so-subtle reminder that we can.) Once we have this reference to the `img` element object, we can access the `src` attribute of the `img` element with the usual dot-notation syntax (`imageObject.src`) and assign to it the filename of the current image from our array of images (`imageArray[imageCounter]`). The browser then takes care of updating the home page display with that image.

Before leaving the `rotate()` function, we must increment the `imageCounter` variable so that the next time `rotate()` is called the next image in the sequence will be displayed. And finally, note that when `imageCounter` reaches 6 we have to set it back to 0, for two reasons: first, to get our "rotational" effect, and second, to prevent our array index from quickly getting out of bounds and trying to access images that don't exist.

Now that we know what `rotate()` does when called, the only remaining question is this: When, exactly, *is* it called? And that's the job of the `startRotation()` function, so let's look at it.

The `startRotation()` function does two things. First, it chooses an initial image for display, before `rotate()` is called to begin the rotation, for reasons we explained above. We opt to display the last image in the sequence first, as this initial image, so that the first image seen as the rotation begins appears in its proper place in the rotation.

The second and last action of `startRotation()` is to call the `setInterval()` function. This is a built-in JavaScript function that takes two parameters. The first parameter is a string containing an action to be performed (often a function call, as in this case), and the second parameter is the length, in milliseconds, of a time interval. A call to `setInterval()` with these two input values causes the action to occur after each time interval of the given length. Thus the call made by our `startRotation()` (namely, `setInterval('rotate()', 2000)`) causes our `rotate()` function to be called every 2 seconds (2000 milliseconds). This, in turn, causes the image on our home page to change every 2 seconds.

7.3 Implementing Our Dropdown Menus

In this section, we discuss the details of the second major new feature of our sample website in this chapter, the dropdown menu options. We are again dealing with the "stripped down" first version of the site found in the `nature1` subdirectory. In this version, none of the links on our home page are active, but the dropdown feature is fully functional in all cases, which is all we need for our discussion. Section 7.4 discusses the more complete `nature2` version of our site, in which all the links are active and lead to other pages, but there is no functionality to be seen there that we have not seen before, except for the enhancements to our BMI and feedback forms, which we also discuss in section 7.4.

To follow the discussion in this section, you will need to refer to four different files from this chapter:

▶ `nature1/index.html` (see Figure 7.2)
▶ `nature1/common/menus.html` (Figure 7.4)
▶ `nature1/css/default.css` (excerpt) (Figure 7.6)
▶ `nature1/scripts/menu.js` (Figure 7.7)

7.3.1 An Overview of How Our Dropdown Menus Work

Let's begin with a brief overview of how our dropdown menus work, and start by examining the HTML markup structure that gives us those menus. This markup is in `menus.html`, shown in Figure 7.4, and as you can see by looking at line 6 of `index.html` in Figure 7.2, `menus.html` is included, via SSI, right after the logo on our home page.

Perhaps the first thing we should point out is that our "dropdown" menus don't really "drop down" in the literal sense, so this can be confusing. In fact, they are always sitting there, just where you see them when they are "dropped down", but they are "invisible" most of the time. When a user hovers the mouse over a menu bar with a hidden "dropdown" menu, the "dropdown" does not "drop down"; it simple "appears" (becomes visible).

So, now to continue our discussion. The menu that sits below the logo on our home page now consists of two kinds of menu options, that is, two kinds of links to other pages. The first kind of "high level" option is illustrated by the seven options that show up on the menu when the page is displayed. Not all of these options are "created equal", since some (but not all) of them have dropdown suboptions. So, the second kind of menu option link is illustrated by the dropdown list of suboptions that appears ("drops down") when the mouse is placed over an option of the first kind, if that option actually has the dropdown feature. This only happens for the third to the sixth options on this menu (**Products+Services**, **Your Health**, **About Us**, **Contact Us**). The first two menu options (**Home**, **e-store**) and the last (**Site Map**) do not have any dropdown suboptions.

Figure 7.4 shows that the entire main menu "strip" on our home page is enclosed in a new HTML5 semantic nav element. Within this nav element is an unordered list containing seven list elements corresponding to the seven high-level menu options on our menu. Finally, under each of these menu options that has a dropdown submenu (the third to the sixth) there is a div element containing a number of anchor elements corresponding to the number of dropdown options for that particular submenu. As you can see from the markup, three of the submenus contain four options (lines 9–12, 18–21, and 27–30), and the remaining one contains two options (lines 36–37).

Note that, for simplicity, we have followed the standard approach of making the hyperlinks "defunct" by using a value of '#' for their href values, which simply means that the links will not actually take us anywhere. This is what we mean by saying that the links on this page are "inactive". We will have more to say about these links in section 7.5 when we compare the menus.html markup for nature1 with the corresponding markup for nature2.

7.3.2 The onmouseover and onmouseout Attributes: Showing and Hiding Dropdown Menu Options

Continuing our examination of Figure 7.4, we note the appearance of two new *event attributes*: onmouseover (lines 4, 5, 7, 8, 16, 17, 25, 26, 34, 35, and 40) and onmouseout (line 2). Each onmouseover attribute appears as the attribute of a list element containing one of the seven "high-level" menu options, or as the attribute of a div element containing a group of dropdown options.

Because the value of each onmouseover attribute is a call to the show() function, when the mouse pointer is placed over any of the main menu options, a call to show() is made. Depending on which menu option the mouse pointer is over, that call is one of show('m1'), show('m2'), show('m3'), show('m4'), show('m5'), show('m6'), or show('m7'). The parameter is the id value of the corresponding div element containing the associated dropdown submenu option group. However, you will note that there are only four groups of submenu options. In fact, there is no div with an id of m1 or m2 or m7, so the call to show() in any one of these cases has no effect since there is no submenu to drop down. We could explain this by saying we are "future proofing" our code: If we ever do add submenu divs with these id values, they will drop down automatically without further code modification.

The purpose of a function call like `show('m3')` (for example) is to make visible the dropdown menu contained within the `div` element whose `id` is `m3`, which is the one under the menu item **Products+Services**. We shall look at the details of this function later in this chapter. As long as the mouse pointer is over the main menu option or the dropdown menu underneath it, that dropdown menu will remain visible.

The `onmouseout` attribute of the outermost `nav` element (line 2) has as its value a call to the function `hide()`. The purpose of `hide()` is to make invisible any currently showing dropdown menu, which it does when the mouse pointer moves away from the `nav` element, that is, away from all of the "high-level" menu options and their dropdown submenus.

7.3.3 The CSS for Our Dropdown Menus

Much of the CSS for our home page in this chapter we have already discussed in Chapter 4. However, our dropdown menu setup makes use of some CSS features that we have not discussed previously, so we introduce them here. For purposes of the discussion, we include, in Figure 7.6, only the relevant portion of the current chapter's `desktop.css` file, in which we see, of course, some familiar CSS along with the new features.

Here are the things to note about the CSS shown in Figure 7.6:

▶ We use a single class called `Links`, combined with various descendant selectors, to style both the "high-level" menu options, which are always visible in the menu bar, and the dropdown submenu options, which only appear when the mouse pointer hovers over one of the "high-level" menu options that actually *has* a dropdown submenu. Comments indicate which styles apply to which menu options.

▶ The .Links li style in lines 42–50 removes the markers from list elements and floats them left, setting up a horizontal main menu, just as we had in Chapter 4.

▶ The style `.Links li:last-child` makes use of the `:last-child` *pseudo-class* to style the last `li` element (the last item in the menu bar) a little bit differently than the others (a slightly different width and no right border). When applied to an element, the `:last-child` pseudo-class identifies the last element of that type that is a direct child of its parent (in this case, the last `li` element that is a child of the `ul` parent element).

▶ In the style for `.Links li a` in lines 58–65 you see something you have not seen before: the style rule `display: block`. An a element is by default an inline element, but turning these anchors (links) into block elements allows us to give them a width, padding, and margins, something we cannot easily do with inline elements.

▶ The style `.Links li a:hover` in lines 67–70 provides a different background color for the menu links as well as the submenu links, when the mouse pointer is hovering over those links.

▶ The .Links div style in lines 73–77 contains three items of interest. First is the style rule `position: absolute`, which takes the menu strip out of the "normal flow" of the page and, in this case, allows the following blocks to rise up under the menu and close up the space that would otherwise be there to accommodate the dropdown submenus when they are activated. Second is the `border: 1px solid #048018` "shorthand" style rule, which gives us a 1-pixel, solid green border all around our dropdown submenu options. And finally, the `visibility` property is set to `hidden` to hide the submenu options when the page is first displayed.

▶ The `.Links div a` style in lines 79–87 styles the anchors (links) in our dropdown menus. The key thing to note here once again is the `display: block` style rule. As before, this allows us to give them all a uniform width. But this is needed here for an even more important reason. Normally an `a` element is inline, and without this rule the submenus would appear in a horizontal row across the page, instead of one under the other as we would like.

You may have to read through the above list several times while referring to Figure 7.6. An even better approach is to view the `nature1/index.html` file in a browser while you have the `nature1/css/desktop.css` file open in an editor. Then you can comment out or alter each style rule in some other way as that rule is mentioned, and then refresh the browser display to see the effect of your actions. There is no better way to learn quickly the real effects or purpose of a particular CSS style. One of the end-of-chapter exercises guides you through a number of such activities.

7.3.4 The JavaScript for Our Dropdown Menus: The `show()` and `hide()` Functions

Finally, we are now ready to look at the JavaScript code that causes the visibility state of the menu suboptions to alternate between visible and hidden. This code is found in the file `menus.js`, which is shown in Figure 7.7. It is a much-simplified version of the code from `http://javascript-array.com/`.

This short script contains, once again, two global variables. One of these is called `isShowing` and the other is called `dropdownMenu`. The rest of the script consists of two short function definitions. One function is called `show()` and the other `hide()`. The names of the variables and the functions have been chosen to suggest their purpose, always a good programming practice.

When this script is run, the global variable `isShowing` is initialized to `false` to indicate that none of the submenu options is showing, and the `dropdownMenu` global variable is initialized to `null` to indicate that no dropdown submenu has yet been chosen. Remember that these global variables are accessible from any part of the script and therefore, in particular, from each of the two functions.

If you now look again at the `menus.html` file in Figure 7.4, you can see that the `show()` function is called when the user places the mouse over one of the "high-level" menu items in the menu bar, and at that point the `show()` function is also passed the `id` value of the `div` of the corresponding submenu, as discussed earlier. This passed value will be one of `'m1'`, `'m2'`, `'m3'`, `'m4'`, `'m5'`, `'m6'`, or `'m7'`, corresponding to the position of the menu item in the menu bar, although (as we pointed out earlier) there are currently no dropdown menus corresponding to either `'m1'` or `'m2'` or `'m7'`.

The first action of the `show()` function is to hide any submenu that may be currently displayed by calling the `hide()` function. It then retrieves the DOM element whose `id` value it has been passed by calling the `getElementById()` method and passing along the same `id` that it received. The `visibility` property of that DOM element is then given the value `visible` and the global variable `isShowing` is set to `true` to indicate that this menu item now indeed "is showing".

The function `hide()` is even simpler. It checks to see if any DOM element is visible by looking at the variable `isShowing`, and if there is such a visible DOM element, it is made invisible by setting its `visibility` property to a value of `hidden`.

7.4 Notes on the `nature2` Version of Our Nature's Source Website

We pointed out at the beginning of the chapter that the `nature1` version of our website in this chapter had no active links, since we were using it solely for demonstrating our slide show and drop-down menus. The `nature2` version, on the other hand, is the most complete version of our site to date.

First, the home page looks the same as the home page for the `nature1` version, except that all links are now active, so the `nature2` directory includes an HTML document file to be displayed whenever the user clicks on any of the now-active links. With two exceptions, these pages contain essentially the same content as they did in Chapter 4, except that all pages have been modified to show the same main menu and footer (but not the rotating images) of the home page. The two exceptions are the **Compute Your BMI** dropdown submenu option found under the "high-level" menu option **Your Health**, and the **Feedback Form** dropdown submenu option found under the "high-level" **Contact Us** menu option. These two links bring up the latest versions of our BMI and feedback forms, and we will say more about them in a moment.

The contents of the `images` and `scripts` subdirectories are the same for both `nature1` and `nature2`. The `desktop.css` and `tablet.css` style files for `nature2` contain the full contents of those files for `nature1`, plus a few additional styles to help with the styling of the newly revised BMI calculator form and feedback form pages.

It would be useful at this point for you to make yourself thoroughly familiar with this up-to-date version of our sample site before we enhance it further with server-side processing using PHP in the next chapter. However, just before you do that, let's take a moment to mention a few enhancements that we have applied to our two forms, which also invite some experimentation on your part.

7.4.1 What's New in Our BMI Form?

Recall from the previous chapter that when a user successfully completed a BMI form and clicked the **Compute your BMI** button, the resulting report was presented in a JavaScript popup window, and that window had to be dismissed before the user could return to using the browser.

The report returned upon completion of the BMI form in `nature2` of this chapter contains the same information as before, but is presented in a new web page, which therefore does not have to be dismissed before continuing to work in the browser. **FIGURE 7.8** shows the result when the user has asked for a detailed report, and **FIGURE 7.9** shows the relevant modified code from `nature2/scripts/bmiCalculate.js` that does the job.

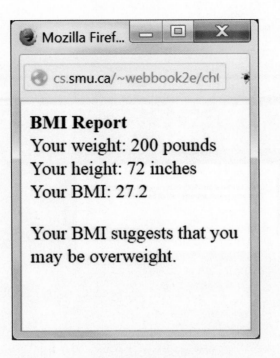

FIGURE 7.8 `graphics/ch07/nature2/displayBMIReport.jpg`
A Firefox browser display of the BMI report produced as a separate web page instead of a
JavaScript popup.

```
70    var bmiDisplay = window.open("", "",
71        "width=200, height=200, top=300, left=300");
72        bmiDisplay.document.write(textToDisplay);
```

FIGURE 7.9 `ch07/nature2/scripts/bmiCalculate.js` **(excerpt)**
The JavaScript code segment that displays a BMI report as a new web page.

In this version of the script we call the `window.open()` JavaScript method (line 70 of
Figure 7.9) rather than the `alert()` method. For our usage of the method we supply three
parameters. The first parameter is the URL of the page to load. Since we are not loading any page,
but instead just writing our report to an empty window, we supply an empty string for this value.
The empty string for the second parameter is the default value and indicates that we want a brand
new window (as opposed to replacing the contents of the current window, for example). The third
parameter is the most interesting one. It too is a string, and contains a comma separated list of
values. More values are possible, but we have used only four: the width and height of the new
window, and the distance of the top left corner of our new window from the top and left sides of
the browser window. All measurements are in pixels.

The other new feature of our BMI form is illustrated by the display in **FIGURE 7.10**. What is
different this time around is that this popup message appears the moment the user clicks on the

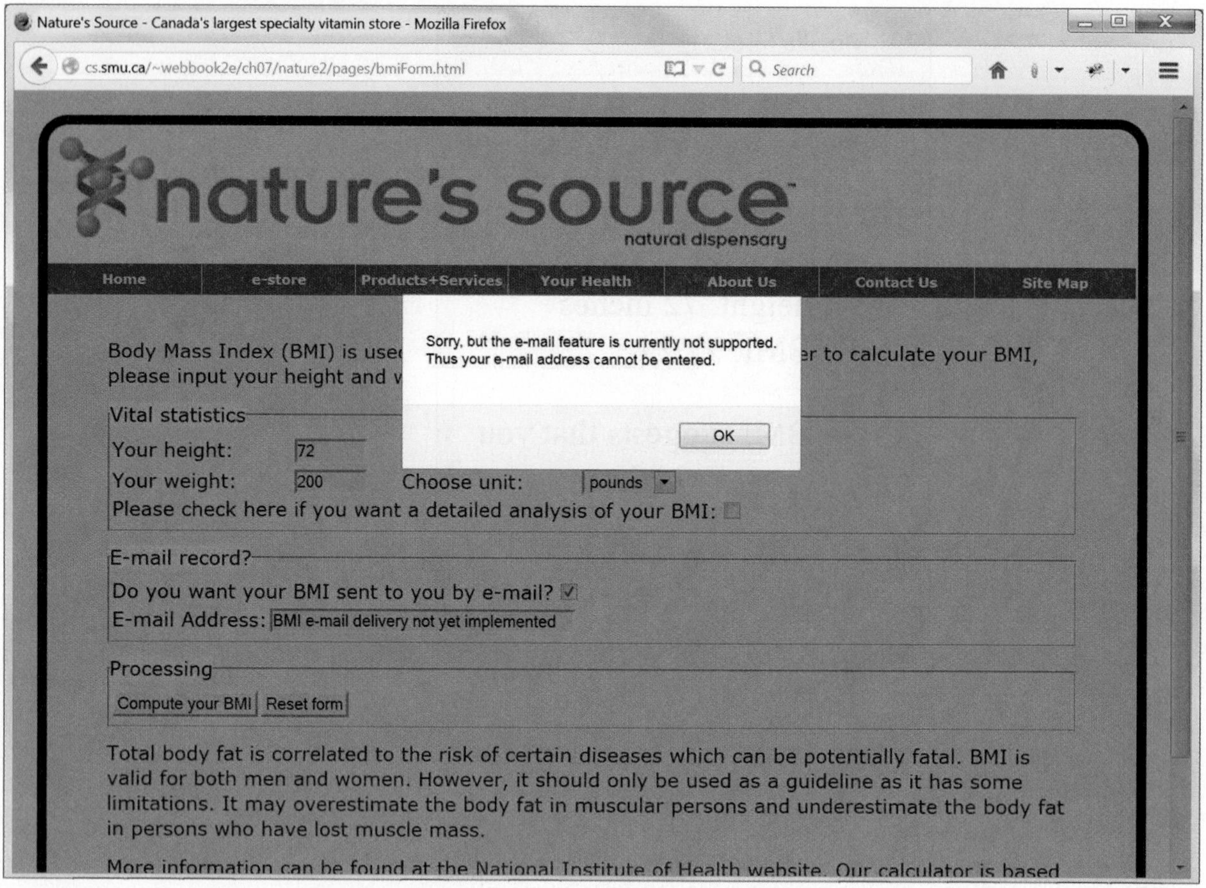

FIGURE 7.10 `graphics/ch07/nature2/displayBMInoEmail.jpg`
A Firefox browser display showing the popup message that appears when the user clicks on the checkbox that requests the BMI report to be sent by email.

checkbox to request an email report. In other words, the user is spared the frustration of clicking on the check box, typing in an email address and *then* being told that email is not yet implemented. In fact, if you look closely you can see that the textbox where the email would be typed actually contains a similar message, so the user should not be clicking the checkbox in any case! As you can see in line 60 of **FIGURE 7.11**, this message shows up because it's the string assigned to the `value` attribute of that textbox, and in fact no email address can be entered because we have given this textbox the `readonly` attribute (see line 61 of Figure 7.11).

Implementing this latest feature requires some new markup, as well as some new JavaScript. The new markup is shown in Figure 7.11, and the new JavaScript in **FIGURE 7.12**. In Figure 7.11 we show the complete `fieldset` element containing the markup for dealing with email, so that we can see the context of the changes.

```
46                <fieldset class="SectionBackground">
47                  <legend class="LegendBackground">E-mail record?</legend>
48                  <table>
49                    <tr>
50                      <td colspan="2"><label for="wantMail">Do you want your
51                      BMI sent to you by e-mail?</label>
52                      <input id="wantMail" type="checkbox"
53                        name="wantMail" value="yes"
54                        onchange="handleBMIEmailRequest()"></td>
55                    </tr>
56                    <tr>
57                      <td><label for="email">E-mail Address:</label></td>
58                      <td><input id="email" type="text"
59                        name="email" size="40"
60                        value="BMI e-mail delivery not yet implemented"
61                        readonly></td>
62                    </tr>
63                  </table>
64                </fieldset>
```

FIGURE 7.11 `ch07/nature2/pages/bmiForm.html` **(excerpt)**
The HTML markup for the revised `fieldset` element of the BMI form that handles the user's request for a BMI report via email.

```
92   function handleBMIEmailRequest()
93   {
94      var bmiFormObj = document.getElementById("bmiForm");
95      if (bmiFormObj.wantMail.checked)
96      {
97        alert("Sorry, but the e-mail feature is currently not supported."
98            + "\nThus your e-mail address cannot be entered.");
99      }
100     bmiFormObj.wantMail.checked = false;
101  }
```

FIGURE 7.12 `ch07/nature2/scripts/bmiFormValidate.js` **(excerpt)**
The JavaScript function that handles the event that occurs when the user clicks on the checkbox that requests a BMI report via email.

Note that the `input` element with `"type=checkbox"` also has a new event attribute, namely `onchange="handleBMIEmailRequest()"`, and we can see the definition of this function in Figure 7.12. When called, this function displays the popup message window that we see in Figure 7.10, and then makes sure the checkbox is unchecked. So, when is the function called? It's called the moment there is any "change" in the status of the corresponding `input` element, in other words the moment the user tries to get an emailed BMI report by clicking on the checkbox.

7.4.2 What's New in Our Feedback Form?

Although in the previous chapter we mentioned the new HTML5 `pattern` attribute and how it could help with form data validation, we did not use it at that time since our focus then was on validating form data with JavaScript. In this chapter's version of our feedback form, we remedy that omission by using the `pattern` attribute to validate first name, last name, email address, and phone number. We have already discussed the regular expressions involved, and you can see how these are used as values of the `pattern` attribute by studying the excerpt from the current feedback form markup shown in **FIGURE 7.13** (lines 27, 33, 40–41, and 48). Note from that figure

```
23        <tr>
24          <td>First Name:</td>
25          <td><input type="text" name="firstName" size="40"
26              title="Initial capital, then lowercase and no spaces"
27              pattern="^[A-Z][a-z]*$" required></td>
28        </tr>
29        <tr>
30          <td>Last Name:</td>
31          <td><input type="text" name="lastName" size="40"
32              title="Initial capital, then lowercase and no spaces"
33              pattern="^[A-Z][a-z]*$" required></td>
34        </tr>
35        <tr>
36          <td>E-mail Address:</td>
37          <td><input type="text" name="email" size="40"
38              title=
39              "x@y.z, x and y can have . or -, z only 2 or 3 letters"
40              pattern=
41              "^\w+([.-]?\w+)*@\w+([.-]?\w+)*(\.\w{2,3})$"
42              required></td>
43        </tr>
44        <tr>
45          <td>Phone Number:</td>
46          <td><input type="text" name="phone" size="40"
47              title="xxx-yyy-zzzz, area code optional"
48              pattern="^(\d{3}-)?\d{3}-\d{4}$" required></td>
49        </tr>
50        <tr>
51          <td>Subject:</td>
52          <td><input type="text" name="subject" size="40" required></td>
53        </tr>
```

FIGURE 7.13 `ch07/nature2/pages/feedbackForm.html` **(excerpt)**
The HTML markup from the current version of our feedback form showing how we use a `pattern` attribute with a regular expression for its value to help us validate our form data, and also the use of the `required` attribute.

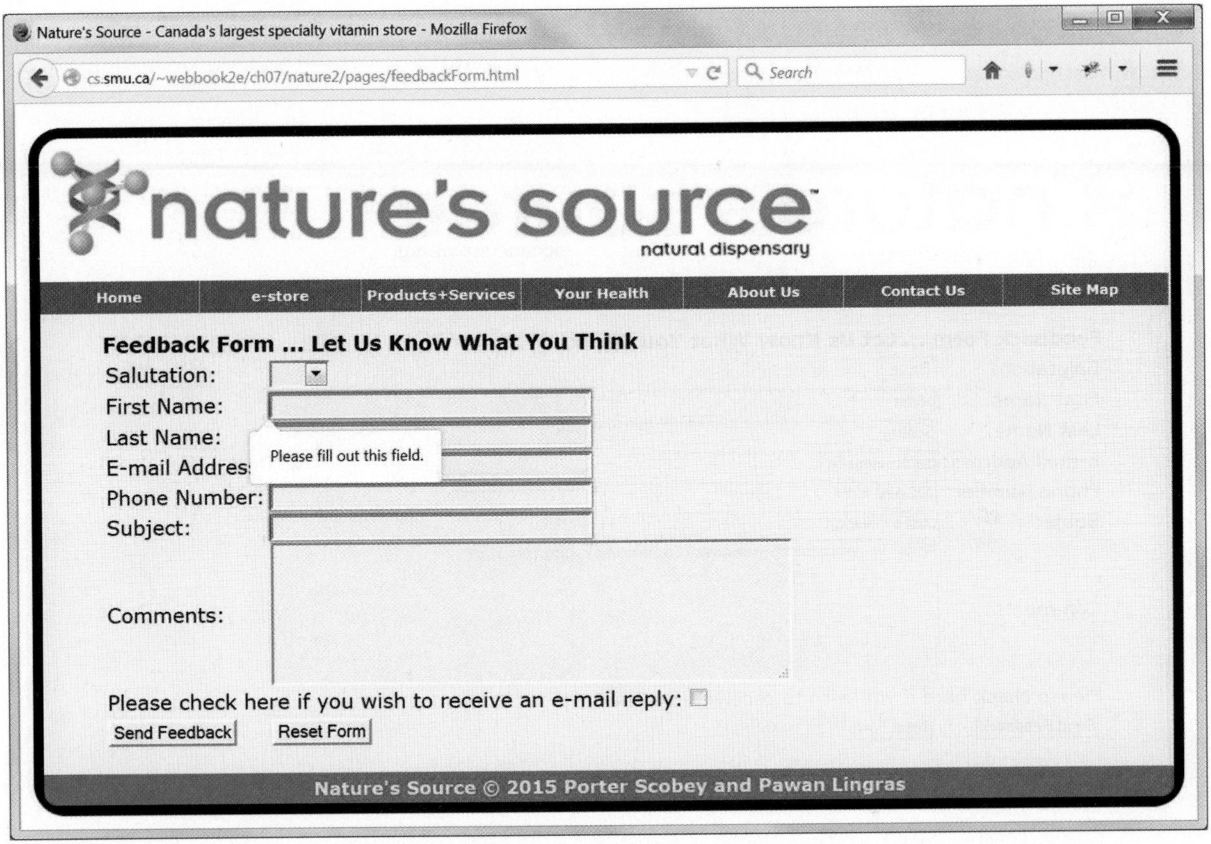

FIGURE 7.14 `graphics/ch07/nature2/displayEmptyFeedbackFormHtml.jpg`
A Firefox browser display showing that all the empty input elements that have a `required` attribute are outlined in red, with an HTML5 generated request to fill in the first one. This occurs when we try to submit a completely empty form.

that we have given all of our `input` elements with `type="text"` the `required` attribute as well (lines 27, 33, 42, and 48). Thus we have implemented a "double whammy" in terms of validation: the `required` attribute insists that something go into the textbox, and the regular expression in the `pattern` attribute value insists that it be the "right thing". Although the textbox for the feedback subject does not have a `pattern` attribute, it must not be left empty.

The effects of these changes can be seen in **FIGURES 7.14** and **7.15**. In Figure 7.14 we have clicked on the Send Feedback button when the form is empty. The result is that all the textboxes created by the `input` elements in our markup are outlined in red, indicating that they need to be filled in, and there is a popup message to that effect pointing at the first of those textboxes. All this has been achieved simply by giving each input element a `required` attribute. Compare that with what would be needed to achieve the same thing with JavaScript!

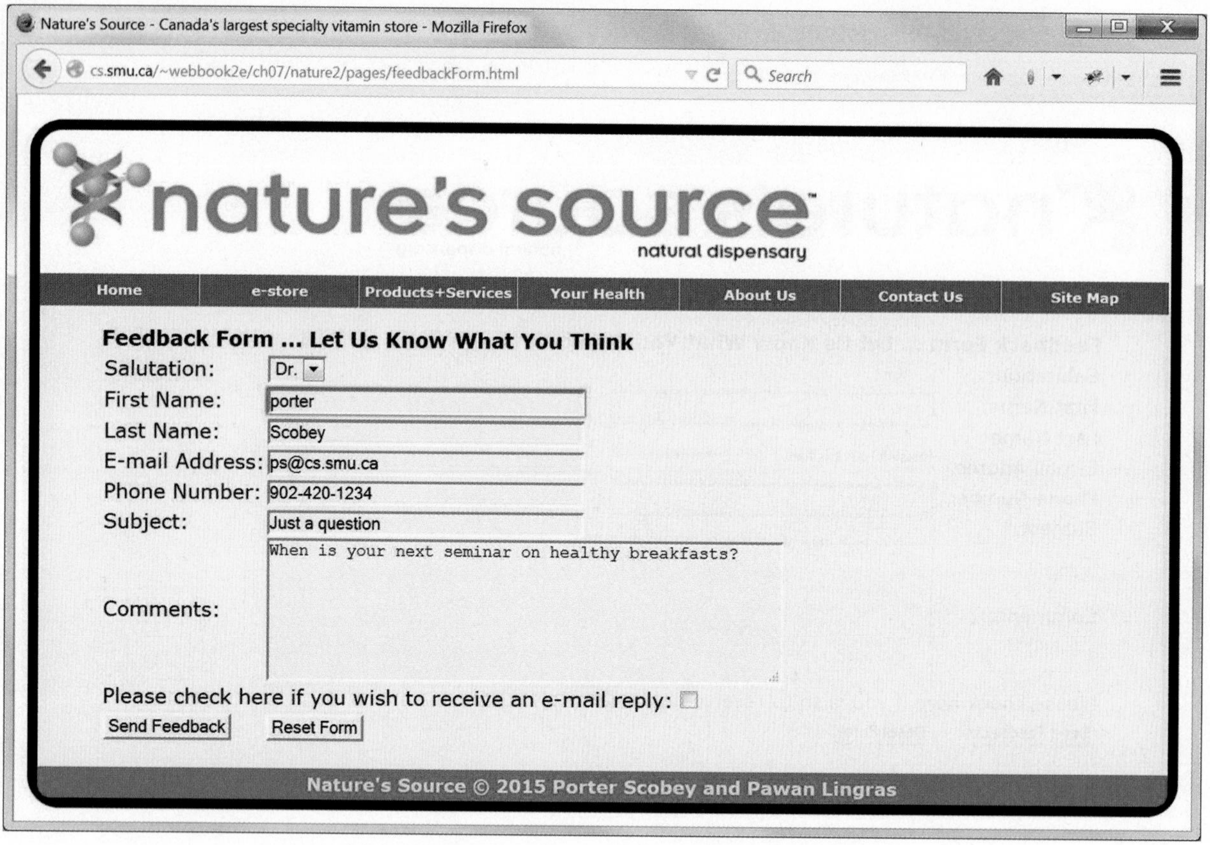

FIGURE 7.15 `graphics/ch07/nature2/displayErrorFeedbackFormHtml.jpg`
A Firefox browser display showing a feedback form that is correctly filled out except that the first name does not begin with a capital letter.

In Figure 7.15 all the required information has been entered and we have again clicked on the Send Feedback button. This time there is a problem with the first name, since our regular expression (line 27 of Figure 7.13) requires that it start with a capital letter. Thus the textbox is again outlined in red and, though it is not shown in the figure, if you hover your cursor over the textbox you will see the advisory popup message given as the value of the `title` attribute of that `input` element (see line 26 of Figure 7.13):

```
"Initial capital, then lowercase and no spaces"
```

Our use of the `pattern` and `required` attributes in our HTML markup in `feedbackForm.html` means that we have a much simpler version of the file `feedbackFormValidate.js` (see **FIGURE 7.16**), which now contains only two short functions. The first is `feedbackFormValidate()`. Once all the input data has been validated, this

```
1    //feedbackFormValidate.js
2    //Now, since the actual validation has been shifted to the
3    //pattern attribute of the input elements in the HTML file,
4    //all this script has to do is report that all went well and,
5    //if required, mention that e-mail replies are not yet available.
6
7    function feedbackFormValidate()
8    {
9        textToDisplay = "<p>All the information looks good.<br>Thank you!</p>"
10       var feedbackDisplay = window.open("", "",
11           "width=250, height=100, top=300, left=300");
12       feedbackDisplay.document.write(textToDisplay);
13   }
14
15   function handleFeedbackEmailRequest()
16   {
17       var contactFormObj = document.getElementById("contactForm");
18       if (contactFormObj.reply.checked)
19       {
20           alert("Sorry, but the e-mail reply feature is currently not "
21               + "supported.\nBut we do validate your email address "
22               + "(syntax only) in any case.");
23       }
24       //User has clicked the checkbox if the above message has been
25       //displayed, so uncheck the checkbox
26       contactFormObj.reply.checked = false;
27   }
```

FIGURE 7.16 `ch07/nature2/scripts/feedbackFormValidate.js`
The limited JavaScript code now needed for our feedback form validation, which is much less than we used previously because we are now using the `pattern` attribute.

function simply displays a message saying everything is OK in a new browser window, much like our revised BMI report was presented in the revised version of our BMI form discussed above.

The second function is `handleFeedbackEmailRequest()`. The user's request for an email response in this form is handled somewhat differently from the way it was handled in the BMI form. In this case, the user is actually allowed to enter an email address because even though email itself is not yet implemented, we still want to validate it with our regular expression, and the user is so advised by a popup message when the checkbox is checked.

7.4.3 What's Different about the `nature2` Markup for Our Menu Bar?

One more difference we should point out concerns the markup for our menu bar in `nature2`, as compared with the analogous markup for `nature1`. In `nature1`, none of the links were active, which meant that we could, and did, simply give all links (main menu options as well as dropdown menu options) the `href="#"` attribute.

However, in `nature2` some of the "options" on the main menu bar are actually live options, and some are not. In particular, **Home, e-store**, and **Site Map** are "actual" links, but **Products+Services**, **Your Health**, **About Us**, and **Contact Us** are not. In these last four cases, only the dropdown options under each heading are active links.

What this means is that, since these last four headings on our menu bar are no longer links, they have to be marked up and styled differently. As you can see in **FIGURE 7.17**, each of the first, second, and last main menu options (lines 4, 5, and 41) is still an `a` element within a `li` element, but the third to sixth main menu options (lines 8, 17, 26, and 35) are now just `span` elements. The best way to "experience" the difference is to compare what happens when you hover your mouse over **Products+Services** (for example) in `nature1` and then in `nature2`. The CSS for these `span` elements is not shown in the text, but for the sake of completeness you should check `desktop.css` to see how they are styled, and also compare the two versions of `menus.html` shown in Figures 7.4 and 7.17.

Summary

In this chapter you have seen how JavaScript can be used to provide a simple "slide show" of rotating images on our home page, and, in conjunction with CSS styles, to create a dropdown menu of options for navigating around our website that appears on every page of the website.

In the case of the rotating images, you saw how the value of the `onload` event attribute of the `body` element of a page could be set to a JavaScript function that is invoked when the page is fully loaded. In our case, this arrangement caused a sequence of images to be displayed in a rotational order that repeated until the page was closed.

In the case of the dropdown menus, you saw how the values of the `onmouseover` and `onmouseout` event attributes of an element can be set to JavaScript functions that are triggered to execute and either show or hide menu options, depending on whether the user's mouse is hovering over an element or has moved away from it. The new CSS concepts we found useful in this context were the `display`, `visibility`, and `position` properties.

In the course of these discussions we also learned more about some basic JavaScript features, including the `Date` and `Array` data types, the `switch`-statement, the `for`-loop, and the `set-Interval()` function.

We also updated our BMI and feedback forms with some enhancements. The results from submitting these forms were displayed in a new web page, thus eliminating the `alert()` popups. Much of the JavaScript validation was replaced by use of the new HTML5 `pattern` attribute, and we also made good use of the `required` and `readonly` attributes for `input` elements, as well as the `onchange` event attribute. Finally, we used the built-in JavaScript `window.open()` method to display to the user the reports from our BMI and feedback forms in a new browser window.

```
1   <!-- menus.html -->
2       <nav onmouseout="hide()">
3         <ul class="Links">
4           <li><a href="index.html" onmouseover="show('m1')">Home</a></li>
5           <li><a href="pages/estore.html"
6                   onmouseover="show('m2')">e-store</a></li>
7           <li>
8             <span onmouseover="show('m3')">Products+Services</span>
9             <div id="m3" onmouseover="show('m3')">
10            <a href="pages/catalog.html">Product Catalog</a>
11            <a href="pages/featured.html">Featured Products</a>
12            <a href="pages/services.html">Services</a>
13            <a href="pages/suppliers.html">Suppliers</a>
14            </div>
15          </li>
16          <li>
17            <span onmouseover="show('m4')">Your Health</span>
18            <div id="m4" onmouseover="show('m4')">
19            <a href="pages/bmiForm.html">Compute Your BMI</a>
20            <a href="pages/tools.html">Tools+Resources</a>
21            <a href="pages/expert.html">Ask An Expert</a>
22            <a href="pages/links.html">Useful Links</a>
23            </div>
24          </li>
25          <li>
26            <span onmouseover="show('m5')">About Us</span>
27            <div id="m5" onmouseover="show('m5')">
28            <a href="pages/about.html">Nature's Source</a>
29            <a href="pages/vision.html">Vision+Mission</a>
30            <a href="pages/employment.html">Job Opportunities</a>
31            <a href="pages/news.html">News Archive</a>
32            </div>
33          </li>
34          <li>
35            <span onmouseover="show('m6')">Contact Us</span>
36            <div id="m6" onmouseover="show('m6')">
37            <a href="pages/locations.html">Locations</a>
38            <a href="pages/feedbackForm.html">Feedback Form</a>
39            </div>
40          </li>
41          <li><a href="pages/sitemap.html" onmouseover="show('m7')">Site
42          Map</a></li>
43        </ul>
44      </nav>
```

FIGURE 7.17 `ch07/nature2/common/menus.html`
The markup for the menus in the `nature2` version of our website. Note the difference in the markup for the main menu bar items that have a dropdown submenu (lines 8, 17, 26, 35), as compared to the markup for those same menu items in the `nature1` version of the same file, shown in Figure 7.4.

Quick Questions to Test Your Basic Knowledge

1. We have not actually used the term *dynamic HTML document*, but what do you suppose we would mean by that term if we did use it?
2. What kinds of values can be used for the case labels in a JavaScript `switch`-statement?
3. What is the name of the element attribute whose value you would set if you wanted something to happen when a web page is fully loaded, and what kind of value would it have?
4. What is the name of the element attribute whose value you would set if you wanted something to happen when the user moved the mouse over that element?
5. What is the name of the element attribute whose value you would set if you wanted something to happen when the user moved the mouse away from that element?
6. How do you put text in a textbox (instructions for the user, let's say) but prevent the user from editing that text?
7. How do you prevent a user from submitting a form with an empty textbox if you really wanted the user to put something into that textbox?
8. What would you do if you wanted to make sure that, before submitting a form, the user actually entered a six-digit integer into a particular textbox?
9. What event attribute would you use if you wanted to notify the user of something the moment that use clicked on a checkbox?
10. What is the usual symbol used as the value of the `href` attribute of an a element if you do not want the link to go anywhere?
11. Why did we change the markup on some of the menu options (but not others) for our main menu bar in going from the `nature1` website to the `nature2` website in this chapter?
12. What JavaScript function would you use if you wanted a function you had written to be called every five seconds and what would that function call look like if your function was called `doIt()`?
13. What is the JavaScript statement that would create an array called a of size 10?
14. Our "dropdown menus" don't actually "drop down". Explain this statement.
15. What is the output of the following JavaScript code segment? And note that the answer depends on the day you are answering this question!

```
var today = new Date();
document.write(today.getDay());
```

Short Exercises to Improve Your Basic Understanding

1. The `switch`-statement that we used in our `rotate.js` script is certainly not the only way, and you could argue that it's not even the best way, to write this particular `switch`-statement. It does the job, but instead of using the `default:` option to handle the weekday cases, it might make the code a little clearer if we had one group of explicit cases to handle the weekend days (which we do), another group of explicit cases to handle the weekday cases (which we don't), and use the `default:` option for something that is extremely unlikely to happen, such as displaying for the user a message via the `alert()` function to inform the user that something has gone wrong. Revise `rotate.js` to implement the `switch`-statement in this way, and test to make sure the revision works.

2. Revise the script in `rotate.js` so that the images are shown in random order, rather than always repeating the sequence in the same order, and test to make sure the revision works.

3. The generic `switch`-statement discussed in this chapter is equivalent to the following generic nested `if`-statement:

```
if (expression == value_1)
{
    statements;
}
else if (expression == value_2)
{
    statements;
}
...
else if (expression == value_n)
{
    statements;
}
else
{
    statements;
}
```

Revise `rotate.js` by replacing its `switch`-statement with an equivalent nested `if`-statement of the above form, and test it to make sure it works.

4. The `switch`-statement in `rotate.js` can also be replaced by the following `if..else`-statement:

```
if (today.getDay()==0 || today.getDay()==5 ||
    today.getDay()==6)
  prefix += "outdoor";
else
  prefix += "indoor";
```

Revise `rotate.js` by replacing its `switch`-statement with an equivalent `if..else`-statement of the above form, and test it to make sure it works. This exercise and the previous one should be a reminder that even for very short and simple code, it's often worthwhile to stop and think about the "best" way to write the code, rather than going with the first thing that comes to mind.

5. JavaScript provides two other loops in addition to the `for`-loop: the `while`-loop and the `do..while`-loop. Though you can use whatever loop you like in most situations, the kind of loop you actually choose in a particular situation will often depend on the logic, since some loops can be more "readable" than others in certain cases.

    Here, in generic form, are those other two loops:

```
initialization;              initialization;
while (condition)            do
{                            {
    statements;                  statements;
}                            }
                             while (condition);
```

The major difference between these two loops is that the body of the `do..while`-loop is guaranteed to execute at least once, since the `condition` is not checked until that has happened. The body of the `while`-loop, on the other hand, may never execute, since the check of the `condition` is made at the beginning.

    In order for the body of either loop to execute properly, the `initialization` must be done correctly, and for either loop to terminate properly the body must contain an action that eventually causes `condition` to become false. In the case of the `for`-loop, the `initialization` and `update` are handled by the loop structure itself. In the other two loops, it is the programmer's responsibility to ensure that proper initialization and updating are performed.

    As a simple example, here is a version of each of the three loops that adds the positive integers from 1 to 10, inclusive:

```
var sum = 0;            var sum = 0;            var sum = 0;
var i;                  var i = 0;              var i = 0;
for (i=1; i<=10; i++)   while (i < 10)          do
```

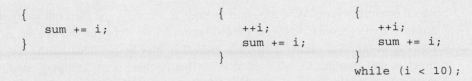

```
{                              {                              {
    sum += i;                      ++i;                           ++i;
}                                  sum += i;                      sum += i;
                               }                              }
                                                              while (i < 10);
```

We used the `for`-loop in this chapter to build our array of images. A `for`-loop was the appropriate choice in that case, because we knew exactly how many times we wanted the loop to execute (the number of images we had), and this is the kind of scenario for which the `for`-loop is well suited. However, either of the other loops could have been used.

Revise `rotate.js`, first of all, to replace the `for`-loop with an equivalent `while`-loop to build the image array. Then revise it a second time to use an equivalent `do..while`-loop. In each case, test to make sure everything still works.

6. In our `rotate.js` script we defined two separate functions, `rotate()` and `start-Rotation()`, to handle the slide show. We can also perform our image rotation with a single `rotate()` function if we implement it somewhat differently, making it a `recursive function`, which is a somewhat advanced concept. Here is that implementation:

```
var i = 0;
function rotate()
{
    document.getElementById('placeholder').src=imageArray[i];
    i++;
    if(i >= imageArray.length) i = 0;
    setTimeout('rotate()', 2000);
}
```

In this version of the image rotation, we begin by initializing the variable `i` to 0. This variable will again keep track of the subscript (or index) of the array element that provides the filename of the current image. This time around the function `rotate()` itself must be the value of the `onload` attribute of the `body` element in `index.html` and performs the image rotation starting when the page has loaded by proceeding as follows.

As before, we access the `img` tag as a DOM element by using the `id('placeholder')` of the tag, and set its `src` attribute to the filename given by `imageArray[i]`. This makes sure that the image given by `imageArray[i]` is displayed in the web page.

We then increment `i` to prepare for loading the next image in the sequence when the time comes and, as before, we have to make sure the value "wraps to 0" when the time comes. Finally, we have to answer this question: When *does* the time come to load the next image? And this is where the major departure from the way we previously did things takes place. The last statement in our `rotate()` function is

```
setTimeout('rotate()', 2000);
```

which essentially says, "Wait 2000 milliseconds (2 seconds) and then call yourself again." Students coming from C, C++, or Java will immediately recognize this as a *recursive function* call (a function calling itself), but even they may be bothered by the fact that the function will continue to call itself forever. That is, there is no "stopping condition" for the function. But this is a case where that is not a major concern, since we do in fact want the images to keep rotating for as long as the user is viewing the page, which may be a long time. If the user displays our page and then goes home for the night, the images should still be rotating the next morning. Of course, if the user closes our page, or browses to another site, the function (and everything else associated with our page) goes away.

So, revise the rotating-image feature of the website to incorporate this recursive version of the rotation function.

7. One of the files our markup file `nature1/index.html` links to is the CSS style file `nature1/css/desktop.css`, and the part of this file dedicated to styling our menus is seen in Figure 7.6.

Make the following changes and perform the suggested actions to observe the changes in the display of `nature1/index.html` when you do so. This will give you a good sense of which style rules are affecting which parts of the display.

a. Comment out the "mini-reset" style rule at the beginning of `desktop.css` (lines 7–10, not shown in Figure 7.6) that sets all margins and padding to 0, and then reload to see what effect, if any, this has had.

b. There are a number of different colors, specified with hex values, in the CSS shown in Figure 7.6. Change each of these values, one at a time, to red. First predict what the effect will be, then reload the page to check your prediction.

c. Comment out the `float: left` style in line 43.

d. Comment out the `list-style: none` style in line 49.

e. Comment out the `display: block` style in line 59.

f. Comment out the `width: 127px` style in line 44.

g. Comment out the `visibility: hidden` style in line 76.

h. Comment out the `width: 124px` style in line 81.

Exercises on the Parallel Project

The website for your business has now developed to the point where it has information about the business itself and some more detailed information about its products and/or services, as well as some data-validated forms for placing an order and for gathering feedback from your users. Now it's time to improve the "look and feel" of your site by adding some additional "rotating" images and some dropdown menus. Once again, of course, this "parallels" the look and feel of our own **Nature's Source** sample website.

1. Find some more images relating to your business that you can legally copy and use on your website (at least six, let's say) and replicate for your site the rotating image feature illustrated by our own example when you display the home page of either the `nature1` website or the `nature2` website of this chapter.

2. Create a version of your website that "parallels" our `nature1` example of this chapter. That is, your site must have only a home page, but it must also have the rotating images and dropdown menus analogous to what you see in Figure 7.1 of the text. Or, if you wish, give it a fancier dropdown menu. The one in the text can be regarded as a "minimal" dropdown menu whose functionality you should be able to replicate using the text code as a model and making appropriate changes for your particular situation. On the other hand, there are lots of dropdown menu options "out there" on the Internet, and you may find one more to your liking. If you do, and it's not illegal to do so, go ahead and use it instead. The menu options and suboptions will, of course, depend on the nature of your business, but most of them should be the same or similar to those in the text example. In this part of these exercises, none of the menu options on either the main menu bar or the dropdown submenus should be active. In other words, your resulting website should "parallel" our `nature1` example, in which none of the links are active.

3. Make a copy of your website from exercise 2 above, and revise it so that all menu links become active and the same header with menu bar and associated dropdown menu options appear on all pages. The rotating images are to appear only on your home page, since you don't want to distract the user from the serious business of buying your products once that user has started to browse your site. The appearance of the business logo and menu bar on all pages helps to give your visitors a feeling of consistency in the "look and feel" of your site as they browse from page to page. In any case, your result this time should "parallel" our `nature2` example, in which all of the links are active on all pages.

4. A final (optional, unless your instructor requires it or some variation of it) exercise: In this version of your website, you may also wish to implement some of the form enhancements we discussed in section 7.4, and you may do that as well.

5. And, of course, everything should validate as HTML5 and CSS3.

What Else You May Want or Need to Know

1. A significant difference between arrays in JavaScript and arrays in more "conventional" languages such as C, C++, and Java is that in JavaScript the size of an array is not fixed once the array is created. You can change the size of an array at any time. You can even assign a variable to an array location with a subscript that is beyond the current last

element of the array. For example, if we only have a six-element array of images to begin with, we could nevertheless say

```
imageArray[20] = "pawan.jpg";
```

and the length of the array will be extended to 21 (remember that indices start at 0). That you can do this is not necessarily a good thing, and there are good reasons why those other languages won't let you do it, even though you may find it convenient from time to time.

2. You should be aware, particularly if you plan to do any extensive JavaScript programming for your website, that there are many sources for JavaScript code on the web, and it is always a good idea to avoid "reinventing the wheel" if at all possible. First of all, if you see a site that exhibits some behavior that you admire and would like to use on your own site, that behavior may be produced by JavaScript and the code may (or may not, remember) be freely available for use by others. In the (reasonably frequent) cases where the code is available, often all the writer will ask is that acknowledgment be placed in the code wherever you use it. Also, there are many JavaScript code libraries (or "frameworks") that are also freely available and contain a great deal of ready-made functionality that you may find useful when designing your site. Many of these were listed in the **References** section of the previous chapter.

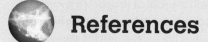

References

1. The **W3Schools** JavaScript tutorial start page is located here:

    ```
    http://www.w3schools.com/js/default.asp
    ```

2. The **W3Schools** JavaScript reference site, which contains lots of examples on both JavaScript itself and the HTML DOM, can be found here:

    ```
    http://www.w3schools.com/jsref/default.asp
    ```

3. In particular, for further information on the JavaScript `Date` and `Array` data types, see:

    ```
    http://www.w3schools.com/jsref/jsref_obj_date.asp
    http://www.w3schools.com/jsref/jsref_obj_array.asp
    ```

4. Here is another site you may find helpful when investigating JavaScript features:

    ```
    http://www.javascriptkit.com/jsref/
    ```

5. The following page contains a table showing many JavaScript frameworks and their features:

    ```
    http://en.wikipedia.org/wiki/Comparison_of_JavaScript_framework
    ```

CHAPTER **EIGHT**

PHP for Server-Side Preprocessing

CHAPTER CONTENTS

Overview and Objectives

The client-side JavaScript programming that we looked at in the previous two chapters is limited to computing that can be safely executed within the confines of the browser. These limitations aside, client-side computing has certain advantages. For example, it limits the amount of data transfer by taking care of simple computing requests on the client computer, instead of transmitting those computational requests to the server, having the server perform them, and then sending the results back to the client. This relieves the server from servicing a large number of requests for minor computational tasks and cuts down on bandwidth consumption as well. Equally important is that client-side computing is very useful for filtering out potentially malicious data, or simply malformed data, on its way to the server.

However, client-side computing using JavaScript is not up to the task of performing much of the computation that is necessary on the contemporary web. Our websites need to serve dynamically created web pages based on the data from users' input devices, files on both the client and server computers, and information contained in databases stored on servers. In general, for the sake of efficiency, it is better to have calculations on data performed wherever the data lives, so clearly you will want to do some serious computing on the server side as well.

Four of the most popular technologies for providing server-side computing are Active Server Pages (ASP), Java Server Pages (JSP), Perl, and Personal Home Page (PHP). The use of ASP requires a relatively intensive study of languages such as Visual Basic, C#, or C++ on Microsoft's .NET platform. A study of JSP requires a reasonable prior exposure to the Java programming language. On the other hand, Perl and PHP are both interpreted scripting languages that, by comparison, are much easier to learn, especially for those with no prior programming experience. These languages make it possible for you to get onto the server side of the web programming highway relatively quickly.

Of the two, PHP is the easier to learn and use, and is currently the one in wider use. So, it is our language of choice, and in this chapter we will discuss the following:

▶ A brief history of the PHP language, and why it is a reasonable choice for our server-side processing (or "preprocessing", as we often call it, since the PHP processing for a given page takes place *before* that page is sent to the browser for display)

▶ How PHP fits into the overall web picture as a scripting language, with the help of a simple initial example that introduces one of PHP's many useful built-in functions, the `date()` function

▶ The features of the PHP language required for our purposes, which include comments, variables, and *superglobals* (a special kind of variable), numerical and string data types, expressions and operators, arrays, built-in and programmer-defined functions, file output, and using PHP to accomplish server-side inclusion of files

▶ PHP script development and testing

▶ How to incorporate in our page header a PHP-generated welcome message that uses Asynchronous JavaScript And XML (AJAX) to retrieve the current date and time from the server and update it every sixty seconds

▶ How to implement the server-side functionality of our feedback form by first uploading the user's input data to the server and then performing the following actions on the server side:

    a. sending the user's feedback to the business via email

    b. sending a copy of the email to the client

    c. confirming the submission to the client via a browser display, and

    d. storing a copy of the feedback on the server

▶ How to implement an alternate version of our BMI calculator by shifting the computation from client-side JavaScript to server-side PHP, allowing us to email the user a permanent record, if requested, in addition to providing the immediate browser display of the result

▶ How to send HyperText Markup Language (HTML)-encoded email, as we do when delivering our BMI report

▶ The GET and POST values of the method attribute of the form element, and how they determine the way in which data is passed to a PHP script on the server, either from a form or via a Uniform Resource Locator (URL)

The updated version of our **Nature's Source** website for this chapter will require several new scripts written in PHP, which we will, of course, place in our ch08/nature/scripts subdirectory, alongside the JavaScript scripts we have already introduced. We shall discuss each script in detail as we encounter it, and there will be some changes in the JavaScript because, for example, PHP will take over the BMI calculation. And, of course, we will also have to (finally) provide an action attribute in the opening form tags that now appear in bmiForm.php and feedbackForm.php so that the data from these forms is now processed by the new PHP scripts. Along with the form's action attribute we will also need a method attribute to specify how the data will be transferred.

To get the welcome message that appears in the banner at the top of our website's pages to the right of our logo, we will replace our logo.html "include file" with a new include file called banner.php, which is comprised of the former content of logo.html plus some additional markup and code to handle this new welcome message.

Since SSI (as we have used it in previous chapters) and PHP do not always play well together without reconfiguring the server, which is beyond the scope of our discussion, we now use a different (and simpler) approach to get our server-side includes. The `include()` function of PHP can be used to include into our `index.php` (formerly `index.html`) our new `banner.php`, as well as the files `menus.html` and `footer_content.html`, which are unchanged except for the `href` values that now contain links to files with a `.php` extension. Analogous changes need to be made to all of the other files to which we link from our menu options, and to indicate this change we alter the extensions of these files from `.html` to `.php` to reflect the fact that each one now contains some PHP code that needs to be "preprocessed" on the server.

Finally, we need a few modifications to our Cascading Style Sheets (CSS) to take care of our new Welcome message, but this does not involve anything we have not seen before. Check the styles at the end of `desktop.css` and `tablet.css` to see what we've added.

8.1 Some PHP History

In the early days of the web, prior to the appearance of PHP, Perl was by far the most popular language of choice for server-side web programming. In recent years, PHP has gained immense popularity and has become a versatile and robust language with more than enough capability to meet the needs of any aspiring web developer.

The current version of PHP has its roots in the C and Perl programming languages, and many of its features reflect those origins. Many of its most commonly used features are also similar to those of JavaScript, which we have already seen, so our discussion of PHP will focus on pointing out those similarities and highlighting the differences.

Unlike Perl, which is a "standalone" programming language that can be used to write virtually any kind of software, PHP is designed specifically for web page development. In this chapter and the next two, you will gain enough experience with PHP and the MySQL database management system to create a prototype e-commerce system.

The acronym PHP originally stood for *PHP*, and the set of Perl scripts that comprised its original implementation was written by Rasmus Lerdorf in 1995. He used his PHP tools for tracking accesses to his online résumé. A revised version of the original product was called PHP/FI, where FI stood for "Forms Interpreter".

Lerdorf posted his work on the web, where it very quickly caught the attention of other developers, and the system soon took on a life of its own. To support increased functionality, Rasmus then wrote a much larger C implementation. This major revision added abilities to communicate with databases, which led to even more interest in the software, and it eventually expanded to the point where it was no longer possible for a single individual to maintain it. Nowadays there is a worldwide community involved in PHP maintenance and development, and you can follow their progress on, and freely download the latest updates for many different platforms from, the home website for PHP, located at `http://php.net/`.

TABLE 8.1 A brief summary of PHP history (with many intermediate versions and details missing).

Date	Version	Notes
1994	Original (private)	Rasmus Lerdorf writes first incarnation of PHP for personal use and calls it "Personal Home Page Tools"
June 1995	1.0	Lerdorf releases source code to the public
November 1997	2.0	Now called PHP/FI2 (FI = "Forms Interpreter"), and contained many features that are still part of PHP
June 1998	3.0	Development has moved from one person to a team
May 2000	4.0	Based on a new parser called the Zend Engine
July 2004	5.0	Based on the new Zend Engine II
August 2014	5.6	Many improvements over 5.0
N/A	6.0	This version, which was supposed to incorporate core Unicode support, was eventually abandoned
November 2015	7.0	Based on Zend Engine III, with many more improvements

See the end-of-chapter **References** for further information, and **TABLE 8.1** for more details of the PHP language development timeline.

Web developers owe a debt of gratitude to Rasmus Lerdorf for making the source code of PHP public, since the resulting vibrant online PHP community has produced many significant improvements in the language itself, as well as facilities that permit PHP to communicate with a wide variety of database implementations. The use of PHP has far outgrown its original motivation of creating PHPs. In fact, that original name has receded into obscurity, since more users now prefer to use the recursive name *PHP: Hypertext Preprocessor*. This definition describes the role of PHP more accurately, since PHP scripts are used for "preprocessing" a web page (on the server) to dynamically create a hypertext document (before it is sent to the browser). HTML markup constructed via PHP, using data from server-side databases that is also obtained via PHP, allows programmers to develop very dynamic and timely web pages.

8.2 PHP as a Server-Side Scripting Language

All current major web server software packages are capable of providing access to a PHP interpreter on the server side of the client-server architecture. This does not mean that you, as a web developer, automatically have access to PHP, even if you have an Internet Service Provider. PHP has to be activated and configured on the server, so you need to check with your system administrator to make sure that PHP is enabled for your web server.

A web server may spawn a separate operating system "process" to handle PHP requests, or the server software itself may have an "internal" module that deals with PHP scripts. As long as PHP is available, which of these options is actually in use will generally be "transparent to the user".

Because of its PHP requirement, this chapter's version of our **Nature's Source** website (found in ch08/nature) cannot be properly viewed unless it's being "served" by a PHP-aware web server. If you wish to test your PHP pages "locally", before uploading them to your server (always a good idea, of course), you can install a web server such as Apache, as well as PHP, on your personal computer, and place our files, with any modifications you have made to them, in a location accessible to that server. See the end-of-chapter **References** for further information. And, of course, you can always view and interact with, but not modify, the authors' installation at http://cs.smu.ca/webbook2e/ch08.

A typical PHP web page will contain the usual HTML markup you have seen, but this markup will also be interspersed with instructions in the PHP programming language. A PHP-enabled web server will run all the embedded PHP instructions in a web page document as part of its "preprocessing" of that web page. These PHP instructions will create additional HTML markup. All of the HTML—that generated by PHP, plus whatever other markup was present on the web page—is then sent to the client. Note immediately this major difference between JavaScript and PHP: JavaScript code is downloaded from the server with the HTML and run in the browser, while PHP code is run on the server and it is the output of this run, along with whatever other HTML the document contains, that is downloaded to the browser. When PHP is processing a document, at any given time it may be in one of two modes:

a. *read mode* (also called *copy mode*), if it is just reading HTML markup from the document, or

b. *interpret mode* (also called *execute mode* or *translate mode*) if it is interpreting an embedded PHP script to generate additional markup for inclusion into the page

This means that the client computer is not aware of any of the embedded PHP instructions, since they have "disappeared" by the time the client receives the page from the server. It also means that the use of PHP does not require any special plug-ins on the client side to work with PHP script output. Finally, all the PHP programming code is "hidden" from the client, which helps with the security issue since that code may contain additional information about data storage on the server, or other sensitive information.

8.3 PHP Script Structure and General Syntax: A Simple First Example

Before we start incorporating PHP into the pages of our **Nature's Source** website, it will be useful to examine a simple example in isolation. Moreover, we shall later incorporate the output of code similar to what we see in this example into our web pages. The example in question is found in the

```
1   <!DOCTYPE html>
2   <!-- welcome.php -->
3   <html lang="en">
4     <head>
5       <meta charset="utf-8">
6       <title>Welcome Message with Date and Time</title>
7     </head>
8     <body>
9       <h2>Welcome!</h2>
10      <?php
11      echo "<h3>It's ".date("l, F jS").".".<br>\r\n";
12      echo "The time is ".date("g:ia").".</h3>\r\n";
13      echo "<h3>Or at least that's our time, though ".
14          "it may not be yours.</h3>\r\n";
15      ?>
16      <h6>Pedagogical Note:<br>This page is static,
17      and therefore will not change once displayed.</h6>
18    </body>
19  </html>
```

FIGURE 8.1 ch08/welcome.php
A very short PHP script embedded in the body of an HTML document. The script places a Welcome message, with the current date and time, into the markup, on the server, before the page is sent to the browser for display.

file ch08/welcome.php, which is shown in **FIGURE 8.1**. The browser display of this file can be seen in **FIGURE 8.2**.

From Figure 8.1 we see that the content of welcome.php is a normal HTML document, except for the content of the body element, which contains some "ordinary" HTML (an h2 element in line 9 and an h6 element in lines 16–17), as well as a short PHP script in lines 10–15. This is typical, but in a more complicated example there could also be JavaScript code and several additional PHP scripts embedded in the document body. Note that any HTML document file that contains PHP code should be given a .php extension, as we have done in this case. This is a helpful visual aid to programmers and an essential indicator to the server that the file must be processed by the PHP interpreter before the page is sent to the browser.

The first thing to note about the PHP script in Figure 8.1 is that the programming language statements in a PHP script are enclosed within a <?php delimiter at the beginning (line 10) and a ?> delimiter at the end (line 15). For readability these are generally placed on lines by themselves, though this is not necessary. This particular script contains just three PHP echo statements. Note that PHP statements, like JavaScript statements, are terminated by a semicolon. The purpose of an echo statement is to "echo" (or print) some output that will become part of the final HTML document that will be generated by the PHP processor and sent to the browser from the server.

In this case, the output in question consists of two HTML h3 elements. The first h3 element, which is output by the first two PHP echo statements, is the more interesting of the two.

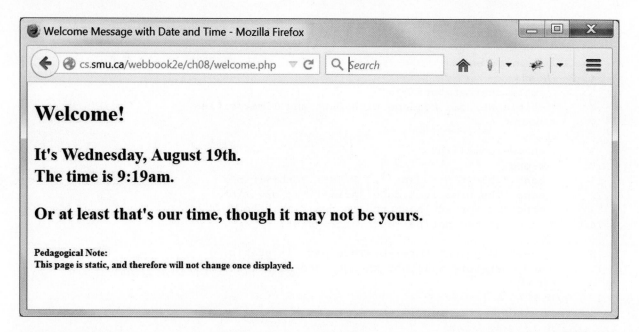

FIGURE 8.2 `graphics/ch08/displayWelcomePhp.jpg`
A Firefox browser display of the final markup after the PHP script embedded in ch08/welcome.php has run.

The content of this h3 element includes some ordinary text, an instance of the HTML `<br>` element, the output from two calls to the PHP built-in `date()` function, and two occurrences of the character combination `\r\n`.

It is important to note here that the period (.) is the PHP *concatenation operator* for strings (the operator that combines two strings into a single string). This may take some getting used to, since many other languages, including JavaScript, use the + operator for this purpose. Study the code in Figure 8.1, compare it carefully with the corresponding display in Figure 8.2, and make sure you identify which periods in the code are concatenation operators used to join PHP strings (text enclosed in double quotes, as usual, and/or `date()` function return values, which are also strings), and which periods are simply part of the text output to be displayed.

The first call to the `date()` function returns the current day of the week and date, and its string input parameter indicates how we want this information formatted. Similarly, the second call to `date()` returns the time of day. We'll examine the details of these function calls in a moment. Once we get the date and time information in our requested formats, and these strings have been combined with the rest of the HTML markup, the final result becomes the body of the HTML document sent to the browser.

One other thing: The two-character combination `\r\n` as we have used it here is not really necessary, since the output from the PHP echo statements in this case is HTML markup and, as we know, end-of-line markers other than `<br>` are generally ignored by HTML. So these characters may sometimes be stripped out along the way, or simply ignored at the destination. On the other hand, if the output is going to a destination that is not HTML (just ordinary text output, for example), and other end-of-line markers are in fact needed, then including this character combination should do the job of ensuring that proper line breaks will occur at the necessary places on most any platform where the message might have to be displayed. Some platforms may require both \r and \n, while others may require just one of the two. On any platform requiring only one of the two, the other of the two should, and with any luck will, simply be ignored.

8.3.1 The PHP `date()` Function

Since we have found it so useful, and you may too, let's take a moment to discuss the built-in PHP `date()` function as we have used it. It is, of course, just one of many built-in functions provided by PHP, but a very handy one. The `date()` function can be quite complex, and you may wish to pursue further details about it and other frequently used, predefined PHP functions that we will discuss later.

In the meantime, let's see what our calls to the `date()` function actually do. The function expects as input a string that specifies the format of the output string (i.e., the returned string value, since this is a value-returning function). The format string that we supplied in our first call to the function was `"l, F jS"`. Unfortunately, the meaning of these symbols is not very mnemonic, and thus not easy to "guess", so let's explain what they mean.

First, the lowercase letter `'l'` (*not* the digit 1, which is the first potential point of confusion) says that we want a full textual representation of the day of the week, such as Sunday, Monday, and so on. The next two characters (the comma and the blank space) are to be interpreted literally to give us a comma and a blank space following the day of the week in the output. Then the character F says we also want the full textual representation of the month, such as January, February, and so on. This is again followed by a literal blank space. Finally, the two-character sequence j S gives us the numerical date with an appropriate suffix appended, such as 1st, 2nd, 3rd, or 4th. The character j gives us the date, while the S character gives us the appropriate suffix (st, nd, rd, or th). As we said, somewhat demonic, rather than mnemonic.

Our second call to `date()` has as its input parameter the string `"g:ia"`, which in fact gives us a time rather than a date, and things are no better here on the mnemonic front. The g gives us the current hour using a 12-hour format, *without* leading zeros, the i gives us the minutes in the current hour, *with* a leading zero if required, and the a appends a lowercase am or pm, as appropriate. The colon (:) is a literal value used to separate hours and minutes in the output.

See the end-of-chapter **References** for a link to a description of all the many ways you can describe the kind of output you want from the PHP `date()` function.

8.3.2 Generating and Displaying the Output from `welcome.php`

If you view the web page generated by `welcome.php` now, you should see something like what is shown in Figure 8.2. But, if you then choose the "view source" option of your browser, you will *not* see any PHP code. This should not be surprising, given what we have said earlier. Only the

HTML markup resulting from the execution of the PHP code will appear as the source of the web page. As mentioned before, this ensures that clients cannot access the PHP code, which may reveal confidential information about the data stored on the server.

8.4 Why We Need AJAX and How We Use It: Two More Examples

In this section we introduce the basic ideas and functionality of AJAX, and show how a very simple application of these ideas can be very useful on our **Nature's Source** website.

8.4.1 What Is AJAX?

Under "normal" circumstances, when a browser sends information to a server and the server responds by sending a page back to the browser, the entire page must be redisplayed in the browser, even if only a small portion of that page has actually changed. This can cause browser response to slow down and generally appear to be much less satisfying to a user than a typical desktop application. A technology called *AJAX* can be used to help alleviate this situation. Java-Script (in conjunction with XML, which we will introduce briefly in a later chapter) can be used to communicate with the server and update only the changed part of a web page, thus speeding up the page-refresh process.

Note that AJAX is not a distinct new technology, but simply a way of combining a number of previously existing technologies. For the insight that spawned AJAX we are indebted (as we have pointed out in Chapter 6) to Jesse James Garrett, who also gave us the acronym.

8.4.2 A Problem We Need to Solve: A "Page Refresh" Example

We are now going to use the web page shown in **FIGURE 8.3** (HTML markup and PHP script) and **FIGURE 8.4** (corresponding browser display) to illustrate several things, only one of which is our need for AJAX.

Let's begin by explaining how this page works. If you load the page into a browser, all the text will be black, but if you wait for a minute all the text will change color. At the end of each subsequent minute, one of four random colors is chosen and the text appears in that color. This is because the entire page is being "refreshed" every 60 seconds, which is accomplished by the `meta` element in line 17, whose two attributes (`http-equiv="refresh"` and `content="60"`) should be self-explanatory. You can arrange for any web page to be refreshed with whatever frequency you desire with a similar `meta` element and the value of its `content` attribute set to the required time interval in seconds.

The "problem" with this is that the entire page is refreshed. It's not a problem if that's what we want, but if only a small part of a page (the date and time, for example) needs to be updated

```php
1   <?php
2   /*welcome_refresh.php
3   This page displays a welcome message and the complete page
4   is refreshed every seconds. Initially the text color is
5   black, but each refresh uses a randomly chosen text color
6   from red, green, blue or maroon. Because the color choice
7   is random, the same color may repeat after a refresh.
8   */
9   session_start();
10  if (!isset($_SESSION['pageRefreshCount']))
11      $_SESSION['pageRefreshCount']=0;
12  ?>
13  <!DOCTYPE html>
14  <html lang="en">
15    <head>
16      <meta charset="utf-8">
17      <meta http-equiv="refresh" content="60">
18      <title>Welcome Message with Date, Time, and 60-Second Refresh</title>
19    </head>
20    <body id="welcome">
21      <h2>Welcome!</h2>
22      <?php
23      $greetingColor = "black";
24      if ($_SESSION['pageRefreshCount'] != 0)
25      {
26          $colorPicker = rand(1, 100);
27          if ($colorPicker > 75)
28              $greetingColor = "red";
29          else if ($colorPicker > 50)
30              $greetingColor = "green";
31          else if ($colorPicker > 25)
32              $greetingColor = "blue";
33          else
34              $greetingColor = "maroon";
35      }
36      $_SESSION['pageRefreshCount'] = $_SESSION['pageRefreshCount'] + 1;
37      echo "<p hidden id='colorChoice'>$greetingColor</p>";
38      echo "<h3>It's ".date("l, F jS").".<br>\r\n";
39      echo "The time is ".date("g:ia").".</h3>\r\n";
40      echo "<h3>Or at least that's our time, ".
41      "though it may not be yours.</h3>\r\n";
42      ?>
```

FIGURE 8.3 `ch08/welcome_refresh.php`
A second version of our Welcome message page, in which the entire page is "refreshed" every 60 seconds. The time is updated, as is the date (if necessary), and a randomly chosen text color is applied to the entire page. The $_SESSION array is used to monitor the refresh count.

```
43      <h6>Pedagogical Note:<br>This page starts off using the
44      default text color of black to display all text. Then
45      the page refreshes<br>every seconds, and each time it
46      does, everything (including this note) is displayed in
47      one of four<br>randomly chosen alternate colors (red, green,
48      blue or maroon) and the date and time are updated.</h6>
49      <script>
50      var hiddenParagraph = document.getElementById("colorChoice")
51      document.getElementById("welcome").style.color=
52          hiddenParagraph.innerHTML;
53      </script>
54    </body>
55  </html>
```

FIGURE 8.3 `ch08/welcome_refresh.php` *(continued)*

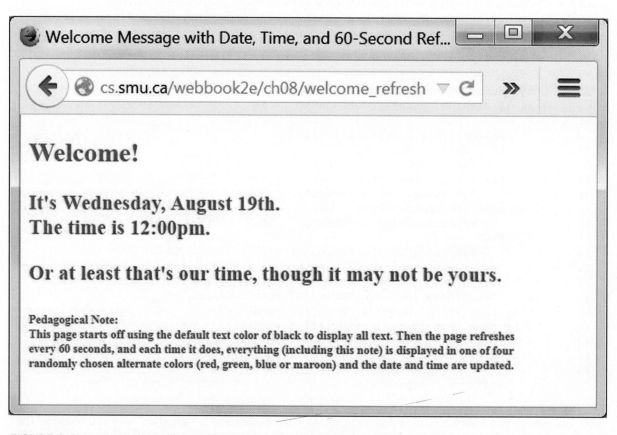

FIGURE 8.4 `graphics/ch08/displayWelcome_RefreshPhp.jpg`
A Firefox browser display of ch08/welcome_refresh.php after at least one refresh has taken place and the color green has been applied to all text on the page.

periodically, then refreshing the entire page represents a lot of wasted effort (and bandwidth). Sometimes the "problem" is just this wasted effort and bandwidth, but a complete page refresh can be a problem in other ways as well. For example, if a user is filling out a form and suddenly the page refreshes, the user may lose some or all of the data entered into the form and will need to start over and try to enter all the form data and submit it before the next refresh. This is likely to generate unhappy users, something no e-commerce website should have.

This is the problem that AJAX solves for us, as we will see in the next example. However, before we leave this example we want to discuss some other aspects of PHP that it illustrates for us.

PHP Sessions and the PHP $_SESSION Superglobal Array Variable

Web pages have no memory. That is, if you load a web page into your browser and then load a second page by clicking on a link in the first page (or by just entering a new URL in your browser's address box), the new page has no idea how you got there or where you came from. This is the default situation, which is sometimes expressed more formally by saying that the HyperText Transfer Protocol (HTTP) protocol is a *stateless protocol*. This default behavior can be quite limiting, since it does not allow information to be passed from one page to another as a user browses around a given website. However, e-commerce websites in particular, among many other kinds of websites, do need to keep track of what users are doing as they move from page to page while viewing, choosing, and buying products, for example.

This is another problem for which we need a solution, and in our case the solution is a PHP *session*. When a PHP session is created, a PHP *superglobal variable* named $_SESSION is also created on the server. This variable is a PHP array variable that can be used by the current and subsequent PHP scripts during the same "session" to store and retrieve information. In other words, this $_SESSION array variable provides a mechanism that allows web pages to communicate as the PHP scripts on those pages execute. It can also give a page "memory", since if a page that was previously loaded is loaded again, it can "recall" (i.e., refer to) information that was previously stored in the $_SESSION array, either by itself or some other page.

In line 9 of Figure 8.3 the call to the session_start() function sets up a PHP session and the $_SESSION array becomes available. If there is already a session in progress, this call means that this current script simply "joins the session" and has full access to the already-existing information in the $_SESSION variable.

Note that the array variable name $_SESSION begins with a $. This is true of all PHP variables and is part of the Perl legacy. For another example, the "ordinary" (non-array) variable $greetingColor in line 23 also begins with a $. Like JavaScript variables, PHP variables are case-sensitive and "enjoy" the convenience of dynamic typing. That is, a variable takes on the type of whatever value is currently assigned to it. Superglobals like $_SESSION also have an underscore (_) as their second character, and all letters in the name are uppercase. We discuss two other superglobals, $_GET and $_POST, in a later section.

Arrays in PHP can be used just like the arrays in JavaScript, but PHP arrays are actually much more flexible. In particular, we can treat them as *associative arrays*. This means that we don't have to restrict ourselves to using non-negative integers as index values. We can also use strings, as we do when we perform the initialization in line 11 of Figure 8.3:

```
$_SESSION['pageRefreshCount'] = 0;
```

Think of this either as "associating" the numerical value 0 with the string value 'pageRefresh-Count', or as creating a *key/value pair* in which 'pageRefreshCount' is the key and 0 is the value. Note that before doing this initialization we use the PHP built-in function isset() to make sure the location in the array where we'd like to store the 0 does not already have a value. We make the test using a PHP if-statement. The syntax of the if-statement (or the if..else-statement) in PHP is the same as it is in any C-based programming language, and we have already seen that syntax in JavaScript.

How the Page Works

In the script of Figure 8.3 we have a simple use for the $_SESSION superglobal. We just want to keep track of how many refreshes have taken place. Let's describe the execution flow. The first time the page is loaded we start (or join) the session and initialize the refresh count to 0 in lines 9–11. Then, in line 23, we explicitly set the color to be used for the page text to be black, though this is in fact the default color. Next, the test in the if-statement in line 24 fails because the "refresh count" at this point is 0, so we do not change the color of the text. (We discuss how the text color is changed by this if-statement shortly.)

Next, in line 36 the refresh count is incremented so that it will not be 0 on any subsequent loading of this page. Then the date and time information is displayed (lines 38–41), using black as the text color.

The next question to be answered is this: How will the browser know what color to use for the text when it displays the date and time information? The answer lies in the rather mysterious line 37 of Figure 8.3. In that line the PHP script sends to the browser (via an echo-statement) a "hidden" p element, which is not displayed in the browser because of its hidden attribute, but whose content will be the color the browser is to use for the page text when the page is displayed. The browser retrieves this color via the JavaScript in lines 49–53, that is, by first getting a DOM object reference to the "hidden" paragraph in the usual way using getElementByID() and the id value of that hidden paragraph, after which the innerHTML property of that object gives the required color. It is hiddenParagraph.innerHTML that refers to the content of the hidden paragraph where the required color is stored. That color is then used to set the text color of the entire page (in lines 51–52), since it is the body element that has the id value "welcome".

Actually there is a little more than this going on in line 37. First, note the use of both double quotes and single quotes. This kind of usage is common and often necessary (as in this case) in scripting languages like JavaScript and PHP that allow strings to be delimited by either type of quotation mark. But the other really important thing that shows up here for the first time is *variable interpolation*, which is something that takes place in PHP (but not in JavaScript). What this means (in this case, as in any analogous situation, of which we will see many more as we go along) is that the string sent by the echo statement in line 37 does not contain the name of the variable `$greetingColor`; it will contain instead the *value* of that variable. This is what happens when the variable appears inside double quotes. Note, however, that this *variable interpolation* (*replacement of a variable by its value*) does not happen if a variable appears inside single quotes.

Finally, let's look at how the text color is chosen in the body of the if-statement in lines 26–34. This code will be executed every time the page is loaded *after the first time*. The first thing that happens is the call to the `rand()` function in line 26, which returns a value in the range from 1 to 100 (inclusive of both). The following nested `if`-statement (lines 27–34) then checks to see where within that range of values the generated random value falls, and sets the color accordingly. It is now that randomly chosen color that is passed as the content of the hidden paragraph element, as discussed above.

8.4.3 The Solution to Our Problem: An AJAX Example

In the previous section we discussed an example in which an entire page was refreshed, even though only a part of the page actually needed refreshing. In this section you will see how AJAX helps us to refresh just the part of the page that needs updating.

For this discussion we need to refer to **FIGURES 8.5** and **8.6** for the markup and code, and to **FIGURE 8.7** for the corresponding browser display. We begin with a high-level view. In Figure 8.5 we have a `script` element within the `head` element. This `script` element contains the definitions of the two JavaScript functions `getCurrentTime()` (lines 25–32) and `updatePage()` (lines 33–42) that we call later on in the second script that appears at the end of the `body` element in our document (lines 61–64).

```
1   <?php
2   /*welcome_ajax.php
3   This page displays a welcome message in which the date and
4   time are refreshed every 60 seconds via AJAX communication
5   with the server. Initially the text color of the entire page
6   is black, but each refresh uses a randomly chosen text color
7   from red, green, blue or maroon just for the two lines containing
8   the date and time information. Because the color choice is
9   random, the same color may repeat after a refresh. The rest
10  of the page is not refreshed, so its text color remains black.
11  */
12  session_start();
13  if (!isset($_SESSION['timedateRefreshCount']))
14      $_SESSION['timedateRefreshCount'] = 0;
15  ?>
```

FIGURE 8.5 ch08/welcome_ajax.php
A third version of our Welcome message page, in which only the date and time information is updated and given a randomly chosen color every 60 seconds, this time via AJAX communication with the server.

```
16  <!DOCTYPE html>
17  <html lang="en">
18    <head>
19      <meta charset="utf-8">
20      <title>Welcome Message with Server-Time Updates via AJAX</title>
21      <script>
22      //This script sets up the AJAX infrastructure for requesting
23      //date, time and random display color updates from the server.
24      var request = null;
25      function getCurrentTime()
26      {
27          request = new XMLHttpRequest();
28          var url = "time.php";
29          request.open("GET", url, true);
30          request.onreadystatechange = updatePage;
31          request.send(null);
32      }
33      function updatePage()
34      {
35          if (request.readyState == 4)
36          {
37              var dateDisplay = document.getElementById("datetime");
38              dateDisplay.innerHTML = request.responseText;
39              var hiddenParagraph = document.getElementById("colorChoice");
40              dateDisplay.style.color = hiddenParagraph.innerHTML;
41          }
42      }
43      </script>
44    </head>
45    <body id="welcome">
46      <h2>Welcome!</h2>
47      <?php
48      echo "<h3 id='datetime'>It's ".date("l, F jS").".<br>\r\n";
49      echo "The time is ".date("g:ia").".</h3>\r\n";
50      ?>
51      <h3>Or at least that's our time, though it may not be yours.</h3>
52      <h6>Pedagogical Note:<br>When this page is first displayed,
53      all text is displayed in the default text color of black.
54      Then the time<br>and date are dynamically updated every 60
55      seconds, and each time this happens the two lines of text<br>
56      containing the date and time are shown in a color chosen
57      randomly from one of these four colors: red,<br>green, blue
58      or maroon. The remaining lines of text on the page
59      (including this note) retain their (static)<br>default
60      color black.</h6>
61      <script>
62      getCurrentTime();
63      setInterval('getCurrentTime()', 60000)
64      </script>
65    </body>
66  </html>
```

FIGURE 8.5 ch08/welcome_ajax.php *(continued)*

```php
1   <?php
2   /*time.php
3   Returns server time and a random display color
4   in response to an AJAX request
5   */
6   session_start();
7   if ($_SESSION['timedateRefreshCount'] == 0)
8   {
9       $greetingColor = "black";
10  }
11  else
12  {
13      $colorPicker = rand(1, 100);
14      if ($colorPicker > 75)
15          $greetingColor = "red";
16      else if ($colorPicker > 50)
17          $greetingColor = "green";
18      else if ($colorPicker > 25)
19          $greetingColor = "blue";
20      else
21          $greetingColor = "maroon";
22  }
23  $date = date("l, F jS");
24  $time = date('g:ia');
25  echo "It's $date.<br>
26      The time is $time.";
27  echo "<p hidden id='colorChoice'>$greetingColor</p>";
28  $_SESSION['timedateRefreshCount'] = $_SESSION['timedateRefreshCount'] + 1;
29  ?>
```

FIGURE 8.6 `ch08/time.php`
The PHP script that produces the date, time, and color choice (on the server) that is sent to the browser for inclusion in our Welcome message. This is the PHP script response to the AJAX request seen in the code of Figure 8.5.

Now let's itemize the things that take place when this page loads:

1. As in the previous example, we start a PHP session and initialize a counter (lines 12–14). Note that this time around we call our counter key `timedateRefreshCount` rather than the former `pageRefreshCount` because in this example it is only the time and date information that will be refreshed, not the entire page.

2. The `script` element in the `head` element of the document defines two JavaScript functions that we call later.

3. The complete page is displayed for the first (and only) time by lines 46–60. This display includes the content produced by the short PHP script in lines 47–50, which we have discussed previously. Note in passing, however, that the value of the `id` attribute of the h3 element in the PHP script output is `"timedate"`, since we will want to refer to this later.

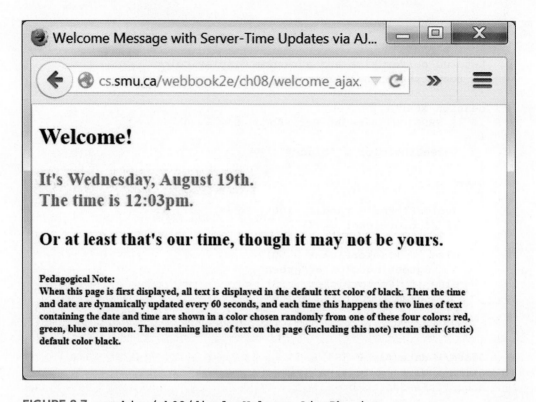

FIGURE 8.7 `graphics/ch08/displayWelcome_AjaxPhp.jpg`
A Firefox browser display of `ch08/welcome_ajax.php` after at least one AJAX request has taken place and the color red has been applied to just the (updated) date and time information lines on the page.

4. Now we come to the script element in lines 61–64. The first thing this script does is call the JavaScript `getCurrentTime()` function, defined above in lines 25–32. This function, in turn, begins by creating an object reference of type `HttpXmlRequest` (line 27) and assigning it to the variable `request`. This is the object that will make our AJAX request to the server. To do this it needs to know the name of the script on the server to which it should make its request. We supply the name of the script to the variable `url` in line 28 and use this variable as one of the parameters in the function call on the next line. There is a bit of subtlety in calling the variable `url`, even though its value is just the name of a PHP script file. We can use only the file name because that script file is located in the same directory as the web page from which it is being called. But it could be a script that is located elsewhere at a location that would have to be given as a "real" URL for the value of the `url` variable.

    Next (line 29) a call to the `request.open()` function opens a connection to the script at the given `url` value (the second parameter), indicating the method for passing the data will be the `GET` method (the first parameter in the function call, and discussed in detail in section 8.6). The third parameter in the function call is the boolean value `true`, which in this case indicates that the connection is to be *asynchronous*. This means that once the connection has been made, the browser can carry on with other business and doesn't have to wait until the connection is finished doing whatever it has to do and closes.

The browser needs to know what to do when it hears back from the server. In this case we assign to the `request.onreadystatechange` property of our request object a reference to our JavaScript `updatePage()` function (line 30). But note that there are no parentheses following the function name in line 30 because we are not *calling* the function at that point. The function will be called only when the "ready state" of the function changes, in other words only when the browser hears back from the server.

Finally, now that we are all set up, the AJAX request is sent to the server in line 31. The parameter is `null` in `request.send(null)` because we have no additional information to send to our server-side script.

5. Let's shift to a server-side view and look at the server-side PHP script `time.php` shown in Figure 8.6. There is really nothing here we haven't seen before; we have just grouped, consolidated, and rearranged some of the PHP code shown in Figure 8.3. But let's describe what it does in this new context.

   The script begins by "joining" the PHP session that has already been started by lines 12–14 in Figure 8.5. Since this is the first call to the `time.php`, the "time date refresh count" will be 0, so the "greeting color" will be reaffirmed to be black. The date and time are then computed and sent back to the browser, along with the hidden paragraph containing the text color. Then, just before the script ends, the count is incremented so that on subsequent runs of this script it will not be 0, and a random color will be chosen for the text of the date and time display.

6. Now we go back to what's happening in the browser and look again at Figure 8.5. When the `time.php` script sends its information back to the browser, the "ready state" of the `request` object will change, and that's when our second JavaScript function `updatePage()` is called. The body of this function (lines 35–41) consists of a single `if`-statement that tests the `readyState` value of the `request` object. It can have several values, but we want it to have the value 4, which essentially means "everything's OK". In that case the body of the if-statement is activated, so we get a reference to the h3 element with `id` value `"datetime"` and change its text color to whatever color came back from the server as the content of the hidden paragraph.

7. The call to the global JavaScript function `setInterval()` in line 63 of Figure 8.5 says, "Call the `getCurrentTime()` function every 60000 milliseconds (every minute), from now on." Henceforth, then, the whole process will repeat, and from now on some color other than black will be used. Note, however, that although a "new" random color is chosen every minute, because there are only four colors from which to choose it may well be the case that the same color appears for two (or even more) intervals in a row.

8.5 Incorporating the Welcome Message into Our Home Page with AJAX

We are now ready to incorporate our welcome message, along with the current date and time, into the home page for our **Nature's Source** website, as shown in **FIGURE 8.8**. As you can see from that figure,

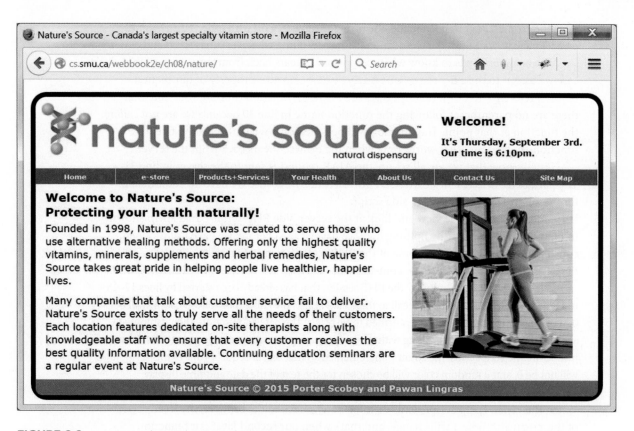

FIGURE 8.8 `graphics/ch08/nature/displayIndexPhp.jpg`
A Firefox browser display of `ch08/nature/index.php` containing our Welcome message, which includes the current date and time produced by a client-side AJAX request and the corresponding server-side PHP script response, and is refreshed every 60 seconds. Photo: © coloroftime/iStockphoto

this information appears at the upper right of the page, next to the logo. You have already seen, in an isolated example in the previous section, how this can be accomplished using AJAX. So here you need only to look at how the necessary code is incorporated into our **Nature's Source** website.

First, look at our revised index file in **FIGURE 8.9**. This file is now called `index.php` rather than `index.html`, because it now contains embedded PHP code. Note that the file contains two short PHP scripts, one in lines 5–8 and the other in line 33. These scripts contain only calls to the PHP `include()` function that is now being used to perform our "server-side includes", but the presence of these two PHP scripts is the reason we have changed the name of the file from `index.html` to `index.php`. Note that we can use the PHP `include()` function to include either strictly HTML files, like `menus.html` and `footer_content.html`, or an HTML file that itself contains an "embedded" PHP script, like `banner.php`.

Second, look at `banner.php` in **FIGURE 8.10**, which replaces the previous `logo.html`. We see that it contains two `div` elements and a `script` element whose body is our AJAX-related JavaScript code. The first `div` is just the `div` with `id` value `"logo"` from our previous

```
1    <?php include("common/document_head.html"); ?>
2    <!-- index.php for ch08/nature -->
3    <body onload="startRotation()">
4      <header>
5        <?php
6        include("common/banner.php");
7        include("common/menus.html");
8        ?>
9      </header>
10     <main>
11       <article id="textLeft">
12         <h3>Welcome to Nature's Source:<br>
13           Protecting your health naturally!</h3>
14         <p>Founded in 1998, Nature's Source was created to serve those who
15         use alternative healing methods. Offering only the highest quality
16         vitamins, minerals, supplements and herbal remedies, Nature's
17         Source takes great pride in helping people live healthier, happier
18         lives.</p>
19         <p>Many companies that talk about customer service fail to deliver.
20         Nature's Source exists to truly serve all the needs of their
21         customers. Each location features dedicated on-site therapists
22         along with knowledgeable staff who ensure that every customer
23         receives the best quality information available. Continuing
24         education seminars are a regular event at Nature's Source.</p>
25       </article>
26       <div id="image">
27         <img id="placeholder" src=""
28              alt="Healthy Lifestyle"
29              width="256" height="256">
30       </div>
31     </main>
32     <footer>
33       <?php include("common/footer_content.html"); ?>
34     </footer>
35   </body>
36 </html>
```

FIGURE 8.9 `ch08/nature/index.php`
The HTML markup for the index file of this chapter's version of our complete **Nature's Source** website. Note that the `header` element now includes both an external PHP file and an external HTML file.

`logo.html` file. The second `div`, with `id` value `"welcome"`, has the same content we saw in the `body` element of `welcome.php`, except that we changed "The time" to a friendlier "Our time" and changed the header sizes to better accommodate the message location.

Finally, as we mentioned earlier, although we do not show it in the text, we have slightly modified the CSS files for this version of the site to style the new contents of `banner.php`.

```
1    <!-- banner.php -->
2        <div id="logo">
3            <img src="images/naturelogo.gif"
4                alt="Nature's Source"
5                width="608"
6                height="90">
7        </div>
8        <div id="welcome">
9          <h3>Welcome!</h3>
10         <h5 id="datetime"><?php
11         echo "It's ".date("l, F jS").".<br>";
12         echo "Our time is ".date('g:ia').".";
13         ?></h5>
14       </div>
15       <script>
16         //This script sets up the AJAX infrastructure for
17         //requesting time updates from the server.
18         var request = null;
19         function getCurrentTime()
20         {
21             request = new XMLHttpRequest();
22             var url = "common/time.php";
23             request.open("GET", url, true);
24             request.onreadystatechange = updatePage;
25             request.send(null);
26         }
27         function updatePage()
28         {
29             if (request.readyState == 4)
30             {
31                 var dateDisplay = document.getElementById("datetime");
32                 dateDisplay.innerHTML = request.responseText;
33             }
34         }
35         getCurrentTime();
36         setInterval('getCurrentTime()', 60000)
37       </script>
38
```

FIGURE 8.10 `ch08/nature/common/banner.php`
The HTML markup and JavaScript code of our new banner file, which essentially replaces the previous `logo.html` and includes that logo as well as the necessary code to handle the AJAX request for a time and date update.

The net effect of all these changes is that the `Welcome!` greeting (with the periodically updating date and time) that we see in Figure 8.8 appears to the right of our logo on each of our website's pages because `banner.php` is included at the beginning of each page.

8.6 Understanding the GET and POST "Methods"

In the next section we will begin our discussion of the "back end" or "server-side" of our website functionality. We will start with our feedback form, but for that discussion, as well as for the discussion of our revised BMI form later in this chapter, and our e-store scripts in Chapter 10, we need to understand more about how data is transmitted from client to server.

When data is transmitted from a form on the client to the server, the opening form tag will have two essential attributes that relate to the processing of the form data: the `action` attribute and the `method` attribute. Here is the opening form tag from the current version of our feedback form, found in lines 13–14 of `ch08/nature/pages/feedbackForm.php`:

```
<form id="contactForm"
    action="scripts/feedbackFormProcess.php"
    method="post">
```

The value of the `action` attribute is the server-side program (a PHP script in our case) that will process the data from the form, and the value of the `method` attribute determines how the data from the form will be passed from the client and made available to that script on the server. We will come back to this `feedbackForm.php` later, but in this section we want to discuss several small examples isolated from any other distractions on our **Nature's Source** website to highlight just the data-transfer process.

The two values of the `method` attribute that we need to understand in this context are `"GET"` and `"POST"`, which we often refer to as "the GET method" and "the POST method". These values are case-insensitive, but when we discuss them here and later in the text we use all caps to help them stand out. In actual markup you may see either (uppercase in line 23 of Figure 8.10 and lowercase in line 18 of **FIGURE 8.11**). Note that the term *method* as used here has nothing to do with the way we use the term when we speak of "calling a method" in a programming language such as PHP or JavaScript. That's why we put the word in quotes in the title of this section.

8.6.1 An Example Illustrating the GET Method

Look first at `test_get.html` in Figure 8.11, in which the important things to note are `method="get"` in line 18, and `"value1"` and `"value2"` as the values of the `name` attributes for the two `input` elements (lines 19 and 20). Second, look at the corresponding display in **FIGURE 8.12**, in which the numerical values 2 and 5 have been entered into the form. If we now click on the Submit button, we will get the web page response shown in **FIGURE 8.13** that is produced by the PHP script shown in **FIGURE 8.14**.

Look carefully at the content of the browser address bar in Figure 8.13, where you see this:

```
cs.smu.ca/webbook2e/ch08/test_get.php?value1=2&value2=5&submit=Submit
```

This is the URL of the script that processes the form data from `test_get.html`, but with some additional information tacked onto its end. What you're seeing here is a typical example of how

```
1    <!DOCTYPE html>
2    <!-- test_get.html -->
3    <html lang="en">
4      <head>
5        <meta charset="utf-8">
6        <title>Test Get</title>
7      </head>
8      <body>
9        <p>Perform the following steps:<p>
10       <ol>
11         <li>Enter two integers into the form below.</li>
12         <li>Click the form's submit button.</li>
13         <li>View the resulting display (of course).</li>
14         <li>But also look carefully at the contents of the
15           <br>display page's address bar to see how the form
16           <br>input data is passed to the PHP script for processing.</li>
17       </ol>
18       <form method="get" action="test_get.php">
19         <p>Value 1: <input type="text" name="value1"></p>
20         <p>Value 2: <input type="text" name="value2"></p>
21         <p><input type="submit" name="submit" value="Submit"></p>
22       </form>
23     </body>
24   </html>
```

FIGURE 8.11 `ch08/test_get.html`
The HTML markup for a page with a simple form requesting two input values, as shown in Figure 8.12.

the GET method transfers form data from client (the browser) to server. Note first the two key/value pairs: value1=2 and value2=5. Now value1 and value2 are the "values" of the name attributes of the two input elements that accept the two numbers seen in the form of test_get.html (lines 19 and 20 of Figure 8.11), and 2 and 5 are the numbers we have entered into the textboxes created by those two form elements (see Figure 8.12).

If more form data was being submitted by the GET method, you would see more of these key/value pairs. The other important part of the syntax is this: The key/value pairs are separated by an ampersand character (&), and the sequence of key/value pairs is separated from the URL itself by a question mark character (?). Note that you also see at the very end of the URL the key/value pair submit=Submit. Even though we do not use this data on the server side, the information is sent simply because the corresponding input element has a name attribute (line 21 of Figure 8.11). From this you should be able to see why it is so important for any form control that has data that *needs* to be transferred to the server to have a name attribute.

So that's one way that data can be transferred from client to server. How is this data received on the server side? Now you need to look at the PHP script in Figure 8.14 that receives and processes the data, and this is where another superglobal variable, namely $_GET comes into

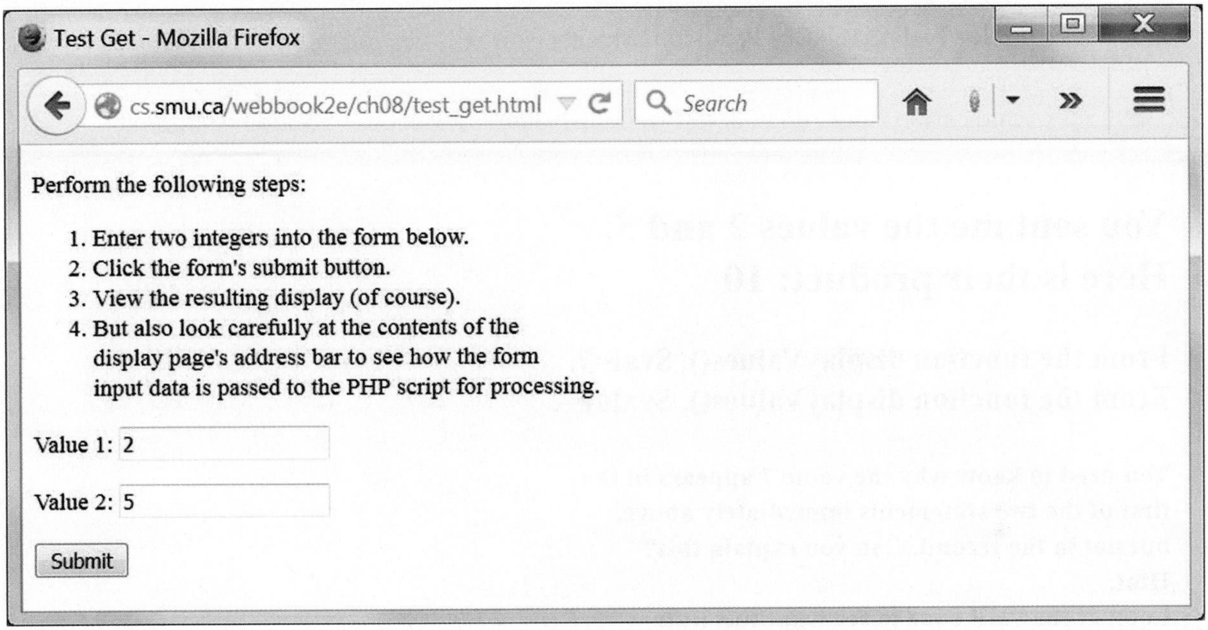

FIGURE 8.12 `graphics/ch08/displayTest_GetHtml.jpg`
A Firefox browser display of `ch08/test_get.html`, with the two requested values filled in and the form ready to be submitted.

play. When we use the GET method to transfer our form data, the key in each key/value pair becomes a key (or "string index") in the superglobal $_GET on the server side If this variable does not exist, it will be created. And, probably not surprisingly, the value associated with that key in the $_GET array is the value assigned to that key in the corresponding key/value pair that was passed at the end of the URL when we submitted the form. In other words, for example, in the particular example we discussed above, the value of $_GET['value1'] is 2 and the value of $_GET['value2'] is 5.

In line 12 of Figure 8.14 we use these values to perform a simple calculation and output the result. Nothing unusual there. However, note carefully line 10 of Figure 8.14, in which we simply display these two values. In this case the array values appear within a double-quoted string and now it is important that the key values of the array components within the square brackets *not* be quoted, if we want to be sure the interpolation happens properly.

You will encounter this difference in the use of quotes quite frequently as time goes on, so you may want to come back and revisit this example. Be sure to read the comments in lines 14–19 of Figure 8.14, which also summarize what we might think of as a "best practice" for this situation.

Before we leave this example, we should point out that we also use it to illustrate the scope of a variable declared within a PHP function (even though this has nothing to do with GET or POST). Unlike JavaScript, PHP has no var keyword. In JavaScript we recommended always declaring a variable with the var keyword. This would ensure that a variable declared and used inside a

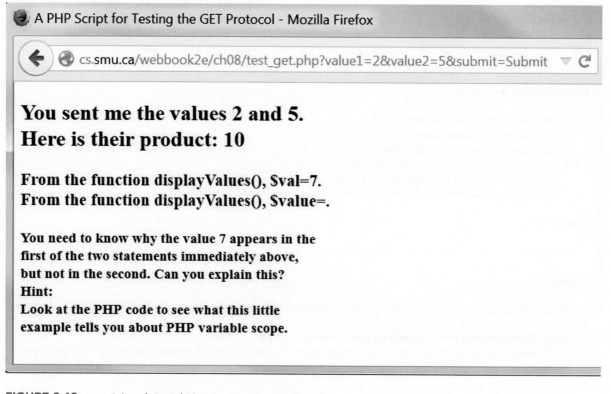

FIGURE 8.13 `graphics/ch08/displayTest_GetPhp.jpg`
A Firefox browser display of the page output produced by the script in Figure 8.14 when the form in Figure 8.12 is submitted.

function could only be seen inside that function and thus could not be inadvertently changed by something outside the function. Even without a `var` keyword, a variable declared inside a PHP function is still "local" to that function and cannot be seen outside the function. You should convince yourself that the rest of the script in Figure 8.14 (lines 21–33) illustrates this fact. Note in particular the definition of a simple PHP user-defined function, which is completely analogous to function definitions in JavaScript.

8.6.2 An Example Illustrating the POST Method

In Figures 8.11 to 8.14 we illustrate the `GET` method for transferring data from client to server. We also have a similar example illustrating the `POST` method, but the differences are not sufficient to justify another four figures here in the text. However, you should run the example, study the corresponding files, compare what you see with the analogous displays in Figures 8.11 to 8.14, and we will point out here the only major differences you should observe.

The two files that comprise the example are `test_post.html` and `test_post.php`, which correspond to the `test_get.html` and `test_get.php` files from the previous

```
1    <!DOCTYPE html>
2    <!-- test_get.php -->
3    <html lang="en">
4      <head>
5        <meta charset="utf-8">
6        <title>A PHP Script for Testing the GET Protocol</title>
7      </head>
8      <body>
9        <?php
10       echo "<h2>You sent me the values $_GET[value1] and $_GET[value2].
11           <br>Here is their product: ";
12       echo $_GET['value1'] * $_GET['value2'];
13       echo "</h2>";
14       //Note in the above code that within the double quoted string
15       //there are no single quotes surrounding value1 or value2, but
16       //outside double quotes value1 and value2 are surrounded by
17       //single quotes. There are other ways to structure this code
18       //while achieving the same output, but this is probably the
19       //simplest and least likely to cause hard-to-find bugs.
20
21       $value = 7;
22       displayValues($value); //Note: function call (this line)
23                              //can precede function definition:
24       function displayValues($val)
25       {
26           echo "<h3>From the function displayValues(), \$val=$val.";
27           echo "<br>From the function displayValues(), \$value=$value.</h3>";
28           echo "<h4>You need to know why the value 7 appears in the
29               <br>first of the two statements immediately above,<br>
30               but not in the second. Can you explain this?<br>Hint:
31               <br>Look at the PHP code to see what this little<br>
32               example tells you about PHP variable scope.</h4>";
33       }
34       ?>
35     </body>
36   </html>
```

FIGURE 8.14 ch08/test_get.php
The PHP script that produces the page shown in Figure 8.13 when the form shown in Figure 8.12 is submitted.

example. If you now load test_post.html, you will get a display with a form similar to what you see in Figure 8.12. The markup in test_post.html will, of course, have method="post" instead of method="get" in its opening form tag. If you enter two values and click Submit, you will get a display that looks like just the first two lines of Figure 8.13, since we do not repeat the last part of that example.

The important thing to do at this point is to look at the content of the browser address window of your display. This time you will see only the URL of the test_post.php file, *with no data attached to the end of that URL*. That's the major visible difference between GET and POST. In the case of the POST method, the data is transferred "behind the scenes" and is not visible in the address window.

8.6.3 An Example Illustrating That a Form Is Unnecessary and GET Is the Default

In the previous two examples we have illustrated how to submit form data to a script on the server, first by the `GET` method, and second by the `POST` method. However, it is possible to pass data directly to a PHP script without using a form, and often very convenient and useful to be able to do so. All we have to do is attach the data to the end of the script URL using the same syntax that we have already seen in the context of the `GET` method. The script can then access the passed data using the `$_GET` superglobal. We sometimes refer to this scenario by saying that `GET` is the "default" data-transfer mechanism, since we do not have to specify anywhere that we are actually using the `GET` method. This technique is very useful if several scripts are running on the server, are cooperating to perform a particular task, and some data needs to be passed from one script to another. Chapter 10 will illustrate this at several points.

This is illustrated by **FIGURE 8.15** (display) and **FIGURE 8.16** (script). Figure 8.15 is obtained by loading the script in Figure 8.16 with the data you see at the end of its URL in the browser address window shown in Figure 8.15. The output in Figure 8.15 is produced by the PHP code in lines 29–37 of Figure 8.16. The new thing in this code is line 33. We said previously that superglobal array keys should not be single-quoted when they appear within double quotes. However, the required interpolation will happen if we enclose the array component within braces

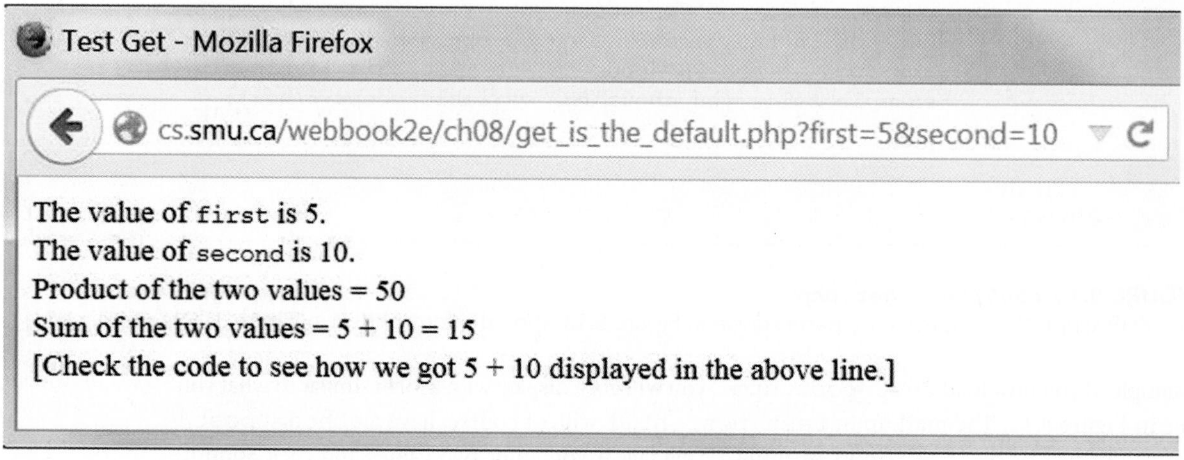
Test Get - Mozilla Firefox
cs.smu.ca/webbook2e/ch08/get_is_the_default.php?first=5&second=10
The value of first is 5.
The value of second is 10.
Product of the two values = 50
Sum of the two values = 5 + 10 = 15
[Check the code to see how we got 5 + 10 displayed in the above line.]

FIGURE 8.15 `graphics/ch08/displayGet_Is_The_DefaultPhp.jpg`
A Firefox browser display of the output of the PHP script shown in Figure 8.16 when it is run with the input data seen at the end of the URL in the browser address box of Figure 8.15.

```
1    <!DOCTYPE html>
2    <?php
3    /*get_is_the_default.php
4    This little script is designed to show that data can
5    be passed directly to a script at the end of its URL.
6    In other words, it is not necessary to use a form to
7    pass the data. When data is passed in this way it is
8    is the GET protocol that is in play.
9    */
10   ?>
11   <html lang="en">
12     <head>
13       <meta charset="utf-8">
14       <title>Test Get</title>
15     </head>
16   <body>
17   <?php
18   if (count($_GET) == 0)
19   {
20       echo <<<INFO
21   You have run this script without any input data.<br>
22   The URL of the script will be in the address bar of your browser.<br>
23   So ... add the following to the end of that URL and refresh:<br>
24   <pre>?first=5&amp;second=10</pre>
25   Then try other values for <code>first</code> and <code>second</code>.
26   INFO;
27       exit(0);
28   }
29   echo "The value of <code>first</code> is $_GET[first].<br>
30       The value of <code>second</code> is $_GET[second].<br>";
31   $product = $_GET['first'] * $_GET['second'];
32   echo "Product of the two values = $product<br>
33       Sum of the two values = {$_GET['first']} + {$_GET['second']} = ";
34   //Note the use of braces to achieve interpolation in the above line.
35   echo $_GET['first'] + $_GET['second'], "<br>";
36   echo "[Check the code to see how we got 5 + 10
37       displayed in the above line.]";
38   ?>
39     </body>
40   </html>
```

FIGURE 8.16 ch08/get_is_the_default.php
A PHP script that illustrates (among other things) that GET is the default method used to transfer data to a server-side script when that data is attached to the end of the URL of the script.

(curly brackets), as we do here. We do not recommend this; we show it only because you may run into it and wonder what on earth is going on.

And finally, before leaving this example, note that we have again taken the opportunity to illustrate a couple of new and useful PHP features, in this case to make our script a little more "user-friendly". You can see what we mean if you just load the script with no data at the end of its URL.

First, if you look at the `if`-statement starting in line 18 of Figure 8.16, you will see the built-in PHP `count()` function being used to check the size of the superglobal array `$_GET`. If the function returns a value of 0, that means the array is empty, and thus no data has been passed to the script. In this case, the body of the `if`-statement is executed, so the user instructions are output by the `echo`-statement and then the script terminates immediately with the `exit(0)` function call.

Here the `echo`-statement itself (lines 20–26) is perhaps more interesting than any we've yet seen, and contains what PHP (and some other languages) call a *here document*. This is kind of an odd name, so just think of it as saying this: *here*'s some text . . . just output it! Note that the text to output is not a string in the usual sense; that is, it is not enclosed in quotes of any kind. Instead, its beginning is indicated by the `<<<INFO` marker, and its end by the `INFO;` marker, where `INFO` is just a programmer chosen name, capitalized for easier visibility. The text is output "as is", but note that in this case the text is going to an HTML document, which means that we can include HTML tags (like `<pre>` and `<code>`) and expect to have them properly dealt with at the destination.

This example also illustrates the usual syntax for a here document, but we should point out that the closing delimiter (`INFO;` in this case) must use the same name as the opening delimiter, must be on a line by itself, must start at the left margin, and must have a semicolon (`;`) at the end (see line 26 of Figure 8.16).

8.6.4 Guidelines for Using GET and POST

Since we now have these two methods—`GET` and `POST`—for transferring data, an obvious question arises: When do we use each? If you think back to the examples we used to illustrate these two methods, you may be able to make an intelligent guess at the answer.

Recall that when we use `GET`, the information sent appears in the browser address window at the end of the relevant URL. From this we can conclude that we should *not* use GET for any situation in which we would not want a user (or someone looking over a user's shoulder) to see the information we are sending. This is just a simple common-sense security precaution.

Somewhat less obvious, but also true, is that when using GET the amount of data we can send is subject to a limit that may depend on both the client and the server, but essentially (once again) because all the data has to be tacked on to the end of the URL.

Both of these problems are solved by using `POST`. The GET security issue is not present when using POST, because the data transferred is not seen by the user. And the limitation on the amount of data transferred when using GET is not an issue either, since there is virtually no limit on the amount of data that can be transferred using the POST method.

And now you'll be asking the following question: So why don't we always just use POST? Well, it has to be admitted that GET is very convenient, especially since we can use it without the bother of setting up a form from which to send the data.

So, the web community seems to have settled on the following guidelines for the use of GET and POST:

1. Use POST if you are transferring a lot of data.
2. Use POST if you don't want the information you are sending to be visible in the browser's address box.
3. Use POST if the information you are sending is going to change something at the destination (the content of a database, for example).
4. Use GET if you are just retrieving some information from the destination (getting information from a database, for example).
5. Use GET for short communication between scripts on the server.
6. Definitely use GET if you are sending small amounts of data, you don't care who sees it, and you don't want or need to bother setting up a form.

8.7 Implementing the Server-Side Functionality of Our Feedback Form

Now we continue putting PHP to work in the ongoing development of our e-commerce website. We start by implementing the remaining part of our website's feedback facility. This will involve sending emails (to both the business and the client), preparing a browser display for immediate confirmation to the client, and storing information on disk (on the server) for future reference by the business, if required.

Recall that we created the feedback form itself in Chapter 5 and then, in Chapters 6 and 7, we showed how we could provide data validation support for that form using JavaScript and/or HTML5. However, when a user "submitted" the feedback form, all that happened was the validation of the data followed by a brief report to the user that the data was "OK"; there was no actual "submission" or any other communication between the customer and the business.

Client-side JavaScript programming does not allow you either to send emails or to upload information to the server, and there is good reason for such restrictions. If such activities were permitted, malicious web programmers could entice clients to their websites and when those users downloaded web pages from such sites, those pages could contain JavaScript that would use the client computer to send out spam, worms, viruses, or other kinds of malware. The origin of such emails could only lead forensic investigators back to the client's computer, and it might be very difficult to establish the true origin of such unwelcome software. Hence, any emails that are triggered by a user's interaction are best sent directly from the web server. This is achieved through server-side programming. So, we will now use our feedback form to demonstrate the following:

▶ How to upload to the web server the information that has been entered into the form
▶ How to send email based on that information (to the business, as well as to the user)
▶ How to confirm to the user that the submission has been made, with a browser display based on the submitted data
▶ How to store the uploaded information in a file on the web server, for future reference by the business if desired

8.7.1 What Happens When the User Clicks `Send Feedback`

FIGURE 8.17 shows this chapter's feedback form all filled out and ready to be submitted. When the user clicks the `Send Feedback` button, the first thing that happens is the validation of the form data. If there is a problem with any of the data items being validated, the form data will not be submitted. Instead, the user will get a message of the type previously seen, and will have to correct the offending data item and resubmit.

On the other hand, if all of the data is valid, the data from the form will be sent to the server for processing by the PHP script shown in **FIGURE 8.18**, after which the following four things will happen:

▶ The PHP script sends an email to the business, like the one shown in **FIGURE 8.19**.
▶ The PHP script also sends a second email to the client as a permanent confirmation of the feedback submission. This consists of a message like the one shown in **FIGURE 8.20**.

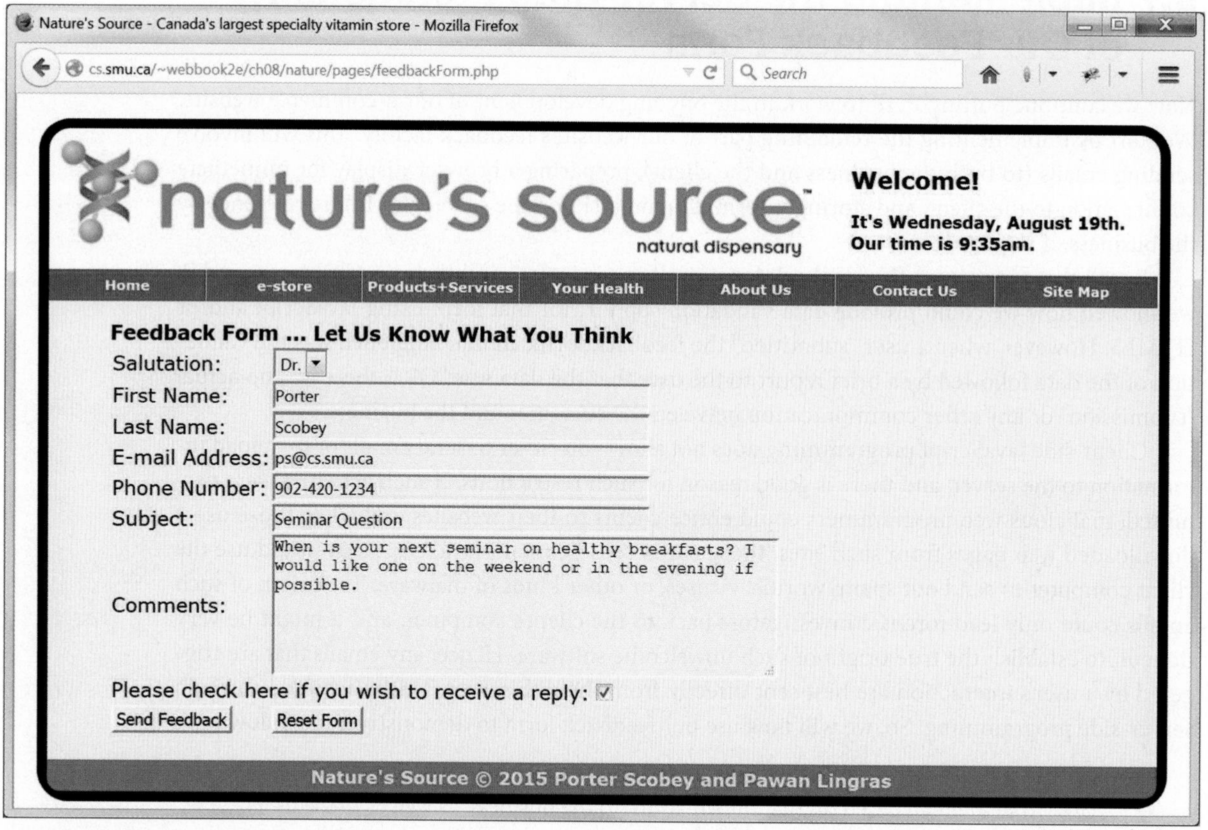

FIGURE 8.17 `graphics/ch08/nature/displayFeedbackFormPhp.jpg`
A Firefox browser display of ch08/nature/pages/feedbackForm.php, with the form completely filled out with valid information and ready to be submitted.

```php
1   <?php
2   /*feedbackFormProcess.php
3   Processes feedback form data by first constructing a
4   message of response from the user's input, and then
5   - sends an e-mail message to the business
6   - sends a sligtly modified e-mail message to the client
7   - returns a confirmation message to the client's browser
8   - logs the feedback in a file on the server
9   */
10
11  //Construct message to be sent to the business
12  $messageToBusiness =
13      "From: $_POST[salute] $_POST[firstName] $_POST[lastName]\r\n".
14      "E-mail address: $_POST[email]\r\n".
15      "Phone number: $_POST[phone]\r\n".
16      "Subject: $_POST[subject]\r\n".
17      "$_POST[message]\r\n";
18
19  //Send e-mail feedback message to the business
20  //(but here, to the text's website)
21  $headerToBusiness = "From: $_POST[email]\r\n";
22  mail("webbook2e@cs.smu.ca", $_POST['subject'],
23      $messageToBusiness, $headerToBusiness);
24
25  //Construct e-mail confirmation message for the client,
26  //which is just a sligtly modified version of the message
27  //that went to the business
28  $messageToClient =
29      "Dear $_POST[salute] $_POST[lastName]:\r\n".
30      "The following message was received from you
31      by Nature's Source:\r\n\r\n".
32      $messageToBusiness.
33      "-----------------------\r\n".
34      "Thank you for the feedback and your patronage.\r\n".
35      "The Nature's Source Team\r\n".
36      "-----------------------\r\n";
37
38  if (isset($_POST['reply'])) $messageToClient.=
39      "P.S. We will contact you shortly with more information.";
40
41  //Sends e-mail confirmation message to the client
42  $headerToClient = "From: webbook2e@cs.smu.ca\r\n";
43  mail($_POST['email'], "Re: $_POST[subject]",
44      $messageToClient, $headerToClient);
45
46  //Transforms confirmation message to HTML5 format for
47  //display in the client's browser
48  $display = str_replace("\r\n", "\r\n<br>", $messageToClient);
```

FIGURE 8.18 `ch08/nature/scripts/feedbackFormProcess.php`
The PHP script that processes submitted feedback form data such as that shown in Figure 8.17.

```
49    $display = "<!DOCTYPE html>
50        <html lang='en'>
51        <head><meta charset='utf-8'><title>Your Message</title></head>
52        <body><code>$display</code></body>
53        </html>";
54    echo $display;
55
56    //Logs the message in data/feedback.txt on the web server
57    //Note: directory "data" is at same level as directory "scripts"
58    $fileVar = fopen("../data/feedback.txt", "a")
59        or die("Error: Could not open the log file.");
60    fwrite($fileVar,
61        "\n-------------------------------------------------------\n")
62        or die("Error: Could not write divider to the log file.");
63    fwrite($fileVar, "Date received: ".date("jS \of F, Y \a\\t H:i:s\n"))
64        or die("Error: Could not write date to the log file.");
65    fwrite($fileVar, $messageToBusiness)
66        or die("Error: Could not write message to the log file.");
67    ?>
```

FIGURE 8.18 `ch08/nature/scripts/feedbackFormProcess.php` (*continued*)

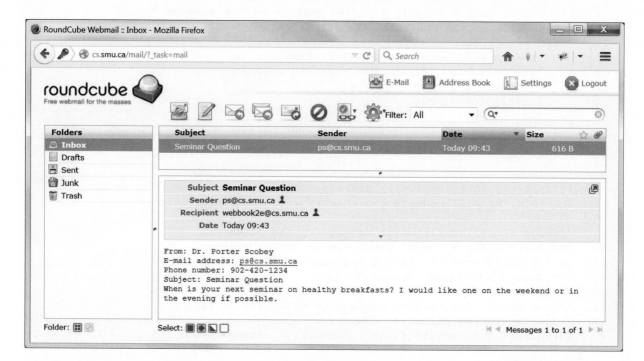

FIGURE 8.19 `graphics/ch08/nature/displayFeedbackFormProcessPhpEmailBusiness.jpg`
A **roundcube** web email client display showing the email received by the business as a result of submitting the form data shown in Figure 8.17.

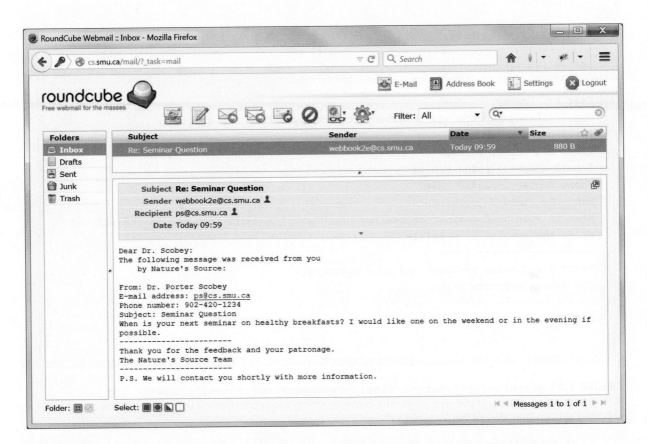

FIGURE 8.20 `graphics/ch08/nature/displayFeedbackFormProcessPhpEmailClient.jpg`
A **roundcube** web email client display showing the email received by the user (the business client) as a result of submitting the form data shown in Figure 8.17.

▶ The user also gets an immediate browser-display confirmation that the feedback submission has been received, which is shown in **FIGURE 8.21**.

▶ Finally, a copy of the email message shown in Figure 8.19 is appended to a textfile on the server's disk, which contains all previous user feedback submissions from this form. This version of the message looks like the sample shown in **FIGURE 8.22**. Note that the date of submission has been prepended to the version of the message stored on disk.

In the following sections we discuss in detail how each of these items is constructed and sent to its required destination.

8.7.2 Uploading the Feedback Form Data from the Client to the Server

We developed our feedback form and its data validation over Chapters 5, 6, and 7, but only now do we get to finally submit the form and have it processed on the server. The current version of our form is found in the file `ch08/nature/pages/feedbackForm.php`. We do not

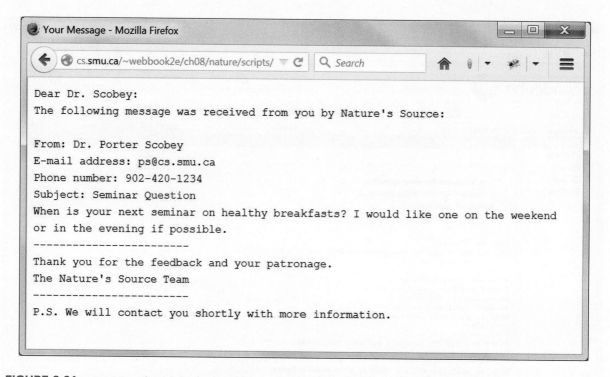

FIGURE 8.21 `graphics/ch08/nature/displayFeedbackFormProcessPhpBrowser.jpg`
A Firefox browser display of the web page that provides immediate confirmation that feedback has been received, after submission of the form data shown in Figure 8.17.

```
1
2      ------------------------------------------------------
3      Date received: 19th of August, 2015 at 09:59:48
4      From: Dr. Porter Scobey
5      E-mail address: ps@cs.smu.ca
6      Phone number: 902-420-1234
7      Subject: Seminar Question
8      When is your next seminar on healthy breakfasts?
9      I would like one on the weekend or in the evening if possible.
```

FIGURE 8.22 `ch08/nature/data/feedback.txt`
The feedback message, with date of submission, as it is stored (for the business) on the server in the log file `ch08/nature/data/feedback.txt`.

reproduce that entire file here. Instead we just remind you that, as we mentioned earlier, the opening form tag now looks like this (lines 13–14 of the file):

```
<form id="contactForm"
  action="scripts/feedbackFormProcess.php"
  method="post">
```

Note the absence of an `onsubmit` attribute and any call to a JavaScript function, because the validation is now being done via the HTML5 `pattern` attribute. The value of the `action` attribute of the `form` element is now a call to the PHP script `feedbackFormProcess.php`, which lives on the server (in `ch08/nature/scripts`), and which will process the data that is sent to the server from this form. And also, as we discussed in detail earlier, the `method` attribute of the `form` tag has the recommended value of `"post"` when we are sending information that is going to be stored on the server.

8.7.3 An Overview of the PHP Code That Processes the Feedback Form Data

It's now time to look closely at the PHP code that makes all of this possible: the two emails, the browser display confirming the submission, and a log of the submission being recorded on the server. The relevant PHP script is `ch08/nature/scripts/feedbackFormProcess.php`, shown in Figure 8.18.

Remember as well that in this context we will *not* use an integer index on the server side to access any value in the `$_POST` array. Instead we will think of the names we gave the form controls in our HTML document form (using their `name` attributes) as the keys to provide access to the corresponding data values input by the user. For example, we will use `$_POST['firstName']` for access to the user's first name because we gave the attribute `name='firstName'` to the `input` element into which the user entered his or her first name.

The script essentially consists of string manipulations to dynamically create the two email messages, the web page reply, and the log message. The message is slightly different in each case, depending on the recipient and where it is to be sent. Note that we have inserted descriptive comments to describe the script as a whole, as well as the various logical subsections of the script. The two forward slashes (`//`) that we used in JavaScript to give us a single-line comment are available for the same purpose in PHP as well, and the `/* ... */` delimiters for multi-line comments are also available.

8.7.4 Building the Feedback Message to the Business with PHP String Literals and the `$_POST` Array Values

In this section we discuss the code segment in lines 12–17 of Figure 8.18 and the content of the corresponding email message of Figure 8.19. These lines construct the basic message that is sent via email to the business, and that forms the basis of all the messages we will build. This message is constructed using the text values from the `input` controls of our HTML feedback form, which are available as values of the `$_POST` array, as discussed earlier. Note once again, as we illustrated in our discussion of GET and POST, when either `$_GET` or `$_POST` is used inside double quotes, the key values inside the square brackets used with them should not be enclosed in quotes.

The complete result that is assigned to the variable `$messageToBusiness` is formed by joining the values from the `$_POST` array to the necessary "infrastructure" text items, such as

```
"From: "
"Email address: "
```

and so on. We are, in effect, putting email header information in front of the message text, because we are, after all, constructing a complete email.

Once the message has been constructed by joining all the required text items with the period (.) concatenation operator, we then assign the completed result to the variable `$messageToBusiness`.

8.7.5 Sending an Email Feedback Message to the Business with PHP's `mail()` Function

We are now ready to send our message via email, and in this section we discuss the code segment from lines 21–23 of Figure 8.18, which deal with the actual sending of the email to the business, as shown in Figure 8.19.

The email is sent using the PHP built-in `mail()` function. The `mail()` function creates a message based on the *Simple Mail Transfer Protocol (SMTP)* specifications. SMTP is an Internet standard for sending email. The `mail()` function creates an SMTP-conforming email message using the following parameters:

▶ The email address of the recipient
▶ The subject of the message
▶ The message itself
▶ Additional strings that you may want to be appended to the header, such as `From:`, `CC:` (Carbon Copy), or `BCC:` (Blind Carbon Copy) fields. These fields have to be separated from the other fields, and from each other, by the `\r\n` sequence.

Under normal circumstances the business would be the recipient of this email message, but here we are using the email address of the book's website as a temporary placeholder for "the business", since we do not have an actual business email address. The subject for the email is whatever the client entered into the `input` element of the form with `name='subject'`, so it is available from `$_POST['subject']`, and note that here the quotes enclosing the key value are needed. The message we want to send is the one we constructed above and is now the content of the variable `$messageToBusiness`.

The only thing still missing is any additional header lines that we may wish to add. We choose to add just a `"From: "` field by supplying the variable defined in line 21 as the fourth (optional) parameter to the `mail()` function:

```
$headerToBusiness = "From: $_POST[email]\r\n";
```

Although this fourth parameter is optional, it is a good idea to include it with at least a `"From: "` field, because this will indicate, in the recipient's mail program, who *sent* the message. This information is in the body of the message as well, of course, but without this "header" information, the mail message may appear, in the recipient's mail program, to have been sent by a web server and may run the risk of being deleted or sent to a spam folder.

It won't hurt to point out that in line 21 you are again seeing PHP's *variable interpolation* in action, and this is a case where the key value within the square brackets should *not* be enclosed in single quotes.

Now that we have all four required parameters for the `mail()` function, we can issue the function call that sends the email message to the business, which we do in lines 22–23. This results in the "business" receiving the email message shown in Figure 8.19.

Of course, PHP also has to be able to access the email system on your server, which is another aspect of PHP configuration and you should confirm with your system administrator that your PHP installation has this access.

8.7.6 Modifying the Previous Message to the Business to Get One Suitable for the Client

In this section we discuss the code segment from lines 28–36 of Figure 8.18, which deal with the construction of the email to the client seen in Figure 8.20.

This part of the script builds an additional email message, based on the previous one sent to the business. This time the message is a confirmation to the client. We create this confirmation message by first *prepending* the message with additional text that includes a greeting to the user using the salutation chosen by the user when filling out the form and the user's last name (lines 29–31). We finish by *appending* a string containing a thank-you message and a company "signature" (lines 33–36).

Our feedback form has also given the user the option of asking for a reply by checking the appropriate form checkbox whose `name` attribute has the value `"reply"`. Thus in our PHP script we can check whether the variable `$_POST['reply']` has been set (line 38), and, if so, deduce that the user wants a reply and thus append another string to our email that informs the user that a reply will be forthcoming (lines 38–39).

The appending is done with the special operator `.=` in lines 38–39. The behavior of this operator is analogous to that of other similar operators like `+=`, `*=`, and so on, that appear in most of the C-based languages, such as JavaScript, in the sense that

```
$string1 .= $string2
```

is equivalent to this:

```
$string1 = $string1 . $string2
```

8.7.7 Sending an Email Feedback Confirmation Message to the Client with PHP's `mail()` Function

In the code segment from lines 42–44 of Figure 8.18 we create the header for sending to the client the email message we constructed in the previous section, and then call `mail()` to actually send it.

There is nothing new going on here, but we should mention the following slight variation: For this version of the email, the subject is modified by preceding it with the string "Re : ", just to help distinguish it more quickly if, during testing, you are sending both emails to the same address, as we have done in our own testing.

8.7.8 Returning a Browser Display to the User for Immediate Confirmation of Feedback Submission

In this section we discuss the code segment from lines 48–54 of Figure 8.18, which produces the browser display for immediate feedback to the client seen in Figure 8.21, and which contains exactly the same textual content as the email message to the client.

However, to convert that plain text into HTML markup appropriate for display in a browser there are at least two things we need to do.

First, we need to add to each instance of \r\n the HTML tag <br> to get line breaks in the right places when the page is displayed in the browser. This we accomplish with the built-in PHP str_replace() function like this:

```
$display = str_replace("\r\n", "<br>\r\n", $messageToClient);
```

The str_replace() function takes three parameters. The first parameter is the "old" string that needs to be replaced; in this case that is "\r\n". The second parameter is the new string that will replace the old string; in this case that is "
\r\n". Finally, the third parameter is the original containing string that is to be modified by the replacement; in this case that is the string contained in the variable $messageToClient. The string that is returned by the call to the function str_replace() is stored in a variable called $display.

Second, in lines 49–53 we surround the contents of $display with appropriate HTML markup so that the displayed page will be a complete and valid HTML5 document. The final value of $display is "echoed" back to the browser for display, resulting in the (very simple) web page shown in Figure 8.21.

8.7.9 Saving the User's Feedback on the Server with PHP File Output

In this section we discuss the final code segment of our feedbackFormProcess.php script, lines 58–66. The purpose of this final part of the script is to write the user's feedback to a file on the server.

A distinguishing feature of server-side programming is its ability to store information obtained from the user on the server, something that cannot be done with client-side technology like JavaScript. This information storage can be achieved in at least two ways:

▶ By placing the information directly into a file on disk
▶ By setting up communication with some kind of database and storing the data in the form required by that database

We will be looking at the database option in the following two chapters. In this section, we will look at the simpler case of file storage.

The feedback submitted by the user has already been sent to our business via email. However, it is also a good idea for our business to log all client feedback in a file on the server, so that we have it all in one place and can go through it at a later date to process it in some way, if we wish. We will store all user feedback in a file called `feedback.txt` in a subdirectory called `data`.

Whenever we wish to use a PHP script to write data to, or read data from, a file, the first step is opening the file. We accomplish this with another built-in PHP function called `fopen()`. Typically this function takes these two parameters

▶ The name of a file or a URL containing the name of a file
▶ The *mode* in which the file is to be opened

and returns a file variable that can be used to work with the file once it has been opened.

The mode depends on the type of operation(s) we want to perform on the file once it has been opened. In our case, we are opening the file `data/feedback.txt` with the mode value `"a"` (line 58). This mode means that the file will be opened in "append mode", which in turn means that any new writing we do will take place *after* the existing last character of the file. In other words, we're adding to the end of the file. If the file does not exist, it will be created and then opened for writing. TABLE 8.2 shows a list of other modes that can be used for opening a file.

Let's get back to our usage of this function. The value returned by the function call in line 58 is stored in a variable called `$fileVar`. From this point on, we can refer to the file by using the variable name `$fileVar`, in a read or write operation for example.

TABLE 8.2 Various modes for PHP file I/O.

Mode	Description	Notes
"r"	Read from the beginning of the file	
"r+"	Read and write from the beginning of the file	
"w"	Write from the beginning of the file	Previous contents are destroyed and file is created if it does not exist already
"w+"	Read and write from the beginning of the file	Previous contents are destroyed and file is created if it does not exist already
"a"	Write from the end of the file	Create file if it doesn't exist
"a+"	Read and write from the end of the file	Create file if it doesn't exist
"x"	Create a file for writing from the beginning	Return an error if file already exists
"x+"	Create a file for reading and writing from the beginning	Return an error if file already exists

We also have another interesting (and somewhat scary) appendage to the function call (line 59):

```
or die("Error: Could not open the log file.")
```

This is actually just a handy way of saying that if the function returns an error, terminate the script after displaying the message shown in the argument of the `die()` function.

Note the path to the `feedback.txt` file in line 58. Because the script that is writing to this file is in the `scripts` subdirectory, and the `data` subdirectory containing `feedback.txt` is at the same level as the `scripts` subdirectory, we have to move up one level from `scripts` and then go down into `data` to reach `feedback.txt`.

Because we have opened the file for writing, we can use the function `fwrite()` to write to the file. The function `fwrite()` also takes two parameters:

▶ The first parameter is the file variable returned by the call to `fopen()`. In our case, this is the variable `$fileVar`.

▶ The second parameter is the string that you want to write to the file.

Now, of course, we want to write to the log file the message string stored in the variable `$messageToClient`. However, before writing the message itself we want to write a blank line followed by a line of dashes to signal the start of a new log entry and then the date of this entry, and only *then* the actual message. Thus we have three calls to `fwrite()` (lines 60–66), and, as before, we use the function `die()` to terminate the program with an error message if any one of the writing operations fails for any reason. A typical entry in this log file is shown in Figure 8.22, which also illustrates an alternate date/time format.

This completes our discussion of the server-side processing of our feedback form.

8.8 Revising the Implementation of Our BMI Calculator to Calculate Server-Side

In the previous discussion of our feedback form submission, all of our server-side processing was done by a PHP script contained in the single file `feedbackFormProcess.php`. In this and the following sections, you will learn how to write programmer-defined PHP functions that may be stored in a separate file and then included into your main "driver" script from that file. Breaking up even a relatively small script in this way makes it more modular and helps you deal with error tracking and updating if required. In other words, it makes "script maintenance" much easier.

So, let us revisit our BMI calculator developed over Chapters 5 to 7. The actual BMI calculation in those versions of the calculator was implemented using JavaScript. The calculator accepted the user's height and weight and displayed the user's BMI after a short JavaScript calculation. We gave the user the option of getting a detailed BMI report, and another option of receiving it by email. Since we were working entirely within the limitations of JavaScript, we displayed the BMI information with the help of a JavaScript popup window or a new web page created by JavaScript, and were forced to omit the sending of any emails.

In this chapter, we will retain our client-side data validation, which is best done on the client side to avoid unnecessary and potentially harmful data being transferred to the server. However, once we are certain the data is valid, we will transfer that data to the server and perform the BMI computations on the server side,[1] with PHP functions that are stored in a file separate from our main script. Then we will send out an email if requested, as well as return a browser display of the BMI calculation result. We will also implement the email functionality this time by using HTML encoded messages, rather than just plain text.

Thus our remaining objectives of this exercise are:

▶ To write programmer-defined PHP functions, store them in a file of their own, and include that file into a main "driver" script where they can then be used
▶ To perform numerical calculations in PHP
▶ To learn how to send HTML-encoded email messages

8.8.1 What Happens When the User Clicks
`Compute your BMI`

A browser display of our BMI form is shown in **FIGURE 8.23**, where we have entered reasonable values for the form fields. Note that we have chosen one unit from the metric system (kilograms, for weight) and one non-metric unit (inches, for height), just to remind ourselves that it doesn't matter.

As with our feedback form, when the user clicks the `Compute your BMI` button on the BMI calculator form, the first thing that happens is the validation of the form data. Only if all the input data is valid will the form data be uploaded to the server for processing. Otherwise the user will have to correct the invalid data and resubmit.

If all of the input data *is* valid, the data from the form is sent to the server. Then the following two actions are performed by our PHP script:

▶ Either a simple report containing the user's BMI value, or a more detailed report if the user has requested one, is constructed and displayed in the browser. To get the more detailed report, the user must check the box indicating that choice on the form. An example of the detailed version is shown in **FIGURE 8.24**. In this case, note that the user has also checked the box requesting an email report, as the last line of the display indicates.
▶ If the user has requested it by checking the corresponding checkbox, an email message containing the chosen BMI report is now sent as well. An example of the email version of the detailed report being read by the **roundcube** email client is shown in **FIGURE 8.25**. Note that this email message is in HTML form, not just a plain text email. We will discuss the creation of such messages shortly. Note that if you try the form yourself from the book's website, for example, and cannot find the email in your INBOX, you should check your

---

[1] Revalidating form input data on the server side is also a good idea, but for simplicity we have omitted that step.

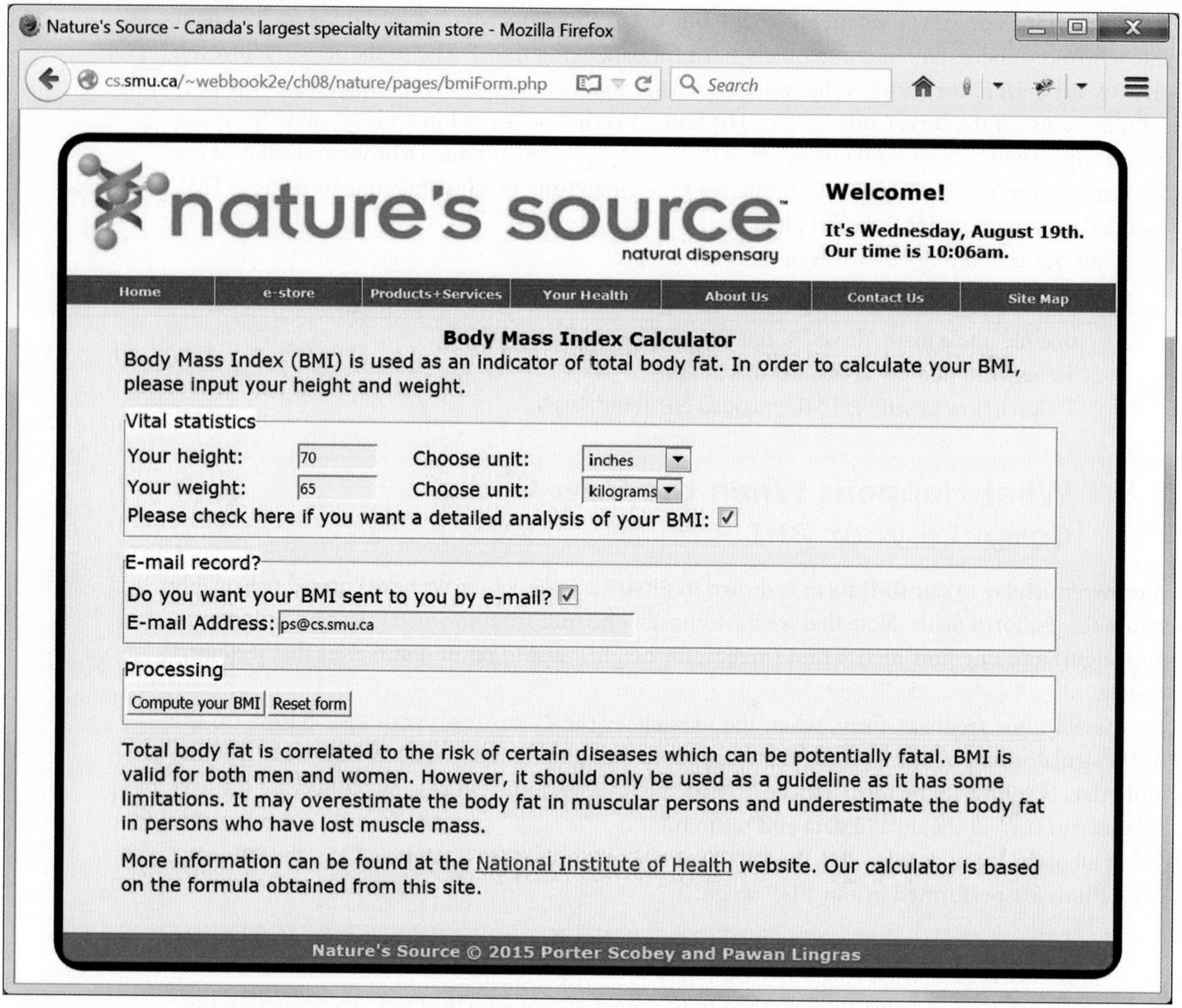

FIGURE 8.23 `graphics/ch08/nature/displayBmiFormPhp.jpg`
A Firefox browser display of `ch08/nature/pages/bmiForm.php`, with the form completely filled out with valid information and ready to be submitted.

SPAM box. Email messages that are coded using HTML are often subjected to stricter spam filtering scrutiny. The problem is further exacerbated by the fact that the sender address may not match the server that is sending the email message, which is yet another reason for the spam filter to be suspicious. This is one of the curses of the proliferation of email messages. You want to make sure that the email is as user-specific as possible, so that the spam filter does not suspect a mass emailing. Also, if you experiment with the BMI form many times, a spam filter may suspect that an automatic mailer is trying to bombard you with multiple copies of the mail and start blocking the message.

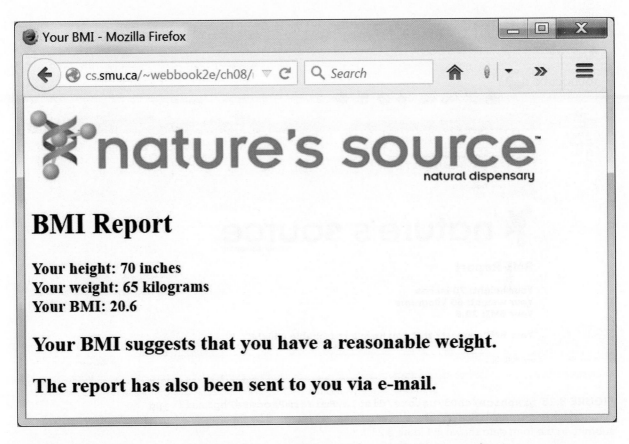

FIGURE 8.24 `graphics/ch08/nature/displayBmiFormProcessPhpBrowser.jpg`
A Firefox browser display of the web page report received by the user as the result of the script in Figure 8.27 processing the form data shown in Figure 8.23 after it has been submitted.

In the following sections, we discuss in detail the script that makes the decisions described in the above list and performs the required actions. But first, for the sake of completeness, let's review the uploading of our BMI form data.

8.8.2 Uploading the BMI Form Data from the Client to the Server

As was the case with our feedback form, we also developed our BMI form and its data validation over Chapters 5, 6, and 7, but only now do we get to finally submit the form and have it processed on the server. The current version of our form is found in the file `ch08/nature/pages/bmiForm.php`. Once again we do not reproduce that entire file here, but instead just show the revised opening form tag (from lines 16–17 of the file):

```
<form id="bmiForm" onsubmit="return bmiFormValidate()"
  action="scripts/bmiFormProcess.php" method="post">
```

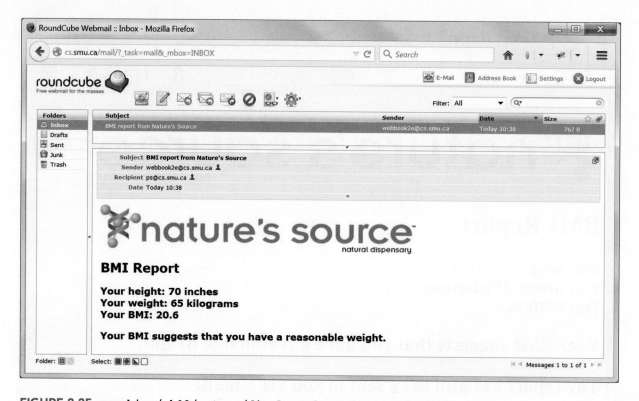

FIGURE 8.25 `graphics/ch08/nature/displayBmiFormProcessPhpEmail.jpg`
A **roundcube** web email client display showing the email received by the user (the business client) as a result of submitting the form data shown in Figure 8.23.

Unlike our feedback form, this form retains an `onsubmit` attribute since its data is still being validated by JavaScript. Note in particular the keyword `return` in front of the call to `bmiFormValidate()` in the value of the `onsubmit` attribute. The form will not be submitted if this `return` is not present, even if the function returns a value of `true`.

The value of the `action` attribute of the `form` element is now a call to the PHP script `bmiFormProcess.php`, which lives on the server (in `ch08/nature/scripts`), and which will process the data that is sent to the server from this form. And once again the `method` attribute of the `form` tag has the recommended value of `"post"` when we are sending information that is going to be stored on the server.

As you will see shortly, our complete PHP script on this occasion is actually split over two files—`bmiFormProcess.php` and `bmiCalculate.php`—but only our higher-level "driver" script in `bmiFormProcess.php` appears as the value of the `action` attribute, since the driver script itself takes care of the necessary access to the other script file.

8.8.3 An Overview of the "Driver" Script That Processes the BMI Form Data

Begin by looking at our PHP "driver" script in the file `bmiFormProcss.php`, which is shown in **FIGURE 8.26**. Note first of all that in line 14 of Figure 8.26 we perform a PHP *server-side include* that includes into this script the contents of the file `bmiCalculate.php`, which is shown in **FIGURE 8.27**, and which lives in the same directory as `bmiFormProcss.php`.

We have already seen how one PHP script can include another. In this case, we can view our use of this server-side include facility as helping us to practice *information hiding*, since we are, in effect, "hiding" some of our implementation details (some programmer-defined functions, in fact) in the included file.

```
1   <!DOCTYPE html>
2   <!-- bmiFormProcess.php
3   The driver script for the BMI calculation based on the
4   user data entered into the BMI form.
5   -->
6   <html lang="en">
7     <head>
8       <meta charset="utf-8">
9       <title>Your BMI</title>
10    </head>
11    <body>
12      <p>
13      <?php
14      include 'bmiCalculate.php';
15      if (isset($_POST['details']))
16          $message = detailedMessage($_POST['height'], $_POST['heightUnit'],
17                                     $_POST['weight'], $_POST['weightUnit']);
18      else
19          $message = simpleMessage($_POST['height'], $_POST['heightUnit'],
20                                   $_POST['weight'], $_POST['weightUnit']);
21      echo $message;
22      if (isset($_POST['wantMail']))
23      {
24          mailBMI($_POST['email'], $message);
25          echo "<h2>The report has also been sent to you via e-mail.</h2>";
26      }
27      ?>
28      </p>
29    </body>
30  </html>
```

FIGURE 8.26 `ch08/nature/scripts/bmiFormProcess.php`
The high-level "driver" PHP script, which processes form data such as that shown in Figure 8.23 after the form is submitted.

```
1   <?php
2   /*bmiCalculate.php
3   Functions to perform the BMI value calculation,
4   to one place after the decimal, assuming all data
5   input by the user has been validated, and to assemble
6   the text including this value to be returned to the
7   browser for display to the user
8   */
9
10  //Constructs and returns the simple form of the BMI message
11  function simpleMessage($height, $heightUnit, $weight, $weightUnit)
12  {
13      $bmi = sprintf("%1.2f", calculateBMI($height, $heightUnit,
14                                      $weight, $weightUnit));
15      $text = "<h1>BMI Report</h1><h3>Your BMI is $bmi.</h3>";
16      return $text;
17  }
18
19  //Constructs and returns the detailed form of the BMI message
20  function detailedMessage($height, $heightUnit, $weight, $weightUnit)
21  {
22      $bmi = sprintf("%.1f", calculateBMI($height, $heightUnit,
23          $weight, $weightUnit));
24      $text = "<p><img src='http://cs.smu.ca/webbook2e/images/naturelogo.gif'
25          alt='Nature's Source Logo'></p>
26          <h1>BMI Report</h1>
27          <h3>Your height: $height $heightUnit<br>
28          Your weight: $weight $weightUnit<br>
29          Your BMI: $bmi</h3>";
30      if ($bmi < 18.5)
31          $text .= "<h2>Your BMI suggests that you
32                      are underweight.</h2>";
33      else if ($bmi < 25)
34          $text .= "<h2>Your BMI suggests that you
35                      have a reasonable weight.</h2>";
36      else if ($bmi < 29)
37          $text .= "<h2>Your BMI suggests that you
38                      are overweight.</h2>";
39      else
40          $text .= "<h2>Your BMI suggests that you
41                      may be obese.</h2>";
42      return $text;
43  }
44
```

FIGURE 8.27   `ch08/nature/scripts/bmiCalculate.php`
The lower-level PHP functions that now perform, on the server side, the BMI calculations that were formerly performed on the client side

```
45   //Simple conversion functions
46   function inchesToCentimetres($height) { return $height*2.54; }
47   function poundsToKilograms($weight) { return $weight/2.2; }
48
49   //Computes and returns the BMI value. Note that it does not matter
50   //whether both units are metric or non-metric or mixed.
51   function calculateBMI($height, $heightUnit, $weight, $weightUnit)
52   {
53       if ($heightUnit == "inches") $height = inchesToCentimetres($height);
54       if ($weightUnit == "pounds") $weight = poundsToKilograms($weight);
55       $height /= 100.0; //Convert height from centimeters to meters
56       $bmi = $weight/($height*$height);
57       return $bmi;
58   }
59
60   //Constructs and sends the e-mail message as HTML
61   function mailBMI($email, $message)
62   {
63       $header = "MIME-Version: 1.0\r\n";
64       $header .= "Content-type: text/html; charset=utf-8\r\n";
65       $header .= "From: webbook2e@cs.smu.ca\r\n";
66       mail($email, "BMI report from Nature's Source", $message, $header);
67   }
68   ?>
```

FIGURE 8.27 `ch08/nature/scripts/bmiCalculate.php` (*continued*)

The "higher-level" functions `detailedMessage()`, `simpleMessage()`, and `mailBMI()` that are called by the "driver" script in `bmiFormProcess.php` are defined in the file `bmiCalculate.php`, along with some auxiliary "lower-level" functions used by these higher-level functions but not called directly from our driver script. We will discuss all of these functions in detail in subsequent sections, but before doing that we need to make some general remarks about programmer-defined functions in PHP.

The first thing to note is that the general format of a function definition in PHP is completely analogous to what we saw in JavaScript:

```
function nameOfFunction(parameter_list)
{
   ... PHP code to perform whatever the function does ...
}
```

The first line is the header of the function, and again it begins with the *keyword* `function`, which indicates the beginning of a function definition. This keyword is followed by the name of the function, which should (as always) be well chosen to indicate the purpose of the function. This, in turn, is followed by a comma-separated list of parameters the function should receive when it is called, enclosed in parentheses.

The parameters listed in the parentheses differ from their JavaScript equivalents in that each name has to be preceded by a $ sign. In this respect PHP parameters are just like PHP variables. The PHP code that actually performs the task of the function is, as usual, called the *function body* and is enclosed in the usual pair of braces {. . .} immediately following the function header.

The rest of the PHP script in `bmiFormProcess.php` is relatively simple. The variable `$message` is used to store the HTML markup that will be used for browser display as well as for emailing. If the user has requested a detailed report, the variable `$_POST['details']` will be set, and we will assign the value returned by the call to the function `detailedMessage()` to the variable `$message` (lines 16–17). On the other hand, if the user did not check the checkbox named `details`, the value of the variable `$_POST['details']` will not be set, and the variable `$message` will be assigned the value returned by the call to the function `simpleMessage()` (lines 19–20). In either case, the variable `$message` is then echoed to a dynamically generated web page similar to the one displayed in Figure 8.24.

The next decision to be made in our `bmiFormProcess.php` script is whether to send an email or not. This decision is based on whether the user has checked the checkbox named `wantMail`. If it *is* checked, then the corresponding variable `$_POST['wantMail']` in our PHP script will be set, and we therefore call the function `mailBMI()` to build and send an HTML-encoded email report (line 24). The function takes two parameters:

▶ `$_POST['email']`, which contains the value from the textbox named `email` in the form
▶ `$message`, which contains the message we just generated by one or the other of the two message-generating function calls

In this case we also echo a message to the end of the dynamically created web page saying that the BMI report has also been sent via email (line 25).

This completes the overview discussion of our driver script. In the following sections we proceed with a top-down discussion of the programmer-defined functions called by this driver script, namely `detailedMessage()`, `simpleMessage()`, and `mailBMI()`, as well as the lower-level programmer-defined functions that compute the BMI value.

8.8.4 Building the BMI Report Message with Programmer-Defined PHP Functions

We begin our study of the code from `bmiCalculate.php` by looking at the two functions `simpleMessage()` and `detailedMessage()`, shown in lines 10–43 of Figure 8.27.

Consider the function `detailedMessage()` in lines 19–43 first. This function takes four parameters: `$height`, `$heightUnit`, `$weight`, and `$weightUnit`. In the body of the function, the very first statement (line 22) is a call to the built-in PHP function `sprintf()`. We use it here to format the numerical value and return the result as a string. We should mention that this function is similar to the function by the same name in the programming language C, on the off chance you may have seen it there. Note that here we are making good use of the appropriate built-in PHP function for this particular task, while in JavaScript we wrote our own (for purposes of illustration, as you may recall).

The function can take a variable number of parameters. In our case, we have two:

▶ The first parameter must be a string indicating a format specification for the number to be printed (the second parameter). We are using the string `"%.lf"`, which means that the value given by the second parameter should be printed as a floating-point value (real number) with one place after the decimal. For a link to details on other formatting options, see the end-of-chapter **References**.

▶ The second argument in our case is the actual value that will be printed. It will be the value returned by a call to another programmer-defined function called `calculateBMI()`, which also takes four parameters, `$height`, `$heightUnit`, `$weight`, and `$weightUnit`, and returns the value of the BMI. We discuss this function in the following section.

The string returned by the call to the function `sprintf()` is stored in a variable called `$bmi` (line 22). The next statement in the function `detailedMessage()` (lines 24–29) builds the HTML-encoded message (i.e., a message containing HTML markup) using the four values that were passed to the function as well as the properly formatted value of the BMI given by the variable `$bmi`. The complete string thus formed is stored in a variable called `$text`. Note that in this case, in the interests of brevity and simplicity, we do not bother to create a valid HTML5 page for the display.

Next, based on the range within which the BMI value lies, a message about whether the BMI is low, high, or reasonable is appended via a compound conditional statement. This conditional is really a sequence of nested `if`-statements of the kind also available in JavaScript.

The final message in the variable `$text` is returned to the calling function.

The function `simpleMessage()` returns a simpler report, but does similar computations. It contains nothing that requires further discussion, but you should confirm this by reading through its code in any case.

Before we leave this part of the discussion, line 24 of Figure 8.27 deserves some additional comment. Note that the value of the `src` attribute is an absolute path to the logo image file. In fact, it is a complete URL to that file. As you know, in earlier chapters we have emphasized that relative paths are always to be preferred to absolute paths, but sometimes you just cannot use a relative path, and this is one of those times. Remember that we are preparing some text that may be sent as part of an email message to a user who could be anywhere, and a relative path in that user's email will be meaningless to that user, so the user's email program needs to know where (on the Internet) the image file is located. We could have used the full URL to the logo image file in `ch08/nature/images`, but to make the URL somewhat shorter we have made a new `images` directory in our home directory and placed a copy of the logo image file there.

8.8.5 Computing the BMI Value: Numerical Computations in PHP, and More Programmer-Defined Functions

In previous sections, we dealt primarily with the string manipulations needed to create dynamic web pages and send emails. In this section, we will look more closely at numerical computations in PHP, which we choose to perform with programmer-defined functions in the same way we did in JavaScript. In fact, what we do here is remarkably similar to what we already did in JavaScript.

As we have already observed, the numerical computations used by the functions `simple-Message()` and `detailedMessage()` are performed by the function `calculateBMI()` (lines 51–58 of Figure 8.27), which takes the four parameters, `$height`, `$heightUnit`, `$weight`, and `$weightUnit`, and returns the BMI value. Note that prior to calling this function, all input data entered by the user has been validated client-side, so we can assume that the fields `height` and `weight` are numbers lying within a reasonable range.

The BMI calculation can be done in various ways, but before doing any calculations we choose to convert all values to the metric system, if they are not metric already. Hence, if the user has entered the height in inches, it is converted to centimeters using the function `inchesToCentimetres()` (line 46) in the first conditional statement (line 53). Similarly, if the user has entered weight in pounds, it is converted to kilograms using the function `poundsToKilograms()` (line 47) in the second conditional statement (line 54). The function `calculateBMI()` then converts the centimeters to meters by dividing the height by 100 and the BMI is simply calculated (in a metric-unit calculation) as the ratio of the weight to the square of the height (lines 55–56).

The functions `inchesToCentimetres()` and `poundsToKilograms()` return the centimeter or kilogram equivalent of inches or pounds using appropriate factors.

In these functions you see the arithmetic operators for multiplication (`*`) and division (`/`) in action, and you will be relieved to learn that the usual operators for addition (`+`), subtraction (`-`), and modulus (`%`) are also available in PHP, all conforming to the usual precedence rules, again as in JavaScript.

8.8.6 Building and Sending an HTML-Encoded Email BMI Report to the User with Another Programmer-Defined Function

The email messages that we sent to the business (Figure 8.19) and the client (Figure 8.20) from our feedback form were simple text messages. However, the email message shown in Figure 8.25 is in HTML format. The built-in PHP function `mail()` can actually be used to send any type of mail that is normally sent through most email clients (including HTML email).

Our programmer-defined function `mailBMI()` to handle this is shown in lines 60–67 of Figure 8.27. This function has a little more work to do before it calls the built-in function `mail()` that sends the HTML version of the BMI report, so it needs the following two parameters:

▶ The email address of the recipient (obtained directly from the submitted form in `$_POST['email']`, as shown in the call to this function in line 24 of Figure 8.26)
▶ Our HTML-encoded BMI report

To get the second parameter in the proper form so that the message is sent as HTML rather than plain text by `mail()`, we need to make that message conform to the requirements of the SMTP for such messages.

Here this means that we have to provide an appropriate header, which we do in lines 63–64 of Figure 8.27, which will have the effect of notifying the recipient's email client that this is an

HTML email. The rest of the header is the same as before, and again contains the `"From: "` address (line 65).

Finally, our programmer-defined function `mailBMI()` then calls the built-in PHP function `mail()` to send the message. You should note that some recipients may not receive the message as HTML, either because their email program cannot handle it or because they have this feature turned off in that program. This is less of a problem nowadays but still one to consider.

This completes our discussion of the programmer-defined functions called either directly or indirectly from our driver script `bmiFormProcess.php`.

8.9 PHP Development and Testing

As with any programming language, writing PHP code will not always go smoothly. You will occasionally discover, sadly, that your code does not do what you wanted it to do. Or, even worse, it may cause your page to "crash" and not display properly or not display at all.

PHP does not as yet have a built-in debugger, so if there are semantic errors that simply cause your script to behave improperly you may find the old-fashioned debugging method of inserting output statements to display variable values at various execution points very helpful.

On the other hand, when you are beginning to program in PHP you may find that your problems tend to be syntax-related issues, and here PHP can be quite helpful by displaying an appropriate error message. For example, suppose that in line 12 of Figure 8.1 you change the name of the `date()` function to `datf()`. Then, instead of the complete page, including the welcome message and date shown in Figure 8.2, you will likely see only a partially displayed page, and then an error message something like the following:

```
Fatal error: Call to undefined function datf() in
welcome.php on line 12
```

This happens because you asked the PHP processor to call a function that it does not recognize, and the result is that the page rendering stops at that point. This can be frustrating, but you should regard it as a good thing, since you would not want your pages showing up on your users' screens with incorrect and potentially embarrassing information on them. It's much better to catch such problems at the development stage, and when PHP is set up to show us such errors we should take advantage of the assistance it provides. See the end-of-chapter **References** section for more on PHP error levels and error reporting.

Another "quick and dirty" (though quite useful) technique is the use of the "`or die()`" construct as illustrated in lines 58–66 of Figure 8.18. This can be useful if something is going wrong with your server-side activity, such as your attempt to open, read from, or write to, a file, or to access a database. These sorts of errors are the kind we will encounter and have to deal with when we start using PHP to communicate with our database in Chapter 10.

If your PHP script fails for any reason, it will (by default, if configured to do so) send to the browser a message containing the name of the file in which the offending script is located, the line number where the error occurred, and a message that (one hopes) describes the problem, as mentioned above. This is excellent default behavior to leave in place, but if you wish to do so there are ways to adjust the "level" of error reporting that PHP provides, and there may be some errors you wish to ignore from time to time. The `error_reporting()` function allows you to set the error level for a particular script, and even turn it off completely should you really wish to live dangerously and do so. Follow the link given in the **References** for further information on this function.

For the sake of brevity, we did not revalidate on the server any of the data sent from our forms on the client side. However, you can never be too careful, and server-side validation as well as client-side validation of user-entered data is something you should consider implementing in a production website.

Summary

Note that in this summary we state some comparisons with JavaScript that assume you are familiar with that language up to the level of the coverage in the earlier chapters of this text.

PHP, invented by Rasmus Lerdorf in the mid-1990s, is one of the most widely used nonproprietary server-side technologies in use on the web today. It is an interpreted programming language designed specifically for preprocessing data on the server side and sending the results of that preprocessing back to a browser on the client side as HTML markup. As a programming language, it is another in the C-based category of languages, though it inherits much of its syntax more directly from Perl and has much in common with JavaScript as well.

One or more PHP scripts may be embedded within HTML markup, as long as each one is enclosed in `<?php...?>` delimiters, in which case the script is executed on the server and its output is returned to the browser, along with whatever normal HTML was in the document, to be rendered for viewing by the user. Thus the user cannot see the PHP script code by choosing the "view source" option in the browser. Additional scripts or portions of a script may also be contained in one or more separate files and included into another script located within an HTML page.

All of the standard decision making and looping control constructs from JavaScript are available in PHP. PHP also has the usual arithmetic operators and the two scalar numerical types `integer` and `double`. The two other scalar types in PHP are `string` and `boolean`, and there are two compound types, `array` and `object`. We have not used `object`. Like JavaScript, PHP is dynamically typed, which means that a variable has the type of the value most recently assigned to it, and if a variable has no value at all its type is the special type `null`. The `null` type has only a single value, which is also `NULL` (or `null`, since keywords are case-insensitive).

Text output from a PHP script is usually accomplished with the `echo`-statement. A *here document* is a very convenient way of outputting a large amount of text. PHP strings can use single or double quotes, but you must remember that variables within double quotes are replaced by their values, a process called *variable interpolation*.

PHP also has functions, both built-in and programmer-defined, which are similar to those found in JavaScript and which can and should be used to modularize your code for enhanced readability. Variables declared in a function are local to that function. Some useful PHP built-in functions, listed alphabetically rather than in the order we encountered them, include `count()`, `date()`, `die()`, `error_reporting()`, `exit()`, `fopen()`, `fwrite()`, `include()`, `mail()`, `rand()`, `replace()`, and `sprintf()`.

We again used the JavaScript function, `setInterval()` to execute another JavaScript function periodically. In this case it was in the context of the AJAX technology, which we put to good use to refresh the time and date on the pages of our **Nature's Source** website.

The PHP script that will process the form data submitted from the browser on the client side must be supplied as the value of the `action` attribute of the HTML `form` element. The POST method is the recommended method for submitting form data. The GET method, in which the passed data appears at the end of the processing script's URL, can also be used for small amounts of data if security is not an issue, especially if you don't want the bother of setting up a form to collect the data.

On the server side, data passed to a script should be accessed via the superglobals `$_POST` or `$_GET` (depending on which method was used to pass the data). These are associative arrays in which we access the values by keys, which may be strings. We must be careful how we use quotes when working with these arrays.

We introduced the idea of a PHP *session*, and used one to keep track of the date and time refreshes on our website. This required using another superglobal, namely `$_SESSION`.

It is a good idea to validate form data on the client side before submitting it to the server for processing. When doing this with a boolean validation function as the value of the `onsubmit` attribute of the `form` element, you must remember to include the keyword `return` in front of the function name. Without it, the data will not be uploaded even if the function returns `true`. Though we did not do it, it is also a good idea to validate, or revalidate, form data on the server side.

You also saw how to create and send an email message that appears as an HTML page in the user's email client.

Some differences in PHP, as compared with JavaScript, include the following:

1. PHP has an additional kind of single-line comment introduced by the # character (i.e., in addition to the `//` and `/*...*/` comments found in JavaScript that are also available in PHP).
2. All PHP variables, including array names, begin with the dollar sign character (`$`).
3. PHP has case-sensitive variable names, but reserved words and function names that are case-insensitive.
4. The string concatenation operator is the period (`.`), not the plus operator (`+`).
5. PHP arrays are unlike arrays in JavaScript or any other language. Among the differences is the fact that you can arrange to access elements of the same array with either a numerical or string index.
6. The contents of an external JavaScript file are *not* enclosed in a `<script>`...`</script>` tag pair, but the contents of an external PHP file *are* enclosed in `<?php...?>` delimiters.

Quick Questions to Test Your Basic Knowledge

1. Who was the original developer of PHP?
2. What did the acronym PHP stand for in the beginning, and what do most people think it stands for now?
3. What is the major difference between how JavaScript is used and how PHP is used in web programming? Hint: Perhaps we should ask what the major difference is in *where* they are used.
4. What are the opening and closing delimiters for a PHP script?
5. We have seen that there is more than one way to make CSS styles available to our HTML documents and more than one way to make JavaScript scripts available to our HTML documents. How many ways can you think of to make a PHP script available to your HTML documents, what are they, which is preferred, and why?
6. What is the difference between the case-sensitivity of PHP and that of JavaScript?
7. What is the major difference between variable names in PHP and variable names in JavaScript?
8. What is the difference between the way two strings are combined (concatenated) in JavaScript and in PHP?
9. How does the . = operator work?
10. We could have used JavaScript to display the date and time on our pages so that the pages would look the same as they do using our PHP scripts. Why would this not be a good idea?
11. Why did we "feel the need" to employ AJAX with PHP on our web pages?
12. What is the name of the type of object that we need to create in order to make an AJAX request?
13. What is a PHP session?
14. What is a PHP superglobal?
15. What is the name of the superglobal we use when working with a PHP session?
16. What are the names of the two "methods" used to transfer data from a form in the browser to a server-side PHP script that will process the data?
17. What is the name of the superglobal we would use to access the data that had been passed to a PHP script by appending it to the end of the script's URL?
18. What was the purpose of inserting the two-character combination \r\n into some of the text output of our PHP scripts?
19. What happens, or at least what *should* happen, in a testing environment when your PHP script contains a syntax error?
20. In what context might we use the PHP die() function?

21. For what purpose did we use the JavaScript `setInterval()` function this time?
22. How, and for what reason, did we use a "hidden" HTML element?
23. What are the possible values that might be returned by the PHP function call `rand(15, 20)`?
24. When we have a reference to an HTML DOM object, and want the content of the corresponding HTML element, what property of that object do we use?

 # Short Exercises to Improve Your Basic Understanding

1. Revise `ch08/welcome.php` so that the script contains just a single `echo` statement.
2. Confirm our claim that a misspelling of the `date()` function (in `ch08/welcome.php`, for example) will generate a PHP error similar to the one described. If this does not happen, your PHP installation may not be set up to display such errors, and you may want to speak to your administrator, or take steps yourself to make this happen.
3. This exercise is best done on a desktop PC where you have more "real estate". Open three different browser windows, and enter one of the three URLs—of `welcome.php`, `welcome_refresh.php`, and `welcome_ajax.php`—in each of the three windows, without actually loading any of the three pages just yet. When you have done this, load all three pages as quickly as you can and start counting. After about a minute, the first page will still be black, the second page should be entirely in some new color, and the third page should have just the two lines with the date and time in some new color. Wait a couple more minutes at least, and make sure you understand what you are seeing.
4. In both our "full-page" refresh example and our "time-and-date-only" refresh example using AJAX, we used a counter in the `$_SESSION` array to keep track of the number of refreshes. However, we were really only interested in whether the page had been refreshed or not. Rewrite either or both of these examples to use a boolean array value rather than the counter array value that we did use.
5. In `test_get.php` as shown in Figure 8.14, insert single quotes from around `value1` and `value2` in line 10 and try the example again to see if that makes any difference. Then undo that change and next remove the single quotes from around `value1` and `value2` in line 12 to see if that makes any difference when you run the example one more time.
6. We went to some extra effort to make the browser display page confirming a feedback form submission a valid HTML5 page, but we did not do this for the browser display page reporting the BMI calculation. Revise the `bmiCalculate.php` script shown in Figure 8.27 so that the resulting page shown in Figure 8.24 is a valid HTML5 page.

7. Trace through all the decision paths in the filling out both the feedback form and the BMI form.

8. Confirm that you need the `return` in `return bmiFormValidate()` in line 16 of the file `ch08/nature/pages/bmiForm.php`.

9. Check to see what, if anything, happens when you remove the `<?php...?>` delimiters from the included file `ch08/nature/scripts/bmiCalculate.php`.

10. Remove line 14 containing the `include()` function call in `bmiFormProcess.php` from its current location and put it in a new one-line PHP script in the head of the file. Test the revised script to see if it works as before. If not, explain why not; if so, explain why we might want to do this.

Exercises on the Parallel Project

1. Modify the pages of your developing business website to include a welcome message with the date and time at your business location that is dynamically produced on the server for display in the user's browser. This feature is analogous to what is seen in this chapter's version of our Nature's Source website, and your version should use both PHP and AJAX in the same way that we did.

2. Implement server-side PHP processing for your own feedback form that is analogous to what we described in this chapter. That is, when the user fills out and submits your feedback form, the following things should happen:
   • Your business receives an email version of the feedback.
   • The user receives an email confirmation of the feedback.
   • The user gets an immediate browser display confirming the feedback submission.
   • A dated copy of the feedback is stored on the server.
   Use a textfile called `feedback.txt` in a subdirectory called `data` to log your feedback messages. Also, since your business may not yet actually be up and running and have a bona fide email address, the "business email address" can be your own email address. In fact, for testing purposes, you can be both customer and business, but the messages received should be at least slightly different in each case so that they may be distinguished from one another. This too is what we did in the text.

3. If there is time, implement in a similar manner the server-side PHP processing for your previously developed order form that provides the same four features described above for your feedback form. In this case, the output should include a summary of the input data, as well as the results of any calculations involving that input data. Each part of the output should be presented in a reasonable format appropriate for that part of the output (email, web page, or file on disk).

What Else You May Want or Need to Know

1. We have used the PHP script delimiters `<?php . . . ?>` to separate PHP code from non-PHP code. We recommend consistent use of these delimiters, though you can also expect to see the short-form delimiters `<? . . . ?>` used as well. However, these are less portable since their use can be disabled in the PHP configuration.

2. The use of # as a single-line comment delimiter, the use of the $ to start a variable name, and the here document are all features that are inherited directly from the Perl programming language, of which PHP may be regarded as a direct descendant.

3. When you are trying to understand how a PHP script works, be careful to distinguish between PHP's *read mode* and its *execution mode*. Only PHP code that is enclosed between proper PHP code delimiters will cause the PHP processor to be invoked to process that code. This is *execution mode*. Anything else is simply read and forwarded on to the browser (this is *read mode*).

4. We have used the `include()` function to include external files into our HTML files or into PHP scripts. An alternative is the `require()` function. The main difference is that if there is a problem, `require()` will report an error and terminate the script, while `include()` will report a warning and let the script continue. Thus `include()` takes a more "relaxed" approach and is perhaps more useful from a development standpoint.

5. Before version 4.1 of PHP, it was common (and perhaps still is) to make use of the fact that a value of a `name` attribute of a form element from a form on the client side will show up as a variable name (beginning with a $, of course) in your PHP script on the server side, and the value of that variable will be the data submitted by the user via that element. For example, if we were making use of this facility, instead of accessing$_POST['firstName'] we would simply access $firstName.

    This may seem to be very convenient, in fact more convenient than using a super-global, but it also turns out to be less secure. For that reason, in order to make use of this feature, the `register_globals` directive must be turned on in the PHP configuration file, and starting with PHP 4.2, `register_globals` has been turned off by default. Moreover, by the time you read this, if PHP 6 or a later version is available, and you are using it, you may find that this feature has simply gone away entirely.

6. Recall that JavaScript is not permitted to read from and write to files, for obvious security reasons, since it is downloaded from the web and runs in the user's web browser. PHP, on the other hand, runs on the server and, therefore, is not subject to the same restrictions. We used PHP for very simple file output, appending each new feedback item to a file of text, but other file operations are possible, as indicated by various I/O modes shown in Table 8.2.

7. Just as there are many JavaScript frameworks freely available for download, as we mentioned in previous chapters, there are also numerous PHP frameworks available for download as well, such as CakePHP and Zend. On the other hand, one cannot obtain PHP code from sites on the web in the same way one can find JavaScript code, because PHP code has "disappeared" from a web page by the time that page has reached the browser. Nevertheless, there are also many PHP scripts that you might find useful and which are freely available for download from various web repositories. See the **References** for some relevant links.

 # References

1. We refer you again to the authors' version of our **Nature's Source** website, since you cannot get the full effect of this chapter's version of the website simply by loading the home page from a copy of the website on your PC, unless it is being "served" by a web server on that PC. This is because the PHP these pages contain will not be activated unless the pages are served from a PHP-aware web browser. This is analogous to the situation back in Chapter 3 when we first started using SSI. If you have the necessary setup of your own, or if your instructor has set one up and installed our files, fine. If not, you can go to our website and load the index file for the Chapter 8 version of our **Nature's Source** website from this location:

    ```
    http://cs.smu.ca/webbook2e/ch08/nature
    ```

2. The ultimate source of PHP information, including the latest downloads and up-to-date information on language and library developments is, of course, the "home" of PHP, which you can find here:

    ```
    http://www.php.net
    ```

    For example, a comprehensive listing of PHP functions can be found at this location:

    ```
    http://www.php.net/manual/en/language.functions.php
    ```

    Information on some of the particular functions we have used can be found at these locations:

    ```
    http://ca.php.net/manual/en/function.date.php
    ```

    ```
    http://ca.php.net/manual/en/function.include.php
    ```

    ```
    http://ca.php.net/manual/en/function.sprintf.php
    ```

    ```
    http://ca.php.net/manual/en/function.mail.php
    ```

And, from the form of these few links, if there is another PHP built-in function about which you need information, you can probably guess where to go for that information. Also, information on the here document (or *heredoc*) and the use of quotes when working with arrays can be found here:

```
http://php.net/manual/en/language.types.string.php
```

```
http://php.net/manual/en/language.types.array.php
```

3. As they usually do for important web technologies, the W3Schools folks provide a PHP tutorial with lots of useful examples and a PHP reference at their site:

    ```
    http://www.w3schools.com
    ```

4. Another PHP tutorial site, similar in approach to that of W3Schools but perhaps with some additional detail, can be found here:

    ```
    http://www.tizag.com/phpT/
    ```

5. Here is a page containing a table showing a number of different PHP frameworks and their features:

    ```
    http://www.phpframeworks.com/
    ```

6. Here are a couple of links to sites containing free PHP scripts that you might find useful:

    ```
    http://gscripts.net/
    ```

    ```
    http://www.hotscripts.com/
    ```

    A Google search will turn up many other similar sites.

7. Our Table 8.1 gives just a very brief summary of PHP history. Like many other web technologies, its history can reasonably be described as "tortured". You may find it interesting to check out further details on Wikipedia at this link:

    ```
    https://en.wikipedia.org/wiki/PHP#History
    ```

CHAPTER NINE

MySQL for Server-Side Data Storage

CHAPTER CONTENTS

Overview and Objectives

From the dawn of the computer age, computers have been required to deal with large amounts of data. In the beginning, much of that data was in the form of results from numerical calculations that scientists at universities and other research institutions wanted to perform. But it was not long before companies large and small doing business of all kinds, governments, and other organizations wanted to get in on the action. And all of them had data, lots and lots of data.

In the early years, data was simply stored in files, but that was soon recognized as an inadequate solution to the problem of organizing data and keeping it organized. Indeed, this problem was recognized early in the game as one that would be of long-term and great significance, and much effort has been devoted to the topic over the last half-century.

A major problem that needed to be solved was the duplication of data, which made it a nightmare to keep all versions of the data up to date. Moreover, duplication required additional storage, at a time when storage was relatively expensive. But the real problem was that humans had to be intimately involved in the various processes needed to maintain the data. And humans make mistakes.

In this chapter we will once again give just a brief introduction to a topic of enduring interest to both researchers in computing science and end users of computers and the software that runs on them. That topic is the solution to many of those early problems that cropped up in the history of computing: the *database*. We begin by looking at the most widely used form of database, the *relational database*, and then move on to get some exposure to one of the major software packages for dealing with that kind of database, namely **MySQL**. This is a powerful, public-domain relational database management software system that can be used on a wide variety of computing platforms, and one that is freely available by download over the Internet. It is especially popular for website development using PHP. Databases like MySQL, as well as other (proprietary) systems from companies like Oracle and IBM, now play a major role in virtually all business applications that run on computers.

In particular, this chapter covers the following topics:

▶ A brief discussion of the history and a high-level view of the relational database model, including tables and their rows (*records* or *objects*) and their columns (*fields* or *attributes*)

▶ Some high-level goals to keep in mind when you are designing your own database

▶ A brief discussion of some important aspects of the "preferred" structure of a relational database, including *normalization*, table *keys*, the possible relationships between tables, and the *functional dependencies* between record attributes

▶ Making use of online resources to help you set up a suitable database for your needs

▶ The **phpMyAdmin** interface to a **MySQL** database system, and setting up a MySQL database for our **Nature's Source** website using this interface

▶ Using the *Structured Query Language* (*SQL*) to manipulate a database in various ways

▶ A brief look at the command-line interface of MySQL

▶ Importing and exporting tables and databases to and from MySQL

9.1 Relational Databases

At the highest level, a *database* is simply a place where you store data. And again, at the highest level, the first rule of databases is to think about what should go into one, and what you expect to get out of it, before you start putting one together. Most people are familiar with "tables" of data, and the first impulse might be to put all of your data into one giant table. You should resist this urge if you have it, since you might wind up with a *spreadsheet* (which is *not* a database) containing all of your data, and if you do you will eventually have a great deal of trouble getting the kind of access you want to the information you have stored.

So, one of the primary design issues in creating a database is deciding what representation model to use when doing so. Such a model must provide a theory or specification describing how the database is to be structured and used.

Early databases used somewhat unstructured hierarchical and network models. In 1970, Edgar F. Codd from IBM introduced the *relational database model*, which revolutionized the database world. Some of the newer models, such as the *object model*, the *object-relational model*, and the more recent *NoSQL models*, may be advantageous in some cases, but the relational database remains the most widely used model. It is the one we will use in all of our discussions in this book.

If you permit us a few words of formal-speak, we can say that data in the relational model is represented as *mathematical relations*. The data is manipulated using *relational calculus* (or *relational algebra*). The mathematical basis for the relational database model makes it possible to minimize *data redundancy* and verify *data integrity*. Although there are many subtleties involved, and nonobvious aspects to all of this, it is not quite as scary as it sounds.

In fact, we can say, somewhat more informally but still with complete accuracy, that data in a relational database is stored in tables, and a table is just what you thought it was. Each row of the table, called a *tuple* in relational algebra, corresponds to a *record* or an *object* (such as an item to be sold, or a service to be rendered). Each *field* in the record is called an *attribute* in database terminology and represents a *property* of an entity stored in a record (such as the color of an item to be sold or the price of a service to be rendered).

It is in making the decisions as to what goes into the various tables, and what the relationships between those tables should be, that you must be careful if you are to have a good *database design*.

9.2 Database Design Goals

Virtually every business needs to store its data in some form, and in deciding what that form should be, you should keep certain goals in mind:

▶ All data necessary for the smooth operation of the business needs to be recorded with whatever frequency the business deems appropriate.

▶ Data integrity must be maintained as new information is added, information currently stored is updated, and (perhaps) some information is deleted.

▶ The data must be stored in such a way that the business can easily retrieve whatever information it needs, in whatever form it is needed, and whenever it is required. This process is referred to as "querying the database", or submitting "queries" to the database. You do this using a special language called *SQL*, which we discuss later in this chapter.

▶ And finally, in the best of all worlds, the database would also occupy minimal storage, have lightning-fast response times to all queries, and be easily modifiable and extensible when the needs of the business change and grow.

An obvious question, of course, is this: What exactly are you trying to achieve by working toward these goals? One answer is that you are trying to have a database that avoids certain kinds of "anomalies" that tend to crop up with depressing regularity when you are working with a poorly designed database. These include:

▶ The *insertion anomaly*, which occurs when you are entering a new record, but not all fields of that record can be filled in because some of the required data is missing.

▶ The *update anomaly*, which occurs when information is updated in one place in the database, but the same information is not updated in some other database location. Elimination or minimization of redundant data in the database can help alleviate this problem, and also help to ensure more logical and efficient storage.

▶ The *deletion anomaly*, which occurs when deletion of one piece of information from the database forces the deletion of something else that you perhaps would not want deleted.

Achieving all of the above goals is a tall order, seldom realized by any real-world business, but if you are careful with your design, even to the point of just applying some common sense (that rare commodity) during setup, you may be able to avoid some major headaches down the road.

9.3 Some Architectural Aspects of a "Good" Database

We are all familiar with tables of data, and if we have some data to organize, one "quick and dirty" first-impulse solution might be to put it all into one large table, as we have already mentioned. The trouble with this approach is that the same data winds up being stored in several different places (data redundancy), we soon lose track of what we have stored, and it becomes more and more difficult over time to add new data or update the data we already have.

9.3.1 Database Normalization

To deal with this problem, Codd did something more than simply invent the relational database. He also developed the concept of *normalization* for a relational database, a process that can help us to achieve at least some of the above goals.

A database is said to be in a particular *normal form* if the relationships between the attributes of the entities represented by the records in the tables of the database are rigorously defined in a certain way. Originally, in 1970, Codd specified three normal forms. These have the somewhat unimaginative, but easy-to-remember, names *First Normal Form*, *Second Normal Form*, and *Third Normal Form*, which are often abbreviated *1NF*, *2NF*, and *3NF*.

Since Codd's original proposal, several additional normal forms have been described, including the Boyce-Codd Normal Form (BCNF), as well as 4NF and 5NF, and a 6NF for "temporal" databases, for example. Clearly you can take the normalization process some distance, but going beyond the second or third normal form is often unnecessary, and may even, in some cases, be counterproductive. There are even "denormalization" procedures that can be applied if it is discovered that more normalization than is desirable has been performed, and some needs to be "undone"! In any case, we will have no need to discuss any of these "higher-level" normal forms. For further information see the end-of-chapter **References**.

One important aspect of these normal forms to remember is that they are *cumulative* in the sense that to be in 2NF, a database must first be in 1NF, and to be in 3NF it must first be in 2NF, and so on. Also, a database is said to be in 1NF if each table in the database is in 1NF, and similarly for the higher normal forms.

The first normal form essentially deals with the "shape" of a record type. For a database to be in 1NF, each row of a table must have the same number of columns of information (i.e., each record must have the same number of attributes) and each attribute value must contain a single piece of information. A short way of describing the latter requirement is to say that each attribute value must be *atomic*.

You need to keep in mind, however, that just what *atomic* means in any given database can depend significantly on the nature of the data and the viewpoint of the database designer. For example, in one database the name of a customer might have the customer's first name, middle initial, and last name all together in one column and be regarded as being a single "atomic" value because there is no perceived need to have a name broken down into its constituent pieces. In another database, each of those three pieces of a name might be placed in its own column because there might well be a need for each part of the name to be accessible at one time or another, and having each name part in its own column makes that access much easier.

As a simple example, assume that we want to keep a list of products bought by a customer by using just two attributes (two fields per table row): `Customer` and `Product`. If a customer, say `Pawan`, buys two products, say `Vitamin B` and `Vitamin C`, the corresponding row of our table would look like the row shown in **TABLE 9.1**. The problem here is that the `Product` attribute value is not atomic (we cannot have a single record with `Customer = Pawan` and `Product = Vitamin B, Vitamin C`). Instead, we need two records with the same `Customer` value, but different `Product` values, as shown in **TABLE 9.2**. In other words, from the point of view of what's in a table, each column must contain a *single* value (whatever that means within the given context) in each row.

TABLE 9.1 A simple illustration of 1NF violated.

Customer	Product
Pawan	Vitamin B, Vitamin C

TABLE 9.2 A simple illustration of 1NF satisfied.

Customer	Product
Pawan	Vitamin B
Pawan	Vitamin C

Before discussing 2NF we need to say something about *keys* for our tables, and the *functional dependency* that may or may not exist between key and non-key record attributes in our tables.

9.3.2 Database Keys: Primary and Foreign, Natural and Surrogate, Simple and Composite

Placing appropriate *keys* in our database tables is an important step in setting up our database. A table column in which the attribute value is used to uniquely identify the record in its row, and serve, in effect, as a "lookup" value for that row, contains what we call the *primary key* for that table. Such a primary key must satisfy the following properties:

▶ It must be unique for every record in the table, and here it is important to remember that the uniqueness must apply to every *possible* entry that might be put into the table, *not* just the entries in the table at some particular time.

▶ It must always have a value and, moreover, a value that will never change.

A primary key column from Table A, say, may also appear in a second table, say Table B, and thus serve to "connect", or establish a "relationship" between those two tables. In this case, in Table B the primary key from Table A is called a *foreign key*.

Sometimes we have a "natural" choice for a primary key, such as the social security number, which will be unique for each person in a table, for example. Other times we may simply want to generate an artificial (or *surrogate*) identifier to use for the primary key. For example, we could use something as simple as a sequence of positive integers. This has the dual advantage of being totally under the control of the database designer, and many database management systems can generate such values automatically as data is entered into the database.

A simple key value that appears in a single column is perhaps the most frequent and convenient kind of primary key, but sometimes the concatenation of the attribute values in two (or more) columns can be also used as the primary key, in which case we refer to it as a *compound* (or *composite*) primary key.

9.3.3 Functional Dependencies and 2NF

The second and third normal forms (2NF and 3NF) deal with the relationship (or the *functional dependency*) between key and non-key attributes in a table.

In particular, 2NF is violated when a non-key attribute is a fact about a *subset* of the primary key (i.e., there is a functional dependency from an attribute that is only part of the primary key to the non-key attribute). Thus this is only relevant when the primary key is composite (consisting of more than one attribute). Another way of saying this is that for 2NF we want each non-key attribute in a table to be information "about the primary key, about the whole primary key, and about nothing but the whole primary key".

Let us illustrate what we mean by taking a simple example of a database that violates 2NF and converting it into one that satisfies 2NF.

Compare what you see in **TABLE 9.3** with what you see in **TABLE 9.4**. Table 9.3 shows a single-table database with four attributes for purchases made in a store: Customer, email,

TABLE 9.3 A simple illustration of 2NF violated.

Customer	Email	Product	Price
Pawan	pawan@yahoo.ca	Vitamin B	$19.99
Pawan	pawan@yahoo.ca	Vitamin C	$24.99
Paul	paul@gmail.ca	Vitamin C	$24.99
Robert	robert@halifax.ca	Vitamin B	$19.99

TABLE 9.4 A simple illustration of 2NF satisfied.

Customer	Email
Pawan	pawan@yahoo.ca
Paul	paul@gmail.ca
Robert	robert@halifax.ca

Customer	Product
Pawan	Vitamin B
Pawan	Vitamin C
Paul	Vitamin C
Robert	Vitamin B

Product	Price
Vitamin B	$19.99
Vitamin C	$24.99

`Product`, and `Price`. Suppose we are using the combination of the customer name attribute (the `Customer` field) and the product name attribute (the `Product` field) as the primary key. There are four records in the database. Clearly there is a functional relationship between the attribute `Customer`, which is part of the primary key, and the non-key attribute `email`, since a customer's email address provides a fact about that customer. However, the `Customer` attribute is only part of the primary key and the customer's email has nothing to do with any product the customer may be buying (the other part of the primary key).

A similar functional dependency also applies from the attribute `Product`, which is part of the primary key, to the non-key attribute `Price`.

Now suppose we split the single table of the original database of Table 9.3 into three tables, as shown in Table 9.4. The first thing we achieve by doing this is that we save some storage. This may not be obvious in this example, because we have so few records, but note, for instance, that in the single-table database of Table 9.3 the product Vitamin C and its price appeared twice, but in the new arrangement this pairing occurs only once, so think about the implications of this for a much larger data set.

We are also moved toward our goal of maintaining database integrity. For example, if we had to change the price of `Vitamin C` to $29.99, then in the configuration of Table 9.4 we would need to make the change for only one record (the one in the table containing the record with the product Vitamin C and its price). That means we could not create an "update anomaly" by making the mistake of changing the price of `Vitamin C` in one place and not in the other (Vitamin C and its price appeared twice in the original table).

Note that these three tables can be "joined" together to recover the original table, and hence the decomposition shown in Table 9.4 is *lossless*. You will see how two or more tables can be joined in various ways using MySQL *queries* later in this chapter.

Though we will not pursue the discussion any further, let us say here simply that 3NF is violated when a non-key attribute provides a fact about another non-key attribute. The creation of further tables from the existing ones may be necessary to achieve 3NF.

9.3.4 Table Relationships in a Database

Another important aspect of a database design to think about during setup is the nature of the relationships that the tables in the database will have to one another, as the above discussion suggests. There are essentially three possibilities:

- ▶ *one-to-one*: There is a one-to-one relationship between Table A and Table B if each record in Table A corresponds to one and only one record in Table B, and vice versa. For example, in your company there might be a one-to-one relationship between each employee and his or her desktop computer, if in fact each employee has a single desktop computer.
- ▶ *one-to-many*: A one-to-many relationship from Table A to Table B means that each record in Table A will correspond (potentially at least) to several and perhaps many records in Table B, and several records in Table B can correspond to a single record in Table A. For

example, a single customer may have placed several orders, so a perfectly "natural" relationship between a Customer table and an Order table might be one-to-many.

▶ *many-to-many*: A many-to-many relationship from Table A to Table B means that at least one record in Table A corresponds to several (or many) records in Table B and at least one record in Table B corresponds to several (or many) records in Table A. Without going into detail, we should say that such relationships often create redundant data in your database and lead to problems in other ways, and so are best avoided.

In all cases, the relationships between tables are established with the help of table keys, the primary key of one table becoming a foreign key in a second table, for example. Sometimes it may prove to be convenient to set up a table containing nothing but keys, just to help "connect" other tables, particularly when you are trying to simplify a many-to-many table relationship.

9.3.5 Some General Advice

So, the first step in creating a database application for a business, or for any other endeavor, is to create a data model that contains all relevant attributes that need to be stored. The next step is to use the functional dependencies among the attributes to create an appropriate set of tables, and then establish the relationships between these tables using keys. The resulting set of tables should minimize data redundancy and preserve data integrity as various operations are performed on the database.

As a best practice, you should ensure that the resulting database model is at least in 2NF. But, as we have pointed out, 2NF is not a concern unless you are using a composite primary key. A normalized database tends to make general-purpose querying easier and faster, while a non-normalized database can favor some queries over others. However, keep in mind that normal forms represent only guidelines for the design of the records in the tables of your database. Though generally a good thing, they are just that—guidelines and *not* rules—and sometimes business requirements become the overriding factor in how a database is actually constructed. Nevertheless, some attempt at normalization is always a good starting point.

9.4 Make Use of Online Resources and Don't Reinvent the Wheel

The previous discussion was intended to give you a brief glimpse into some of the considerations that go into the setting up of a suitable database for any enterprise, but it did not provide enough detail to use as a guide for serious, hands-on database development. In fact, as a practical matter, many entrepreneurs simply do not have the time, energy, or expertise to make use of the theoretical underpinnings of database design when it comes to the actual real world task of doing so. Fortunately, help can be found online, and unless you have very special needs for your particular

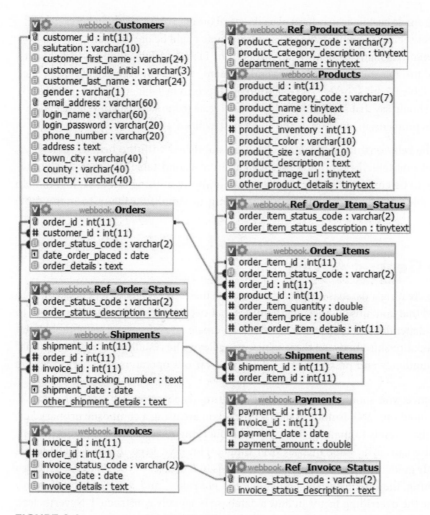

FIGURE 9.1 `graphics/ch09/dbSchema.jpg`
Data Model for an e-commerce website based on models from DataBaseAnswers.org.

situation it may be a good idea to go looking for a database design that will serve your purposes. For example, the website **Database Answers** at `http://databaseanswers.org/` describes data models for a wide variety of applications, and you may want to browse this website for a data model that might be suitable for your situation.

For our own e-commerce development, we have chosen a design that uses a combination of two of their data models, and we are actually using a subset of the combined data model. Furthermore, we have added and deleted attributes to suit our needs. **FIGURE 9.1** shows the data model used in our database. The figure is drawn using the designer utility provided by phpMyAdmin, one of the GUI (Graphical User Interface) "front ends" for the MySQL database management software.

9.5 The Data Model for Our Nature's Source Database

Let us take a few moments to examine our data model, which is illustrated in Figure 9.1. The figure shows that our database will consist of a total of 12 tables, with each box in the figure representing one of those tables. The rows in each box of the figure represent, in turn, the attributes of a record in the corresponding table. A common naming convention in the database world is to use multiple words to name an attribute, with the words joined by an underscore character (_), as in `customer_id`, for example.

On the left-hand side of each attribute you will see an icon that suggests the role and properties of that attribute. For example, an icon that looks like a key indicates that the corresponding attribute is a primary key for the table in which it appears. Recall that the primary key of a table uniquely identifies each record in that table, and it can be either of the following:

▶ A single attribute that is guaranteed to be unique. For example, `customer_id` in the `Customers` table is unique in the sense that there is no more than one record in the table corresponding to any particular value of `customer_id`. It is possible to generate these unique values automatically when inserting records into the table.

▶ A concatenation of multiple attributes. For example, in the `Shipment_Items` table the `shipment_id` and the `order_item_id` attributes are combined to form the primary key.

Other icons that we see on the left of an attribute include these:

▶ A # sign, indicating a type whose values are numeric
▶ A text page icon, indicating a type whose values are character strings
▶ A date icon, indicating a type whose values represent dates

These icons are actually redundant, because on the right of each attribute name, after the colon, we have text that describes the type of the attribute.

MySQL supports a wide range of data types. Like other keywords in MySQL, their names are case-insensitive. In Figure 9.1 we show them in lowercase, but in the text discussion we show them in uppercase to help them stand out. So, here are the ones we use in our data model shown in Figure 9.1:

▶ `INTEGER` (or its synonym `INT`, which can also be used), a numeric data type capable of storing 32-bit integer values
▶ `DOUBLE`, a numeric data type capable of storing 64-bit floating point values (values containing a decimal point, i.e., "real numbers")
▶ `VARCHAR(M)`, an efficient data type for storing variable-length strings (At the time of this writing, the maximum size `M` of such a string is 65,535 characters, but the effective maximum length is also subject to the maximum row size—also 65,535 characters, and shared among all columns—and the character set in use.)
▶ `TINYTEXT`, another data type for storing strings of length not exceeding 255 characters
▶ `TEXT`, for storing large amounts of text (up to 65,535 characters)
▶ `DATE`, for storing date values

See the end-of-chapter **References** section for links to further information on these and other data types available in MySQL.

Let's dig a little deeper into the structure of our database by discussing some of the table relationships. Each table is connected to another table through a common attribute. Usually the common attribute is the primary key in one of the two connected tables, and that same key is therefore a *foreign key* in the other table. It may be a good idea to make the foreign keys *indexed* in a table. Indexing an attribute allows for faster searching based on that attribute.

Figure 9.1 shows the connections from the primary key to the foreign keys. Lines with a small, filled-in semicircle at one end and a larger, filled-in semicircle at the other make these connections. The end with the smaller semicircle points to the primary key, while the end with the larger semicircle indicates the foreign key.

We have three main tables:

1. `Customers` This table contains all the relevant information for each customer. Note that it is linked to the `Orders` table through its `customer_id` primary key attribute. For every order, there will be a `customer_id` foreign key in the `Orders` table identifying the customer in the `Customers` table who placed that order. On the other hand, a particular customer may typically have placed multiple orders, so there is a one-to-many relationship from the `Customers` table to the `Orders` table.

2. `Products` This table contains all the relevant information for each product. Note that it is connected to the `Ref_Product_Categories` table, which provides information about the category of each product. Note that we are using the convention from the **Database Answers** website, according to which tables that start with the prefix `Ref_` are essentially for reference. There is no physical object corresponding to one of the rows in such a table. Examples of product categories listed in `Ref_Product_Categories` include exercise equipment, stomach remedies, vitamins, and so on. Each category will contain many products that are listed in the `Products` table, so again we have a one-to-many relationship, this time from a product category to the products in that category.

3. `Orders` This table contains some basic information about each order but is also connected to a number of other tables that provide additional information about each order. In particular, through its `order_id` primary key, which appears as a foreign key in those other tables, the `Orders` table is connected to each of the following tables:
   - `Shipments` This table keeps track of shipments. It is in turn connected to the `Shipment_Items` table to follow the details of the shipment of individual items.
   - `Order_Items` This table contains information relating to the individual items in a particular order. The attributes for an "order item" include the `order_item_quantity` and the `order_item_price` for that item.
   - `Invoices` This table contains invoice information and is connected to a number of other relevant tables, such as the `Payments` table.

Study Figure 9.1 until you have a reasonable sense of our data model. Once you have some understanding of the structure we are going to use for our database, we can proceed to implement that database using MySQL, and that is our next task.

9.6 MySQL, phpMyAdmin, and SQL

Our choice of MySQL is based on the fact that it is the most popular open source relational database management software for web programming. TABLE 9.5 gives a brief summary of its history. We will begin by using the phpMyAdmin GUI for MySQL, but we will always provide corresponding commands in SQL that we would enter directly if we were using the command-line interface to MySQL. In fact, we shall also discuss that command-line interface and how to enter these commands later in the chapter.

And by the way, these SQL commands tend to be the same for all the major database management systems. Using these commands is how you "talk to" a database system. There are various ways of doing this: using phpMyAdmin or the command-line interface, as we do in this chapter, or using an API (Application Programming Interface) provided by some programming languages such as Java or (in our case) PHP. We will make use of the PHP approach in the following chapter.

SQL commands are very often called *queries*, whether or not they are actually asking a database for information, and we will use the terms interchangeably. So, a "query" might also be creating a table, putting some information into a table, or updating that information as well.

At this point we assume that you have the necessary access to both MySQL itself and the phpMyAdmin interface to MySQL. You may wish to install both of these software packages on your own computer, and there are some links to information that will prove helpful in doing so in the end-of-chapter **References** section.

TABLE 9.5 A brief history of MySQL.

Date	Version	Notes
1994		Original development by Michael Widenius and David Axmark
May, 1995		First internal release
1996	3.19	First numbered release, according to Wikipedia
January 1998		Released for Windows
January 2001	3.23	Last 3.xx production release
March 2003	4.0	First 4.xx production release
October 2005	5.0	First 5.xx production release
2008		Sun Microsystems acquires MySQL
2010		Oracle acquires Sun Microsystems, causing Widenius to fork MySQL and launch MariaDB, perhaps fearing what Oracle would do with MySQL
October 2015	5.7	MySQL still alive and well . . .

More realistically, particularly if you are working in an academic environment, your instructor may have arranged for your system administrator to create an account and an empty database for you. Then, once you log in to the system and choose that database, you will be ready for the next step of creating and "populating" the database tables based on the design from Figure 9.1, or based on a design of your own.

If you are working with some other database system, much of what we say will still be meaningful and useful, but the screenshots shown in the text will not be as relevant. Although the vast majority of screenshots and figures in this second edition of the text have been updated, our **Nature's Source** database has not changed, so the screenshots, figures, and tables in this chapter remain the same. This means that you will occasionally see references to webbook, the name we used for our account and database in the first edition. For this second edition this name became webbook2e, but the **Nature's Source** database content for our **Nature's Source** sample website and for the text has not changed.

9.7 Using phpMyAdmin and SQL to Set Up the MySQL Database for Our Nature's Source Website

The phpMyAdmin software is a web-based tool, so to use it for accessing your MySQL installation you will need a URL for phpMyAdmin on the server on which your MySQL and phpMyAdmin have been installed, and on which you have a MySQL account. For example, in our case that URL is

```
http://cs.smu.ca/phpmyadmin
```

and we simply browse to that web address and respond to the login window we get by entering our MySQL username and password. You would do the same, and you would then get the local "home page" of your phpMyAdmin. At that point you would have whatever access your system administrator has established for you. We assume you have a local copy of our text website and have progressed to this point, if you wish to follow along with the discussion that comes next in the text.

We also assume that you are starting with an empty database (here called webbook in what follows). Once again, that is a likely scenario in an academic environment, though if you don't have such a database but do have permission to create one, it is easy enough to do so, as we shall see shortly.

So, we want to start creating and populating tables within our webbook database, based on our design from Figure 9.1, and using phpMyAdmin. **FIGURE 9.2** shows a typical dialog box that appears by default once you have logged in to phpMyAdmin, have chosen the database that you are building, and issued a request to create a table. We have filled in the necessary information to create a table called Customers, in which each row will have 13 fields. That is, each customer will have 13 attributes. The observant reader may notice that we actually have 14 attributes in the Customers table of our data model. An error like this during database construction is not uncommon, and we will see a bit later how we can fix such a mistake after the table has been created.

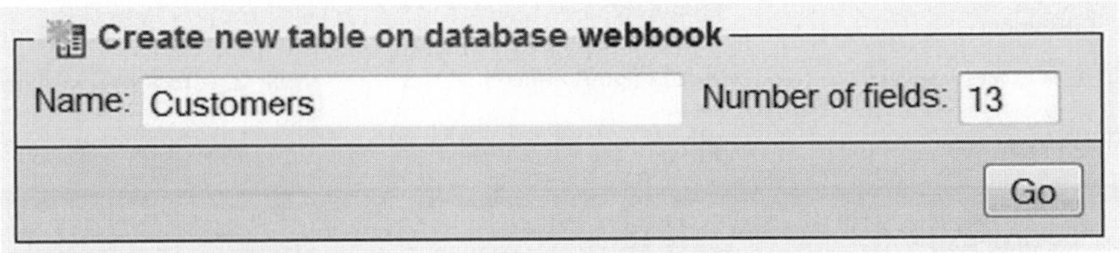

FIGURE 9.2 `graphics/ch09/displayCreateTableCustomers.jpg`
Specifying the name and size of the `Customers` table using phpMyAdmin.

Once you click on the `Go` button shown in Figure 9.2, you will get a screen like the one shown in **FIGURE 9.3**. Here we enter the names of the customer attributes and their types, according to our design shown in Figure 9.1. Then, clicking on the `Save` button causes the table to be created, as shown in **FIGURE 9.4**. This figure shows the complete structure of the table. Also, in the `Indexes:` part of the figure (at the bottom) we see a list of our primary and unique keys, as well as other indexed attributes. Finally, the figure also shows (partially) the actual SQL statement that was used to create the table.

If you are using another database management software system, the same query should still be able to create this table for you. We have reproduced the query separately in **FIGURE 9.5**.

SQL commands, or queries, can be grouped into various categories. Below we provide a list of the major groupings, together with an indication of the category to which each command of interest to us belongs. In the text we introduce and discuss each command as and when we need it. There are, of course, many additional MySQL commands that we do not discuss, and many options for using the commands that we do discuss for the simple reason that we do not have the time or space and have no immediate need for them. See the end-of-chapter **References** section for links to the MySQL documentation. Here are the categories:

▶ Commands for data definition (`CREATE`, `ALTER`, `DROP`) that are most frequently used to create, modify, and delete database tables
▶ A command for data retrieval (`SELECT`) used to query the database and retrieve useful information stored in it (probably the most-used command)
▶ Commands for data manipulation (`INSERT`, `LOAD`, `UPDATE`, `DELETE`, `TRUNCATE`) that are used to enter data into tables, modify data that is already in those tables, and to remove data from tables
▶ Commands for data transaction, and commands for data control, neither of which we will need to discuss

9.7.1 The `CREATE` Command

The `CREATE` command is most often used to create a table within a database, but it can also be used to create the database itself. For example, the command

```
CREATE DATABASE webbook;
```

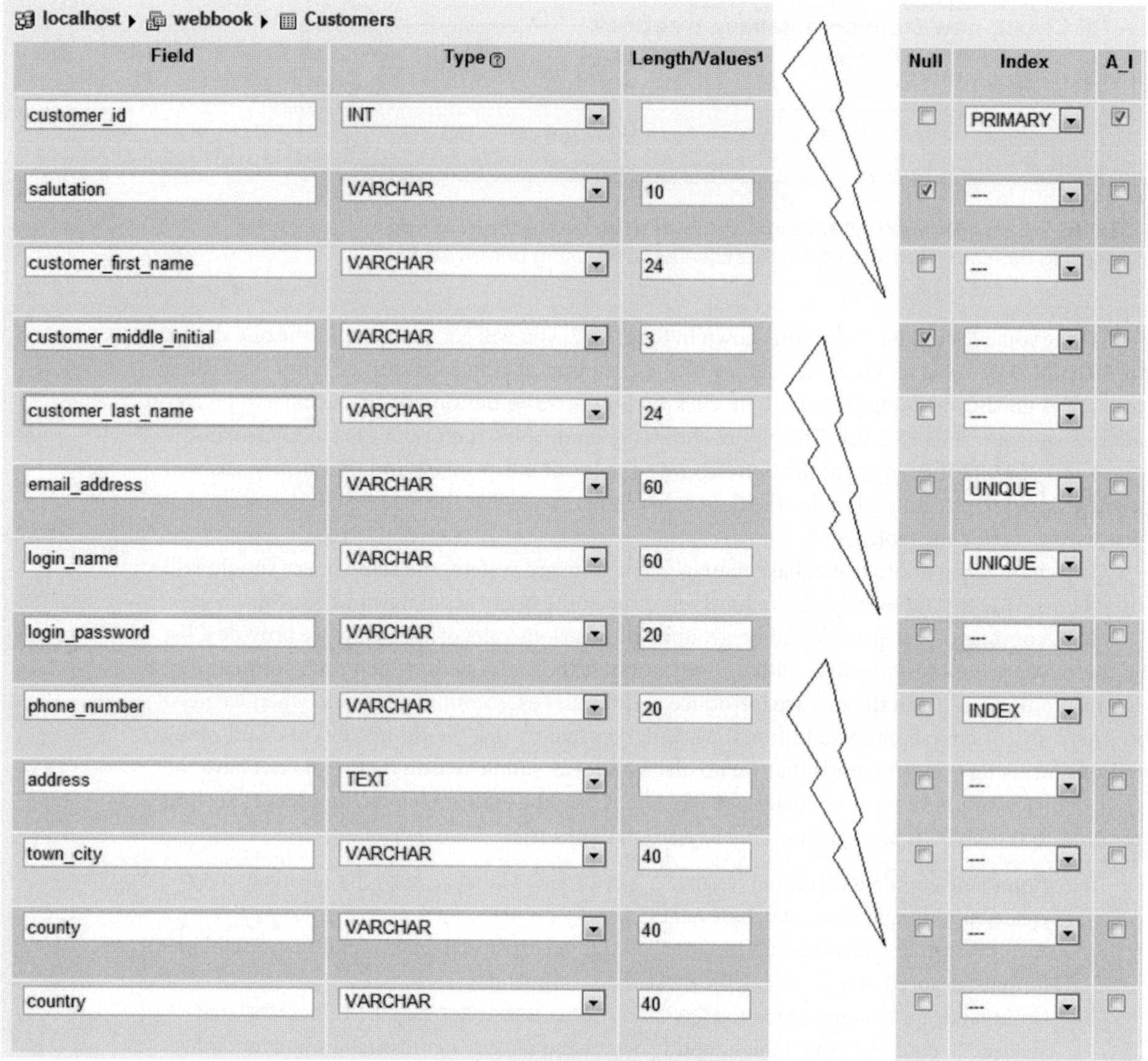

FIGURE 9.3 `graphics/ch09/displaySpecifyAttributeCustomers.jpg`
Specifying the attributes for the `Customers` table using phpMyAdmin.

could be used to create our webbook database, provided we have the necessary MySQL permissions to do so. These permissions are under the control of the MySQL administrator. That administrator will be you if you have installed MySQL on your own machine. However, many users in an academic environment may not have the authority to create their own databases. If this is the case for you, your system administrator would probably have created a database for you, based on information provided by a course instructor.

🔲 Browse 📝 Structure 📊 SQL 🔍 Search ➕ Insert 📤 Export 📥 Import ⚙ Operations 🗑 Empty ❌ Drop

✔ Table `webbook`.`Customers` has been created.

```
CREATE TABLE 'webbook'.'Customers' (
'customer_id' INT NOT NULL AUTO_INCREMENT PRIMARY KEY ,
'salutation' VARCHAR( 10 ) NULL ,
'customer_first_name' VARCHAR( 24 ) NOT NULL ,
'customer_middle_initial' VARCHAR( 3 ) NULL ,
'customer_last_name' VARCHAR( 24 ) NOT NULL ,
'email_address' VARCHAR( 60 ) NOT NULL ,
'login_name' VARCHAR( 60 ) NOT NULL ,
'login_password' VARCHAR( 20 ) NOT NULL ,
```

	Field	Type	Collation	Attributes	Null	Default	Extra	Action					
🔲	**customer_id**	int(11)			No	None	auto_increment	🔲	✏	✖	🔲	🔲	🔲	🔲
🔲	salutation	varchar(10)	latin1_swedish_ci		Yes	NULL		🔲	✏	✖	🔲	🔲	🔲	🔲
🔲	customer_first_name	varchar(24)	latin1_swedish_ci		No	None		🔲	✏	✖	🔲	🔲	🔲	🔲
🔲	customer_middle_initial	varchar(3)	latin1_swedish_ci		Yes	NULL		🔲	✏	✖	🔲	🔲	🔲	🔲
🔲	customer_last_name	varchar(24)	latin1_swedish_ci		No	None		🔲	✏	✖	🔲	🔲	🔲	🔲
🔲	email_address	varchar(60)	latin1_swedish_ci		No	None		🔲	✏	✖	🔲	🔲	🔲	🔲
🔲	login_name	varchar(60)	latin1_swedish_ci		No	None		🔲	✏	✖	🔲	🔲	🔲	🔲
🔲	login_password	varchar(20)	latin1_swedish_ci		No	None		🔲	✏	✖	🔲	🔲	🔲	🔲
🔲	phone_number	varchar(20)	latin1_swedish_ci		No	None		🔲	✏	✖	🔲	🔲	🔲	🔲
🔲	address	text	latin1_swedish_ci		No	None		🔲	✏	✖	🔲	🔲	🔲	🔲
🔲	town_city	varchar(40)	latin1_swedish_ci		No	None		🔲	✏	✖	🔲	🔲	🔲	🔲
🔲	county	varchar(40)	latin1_swedish_ci		No	None		🔲	✏	✖	🔲	🔲	🔲	🔲
🔲	country	varchar(40)	latin1_swedish_ci		No	None		🔲	✏	✖	🔲	🔲	🔲	🔲

↑__ Check All / Uncheck All *With selected:* 🔲 ✏ ✖ 🔲 🔲 🔲 🔲

📄 Print view 📑 Relation view 📊 Propose table structure ⓘ

➕ Add `1` field(s) ⦿ At End of Table ⦾ At Beginning of Table ⦾ After `customer_id` ⯆ `Go`

Indexes: ⓘ

Action	Keyname	Type	Unique	Packed	Field	Cardinality	Collation	Null	Comment
✏ ✖	**PRIMARY**	BTREE	Yes	No	customer_id	0	A		
✏ ✖	**email_address**	BTREE	Yes	No	email_address	0	A		
					login_name	0	A		
✏ ✖	**phone_number**	BTREE	No	No	phone_number	0	A		

Create an index on `1` columns `Go`

FIGURE 9.4 `graphics/ch09/displayResultCreateTableCustomers.jpg`
Result of creating the (empty) Customers table using phpMyAdmin.

As for creating a table in an already existing database, the general syntax of the required command looks like this:

```
CREATE TABLE table_name (col_name col_type col_constraints[,...]);
```

Figure 9.5 shows the CREATE command used to create our Customers table. This command, as shown, could be typed in directly if we were using the command-line interface to MySQL, a

```
1   CREATE TABLE 'webbook'.'Customers' (
2       'customer_id' INT NOT NULL AUTO_INCREMENT PRIMARY KEY,
3       'salutation' VARCHAR(10) NULL,
4       'customer_first_name' VARCHAR(24) NOT NULL,
5       'customer_middle_initial' VARCHAR(3) NULL,
6       'customer_last_name' VARCHAR(24) NOT NULL,
7       'email_address' VARCHAR(60) NOT NULL,
8       'login_name' VARCHAR(60) NOT NULL,
9       'login_password' VARCHAR(20) NOT NULL,
10      'phone_number' VARCHAR(20) NOT NULL,
11      'address' TEXT NOT NULL,
12      'town_city' VARCHAR(40) NOT NULL,
13      'county' VARCHAR(40) NOT NULL,
14      'country' VARCHAR(40) NOT NULL,
15      INDEX ('phone_number'),
16      UNIQUE (
17          'email_address',
18          'login_name')
19  ) ENGINE = MyISAM;
```

FIGURE 9.5 `graphics/ch09/createCustomers.sql`
The complete SQL command for creating our `Customers` table.

topic for later discussion in this chapter. For the moment, we are happy to have phpMyAdmin "construct" this command for us "behind the scenes", based on information we enter into the form it displays for us. This particular command illustrates almost all of the useful features of the CREATE command. In the first line, `'webbook'.'Customers'` tells that we are creating a table called `Customers` in the database `webbook`. The use of single quotes is not always necessary, but phpMyAdmin has put them in for us. Within the parentheses we specify the list of attributes, along with their types, and their lengths and other constraints wherever appropriate (such as NOT NULL, which means that the attribute *must* have a value).

At the end of the list of attributes, we specify that `customer_id` is the primary key, that the table should be indexed based on `phone_number`, and that the attribute values of `email_address` and `login_name` should be unique. Outside the parentheses, the "storage engine" is specified to be MYISAM, a specification that was not really necessary since MYISAM was the default storage engine at the time of this writing, though this may have changed by the time you read this and is likely to be irrelevant for our purposes in any case.

Now that we have created the `Customers` table using the CREATE command, let us move on to our next *data definition command* of interest, ALTER, and see how to make changes in the structure of our table.

9.7.2 The ALTER Command

The ALTER command allows us to modify an existing object in our database. For example, we can use it to add a column to, or delete a column from, an existing table. This is different from,

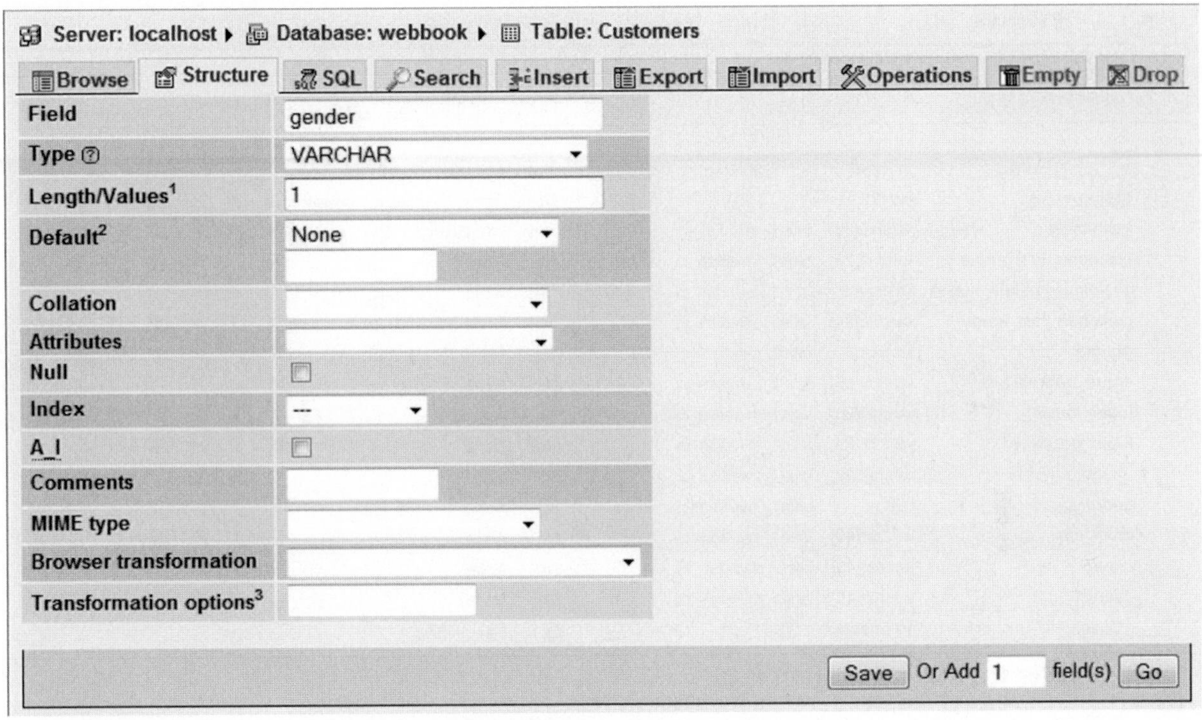

FIGURE 9.6 `graphics/ch09/displayChangeAttributeProperty.jpg`
Altering the `Customers` table using phpMyAdmin.

and should not be confused with, the UPDATE command, which is used to change the values of attributes in the rows of our tables, and which we discuss later.

Recall that we had made a mistake in creating the `Customers` table by omitting the `gender` attribute. We will now add this attribute. Let us say that we realized our error as soon as we looked at the results returned by the CREATE command in Figure 9.4. Notice at the bottom of the figure that we have the option of adding an attribute. We can indicate that we want to add an attribute after `customer_last_name` and click on the `Go` button.

FIGURE 9.6 shows the page that will come up for specifying the properties of the new attribute. We indicate that the name of the attribute is `gender`, and it will be of type VARCHAR with a length of 1, and then click the `Save` button.

FIGURE 9.7 shows the structure of the altered `Customers` table, as well as the SQL ALTER command that was used to add the `gender` attribute. This command is also shown, more clearly, in **FIGURE 9.8**. ALTER is a very versatile command, which allows us to add, change, or delete attributes (as opposed to *values* of attributes, done with UPDATE, as we mentioned above). In our case, we have simply used the ADD "subcommand" to add `gender` after `customer_last_name`.

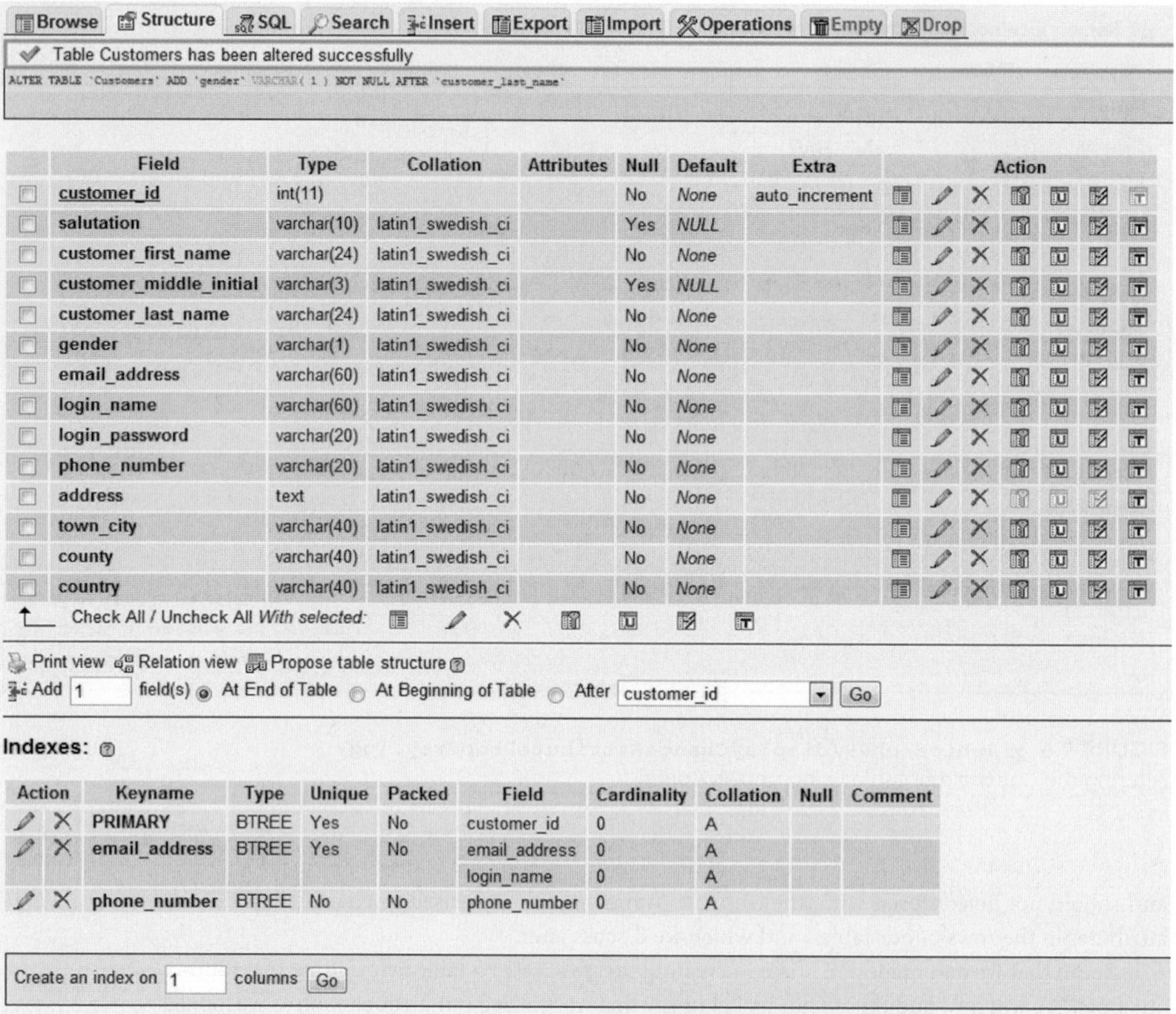

| Browse | Structure | SQL | Search | Insert | Export | Import | Operations | Empty | Drop |

✔ Table Customers has been altered successfully

`ALTER TABLE 'Customers' ADD 'gender' VARCHAR( 1 ) NOT NULL AFTER 'customer_last_name'`

	Field	Type	Collation	Attributes	Null	Default	Extra	Action						
☐	customer_id	int(11)			No	None	auto_increment			✕				
☐	salutation	varchar(10)	latin1_swedish_ci		Yes	NULL				✕				
☐	customer_first_name	varchar(24)	latin1_swedish_ci		No	None				✕				
☐	customer_middle_initial	varchar(3)	latin1_swedish_ci		Yes	NULL				✕				
☐	customer_last_name	varchar(24)	latin1_swedish_ci		No	None				✕				
☐	gender	varchar(1)	latin1_swedish_ci		No	None				✕				
☐	email_address	varchar(60)	latin1_swedish_ci		No	None				✕				
☐	login_name	varchar(60)	latin1_swedish_ci		No	None				✕				
☐	login_password	varchar(20)	latin1_swedish_ci		No	None				✕				
☐	phone_number	varchar(20)	latin1_swedish_ci		No	None				✕				
☐	address	text	latin1_swedish_ci		No	None				✕				
☐	town_city	varchar(40)	latin1_swedish_ci		No	None				✕				
☐	county	varchar(40)	latin1_swedish_ci		No	None				✕				
☐	country	varchar(40)	latin1_swedish_ci		No	None				✕				

↑ Check All / Uncheck All *With selected:* ▤ ✎ ✕ ▥ ▨ ▧ ▦

🖨 Print view Relation view Propose table structure ⓘ

Add `1` field(s) ⦿ At End of Table ⦾ At Beginning of Table ⦾ After `customer_id` ▾ [Go]

Indexes: ⓘ

Action		Keyname	Type	Unique	Packed	Field	Cardinality	Collation	Null	Comment
✎	✕	PRIMARY	BTREE	Yes	No	customer_id	0	A		
✎	✕	email_address	BTREE	Yes	No	email_address	0	A		
						login_name	0	A		
✎	✕	phone_number	BTREE	No	No	phone_number	0	A		

Create an index on `1` columns [Go]

FIGURE 9.7 `graphics/ch09/displayResultChangeAttributeProperty.jpg`
Result of altering the Customers table using phpMyAdmin.

```
1   ALTER TABLE 'Customers'
2   ADD 'gender' VARCHAR ( 1 )
3   NOT NULL AFTER 'customer_last_name'
```

FIGURE 9.8 `graphics/ch09/changeAttributeProperty.sql`
The SQL command for altering our Customers table by adding a new attribute.

9.7.3 The DROP Command

The last SQL data definition command we want to look at is the DROP command. The DROP command can be used to remove an attribute from a table, a table from your database, or even to remove the complete database. Caution should be exercised when using this command, because the deletion is irreversible and the "dropped" data is therefore irretrievable. A GUI interface to MySQL, like php-MyAdmin, will generally warn you and ask you to confirm deletions, but remember later on when you are using the command-line interface to MySQL that you will not get any such warnings, the idea being that if you are at the command-line you know what you are doing, and you are doing it carefully.

We will study this command with the help of a table called temp. We have created such a table in our database with two attributes called dummy1 and dummy2, as shown in **FIGURE 9.9**. If you click on the red X icon in the row containing the dummy1 attribute, a dialog box will appear. This is also shown in Figure 9.9. The corresponding SQL query uses this ALTER command with a DROP subcommand:

```
ALTER TABLE 'temp' DROP 'dummy1';
```

As soon as you click on OK, the attribute dummy1 will disappear from the table. If we want to delete the entire table temp from the database, we can click on the database and then click on the red X icon in the row corresponding to that table, as shown in **FIGURE 9.10**. The required SQL query is:

```
DROP TABLE 'temp';
```

Clicking on the OK button will permanently delete the table temp from our database.

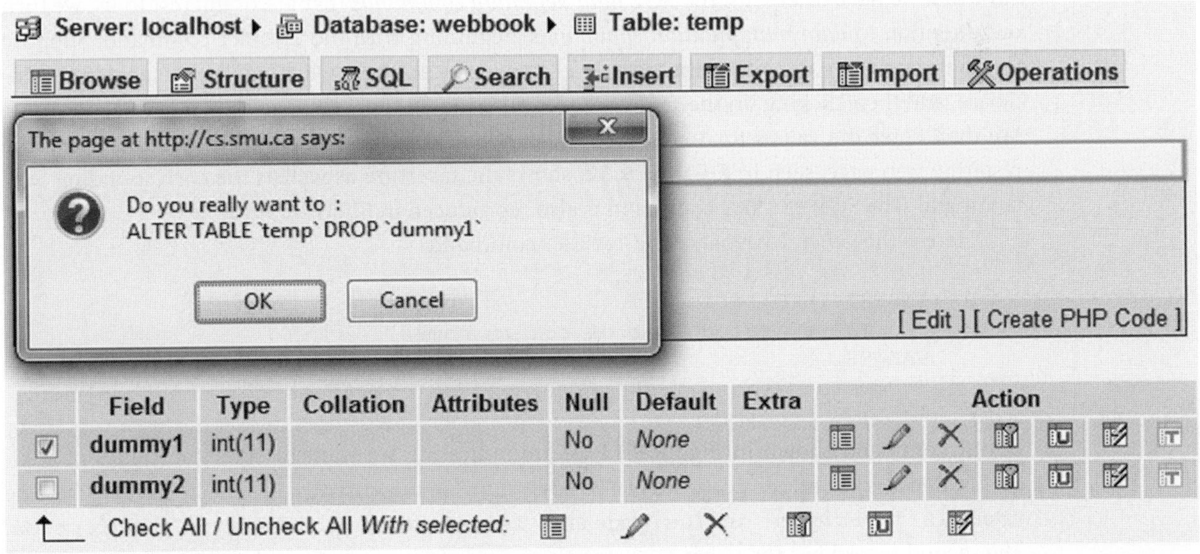

FIGURE 9.9 `graphics/ch09/displayDropDummy1.jpg`
Dropping an attribute from a table.

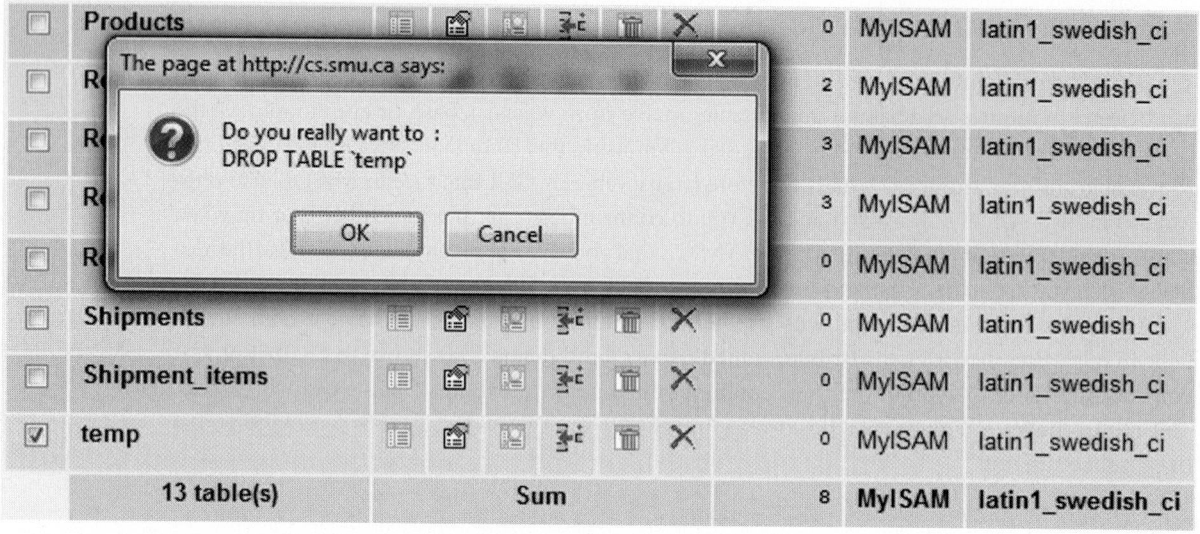

FIGURE 9.10 `graphics/ch09/displayDropTemp.jpg`
Dropping a table from a database.

9.7.4 The `INSERT` Command

Now that we have dealt with the SQL *data definition commands* that are of interest to us, we turn our attention to *data manipulation commands*, beginning with the `INSERT` command. Suppose we want to add two records to the table `Ref_Invoice_Status`. Clicking on that table in the database, and then clicking on the `Insert` link will bring up the web page shown in **FIGURE 9.11**. We then enter the values for the two records and click the `Go` button at the bottom right. The resulting web page, seen in **FIGURE 9.12**, shows the insertion as well as the corresponding SQL command. The SQL `INSERT` command is also reproduced in **FIGURE 9.13**.

Here is the general format of the `INSERT` command:

```
INSERT INTO table_name
(comma-separated list of column names)
VALUES
(comma-separated list of corresponding values for those columns)
```

In our command shown in Figure 9.13 we are indicating we want to enter the values of attributes `invoice_status_code` and `invoice_status_description`. The first record has the value `'IS'` for `invoice_status_code` and `'Issued'` for `invoice_status_description`. The second record has the value `'PD'` for `invoice_status_code` and `'Paid'` for `invoice_status_description`.

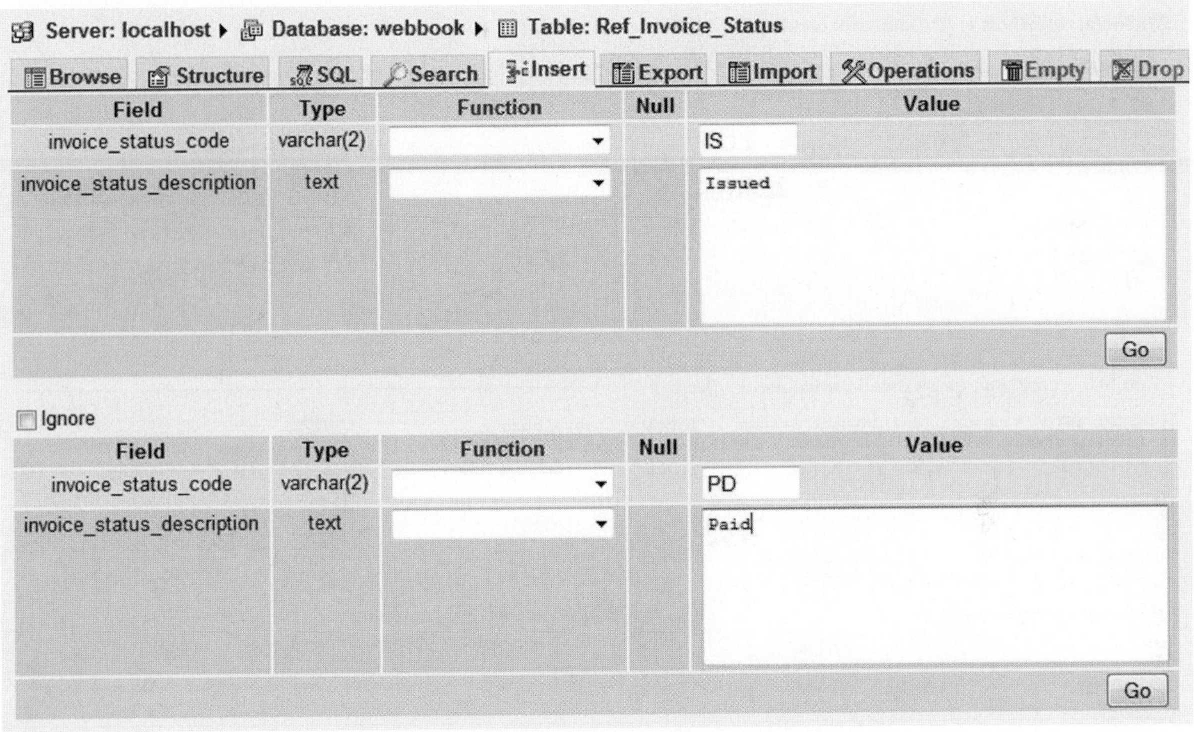

FIGURE 9.11 `graphics/ch09/displayInsertRecords.jpg`
Inserting records into the `Ref_Address_Types` table using phpMyAdmin.

The INSERT command is quite useful for loading a small number of records into our database. But what if we want to insert a large number of records from a file? In this case we can run the INSERT command for each record automatically using SQL programming. This can also be achieved using a GUI interface such as that provided by phpMyAdmin, a process we now describe.

In the `ch09` subdirectory of the text website (or text files) you will find a data file called `products870.csv`, which contains 870 product records. Note that these are not real products; they are generated by changing the names of some of the products that one usually finds in a health products store. A typical store would carry many more products than this. The first 20 records from the file are shown (partially) in **FIGURE 9.14**, with the lines truncated so the display will fit on the page. The value for each attribute is enclosed in a pair of single quotes and values are separated by commas. That is why we use the (conventional) file extension `.csv`, which stands for "comma-separated values".

We can import these records into our `Products` table using phpMyAdmin. If we click on the `Products` table, we will see a link called `Import`. Clicking on the `Import` link brings up

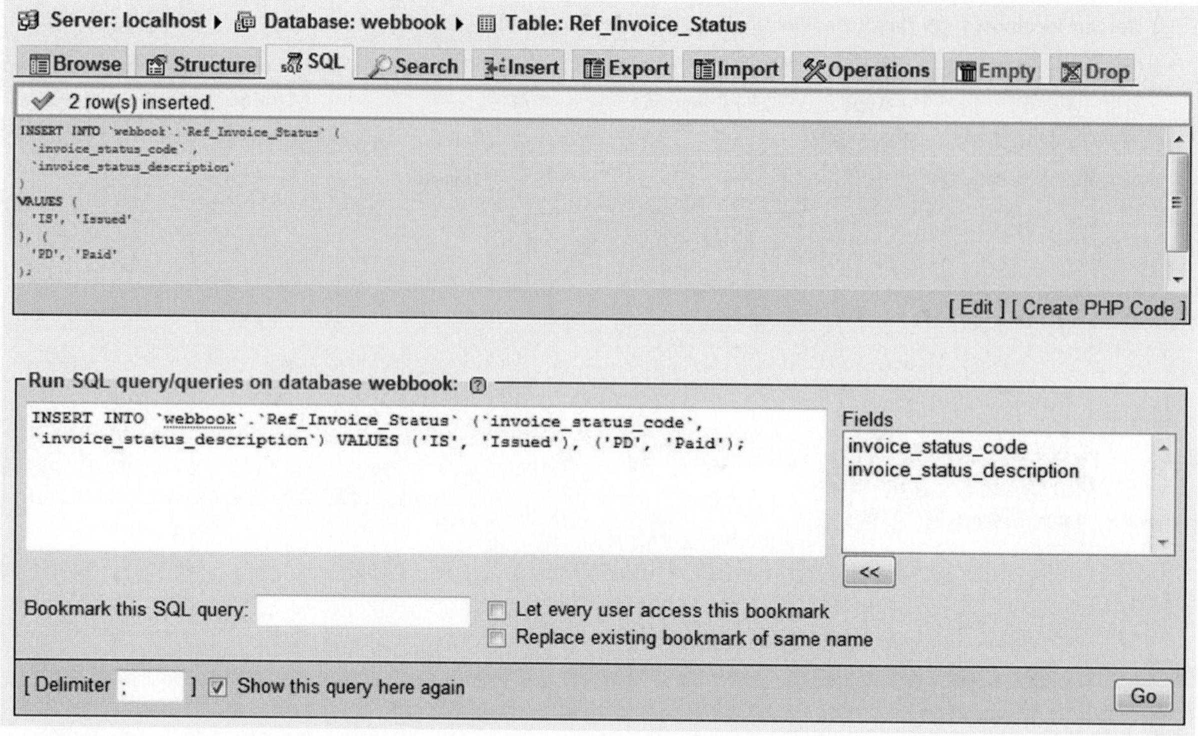

FIGURE 9.12 `graphics/ch09/displayResultInsertRecords.jpg`
Result of inserting records into the `Ref_Address_Types` table using phpMyAdmin.

```
1   INSERT INTO 'webbook'.'Ref_Invoice_Status' (
2       'invoice_status_code' ,
3       'invoice_status_description'
4   )
5   VALUES (
6       'IS', 'Issued'
7   ), (
8       'PD', 'Paid'
9   );
```

FIGURE 9.13 `graphics/ch09/insertRecords.sql`
The SQL command for inserting two records into our `Ref_Invoice_Status` table.

a web page similar to the one shown in **FIGURE 9.15**, where we have entered the name of our data file and clicked on the CSV radio button. We have also indicated that the fields are enclosed in single quotes and separated by commas. Finally, we use the default value \ for the *escape character*. This means that any occurrences of tab, newline, or \ that are preceded by \ should

```
 1  '707689','ACID','HMF PRE+PROBIO 250G','39','28','','','HMF PRE+PROBIO 250G
       for Acidic suppleme
 2  '707690','ACID','LACTOBACILLUS 60C','20','2','','','LACTOBACILLUS 60C for
       Acidic supplements',
 3  '707691','ACID','100 ACIDOPHILUS WITH FOS','26.99','67','','','100
       ACIDOPHILUS WITH FOS for Ac
 4  '707692','ACID','S STRNGTH 5 LOZENGES 60T','16.99','14','','','S STRNGTH
       5 LOZENGES 60T for Ac
 5  '707693','ACID','PLUS ACID- BIFID-FOS 100VC','29.99','8','','','PLUS
       ACID- BIFID-FOS 100VC for
 6  '707694','ACID','PLUS 100ML','55','46','','','PLUS 100ML for Acidic
       supplements','images/produ
 7  '707695','ACID','HMF NATOGEN (NEOGEN)','29','74','','','HMF NATOGEN
       (NEOGEN) for Acidic supple
 8  '707696','ACID','MEGA ACID 75GM','11.99','21','','','MEGA ACID 75GM for
       Acidic supplements','i
 9  '707697','ACID','PCA-RX 30ML','199.99','26','','','PCA-RX 30ML for Acidic
       supplements','images
10  '707698','ACID','LACTOVIDEN ID 60C','40','16','','','LACTOVIDEN ID 60C for
       Acidic supplements'
11  '707699','ACID','S INFANTS BLEND 75G','24.99','16','','','S INFANTS BLEND
       75G for Acidic suppl
12  '707700','ACID','LEAF ACIDOPHILUS 120C','44.99','7','','','LEAF ACIDOPHILUS
       120C for Acidic su
13  '707701','ACID','ULTRA FLOR+ DF 50G','42','48','','','ULTRA FLOR+ DF 50G
       for Acidic supplement
14  '707702','ACID','FEM DOPHILUS 30CT','30','57','','','FEM DOPHILUS 30CT for
       Acidic supplements'
15  '707703','ACID','S STRNGTH 8 60C','36.99','3','','','S STRNGTH 8 60C for
       Acidic supplements','
16  '707704','ACID','YOGOURT STARTER 49GM','19','89','','','YOGOURT STARTER
       49GM for Acidic supple
17  '707705','ACID','KAPS CAPS 30C','39.99','43','','','KAPS CAPS 30C for
       Acidic supplements','ima
18  '707706','ACID','S ADULT BLEND 60C','26.99','79','','','S ADULT BLEND
       60C for Acidic supplemen
19  '707707','ACID','S CHILDRENS BLEND 60C','19.99','16','','','S CHILDRENS
       BLEND 60C for Acidic s
20  '707708','ACID','S DIGESTIVE ENZYME 120C','39.99','21','','','S DIGESTIVE
       ENZYME 120C for Acid
```

FIGURE 9.14 `graphics/ch09/products870Truncated.csv`
Partial view of a file of comma-separated values containing product records.

be treated as literal characters. For example, \\ will be treated as a single \ . Clicking on the Go button will add all 870 records to the table, using 870 INSERT queries, as confirmed by the message shown in **FIGURE 9.16**.

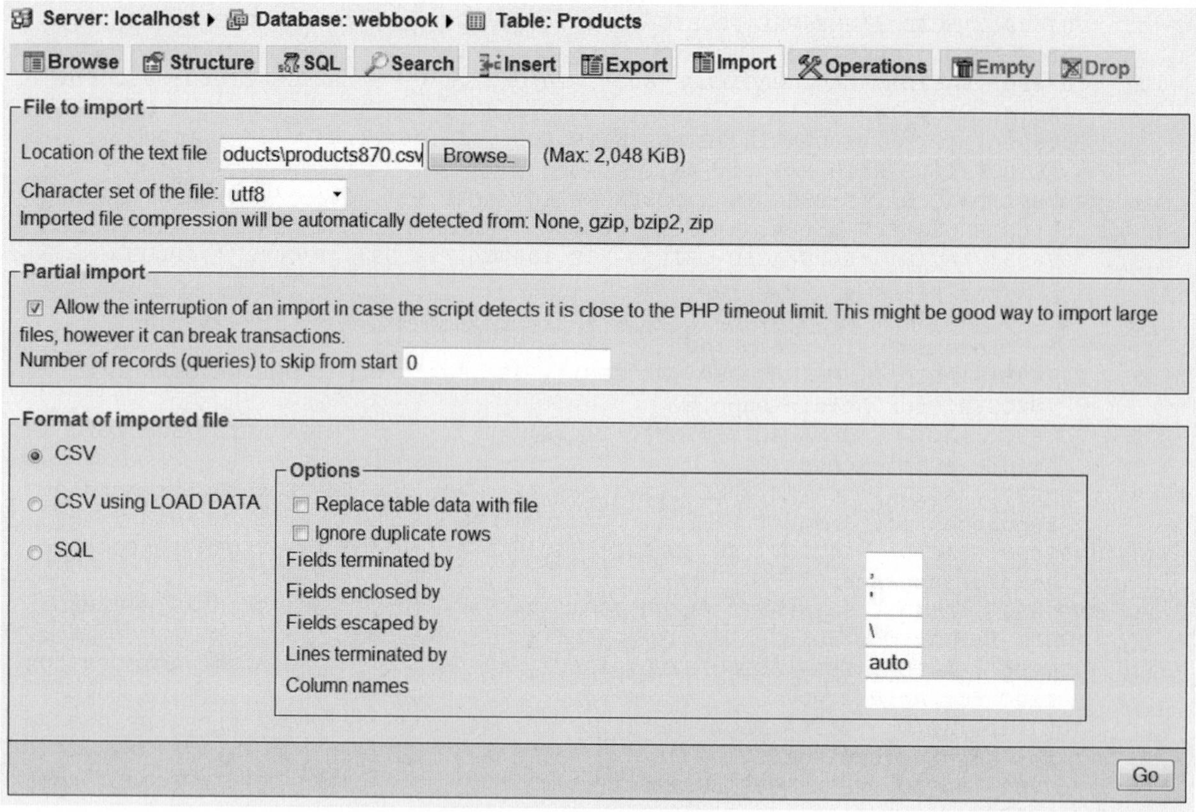

FIGURE 9.15 `graphics/ch09/displayInsertManyRecords.jpg`
Inserting multiple records in the `Products` table using phpMyAdmin.

FIGURE 9.16 `graphics/ch09/displayResultInsertManyRecords.jpg`
Result of inserting multiple records in the `Products` table using phpMyAdmin.

9.7.5 The `LOAD` Command

There is a more efficient way to import a large number of records, by using the `LOAD` command. Let us explore this option with the help of the same `Import` interface, but this time we will use the `Customers` table. The data file we will import contains 10,000 customers, is called

```
 1   '100005','Mr.','Michael','P.','McClune','M','Michael0@webbook.com',
         'Michael0','Michael0','607-
 2   '100007','Mr.','Michael','P.','Young','M','Michael1@webbook.com',
         'Michael1','Michael1','470-64
 3   '100009','Mr.','Jordan','I.','Ore','M','Jordan2@webbook.com',
         'Jordan2','Jordan2','882-551-3892
 4   '100011','Mr.','Bjorn','A.','Ditty','M','Bjorn3@webbook.com','Bjorn3','Bj
         orn3','846-305-8131',
 5   '100013','Ms.','Riza','U.','Zalameda','F','Riza4@webbook.com','Riza4',
         'Riza4','570-476-7282','
 6   '100015','Ms.','Jacqueline','M.','Goldfeld','F','Jacqueline5@webbook.com',
         'Jacqueline5','Jacqu
 7   '100017','Mr.','Scoville','E.','Lepchenko','M','Scoville6@webbook.com',
         'Scoville6','Scoville6'
 8   '100019','Mr.','Nathan','T.','Blake','M','Nathan7@webbook.com','Nathan7',
         'Nathan7','524-687-39
 9   '100021','Mr.','Ryan','R.','Smyczek','M','Ryan8@webbook.com','Ryan8',
         'Ryan8','576-452-5110','7
10   '100023','Ms.','Angela','C.','Nguyen','F','Angela9@webbook.com','Angela9',
         'Angela9','474-367-1
11   '100025','Ms.','Ester','Z.','Muhammad','F','Ester10@webbook.com','Ester10',
         'Ester10','511-803-
12   '100027','Ms.','Abigail','K.','Harrison','F','Abigail11@webbook.com',
         'Abigail11','Abigail11','
13   '100029','Mr.','Mike','K.','DeHeart','M','Mike12@webbook.com','Mike12',
         'Mike12','621-815-4208'
14   '100031','Mr.','Gonzalas','M.','Russell','M','Gonzalas13@webbook.com',
         'Gonzalas13','Gonzalas13
15   '100033','Mr.','Alexander','T.','Buchanan','M','Alexander14@webbook.com',
         'Alexander14','Alexan
16   '100035','Mr.','Michael','X.','Rolle','M','Michael15@webbook.com',
         'Michael15','Michael15','782
17   '100037','Mr.','Junior','S.','Martin','M','Junior16@webbook.com',
         'Junior16','Junior16','548-76
18   '100039','Ms.','Abigail','X.','Vandeweghe','F','Abigail17@webbook.com',
         'Abigail17','Abigail17'
19   '100041','Mr.','Jordan','P.','Venus','M','Jordan18@webbook.com','Jordan18',
         'Jordan18','786-454
20   '100043','Mr.','Johannes','K.','Kendrick','M','Johannes19@webbook.com',
         'Johannes19','Johannes1
```

FIGURE 9.17 `graphics/ch09/customers10000Truncated.csv`
Partial view of a file of comma-separated values containing customer records.

`customers10000.csv`, and a copy is also provided in the `ch09` subdirectory of the text files. As with our products data file, a truncated version is shown in **FIGURE 9.17**.

This time we choose the `CSV using the LOAD DATA` radio button, but the rest of the selections are the same as before. Clicking on the `Go` button in **FIGURE 9.18** will add all 10,000 records

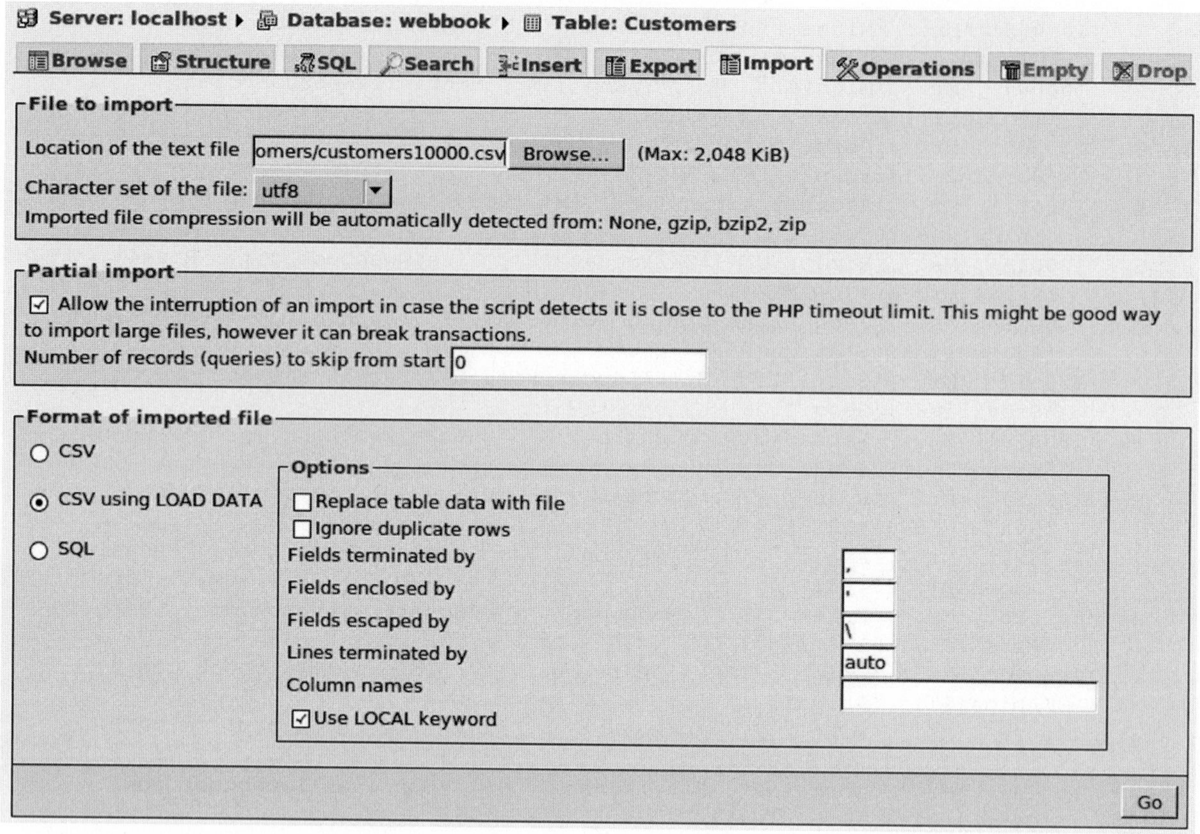

FIGURE 9.18 `graphics/ch09/displayLoadFile.jpg`
Loading multiple customer records from a CSV file into the `Customers` table using phpMyAdmin.

using a single query based on the LOAD command in SQL, as shown in **FIGURE 9.19**. Caution should be exercised when loading large files through the phpMyAdmin interface. There may be a limit of 2MB. Even if your file is smaller than 2MB, the LOAD command may not be successful. We recommend that you upload the file through other means to the server that hosts your MySQL server. Then execute the SQL query preferably through the command-line interface that we will look at shortly.

In the meantime, look at the SQL query shown in **FIGURE 9.20**, which uses the SQL LOAD command. Here is the abbreviated (and generic) format of the LOAD command that we used for our example:

```
LOAD DATA LOCAL INFILE 'file_name'
     INTO TABLE tbl_name
     FIELDS TERMINATED BY 'string'
     ENCLOSED BY 'char'
     ESCAPED BY 'char'
     LINES TERMINATED BY 'string';
```

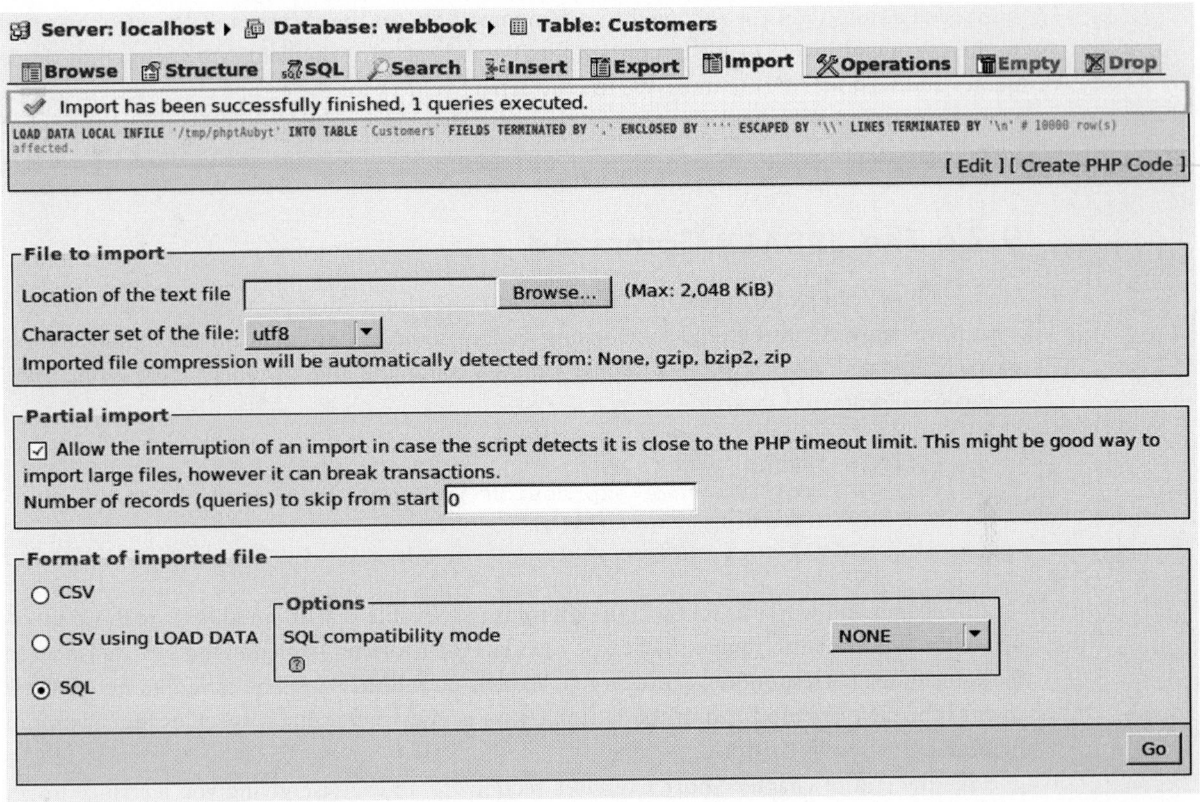

FIGURE 9.19 `graphics/ch09/displayResultLoadFile.jpg`
Result of loading multiple customer records from a CSV file into the `Customers` table using phpMyAdmin.

```
1    LOAD DATA LOCAL INFILE '/tmp/phpvBgdxT'
2    INTO TABLE 'Customers'
3    FIELDS TERMINATED BY ','
4    ENCLOSED BY ''''
5    ESCAPED BY '\\'
6    LINES TERMINATED BY '\n';
```

FIGURE 9.20 `graphics/ch09/loadFile.sql`
The SQL command for loading multiple customer records from a CSV file into the `Customers` table.

Here we see only the options that we actually used in loading our customer records. See the MySQL manual for details about many other options.

First, the keyword LOCAL means that the file needs to be copied to the server that hosts MySQL. That is why we have a funny filename in the command shown in Figure 9.20. Our file `customers10000.csv` was copied to a temporary file on the server, and the filename used in the command is that of the temporary file. We indicate that the fields are enclosed in single quotes and separated by commas. We use the default value \ for the escape character. As before, that means all occurrences of `tab`, `newline`, or \ that are preceded by \ should be treated as literal characters.

9.7.6 The `UPDATE` Command

We have now seen two commands (`INSERT` and `LOAD`) for getting data into our database. But what if we inadvertently entered some wrong data, or some piece of data already in the database has to be updated? Clearly we also need an `UPDATE` command and, of course, there is one. Here is its general syntax:

```
UPDATE 'table_name'
    SET column1_name=expression [column2_name=expression2,...]
    [WHERE where_expression]
    [LIMIT n]
```

The command works as follows. The columns in the table that are modified are those specified in the `WHERE` clause, and each of those rows has each column named in the `SET` clause set to the value of the corresponding expression. If there is no `WHERE` clause, be careful to note that *all* rows of the table are modified. If the `LIMIT` clause is given, the value n specifies the maximum number of rows to be modified.

See the end-of-chapter **Short Exercises** section for an exercise giving you a chance to get familiar with this command.

9.7.7 A First Look at the `SELECT` Command

We now know how to "populate" our database using two data manipulation commands, `INSERT` and `LOAD`. Two other commands, `DELETE` and `TRUNCATE`, will allow us to "de-populate" our database. Before looking at these two destructive commands, we will take a brief look at the most important data retrieval command, `SELECT`. It will be discussed in more detail later in the chapter when we discuss the command-line interface. However, in order to delete records, we will have to browse our tables and find what to delete. So a simple introduction to data retrieval is in order.

The records we have in our database allow us to experiment with the `SELECT` command. We can simply click on the `Browse` link when we are in the `Customers` table, and we will get (by default) the first 30 records in the table, as shown in **FIGURE 9.21**. The corresponding SQL query is shown in **FIGURE 9.22** and you can see that these records have been retrieved from the database using a `SELECT` command.

In Figure 9.22 we show the use of the `SELECT` command in its simplest form to select the complete record by specifying `'*'` after the keyword `SELECT`. The word `Customers` after `FROM` indicates the table, and the range of 0 to 30 records appears after the keyword `LIMIT`. We will be

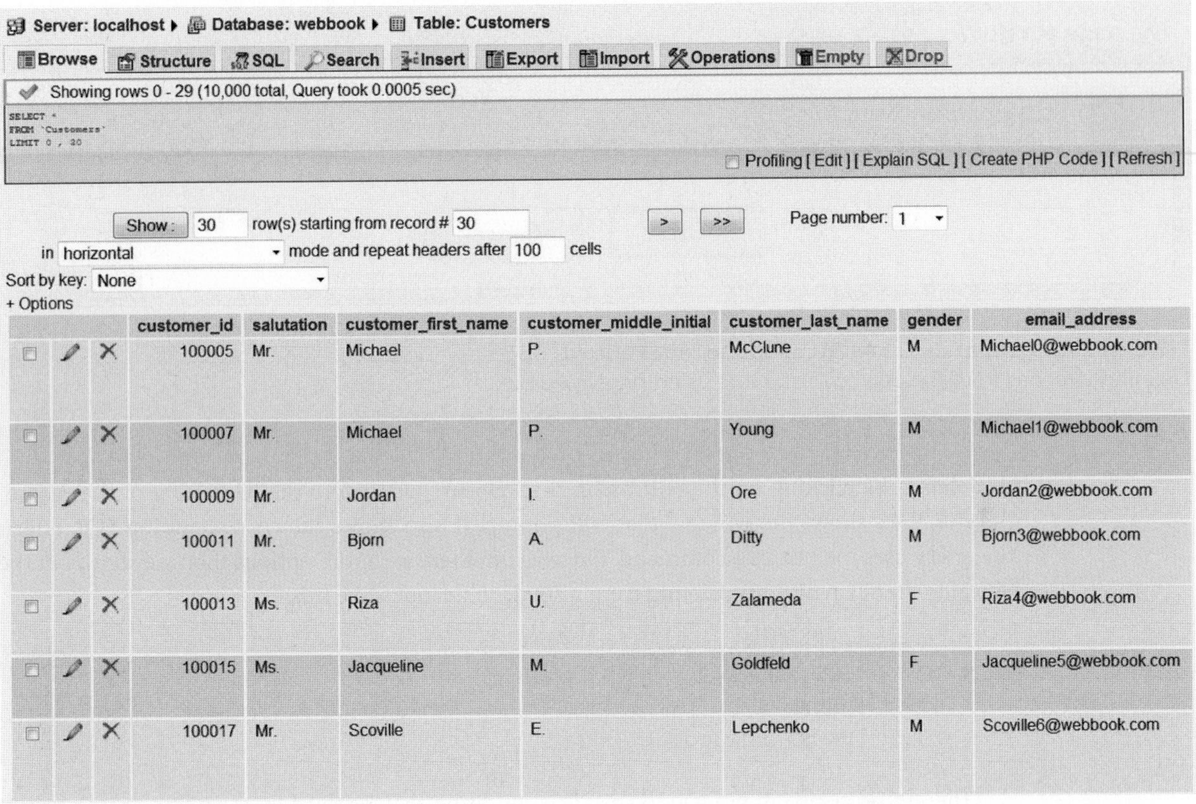

FIGURE 9.21 `graphics/ch09/displaySelectAll.jpg`
Selecting records from the `Customers` table using phpMyAdmin.

```
1    SELECT *
2    FROM `Customers`
3    LIMIT 0 , 30
```

FIGURE 9.22 `graphics/ch09/selectAll.sql`
Selecting records from the `Customers` table using SQL.

experimenting with more sophisticated SELECT statements later on in this chapter, but for the moment we just look at how to delete a few, or all, of the records from a database.

9.7.8 The DELETE Command

The `Customers` table shown in Figure 9.21 has one of the records highlighted with a different color, because we are hovering our mouse over that record. We are going to pick the record

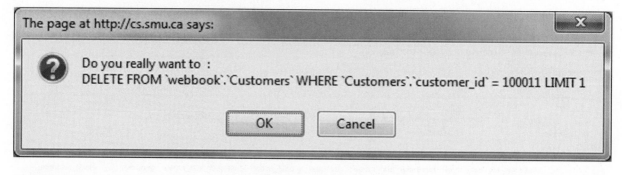

FIGURE 9.23 `graphics/ch09/displayDeleteRecord.jpg`
Deleting a record from the `Customers` table using phpMyAdmin.

for deletion by clicking on the red X icon that appears just before the beginning of the record. **FIGURE 9.23** shows the window that will pop up. It also shows the corresponding SQL query. The query uses the DELETE command. Once again, there are more options than we show, but the typical (generic) syntax for deleting from a single table looks like this:

```
DELETE FROM table_name
    [WHERE where_condition]
    [ORDER BY...]
    [LIMIT row_count]
```

The WHERE clause allows you to specify a condition that a record must satisfy for it to be deleted. In our case, we specified that the `customer_id` must match the specified value. The ORDER BY option allows us to specify the attributes that should be used to order the records for deletion. The ordering is especially relevant if we were going to limit the number of records that should be deleted using the option LIMIT. In our example query, we are limiting the number of deletions to a single record. This is redundant, since `customer_id` is unique, and there will be only one record that will match the WHERE clause in any case.

9.7.9 The TRUNCATE Command

Since we have started deleting records, why stop at one record? Let us delete all the records and then rebuild our data—we now have the power. The command TRUNCATE TABLE allows us to delete all the records in a table. We can invoke it from phpMyAdmin by clicking on the database and then clicking on the red X next to the table name. A warning window including the SQL query will pop up as shown in **FIGURE 9.24**. Click the OK button and all the data in the table will be deleted. Most database engines implement the TRUNCATE TABLE command by dropping the table and recreating an empty table. It is much faster than deleting individual records when the tables are large. Should we spare you the obvious warning about exercising caution while using DELETE and TRUNCATE TABLE commands?

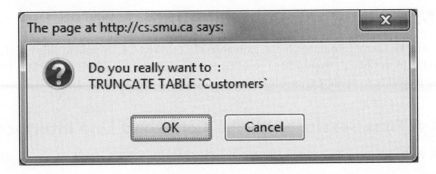

FIGURE 9.24 `graphics/ch09/displayTruncateTable.jpg`
Truncating the `Customers` table using phpMyAdmin.

9.7.10 Inventory Management Systems

Most retail businesses will have some kind of *inventory management system* that will be part of the "back office" for the use of store management. It will handle the wholesale purchase of items from suppliers and maintain the data necessary to keep track of inventory.

Systems like this are not unique to e-commerce businesses. Our system can work with such an inventory management system simply by interacting with the product-related tables. We have chosen to limit the scope of our system, since the inclusion of many additional tables would not help us learn any new features of web programming. However, for the business you are working on in the "parallel project", you may find it convenient to add a number of additional tables to deal with the specific activities in which your business is involved. Be thinking about the possibilities as you work on the next iterations of the parallel project at the end of this chapter and the next.

In the absence of a complete inventory management system, we have filled as many tables as necessary for experimenting with the database. Readers are encouraged to browse through the populated tables from the book's website.

Later on in this chapter we will also describe how you can import our entire database into your own MySQL system so that you can experiment with it. In the next chapter, we will also see how to populate other tables using simulated e-commerce, when we process online "purchases" of our products by our customers.

However, our limited discussion of database management is not yet complete. We need to look at the command-line interface to MySQL. The command-line interface is generally less user-friendly than phpMyAdmin, but much faster to use for those who know what they are doing, especially when queries are more complicated. It is also less forgiving than the GUI counterpart, and is therefore meant for more knowledgeable users. To become comfortable with database management, it is necessary for all web programmers to learn how SQL queries are executed via the command-line interface, since when such queries are sent through a programming language API the commands have essentially the same form as when they are entered directly by typing them in at a command-line prompt.

9.8 MySQL's Command-Line Interface

We will use the Linux command line to gain access to our MySQL command-line interface. You can also log in to MySQL from other operating systems such as Windows or the Mac OS. Once you have logged in to MySQL from any operating system, you use essentially the same interface.

9.8.1 A First Session with the Command-Line Interface

FIGURE 9.25 shows our first command-line interaction with MySQL. In line 1 we use the Linux command[1]

```
mysql -u webbook -p
```

to log in to our MySQL system. Note that the command to access the MySQL system under Linux is an all-lowercase `mysql`. The name following the `-u` option is the username by which MySQL identifies the user. The `-p` option indicates that the username requires a password, which will be entered in response to the prompt from MySQL on line 2.

As is always the case in these situations, when the password is typed, it does not show up on the screen. Once the password is verified and accepted, the prompt

```
mysql>
```

appears, and we are then ready to enter our commands at the command-line interface.

The first thing we have to do is tell MySQL which database we would like to use. That is the purpose of the USE command in line 9:

```
USE webbook;
```

We continue to capitalize MySQL commands, for emphasis, in our discussions of them, but we have saved time when entering them at the command line by using lowercase. Note that most commands in MySQL have to be terminated with a semicolon (;). Some commands do not actually require the semicolon, but having a semicolon at the end of those commands does not cause an error, so it is much safer, and a recommended "best practice", simply to put a semicolon at the end of every command.

With the command

```
SHOW tables;
```

in line 13 we can find out what tables are currently in the database we have said we want to use. In this case, we see the 12 tables of our own **Nature's Source** database that we have been discussing.

---

[1] You may or may not need to supply the `-u` command-line parameter, since it may be assumed by default. However, we should point out that if the LOAD command does not work as we indicated here in the text that it should, you may have a version of MySQL that requires you to log in from the (Linux) command line with the following additional command-line parameter: `--local-infile name_of_your_database`

```
 1  ok > mysql -u webbook -p
 2  Enter password:
 3  Welcome to the MySQL monitor.  Commands end with ; or \g.
 4  Your MySQL connection id is 28603
 5  Server version: 5.0.75-0ubuntu10.2 (Ubuntu)
 6
 7  Type 'help;' or '\h' for help. Type '\c' to clear the buffer.
 8
 9  mysql> use webbook;
10  Reading table information for completion of table and column names
11  You can turn off this feature to get a quicker startup with -A
12  Database changed
13  mysql> show tables;
14  +------------------------+
15  | Tables_in_webbook      |
16  +------------------------+
17  | Customers              |
18  | Invoices               |
19  | Order_Items            |
20  | Orders                 |
21  | Payments               |
22  | Products               |
23  | Ref_Invoice_Status     |
24  | Ref_Order_Item_Status  |
25  | Ref_Order_Status       |
26  | Ref_Product_Categories |
27  | Shipment_items         |
28  | Shipments              |
29  +------------------------+
30  12 rows in set (0.00 sec)
31  mysql> select * from Ref_Invoice_Status;
32  +---------------------+----------------------------+
33  | invoice_status_code | invoice_status_description |
34  +---------------------+----------------------------+
35  | IS                  | Issued                     |
36  | PD                  | Paid                       |
37  +---------------------+----------------------------+
38  2 rows in set (0.01 sec)
39
40  mysql> quit
41  Bye
42  webbook >
```

FIGURE 9.25 `graphics/ch09/mysqlSession1.txt`
A first look at the command-line interface for MySQL.

Next, we execute a simple `SELECT` command (line 31) to retrieve all the records from the table `Ref_Invoice_Status`:

```
SELECT * FROM Ref_Invoice_Status;
```

There are only two such records, as the display shows (lines 32–38). The use of * in this context means that we want to see all the fields from each record. This `SELECT` command is similar to the one we saw earlier. Note the format of the output for each of the queries we have seen here, which is typical.

In fact, all the SQL commands we saw in the previous section can be executed using the command-line interface, but in some cases—such as creating a table or adding one or two records—it may be easier to use the phpMyAdmin GUI.

9.8.2 A Closer Look at the `SELECT` Command

Unfortunately, the phpMyAdmin GUI may be of limited use when we are specifying more complex data retrieval queries using `SELECT`. Let's now investigate some more sophisticated retrievals using the command-line interface. In a `SELECT` query, the user describes only the desired *result set*. The following are keyword modifiers commonly used with a `SELECT` command:

▶ `FROM`, which is followed by a comma-separated list of the names of the tables from which the data is to be taken

▶ `WHERE`, which is followed by a comma-separated list of the conditions that specify which rows are of interest for the retrieval

▶ `GROUP BY`, which is followed by information indicating how the data in rows with related values is to be combined

▶ `ORDER BY`, which is used to identify which columns are used to sort the retrieved data

▶ `LIMIT`, which specifies a range of records for which the data is to be retrieved

We will explore these keywords with the help of some queries. Note that in the text discussion we continue to use all uppercase for the names of MySQL commands and their modifiers to distinguish them from the (user-chosen) names of other entities. When typing them into the command-line interface, however, it is easier to take advantage of the case-insensitivity of MySQL and use all lowercase. Keep in mind, however, that the user-chosen names (for tables and attributes, for example) *will* be case-sensitive, at least on Linux and other Unix-based systems.

Calling Built-In MySQL Functions and Performing Simple Arithmetic During Data Retrieval

MySQL has some built-in functions that can be very useful in data retrieval. Let us begin by illustrating `COUNT()`, a function that retrieves just the total number of records, instead of the records themselves. So in **FIGURE 9.26** our first query (line 1) is

```
SELECT COUNT(*) from Customers;
```

```
 1  mysql> select count(*) from Customers;
 2  +----------+
 3  | count(*) |
 4  +----------+
 5  |    10000 |
 6  +----------+
 7  1 row in set (0.00 sec)
 8
 9  mysql> select country,count(*) from Customers group by country;
10  +---------+----------+
11  | country | count(*) |
12  +---------+----------+
13  | Canada  |     1791 |
14  | USA     |     8209 |
15  +---------+----------+
16  2 rows in set (0.01 sec)
```

FIGURE 9.26 `graphics/ch09/countSQL.txt`
Use of the COUNT() function in SQL.

and the result shows the total number of records in the Customers table. You may recall that phpMyAdmin generated queries that used single quotes around table and attribute names. We are not using single quotes around the table names here, since they are unnecessary if the names do not contain any spaces. But if we had a table with a name like Our Customers, for example, we would have to enclose it in single quotes. However, best practice would dictate that we avoid such names.[2]

The second query in Figure 9.26 is

```
SELECT country, COUNT(*) FROM Customers GROUP BY country;
```

and uses the GROUP BY option (line 9), where the records are grouped by the values in the specified list of attributes. We are grouping by the country, so there will be a separate record for each country. That is why we get two records for two countries in our table, one for Canada and the other for the USA (we only have customers in those two countries).

Another useful MySQL function is SUM(). **FIGURE 9.27** shows its use with the following query from line 1:

```
SELECT SUM(product_inventory) FROM Products;
```

This query sums up the values of the attribute product_inventory for every record in the Products table. So we see that there are 43,097 items in our inventory (line 5).

---

[2] In fact, Microsoft Windows notwithstanding, if you consistently avoid using names containing blank spaces when you are naming things on your computer, there are several kinds of problems you will never have.

```
 1  mysql> select sum(product_inventory) from Products;
 2  +------------------------+
 3  | sum(product_inventory) |
 4  +------------------------+
 5  |                  43097 |
 6  +------------------------+
 7  1 row in set (0.01 sec)
 8  mysql> select sum(product_inventory)/count(*) from Products;
 9  +---------------------------------+
10  | sum(product_inventory)/count(*) |
11  +---------------------------------+
12  |                         49.5368 |
13  +---------------------------------+
14  1 row in set (0.00 sec)
```

FIGURE 9.27 `graphics/ch09/sumSQL.txt`
Use of the SUM() function in SQL.

The second query in Figure 9.27 also shows that we can do simple arithmetic during data retrieval using SQL (line 8):

```
SELECT SUM(product_inventory)/COUNT(*) FROM Products;
```

This query gives us the average number of items per product (line 12).

9.8.3 Restricting the Set of Records from Which We Retrieve Our Data

So far each of our queries has dealt with all of the records in a given table. We can restrict the scope of our retrieval by using a WHERE clause similar to the one we used for DELETE. Let us say we wanted to find out how many products in the Products table have fewer than 10 items in stock. As **FIGURE 9.28** shows, we can use the query (line 1)

```
SELECT COUNT(*) FROM Products WHERE product_inventory < 10;
```

which gives a result of 96 (line 5).

If we want to sort the records, we can use the ORDER BY option, as shown in **FIGURE 9.29** (line 4). In this case we want to retrieve a list of the products with inventory size greater than 90 and have it sorted based on the value of the attribute product_inventory. The DESC option indicates that we want the sorting performed in descending order. We also used the LIMIT option here so that we only see the top 10 records in the list. The LIMIT option has two (comma-separated) values in this case, 0 and 10. The first indicates how many records to skip before starting the retrieval, and the second tells how many records to retrieve. Since the first value is 0, it is actually redundant in this case, and we could have used the single value 10.

```
 1  mysql> select count(*) from Products where product_inventory < 10;
 2  +----------+
 3  | count(*) |
 4  +----------+
 5  |       96 |
 6  +----------+
 7  1 row in set (0.00 sec)
```

FIGURE 9.28 `graphics/ch09/conditionSQL.txt`
An SQL query illustrating "conditional retrieval".

```
 1  mysql> select product_name, product_inventory
 2      -> from Products
 3      -> where product_inventory > 90
 4      -> order by product_inventory desc
 5      -> limit 0,10;
 6  +----------------------------+-------------------+
 7  | product_name               | product_inventory |
 8  +----------------------------+-------------------+
 9  | LACTOBACILLUS      30 C     |                99 |
10  | ALLERGY RELIEF     30C      |                99 |
11  | QUERCETIN 90C              |                99 |
12  | GOOD STRNGTH CARNOSINE     |                99 |
13  | AS MEDICINE                |                99 |
14  | LINEN FOUNDATION           |                99 |
15  | CHAMMOMILE TEA             |                99 |
16  | D 400IU 100T               |                99 |
17  | VEGETARIAN BOOSTER 90C     |                98 |
18  | STRNGTH AO FORMULA         |                98 |
19  +----------------------------+-------------------+
20  10 rows in set (0.00 sec)
```

FIGURE 9.29 `graphics/ch09/orderSQL.txt`
Ordering retrieved records using SQL.

Note that this (somewhat longer than usual) query is entered over several lines, and the prompt from MySQL changes to `->` from the second line on, until we enter the terminating semicolon.

9.8.4 Retrieving Data from More Than One Table with a Join

So far, in making our queries, we have only dealt with a single table. Our retrievals can also collect information from multiple tables at the same time, which is referred to as a *join*. We illustrate this in **FIGURE 9.30**. The query in this figure is our most complex query to date.

```
1    mysql> select product_category_description as category,
2         -> count(*) as products,
3         -> sum(product_inventory) as product_inventory
4         -> from Products as P, Ref_Product_Categories as R
5         -> where P.product_category_code = R.product_category_code
6         -> group by category
7         -> order by products desc
8         -> limit 0,10;
9    +----------------------+----------+-------------------+
10   | category             | products | product_inventory |
11   +----------------------+----------+-------------------+
12   | Adult multi-vitamins |      128 |              6063 |
13   | Nutritional bars     |       68 |              3311 |
14   | Body enhancement     |       64 |              3067 |
15   | Anti-oxidants        |       62 |              3431 |
16   | Acidic supplements   |       55 |              2295 |
17   | Application products |       34 |              1660 |
18   | Hair treatment       |       32 |              1741 |
19   | Aromatic therapy     |       28 |              1312 |
20   | Baby products        |       27 |              1414 |
21   | Relief from allergies|       26 |              1350 |
22   +----------------------+----------+-------------------+
23   10 rows in set (0.02 sec)
```

FIGURE 9.30 `graphics/ch09/multiTableSQL.txt`
Retrieving data from multiple tables using join in SQL.

In this example, we want to list the number of products in each product category as well as the total number of items in each category. We want to use the category description as the first column in our retrieved data. The category description is in the `Ref_Product_Categories` table, while the rest of the information is in the `Products` table.

This query also employs another useful feature of SQL that allows us to assign temporary aliases to certain entities, which provide more meaningful or concise names to be used within the query itself. Here, for example, we are indicating that the `product_category_description` will also be known as `category`, by using the keyword `AS` (line 1). Similarly, the count of products will also be known as `products`, and the sum of the product inventory will be known as `product_inventory`. We further abbreviate the `Products` table simply as `P` and the table `Ref_Product_Categories` as `R` (line 4).

These two tables are "joined" by requiring the following condition, which connects them via their common keys, to be satisfied (line 5):

```
P.product_category_code = R.product_category_code
```

The records are then grouped by category (line 6), and finally they are sorted in descending order based on the value of `products` (line 7), and we are also limiting ourselves to viewing the first

10 records (line 8). The *join* we have seen in this case is the simplest form of join. SQL allows for more sophisticated joining of tables. See the MySQL manual or the **References** section at the end of this chapter for more information.

The data from any of the SQL queries we might make can be stored in new tables. We will look into that facility in the next section, along with general importing and exporting of both individual tables and entire databases.

9.9 Importing and Exporting Tables and Databases

In this section, we look at some of the SQL commands, as well as the GUI facilities, that we can use to copy, import, and export data in MySQL. You should know how to perform these tasks, since from time to time you may need to make a copy of one or more tables, with or without modifications, or even make a copy of an entire database.

9.9.1 Copying a Table or Part of a Table

Let's illustrate this process by copying just part of a table. We can achieve this by combining the CREATE and SELECT commands, as shown in **FIGURE 9.31**. Suppose we want to make a copy of just a portion of our Customers table. We will only copy the customer_id, customer_first_name, customer_last_name, and login_name to another table called Customers2. First, we have to retrieve the required information, and here is the SELECT command we need:

```
SELECT customer_id,customer_first_name,
       customer_last_name,login_name
       FROM Customers;
```

Now all we have to do is precede this command with

```
CREATE Customers2 AS
```

and the output from the SELECT statement will be stored in the table Customers2. Figure 9.31 shows the complete MySQL session that performs this action. The SHOW tables; command (line 6) shows that the table Customers2 does not exist. We then create it using the above described combination of CREATE and SELECT. We then verify the creation of the table by looking at the first five records in the newly created Customers2 table.

Later, we delete the table with a

```
DROP TABLE Customers2;
```

command (not shown in the session), since we do not want it to be part of our database.

```
 1  mysql> use webbook
 2  Reading table information for completion of table and column names
 3  You can turn off this feature to get a quicker startup with -A
 4
 5  Database changed
 6  mysql> show tables;
 7  +------------------------+
 8  | Tables_in_webbook      |
 9  +------------------------+
10  | Customers              |
11  | Invoices               |
12  | Order_Items            |
13  | Orders                 |
14  | Payments               |
15  | Products               |
16  | Ref_Invoice_Status     |
17  | Ref_Order_Item_Status  |
18  | Ref_Order_Status       |
19  | Ref_Product_Categories |
20  | Shipment_items         |
21  | Shipments              |
22  +------------------------+
23  12 rows in set (0.00 sec)
24
25  mysql> create table Customers2 as
26      -> select customer_id,customer_first_name,customer_last_name,login_name
27      -> from Customers;
28  Query OK, 10000 rows affected (0.02 sec)
29  Records: 10000 Duplicates: 0 Warnings: 0
30
31  mysql> select * from Customers2 limit 0,5;
32  +-------------+---------------------+--------------------+------------+
33  | customer_id | customer_first_name | customer_last_name | login_name |
34  +-------------+---------------------+--------------------+------------+
35  |      100005 | Michael             | McClune            | Michael0   |
36  |      100007 | Michael             | Young              | Michael1   |
37  |      100009 | Jordan              | Ore                | Jordan2    |
38  |      100011 | Bjorn               | Ditty              | Bjorn3     |
39  |      100013 | Riza                | Zalameda           | Riza4      |
40  +-------------+---------------------+--------------------+------------+
41  5 rows in set (0.00 sec)
```

FIGURE 9.31 `graphics/ch09/copyTableSQL.txt`
Creating a copy of a portion of the Customers table using SQL.

9.9.2 Copying an Entire Database

Now we will show you how to create a copy of our entire database. First, we will use the php-MyAdmin interface, and then the command-line option.

In phpMyAdmin, you click on the database you want to "export" (webbook in our case) and then click on the Export link at the top. **FIGURE 9.32** shows the web page that will pop up. You

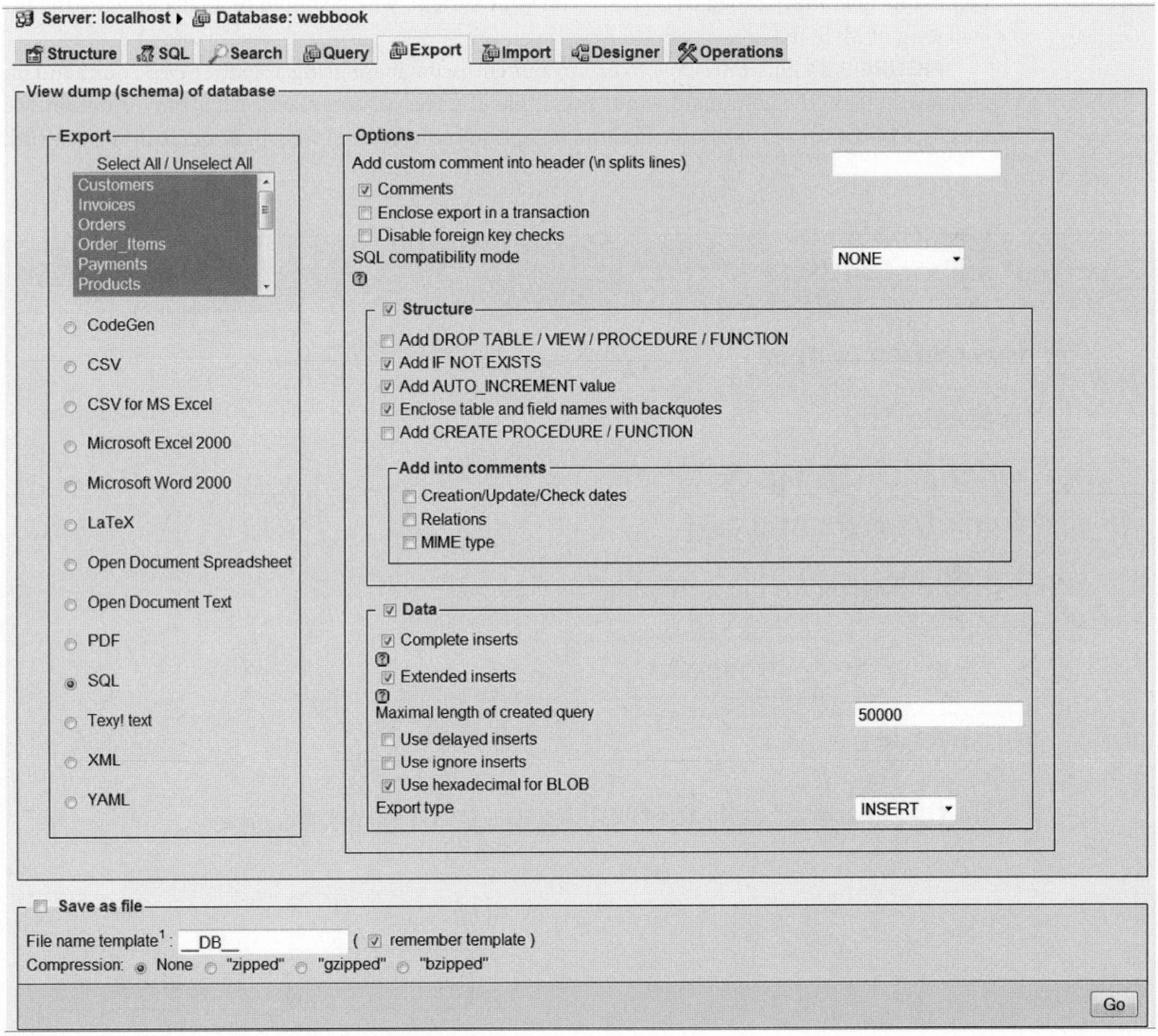

FIGURE 9.32 `graphics/ch09/displayExport.jpg`
Exporting a database using phpMyAdmin.

can select the tables you want to export, as well as the format of the exported file. We will use the default options of exporting all the files and exporting them as an SQL file. Clicking on the Go button will bring up the dialog box that tells you that the file will be saved as webbook.sql, as shown in **FIGURE 9.33**. You can save the file in an appropriate location.

The exporting and importing of large databases using phpMyAdmin can be a problem, as it may result in an unusually high volume of traffic over the Internet. For this reason, the command-line option is the preferred method for performing these tasks. You need a related command-line utility called mysqldump on your system, which should be available with any installation of MySQL.

FIGURE 9.34 illustrates how to export our entire database using a mysqldump command on a Linux system. The command works much like the mysql command. After the –u option, we specify that the user is webbook, and the –p option indicates that we will be entering a password.

FIGURE 9.33 `graphics/ch09/displayResultExport.jpg`
Result of exporting a database using phpMyAdmin.

```
1  webbook > mysqldump -u webbook -p webbook > backupbookSep09.sql
2  Enter password:
3  webbook > ls -l backupbookSep09.sql
4  -rw------- 1 pawan pawan 1751057 2009-09-20 07:01 backupbookSep09.sql
```

FIGURE 9.34 `graphics/ch09/mysqldump.txt`
Exporting a database using `mysqldump`.

The name `webbook` after the `-p` option says that we want to dump the `webbook` database. The `>` sign redirects the output to a file called `backupbookSep09.sql`.

We confirm the existence of this file simply by doing a directory listing (line 3). The file is in place and has approximately 1.8MB worth of data. The format of the file created by exporting from phpMyAdmin and `mysqldump` is identical. We can take a quick peek at the file created by `mysqldump`, as shown in **FIGURE 9.35**.

Note that the most recent version of this file (which you should now use) is called

> `webbook2e_backup20150504.sql`

and is available from the `ch09` subdirectory of the text website.

As we can see, it is really just a file containing SQL commands that can be used to create a database, and you can run these SQL commands to recreate the database. In fact, you can import the entire **Nature's Source** database (that is, the `webbook` database) to your own system using the commands in this file. First, you need to have an empty database with complete manipulation privileges. It can have any name. To illustrate, we will leave the `webbook` database unchanged and import its contents from the most recent version of the backup file into another database called `webbook1` using this backup file. Our system administrator has created this database for us and granted us all the necessary privileges. All we need to do is run the following command:

> `mysql -u webbook -p webbook1 < webbook2e_backup20150504.sql`

After the `-u` option, we are specifying that the user is `webbook`. The `-p` option again indicates that we will be entering a password. The name `webbook1` after the `-p` option tells us that we want to work with the `webbook1` database. The `<` sign redirects the input from our previously created file `webbook2e_backup20150504.sql`, which contains all the commands necessary to replicate the original database.

All of this activity, including the results of the command-line import, is shown in **FIGURE 9.36** and its continuation, **FIGURE 9.37** (except in the figures we are using the original backup file `backupbookSep09.sql` rather than the latest `webbook2e_backup20150504.sql`). We refer to the line numbers in those two figures to help you follow the action. First, we verify that we do in fact have a database called `webbook1` (lines 9–10 of Figure 9.36). There are no tables in the database, since the command `SHOW tables;` comes up empty (lines 11–12 of Figure 9.36). Now

```
 1  -- MySQL dump 10.13  Distrib 5.1.73, for debian-linux-gnu (x86_64)
 2  --
 3  -- Host: localhost    Database: webbook2e
 4  -- --------------------------------------------------------
 5  -- Server version           5.1.73-0ubuntu0.10.04.1-log
 6
 7  /*!40101 SET @OLD_CHARACTER_SET_CLIENT=@@CHARACTER_SET_CLIENT */;
 8  /*!40101 SET @OLD_CHARACTER_SET_RESULTS=@@CHARACTER_SET_RESULTS */;
 9  /*!40101 SET @OLD_COLLATION_CONNECTION=@@COLLATION_CONNECTION */;
10  /*!40101 SET NAMES utf8 */;
11  /*!40103 SET @OLD_TIME_ZONE=@@TIME_ZONE */;
12  /*!40103 SET TIME_ZONE='+00:00' */;
13  /*!40014 SET @OLD_UNIQUE_CHECKS=@@UNIQUE_CHECKS, UNIQUE_CHECKS=0 */;
14  /*!40014 SET @OLD_FOREIGN_KEY_CHECKS=@@FOREIGN_KEY_CHECKS, FOREIGN_KEY_CHECKS=0 */;
15  /*!40101 SET @OLD_SQL_MODE=@@SQL_MODE, SQL_MODE='NO_AUTO_VALUE_ON_ZERO' */;
16  /*!40111 SET @OLD_SQL_NOTES=@@SQL_NOTES, SQL_NOTES=0 */;
17
18  --
19  -- Table structure for table 'Customers'
20  --
21
22  DROP TABLE IF EXISTS 'Customers';
23  /*!40101 SET @saved_cs_client = @@character_set_client */;
24  /*!40101 SET character_set_client = utf8 */;
25  CREATE TABLE 'Customers' (
26    'customer_id' int(11) NOT NULL AUTO_INCREMENT,
27    'salutation' varchar(10) DEFAULT NULL,
28    'customer_first_name' varchar(24) NOT NULL,
29    'customer_middle_initial' varchar(3) DEFAULT NULL,
30    'customer_last_name' varchar(24) NOT NULL,
31    'gender' varchar(1) NOT NULL,
32    'email_address' varchar(60) NOT NULL,
33    'login_name' varchar(60) NOT NULL,
34    'login_password' varchar(20) NOT NULL,
35    'phone_number' varchar(20) NOT NULL,
36    'address' text NOT NULL,
37    'town_city' varchar(40) NOT NULL,
38    'county' varchar(40) NOT NULL,
39    'country' varchar(40) NOT NULL,
40    PRIMARY KEY ('customer_id'),
41    UNIQUE KEY 'email_address' ('email_address','login_name'),
42    KEY 'phone_number' ('phone_number')
43  ) ENGINE=MyISAM AUTO_INCREMENT=120010 DEFAULT CHARSET=latin1;
44  /*!40101 SET character_set_client = @saved_cs_client */;
45
46  --
47  -- Dumping data for table 'Customers'
```

FIGURE 9.35 `ch09/webbook2e_backup20150504.sql` **(excerpt)**
Exported database in an SQL file.

we exit from MySQL and run the MySQL command that imports the database from the Linux command-line interface (lines 14–17 of Figure 9.36). As Figure 9.37 now shows, by going back into the database we can see that all the tables are in place. We also perform two SELECT queries (lines 50 and 62 of Figure 9.37) to do a "spot check" to convince ourselves that the records have been imported and we have the right number of customers. All of this takes place in lines 18–72 of Figure 9.37.

9.9.3 Potential Problem with Importing via phpMyAdmin

As we cautioned before, using phpMyAdmin over the Internet can be problematic for importing large databases. Our database is of moderate size—less than 2MB. Let us see what happens if we

```
 1  webbook > mysql -u webbook -p
 2  Enter password:
 3  Welcome to the MySQL monitor. Commands end with ; or \g.
 4  Your MySQL connection id is 37531
 5  Server version: 5.0.75-0ubuntu10.2 (Ubuntu)
 6
 7  Type 'help;' or '\h' for help. Type '\c' to clear the buffer.
 8
 9  mysql> use webbook1;
10  Database changed
11  mysql> show tables;
12  Empty set (0.00 sec)
13
14  mysql> quit
15  Bye
16  webbook > mysql -u webbook -p webbook1 < backupbookSep09.sql
17  Enter password:
```

FIGURE 9.36 `graphics/ch09/importSQL.txt (Part 1)`
Importing a database using the command-line interface to MySQL (up to the actual import).

```
18  webbook > mysql -u webbook -p
19  Enter password:
20  Welcome to the MySQL monitor. Commands end with ; or \g.
21  Your MySQL connection id is 37533
22  Server version: 5.0.75-0ubuntu10.2 (Ubuntu)
23
24  Type 'help;' or '\h' for help. Type '\c' to clear the buffer.
25
```

FIGURE 9.37 `graphics/ch09/importSQL.txt (Part 2)`
Importing a database using the command-line interface to MySQL (confirming the import).

```
26  mysql> use webbook1;
27  Reading table information for completion of table and column names
28  You can turn off this feature to get a quicker startup with -A
29
30  Database changed
31  mysql> show tables;
32  +------------------------+
33  | Tables_in_webbook1     |
34  +------------------------+
35  | Customers              |
36  | Invoices               |
37  | Order_Items            |
38  | Orders                 |
39  | Payments               |
40  | Products               |
41  | Ref_Invoice_Status     |
42  | Ref_Order_Item_Status  |
43  | Ref_Order_Status       |
44  | Ref_Product_Categories |
45  | Shipment_items         |
46  | Shipments              |
47  +------------------------+
48  12 rows in set (0.00 sec)
49
50  mysql> select customer_first_name,customer_last_name from Customers limit 0,5;
51  +---------------------+--------------------+
52  | customer_first_name | customer_last_name |
53  +---------------------+--------------------+
54  | Michael             | McClune            |
55  | Michael             | Young              |
56  | Jordan              | Ore                |
57  | Bjorn               | Ditty              |
58  | Riza                | Zalameda           |
59  +---------------------+--------------------+
60  5 rows in set (0.00 sec)
61
62  mysql> select count(*) from Customers;
63  +----------+
64  | count(*) |
65  +----------+
66  |    10000 |
67  +----------+
68  1 row in set (0.01 sec)
69
70  mysql> quit
71  Bye
72  webbook >
```

FIGURE 9.37 `graphics/ch09/importSQL.txt (Part 2)` *(continued)*

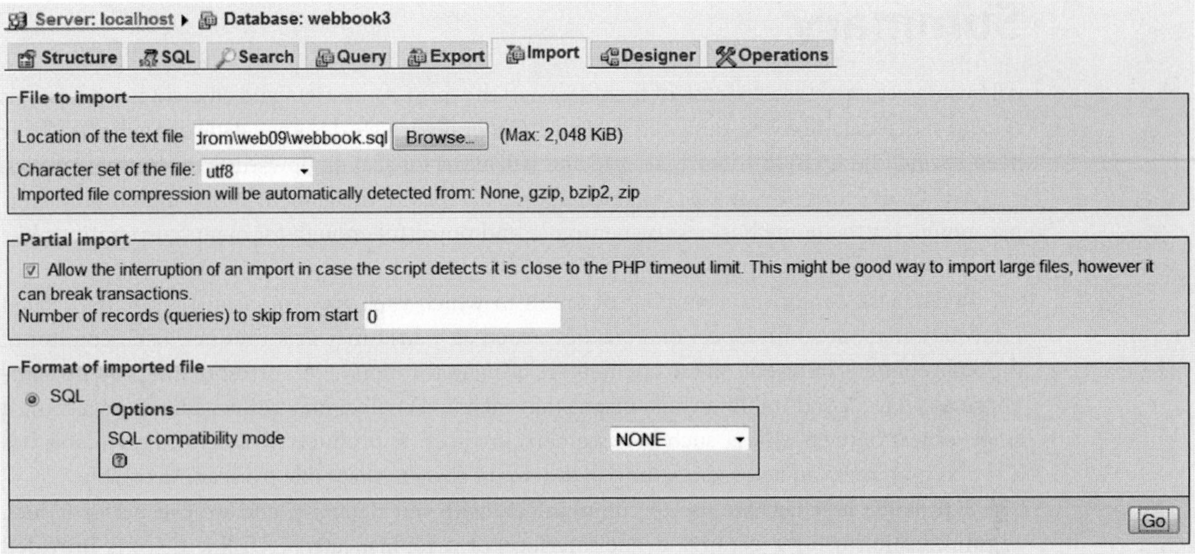

FIGURE 9.38 `graphics/ch09/displayImport.jpg`
Importing a database using phpMyAdmin.

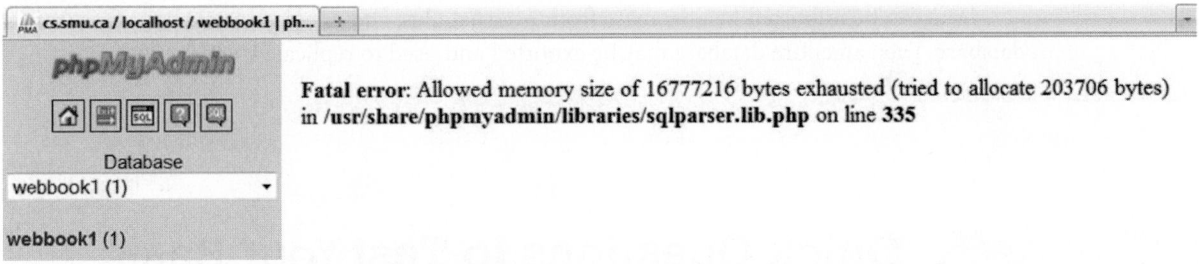

FIGURE 9.39 `graphics/ch09/displayResultImport.jpg`
Result of importing a database using phpMyAdmin.

try to import it using phpMyAdmin. **FIGURE 9.38** shows what will happen if we click on a database such as `webbook3`, which is currently empty. We indicate that we want to import from the file `webbook.sql` that we had saved earlier by exporting through phpMyAdmin. Clicking on the `Go` button starts the importing process.

Unfortunately, as shown in **FIGURE 9.39**, phpMyAdmin returns an error saying that it does not have the resources to carry out the importing task. Given what we have said, this is not entirely surprising. It follows that your best option may well be to work at the command line when you are importing a database, as shown in Figures 9.36 and 9.37.

Summary

All businesses need to keep track of their data and the most convenient and efficient way to do this is to keep that data in a well-designed database. Generally, a well-designed database will often have been *normalized* up to third normal form and will allow for scaling upward as the business grows.

MySQL is (currently, at least) an open-source database management system that is both simple enough for the home business owner to use and powerful enough for major corporations like Google and YouTube to employ as well.

A database comprises a number of tables in which each row (or record) contains related information about some aspect of a business, such as a customer or a product. Each column of the table contains information (an attribute) relating to the item in its corresponding row. It is important to have "good" tables, which means that each table will contain information concerning a single aspect of the business, such as customers, invoices, or products for sale, and each table has a key column that can be used if you wish to refer to rows in that table from another table.

SQL is the language we use to communicate with our database, and we can perform such communication using a command-line interface, or a sophisticated GUI like the one provided by phpMyAdmin, or one or more simple PHP scripts that we can write ourselves. There are SQL commands for creating databases, creating tables within those databases, adding information to the tables, modifying information that has already been stored, deleting some or all of that information, retrieving information and displaying it in various ways, and so on. We can also use SQL to perform numerical calculations on our data during the retrieval process.

Data can be imported to a database from external files, and exported to external files from a database. Even an entire database may be exported and used to replicate itself elsewhere.

Quick Questions to Test Your Basic Knowledge

1. Can you think of at least three reasons why storing large amounts of data in "ordinary" files turned out not to be a good idea? Here are some keywords to guide your thinking: *duplication, maintenance, excessive human involvement*.
2. What would you say to a business owner who had decided to keep all of the data for his business in one large table?
3. How would you describe what it means for a database to be in *first normal form*?
4. How would you describe what it means for a database to be in *second normal form*?
5. How would you describe what it means for a database to be in *third normal form*?
6. What has happened to MySQL that may (or may not) affect its future as a freely available, open-source database management system?

7. What is the MySQL command for creating a database? Can you always expect this command to work on any system?
8. What is the MySQL command that says you are going to use a database called `my_business`?
9. What MySQL command would you use to create a table called `Customers` with the following five fields: a unique identification number, first name, last name, telephone number, and email address? Choose good names for the columns in your table.
10. Give a typical command for inserting a record in the table created in the previous exercise.
11. If you wanted to import a lot of data into this table from an external file, what would a typical line in that file look like?
12. What is the MySQL command for displaying all the information in this table?
13. What is the command for displaying just the names of the customers in the table?

Short Exercises to Improve Your Basic Understanding

The following exercises assume you have access to an installation of MySQL and that installation either has at least one database to which you also have access, or you have permission to create databases on the system. These are just a few suggestions to get you started on the road to becoming comfortable working with a database. Some of the exercises will take more time and effort than others, but all are well worth the effort. In fact, we do not specify whether to use the command-line interface or the GUI interface to perform any particular activity, and you should use both, preferably, to do the same exercise.

1. Log in to your MySQL and give the command that shows you all of the databases you are allowed to "see".
2. Decide whether you will work with an already existing database, or create a new one. If you are going to create a new one, first do that. Then, in either case, give the command that sets you up for using whatever database you plan to use.
3. Create a table called `Customers` that will hold, for each customer, that customer's first and last name, telephone number, email address, and a unique identification number.
4. Modify your `Customers` table using the `ALTER` command to add a `city` attribute for each customer.
5. Enter some imaginary customers into your `Customers` table. First, use the `INSERT` command to enter just a couple of customers. Then create a file of customers and use the `LOAD` command to enter them.
6. Create a second table called either `Products` or `Services` that contains products or services that might be purchased by one or more of these customers. Enter some imaginary products or services into the table, based on the kind of business you are working on in your "parallel project".

7. Create a third table called `Orders` that "connects" the customers and the products that they have purchased. Enter some imaginary orders into the table.

8. Practice some SQL retrieval commands to display information from one or more of these tables in various forms.

9. Experiment with the `UPDATE` command by changing some attribute values. Then confirm the changes using a `SELECT` query. Finally, use `UPDATE` again to change the values back to what they were.

10. When you have finished the above experimentation, continue by experimenting with the `DELETE`, `DROP`, and `TRUNCATE` commands until all of your sample tables have been removed from your database.

Exercises on the Parallel Project

1. Rethink the objective(s) of your business, from the point of view of the kind of data that you will need to handle, and the kind of information you will need to store and later retrieve. Virtually every business has products and/or services to sell and needs to have some kind of inventory management system to deal with all aspects of information relating to those products and services. Time constraints may limit the scope of your effort, but give some thought to what is both reasonable and feasible to implement, given your particular situation.

2. Decide what tables you will need for your data, and the relationships between them.

3. Decide what attributes should go into each table, what data type each attribute should have, and what keys should be used to identify the rows in individual tables and connect the tables.

4. Think about any "business rules" that may be peculiar to your business and make sure they do not "break" your design. If you discover a business rule that is inconsistent with your database design, revise your design accordingly.

5. Implement your design in MySQL, using any combination of phpMyAdmin and the command-line interface, but try to use both enough to enhance your familiarity with each.

6. Add enough data to each table so that you can perform some meaningful queries, and test your database until you are satisfied it is going to help you perform the necessary tasks your business requires.

What Else You May Want or Need to Know

1. MySQL started life as an open-source, freely available, database system. As of this writing, that is still true. However, MySQL was taken over by Sun Microsystems which, in turn, has been acquired by Oracle, who owns one of the largest proprietary database systems.

Some believe that this does not bode well for the future of MySQL as a freely available system, and some of the MySQL websites are taking on a decidedly commercial look and feel. Nevertheless, until you hear differently, you should assume you will be able to download and install a free version of MySQL.

2. When you first begin to work with an RDBMS (Relational Database Management System) it can be an intimidating experience. Even the installation of such a system on your home computer can seem like a daunting undertaking, especially since to get the full advantage of the installation you will want to have a web server, the PHP programming language, and phpMyAdmin all installed as well. Fortunately, some very clever and helpful people have worked long and hard to make all this "easy" for you, and you should know that it's not as bad as it may seem. This is not to say you will not encounter the odd bump in the road during the setup, but it should be nothing you cannot overcome with a quick search on the web or a question to a more knowledgeable friend. See the following **References** section for some relevant links.

3. In this chapter we have dealt only with the relational database and the MySQL version of that kind of database, as well as the SQL used to communicate with such databases. These databases and even MySQL are very widely used and are not going away anytime soon. However, you should be aware that there are many other kinds of databases and that recently the so-called NoSQL databases such as **MongoDB** and **Couchbase** have been gaining much influence on the web. You should keep an eye out for further developments in this area.

 # References

1. Whatever information and software you need to get started with MySQL should be available at one or both of the following links:

    ```
    http://www.mysql.com/
    ```

    ```
    http://dev.mysql.com
    ```

2. The home page for phpMyAdmin can be found here:

    ```
    http://www.phpmyadmin.net/home_page/index.php
    ```

3. You can download MySQL, PHP, phpMyAdmin, and the Apache web server software in a single package as well. Such a package may also include other useful pieces of software. If you wish to pursue this option, check out one or both of the following sites:

    ```
    http://www.apachefriends.org/en/xampp.html
    ```

    ```
    http://www.wampserver.com/en/
    ```

4. The W3Schools tutorial on SQL starts here:

    `http://www.w3schools.com/sql/default.asp`

5. Wikipedia has articles on database normalization, functional dependency, and SQL:

    `http://en.wikipedia.org/wiki/Database_normalization`

    `http://en.wikipedia.org/wiki/Functional_dependency`

    `http://en.wikipedia.org/wiki/SQL`

6. All of the following links will take you to articles that discuss the database normalization process:

    `http://agiledata.org/essays/dataNormalization.html`

    `http://databases.about.com/od/administration/u/database_basics.htm`

    `http://www.bkent.net/Doc/simple5.htm`

    `http://www.phlonx.com/resources/nf3/nf3_tutorial.pdf`

7. Here is a link to a tutorial article on the `Database Answers` site entitled *How to Understand a Database Schema*:

    `http://www.databaseanswers.org/tutorial4_db_schema/index.htm`

8. For a tutorial on joins in MySQL see:

    `http://www.tizag.com/mysqlTutorial/mysqljoins.php`

9. For information on NoSQL databases, and MongoDB and Couchbase in particular see:

    `https://en.wikipedia.org/wiki/NoSQL`

    `https://www.mongodb.org/`

    `http://www.couchbase.com/`

CHAPTER **TEN**

PHP and MySQL for Client-Server Database Interaction

CHAPTER CONTENTS

Overview and Objectives

We have now arrived at the pinnacle of our e-commerce website development. In this chapter we combine all the knowledge we have learned so far to create a "complete" e-commerce solution for our business that will allow a user to visit our online e-store and perform each of the following tasks:

▶ Browse through our product catalog "anonymously" (as a casual web surfer, without registering—recall that a casual visitor to our site can also perform a Body Mass Index (BMI) calculation or send feedback to the company)

▶ Open an account by registering with our website

▶ Log in to our website as a registered user, and later (after browsing and shopping, we hope) log out

▶ Browse through our product catalog as a registered user who can now manage an online "shopping cart" by adding and removing items

▶ And, finally, "check out" and "purchase" the shopping cart items (Actually, our system stops short of accepting payment and shipping items, since in reality it has no items to ship and besides, that would involve connecting to other businesses under false pretenses . . .)

We can customize the Personal Home Page (PHP) scripts that allow users to connect to our MySQL database and perform the various new tasks that require such a connection. Note that phpMyAdmin and the command-line interface that we examined in the last chapter are tools to be used by a business owner or designated administrator to maintain the database for the business. These are not tools we want our site visitors to be using for access to our database. Instead, it is more appropriate (and safer) to provide our own specialized PHP scripts to control user interaction with our website and its database in very specific ways.

In the previous two chapters we laid the groundwork for what we are about to do now by introducing the PHP programming language and the MySQL database system. In this chapter we need to expand that discussion by covering the following topics:

▶ How a PHP script connects to a MySQL database

▶ How a PHP script issues *queries* (requests for information) to a MySQL database and then receives the requested information and processes it in the appropriate way (A "query" does not have to be a request for information; it can also be an instruction to the database to perform some action not related to the retrieval of information.)

▶ More about PHP arrays, which must be well understood and used properly if we expect our scripts to function as intended

▶ How to use a PHP session (introduced in Chapter 8) to keep track of a user's activity during a visit to our website

FIGURE 10.1 `graphics/ch10/nature/displayIndexPhp.jpg`
The latest version of our home page, showing our e-store dropdown menu options and a handy login link at the upper right. Photo: © LUNAMARINA/iStockphoto

FIGURE 10.1 shows our revised home page, in which the former e-store menu option has been replaced with several dropdown menu items. Those dropdown menu items are also shown. They are all e-store related, are essentially self-explanatory, and summarize the new functionality that we intend to implement in this chapter.

A user who clicks on the first item (`e-store Options`) in the dropdown menu shown in Figure 10.1 is taken to the starting page for our e-store shown in **FIGURE 10.2**, which provides a little more information about some of our e-store links.

10.1 PHP and MySQL

It is interesting to note how, in the history of computing, certain programming languages and other products have evolved together and now give the impression that they were "made for each other". In early business computing, you could see such symbiotic relationships illustrated by the association between COBOL and IBM's System/360 and its successor MVS. Computing enthusiasts

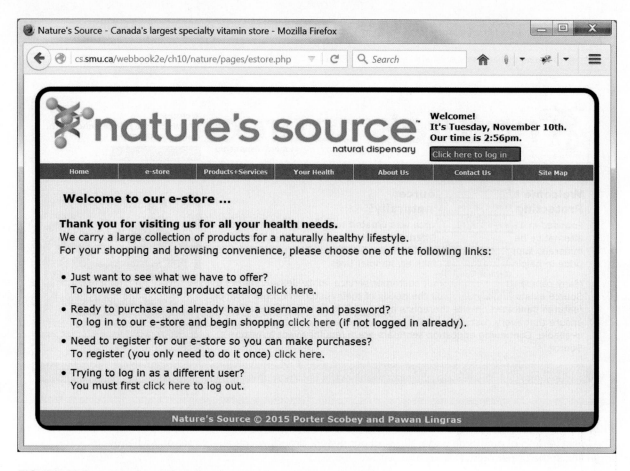

FIGURE 10.2 `graphics/ch10/nature/displayEstorePhp.jpg`
Our e-store page, giving a bird's eye view of our e-store functionality.

also reveled in the compatibility between Unix and the C programming language in the 1970s and 1980s. While the pairing of PHP and MySQL may not yet have attained the status of some of these earlier "marriages made in heaven", in this chapter we should come to appreciate the ease with which programming MySQL database management for the web can be achieved using PHP.

We begin by assuming that you have access to a computing platform with both PHP and MySQL installed. Furthermore, the system must be able to establish a connection between the two. Usually, such installation and configuration tasks are left to more sophisticated users or system administrators, but they may also be performed on a PC by any dedicated and reasonably competent user who refuses to be intimidated, as we have pointed out in the previous chapter.

As we know, connecting to a MySQL system as an authorized user and selecting an appropriate database can be done using phpMyAdmin or the command-line interface, but we are now interested in more direct control of our web pages using our own PHP scripts as the interface. This gives us business-specific solutions that allow our users access to our database in a more controlled fashion.

```php
1    <?php
2    /*connectToDatabase.php
3    Handles the connection to the Nature's Source database.
4    Values for $dbLocation, $dbUsername, $dbPassword, and
5    $dbName are assigned in the file database.inc, which
6    must be included from a "safe" (but readable) location
7    which is outside public_html, for security reasons.
8    */
9
10   include("../../../../htpasswd/database.inc");
11
12   if (!isset($dbLocation))
13   {
14       echo "Database location is missing.<br>
15           Connection script now terminating.";
16       exit(0);
17   }
18
19   if (!isset($dbUsername))
20   {
21       echo "Database username is missing.<br>
22           Connection script now terminating.";
23       exit(0);
24   }
25
26   if (!isset($dbPassword))
27   {
28       echo "Database password is missing.<br>
29           Connection script now terminating.";
30       exit(0);
31   }
32
33   if (!isset($dbName))
34   {
35       echo "Database name is missing.<br>
36           Connection script now terminating.";
37       exit(0);
38   }
39
40   $db = mysqli_connect($dbLocation,
41                        $dbUsername,
42                        $dbPassword,
43                        $dbName);
44   if (mysqli_connect_errno() || ($db == null))
45   {
46       printf("Database connection failed: %s<br>
47           Connection script now terminating.",
48           mysqli_connect_error());
49       exit(0);
50   }
51   ?>
```

FIGURE 10.3 `ch10/nature/scripts/connectToDatabase.php`
Typical PHP code for connecting to MySQL. For security reasons we do not show the content of the file `database.inc` referenced in line 10, but we discuss its contents (generically) in the text.

The first thing we need to know, as web programmers, is how to use PHP to connect to the MySQL system as an authorized user and select an appropriate database. **FIGURE 10.3** shows the necessary PHP code, which is stored in a file called `connectToDatabase.php` (found in `ch10/nature/scripts`)[1]. We can use this or similar code in any one of our scripts that needs to make such a connection.

The script begins by including the file `database.inc`. The first thing to note about this file is that it must be outside the publicly accessible part of your website (outside your `public_html`, for example), but in a location accessible by PHP. The reason for this is that the file contains the necessary (sensitive) information for access to your database. Here is what our file looks like, and yours should look the same, except (of course) the values of the variables must be what you need for your particular setup:

```php
<?php
$dbLocation = "localhost";
$dbUsername = "webbook2e";
$dbPassword = "our_password";
$dbName = "webbook2e";
?>
```

The variable `$dbLocation` contains the name or the IP address of the computer that hosts the MySQL system we wish to access. It can be the same as, or different from, the computer that hosts the web server. In our case, both are the same so we use the value `"localhost"` for this variable. Next, the variable `$dbUsername` has the value `"webbook2e"`, which is our username for our MySQL system. We show here only a dummy password being assigned to the variable `$dbPassword`, and finally our database name (also `webbook2e`) is stored in the variable `$dbName`.

Once this file has been included and the variables it contains are available, the rest of the script can proceed.

Lines 12–38 of the script in Figure 10.3 contain a sequence of `if`-statements that check to make sure each of the four required variables has a value (via calls to the PHP `isset()` function). The script terminates with a call to the `exit(0)` function after issuing an appropriate message if any of the four variables has no value. Note in passing that each of the message strings in the `echo` statements extends over two lines, which is permissible without using a concatenation operator in PHP.

The connection to the MySQL server is established from PHP by calling the built-in function `mysqli_connect()`, which takes as its four parameters the values of the variables in the `database.inc` file:

▶ The location of the MySQL server (`$dbLocation`)
▶ The user's MySQL username (`$dbUsername`)
▶ The user's MySQL password (`$dbPassword`)
▶ The MySQL database name (`$dbName`)

---

[1] Since this chapter discusses exclusively the version of our website found in the `nature` subdirectory of `ch10`, we will generally omit the `ch10/nature` prefix in any future file paths where no confusion is likely to result.

If the connection does not succeed, we output an appropriate message (this time using the `printf` alternative to `echo`), and again terminate the PHP script, once more with a call to `exit(0)`. If the connection succeeds, we save the result returned by `mysqli_connect()` in a variable called `$db`. This variable gives us a reference to our database, on which subsequent actions can now be performed. That is, we are now in position to run almost any SQL query that we saw in the previous chapter, but this time we will run the queries from our PHP scripts.

When writing PHP scripts that deal with MySQL, you can leverage your knowledge of SQL queries, since this is the form in which PHP delivers these queries to MySQL. The following sections look at how PHP performs database retrieval and manipulation operations to help us carry out the e-commerce tasks required by our business. And, of course, we shall be using several additional built-in PHP functions, like the `mysqli_connect()` function used above, in dealing with our MySQL database. Their names all begin with the `mysqli_` prefix.

Before we proceed, we should remind you that unless you have installed PHP and MySQL on a local machine (your own, or your school's, for example), you will have to view the pages we are discussing on the book's website. Even on the book's website, we will have certain restrictions. Any manipulations to the database may be difficult or impossible to manage on our server. We strongly recommend, therefore that readers import the database provided in the previous chapter on their own MySQL server and set up PHP so that it can access this database. As is our practice, however, we will continue to provide detailed screenshots of various web interactions to ensure that the reader can follow the exposition in the text without having to access a computer.

10.2 Registration

While casual visitors to our website can browse through our catalog anonymously, we do not permit any actual e-commerce transactions until we know we are dealing with an "authorized" user. The first step in establishing a user's identity for an e-commerce website is, usually, to have the user complete and submit a registration form such as the one shown in **FIGURE 10.4**.

During the registration process we must be prepared to deal with at least the following possible scenarios:

- ▶ The typical case where the user enters data that causes no problem and simply completes a successful registration
- ▶ The case where the user enters something on the form that does not pass validation on the client side
- ▶ The case where a user has already registered and has perhaps forgotten they have done so, which will be recognized when the user is discovered to be in the database already
- ▶ The case where the user attempts to choose a login name that is already in use by a previously registered customer

In the discussion that follows it will be useful to keep in mind this distinction: Data that is OK on the client side may turn out to be not OK on the server side. For example, a perfectly valid login name (as far as the client-side validation is concerned) may turn out to be invalid upon being sent to the server and checked against the MySQL database, for the reason that it is already in use.

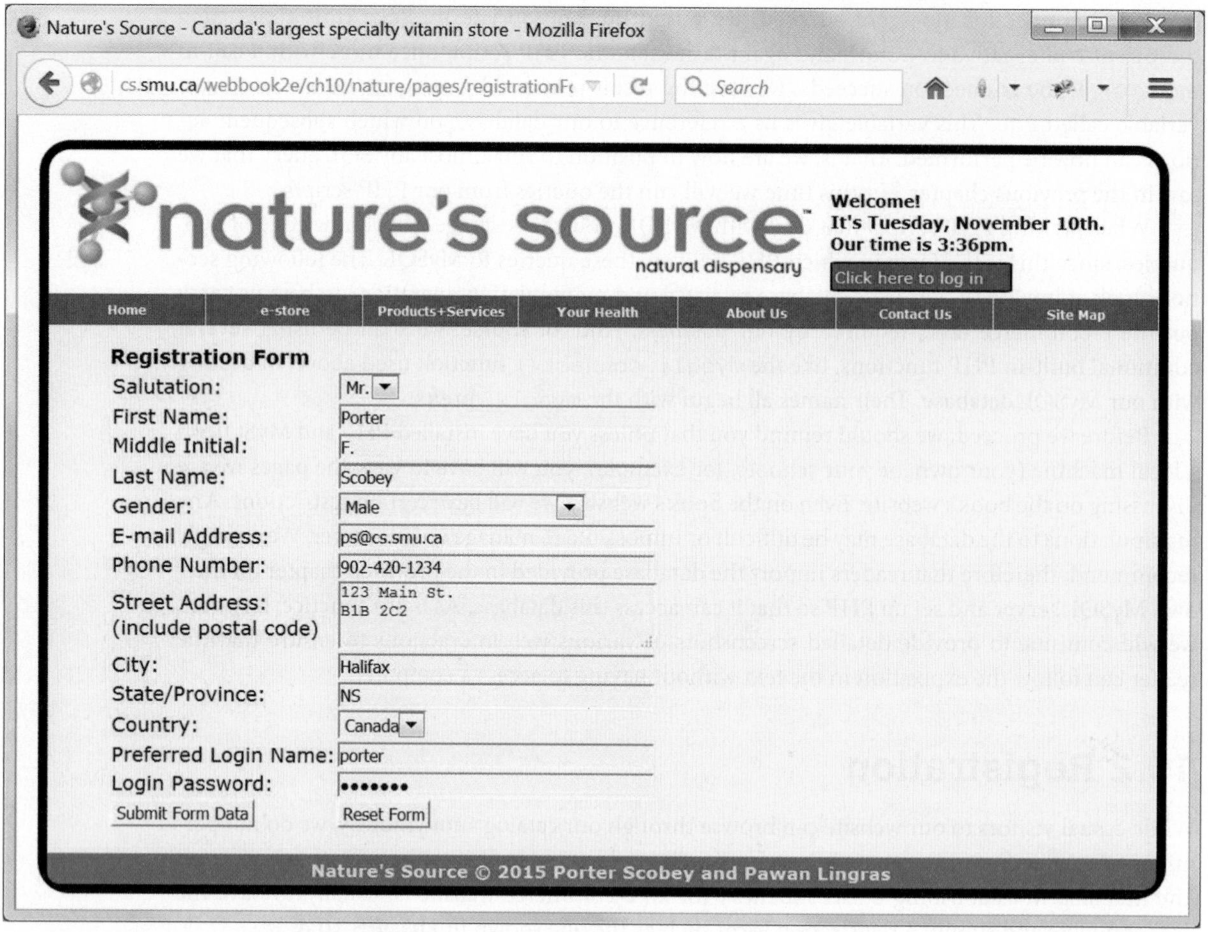

FIGURE 10.4 `graphics/ch10/nature/displayRegisterPhp1.jpg`
The registration form a user must complete and submit to register with our website in order to be authorized when making future online purchases from our e-store.

10.2.1 Getting Valid Registration Form Data from the User

The web page containing our registration form shown in Figure 10.4 is produced by the file `pages/registrationForm.php`, an excerpt of which is shown in **FIGURE 10.5**. The registration form itself is not very different from other HTML forms we have seen in previous chapters, such as our feedback form, except that in order to reduce the amount of markup, we are not using label elements for accessibility in this chapter.

As we did with our previous forms, we continue to validate the user's data entries on the registration form, in this case using both client-side JavaScript and the HTML5 `pattern` attribute on form controls.

```
13    <main>
14      <article class="Registration">
15        <h4>Registration Form</h4>
16        <form id="registrationForm"
17              onsubmit="return registrationFormValidate();"
18              action="scripts/registrationFormResponse.php"
19              method="post">
20          <table>
21            <tr>
22              <td>Salutation:</td>
23              <td><select name="salute">
24                <option> </option>
25                <option>Mrs.</option>
26                <option>Ms.</option>
27                <option>Mr.</option>
28                <option>Dr.</option>
29              </select></td>
30            </tr>
31            <tr>
32              <td>First Name:</td>
33              <td><input required type="text" name="firstName" size="40"
34                  title="Initial capital, then lowercase and no spaces"
35                  pattern="^[A-Z][a-z]*$"></td>
36            </tr>
```

FIGURE 10.5 `ch10/nature/pages/registrationForm.php` **(excerpt)**
A partial display of the markup that produces our registration form.

First, from line 17 in Figure 10.5 you can see from the value of the onsubmit attribute that we are calling the JavaScript function registrationFormValidate() when the form is submitted. (Note the presence of return, which is necessary even though the function itself "returns" a boolean value.) This function is contained in the JavaScript file scripts/registrationForm-Validate.js, which contains only the definition of this single function. The function, in turn, only checks to ensure that we do no try to submit a completely empty registration form. This is really a bit of validation redundancy, since we can achieve the same effect by placing a required attribute on each of our form controls.

Second, note that the input element in lines 33–35 of Figure 10.5 has both the above-mentioned required attribute, as well as a pattern attribute whose value describes the kind of input we will accept for the user's first name (in this particular case).

Both JavaScript validation and validation via the HTML5 pattern attribute have been discussed previously, so we do not go into any further detail here. However, it may be useful to look over, for the sake of completeness, the full contents of both registrationForm.php and reg-istrationFormValidate.js.

10.2.2 Submitting the Form Data: Possible Outcomes

The sequence of events related to the filling out and submission of the registration form goes something like this. First, the user fills in the form and clicks on the **Submit Form Data** button. If the form data validates, the form data is sent to the server. If the form data does not validate, the data is not forwarded to the server. If the form data makes it to the server, it is "handled" by the script in `scripts/registrationFormResponse.php`. This file is given in the value of the registration form's `action` attribute, as seen in line 18 of Figure 10.5, and note that its path there is relative to the home directory of this version of our website (`ch10/nature`). The final processing of the submitted data is done by the script in `scripts/registrationFormProcess.php`, and the final outcome of submitting the registration form data will depend on the nature of the data submitted, as we describe in what follows.

At the highest level, any one of the following scenarios may occur.

Scenario 1: A Typical Problem-Free Registration

If all the data entered into our registration form as shown in Figure 10.4 validates, and the user clicks the **Submit Form Data** button, the form data is sent to the server. If there are no problems on the server side, we get a display like the one shown in **FIGURE 10.6**.

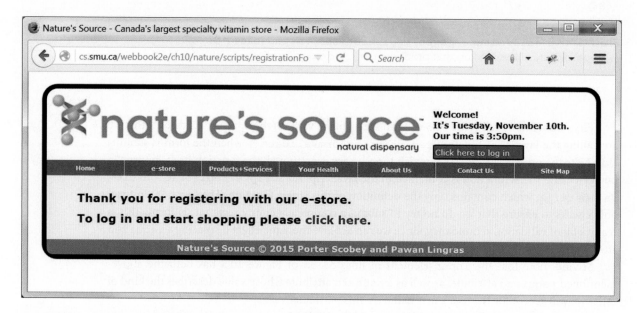

FIGURE 10.6 `graphics/ch10/nature/displaySuccessfulRegistrationFormResponsePhp.jpg`
The resulting display when a new user registers successfully for our website.

Scenario 2: A Problem with Invalid Data Entered into the Form by the User

If one or more of the form data entries causes the form data not to validate on the client side, the user will be so informed in some way, and will have to make corrections and try again. As indicated above, we will not illustrate this scenario any further here.

Scenario 3: A Problem with Duplicate Registrations (Duplicate Email Addresses)

This scenario occurs when the user (i.e., the user's email address, which is used to identify every user uniquely) is already in our server-side database. As we have indicated in Chapter 9, the email address in the Customers table of our database must be unique. If a user tries to enter the same information again, the user should get an error because an attempt is being made to duplicate the email address. **FIGURE 10.7** shows the reaction from our PHP processing to such an attempt. You may be able to obtain this page easily by clicking on the refresh button in your browser, immediately after a successful registration. In that case, if the browser attempts to send the same form information again, the page shown in Figure 10.7 should appear.

FIGURE 10.7 `graphics/ch10/nature/displayUnsuccessfulRegistrationFormResponsePhp.jpg`
The resulting display when a potential new user fails to register because the email address entered into the registration form was already in the database. All email addresses in our database must be unique.

Scenario 4: A Problem with Duplicate Login Usernames (Login Username has Already Been Chosen by Another User)

The Customers table of our database also requires that the login username be unique. However, it might be quite natural for another user named Porter, with a different email address, to ask for porter as a username. What should our PHP script do in such a case? A reasonable course of action might be to create a new username by simply appending a digit to the preferred username. If we do, in fact, attempt to specify a username of porter from a different email address, as shown in **FIGURE 10.8**, our PHP script processing results in the output shown in **FIGURE 10.9**. The registration was accepted, but the login username was changed to porter0.

FIGURE 10.8 graphics/ch10/nature/displayRegistrationFormPHP2.jpg
Another registration form in which the user is "unknown" to the database because his email address is not in the database, but he is attempting to use a login username that is already in use.

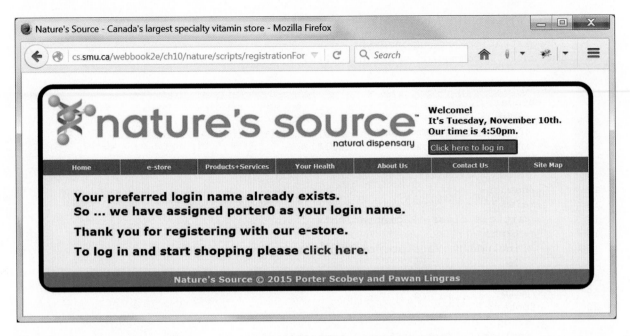

FIGURE 10.9 `graphics/ch10/nature/displaySuccessfulRegistrationFormResponsePhp2.jpg`
The resulting display when a new user registers successfully for our website, despite having chosen a login username that is already in use.

An alternate approach might be to suggest the new username, ask the user to re-register, and use the new (suggested) username. The logic for either of these two approaches is essentially the same.

10.2.3 Actual Processing of the Registration, with Valid Form Data

We are now ready to look at the PHP processing of the registration form data, given that valid form data has been uploaded to the server. There are actually two files involved: `scripts/registrationFormResponse.php` (shown in **FIGURE 10.10**) and `scripts/registrationFormProcess.php` (shown in **FIGURES 10.11** and **10.12**). The registrationFormResponse.php script appeared as the go-to script in the `action` attribute of the registration form, and is actually a "high-level" script that does three things for us:

1. Its overall task is to set up the "infrastructure" for the HTML page that will be displayed to the user as the response to the processing of the registration form data.
2. In line 10 it includes our `scripts/connectToDatabase.php` script, which runs and connects us to our database so that we can enter the user's information.
3. In line 16 it includes the second script, `registrationFormProcess.php` (Figures 10.11 and 10.12), which does all of the actual work.

```
1   <?php
2   //registrationFormResponse.php
3   include("../common/document_head.html");
4   ?>
5     <body>
6       <header>
7         <?php
8         include("../common/banner.php");
9         include("../common/menus.html");
10        include("../scripts/connectToDatabase.php");
11        ?>
12      </header>
13      <main>
14        <article class="Registration">
15          <?php
16          include("../scripts/registrationFormProcess.php");
17          ?>
18        </article>
19      </main>
20      <footer>
21        <?php
22        include("../common/footer_content.html");
23        ?>
24      </footer>
25    </body>
26  </html>
```

FIGURE 10.10 `ch10/nature/scripts/registrationFormResponse.php`
The file that handles, at a high level, the response to the user when the user submits the registration form in
`registrationForm.php`.

```
15  //========= main script begins here
16  if (isset($_POST['gender']) && ($_POST['gender'] == "Female"))
17      $gender = "F";
18  else if (isset($_POST['gender']) && ($_POST['gender'] == "Male"))
19      $gender = "M";
20  else $gender = "O"; //for "Other"
21
22  if (emailAlreadyExists($db, $_POST['email']))
23  {
24      echo "<h3>Sorry, but your e-mail
25            address is already registered.</h3>";
26  }
```

FIGURE 10.11 `ch10/nature/scripts/registrationFormProcess.php` **(Part 1 of 2)**
The first part of the script that actually processes the data submitted from the registration form in
`registrationForm.php`.

```
27   else
28   {
29       $unique_login = getUniqueID($db, $_POST['loginName']);
30       if ($unique_login != $_POST['loginName'])
31       {
32           echo "<h3>Your preferred login name already exists.<br>So ...
33               we have assigned $unique_login as your login name.</h3>";
34       }
35
36       $query = "INSERT INTO Customers(
37           customer_id,
38           salutation,
39           customer_first_name, customer_middle_initial, customer_last_name,
40           gender,
41           email_address,
42           login_name, login_password,
43           phone_number,
44           address, town_city, county, country
45       )
46       VALUES (
47           NULL,
48           '$_POST[salute]',
49           '$_POST[firstName]', '$_POST[middleInitial]', '$_POST[lastName]',
50           '$_POST[gender]',
51           '$_POST[email]',
52           '$unique_login', '$_POST[loginPassword]',
53           '$_POST[phone]',
54           '$_POST[address]', '$_POST[city]', '$_POST[state]', '$_POST[country]'
55       );";
56       $success = mysqli_query($db, $query);
57       echo "<h3>Thank you for registering with our e-store.</h3>";
58       echo "<h3>To log in and start shopping please
59           <a href='pages/loginForm.php'
60               class='NoDecoration'>click here</a>.</h3>";
61   }
62   mysqli_close($db);
63   //========== main script ends here
```

FIGURE 10.11 `ch10/nature/scripts/registrationFormProcess.php` **(Part 1 of 2)** (*continued*)

```
64
65    /*emailAlreadyExists()
66    Determines if the e-mail address supplied by the customer
67    upon registration is already in the database.
68    */
69    function emailAlreadyExists($db, $email)
70    {
71        $query =
72          "SELECT *
73          FROM Customers
74          WHERE email_address = '$email'";
75        $customers = mysqli_query($db, $query);
76        $numRecords = mysqli_num_rows($customers);
77        return ($numRecords > 0) ? true : false;
78    }
79
80    /*getUniqueID()
81    Assigns a unique login name to the customer upon registration.
82    If the login name requested by the customer is already in use,
83    the customer will be assigned the login name which is formed
84    by taking the requested login name and appending the lowest
85    positive integer that makes the result unique in the database.
86    */
87    function getUniqueID($db, $loginName)
88    {
89        $unique_login = $loginName;
90        $query =
91          "SELECT *
92          FROM Customers
93          WHERE login_name = '$unique_login'";
94        $customers = mysqli_query($db, $query);
95        $numRecords = mysqli_num_rows($customers);
96        if ($numRecords != 0)
97        {
98            //Try appending non-negative integers 0, 1, 2 ...
99            //till you get a unique login name
100           $i = -1;
101           do
102           {
103               $i++;
104               $unique_login = $loginName.$i;
105               $query =
106                 "SELECT *
107                 FROM Customers
108                 WHERE login_name = '$unique_login'";
```

FIGURE 10.12 `ch10/nature/scripts/registrationFormProcess.php` **(Part 2 of 2)**
The second part of the script that actually processes the data submitted from the registration form in
registrationForm.php.

```
109                 $customers = mysqli_query($db, $query);
110                 $numRecords = mysqli_num_rows($customers);
111             }
112         while ($numRecords != 0);
113     }
114     return $unique_login;
115 }
116 ?>
```

FIGURE 10.12 `ch10/nature/scripts/registrationFormProcess.php` **(Part 2 of 2)** (*continued*)

The Script That Does the Actual Form Data Processing: `registrationFormProcess.php`

This is the script that is included at line 16 of Figure 10.10, is shown in Figures 10.11 and 10.12, and is the one that actually processes the submitted registration form data and produces one of the user-notification displays seen earlier, depending on the results of its analysis.

Figure 10.11 shows what could be called the "main program" for the registration task, while the supporting "helper functions" are shown in Figure 10.12. Let us now discuss the actions taken by this script.

The first nested `if`-statement in our "main program" (lines 16–20 of Figure 10.11) assigns an appropriate letter for the gender, since we shall store only a single letter in our database.

The next item on our agenda is to see if the email address supplied by the user now trying to register is already registered in our database. This check is performed by the function `email-AlreadyExists()`, which we will study in detail shortly. If the function `emailAlready-Exists()` finds the user's email in the `Customers` table of our database, it will return `true`, and we then echo an appropriate error message, which we saw in Figure 10.7. As you know by now, from Chapter 8, it is a relatively simple task to email the login name and password to the user, but we leave this as an exercise for the reader.

On the other hand, if the email address does not exist in our `Customers` database table, we continue with the process of trying to add a new user to the table. We now have to ensure that the user's login name is also unique. The user has specified a preferred login name, but there is a possibility that this login name may already exist in the `Customers` table, and we do not permit duplicate login names. Hence, line 29 calls the function `getUniqueID()`, which takes in the `$login_name` preferred by the user and returns a unique name, which may in fact be the name that was requested by the user, or it may be a variation of that name if the requested name was found to be already in use. In any case, the value of the variable `$unique_login` will not exist in the `Customers` table at this point. Before we go ahead and add the new record into the table, we let the user know if the preferred name had to be changed. This is achieved by the `if`-statement (lines 30–34 of Figure 10.11) that compares `$login_name` with `$unique_login`, and, if these two names do not match, echoes an appropriate message and also displays the login name the user should use from this point on.

The Final Step: Entering the User's Information into the Database

At this point, if we have managed to avoid all potential difficulties, we can now add the user's record to the `Customers` database. We do this by executing the appropriate SQL query from our PHP script, which is a two-step process.

First, we build the query as a string. In our case, we use a variable called `$query` and assign it a string that is constructed using data taken directly from the various form elements, except that we modified the value of `$gender` and in addition we are now using the variable `$unique_login` instead of `$login_name`. The `INSERT` query string shown in Figure 10.11 (lines 36–55) is similar to the `INSERT` queries we studied in Chapter 9.

Second, we have to send the SQL query string that we have just built to our MySQL database. This we do via the call to the PHP function `mysqli_query()` at line 56 of Figure 10.11. Notice that this function takes two parameters. The first parameter is the `$db` variable that references our database and that became available to us when we ran our `connectToDatabase.php` script (see line 10 of Figure 10.10). And the second parameter is the query string itself.

The result of the call to this function is stored in the variable `$success`. On this occasion we do not test this return value from the `INSERT` query, which just means we are assuming it was successful. However, we can always test such return values from SQL queries and may wish to do so for the `SELECT` or other queries that we will be doing later on, if we suspect a problem.

Note that we have not included any error checking in this code. This is not what we recommend, of course, it's just that we have tested our code, are relatively confident in it, and we want to take a minimalist approach to the amount of code we present, for pedagogical reasons. You could, and should, in your own code, include error checking. As you know, again from Chapter 8, you could use the primitive `die()` approach to terminate the script with an error message if the function `mysqli_query()` fails for any reason. If you also want a helpful error message that may assist you in identifying the problem, you can get such an error message via a call to the built-in function `mysqli_error($db)`, which returns a textual description of what went wrong with the previous call to `mysqli_query()`. The parameter is again the `$db` variable containing the reference to our database to which we sent the query. This message can also be incorporated into the output from the call to `die()` if you wish.

The remaining part (lines 57–60) of the "main program" in Figure 10.11 is simple echoing of HTML markup, including a link to `pages/loginForm.php`, which will allow (and encourage) the user to log in to our site (and shop . . .) after successfully registering. And finally, as good programming citizens, in line 62 of Figure 10.11 we close our database once we have finished with it.

The Helper Functions `emailAlreadyExists()` and `getUniqueID()`

Figure 10.12 shows the two functions used by the "main program" of our script to ensure that the email address and login names of the user who is trying to register are unique:

`emailAlreadyExists()` This function accepts an email address as input and returns `true` if that email address already exists in the database. It begins by creating a `SELECT` query that attempts to retrieve a record with the specified email address, and then runs the query with a call to `mysqli_query()`, as before. The result of the query is stored in the variable `$customers`. This time we are trying to retrieve records matching a given -mail address, but we do not really want to look at the records. We only want to know if there *are* any records with the given email address. The function `mysqli_num_rows()` takes the result from the query execution (`$customers` in our case) and returns the number of rows retrieved. We store this number of rows in a variable called `$numRecords`. Our function `emailAlreadyExists()` then returns a value of `true` if `$numRecords` is greater than 0, and `false` otherwise.

`getUniqueID()` This function interacts with the database in a manner similar to the one above, but requires a loop. It tries to retrieve a record with the user's preferred login name by setting `$unique_login` to `$login_name`, and then `SELECT`ing the records from the `Customers` table where the value of the `login_name` field matches the value of `$unique_login`. As before, we store the number of records retrieved in `$numRecords`. If the value of `$numRecords` is not 0, that means the user's preferred login name is already in the database. The function then uses a `do..while`-loop that, on each iteration, adds a new number (starting at 0, and increasing by 1 each time) to the user's preferred login name and continues until it finds a login username of this form that is not in the database. For example, if the preferred login name were `porter`, the loop would try names such as `porter0`, `porter1`, `porter2`, and so on. The process continues until the login name given by `$unique_login` does not exist in the `Customers` table. In that case, the variable `$numRecords` will have the value 0, and the loop will terminate.

In any case, the value of the variable `$unique_login` is returned to the "main program" part of the script in line 29 of Figure 10.11.

10.3 Logging In and Logging Out

Registering for our website provides the user with a login name and password, which can then be used to log in to the site by completing and submitting the form shown in **FIGURE 10.13**. This is a standard HTML form, with two text fields as well as submit and reset buttons. However, the PHP code that processes the form is a little complicated, since we need to take care of a variety of conditions. In fact, the PHP scripts that we are going to use from this point on make critical use of both sessions and arrays, so we need to say a little more about both of these before continuing.

10.3.1 PHP Sessions Revisited: We Need to Know More about Them

So far our programs have not tracked the web browsing activities of our users, since there has been no need to do so. Now, however, we do have a need since, for example, we will have to keep track of who the user is and monitor that user's choices when products are placed into a shopping cart during online shopping.

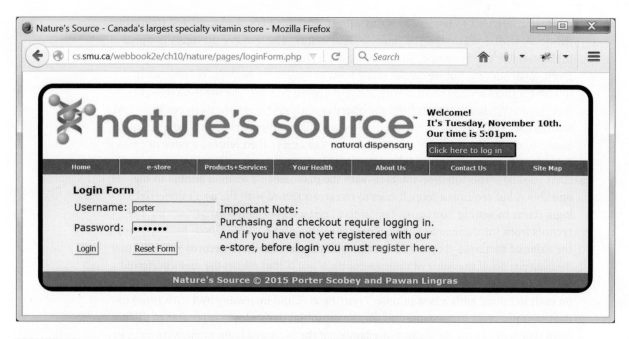

FIGURE 10.13 `graphics/ch10/nature/displayLoginFormPHP.jpg`
The login form a user completes and submits to log in to our website (after having registered) in order to make online purchases.

So, we now have another use for a PHP session, which we introduced and used in a simple way to monitor web page refreshes back in Chapter 8. In the current context a session will provide us with a way to store information in variables on the server, after which those variables can be accessed and their values used (read and written) across multiple pages. Note that these variables are different from *cookies* (about which you may have heard), and which are stored on the user's computer. They also differ from the variables and their values that we have been passing from browser to server in form processing. The session variables are retrieved from the session that is opened (or connected to) at the beginning of each page, and are kept in the same `$_SESSION` superglobal array that we met in Chapter 8.

We must always remember to call the PHP `session_start()` function at the very beginning of each web page that wants to participate in session tracking. A call to this function either creates a new session or resumes (connects to) the currently running session. The real session tracking activity begins once a user logs into our website and, with luck, begins to shop.

10.3.2 PHP Arrays Revisited: We Need to Know More about Them

We have already discussed JavaScript arrays in Chapter 6, and you may have encountered arrays in other programming languages such as Java or C++. However, PHP arrays are quite different from any other arrays you may have used, including those in JavaScript, which were already quite different from those of Java or C++.

A PHP *array*, like other arrays, is essentially a list of elements. Usually, arrays are stored in such a way that each element of the array can be efficiently accessed. The elements of an array are addressed using a *subscript* (or *index*) that appears in a pair of square brackets following the name of the array, and this is true of PHP arrays as well. Moreover, as is usually the case, PHP array indices start at 0. For example, if we have an array called `$a`, the first element of the array is given by `$a[0]`, the second element by `$a[1]`, and so on.

But now we come one of the stranger and more interesting things about PHP arrays. The elements of a PHP array can be accessed not only by using integer indices, but also by using "string indices" (sometimes also called *keys*). Some readers may have encountered such string-indexable containers elsewhere and referred to them by such terms as *associative arrays* or *hash tables* or *maps* or even *dictionaries*. Oddly enough, in PHP the types of array indices are interchangeable. That is, PHP arrays have, or at least can have, this dual personality: an element value can be accessed using either an integer index or a string key. Furthermore, if you do not specify an index (when adding an element to an array, for example), an "appropriate" numeric index will be assumed.

The best way to appreciate and get familiar with the PHP array is to experiment with it in an interactive environment. If you have an account on your server that's running PHP, you can probably enter the PHP interactive environment (PHP interpreter) with the command

```
$ php -a
```

and at the end of the session's activity you can leave the interpreter with the `exit` command. We refer you now to the first exercise in the **Short Exercises** section at the end of this chapter, where you will find a sequence of commands that can be entered into the interpreter and will give the results shown. You should at least study that session now, replicate it if you can, or, even better, make up some commands of your own to experiment with PHP arrays. And look in particular at the end of that exercise where we give a list of some of the most important array properties possessed by PHP arrays that you should know as you continue to work with them.

See the end-of-chapter **References** section for more information.

10.3.3 Logging In: The Logic of `loginForm.php`

One of the design decisions we have made for our e-store is that if a user is logged in, that user cannot log in again using the same identity or, for that matter, any other identity. In other words, the user will have to explicitly log out and then log back in. A currently logged-in user who tries to log in again will simply be directed to our `pages/estore.php` page. This logic is implemented at the beginning of the file `pages/loginForm.php`. **FIGURE 10.14** shows the first part of this file.

```
1    <?php
2    //loginForm.php
3    session_start();
4    if (isset($_SESSION['customer_id'])) header('Location: estore.php');
5    $retrying = isset($_GET['retrying']) ? true : false;
6    include("../common/document_head.html");
7    ?>
8      <body>
9        <header>
10         <?php
11         include("../common/banner.php");
12         include("../common/menus.html");
13         ?>
14       </header>
15       <main>
16         <article class="Login">
17           <h4>Login Form</h4>
18           <form id="loginForm"
19                 onsubmit="return loginFormValidate();"
20                 action="scripts/loginFormProcess.php"
21                 method="post">
```

FIGURE 10.14 `ch10/nature/pages/loginForm.php` **(Part 1 of 2)**
The first part of the markup that produces our login form.

The short PHP script at the beginning of the file starts, or resumes, a session with a call to the function `session_start()` that we have discussed previously. When we have started or are continuing a session with the function `session_start()`, we can use the `$_SESSION` array to store information that can be shared by all the PHP scripts that will be run during that session. Note that it is our responsibility to populate the `$_SESSION` array with appropriate and useful key/value pairs. We will see how to do that when a user is successfully logged in a little later on. In line 4 of Figure 10.14, we are checking to see if there is an element in the `$_SESSION` array with index (or key) `customer_id`. If that is the case, then we may assume that the user is already logged in, and simply redirect the user to our `estore.php` web page.

The redirection is achieved using a built-in PHP function called `header()`. The `header()` function is used to send a "raw" HTTP header to the browser. Here we are using a special case of the `header()` function, where the parameter string begins with `Location:` and is followed by the URL of the web page to which we are redirecting the user. Thus our function call

```
header('Location: estore.php');
```

in line 4 of Figure 10.14 will redirect the browser to the file `estore.php`, which is located in the same directory as `loginForm.php`, so we need only the filename and no additional path information.

We postpone, just for the moment, a discussion of the code in line 5 of Figure 10.14.

The login form shown in Figure 10.13 is also subject to some data input validation. As you can see in line 19 of Figure 10.14, we call the JavaScript validation function `loginFormValidate()` when the form is submitted. This is the only function defined in the file `loginFormValidate.js` (not shown here), which is made available in the usual way by a script element in the head element of this page. All this function does is ensure that the login form is not completely empty when the user tries to submit it. This function is actually needed here because (just for variety) we've left off the required attribute from the text boxes on the login form. As for what goes into those text boxes, we again validate using the HTML5 pattern attribute (see lines 28 and 43 of **FIGURE 10.15**).

```
22          <table class="TableCellSpacer">
23              <tr>
24               <td>Username:</td>
25               <td><input name="loginName"
26                 type="text" size="20"
27                 title="Must be at least 6 letters and or digits"
28                 pattern="^\w{6,}$"></td>
29               <td rowspan="3">
30                 Important Note:
31                 <br>Purchasing and checkout require logging in.
32                 <br>And if you have not yet registered with our
33                 <br>e-store, before login you must
34                 <a href="pages/registrationForm.php"
35                     class="NoDecoration">register here</a>.
36               </td>
37              </tr>
38              <tr>
39               <td>Password:</td>
40               <td><input name="loginPassword"
41                 type="password" size="20"
42                 title="Must be at least 6 letters and or digits"
43                 pattern="^\w{6,}$"></td>
44              </tr>
45              <tr>
46               <td><input type="submit" value="Login"></td>
47               <td><input type="reset" value="Reset Form"></td>
48              </tr>
49
```

FIGURE 10.15 `ch10/nature/pages/loginForm.php` **(Part 2 of 2)**
The second part of the markup that produces our login form.

```
50                    <?php if ($retrying) { ?>
51
52                <tr>
53                  <td colspan="2" class="ErrorMessage">
54                    Sorry, but your login procedure failed.
55                    <br>An invalid username or password was entered.
56                    <br>Please try again to enter correct login information.
57                  </td>
58                </tr>
59
60                <?php } ?>
61
62              </table>
63            </form>
64          </article>
65        </main>
66        <footer>
67          <?php
68          include("../common/footer_content.html");
69          ?>
70        </footer>
71      </body>
72    </html>
```

FIGURE 10.15 `ch10/nature/pages/loginForm.php` **(Part 2 of 2)** (*continued*)

The rest of the file `loginForm.php`, shown in Figure 10.15, consists mostly of the markup for the login form itself, which includes a reminder message and link (lines 30–35) if the user has not yet registered. However, in lines 50–60 there is a PHP script that we will discuss at the end of this section. The main contents of the login form are one text box for the username (with `name="loginName"`) and another for the password (with `name="loginPassword"`), as well as the usual submit and reset buttons.

We now look at the actual processing of the login form. When a user fills out the form and clicks the submit button, the form data will be validated and then control will be transferred to `scripts/loginFormProcess.php`, which is the value of the form's `action` attribute in line 20 of Figure 10.14. This script is shown in **FIGURE 10.16**.

```
1    <?php
2    /*loginFormProcess.php
3    Processes the login form data and sets up the necessary
4    session data for the user to shop. If incorrect login
5    information (bad username and/or bad password) is entered,
6    the user is redirected back to the login form.
7    */
```

FIGURE 10.16 `ch10/nature/scripts/loginFormProcess.php`
The script that processes the data submitted from our login form in `loginForm.php`.

```
 8   session_start();
 9   if (isset($_SESSION['customer_id']))
10       header("Location: ../pages/estore.php");
11   include("connectToDatabase.php");
12
13   $query = "SELECT * FROM Customers
14                   WHERE login_name = '$_POST[loginName]'";
15   $rowsWithMatchingLoginName = mysqli_query($db, $query);
16   $numRecords = mysqli_num_rows($rowsWithMatchingLoginName);
17   if ($numRecords == 0)
18   {
19       //No records were retrieved, so ...
20       header("Location: ../pages/loginForm.php?retrying=true");
21   }
22   if ($numRecords == 1)
23   {
24       $row = mysqli_fetch_array($rowsWithMatchingLoginName, MYSQLI_ASSOC);
25       if ($_POST['loginPassword'] == $row['login_password'])
26       {
27           $_SESSION['customer_id'] = $row['customer_id'];
28           $_SESSION['salutation'] = $row['salutation'];
29           $_SESSION['customer_first_name'] = $row['customer_first_name'];
30           $_SESSION['customer_middle_initial'] =
31               $row['customer_middle_initial'];
32           $_SESSION['customer_last_name'] = $row['customer_last_name'];
33           $productID = $_SESSION['purchasePending'];
34           if ($productID != "")
35           {
36               unset($_SESSION['purchasePending']);
37               $destination =
38                   "../pages/shoppingCart.php?productID=$productID";
39               $goto = "Location: $destination";
40           }
41           else
42           {
43               $destination = getenv('HTTP_REFERER');
44               $goto = "Location: ".$destination;
45           }
46           header($goto);
47       }
48       else
49       {
50           //The password entered did not match the database
51           //password for the login name entered, so ...
52           header("Location: ../pages/loginForm.php?retrying=true");
53       }
54   }
55   mysqli_close($db);
56   ?>
```

FIGURE 10.16 `ch10/nature/scripts/loginFormProcess.php` (*continued*)

The script begins with a call to `session_start()`, followed by an immediate transfer to our e-store page if the user is already logged in. If we are to proceed with a login, the next step is to include the `connectToDatabase.php` script to establish a connection to our database. Then, in lines 13–15, we attempt to retrieve records from the `Customers` table of our database for which the `login_name` attribute matches the name entered in the `loginName` text box of our login form. Next, the variable `$numRecords` is assigned the number of records retrieved from the database by this query, via a call to `mysqli_num_rows()` (line 16). Since `login_name` must be unique in our database, the only possible values for `$numRecords` are 0 and 1.

If the value of `$numRecords` is 0, the user's login name was not found in the database, so the user is redirected back to the login page (lines 17–21). But note in particular line 20, in which we are using the (default) GET method (as discussed in Chapter 8) to communicate the fact to the `loginForm.php` script that the user is "retrying" (making a second or later attempt) to log in.[2] And now look back at line 5 of Figure 10.14, where we check to see if this 'retrying' component of the `$_GET` array has been set. If it has, then the table row in lines 52–58 of Figure 10.15 is included in the markup of the page display of the login form by the PHP `if`-statement of lines 50 and 60, thus informing the user to try again.

On the other hand, if the value of `$numRecords` is 1, then we have managed to find a record from the `Customers` database table for which the `login_name` attribute matches the login-Name field of our login form. The next step is to see if the corresponding password is correct. In order to check the user's password, we must first retrieve it. At this point we know that the code in line 15 of Figure 10.16 has resulted in our (unique) user's information being returned by the call to `mysqli_query()` and stored in the variable `$rowsWithMatchingLoginName`. The value of this variable (the return value of `mysqli_query()`) can be viewed as a table with a "current pointer" pointing to its first row. Of course, in our case there is only a single row because there is only a single user with the given login username.

Now the function call `mysqli_fetch_array()` in line 24 returns the table row pointed to by the "current pointer" in the previously retrieved result as an associative array (that's the effect of the second parameter, `MYSQLI_ASSOC`). Note that this function also advances the "current pointer" to the next row, if there is one, which would not be the case here, but we will want to take advantage of this in later scripts. We store the returned associative array in an appropriately named variable called `$row`, and since values in associative arrays can be accessed by the names of their keys, we can now retrieve the element corresponding to the key (or "index") `login_password` and check to see if it matches the value in the form variable `$_POST['loginPassword']`.

If there is a match, we proceed to wrap up the login process. This involves setting up five elements in the `$_SESSION` array so that they will be available for all other PHP scripts that run during the life of this session. In particular, we want to make this information available so that

---

[2] This is a good illustration of the default use of the GET method to pass information from one PHP script to another, which we noted in Chapter 8 as one of the use cases in which GET should be the data transfer method of choice.

we can personalize our welcome message once a user is logged in. The keys for these $_SESSION array elements are:

- ▶ customer_id
- ▶ salutation
- ▶ customer_middle_initial
- ▶ customer_first_name
- ▶ customer_last_name

Once these variables are set, we only need to decide where to redirect the user. The redirection location is stored in a variable called $goto (lines 39 and 44). We have not yet studied the scripts that handle our shopping cart and product purchases, but when we do we will see that if a user decides to purchase a product without having logged in, we perform the following steps:

1. We set the element of $_SESSION with index 'purchasePending' to the product_id of the product that the customer was trying to buy.
2. We redirect the user to the login page.

If that is the reason why we came to the login page, then we want to take the user to our shopping cart web page pages/shoppingCart.php after login to give the user an immediate opportunity to buy the product of interest. This is done as follows. First we capture, in the variable $productId the value from $_SESSION['purchasePending'] so that we know the product of interest to the user (see line 33 of Figure 10.16). Once we have retrieved this value, we apply the unset() function to $_SESSION['purchasePending'] to delete that component from the $_SESSION array (see line 36 of Figure 10.16), since the user will either buy or ignore the product and in either case it will no longer be "pending". The $goto variable is then set (lines 37–39 of Figure 10.16) to a value that will send the user to our shopping cart page, along with the product identifier of the product in which the user has expressed an interest (attached to the end of the URL as a key/value pair in the usual way). The user is actually redirected to that page by line 46 of Figure 10.16, after coming out of the if-statement.

If there is no purchase pending when we come to the login page, the test in line 34 of Figure 10.16 will fail and we will execute the else portion of that if..else-statement, which simply redirects the user back to the page from which this script was called. In a typical login, with a correct username and password, the user is simply directed back to pages/loginForm.php, but now, being logged in, the user is again redirected to our e-store page as shown in **FIGURE 10.17**. The main difference now is that the Welcome message at the top right of the page has been personalized with the user's information by our revised common/banner.php, the details of which we will discuss shortly.

We still have to answer this question: How do we know which page called our script so we can direct the user back to that page? This page is obtained by retrieving the value of what is called the "referer page", as follows. Whenever we are browsing, our browser keeps track of a set of *environment variables*. We can get a list of these environment variables for our particular environment by making a call to the function phpinfo(). We need the value of the environment variable called HTTP_REFERER, which is the web page our browser was viewing before coming to the current

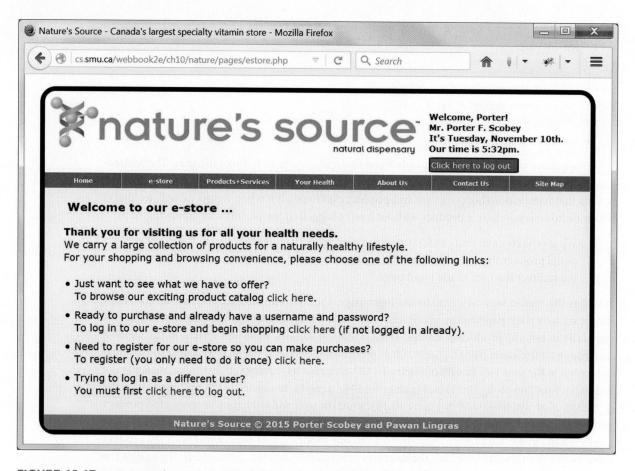

FIGURE 10.17 `graphics/ch10/nature/displayAfterLoginEstorePHP.jpg`
A display of our e-store page after a successful login. Compare with the display in Figure 10.2 and note the addition of the personalized greeting information at the top right in this version, as well as the appearance of a logout button under the greeting.

page. The value of this environment variable can be retrieved using the function getenv(), with a call like this:

```
$ref = getenv("HTTP_REFERER");
```

We then simply prepend the variable $ref with the string "Location:" to create the required value of the $goto variable. Once again, the actual redirection takes place in line 46.

Finally, if the password test in line 25 of Figure 10.16 fails, then we execute the else portion of this if..else-statement in lines 50–52 of Figure 10.16. This code simply redirects the user back to the login form for another try, just as line 20 of Figure 10.16 did when the login username failed to match. **FIGURE 10.18** shows the display received after a failed login attempt.

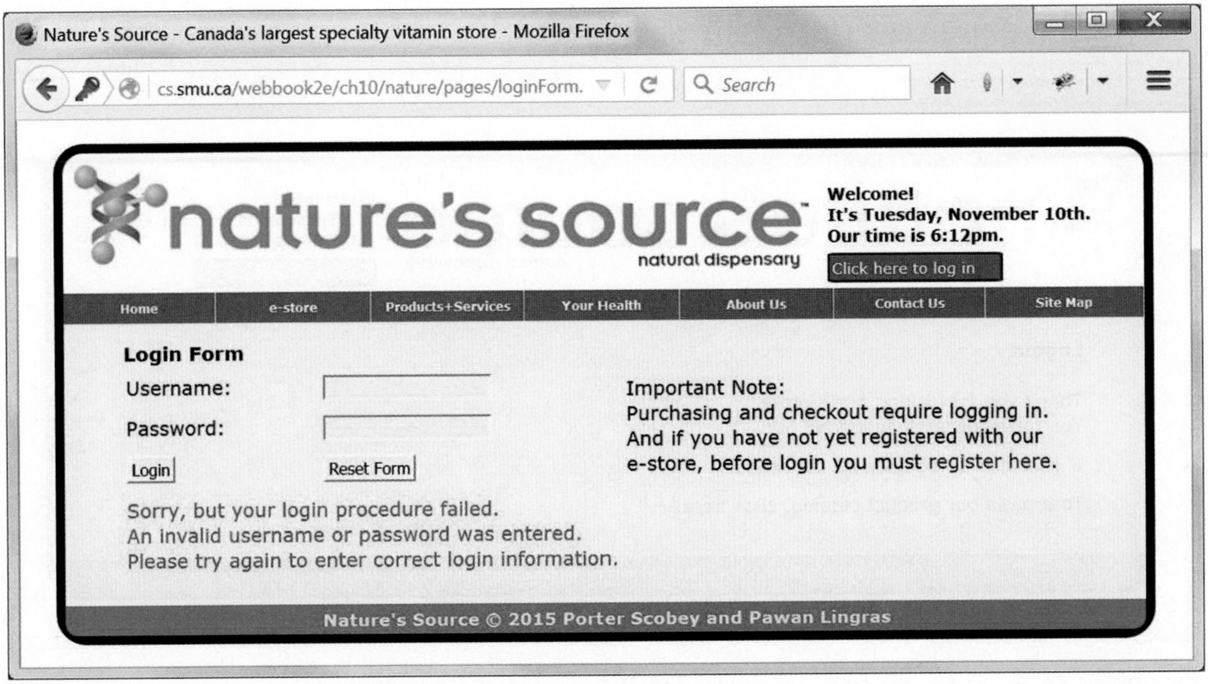

FIGURE 10.18 `graphics/ch10/nature/displayRetryLoginFormPhp.jpg`
The display produced by an unsuccessful login attempt, due to an invalid username or password, or both.

10.3.4 Logging Out: The Logic of `logout.php`

There are two situations in which the user may attempt to log out: first, the "normal" case in which the user has in fact logged in; and second, the case in which the user has not yet logged in. We must be ready for both, since you never know just what a user will do, whether accidentally or intentionally. **FIGURE 10.19** shows the display a logged-in user receives after successfully logging out, while **FIGURE 10.20** shows what the user sees if an attempt is made to log out without having logged in.

The logout page is produced by `pages/logout.php`, which is shown in **FIGURE 10.21**. The overall structure of this kind of page is by now quite familiar, so let's concentrate on the two PHP scripts (lines 1–17 and lines 29–51).

In line 3 of Figure 10.21 we start up a session as usual and then in line 4 we record, in the local variable `$needToUseLoggedInMessage` whether or not the user is in fact logged in, since if the user *is* logged in we will want to use our "thank you for logging in" message upon logout. We need to record this value in a local variable because if the user is logged in, in lines 11–12 we shut down the session in preparation for logout, and once this happens we will no longer have access to any session information that we have not recorded locally. The session would be shut down anyway if we closed our browser, but we should always try to be "good programming citizens" and also keep our logic "clean".

FIGURE 10.19 `graphics/ch10/nature/displaySuccessfulLogoutPhp.jpg`
A display of a successful logout, with options to log back in or simply browse our product catalog.

FIGURE 10.20 `graphics/ch10/nature/displayNoLoginLogoutPhp.jpg`
The display produced when a user attempts to log out without having logged in.

```php
1   <?php
2   //logout.php
3   session_start();
4   $needToUseLoggedInMessage = isset($_SESSION['customer_id']) ? true : false;
5   if (isset($_SESSION['customer_id']))
6   {
7       $customerID = $_SESSION['customer_id'];
8       include("../scripts/connectToDatabase.php");
9       include("../scripts/logoutProcess.php");
10      //Doing this ...
11      session_unset();
12      session_destroy();
13      //... requires that banner.php check to make sure
14      //that $_SESSION values are set before using them.
15  }
16  include("../common/document_head.html");
17  ?>
18    <body>
19      <header>
20        <?php
21        include("../common/banner.php");
22        include("../common/menus.html");
23        ?>
24      </header>
25      <main>
26        <article class="Logout">
27          <h4>Logout</h4>
28
29          <?php if ($needToUseLoggedInMessage) { ?>
30
31          <p><br>Thank you for visiting our e-store.<br>
32             You have successfully logged out.</p>
33          <p>If you wish to log back in,
34             <a href="pages/loginForm.php"
35                class="NoDecoration">click here</a>.</p>
36          <p>To browse our product catalog,
37             <a href="pages/catalog.php"
38                class="NoDecoration">click here</a>.</p>
39
40          <?php } else { ?>
41
42          <p><br>Thank you for visiting Nature's Source.<br>
43             You have not yet logged in.</p>
44          <p>If you do wish to log in,
45             <a href="pages/loginForm.php"
46                class="NoDecoration">click here</a>.</p>
```

FIGURE 10.21 `ch10/nature/pages/logout.php`
The script that processes a user's request to log out, whether or not the user is actually logged in.

```
47        <p>Or, just to browse our product catalog,
48            <a href="pages/catalog.php"
49                class="NoDecoration">click here</a>.</p>
50
51        <?php } ?>
52
53      </article>
54    </main>
55    <footer>
56      <?php
57      include("../common/footer_content.html");
58      ?>
59    </footer>
60  </body>
61 </html>
```

FIGURE 10.21 `ch10/nature/pages/logout.php` (*continued*)

We should also point out that in lines 8–9 we again connect to our database and then include and run `scripts/logoutProcess.php`. This performs some "cleanup" that may or may not be necessary, but we postpone a discussion of this script until later in this chapter after we have had our shopping cart discussion, at which time it should be more meaningful.

In the second script (lines 29–51 of Figure 10.21) we simply use a PHP if-statement to check the value of `$needToUseLoggedInMessage` and activate the appropriate HTML markup, depending on its value.

10.4 An E-Store Session after a Successful Login

Once a user has successfully logged in to our website, all subsequent movements through our e-store will be labeled with the user's relevant personal information. Figure 10.17 shows the web page now produced by `pages/estore.php`, which displays the user's information in the top right corner. The date and time are included, as before, as well as a new link for logging out, which replaces the previous one for logging in. In fact, all of this information will persist, along with the **Nature's Source** logo, as a banner at the top of each page as the user browses around our site.

We are already familiar with much of the basic infrastructure that permits us to do this, but some further comments and changes are in order as we examine in more detail our revised `common/banner.php` script and get set up to permit our site visitors to do some shopping.

First, because we are showing the user's information on every page if that user is logged in, any of our scripts that creates a page display will have to begin with a call to the `session_start()` function, so that the user's information will be available from the `$_SESSION` array, where we will have stored it.

Second, all files that need to interact with our database (for registration, login, product display, and checkout, for example) will have to include at the beginning of the file our PHP "connection code" from `connectToDatabase.php` to make the connection with our MySQL database.

Third, our `banner.php` needs a significant revision to take care of these new requirements. Recall that our original `banner.php` (in Chapter 8) simply displayed a nonspecific `Welcome` message, along with the current date and time. Until the user actually logs in, we essentially want to continue doing this, but now we also add a strategically placed link in this area of our web pages to facilitate easy login, as we have seen in previous page displays.

FIGURES 10.22 and **10.23** show the revised version of our `banner.php` file. Notice first of all the comment in lines 19–25 gives us another reminder about the need for any file that includes this script to call `session_start()` as its first action so that we will be able to extract information from the `$_SESSION` array, which is what the script does as it gets under way. Recall that it was the script shown in Figure 10.16 that handled the user's login and placed the user's information in the `$_SESSION` array for us to use now.

So, we first set the variable `$loggedIn` (line 26 of Figure 10.22) to tell us whether the user is in fact logged in, and which we use later (lines 37–46) to decide whether to display the

```
1   <?php
2   /*banner.php
3   This file handles the "banner display" of our Nature's Source
4   website, which includes the logo and welcome message. The logo
5   is just HTML. A PHP script displays a Welcome and the current
6   date and time, including a personal Welcome if the user has
7   logged in. And finally, a JavaScript script uses AJAX and a
8   second PHP script to update the date and time every 60 seconds.
9   */
10  ?>
11      <div id="logo">
12          <img src="images/naturelogo.gif"
13              alt="Nature's Source"
14              width="608" height="90">
15      </div>
16
17      <div id="welcome">
18          <?php
19          //Ensure that session_start() is called at the
20          //beginning of any file that includes this script
21          //and needs to make use of the $_SESSION array.
22          //Also because logout.php destroys the session
23          //before its final display it is necessary here
24          //to check that the $_SESSION values are actually
25          //set and available before using them.
```

FIGURE 10.22 `ch10/nature/common/banner.php` **(Part 1 of 2)**
The first part of our new "banner script" that now combines the output of our logo and our Welcome message and, if the user is logged in, the message is personalized with some of the user's information.

```
26          $loggedIn = isset($_SESSION['customer_id']) ? true : false;
27          if (isset($_SESSION['customer_id']))
28              $customerID = $_SESSION['customer_id'];
29          if (isset($_SESSION['salutation']))
30              $salutation = $_SESSION['salutation'];
31          if (isset($_SESSION['customer_first_name']))
32              $customerFirstName = $_SESSION['customer_first_name'];
33          if (isset($_SESSION['customer_middle_initial']))
34              $customerMiddleInitial = $_SESSION['customer_middle_initial'];
35          if (isset($_SESSION['customer_last_name']))
36              $customerLastName = $_SESSION['customer_last_name'];
```

FIGURE 10.22 `ch10/nature/common/banner.php` **(Part 1 of 2)** (*continued*)

```
37          if (!$loggedIn)
38          {
39              echo "<h5>Welcome!<br>";
40          }
41          else
42          {
43              echo "<h5>Welcome, $customerFirstName!<br>
44                      $salutation $customerFirstName
45                      $customerMiddleInitial $customerLastName<br>";
46          }
47          $date = date("l, F jS");
48          $time = date("g:ia");
49          echo "<span id='datetime'>It's $date.<br>";
50          echo "Our time is $time.</span>";
51          if ($loggedIn)
52          {
53              echo "</h5><a class='LongerButton'
54                          href='pages/logout.php'>
55                          Click here to log out</a>";
56          }
57          else
58          {
59              echo "</h5><a class='LongerButton'
60                          href='pages/loginForm.php'>
61                          Click here to log in</a>";
62          }
63          ?>
64      </div>
```

FIGURE 10.23 `ch10/nature/common/banner.php` **(Part 2 of 2)**
The second part of our new "banner script" that now combines the output of our logo and our Welcome message.

```
65      <script>
66          //This script sets up the AJAX infrastructure for
67          //requesting date and time updates from the server.
68          var request = null;
69          function getCurrentTime()
70          {
71              request = new XMLHttpRequest();
72              var url = "common/time.php";
73              request.open("GET", url, true);
74              request.onreadystatechange = updatePage;
75              request.send(null);
76          }
77          function updatePage()
78          {
79              if (request.readyState == 4)
80              {
81                  var dateDisplay = document.getElementById("datetime");
82                  dateDisplay.innerHTML = request.responseText;
83              }
84          }
85          getCurrentTime();
86          setInterval('getCurrentTime()', 60000)
87      </script>
```

FIGURE 10.23 `ch10/nature/common/banner.php` **(Part 2 of 2)** *(continued)*

personalized Welcome message or just the generic Welcome message, and again in lines 51–62 to decide whether to display the "login button" or the "logout button".

Next, in lines 27–36 of Figure 10.22 the necessary `$_SESSION` array values are retrieved and assigned to appropriately named local variables for use later on in the script. The rest of the current `banner.php` (lines 65–87) consists of an HTML `script` element containing the JavaScript code that deals with the Asynchronous JavaScript And XML (AJAX) request to the server for the updated date and time, which we have discussed previously.

10.5 Browsing Our E-Store Product Catalog

A user who is logged in to our website will likely want to browse through our product catalog. At least we hope so. In fact, we permit this kind of product browsing even if a site visitor is not logged in, and of course in that case we want our login link to be readily available on each page just in case the user decides it's time to buy. This is why we put that link next to the Welcome message in our page banner.

The **Product Catalog** dropdown link that appears under both the **e-store** and **Products+ Services** headings on our menu strip will take the user to the display shown in **FIGURE 10.24**, which is produced by `pages/catalog.php`, with the help of the included file `scripts/displayListOfCategories.php` shown in **FIGURE 10.25**. We do not show `category.php`

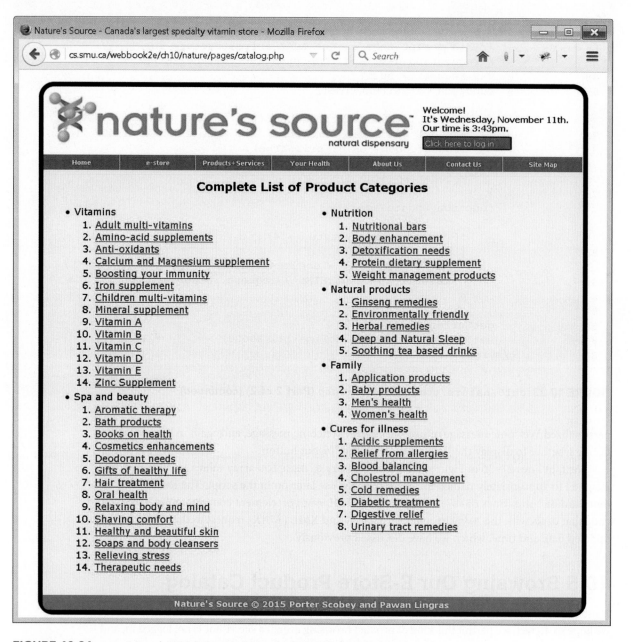

FIGURE 10.24 `graphics/ch10/nature/displayCatalogPhp.jpg`
A listing of the departments and product categories in our e-store.

```php
1    <?php
2    /*displayListOfCategories.php
3    Included in catalog.php
4    This script assumes a connection has already been made
5    to the database, from which it loads and displays all
6    product categories.
7    */
8
9    $query = "SELECT * FROM Ref_Product_Categories
10                      ORDER BY department_name DESC";
11   $categories = mysqli_query($db, $query);
12   $numRecords = mysqli_num_rows($categories);
13   $categoryCount = 0;
14   $currentDepartment = "";
15   echo
16   "<table><tr><td><ul>";
17   for ($i=1; $i<=$numRecords; $i++)
18   {
19       $row = mysqli_fetch_array($categories, MYSQLI_ASSOC);
20       if ($currentDepartment != $row['department_name'])
21       {
22           if ($currentDepartment != "") echo "</ol></li>";
23           if ($categoryCount > $numRecords/2)
24           {
25               echo "</ul></td>\r\n<td class='AlignToTop'><ul>";
26               $categoryCount = 0;
27           }
28           $currentDepartment = $row['department_name'];
29           echo "<li>$currentDepartment<ol>";
30       }
31       $prodCatCode = urlencode($row['product_category_code']);
32       $prodCatDesc = $row['product_category_description'];
33       $categoryURL = "pages/category.php?categoryCode=$prodCatCode";
34       echo "<li><a href='$categoryURL'>$prodCatDesc</a></li>\r\n";
35       $categoryCount++;
36   }
37   echo
38   "</ol></li></ul></td></tr></table>";
39   mysqli_close($db);
40   ?>
```

FIGURE 10.25 `ch10/nature/scripts/displayListOfCategories.php`
The script that displays a complete list of all departments in our e-store and all product categories within each department.

itself, since it is very similar to previously seen files that set up our page infrastructure and there is nothing new to see there, except to note that we have a couple of new CSS classes (`CategoryList` and `ProductHeader`) that have been added to our CSS style sheet and are applied to our product display. In fact, you may have noted already, and you will continue to see, new CSS classes creeping into our markup to style the new features seen on our new pages. These styles do not illustrate anything about CSS that we have not already seen, so we do not show or discuss them further. You can see their effect on our pages, of course, and you should take a few moments to look "behind the scenes" at `desktop.css`, and at `estore.css` in particular, to reconcile what you see with the CSS that produces what you see.

10.5.1 Displaying a Two-Column List of Categories

The script `displayListOfCategories.php` in Figure 10.25 starts by retrieving the list of all product categories from our database table `Ref_Product_Categories`, ordered by the values of the attribute `department_name` in descending alphabetical order (lines 9–11). We also save the number of records returned by the query in the variable `$numRecords` (line 12).

We want to write the names of our product departments as an unordered list, and all the product categories in each department as a nested ordered list under that department. We also want the entire display to appear in two columns, as shown in Figure 10.24. That means our script should create the second column approximately halfway through our listing. We will see how the code in Figure 10.25 produces such a display.

We keep track of the number of categories that have been displayed using the variable `$categoryCount`, initialized to 0 in line 13. When `$categoryCount` exceeds `$numRecords/2` (line 23 is where we make this check), we will start a new column with the next department. Another variable called `$currentDepartment` holds the string value of the current department whose product categories are being listed. To start, we initialize the value of `$currentDepartment` to be an empty string (line 14).

Once we have initialized our variables, we are ready to start the display, which begins by outputting (in lines 15–16) the opening tags for a table with one row in which the first table cell will contain the first column of a two-column unordered list of departments, so we also output a `<ul>` tag to mark the beginning of this list. We then enter a `for`-loop (line 17) that will go through and process all the records retrieved by the preceding database query in lines 9–11. The first thing we do inside the loop (line 19) is retrieve, as an associative array called `$row`, the first row from our list of product categories (and now is a good time to recall that every time we call the function `mysqli_fetch_array()` we move to the next record). Next (line 20), we check if the department for the current record is different from the last value of the department stored in the variable `$currentDepartment`. If it is different, it is time to do the following:

1.   In line 22 we close the ordered list of product categories in the current department by echoing `</ol>`, and also close the unordered list item, which is the current department, by echoing `</li>`. But note that we only do these two things if `$currentDepartment` is not an empty string, since if it *is* an empty string we are still working on the first department.

2. If the number of categories printed so far is greater than or equal to `$numRecords/2` (as determined by the test in line 23), in line 25 we terminate the unordered list of departments in the first column of the display in Figure 10.24 (by echoing `</ul>`), as well as the first table cell (by echoing `</td>`). In that same line 25 we start a second (continuation) column of the unordered list of departments and product categories by outputting a new `<td>` tag and a new `<ul>` tag in the same echo statement.

3. As the last action of the if-statement begun in line 20, in line 28 we re-initialize the value of `$currentDepartment` to the value of `department_name` in the current record, and then display this name of the current department as a list item in line 29. Note carefully that the opening `<li>` tag in line 29 of Figure 10.25 is not closed until immediately after the order list begun by the `<ol>` tag at the end of that line has been terminated, since the ordered list is nested inside a list element of the unordered list. This structure must be done just so if we want our page to validate (and, of course, we do).

Unlike the body of the if-statement begun in line 20, all the statements in lines 31–35 are executed on each iteration of the for-loop. In lines 31 and 32 we retrieve the product code and product description for the most recent product retrieved from the database and store these values in local variables. The use of the PHP `urlencode()` function in line 31 avoids a problem that would be caused when trying to validate the displayed page as HTML5 if a blank space were to occur in a product code. (This actually happens in our database, and this function ensures that a blank space is encoded properly, since the product code will appear in a link and blank spaces are not allowed in links.)

In lines 32–34 the product description and product category code are used to construct a link in which the product category description appears as the clickable text. When the user clicks on that text, and the product category code is then passed, as the value in a key/value pair, to another PHP script, `pages/category.php`. That product category code value will, of course, indicate which category of product items the user wishes to see.

Finally, the last line of our for-loop (line 35) increments the count of the number of categories that have been displayed.

When all results retrieved from the database have been displayed, we exit the for-loop and close, in the appropriate order, all the markup elements that remain open (lines 37–38) and then close the database itself (line 39).

10.5.2 Displaying Individual Products within a Category

A click on any of the "category links" shown in Figure 10.24 will provide the user with a display of the details for each of the products in that particular category. For example, clicking on **Deodorant needs**, which is item 5 in the list under the **Spa and beauty** department, brings up the page shown in **FIGURE 10.26**. As we have just seen, the link itself is one of those links produced by lines 33–34 of Figure 10.25 and thus links to `pages/category.php`. On this occasion the product category code (for the desired product) that is passed in the key/value pair at the end of the URL is DEOD. This particular category contains only the four products shown in Figure 10.26, though many categories will contain a much longer list of items.

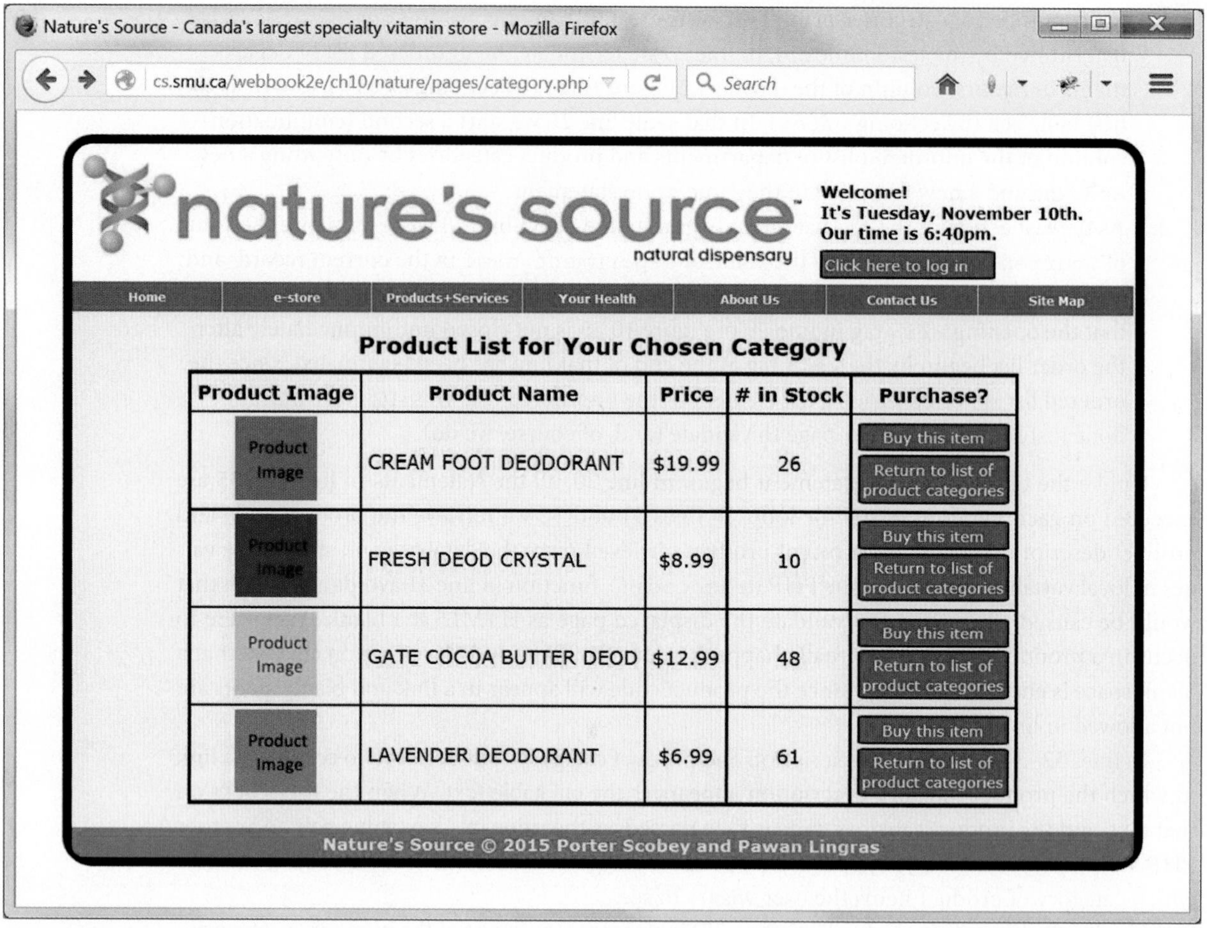

FIGURE 10.26 `graphics/ch10/nature/displayCategoryPhp.jpg`
A listing of the individual products in the `Deodorant` needs category under the Spa and beauty department. Note that we are using simple "placeholder" images of different colors rather than images of actual products.

The information for each product category is presented in a tabular format with each row of the table corresponding to a particular product and these five column headers for the properties of each product: **Product Image**, **Product Name**, **Price**, **# in Stock**, and **Purchase?**. This last column contains both a link to add the given product to the shopping cart and a link to return to the full catalog list and continue shopping.

As was the case with `pages/catalog.php`, the `pages/category.php` file is very similar to previous pages, so for the same reasons we do not show or discuss it here. We shall concentrate instead on `scripts/displayOneCategoryItems.php`, which is included in `pages/category.php` and produces the listing of individual products in a particular category, as shown in Figure 10.26.

The script itself is shown in **FIGURE 10.27** and begins in line 7 by capturing in the local variable `$categoryCode` the code of the product category to be displayed. Lines 8–12 then create

```php
1   <?php
2   /*displayOneCategoryItems.php
3   This script is called when all product categories have
4   been displayed and the user clicks on a link to see all
5   prodcuts in a particular category.
6   */
7   $categoryCode = $_GET['categoryCode'];
8   $query = "SELECT * FROM Products
9                       WHERE product_category_code = '$categoryCode'
10                      ORDER BY product_name ASC";
11  $category = mysqli_query($db, $query);
12  $numRecords = mysqli_num_rows($category);
13  echo
14  "<table>
15    <tr>
16      <th>Product Image</th>
17      <th>Product Name</th>
18      <th>Price</th>
19      <th># in Stock</th>
20      <th>Purchase?</th>
21    </tr>";
22  for ($i=1; $i<=$numRecords; $i++)
23  {
24      $row = mysqli_fetch_array($category, MYSQLI_ASSOC);
25      $productImageURL = $row['product_image_url'];
26      $productName = $row['product_name'];
27      $productPrice = $row['product_price'];
28      $productPriceAsString = sprintf("$%.2f", $productPrice);
29      $productInventory = $row['product_inventory'];
30      $productID = $row['product_id'];
31      $shoppingCartURL = "pages/shoppingCart.php?productID=$productID";
32      $catalogURL = "pages/catalog.php";
33      echo
34      "<tr>
35        <td>
36          <img height='70' width='70'
37               src='$productImageURL'
38               alt='Product Image'>
39        </td><td style='text-align: left;'>
40          $productName
41        </td><td>
42          $productPriceAsString
43        </td><td>
44          $productInventory
45        </td><td>
```

FIGURE 10.27 `ch10/nature/scripts/displayOneCategoryItems.php`
The script that displays a complete list of all products within a single category.

```
46                 <a class='Button' href='$shoppingCartURL'>Buy this item</a>
47                 <a class='Button' href='$catalogURL'>Return to list of
48                                         product categories</a>
49           </td></tr>";
50    }
51    echo
52    "</table>";
53    mysqli_close($db);
54    ?>
```

FIGURE 10.27 `ch10/nature/scripts/displayOneCategoryItems.php` (*continued*)

a query to retrieve all the products from our database `Products` table that match that category code. And, as before, we assign the number of records retrieved (number of products in the category of interest) to the variable `$numRecords`.

The next `echo` statement (lines 13–21) begins a table by outputting an opening table tag and then outputs as the first row of the table an appropriate table header for the display of the products in the chosen category. The for-loop in lines 22–50 goes through each record returned by the query in line 11 and displays each product. The statements after the for-loop ends (lines 51–53) first close off the table by echoing the closing `</table>` tag and then close the database.

Let us examine the for-loop in a little more detail. The body of the loop begins in line 24 by retrieving, as an associative array, all the information for the first (or next) product. Next, in lines 25–32, this information is copied into appropriate local variables. Most of what is going on here we have seen before, but we do have to make two comments.

First, note that our "product images" are not actually images of products. In this second edition of the text we have opted to use simple, colored "image placeholders" in place of actual product images, since having actual product images would not add anything to the discussion. So, in the subdirectory `ch08/nature/images/products` we have 10 of these image placeholder. jpg files and each product is associated with a more or less random one of these images. Along with the other product information, the path to a product's placeholder image is retrieved from the database and placed in its own local variable (line 25). Thus the first column of the table contains these images, and the next three columns contain the product name, product price, and the number in stock.

Second, note that the fifth and final column of a typical table row always displays the same two "button links", one to buy the current item and one to return to the full list of departments and categories. The next section discusses what happens when the user clicks on the first of these links and goes to the URL that was set up in line 31 and now appears in line 46. In fact, most of the rest of this chapter will be devoted to this discussion, as the user switches from "browsing" mode to "shopping" mode. Note in passing that these "button links" are not actually button images, just anchor tags (a tags) styled by our CSS `Button` class, which you will find in our `css/estore.css`.

The echo-statement in lines 33–49 now simply outputs all the information we now have at our disposal as a row of the table, suitably enclosed within appropriate `td` and `tr` elements.

10.6 Purchasing Products

Processing purchases is probably the most complex logic one needs to handle in an e-commerce website. In the discussion that follows, we have tried to ensure that all of the essential features of the purchasing process are illustrated in our prototype, while keeping the logic of the code involved easy enough to follow.

Let's begin with a high-level view. Consider first the display in **FIGURE 10.28**, which shows the "Shopping Cart" web page that appears when a user clicks on the **Buy this item** link for the product in the first row of the display in Figure 10.26. The assumption here is that the customer has logged in and this is the first product that is going to be added to the shopping cart. A customer who clicks on one of these buttons without having logged in will simply be transferred to the login page, since logging in is required before purchasing can proceed.

Assume that the customer enters the quantity 6 into the textbox provided under the **Quantity** column header, and clicks on the **Add to cart** link. The customer is then presented with an updated page like the one shown in **FIGURE 10.29**, containing the total owing for the quantity currently in the shopping cart. Suppose the customer now clicks on **Continue shopping**,

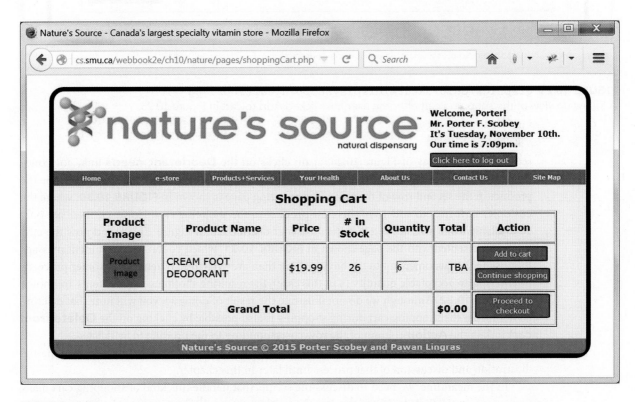

FIGURE 10.28 `graphics/ch10/nature/displayShoppingCartPhp1.jpg`
A view of the shopping cart showing that the user is about to add six of the item shown to the cart.

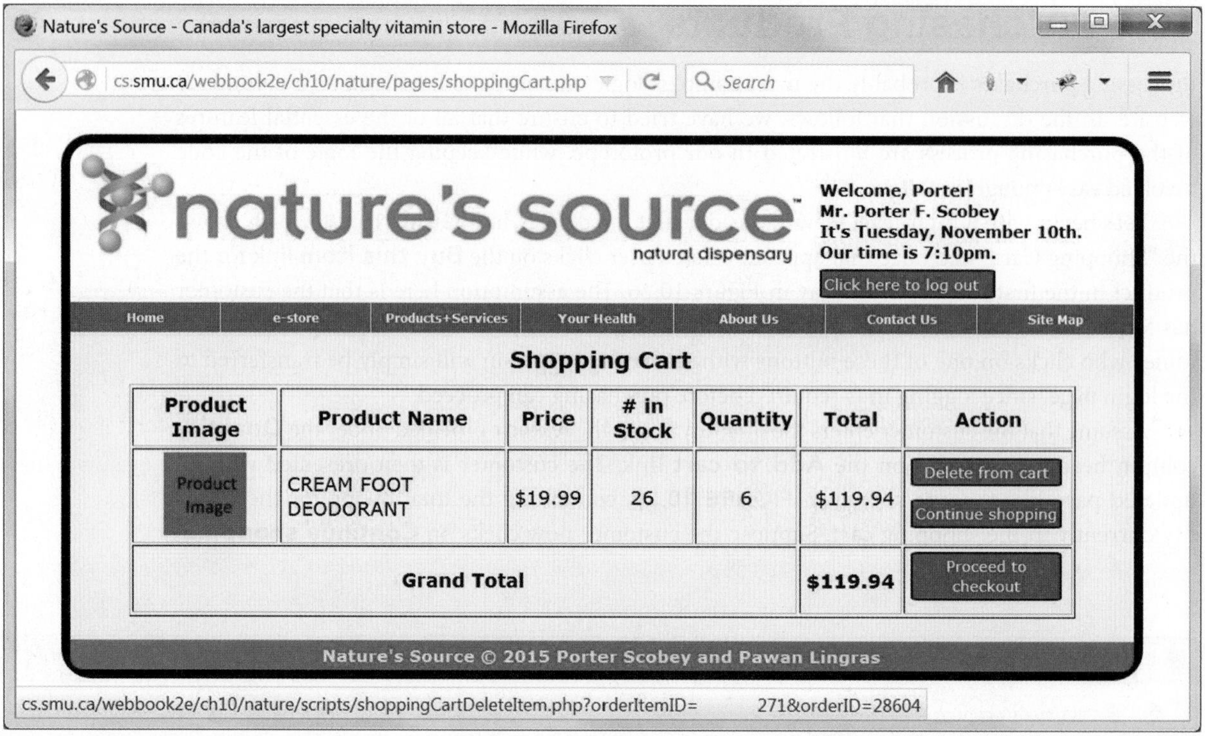

FIGURE 10.29 `graphics/ch10/nature/displayShoppingCartPhp2.jpg`
A follow-up view of the shopping cart after the user has clicked Add to cart in Figure 10.28.

returns to the display of Figure 10.24, again clicks on the **Deodorant needs** link, goes once more to the page seen in Figure 10.26 and this time clicks on the **Buy this item** link for the product in the second row of the table. The resulting page is shown in **FIGURE 10.30**, where the customer now tries to add 12 of this new product to the shopping cart. However, there are only 10 available from inventory (a fact the customer overlooked in Figure 10.30), and now the customer is presented with the page shown in **FIGURE 10.31**, which contains a prominent message reminding the customer not to try buying more than are available. When the customer proceeds by entering an acceptable quantity (4 in this case), the resulting shopping cart contents are shown in **FIGURE 10.32**. Although we do not illustrate the result of doing so, you will note that deleting an item from the shopping cart during shopping is also possible by clicking on the **Delete from cart** link in the **Action** column of the row corresponding to the product to be deleted.

At this point the user can click on the **Proceed to checkout** link, but we postpone the illustration and discussion of that process until later in this chapter.

In the meantime, we need to discuss the scripts that handle this kind of shopping cart management: first, the high-level `pages/shoppingCart.php`, which sets up our shopping cart page infrastructure, and the included `scripts/shoppingCartProcess.php`. This second script is

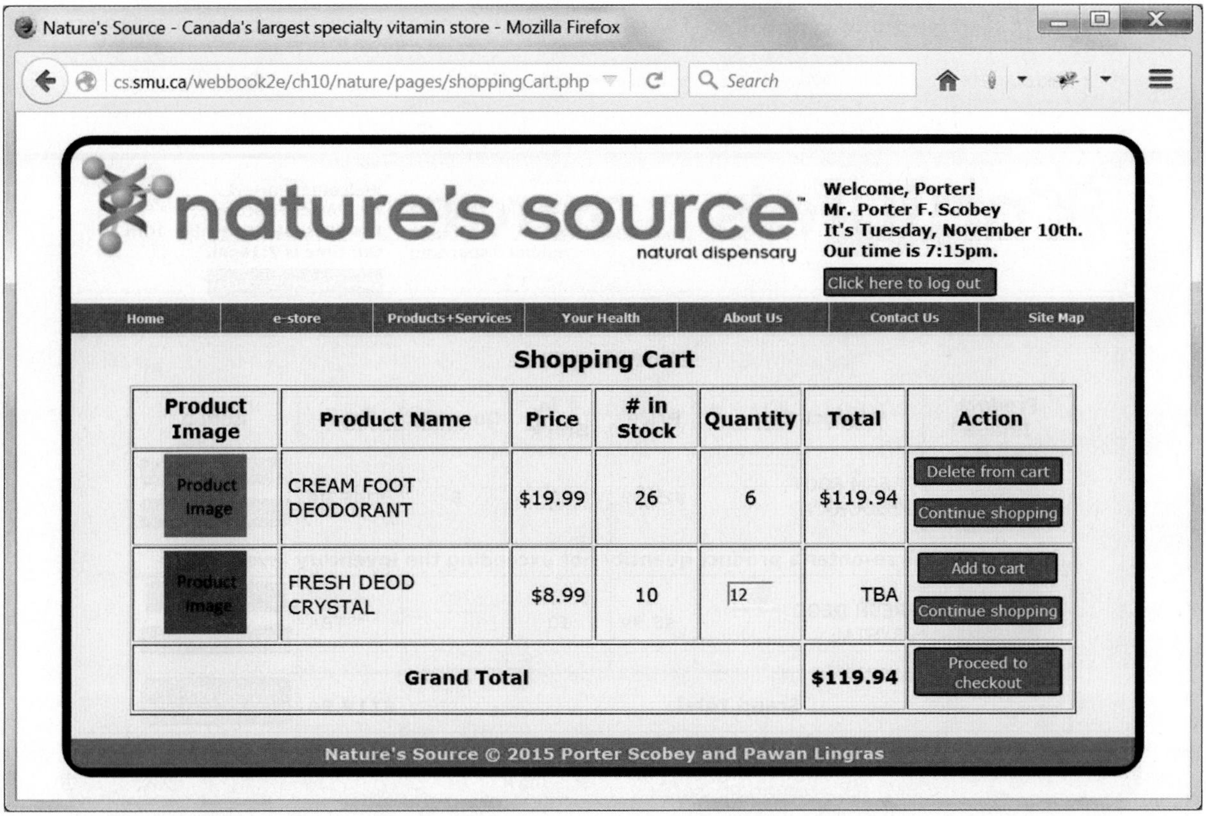

FIGURE 10.30 `graphics/ch10/nature/displayShoppingCartPhp3.jpg`
A view of the shopping cart after the user has clicked Continue shopping in Figure 10.29, has then returned to the Deodorant needs category and is about to try adding 12 of another item to the cart when there are only 10 in stock.

where all the details of managing the shopping cart are handled, and where we will focus our attention. The script is longer and more involved than ones we have seen before, and hence is distributed across multiple figures within the following discussion (see Figures 10.34–10.38).

10.6.1 The `pages/shoppingCart.php` Script

Recall that the `pages/catalog.php` and the `pages/category.php` scripts just set up the "page infrastructure" for our complete catalog list display and our individual category of products display (respectively), while in each case a second (included) script did all the work of preparing the page content. Like those pages, the `pages/shoppingCart.php` script, shown in **FIGURE 10.33**, sets up the infrastructure for our shopping cart page, but here there is a little more going on because now it matters whether the user is logged in or not when the script is invoked.

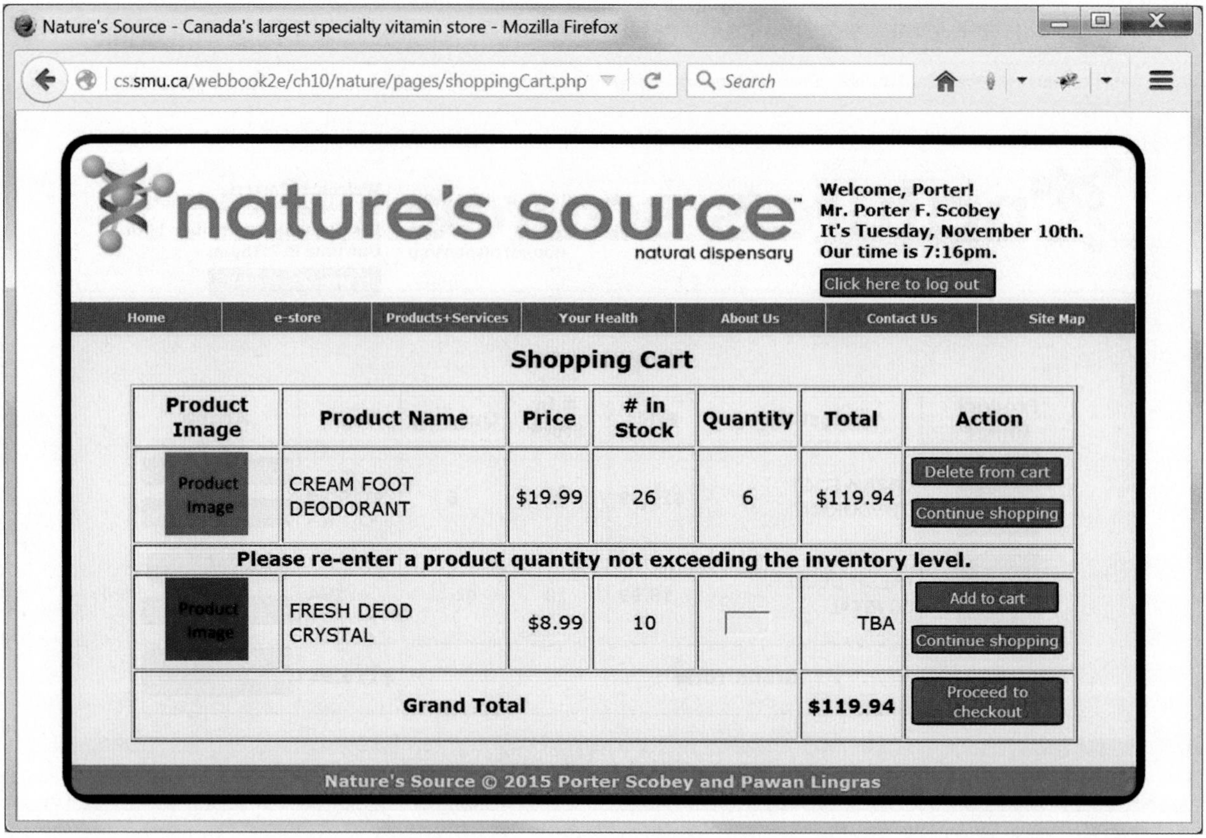

FIGURE 10.31 `graphics/ch10/nature/displayShoppingCartPhp4.jpg`
A view of the shopping cart after the quantity of a particular item that the user has tried to add to the cart exceeded the quantity available from inventory.

The script begins in line 7 of Figure 10.33 with the usual call to `session_start()` and then uses local variables to capture two values from the superglobals `$_SESSION` and `$_GET`. These variables (`$customerID` and `$productID`) will tell us whether the customer is logged in (`$customerID` has a value), and whether we are dealing with an actual product or just in "shopping cart view mode" (`$productID` has the value `'view'`).

If the user is not logged in, the `pages/shoppingCart.php` script can only be invoked in two ways:

1. The user might simply click on the **View Shopping Cart** dropdown link under **e-store**. In this case, the test in line 10 succeeds because the user is not logged in, and the user is redirected to the login page, which contains the reminder about logging in before shopping. Note that `$_SESSION['purchasePending']` is also set to `$productID`, which in this case will be `'view'`, but this value in not actually used in this scenario.

FIGURE 10.32 `graphics/ch10/nature/displayShoppingCartPhp5.jpg`
A view of the shopping cart, which now contains two items and is ready for the user to click on Proceed to checkout.

2. The user may be browsing the product catalog, suddenly see an item of interest, and click on the **Buy this item** link at the end of the table row containing that item. In this case, once again, the test in line 10 succeeds (for the same reason), but this time `$_SESSION ['purchasePending']` is set to an actual product code before the user is redirected to the login page, and after logging in the user is (very conveniently, from the point of view of the business) immediately presented with a shopping cart showing the item of interest just waiting to be purchased. In other words, the user does not have to retrace the steps that led to that product in the first place.

On the other hand, if the user *is* logged in, then the test in line 10 of the script fails, there is no immediate redirection, and we proceed with the rest of the page which, among other things, includes and executes the `scripts/shoppingCartProcess.php` script (line 29). We begin a detailed discussion of this included script in the next section. In the meantime, let's just note that

```php
1   <?php
2   /*shoppingCart.php
3   This page provides the "high-level" shopping cart view, if in
4   fact the visitor has a shopping cart. Otherwise the visitor is
5   redirected to the login page.
6   */
7   session_start();
8   $customerID = isset($_SESSION['customer_id']) ? $_SESSION['customer_id'] : "";
9   $productID = $_GET['productID'];
10  if ($customerID == "")
11  {
12      $_SESSION['purchasePending'] = $productID;
13      header("Location: loginForm.php");
14  }
15  include("../common/document_head.html");
16  ?>
17    <body>
18      <header>
19        <?php
20        include("../common/banner.php");
21        include("../common/menus.html");
22        include("../scripts/connectToDatabase.php");
23        ?>
24      </header>
25      <main>
26        <article class="ShoppingCart">
27          <h4 class="ShoppingCartHeader">Shopping Cart</h4>
28          <?php
29          include("../scripts/shoppingCartProcess.php");
30          ?>
31        </article>
32      </main>
33      <footer>
34        <?php
35        include("../common/footer_content.html");
36        ?>
37      </footer>
38    </body>
39  </html>
```

FIGURE 10.33 `ch10/nature/pages/shoppingCart.php`

The shopping cart page that handles, at a high level, the shopping activity of a user when that user is browsing and buying in our e-store.

a logged-in user can come to the `pages/shoppingCart.php` script in four different ways (the details of which are discussed as we go):

1. As was the case with someone not logged in, the user might simply click on the **View Shopping Cart** dropdown link under **e-store**. In this case, the user's shopping cart, which may or may not have something in it, is displayed.
2. The user may have clicked on a **Buy this item** link for a product, and that request for a purchase of the given product must now be processed.
3. The user may have filled in the number required of a given item and clicked on the corresponding **Add to cart** link. This part of the process is handled by the `scripts/shoppingCartAddItem.php` script shown in Figure 10.39, which causes a redisplay of the shopping cart after the item has been added to it (as you will see later in line 64 of Figure 10.39).
4. The user may have decided to delete a product from the shopping cart and clicked on the corresponding **Delete from cart** link. This part of the process is handled by the `scripts/shoppingCartDeleteItem.php` script shown in Figure 10.40, and it too causes a redisplay of the shopping cart after the item has been deleted from it (as you will see later in line 27 of Figure 10.40).

10.6.2 A High-Level View of the `scripts/ shoppingCartProcess.php` Script

FIGURE 10.34 shows the main part of the script that handles our shopping cart. Once again, since there is no explicit `main()` function in a PHP script, we refer to that part of the total script excluding any function definitions as the "main" part of the script. Each of the functions called by this part of the script, and which we simply mention in passing in this section, is defined later in the script and will be discussed in more detail in the following sections.

```php
1   <?php
2   /*shoppingCartProcess.php
3   Handles interaction between the user and the database
4   for Shopping Cart transactions.
5   Included by pages/shoppingCart.php.
6   Calls these functions (defined below):
7   getExistingOrder()
8   createOrder()
9   displayHeader()
10  displayExistingItemColumns()
11  displayNewItemColumns()
12  displayFooter()
13  */
```

FIGURE 10.34 `ch10/nature/scripts/shoppingCartProcess.php` **(Part 1 of 5)**
The first part of the script that handles the processing of our shopping cart: contains the main (high-level) script.

```
14
15   //========== main script begins here
16   $retrying = isset($_GET['retrying']) ? true : false;
17   $items = getExistingOrder($db, $customerID);
18   $numRecords = mysqli_num_rows($items);
19
20   if ($numRecords == 0 && $productID == 'view')
21   {
22       echo
23       "<p class='Notification'>Your shopping cart is empty.</p>
24       <p class='Notification'>To continue shopping, please
25       <a class='NoDecoration' href='pages/catalog.php'>click here</a>.</p>";
26   }
27   else
28   {
29       displayHeader();
30       $grandTotal = 0;
31       if ($numRecords == 0) //Shopping cart is empty
32       {
33           createOrder($db, $customerID);
34       }
35       else //Shopping cart contains one or more items to display
36       {
37           for ($i=1; $i<=$numRecords; $i++)
38           {
39               $grandTotal += displayExistingItemColumns($db, $items);
40           }
41       }
42
43       if ($productID != 'view') //Display entry row for new item
44       {
45           if ($retrying)
46           {
47               echo
48               "<tr>
49                 <td class='Notification' colspan='7'>Please re-enter a
50                   product quantity not exceeding the inventory level.
51                 </td>
52               </tr>";
53           }
54           displayNewItemColumns($db, $productID);
55       }
56       displayFooter($grandTotal);
57   }
58   mysqli_close($db);
59   //========== main script ends here
```

FIGURE 10.34 `ch10/nature/scripts/shoppingCartProcess.php` (Part 1 of 5) (*continued*)

The script begins in line 16 by recording in a local variable whether the user is "retrying", which will only be the case if the user has tried to buy more of a product than is available. If true, this value is used later in the script to output an appropriate message (lines 45–53).

The user has to be logged in to have reached this point in the script, so $customerID has a value (from line 8 of Figure 10.33), and we can therefore call the getExistingOrder() function and pass this value to it (line 17). This function retrieves all the items in the order that is currently "in progress" (those for which order_status_code='IP') for the customer, and we again store the number of records retrieved by this query in the variable $numRecords.

Note that when we get to this script, the value of $productID is the product code of an actual product if the user is adding a product to, or deleting a product from, the shopping cart, and otherwise $productID has the value 'view', which means that the user will only be viewing the cart's current contents.

If $numRecords is 0 and the customer is only trying to view the cart (line 20), then there is really nothing to display. Therefore, a message to that effect is displayed for the customer, along with a link to pages/estore.php, the start page for our e-store, which returns the customer to "browsing mode" (lines 22–25).

On the other hand, if $numRecords is not zero, or if the customer is adding or deleting an item, or both, we have more work to do. We begin by displaying the header for a table of product information with a call to the function displayHeader() (line 29).

The running total of all the items in the cart will be kept in a variable called $grandTotal, which is then initialized to zero (line 30).

If $numRecords is 0, we need to create a new order for the customer, which we do with a call to the createOrder() function (line 33). Otherwise, we display all the items that are currently in the cart by calling the displayExistingItemColumns() function once for each item within a for-loop (lines 37–40). Note that this function not only displays one item per call, but also returns the total cost of the item, which is added to $grandTotal.

Once all the existing items have been displayed, we check to see if $productID has the value 'view'. If it does not, we have a new item to display. If the variable $retrying is true, that means the previous attempt at adding the item to the cart has failed (because the customer tried to add more of a product to the shopping cart than the company has in stock), so we display an appropriate message. Whether or not this message is displayed, we then display a row of the table for this item using the function displayNewItemColumns() (line 54). Finally, we display the $grandTotal as well as the rest of the footer of the table using the function displayFooter(), to which $grandTotal is passed (line 56).

Now that we have looked at the global logic of the main part of processPurchase.php, let's move on to look at some of the lower-level details by studying the various helper functions mentioned above, beginning with those that work with the database tables. And finally, in any case, we close our database (line 58).

10.6.3 Reviewing the Relevant Tables in Our Nature's Source Database Structure

Before we look at performing any database queries for product purchases by a PHP script, let us review the two relevant tables in our database scheme. The first of the two tables that are used to manage our shopping cart is the `Orders` table, which contains the following attributes:

- ▶ `order_id`
- ▶ `customer_id`
- ▶ `order_status_code`
- ▶ `date_order_placed`
- ▶ `order_details`

The main purpose of the `Orders` table is to keep track of information that is common to all the items that are being purchased by a customer at any given time. We assume that there is at most one order in progress for a customer at any given time. If there is such an order in progress, the `order_status_code` will be `IP`. The list of items in the order is maintained in the second table of interest, `Order_Items`, which contains the following attributes:

- ▶ `order_item_id`
- ▶ `order_item_status_code`
- ▶ `order_id`
- ▶ `product_id`
- ▶ `order_item_quantity`
- ▶ `order_item_price`
- ▶ `other_order_item_details`

10.6.4 Getting the Product Details of an Existing Order with `getExistingOrder()`

The function `getExistingOrder()` is called in line 17 of Figure 10.34 and is shown in lines 67–83 of **FIGURE 10.35**. It takes `$customerID` as a parameter and retrieves all the items for that customer that are "in progress" (i.e., for which the value of `order_status_code` in the Orders table of our database is `'IP'`). The function simply constructs an appropriate query, executes the query, and returns the retrieved results to the main script as the return-value of the function.

The essence of the function lies in the query construction. This particular query is a little more complex than previous ones we have seen, as it involves "joining" the two tables `Orders` and `Order_Items`. The query actually retrieves the first three attributes from the `Orders` table (lines 71–73), and (using the wildcard character * in line 74) all the attributes from the `Orders_ Items` table. However, these attributes are only retrieved from those records satisfying the following criteria, as determined by the `WHERE` clause in lines 77–80 of Figure 10.35:

```
Orders.order_id=Order_Items.order_id and
Orders.order_status_code='IP' and
Orders.customer_id=$customer_id
```

```
62    /*getExistingOrder()
63    Retrieves from the database the items in an existing order,
64    that is, items currently in the shopping cart that have not
65    been purchased by going through checkout.
66    */
67    function getExistingOrder($db, $customerID)
68    {
69        $query =
70            "SELECT
71                Orders.order_id,
72                Orders.customer_id,
73                Orders.order_status_code,
74                Order_Items.*
75            FROM
76                Order_Items, Orders
77            WHERE
78                Orders.order_id = Order_Items.order_id and
79                Orders.order_status_code = 'IP' and
80                Orders.customer_id = $customerID";
81        $items = mysqli_query($db, $query);
82        return $items;
83    }
84
85    /*createOrder()
86    Creates a new order, to which items may be added for purchase.
87    */
88    function createOrder($db, $customerID)
89    {
90        $query = "INSERT INTO Orders
91        (
92            customer_id,
93            order_status_code,
94            date_order_placed,
95            order_details
96        )
97        VALUES
98        (
99            '$customerID',
100            'IP',
101            CURDATE(),
102            NULL
103        )";
104        $success = mysqli_query($db, $query);
105    }
```

FIGURE 10.35 `ch10/nature/scripts/shoppingCartProcess.php` **(Part 2 of 5)**
The second part of the script that handles the processing of our shopping cart: contains one function that will retrieve information for any existing order-in-progress, and another function for creating a new order.

10.6.5 Creating a New Order with `createOrder()`

The second database-related function that may be called from the main part of the script creates a new order if the customer does not have an existing order "in progress". This is the `createOrder()` function, called in line 33 of Figure 10.34 and shown in lines 88–105 of Figure 10.35. This function takes in `$customerID` as a parameter and then inserts a new record into the `Orders` table by creating a query that executes an appropriate `INSERT` command.

Note that we do not specify the value for the `order_id` attribute, because it is generated automatically by MySQL. The value of `customer_id` is set to the one that was passed to the function. The `order_status_code` is set to `'IP'` to indicate that this is an in-progress order item. A built-in PHP function called `CURDATE()` is used to specify the value of the attribute `date_order_placed`. The `order_details` attribute is left `NULL`.

10.6.6 Displaying the Header of the Shopping Cart Table with `displayHeader()`

Lines 110–126 of **FIGURE 10.36** show the function `displayHeader()` which is called in line 29 of Figure 10.34 to display the header of the shopping cart table. The function begins by opening a form, identified as `orderForm`, that can be used to add an item to the shopping cart (lines 113–115). The form is validated (line 114) by the JavaScript function `shoppingCartAddItemForm-Validate()` found in a `scripts` file of the same name. All that needs to be validated in this case is the customer's entry for the quantity of product desired. Note that this validation by JavaScript can only determine whether the user has entered a positive integer quantity. JavaScript cannot determine whether the quantity entered exceeds the current inventory level. The quantity must be sent to the server for that determination to be made.

```
107   /*displayHeader()
108   Displays headers for the seven columns of the shopping cart table.
109   */
110   function displayHeader()
111   {
112      echo
113      "<form id='orderForm'
114            onsubmit='return shoppingCartAddItemFormValidate();'
115            action='scripts/shoppingCartAddItem.php'>
```

FIGURE 10.36 `ch10/nature/scripts/shoppingCartProcess.php` **(Part 3 of 5)**
The third part of the script that handles the processing of our shopping cart: contains one function that will display the header of our shopping cart page, and another that will display the first four columns of a product row in the cart. These four columns are always the same, unlike the last three columns.

```
116          <table border='1px'>
117           <tr>
118             <th>Product Image</th>
119             <th>Product Name</th>
120             <th>Price</th>
121             <th># in Stock</th>
122             <th>Quantity</th>
123             <th>Total</th>
124             <th>Action</th>
125           </tr>";
126   }
127
128   /*displayFirstFourColumns()
129   Displays the first four columns of a row of the shopping cart
130   table. The contents of the last three columns of a row of the
131   table will be different, depending on whether the row contains
132   information for an item that's already in the shopping cart,
133   or an item that has been chosen for adding to the cart but is
134   not yet in it.
135   */
136   function displayFirstFourColumns($db, $productID)
137   {
138       $query =
139         "SELECT *
140         FROM Products
141         WHERE product_id='$productID'";
142       $product = mysqli_query($db, $query);
143       $row = mysqli_fetch_array($product, MYSQLI_ASSOC);
144       $productPrice = sprintf("$%1.2f", $row['product_price']);
145       echo
146       "<tr>
147         <td>
148           <img height='70' width='70'
149               src='$row[product_image_url]' alt='Product Image'>
150         </td><td style='text-align: left;'>
151           $row[product_name]
152         </td><td style='text-align: right;'>
153           $productPrice
154         </td><td>
155           $row[product_inventory]
156         </td>";
157   }
```

FIGURE 10.36 ch10/nature/scripts/shoppingCartProcess.php **(Part 3 of 5)** (*continued*)

The file `scripts/shoppingCartAddItem.php` (shown in Figure 10.39) contains the PHP script that will be called for processing when this form submits its data (line 115). The rest of the function `displayHeader()` simply displays the header row of the table that will display the shopping cart contents. The closing `</table>` and `</form>` tags are provided by the `display-Footer()` function, which we discuss a bit later.

10.6.7 Displaying the Product Information in the Shopping Cart with `displayFirstFourColumns()`, `displayExistingItemColumns()`, and `displayNewItemColumns()`

Now we come to the table display of the product information. There will be one row of the table for each product currently in the shopping cart. Also, if a new item is being added, there will be a row for that product's information as well, and this row will have a textbox form field into which the customer can enter the desired quantity of this product.

As you read the rest of the discussion in this section, you will find it helpful to refer back to the display in Figure 10.30. From that figure you can see that the first four columns for items already in the shopping cart, as well as the first four columns for any new item, are always the same, so we use a separate function to handle these columns in both cases. That function, shown in lines 136–157 of Figure 10.36, is called `displayFirstFourColumns()`, and it takes in `$productID` as its second parameter. The function first retrieves the record for the given product from the `Products` table of the database (lines 138–142), which is then converted to an associative array and stored in `$row` (line 143). Finally, the function outputs the required row of information, with its four columns containing the appropriate table markup and cell content:

▶ The first column contains an `img` element whose `src` attribute value is given by the value obtained from the associative array `$row` containing the retrieved record by using the key `product_image_url`.

▶ The next three columns simply display the values of the attributes `product_name`, `product_price`, and `product_inventory`, again obtained from the `$row` array with the corresponding keys.

Now for the `displayExistingItemColumns()` function, shown in **FIGURE 10.37**. The first three statements of this function (lines 168–170), set up and call the `displayFirstFour-Columns()` function that we have just discussed. This involves retrieving a row of product information from `$items`, which has been passed in as a parameter, putting that information into the associative array `$row`, extracting the product code for that product into `$productID`, and passing this product code on to the `displayFirstFourColumns()` function. Once we have displayed the first four columns for the product, the remaining three columns for an existing item are displayed by the rest of the function. But first, lines 172–173 compute the total price of the

```
159    /*displayExistingItemColumns()
160    Displays the last three columns of information for an item that
161    is alreay in the shopping cart. This information includes the
162    quantity ordered, the total price, and buttons to allow the
163    deletion of the item or continuing to shop by transferring
164    back to the product catalog.
165    */
166    function displayExistingItemColumns($db, $items)
167    {
168        $row = mysqli_fetch_array($items, MYSQLI_ASSOC);
169        $productID = $row['product_id'];
170        displayFirstFourColumns($db, $productID);
171
172        $total = $row['order_item_quantity'] * $row['order_item_price'];
173        $totalAsString = sprintf("$%1.2f", $total);
174        echo
175          "<td>
176            $row[order_item_quantity]
177          </td><td style='text-align: right;'>
178            $totalAsString
179          </td><td>
180            <p><a class='Button'
181                href='scripts/shoppingCartDeleteItem.php?orderItemID=
182                $row[order_item_id]&orderID=$row[order_id]'>
183                Delete from cart</a></p>
184            <p><a class='Button' href='pages/catalog.php'>
185                Continue shopping</a></p>
186          </td>
187        </tr>";
188        return $total;
189    }
```

FIGURE 10.37 `ch10/nature/scripts/shoppingCartProcess.php` **(Part 4 of 5)**
The fourth part of the script that handles the processing of our shopping cart: contains a function that will display the last three columns of information for an item that has already been added to the shopping cart.

current product and then convert it to string form, with two places after the decimal. Then the echo statement in lines 174–187 displays those last three columns (table cells) as follows:

▶ The fifth column (lines 175–177) displays the quantity of product that was placed in the shopping cart, as retrieved from the associative array $row. (The sharp-eyed reader will note here one of the few instances in which we have used a style attribute to tweak the display, not something that should be done often, as you know.)

▶ The sixth column (lines 177–179) displays the total cost for the ordered item in the current row, as computed in lines 172–173.

▶ The seventh and final column contains two "button links". The first one contains the label **Delete from cart**, and clicking on it activates scripts/`shoppingCartDeleteItem`. `php`, to which it also passes the order and order item information necessary to perform the requested deletion. The second button contains the label **Continue shopping** and clicking on it activates `pages/catalog.php`, taking the user back to the view of all of our departments and the product categories within them.

Once we have displayed all of the items already in the user's shopping cart, if we are also adding an item to the cart, then we have to call the function `displayNewItemColumns()` to display the part of the form that allows a user to add another item to the cart (line 54 of Figure 10.34). This function is shown in lines 200–216 of **FIGURE 10.38**. The function receives `$productID` as a parameter and the first statement again calls the function `displayFirstFourColumns()`

```
191   /*displayNewItemColumns()
192   Displays the last three columns of information for an new item
193   that has been chosen for purchase but has not yet been added to
194   the shopping cart. This information includes a box for entering
195   the quantity desired, TBA in the total price spot, and buttons
196   to allow the addition of the item to the shopping cart or just
197   continuing to shop by transferring back to the product catalog,
198   thereby ignoring the given item.
199   */
200   function displayNewItemColumns($db, $productID)
201   {
202       displayFirstFourColumns($db, $productID);
203       echo
204       "<td>
205         <input type='hidden' id='productID' name='productID' value=$productID>
206         <input type='text' id='quantity' name='quantity' size='3'>
207       </td><td style='text-align: right;'>
208         TBA
209       </td><td>
210         <p class='Centered' style='font-size:100%'>
211             <input class='Button' type='submit' value='Add to cart'></p>
212         <p><a class='Button' href='pages/catalog.php'>
213             Continue shopping</a></p>
214       </td>
215       </tr>";
216   }
217
```

FIGURE 10.38 `ch10/nature/scripts/shoppingCartProcess.php` **(Part 5 of 5)**
The fifth and final part of the script that handles the processing of our shopping cart: contains one function that will display the last three columns of information for an item that has been chosen for purchase but has not yet been added to the shopping cart, and another function for displaying the footer of the shopping cart page.

```
218    /*displayFooter()
219    Displays the final row of the shopping cart table, including
220    the grand total cost of items to be purchased and button to
221    permit proceeding to checkout.
222    */
223    function displayFooter($grandTotal)
224    {
225        $grandTotalAsString = sprintf("$%1.2f", $grandTotal);
226        echo
227        "<tr>
228          <td class='Notification' colspan='5'>
229            Grand Total
230          </td><td class='RightAligned'>
231            <strong>$grandTotalAsString</strong>
232          </td><td>
233            <p><a class='Button' href='pages/checkout.php'>
234               Proceed to checkout</a></p>
235          </td>
236        </tr>
237      </table>
238    </form>";
239    }
240    ?>
```

FIGURE 10.38 `ch10/nature/scripts/shoppingCartProcess.php` **(Part 5 of 5)** (*continued*)

to display the first four columns, as before. The remaining three columns now have the following contents:

▶ The fifth column displays a textbox field named `quantity` for accepting the quantity of the product to be added to the order. In addition, a `hidden` form field named and identified as `productId` is added to the form, and used to store the product code. The input element with this `hidden` attribute does not show up on the web page, but serves as a convenient way of passing the product code along to the PHP script `shoppingCartAddItem.php`, where it is needed.

▶ The sixth column displays the string TBA, since when this row is displayed we do not yet know the quantity of the item the user wants, so we cannot display the total cost for that item.

▶ The seventh and final column again contains two button links. Remember that the table containing our shopping cart display is also the content of a form, and if the display contains a last row for adding a new item to the cart, we must also have a submit button to send the form data to the server. The first button in the last column, which contains the label **Add to cart**, is actually the submit button for this form. Thus clicking on it submits the form data, including the "hidden" product code that we mentioned above, to the

PHP script `shoppingCartAddItem.php`. The second button contains the label **Continue shopping**, and clicking on it activates the script `pages/category.php`, taking the user back to the view of all of our departments and the product categories within them. This is the same button that also appears at the end of each row corresponding to an item already in the cart.

So, the PHP script `shoppingCartProcess.php` that we have discussed so far displays the contents of the cart and creates a form for possibly adding an item. The resulting web page needs two database manipulation scripts, one called `shoppingCartAddItem.php` and the other called `shoppingCartDeleteItem.php`. We will discuss these two scripts shortly, but first we look briefly at the script that displays the shopping cart web page footer, and thus completes the display of the shopping cart page.

10.6.8 Displaying the Footer of the Shopping Cart Table with `displayFooter()`

The function `displayFooter()` is called in line 56 of Figure 10.34 and is shown in lines 223–239 of Figure 10.38. It takes in `$grandTotal` as a parameter and displays this value in the last row of the table at the bottom of the **Total** column. This function also places a **Proceed to checkout** button in the **Action** column of this final row of the table. (See, once again, Figure 10.32.)

Note that the script in the value of the `href` attribute of the **Proceed to checkout** button link is, of course, `pages/checkout.php`.

Finally, the function then completes the display of the shopping cart information by outputting the closing `</table>` and `</form>` tags.

10.6.9 Adding an Item to the Shopping Cart with `shoppingCartAddItem.php`

The complete code for the `scripts/shoppingCartAddItem.php` script is shown in **FIGURE 10.39**. The main script begins once again by calling the `session_start()` function, and then includes the script `connectToDatabase.php` to connect to our MySQL database. In lines 9 and 10 we do some by-now-typical "housekeeping". That is, we get the `customer_id` value from the `$_SESSION` array, as well as the product code from the `$_GET` array. It's worth pointing out here that the product code is in the `$_GET` array because it's coming from the form we started to set up back in line 113 of Figure 10.36, and we did not specify a submission method for that form, which makes GET the default data transmission method.

If the customer is adding an item to the shopping cart, that customer will already have an order "in progress", so in lines 13–24 of Figure 10.39 we set up and execute a query to retrieve this order and store its information as an associative array in the variable `$row`, from which we then extract the order id (line 24). This will be the order to which we add the item.

```php
1    <?php
2    /*shoppingCartAddItem.php
3    Adds an item to the user's shopping cart, and redisplays the cart.
4    */
5    session_start();
6    include("connectToDatabase.php");
7
8    //========== main script begins here
9    $customerID = $_SESSION['customer_id'];
10   $productID = $_GET['productID'];
11
12   //Get the order ID for the current order in progress
13   $query =
14      "SELECT
15         Orders.order_id,
16         Orders.order_status_code,
17         Orders.customer_id
18      FROM Orders
19      WHERE
20         Orders.order_status_code = 'IP' and
21         Orders.customer_id = $customerID";
22   $order = mysqli_query($db, $query);
23   $row = mysqli_fetch_array($order, MYSQLI_ASSOC);
24   $orderID = $row['order_id'];
25
26   //Get the quantity in inventory of the requested product
27   $query =
28      "SELECT *
29      FROM Products
30      WHERE product_id = '$productID'";
31   $product = mysqli_query($db, $query);
32   $row = mysqli_fetch_array($product, MYSQLI_ASSOC);
33   $productInventory = $row['product_inventory'];
34
35   $quantityRequested = $_GET['quantity'];
36   if ($quantityRequested > $productInventory)
37   {
38      $gotoRetry = "../pages/shoppingCart.php?
39                    productID=$productID&retrying=true";
40      header("Location: $gotoRetry");
41   }
```

FIGURE 10.39 `ch10/nature/scripts/shoppingCartAddItem.php`.
The script that adds a new item to the shopping cart and redisplays the cart.

```
42    else
43    {
44        $productPrice = $row['product_price'];
45        $query = "INSERT INTO Order_Items
46        (
47            order_item_status_code,
48            order_id,
49            product_id,
50            order_item_quantity,
51            order_item_price,
52            other_order_item_details
53        )
54        VALUES
55        (
56            'IP',
57            '$orderID',
58            '$productID',
59            '$quantityRequested',
60            '$productPrice',
61            NULL
62        )";
63        $success = mysqli_query($db, $query);
64        header("Location: ../pages/shoppingCart.php?productID=view");
65    }
66    //========== main script ends here
67    ?>
```

FIGURE 10.39 `ch10/nature/scripts/shoppingCartAddItem.php`. (*continued*)

Next we set up and execute a similar query (lines 27–33) to get the quantity in inventory of the product in question. If this is less than the quantity the customer is requesting (line 35), we cannot proceed any further, so in lines 36–41 of Figure 10.39 we redirect the customer back to the shopping cart page, with the same product code and the parameter `retrying` with a value of `true` added to the URL to indicate to the receiving script that this is a repeated attempt. The script will take this as an indication to display the reminder message to the user that we have seen earlier about not exceeding the inventory level. (See lines 45–53 of Figure 10.34.)

Alternatively, if the quantity of the item requested by the user is less than or equal to the amount in inventory, we continue with the code given in the `else` block in lines 43–65 of Figure 10.39, in which we (finally) add the item to the `Order_Items` table of our database. We need the price of the product, which we can extract from the most recent `$row` array and we already know the rest of the values required to add this record to the `Order_Items` table. We do not specify any value for the `order_item_id`, which will be automatically determined by MySQL. The `order_item_status` code is set to `'IP'`, and the values of the rest of the attributes are obtained from the available variables, except for `other_order_item_details`, which is set to NULL.

Once the query is executed, the customer is redirected, in line 64, back to `shoppingCart.php`, but with the value of the parameter `productID` set to `view`. This means the customer will only see the items currently in the cart, which will include the recently added item.

Once again we should note that in line 63 we have captured the return value of this particular call to `mysqli_query()` in a variable called `$success`, and observant readers will note that we have once more ignored this value. This means we are assuming the success of the query, but if we were including error-checking code at this point, we could test this value to see if the operation had failed, and issue an appropriate report if something had gone wrong.

10.6.10 Deleting an Item from the Shopping Cart with `shoppingCartDeleteItem.php`

The script `shoppingCartDeleteItem.php` for deleting an existing item from the shopping cart is shown in **FIGURE 10.40**. This script is invoked when the user is viewing the shopping cart containing one or more items and clicks on the **Delete from cart** link, which also provides this

```php
<?php
/*shoppingCartDeleteItem.php
Deletes an item from the user's shopping cart, and
redisplays the cart.
*/
session_start();
include("connectToDatabase.php");

$orderItemID = $_GET['orderItemID'];
$orderID = $_GET['orderID'];
$query =
    "DELETE FROM Order_Items
    WHERE order_item_id='$orderItemID'";
$success = mysqli_query($db, $query);
$query =
    "SELECT COUNT(*) AS numItemsStillInOrder
    FROM Order_Items
    WHERE order_id='$orderID'";
$return_value = mysqli_query($db, $query);
$row = mysqli_fetch_array($return_value, MYSQL_ASSOC);
if ($row[numItemsStillInOrder] == 0)
{
    $query = "DELETE FROM Orders
                WHERE order_id='$orderID'";
    $success = mysqli_query($db, $query);
}
header("Location: ../pages/shoppingCart.php?productID=view");
?>
```

FIGURE 10.40 `ch10/nature/scripts/shoppingCartDeleteItem.php`
The script that deletes an item from the shopping cart and redisplays the cart.

script with the product code of the product to be deleted (as a parameter at the end of the URL, in the usual way). After executing `session_start()` and connecting to the database as usual, the script constructs and executes the necessary query (lines 11–14) for deleting the given product from the `Order_Items` table. Then, in lines 15–26 a second query is constructed and executed to determine if deleting the given item has emptied the cart, and, if so, the order itself is also deleted. Finally, the customer is redirected (line 27) to the shopping cart page to view the revised status of the cart, thus confirming the deletion.

Note that line 16 of Figure 10.40 illustrates something new. It shows how we can create, in the associative array we will get from our query, a key/value pair in which `numItemsStillInOrder` is the key and the value is that obtained by a call to the `MySQL COUNT()` function. This value is retrieved from the array and used in line 21.

10.7 Checkout

We have now come to the final stage of our e-commerce website's shopping cart and product-purchasing functionality: letting the customer "check out", and, in the process, "purchase" the items they have added to their shopping cart. Actually, we do not provide any ability to accept a real payment. Such a payment mechanism would require a secure communication with a payment gateway site, which is beyond the scope of this text. Our checkout script will therefore perform only the following actions:

▶ Display a receipt and thank the customer for shopping with us.
▶ Adjust the proper entries in the `Orders` and `Order_Items` tables to indicate payment.
▶ Reduce inventory as appropriate.

So, let's look at the checkout programming that *is* implemented for our prototype website, short of actual payment for products purchased.

10.7.1 Displaying a Customer Receipt and Updating Our Database

If you look back at Figure 10.32, you will see a shopping cart containing two products that is ready for checking out. If the user now clicks on **Proceed to checkout** in that view, the "receipt page" shown in **FIGURE 10.41** will be displayed, confirming the sale and thanking the customer.

Note that there is no intermediate stage in which the customer provides credit card information for the payment and chooses a shipping method, for example. The `pages/checkout.php` script, which is activated here, simply displays a receipt and a thank-you message.

FIGURE 10.42 shows the web page we would now see if we proceeded as though we wished to make another purchase of the same or similar products by displaying the product category containing the just-purchased product. The main point here is that we can now verify that the checkout process has indeed made the appropriate reduction of the inventory levels for the purchased products by comparing the inventory levels shown for these products in Figures 10.42 and 10.26, with the quantity of products purchased as shown in Figure 10.32.

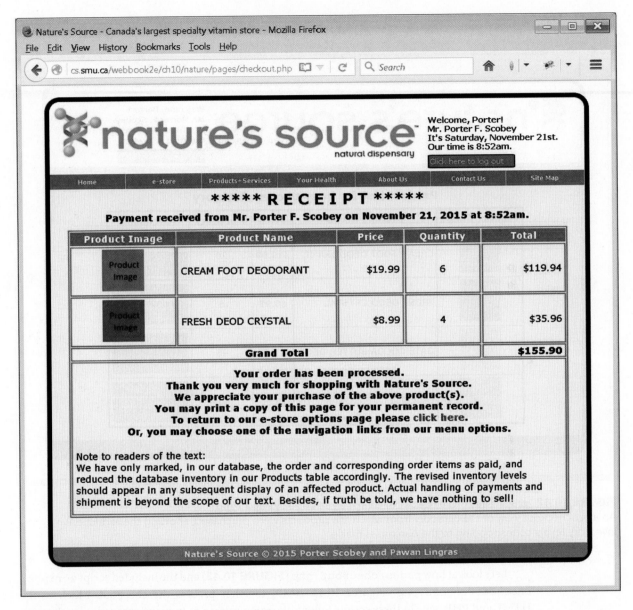

FIGURE 10.41 `graphics/ch10/nature/displayCheckoutPhp.jpg`
A view of the receipt printed after the user has clicked on **Proceed to checkout** in Figure 10.32. Note that since we are not actually selling anything, we do not include an additional form for the collection of payment and shipping information.

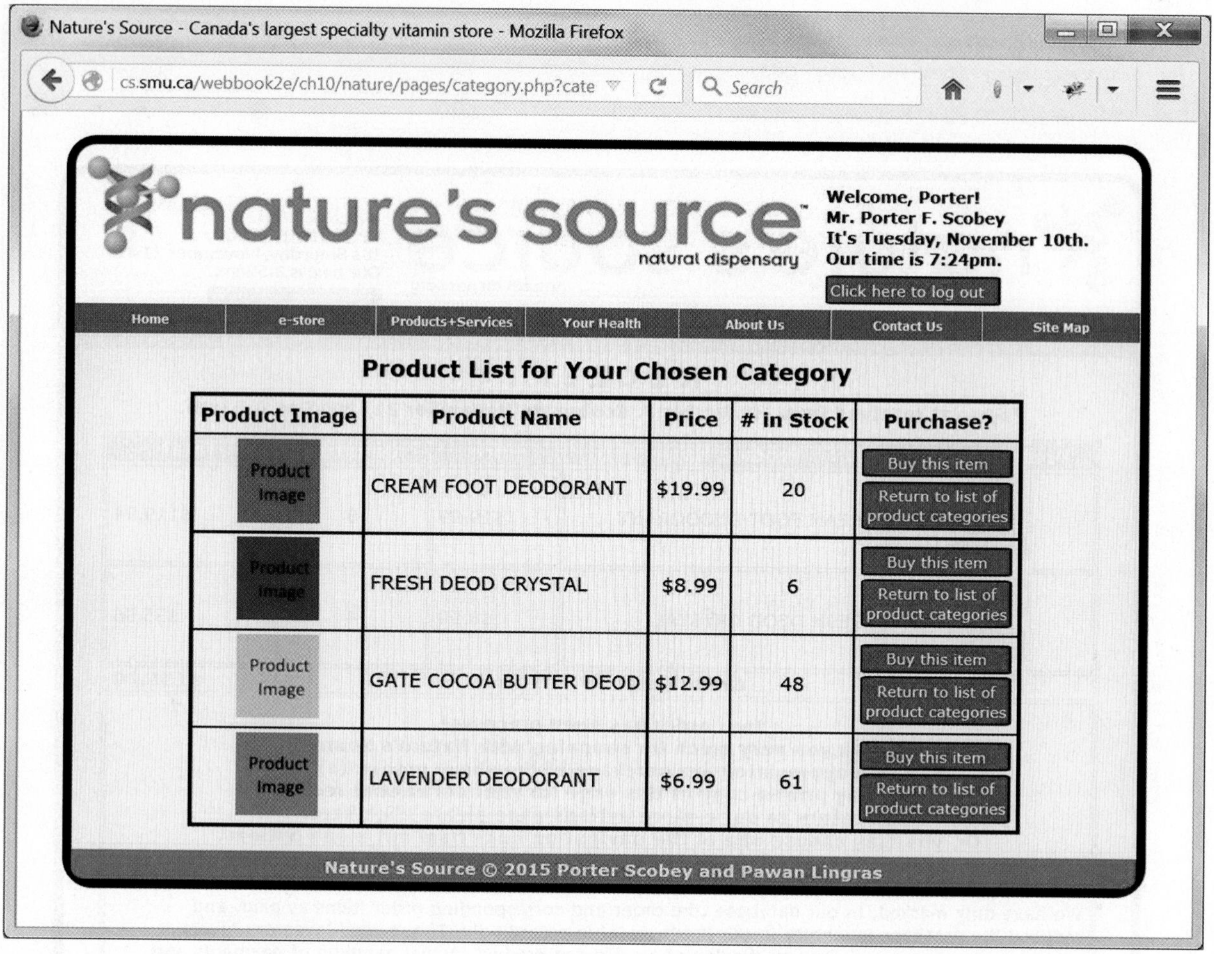

FIGURE 10.42 `graphics/ch10/nature/displayCategoryPhp2.jpg`
An after-checkout view of the category from which the products were purchased, showing the reduction in inventory levels corresponding to the purchases made.

Let's look at how `pages/checkout.php` (**FIGURE 10.43**) and the included script `scripts/checkoutProcess.php` (Figures 10.44–10.49) together process the checkout. Much of the HTML and PHP code in these scripts follows the same pattern as in many other files you have already looked at, so although we include the complete scripts, we focus only on the high-level flow of the action and mention details of interest along the way. As usual, the `pages/checkout.php` script sets up the page infrastructure, and the included `scripts/checkoutProcess.php` does all the work of filling in the page content. However, in this case there is something else going on in lines 9–10 of Figure 10.43 that we need to mention. We first need to say that `$_SESSION['HTTP_REFERER']` will contain the URL of the previous page from which we came to the current page. We use the PHP built-in function `preg_match()` to test whether `shoppingCart.php` occurs in

```php
1   <?php
2   /*checkout.php
3   This page handles the user's checkout process at the highest-level,
4   if that user has come here from his or her shopping cart, and
5   otherwise the user is redirected to a view of the current status
6   of the user's shopping cart.
7   */
8   session_start();
9   if (!preg_match('/shoppingCart.php/', $_SERVER['HTTP_REFERER']))
10       header("Location: shoppingCart.php?productID=view");
11  $customerID = $_SESSION['customer_id'];
12  include("../common/document_head.html");
13  ?>
14    <body>
15      <header>
16        <?php
17        include("../common/banner.php");
18        include("../common/menus.html");
19        include("../scripts/connectToDatabase.php");
20        ?>
21      </header>
22      <main>
23        <article class="Receipt">
24          <?php
25          include("../scripts/checkoutProcess.php");
26          ?>
27        </article>
28      </main>
29      <footer>
30        <?php
31        include("../common/footer_content.html");
32        ?>
33      </footer>
34    </body>
35  </html>
```

FIGURE 10.43 `ch10/nature/pages/checkout.php`
The checkout page that handles, at a high level, the checkout process. In our case this simply consists of producing a receipt-for-purchases-made page for the user, and making appropriate adjustments to our e-store inventory according to the quantity of each item purchased.

the URL of this previous page, in other words to test whether we have just come from a shopping cart page. If a false value is returned, the user has come from some page other than the shopping cart page, so we send the user to view the shopping cart before actually checking out, with a call to the `header()` function. Otherwise we just carry on with the checkout process.

FIGURE 10.44 shows the (very short) "main" part of `scripts/checkoutProcess.php`. This script has two "high level" tasks to perform. First, it displays the customer's receipt for the

```
1    <?php
2    /*checkoutProcess.php
3    Displays a receipt to confirm the client's purchase(s)
4    and adjusts the database inventory levels accordingly.
5    Has a very short main driver, but uses eight helper
6    functions, all of which are defined below.
7    Calls displayReceipt() once, which in turn calls
8    --getExistingOrder() once
9    --displayReceiptHeader() once
10   --displayItemAndReturnTotalPrice() once for each item in the order
11   --displayReceiptFooter() once
12   Calls markOrderPaid() once
13   Calls markOrderItemsPaid() once, which in turn calls
14   --reduceInventory() once for each item in the order
15   */
16   //error_reporting(E_ALL);
17
18   //========== main script begins here
19   displayReceipt($db, $customerID);
20
21   //Get the order ID for the order in progress
22   $query =
23      "SELECT
24         Orders.order_id,
25         Orders.customer_id,
26         Orders.order_status_code,
27         Order_Items.*
28      FROM
29         Order_Items, Orders
30      WHERE
31         Orders.order_id = Order_Items.order_id and
32         Orders.order_status_code = 'IP' and
33         Orders.customer_id = $customerID";
34      $orderInProgress = mysqli_query($db, $query);
35      $orderInProgressArray = mysqli_fetch_array($orderInProgress);
36      $orderID = $orderInProgressArray[0];
37
38   //Now mark as paid both the order itself and its order items
39   markOrderPaid($db, $customerID, $orderID);
40   markOrderItemsPaid($db, $orderID);
41   mysqli_close($db);
42   //========== main script ends here
```

FIGURE 10.44 `ch10/nature/scripts/checkoutProcess.php` **(Part 1 of 6)**
The first part of the script that performs the activities needed for the checkout process: contains the main (high-level) script.

purchases made, with a call to `displayReceipt()` in line 19. Then, in lines 22–36 it sets up and executes a query to retrieve information about the order the customer is checking out, and makes sure (in lines 39–40) that both the order as a whole and the individual items are marked as paid, with calls to the `markOrderPaid()` and `markOrderItemsPaid()` functions. As we will see when we look in more detail at these function calls, marking the order items paid also involves appropriate inventory reductions in our database. Finally, we must make sure to close our database once we are finished with the checkout, which we do in line 41.

The only other thing we should mention in Figure 10.44 is seen in line 16. This is currently a comment, but contains a PHP statement that we could easily activate by removing the comment. Doing so would cause PHP to report any and all errors that might occur as our script executes, provided PHP is configured to report errors. Such errors are the "ugly" ones that just appear as text output in your browser window, often along with other page output. You may wish to incorporate more elegant error-testing by checking to make sure each database query succeeds, for example, and outputting a nicely formatted appropriate message if something goes wrong. We did this in our own code testing, but have removed this code to keep our code displays to a reasonable size and allow the reader to focus more easily on the "meat and potatoes" aspects of each script.

The `displayReceipt()` function called in line 19 of Figure 10.44 is shown in lines 48–73 of **FIGURE 10.45**. This function begins in line 50 by calling the `getExistingOrder()` function (which is also shown in Figure 10.45, lines 79–95, and contains nothing new of interest). If the number of records in the order is 0, there is in fact no order, so in lines 54–60 the customer is

```
44    /*displayReceipt()
45    The "driver" routine for preparing and displaying a receipt
46    for the items purchased in the current order being checked out.
47    */
48    function displayReceipt($db, $customerID)
49    {
50        $items = getExistingOrder($db, $customerID);
51        $numRecords = mysqli_num_rows($items);
52        if($numRecords == 0)
53        {
54            echo
55            "<h4 class='ShoppingCartHeader'>Shopping Cart</h4>
56            <p class='Notification'>Your shopping cart is empty.</p>
57            <p class='Notification'>To continue shopping, please
58            <a class='NoDecoration' href='pages/catalog.php'>click
59            here</a>.</p>";
60            exit(0);
61        }
```

FIGURE 10.45 `ch10/nature/scripts/checkoutProcess.php` **(Part 2 of 6)**
The second part of the script that performs the activities needed for the checkout process: contains one function that acts as a "driver" routine for preparing and displaying the user's receipt, and a second function that gets and returns the items being checked out.

```
62          else
63          {
64              displayReceiptHeader();
65              $grandTotal = 0;
66              for($i=1; $i<=$numRecords; $i++)
67              {
68                  $row = mysqli_fetch_array($items, MYSQLI_ASSOC);
69                  $grandTotal += displayItemAndReturnTotalPrice($db, $row);
70              }
71              displayReceiptFooter($grandTotal);
72          }
73  }
74
75  /*getExistingOrder()
76  Gets and returns the purchased items in the order
77  being checked out.
78  */
79  function getExistingOrder($db, $customerID)
80  {
81      $query =
82          "SELECT
83              Orders.order_id,
84              Orders.customer_id,
85              Orders.order_status_code,
86              Order_Items.*
87          FROM
88              Order_Items, Orders
89          WHERE
90              Orders.order_id = Order_Items.order_id and
91              Orders.order_status_code = 'IP' and
92              Orders.customer_id = '$customerID'";
93      $items = mysqli_query($db, $query);
94      return $items;
95  }
```

FIGURE 10.45 `ch10/nature/scripts/checkoutProcess.php` **(Part 2 of 6)** (*continued*)

informed that the shopping cart is empty and is invited to go view our catalog display, after which the script terminates (line 60). If the number of records is not 0, we execute the `else` block in lines 64–71 of Figure 10.45. This `else` block performs three high-level tasks:

1. It displays the receipt header with a call to `displayReceiptHeader()` (line 64).
2. It executes a loop (lines 65–70) to display a table row for each product purchased, while simultaneously accumulating the grand total of the individual product costs with each call to `displayItemAndReturnTotalPrice()` (line 69).
3. It displays the receipt footer with a call to `displayReceiptFooter()` (line 71).

The `displayReceiptHeader()` function is shown in **FIGURE 10.46**. The function displays the receipt header and customer information, along with the date and time of the transaction. The date and time are obtained with two calls to the PHP `date()` function (lines 103–104), and the customer information is taken directly from the `$_SESSION` superglobal (lines 109–112), without first capturing the values in local variables as we have occasionally done in the past. The function's final action (lines 114–122) is to display the header for the table whose rows will contain the product information for the customer's purchases.

The `displayItemAndReturnTotalPrice()` function is shown in **FIGURE 10.47**. Usually we want a function to do only one thing well, but in this case it is convenient to have this function perform the two tasks that its name suggests. This is the function that is called in the body of the `for`-loop in lines 66–70 of Figure 10.45. Each time the function is called in that loop it is passed a new row of order information. The function first gets the product code from that row (line 131 of Figure 10.47), then constructs and executes a query to retrieve from the `Products` table of our database the required information (lines 132–134). In lines 135–139 we get the product price and

```
97    /*displayReceiptHeader()
98    Displays user information and the date, as well as column
99    headers for the table of purchased items.
100   */
101   function displayReceiptHeader()
102   {
103       $date = date("F j, Y");
104       $time = date('g:ia');
105       echo
106       "<p class='ReceiptTitle'>***** R E C E I P T *****</p>
107       <p class='Notification'>
108           Payment received from
109           $_SESSION[salutation]
110           $_SESSION[customer_first_name]
111           $_SESSION[customer_middle_initial]
112           $_SESSION[customer_last_name] on $date at $time.
113       </p>";
114       echo
115       "<table class='Receipt'>
116           <tr>
117           <th>Product Image</th>
118           <th>Product Name</th>
119           <th>Price</th>
120           <th>Quantity</th>
121           <th>Total</th>
122       </tr>";
123   }
```

FIGURE 10.46 `ch10/nature/scripts/checkoutProcess.php` (Part 3 of 6)
The third part of the script that performs the activities needed for the checkout process: contains a function that displays the header for the user's receipt, including date and time information and the user's name.

```
125   /*displayItemAndReturnTotalPrice()
126   Displays one table row containing the information for
127   one purchased item.
128   */
129   function displayItemAndReturnTotalPrice($db, $row)
130   {
131       $productID = $row['product_id'];
132       $query = "SELECT * FROM Products WHERE product_id ='$productID'";
133       $product = mysqli_query($db, $query);
134       $rowProd = mysqli_fetch_array($product, MYSQLI_ASSOC);
135       $productPrice = $rowProd['product_price'];
136       $productPriceAsString = sprintf("$%1.2f", $productPrice);
137       $totalPrice = $row['order_item_quantity'] * $row['order_item_price'];
138       $totalPriceAsString = sprintf("$%1.2f", $totalPrice);
139       $imageLocation = $rowProd['product_image_url'];
140       echo
141       "<tr>
142         <td class='Centered'>
143           <img height='70' width='70'
144               src='$imageLocation' alt='Product Image'>
145         </td><td class='LeftAligned'>
146           $rowProd[product_name]
147         </td><td class='RightAligned'>
148           $productPriceAsString
149         </td><td class='Centered'>
150           $row[order_item_quantity]
151         </td><td class='RightAligned'>
152           $totalPriceAsString
153         </td>
154       </tr>";
155       return $totalPrice;
156   }
```

FIGURE 10.47 `ch10/nature/scripts/checkoutProcess.php` **(Part 4 of 6)**
The fourth part of the script that performs the activities needed for the checkout process: contains a function that displays one table row containing the information for one purchased item and returns the total price for that item.

format it for output, compute and format for output the total price for the quantity purchased, and capture the location of the (placeholder) product image in a local variable. Lines 140–154 then place all of this information into a row of a table like the one shown in Figure 10.41. Finally, in line 155 the total price of the current product is returned from the function to be accumulated into the grand total price of the order in line 69 of Figure 10.45.

The function `displayReceiptFooter()` is shown in **FIGURE 10.48**. This function finishes off the display of the product table in our receipt, as seen in Figure 10.41. It first displays a row containing the total cost of the customer's order, which it has received as a parameter, followed by a final row containing only text messages for the customer.

```
158    /*displayReceiptFooter()
159    Displays the total amount of the purchase and additional
160    information in the footer of the receipt.
161    */
162    function displayReceiptFooter($grandTotal)
163    {
164        $grandTotalAsString = sprintf("$%1.2f", $grandTotal);
165        echo
166        "<tr>
167          <td class='Notification' colspan='4'>
168            Grand Total
169          </td><td class='RightAligned'>
170            <strong>$grandTotalAsString</strong>
171          </td>
172        </tr><tr>
173          <td colspan='5'>
174            <p class='Notification'>Your order has been processed.
175            <br>Thank you very much for shopping with Nature's Source.
176            <br>We appreciate your purchase of the above product(s).
177            <br>You may print a copy of this page for your permanent record.
178            <br>To return to our e-store options page please
179              <a href='pages/estore.php' class='NoDecoration'>click here</a>.
180            <br>Or, you may choose one of the navigation links from our
181            menu options.</p>
182
183            <p class='LeftAligned'>Note to readers of the text:<br>
184            We have only marked, in our database, the order and corresponding
185            order items as paid, and reduced the database inventory in our
186            Products table accordingly. The revised inventory levels should
187            appear in any subsequent display of an affected product. Actual
188            handling of payments and shipment is beyond the scope of our text.
189            Besides, if truth be told, we have nothing to sell!</p>
190          </td>
191        </tr>
192      </table>";
193    }
```

FIGURE 10.48 `ch10/nature/scripts/checkoutProcess.php` **(Part 5 of 6)**
The fifth part of the script that performs the activities needed for the checkout process: contains a function that displays the footer of the user's receipt, including the total price and additional information.

10.7.2 Updating Our Database

In the previous section we have discussed only what the *customer* sees and experiences during the process of adding items to our shopping cart and then checking out to complete the "purchase" of those items. However, some things must happen "behind the scenes" as well, and we now move on to that discussion.

Three tasks have to be performed on our database when a customer completes a purchase:

1. The customer's order has to be marked as paid in our Orders table.
2. Each individual item in the customer's order has to be marked as paid in our Order_ Items table.
3. For each product purchased, an appropriate inventory reduction must be applied to our Products table.

The three functions that accomplish these tasks are shown in **FIGURE 10.49**: markOrderPaid(), markOrderItemsPaid(), and reduceInventory(). They set up and execute queries appropriate to their individual tasks, and there is not much involved in this process that we have not already seen. We just point out that here we have an excellent opportunity to use the MySQL UPDATE command, since we are only changing the value of a single record field when we are marking something paid or reducing an inventory amount. Note as well that the first two of these

```
195   /*markOrderPaid()
196   Changes the status in the database of the order being checked
197   out from IP (in progress) to PD (paid).
198   */
199   function markOrderPaid($db, $customerID, $orderID)
200   {
201       $query =
202           "UPDATE Orders
203           SET order_status_code = 'PD'
204           WHERE customer_id = '$customerID' and
205               order_id ='$orderID'";
206       $success = mysqli_query($db, $query);
207   }
208
209   /*markOrderItemsPaid()
210   Changes the status in the database of each item purchased
211   from IP (in progress) to PD (paid).
212   */
213   function markOrderItemsPaid($db, $orderID)
214   {
215       $query =
216           "SELECT *
217           FROM Order_Items
218           WHERE order_id = '$orderID'";
219       $orderItems = mysqli_query($db, $query);
220       $numRecords = mysqli_num_rows($orderItems);
```

FIGURE 10.49 `ch10/nature/scripts/checkoutProcess.php` **(Part 6 of 6)**
The sixth part of the script that performs the activities needed for the checkout process: contains one function that marks the user's order as paid, a second function that marks each order item as paid, and a third function that makes the necessary reduction in inventory levels.

```
221     for($i=1; $i<=$numRecords; $i++)
222     {
223         $row = mysqli_fetch_array($orderItems, MYSQLI_ASSOC);
224         $query =
225             "UPDATE Order_Items
226             SET order_item_status_code = 'PD'
227             WHERE order_item_id = $row[order_item_id] and
228                 order_id = $row[order_id]";
229         mysqli_query($db, $query);
230         reduceInventory($db, $row['product_id'],
231                             $row['order_item_quantity']);
232     }
233 }
234
235 /*reduceInventory()
236 Reduces the inventory level in the database of the product
237 purchased by the amount purchased.
238 */
239 function reduceInventory($db, $productID, $quantityPurchased)
240 {
241     $query = "SELECT * FROM Products WHERE product_id = '$productID'";
242     $product = mysqli_query($db, $query);
243     $row = mysqli_fetch_array($product, MYSQLI_ASSOC);
244     $row['product_inventory'] -= $quantityPurchased;
245     $query =
246         "UPDATE Products
247         SET product_inventory = $row[product_inventory]
248         WHERE product_id = $row[product_id]";
249     mysqli_query($db, $query);
250 }
251 ?>
```

FIGURE 10.49 `ch10/nature/scripts/checkoutProcess.php` **(Part 6 of 6)** (*continued*)

functions are called in lines 39–40 of Figure 10.44, while the third function is called by the second (line 230 of Figure 10.49), since every time we mark an order item as paid we want to reduce its inventory level appropriately.

10.7.3 Performing Some "Cleanup" During Logout

It may or may not be the case that we have some "cleanup" to perform when a user logs out. The "cleanup" to which we refer is the removal of any "orphaned" orders that have been created in our database. If we don't perform this cleanup, then over time such orders will certainly "clutter up" our database, and may even overwhelm it.

The problem may occur in two different ways, and the reason it occurs is that in the interest of simplicity we have not made our shopping cart scripts as robust as we might like to have them in a real-world "production" environment.

▶ In the first case, when a site visitor who is not logged in clicks on a **Buy this item** link, an order is created in our database `Orders` table that has a `customer_id` value of 0. This order will never be a "real" order because even if the customer now logs in and continues to shop, a new order will be created and that first order will now become an "orphan", the name we give to orders that have been started and then abandoned. We should arrange for all such orders to be deleted from our database.

▶ In the second case, a logged-in user may start up an order by clicking on a **Buy this item** link, but then decide not to proceed with that order by actually adding the item to the shopping cart. In fact, a logged-in user can create several orders like this, each containing no order items, before creating a "real" order and actually adding one or more items to it. These orders that have no corresponding order items may also be regarded as "orphans", and should also be deleted from our database.

The script that deals with both of these problems is `scripts/logoutProcess.php`, and it is shown in **FIGURES 10.50** and **10.51**. Recall that we mentioned this script earlier since it showed up in line 9 of the `pages/logout.php` script shown in Figure 10.21. We said then that we would come back later to a discussion of that script, when it made more sense to do so, and here we are.

Lines 16–21 of Figure 10.50 set up and execute a query that deletes all the orders having a `customer_id` field with value 0 in the `Orders` table. Note that it does not matter who caused those orders to be created. In fact, we have no knowledge of who might have done so, nor any

```
1    <?php
2    /*logoutProcess.php
3    Handles "clean up" by deleting any orders that
4    have been created by users who have tried to buy
5    items without being registered and logging in,
6    or by users who have logged in and started to
7    buy one or more items but changed their mind.
8    */
9    //error_reporting(E_ALL);
10
11   //First delete all "orphaned" orders created
12   //by not-logged-in customers who tried to buy
13   //an item, but did not follow up when they
14   //discovered registration and login were
15   //required ...
```

FIGURE 10.50 `ch10/nature/scripts/logoutProcess.php` **(Part 1 of 2)**
The first part of the script that performs some "cleanup" of possibly "orphaned" order items when the user logs out.

```
16   $query =
17       "DELETE FROM Orders
18       WHERE
19           customer_id = 0 and
20           order_status_code = 'IP'";
21   $success = mysqli_query($db, $query);
22
23   //Next, see if there is an order "in progress"
24   $query =
25       "SELECT
26           Orders.order_id,
27           Orders.customer_id,
28           Orders.order_status_code,
29           Order_Items.*
30       FROM
31           Order_Items, Orders
32       WHERE
33           Orders.order_id = Order_Items.order_id and
34           Orders.order_status_code = 'IP' and
35           Orders.customer_id = $customerID";
36   $items = mysqli_query($db, $query);
37   if ($items != null)
38       $numRecords = mysqli_num_rows($items);
39   //If $numRecords is non-zero (actually, 1) there is
40   //an order in progress; if it is 0, there is no order
41   //in progress, but there may be any number of orders
42   //that were created by a logged-in user choosing to
43   //"Buy this item" but not actually buying it, and doing
44   //this one or more times before actually starting an
45   //order, thus creating one or more orders without any
46   //corresponding order items,
47   //so ...
```

FIGURE 10.50 `ch10/nature/scripts/logoutProcess.php` **(Part 1 of 2)** (*continued*)

need to have such knowledge. It might be, for example, that three random site visitors each created one or more of these "orphan orders". Then a registered user logs in. These orphans will be deleted when that user logs out.

The rest of the script (lines 23–47 of Figure 10.50 and all of Figure 10.51) deal with the second problem, the orders that have been started by the current logged-in customer but abandoned before any items were added to them. This part of the script deletes those "orphaned" orders.

You may find it interesting to monitor "behind-the-scenes" database updates as you perform the activities described above using the web interface, as both a logged-in user and a user who is not logged in. See the following section for a description of some utility scripts that can help you do this kind of monitoring, and you may wish to create additional scripts for similar purposes, or use phpMyAdmin for similar monitoring.

```
49  if ($numRecords == 0)
50  //If there are "orphaned" orders for which there are no
51  //corresponding order items, find them and delete them ...
52  {
53      $query =
54          "SELECT
55              order_id,
56              customer_id,
57              order_status_code
58          FROM Orders
59          WHERE
60              order_status_code = 'IP' and
61              customer_id = $customerID";
62      $orphanedOrders = mysqli_query($db, $query);
63      if ($orphanedOrders != null)
64      {
65          $numRecords = mysqli_num_rows($orphanedOrders);
66          if ($numRecords != 0)
67          {
68              for ($i=0; $i<$numRecords; $i++)
69              {
70                  $orphanedOrdersArray =
71                      mysqli_fetch_array($orphanedOrders, MYSQLI_ASSOC);
72                  $orphanedOrderID = $orphanedOrdersArray['order_id'];
73                  $query =
74                      "DELETE FROM Orders
75                      WHERE
76                          order_id = '$orphanedOrderID' and
77                          order_status_code = 'IP' and
78                          customer_id = '$customerID'";
79                  $success = mysqli_query($db, $query);
80              }
81          }
82      }
83  }
84  mysqli_close($db);
85  ?>
```

FIGURE 10.51 `ch10/nature/scripts/logoutProcess.php` **(Part 2 of 2)**
The second part of the script that performs some "cleanup" of possibly "orphaned" order items when the user logs out.

10.8 Some Utility Files for Use at the MySQL Command-Line Interface

When you are experimenting with the web interface to the **Nature's Source** website by registering, logging in, adding and deleting items from your shopping cart, and making "purchases", it can be very instructive to keep track of what's going on "behind the scenes" as well. That is, if while doing this you are also logged in to your account and then into the MySQL command-line interface, you can enter commands at the `mysql>` prompt to see what changes have been made to the database tables (after you register or add something to the shopping cart, for example).

FIGURE 10.52 shows the text of five different short files, each of which contains SQL commands that perform a task of the kind just described. These files are all available in the `ch10` directory, and you can run any one of them using a command like

```
mysql> source filename.sql
```

```
 1   #get_me.sql
 2   #Replace 'Scobey' with 'your_name'
 3   #--------------------------------
 4   SELECT customer_id as id,
 5          salutation as sal,
 6          customer_first_name as first,
 7          customer_middle_initial as mid,
 8          customer_last_name as last,
 9          gender as sex,
10          email_address as email,
11          login_name as username,
12          login_password as password
13   FROM   Customers
14   WHERE  customer_last_name='Scobey';
15
16   SELECT phone_number, address, town_city, county, country
17   FROM   Customers
18   WHERE  customer_last_name='Scobey';
19
20   #delete_me.sql
21   #Replace 'Scobey' with 'your_name'
22   #--------------------------------
23   DELETE FROM Customers
24          WHERE customer_last_name='Scobey';
25
26   #get_orders.sql
27   #--------------
```

FIGURE 10.52 `graphics/ch10/utility_files.txt`
Five different utility files that may be helpful to keep track of some "behind-the-scenes" changes in your copy of the database tables when experimenting with your copy of the web interface to the **Nature's Source** website.

```
28  SELECT order_id as id,
29         customer_id as cust,
30         order_status_code as status,
31         date_order_placed as date,
32         order_details as details
33  FROM Orders;
34
35  SELECT order_item_id as id,
36         order_item_status_code as status,
37         order_id,
38         product_id,
39         order_item_quantity as quant,
40         order_item_price as price,
41         other_order_item_details as details
42  FROM Order_Items;
43
44  #delete_orders.sql
45  #----------------
46  DELETE FROM Orders;
47  DELETE FROM Order_Items;
48
49  #get_table_sizes.sql
50  #Replace 'webbook2e' with 'your_database_name'
51  #---------------------------------------------
52  SELECT TABLE_NAME, TABLE_ROWS
53  FROM information_schema.tables
54  WHERE table_schema='webbook2e';
```

FIGURE 10.52 `graphics/ch10/utility_files.txt` (*continued*)

at the `mysql>` command prompt. You will have to make minor modifications to three of the files, as indicated in their comments, and you may be inspired by looking at these files to create some more of your own.

For example, you can use the `get_me.sql` file to get all your registration information after you have registered, if you simply make the name change indicated in the comment and run the file.

Summary

In a very real sense, PHP and MySQL have "grown up together", at least in the sense that much effort has gone into making the two technologies work well together. The fact that this effort has been successful is reflected in the number of major commercial enterprises that use the combination to handle their database activities.

PHP contains many functions for dealing directly with a MySQL database system and, for that matter, for dealing with many other database systems. You can write your own scripts to connect to a MySQL database system, create and populate tables with data, add and remove data after the fact, modify that data, and retrieve it in various ways. Or, if you are the database administrator, you can use a sophisticated PHP-based front-end GUI interface (like phpMyAdmin) to communicate with your database.

Exactly what scripts you will need for your own website will depend on what you want your site visitors to be able to do with the data stored in your database. At a minimum, if you are setting up an online store, you will want them to be able to view your offerings, make choices, and pay for them online. Except for the final step of actually making a payment, we have illustrated the steps needed for such transactions. The idea of a "session", which we first encountered in Chapter 8, allows your site to "remember" what is going on as the user browses from one page to another, and adds items to a "shopping cart", by using values stored in the PHP superglobal array $_SESSION. These items in the shopping cart will be "paid for" at "checkout time". This is in contrast to the simple display of one static page after another, a process which "has no memory".

It is a useful exercise to monitor what is going on "behind the scenes" in your database as the user interacts with that database via the web interface, and we have provided some SQL scripts for doing this from the MySQL command-line interface.

Quick Questions to Test Your Basic Knowledge

1. Some folks regard the combination of PHP and MySQL as a "marriage made in heaven", and certainly it is widely used on the Web, but there are other competing technologies. Can you name some of them?

2. What is the PHP function we used to connect to MySQL from a PHP script, and what are its parameters?

3. What PHP function did we use to check whether or not a PHP variable actually has a value?

4. What is a good way to keep your MySQL login information out of any PHP script that is going to access your MySQL database, and thus "hide" it from anyone who might be able to view your script?

5. What is the PHP function we used to send an SQL query to a MySQL database, and how would you describe the general form of the return value of this function?

6. Suppose your MySQL database contains a table named `Clients`, and suppose among its columns is one named `first_name` and one named `last_name`. Can you quickly perform each of the following tasks, at the MySQL command line as well as from a PHP script?
   - First, compose a query that would retrieve the first and last names (last names first) of all clients whose last name is either `Jones` or `Green`, and then assign the query to a variable named `$query`.
   - Second, send the query to MySQL from a PHP script, assuming the connection has already been made and the database chosen.

7. What PHP function would you use to direct a visitor to one page from another page if, for example, your script on the current page performs a test of some kind and decides the user should go to that other page?

8. What is the PHP feature called that you use to provide a way for certain information to be "remembered" as your site visitors browse from one page to another, and what is the first thing you need to do in a PHP script that wants to take advantage of this feature?

9. When you are using a PHP superglobal array such as $_SESSION or $_GET, and you want to access a value in that array, when would you put single quotes around the key value in the square brackets, and when would you not do this?

10. Suppose you are logged in to MySQL and you are at the command-line interface and connected to the appropriate database. If you are monitoring some "behind-the-scenes" database activity using a script called check_it.sql and that script is in your current directory, what command would you give to execute the script?

11. What do we mean by an "orphan" order, and how might one be created?

Short Exercises to Improve Your Basic Understanding

1. This exercise appears longer than it actually is. It contains an interactive PHP session that you should replicate to help you get more comfortable with how arrays work in PHP. As you go through the exercise it will be useful to keep in mind that PHP arrays may be viewed as both an "ordinary" array with integer indices starting at 0, or as a collection of key/value pairs, depending on the context. And be sure to study the summary of array properties at the end of the exercise.

   We are using the interactive PHP interpreter available on our Linux system to test our PHP code. On this system we start the interpreter with the command

   ```
   $ php -a
   ```

   and at the end of the session we use the exit command to stop the interpreter and return to the Linux prompt. We have added some comments here and there that will help you follow the session:

   ```
   php > //The following command creates a one-element array:
   php > $a[] = "Hello";
   php > //We omitted the subscript so the next available
   php > //subscript is used, which is 0 in this case.
   php > //The echo command can print an array element.
   php > echo $a[0];
   Hello
   php > //Next we add a number of elements to our array.
   php > $a[] = "World";
   ```

```
php > $a[-90] = "This is wild";
php > $a[90] = "This is wild";
php > $a[70] = "This is wild";
php > $a["name"] = "Pawan";
php > //Use the print_r() function to print an entire array.
php > print_r($a);
Array
(
    [0] => Hello
    [1] => World
    [-90] => This is wild
    [90] => This is wild
    [70] => This is wild
    [name] => Pawan
)
php > //As we can see, the indices are not ordered as you would have
php > //expected, since -90 comes after 1, and 70 comes after 90.
php > //If we do not specify the index, it will be one
php > //more than the highest current index, i.e., 90+1 = 91.
php > $a[] = "What is the index?";
php > print_r($a);
Array
(
    [0] => Hello
    [1] => World
    [-90] => This is wild
    [90] => This is wild
    [70] => This is wild
    [name] => Pawan
    [91] => What is the index?
)
php > //You can get numeric indices properly ordered
php > //by using the function array_values().
php > $b = array_values($a);
php > print_r($b);
Array
(
    [0] => Hello
    [1] => World
    [2] => This is wild
    [3] => This is wild
    [4] => This is wild
    [5] => Pawan
    [6] => What is the index?
)
php > //You can delete an element using the function unset.
php > unset($a[-90]);
php > print_r($a);
```

```
Array
(
      [0] => Hello
      [1] => World
      [90] => This is wild
      [70] => This is wild
      [name] => Lingras
      [91] => What is the index?
)
php > //The count() function gives you the size of an array.
php > echo count($a);
6
php > //The "construct" array() (not a function) can be used
php > //to create an entire array.
php > $a = array("This", "is", "different", 5, 6, 7);
php > print_r($a);
Array
(
      [0] => This
      [1] => is
      [2] => different
      [3] => 5
      [4] => 6
      [5] => 7
)
php > //The construct array() also allows you to specify the indices.
php > //Note the secondary prompt "php (".
php > $a=array(7=>"This", 0=>"is", 8=>"different", "five"=>5,
php (6=>6, "eight"=>7);
php > print_r($a);
Array
(
      [7] => This
      [0] => is
      [8] => different
      [five] => 5
      [6] => 6
      [eight] => 7
)
```

In summary, then, here again are the essential array features illustrated by the above session:
- A PHP array index is really just a means of accessing a particular element in an array (the "key" of a "key/value pair", in effect). It does not necessarily suggest an ordering. That is why we can use –90 as an index, which is stored in the array after the index 1.
- If we do not use an index to place a value in an array, the first numeric index greater than the last-used numeric index is used.

- A single array element can be displayed using echo, as in echo($a[3]) for example, but to display an entire array with a single command, use the built-in function print_r($a).
- A call to the built-in function count($a) gives us the size of an array $a.
- An entire array can be created by using the array() construct, by placing within the parentheses a comma-separated list of values (they will have integer indices/keys 0, 1, 2 . . .), or a comma-separated list of key/value pairs (each having the form key=>value, and string keys should be enclosed in quotes).
- If you want to get an array with conventionally ordered numeric indices from an associative array, you can use the function array_values().
- PHP has an amazing number of built-in functions that perform various array-related tasks, as well as a variety of PHP functions with an array as their return value, including functions that return database records as arrays.

2. Write a short PHP script that simply tries to connect to your MySQL database system and reports either success or failure, depending on the outcome of the attempt.

3. Write a short PHP script that connects to your MySQL database system and displays a list of all databases accessible to you. If there is a problem with the connection or with generating the list of databases, your script should report the problem, with an appropriate message.

4. Write a short PHP script that connects to your MySQL database system and then displays a list of all tables in all databases accessible to you. If there is a problem with connection or with generating the list of tables, your script should report the problem, with an appropriate message.

5. Create an HTML form page that lets the user enter the name of a table to be created in a particular MySQL database and the number of fields that this table is to contain. Provide a button that, when clicked by the user, will take the user to a second form page where the user can choose the data type and size for each field of this table. A button on this page, when clicked, should then connect to the database and create the table.

6. Create an HTML form page and corresponding PHP script that will let the user enter a single record into the table created in the previous exercise.

7. Create an HTML page with several links on it. Each link, when clicked, retrieves and displays all or part of the data stored in the table of the previous exercise.

8. Revise the registrationFormProcess.php script shown in Figures 10.11 and 10.12 so that in addition to producing displays like those shown in Figures 10.7 and 10.9, it also sends out appropriate email messages to the client.

9. Make the following two improvements to the registration form shown in Figure 10.4:
   - Ask the user to enter the password twice, to use at least six alphanumeric characters with at least one capital letter and at least one digit, and validate accordingly.
   - Include a separate entry textbox for the zip code, and validate it as well. If you are really ambitious, do a little research to establish the exact possible formats for U.S. zip codes and Canadian postal codes, and validate according to the client's country of origin.

10. Scan the scripts of this chapter to find one place where we captured values from a superglobal array into local variables and then used those local variables elsewhere in the script. Rewrite that script to use the superglobal array values directly, without first capturing them in local variables.

11. Repeat the previous exercise, but in the "opposite direction".

12. Note that in the display of our customer receipt (see Figure 10.41) we still have the personalized Welcome message at the top right and we also repeat the user's name, date, and time just before the table. Suppose we decide to eliminate the Welcome message and personalized information in the top right corner when the receipt is displayed. Think about where we might set, and later use, a variable called `$noWelcomeMessage` to achieve this result, and then implement this feature.

13. Take a look at `scripts/loginFormValidate.js` and note that all the function in that file does is check to make sure we don't have a completely empty form. Eliminate this script by implementing the same functionality using only HTML5 features in `pages/loginForm.php`.

Exercises on the Parallel Project

In this section of the previous chapter you created some data for your business and entered it into a MySQL database. Thus you now have a business-related database containing several tables with which your business website must be able to communicate, so that your users can retrieve, among other things perhaps, at least the information that you would like them to know about what you have to offer them.

Also, for some time now you have had a **Products+Services** link, or a similar link, on the home page of your business. Previously that link would have simply taken you to a static web page display showing what your business offers for sale. Now you must make that page dynamic, as outlined in the following exercises.

1. Your **Products+Services** (or analogous) link must be converted to a dropdown menu list, and the first option on that list must take the user to a new page showing the various categories of products and/or services your business offers for sale, analogous to the page display seen in Figure 10.24. Each of the links on this page will, in turn, be attached to a PHP script that connects to your database, retrieves the necessary product and/or service information for all the products and/or services in a particular category, and displays this information for the user in a new page, using an appropriate format.

2. Design and implement the necessary PHP scripts for the "back-end" processing required to implement the functionality described in exercise 1 above. As a minimum, your website should allow the user to see a full "catalog" list of all categories of products and services that you offer, and clicking on a "category link" should produce a suitable display of all products in that category.

3. Depending on the time available, you should also try, or your instructor may require you, to pursue one or more additional features illustrated in this chapter, which include registering with your business, logging in, and conducting an online session in which several products or services are chosen for purchase, followed by an appropriate "check out" process. You should be able to adapt our scripts for your own particular needs to implement analogous functionality for your own website. The options you should try to implement would be those additional options you see on the **Products+Services** dropdown menu of the **Nature's Source** website.

What Else You May Want or Need to Know

1. There is one aspect of PHP that may cause you some confusion and potentially some problems if you are not aware of how it behaves in this language: *variable scope*. We discussed and illustrated this back in Chapter 8, but it deserves another mention here. The most important thing to remember in this context is that in PHP if a variable has the same name inside and outside a function, it is *not* the same variable. Where this is most likely to cause you a problem is if you are using a variable inside a function and you are thinking it is that variable outside the function that has the same name, with the value you know that "outside variable" to have. You will actually be using a different variable that probably doesn't have any value at all. This is one of the main problems with PHP and many other scripting languages—the lack of strong typing, along with inconsistent and confusing scope rules—and though taking advantage of these somewhat "relaxed" rules can be very convenient at times, they also create a minefield around which you must tread very carefully.

2. We have pointed out in this chapter that it is critical to your business that you keep your database secure. In our `connectToDatabase.php` script, shown in Figure 10.3, the hostname, username, password, and database name are being included from an external file called `database.inc` (line 10). This file should be placed in a location on the server that will permit the file to be included by the PHP `include()` function in the place where it is needed, but that location should not be accessible to anyone with access to your `public_html` (or equivalent) directory. We cannot emphasize this too strongly!

3. You may have observed, or wondered along the way, what might happen if several customers are attempting to buy products from us at the same time. This in fact might be a problem if, for example, there are only three of some product left in inventory and one customer has them in his shopping cart when suddenly another customer in more of a hurry shows up and buys the items while they are still in the first customer's cart. Our simple model does not address this problem, but a real-world store would have to deal with it, of course, by ensuring that pending purchases by one customer are "locked down"

until that customer's session has finished. A more general discussion of *transaction processing*, which considers this entire problem and how to handle it, is beyond the scope of this text.

4. Sometimes, when you are debugging a PHP script that generates and sends some reasonably complex HTML markup to the browser that is not appearing in the expected form (nested lists that aren't coming out right, for example), you may want to include the newline characters \r\n in your PHP output, as we have done from time to time. As you know, this will not have any effect on the browser display, but if you do a "view source" to see what your page looks like "behind the scenes", it may be useful to have appropriately placed line breaks to help you read and debug your markup.

5. We have used a PHP *session* to help us "remember" some information about the customer as that customer browses from page to page on our site during the shopping process. Sometimes it is convenient, when a customer comes back to a site, for the site to "remember" that the customer has been there before, but this cannot be done with a session, since session information generally goes away when the user logs out. However, this can be done even if the site does not force the user to log in and be identified in that way. Another technique is to use a *cookie*, which is a small piece of text sent by the server to the browser and stored on the customer's computer. When that customer returns, from that same computer, the cookie is sent back to the server from which it came, and the information in it can be used to identify the visitor and display a "Welcome Back" message (for example). Cookies may be useful, but should not be relied on for anything too serious, since the browser may be instructed not to accept them.

6. We discussed and used the PHP built-in function urlencode() in this chapter. You should read about this function, as well as urldecode(), stripslashes() and addslashes() in the PHP documentation, in case you need to use them when using PHP and MySQL on your website. See the **References** for the relevant links.

References

1. The home page of PHP can be found at:

```
http://www.php.net
```

and there you will find the most up-to-date documentation on the latest version of the language, as well as links from which you can download various versions of the software for your particular platform.

2. The tutorial part of the above site is here:

```
http://php.net/manual/en/tutorial.php
```

3. The part of the PHP home site that deals explicitly with its interface to MySQL can be found here:

   ```
   http://php.net/manual/en/book.mysql.php
   ```

4. For the official word on PHP arrays, see:

   ```
   http://php.net/manual/en/book.array.php
   ```

5. The PHP manual material on the `printf()` and `sprintf()` formatting functions can be found at these links:

   ```
   http://php.net/manual/en/function.printf.php
   http://php.net/manual/en/function.sprintf.php
   ```

6. As always, the `W3Schools` site is also an excellent resource, and you can start here:

   ```
   http://www.w3schools.com/PHP/php_intro.asp
   ```

7. Check out this site for tutorials on both PHP cookies and PHP sessions:

   ```
   http://www.tizag.com/phpT/phpcookies.php
   http://www.tizag.com/phpT/phpsessions.php
   ```

8. Another tutorial site:

   ```
   http://www.tutorialspoint.com/php/index.htm
   ```

9. Sites with some concise but helpful pages on both cookies and sessions:

   ```
   http://php.about.com/od/advancedphp/qt/php_cookie.htm
   http://php.about.com/od/advancedphp/ss/php_sessions.htm
   ```

10. Here are links to information on `urlencode()`, `urldecode()`, `stripslashes()`, and `addslashes()`:

    ```
    http://php.net/manual/en/function.urlencode.php
    http://php.net/manual/en/function.urldecode.php
    http://php.net/manual/en/function.stripslashes.php
    http://php.net/manual/en/function.addslashes.php
    ```

CHAPTER **ELEVEN**

XML (eXtensible Markup Language) for Data Description

CHAPTER CONTENTS

Overview and Objectives

XML (*eXtensible Markup Language*) is a relatively simple metalanguage derived from the much more complex *SGML* (*Standard Generalized Markup Language*). As a metalanguage, it can be used to describe other languages, and we have already pointed out how it was used to "rewrite" HTML as XHTML. But it can be used for much more than that.

The power, flexibility, and usefulness of XML really does stem from its simplicity. First, it has very few rules that a developer must remember and use. Second, as its name indicates, it is *extensible*. This means that unlike HTML, say, which has tags that can only be used in the way that HTML specifies, XML lets you make up your own tags and decide what they mean and how they will be used. In fact, not only *can* you make up your own tags, you *must* make up your own tags, since XML does not have *any* predefined tags. Of course, by now lots of people and organizations have made up their own tag sets to describe their own kinds of data, and you may wish to avoid making up *your* own tags by using those made up by someone else. See the **What Else** section at the end of this chapter for more on this.

Thus XML can be used to describe almost anything, and the WWW has embraced it as the best way to describe all kinds of different data on any kind of computing platform. XML has become the *lingua franca* of the web, although recently it has lost some ground to JSON.

As with the other technologies we have introduced, we will only have time and space to scratch the XML surface. By the end of this chapter you should have a good idea of what XML is all about and why it may be useful, but if you wish to incorporate it into your website in any significant way you will need to spend some additional time and effort delving further into some of the topics we only touch upon here. See the end-of-chapter **References** for some relevant links.

We will first present the main features of XML, and then see how we can represent some of our data using it. If we have several documents containing the same kind of data, we will also want to verify that they all have the same structure, and for this we will use an appropriate *DTD* (*Document Type Definition*). We may also want to put the XML tags and attributes we have chosen to describe our data in an *XML namespace* to prevent them from being confused with the tags and attributes chosen by others.

One of the things we often want to do, of course, is display our data, and we will see how we can use our Cascading Style Sheets (CSS) knowledge to apply some style when we display data stored in XML format. An alternative to this approach, more in keeping with the XML way of doing things, is to use styles in XSL (*eXtensible Style Language*) format and an XSLT (*eXtensible Style Language Transformation*) to "transform" our data into an HTML page for display in a browser. The power of this simple idea immediately suggests that we might want to use a different XSLT to transform our data into some other useful form, and in fact that is just what the XSLT technology allows us to do.

In this chapter, then, we discuss the following topics:

▶ The few basic syntax rules you must follow when preparing an XML document

▶ What it means for an XML document to be *well-formed*, and what happens when it isn't

▶ What it means for an XML document to be *valid*, and the validation process

▶ The structure and syntax of a *DTD*

▶ What happens when you view a "raw" XML document in a browser

▶ How to style an XML document using *CSS*

▶ A brief introduction to *XSL* and transforming an XML document with *XSL Transformations XSLT* and *XPath*

▶ XML namespaces

11.1 The Basic Rules of XML

In the next section we actually put XML to work describing some of our data. It's a good idea to get ready for that by acquiring some familiarity with the very few things you need to know about XML in order to begin using it effectively. Here's a short list, and if you are already comfortable with HTML, you will feel right at home here:

1. XML is just text, so any editor can be used to create and modify XML markup. There are also XML-specific editors available, with varying degrees of functionality and cost. See the end-of-chapter **References** for links to some possible choices.

2. XML lets you create your own tags to describe elements that have content enclosed by a tag pair, as in `<tagname>... content...</tagname>`, which must be properly nested. Empty elements are possible as well, and have the form `<tagname/>` (note the forward slash following `tagname`). Also, every XML document must contain a single *root element*, within which all of the other elements of the document are contained.

3. XML elements may have attributes. Each attribute must have a value, and that value *must* be enclosed in quotation marks, as in `<tagname attribute="value">`. Either single or double quotes are OK.

4. XML is case-sensitive (like XHTML, but unlike HTML), and names must start with a letter or underscore (_), which can then be followed by any number of alphanumeric characters, hyphens, periods, or underscores.

5. XML has only five predefined *entity references* (special characters), and here they are:

```
&lt;     <     less than
&gt;     >     greater than
&amp;    &     ampersand
&apos;   '     apostrophe (single quotation mark)
&quot;   "     quotation mark (double quotation mark)
```

6. XML has comments, as in `<!-- text of comment -->`, just like those of HTML.
7. XML preserves whitespace (unlike HTML or even XHTML, for example). However, exactly what this means does "depend on the situation".
8. In XML *you have to get it right* if you expect any XML *parser* (processor), including your favorite browser, to process your document. This will come as a shock to those who have been accustomed to having their HTML trespasses forgiven by most browsers. Getting it right means following all of the above rules, of course, but also having a special line as the first line of an XML document, *before anything else appears*, even a single blank space. More on this when we look at our first example.

See what we mean by simplicity? You are now ready to describe some data, which we begin to do in the next section.

11.2 Describing Our Data with Well-Formed XML

To see how we can use XML to describe our data, it is best to begin with an example, so take a look at **FIGURE 11.1**, which shows the contents of the file ch11/sampledata.xml.

The first thing to note is that the file is identified as containing XML data by its .xml file extension. Also, the first line of the file is the *XML declaration* (also called the *XML prolog*), which defines the XML version (1.0) and encoding (ISO-8859-1, which is a Latin-1/West European character set) being used. You will often see UTF-8 as the encoding scheme as well. UTF-8 offers many more characters, but for a unilingual English website ISO-8859-1 is fine, and, for all intents and purposes, equivalent to UTF-8.

The second line of the file is a comment. Note that XML comments are the same as HTML comments. However, there is an important placement distinction here. The XML declaration *must* be the first line of an XML file, which requires our comment containing the filename to be the second line. We had a similar convention of placing the analogous comment in an HTML file immediately following the DOCTYPE declaration.

Line 3 of ch11/sampledata.xml contains the *opening tag* of the *root element* of the XML document in the file. This outermost element is the supplements element in this case. It corresponds to the html element in an XHTML document, since in either case all other elements are contained within the root element.

All XML documents consist essentially of a collection of nested elements, and this one is no exception. Nested within the outermost (root) element supplements we have several vitamin elements containing information about each available vitamin. This information is, in

```
1    <?xml version="1.0" encoding="ISO-8859-1"?>
2    <!-- sampledata.xml -->
3    <supplements>
4      <vitamin product_id="10">
5        <name>Vitamin A</name>
6        <price>$8.99</price>
7        <helps_support>Your eyes</helps_support>
8        <daily_requirement>5000 IU</daily_requirement>
9      </vitamin>
10     <vitamin product_id="20">
11       <name>Vitamin C</name>
12       <price>$11.99</price>
13       <helps_support>Your immune system</helps_support>
14       <daily_requirement>250-400 mg</daily_requirement>
15     </vitamin>
16     <vitamin product_id="30">
17       <name>Vitamin D</name>
18       <price>$3.99</price>
19       <helps_support>Your bones, especially your rate of
20         calcium absorption</helps_support>
21       <daily_requirement>400-800 IU</daily_requirement>
22     </vitamin>
23   </supplements>
```

FIGURE 11.1 `ch11/sampledata.xml`
Some sample data described using XML tags with names chosen appropriately for the data.

turn, contained in a sequence of elements nested within each `vitamin` element. Each element in the sequence specifies one further piece of information associated with the corresponding vitamin.

Note that, just like HTML tags, XML tags can also have attributes, but in the case of XML each attribute *must* have a value, and the value *must* be enclosed in quotes. This is illustrated here by the `product_id` attribute of the `vitamin` tag.

11.2.1 Nested Elements vs. Tag Attributes

One of the more difficult decisions to be made when you are designing an XML document to describe some of your data is the choice of what information should be placed in a nested element and what should be placed in a tag attribute.

For example, in the simple XML document shown in Figure 11.1 we have given the `vitamin` tag an attribute called `product_id`. Although ID numbers often do show up as attributes in XML documents, there is no theoretical, or even practical, reason why we could not have placed this information in another nested element, along with `name`, `price`, and the rest.

So, here are one rule, one guideline, and one "rule of thumb" for what you should do when making these decisions:

Rule   Any binary data (such as an image) *must* be specified by placing its location in a tag attribute, since only text can appear in an XML file. This is analogous to the `src` attribute of the HTML `img` tag.

Guideline   If the information in question might, at some later time, need to be subdivided, placing it in an element rather than an attribute will make this much easier. This is because although nothing can be added to an attribute once it is in place, we can easily add nested tags to any existing tag to reflect the growth of complexity in our data. On the other hand, if it is clear that the information will never need to be subdivided and is simply "information about your information" (in other words, *metadata*), then an attribute is probably the better choice. Identification information like that contained in the HTML `id` or `name` attribute will be a likely candidate for an XML attribute.

Rule of Thumb   This one may be rather vague, but it is, after all, only a "rule of thumb": Use an attribute for information that you would not likely need or want to display to a user of the information.

For example,

```
<customer>
  <name>Pawan Lingras</name>
  <phone>420-5798</phone>
</customer>
```

is much better than

```
<customer name="Pawan Lingras">
  <phone>420-5798</phone>
</customer>
```

because it is much easier to convert, if necessary, to this:

```
<customer>
    <first_name>Pawan</first_name>
    <last_name>Lingras</last_name>
    <phone>420-5798</phone>
</customer>
```

11.2.2 And What Does It Mean for Our XML to Be "Well-Formed"?

In section 11.2 we listed a number of syntax rules that we have to follow when constructing our XML documents (properly nested tags, consistent capitalization, and so on). XML processors are much more stringent in their expectations than HTML processors, and will simply refuse to

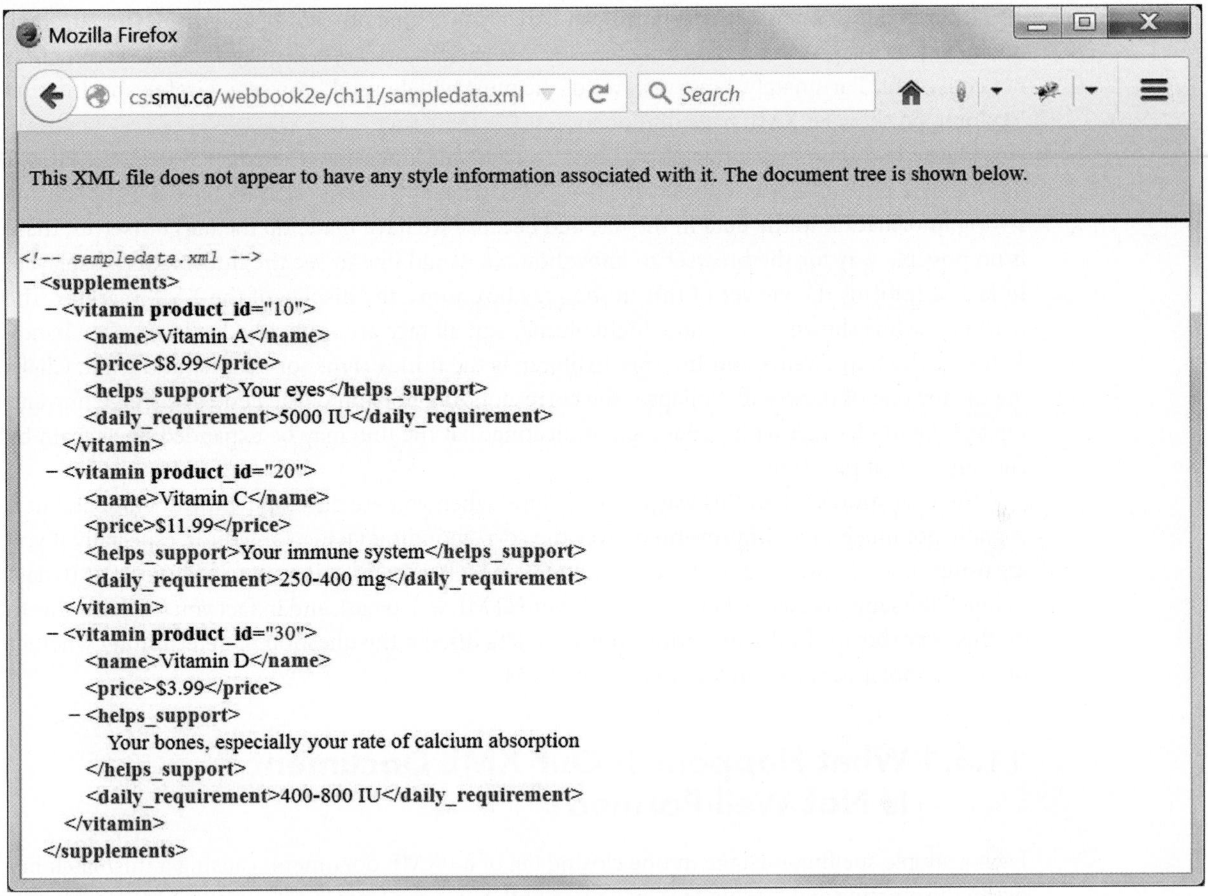

FIGURE 11.2 `graphics/ch11/displaySampledataXml.jpg`
A Firefox browser display of the XML document in `sampledata.xml`.

process our XML documents if we break *any* of these rules. If our XML document does in fact conform to all of the required syntax rules, we say that it is *well-formed*.

11.3 Viewing Our Raw (Unstyled) XML Data in a Browser

You are by now very familiar with the fact that whatever browser you use to "surf the web" contains a *rendering engine* that reads the contents of a web page document and displays it in a browser window for you to view. You also know that this rendering engine is a very "forgiving" machine, since it will often overlook markup errors in a web page and simply do its best to interpret what it sees and try to produce a reasonable display of the content.

It turns out that most modern browsers are also capable of reading and displaying an XML document, although as of this writing the way that various browsers display an XML document is not consistent. Fortunately, however, two of the most widely used browsers, Firefox and Internet Explorer, do show an XML page in more or less the same way.

Figure 11.2 shows what our `sampledata.xml` file looks like when displayed by the Firefox browser. We refer to this as a display of "raw" XML data, in the sense that we have not applied any styling information to the data in the file, and because we have made up the tags ourselves, there is no possible way for the browser to know how we would like to see the information displayed. In fact, it informs the viewer of this in the grey box above the display of the XML markup. The markup itself is shown with syntax highlighting, and all tags are explicitly displayed. One handy feature, at least in Firefox and Internet Explorer, is the minus signs (or dashes) at the left. Clicking on any one of these will "collapse" the corresponding portion of the code to a single line and replace the minus sign with a plus sign, indicating that the line may be expanded once again by clicking on that plus sign.

Viewing your XML in this way can be helpful when you are developing the document, but it is really not much of an improvement over the corresponding view in an editor, especially if you are using an XML-aware editor for development. Most likely you will want to style your XML data in much the same way as we have done with our HTML web pages, and in fact you shall see how to do this very shortly. In the meantime, however, let's discuss the question of determining whether or not our documents are in fact well-formed XML.

11.3.1 What Happens If Our XML Document Is Not Well-Formed?

Even a simple spelling mistake in one closing tag of an XML document, causing a mismatch between the opening and closing tags, will prevent the browser from displaying an XML document. For example, **FIGURE 11.3** shows the error generated and displayed by the browser if we make the closing tag of the first vitamin element `</vitamine>` instead of `</vitamin>`. It should be clear from this example that using an XML-aware editor to prepare your XML documents will be highly advantageous and will help to keep such errors to a minimum.

The file `ch11/sampledataError.xml` is identical to the `ch11/sampledata.xml` file of Figure 11.1 except that it contains this error. You should browse to that file with whatever browsers you have available to see their reaction when asked to display an XML file that is not well-formed.

11.4 Validating Our XML Data with a Document Type Definition

OK, so now you know what a well-formed XML document is—one that does not violate any of the basic XML syntax rules. But we have a researcher friend who's just discovered several new vitamins, and he wants to describe them in an XML document just like the one we've been using. What to do?

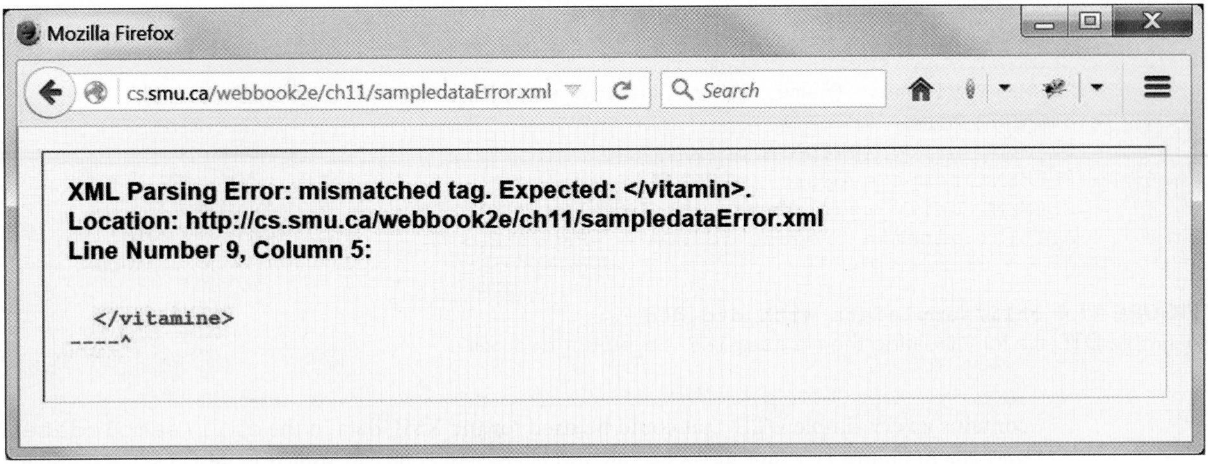

FIGURE 11.3 `graphics/ch11/displaySampledataErrorXml.jpg`
A Firefox browser display of the error message displayed when the XML document in `sampledata.xml` has a misspelled closing tag.

Well, we could send him a copy of our document, which he could study and whose tags and attributes he could try to replicate when he prepares his own document. That might even work for a simple document like ours, but for a larger and more complex XML data description, this approach would be iffy at best. We need a better way.

One such "better way" is to prepare a *Document Type Definition (DTD)*, which describes in unambiguous terms what a document such as ours is allowed to contain, and the form in which its contents must appear. Then we give this DTD to our researcher friend and it is up to him to make sure his document conforms to the specifications that it contains. In fact, he and anyone else using our tag set and our DTD can and should validate their XML documents against our DTD to ensure that they do in fact conform to the required specifications for such documents.

Thus a DTD is a collection of rules, called *declarations*, that describe the structure of a particular kind of XML document. That is, it specifies what elements and attributes are allowed to appear, the order in which they may appear, what elements are allowed to have which attributes, and so on.

The DTD is just one method you can use to specify how your XML document must be constructed. Another approach is to use an *XML schema*, which we will not discuss here, since at the time of this writing DTDs are more widely used and supported than XML schemas for this purpose. It is likely, however, that eventually XML schemas will replace DTDs, so you should at least be aware of them. For one thing, they are more powerful, more flexible, and more expressive when it comes to describing the kinds of data you can place in your XML documents. For another, DTD syntax is quite different from the syntax of XML itself so it cannot be processed by the same processor that is processing the XML. An XML schema, on the other hand, is itself written in XML, so both the schema and the XML it describes can be processed by the same processor.

The best way to get an initial feeling for what a DTD looks like and how it is used is to look at an example. **FIGURE 11.4** shows the file `ch11/sampledata_with_dtd.dtd`, which

```
1    <!-- sampledata_with_dtd.dtd -->
2    <!ELEMENT supplements (vitamin+)>
3    <!ELEMENT vitamin (name, price, helps_support, daily_requirement)>
4    <!ELEMENT name (#PCDATA)>
5    <!ELEMENT price (#PCDATA)>
6    <!ELEMENT helps_support (#PCDATA)>
7    <!ELEMENT daily_requirement (#PCDATA)>
8    <!ATTLIST vitamin product_id CDATA #REQUIRED>
```

FIGURE 11.4 ch11/sampledata_with_dtd.dtd
A simple DTD file for validating the file sampledata_with_dtd.xml.

contains a very simple DTD that could be used for the XML data in the ch11/sampledata.xml file of Figure 11.1. Just as CSS styles and JavaScript code can appear in an HTML document, so can a DTD appear in the same file as the XML data it describes. However, just as we have argued that placing CSS styles and JavaScript code in separate files is a good idea, we will make the same argument for keeping our DTD in a file separate from the XML code, and for pretty much the same reasons. For example, a separate DTD file can be referenced by many different XML files, provided they all need to conform to that particular DTD.

11.4.1 Connecting an XML Document to Its DTD: DOCTYPE Revisited

Before we study Figure 11.4 in detail, take a look at **FIGURE 11.5**, which shows the first few lines of the file ch11/sampledata_with_dtd.xml. This file has the same contents as ch11/sampledata.xml, except for the DOCTYPE declaration in line 3:

```
<!DOCTYPE supplements SYSTEM "sampledata_with_dtd.dtd">
```

Think back to the DOCTYPE declaration you have been seeing and using for some time in HTML5 document files. The DOCTYPE you see here is analogous. Note that the outermost element in the XML file is supplements, so the supplements tag now takes the place of the html tag in an HTML5 DOCTYPE declaration. The SYSTEM keyword indicates that the DTD for

```
1    <?xml version="1.0" encoding="ISO-8859-1"?>
2    <!-- sampledata_with_dtd.xml -->
3    <!DOCTYPE supplements SYSTEM "sampledata_with_dtd.dtd">
4    <supplements>
```

FIGURE 11.5 ch11/sampledata_with_dtd.xml (excerpt)
A file with the same contents as sampledata.xml, except for the DOCTYPE declaration in line 3, which links this file to its DTD.

this document is to be found on the local system, and (of course) the name of a DTD file (which in this case is located in the same directory as the XML file itself) needs to be specified. As we know, it is the DTD file that says what has to be in the XML document, and it is the one we now look at in more detail.

11.4.2 A Simple DTD Anatomy Lesson

Now let's take a closer look at what's in the DTD file shown in Figure 11.4.

The first line is a comment containing the name of the file, as usual. Note that comments in a DTD file are the same as those in an XML (or HTML) file.

The rest of the document contains information, using DTD syntax, to describe what an XML document must "look like" if it is to be a valid document according to this DTD. Each line consists of a *declaration* having the following form:

```
<!keyword additional_information>
```

Line 2 of the file is

```
<!ELEMENT supplements (vitamin+)>
```

which tells us that the highest-level element in our file must have a tag named `supplements`. The `(vitamin+)` part of the declaration tells us that there must be *at least one* element called `vitamin` nested within the supplements element (i.e., in the body of the `supplements` element). The + is thus used here as a numerical qualifier in much the same way as it is used in regular expressions. The * (for zero or more) and the ? (for zero or one) qualifiers may also be used.

Line 3 of the file is

```
<!ELEMENT vitamin (name, price, helps_support,
daily_requirement)>
```

which specifies that a `vitamin` element must, in turn, contain four nested elements—name, price, helps_support, and daily_requirement—and *they must be in the order listed*, because they appear in a comma-separated list.

Line 4 of the file is

```
<!ELEMENT name (#PCDATA)>
```

which specifies that the content (body) of a `name` element will be of type #PCDATA. This is `Parsable Character DATA`. You can think of such data as ordinary text that may (or may not) contain XML entities (such as &) that need to be "parsed" and replaced by their equivalent characters when the file is processed. Lines 5–7 are analogous to line 4.

Line 8 of the file is

```
<!ATTLIST vitamin product_id CDATA #REQUIRED>
```

and it specifies that the `vitamin` element *must* have (because of the `#REQUIRED`) an attribute called `product_id`, whose value will be of type `CDATA`.[1] Think of this kind of data as just ordinary text containing nothing that needs to be "parsed".

11.4.3 More DTD Anatomy

The simple DTD document analyzed in the previous section did not illustrate a great deal about DTDs. In this section we mention a few additional features that you may find useful in your own documents.

User-defined entities   In addition to the five predefined XML entities listed earlier, you can define your own by using the following syntax:

```
<!ENTITY va "Vitamin A">
```

This `ENTITY` declaration is similar to the `ELEMENT` and `ATTLIST` declarations discussed above. It defines the entity `va` so that if we have an XML document that uses the DTD in which this `ENTITY` declaration appears, everywhere we use the entity reference `&va;` it will be replaced by `Vitamin A`.

> *Moreover, when you use a DTD, the five predefined XML entities are no longer defined, so if you want to use one or more of them, you have to redefine them yourself in your DTD.*

Finally, if an entity's definition is not just a word or two but contains a lot of text, you may want to remove it from the main DTD document to reduce clutter. You can do this using the following syntax:

```
<!ENTITY name_of_entity SYSTEM "path/
file_containing_definition">
```

CDATA sections   Since any data of type `CDATA` is not parsed, it may contain metasymbols like < or &, which would otherwise have to appear as entities. Also, any entities that appear in a `CDATA` section will simply remain as themselves. Thus if you have some character data in your XML document that contains a lot of these kinds of items, it is convenient to be able to place this data in a `CDATA` section. Here is an example, which illustrates both the syntax and some typical content:

```
<![CDATA[
A section like this can contain things like << or >>, as well as
```

---

[1] If you are wondering why, for example, #PCDATA has a # at the beginning and CDATA does not, you are not alone. The # is a Reserved Name Indicator (RNI). Although XML does not have "reserved words" in the same sense as programming languages like Java or C++, it does have terms that are used in special ways, and it appears to be convention that some but not all of them are preceded by the # to ensure there is no ambiguity created by a developer deciding to use the same name for some other purpose. The bottom line: having a # in front of a term effectively makes the combination a keyword.

```
& if we wish to use it for "and". This is convenient, since we
don't have to use entities like &lt;, &gt; and &amp;.
]]>
```

Note that neither the nine-character opening delimiter <![CDATA[, nor the three-character closing delimiter]]>, has to be placed on a line by itself in the way we've done in the example, but doing so may enhance readability. In any case, neither delimiter may contain any blank spaces.

Other element data types   In addition to #PCDATA and CDATA data types, a DTD will let you specify EMPTY as a data type to indicate that an element does not contain any data (like an HTML img tag, for example). There is also an ANY data type, signifying that an element's content can be most anything. This is not very helpful, except perhaps during development as a placeholder until you have decided just what you want the content to be. If you want more comprehensive control over the permissible data types for your elements than can be provided by DTDs, you need to use an XML schema.

Other attribute data types   In addition to using the CDATA data type for an attribute value, XML provides a number of other choices. We mention only the ID type (an XML name to be used as a unique identifier) and the ENUMERATED type (a list of possible values for an attribute, with values in the list separated by a vertical bar rather than the usual comma or space).

Default attribute values   When giving an XML element an attribute, you can also give the attribute a value or specify some criterion that the value must satisfy. The general syntax of the ATTLIST declaration is

```
<!ATTLIST element-name
          attribute-name
          attribute-data-type
          attribute-default-value>
```

You have already seen #REQUIRED used in the attribute_default_value position to insist that the product_id attribute of the vitamin element must actually have a value (of type CDATA). There are other possibilities for the attribute_default_value as well. These include

```
#FIXED
```

which means that in every element having the attribute with this default value, the attribute will in fact have this value (which cannot be changed), as well as

```
#IMPLIED
```

which means that, in effect, no default value is specified, so the value may (or may not) be supplied in a given element. You can also simply supply a default value for an attribute without preceding it by a keyword like #FIXED. In this case, the supplied value is used unless another value is given in a particular element.

Numerical qualifiers   You have seen how vitamin+ was used to specify that at least one vitamin element (i.e., one or more) was the requirement for the content of a supplements element. Just as the + is used to mean one or more (required and repeatable), the * may be used to mean zero or more (optional and repeatable), and the ? may be used to mean zero or one (optional and *not* repeatable).

Fine-tuning your choices   A comma-separated, parentheses-enclosed list like (a, b, c) requires the sequence a, b, and c (in that order), while (a|b|c) simply requires a choice of a, b, or c.

Note that numerical qualifiers may be combined with the sequence and choice indicators to construct some reasonably complex descriptors, such as

```
<!ELEMENT person (parent+, spouse?, child*,
(brother|sister)*)>
```

which would be interpreted to mean that a person has one or more parents, possibly a spouse, zero or more children, and any number of brothers and/or sisters.

11.4.4 Do You Really Need a DTD for Your XML Document?

That depends. If your document is just a one-of-a-kind standalone document, maybe not. But if you are going to be creating several or a large number of similar documents, and especially if other people are going to be creating and using similar documents, then you should seriously consider having a DTD against which you and others can test all such documents to ensure that each one conforms to the same set of rules.

In any case, remember that to be useful your document must at the very least be well-formed, even if it has not been validated against a DTD.

11.4.5 Validating Your XML Document Against Your DTD, If You Have One

As we know, most any browser will recognize an XML file that is not well-formed and display an appropriate error. But that is a far cry from actually validating an XML document against its associated DTD, and at the time of this writing it seems that most browsers are not, by default, *validating parsers*. That is, they parse, but they don't validate.

At the time of this writing, you could validate your XML file against a DTD on the w3schools.com site, but only if it was an internal DTD and only if you were using Internet Explorer, but this limitation may no longer apply by the time you get to try it. See the **References** at the end of this chapter for links to validators.

11.5 Styling Our XML Data with CSS

When you load an HTML document into your browser, the browser has prior knowledge of all the HTML tags you've used and can display your document with all the headings, paragraphs, lists, and other items in their proper places and with their default styling. If we wish to change or enhance that styling, as we often do, we know that we can use CSS to do so.

On the other hand, when it comes to XML we have made up our own tags, so there is no way any browser can have prior knowledge of what those tags mean or how we would like to have their content displayed. That's why, by default, the browser simply shows a stylized display of the raw XML markup itself when asked to "display" an XML file.

However, it turns out that we can leverage our knowledge of CSS to help us display our XML data with our choice of fonts, colors, indentation, and other styling features, in much the same way as we did in the case of HTML. We now illustrate this by using a CSS file to provide the style for a display of our `ch11/sampledata.xml` file. To do so, we have yet another minimally modified version of this file in ch11/sampledata_with_css.xml, the first few lines of which are shown in **FIGURE 11.6**.

The CSS file itself is called `supplements.css` and is shown in **FIGURE 11.7**. You should by now be familiar with everything in this file. Note, however, that instead of styling HTML selectors like `h1` and `p`, we are now styling the element tags we have chosen for our own data.

The output of the data content of `ch11/sampledata_with_css.xml`, styled with the CSS in `ch11/supplements.css`, is shown in **FIGURE 11.8**.

11.6 Isolating Our XML Tag Sets within XML Namespaces

Many programming languages have the following problem: Two or more different developers working on the same project choose the same names for different things and when their work is combined they experience a *name clash*. Different languages solve the problem in different ways—Java with *packages* and C++ with *namespaces*, for example. Similar problems, if they occur in languages like JavaScript or PHP, may have to be solved "after the fact", since these languages do not provide elegant facilities for helping developers avoid the problem in the first place.

```
1    <?xml version="1.0" encoding="ISO-8859-1"?>
2    <!-- sampledata_with_css.xml -->
3    <?xml-stylesheet type="text/css" href="supplements.css"?>
4    <supplements>
```

FIGURE 11.6 ch11/sampledata_with_css.xml (excerpt)
A file with the same contents as `sampledata.xml`, except for the `xml-stylesheet` processing instruction in line 3, which links this file to its CSS file.

```
1   /*supplements.css*/
2
3   supplements {
4     background-color: #ffffff;
5     width: 100%;
6     font-family: Arial, sans-serif;
7   }
8
9   vitamin {
10    display: block;
11    margin-top: 10pt;
12    margin-left:0pt;
13  }
14
15  name {
16    background-color: green;
17    color: #FFFFFF;
18    font-size: 1.5em;
19    padding: 5pt;
20    margin-bottom:3pt;
21    margin-right:0;
22  }
23
24  price {
25    background-color: lime;
26    color: #000000;
27    font-size: 1.5em;
28    padding:5pt;
29    margin-bottom:3pt;
30    margin-left:0
31  }
32
33  helps_support {
34    display: block;
35    color: #000000;
36    font-size: 1.2em;
37    padding-top: 3pt;
38    margin-left: 20pt;
39  }
40
41  daily_requirement {
42    display: block;
43    color: #000000;
44    font-size: 1.2em;
45    margin-left: 20pt;
46  }
```

FIGURE 11.7 `ch11/supplements.css`
The CSS style file used to style the display of the data in `sampledata_with_css.xml`.

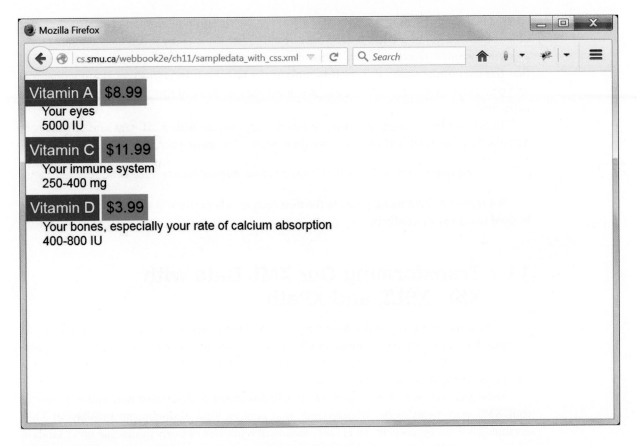

FIGURE 11.8 `graphics/ch11/displaySampledataWithCssXml.jpg`
A Firefox browser display of the XML document in `sampledata_with_css.xml` styled by the CSS in `supplements.css`.

The same sort of problem can happen with XML. Suppose some developer creating his own tag set decides to use one or more names that we have used in our tag set. Then a third developer decides he likes, and wants to use, both tag sets. Once again there will be a name clash, a problem of ambiguity that an XML parser will not be able to resolve on its own.

We can avoid this problem if each developer places his tag set in an *XML namespace*, which is just a particular collection of element and attribute names that has been assigned a name.

In the first part of this text we have been using HTML5, but if we had been using XHTML, our opening html tag would have looked like this:

```
<html xmlns="http://www.w3.org/1999/xhtml">
```

Here, `xmlns` is the *XML namespace attribute* and its value, `"http://www.w3.org/1999/xhtml"`, is the URL of an actual document that describes, among other things, the tags and attributes that can be used for XHTML. However, we should note immediately that the value of `xmlns` need *not* be a URL; it need only be a URI, which is to say it can have the same form as a URL without referring to an actual document. Making it a URI is one way of ensuring that the namespace name will itself be unique. In fact, even though there is a document at `http://www.w3.org/1999/xhtml`, it is better to think of this simply as a name for the namespace.

Thus if we had a large collection of health supplements with XML tags and attributes to describe them all, we might want to place them in an XML namespace, perhaps like this:

```
<supplements xmlns="http://cs.smu.ca/nature/source/supplements">
```

We say more about namespaces in the next section, where you will actually see how they can be used to help avoid conflicts.

11.7 Transforming Our XML Data with XSL, XSLT, and XPath

XSL is the acronym for *eXtensible Style Language,* and the moment you hear that you might suspect that XSL is an XML replacement for CSS. In a way, that may even be true. But XSL is capable of much more than styling the presentational aspects of your XML documents, though that is indeed one of the things it can be used for.

More generally, you should think of an XSL document as describing how you want one of your XML documents to be "transformed" into another kind of document, possibly an XML document but not necessarily. An HTML document is just one of many things that other kinds of documents could be.

Thus we have another acronym, *XSLT,* which stands for *XSL Transformation.* XSLT is more of a programming language[2] than a markup language, and its transformations (functions) are what convert our XML document from one form to another. We can think of an XSLT processor (and many browsers have this capability) as a "black box" taking two inputs and producing a single output, like this:

```
XSLT processor(XML file, XSLT file) => some_kind_of_output
```

Here, `some_kind_of_output` could be anything from plain ASCII text to HTML to another XML document of some kind. We illustrate the process with the HTML output shown in **FIGURE 11.9**, which is once again based on the same input from `ch11/sampledata.xml` that we have been using all along, but this time "transformed" by an appropriate XSLT.

---

[2] But not a language you might be used to, like Java or C++. It is more like a "functional" language such as LISP.

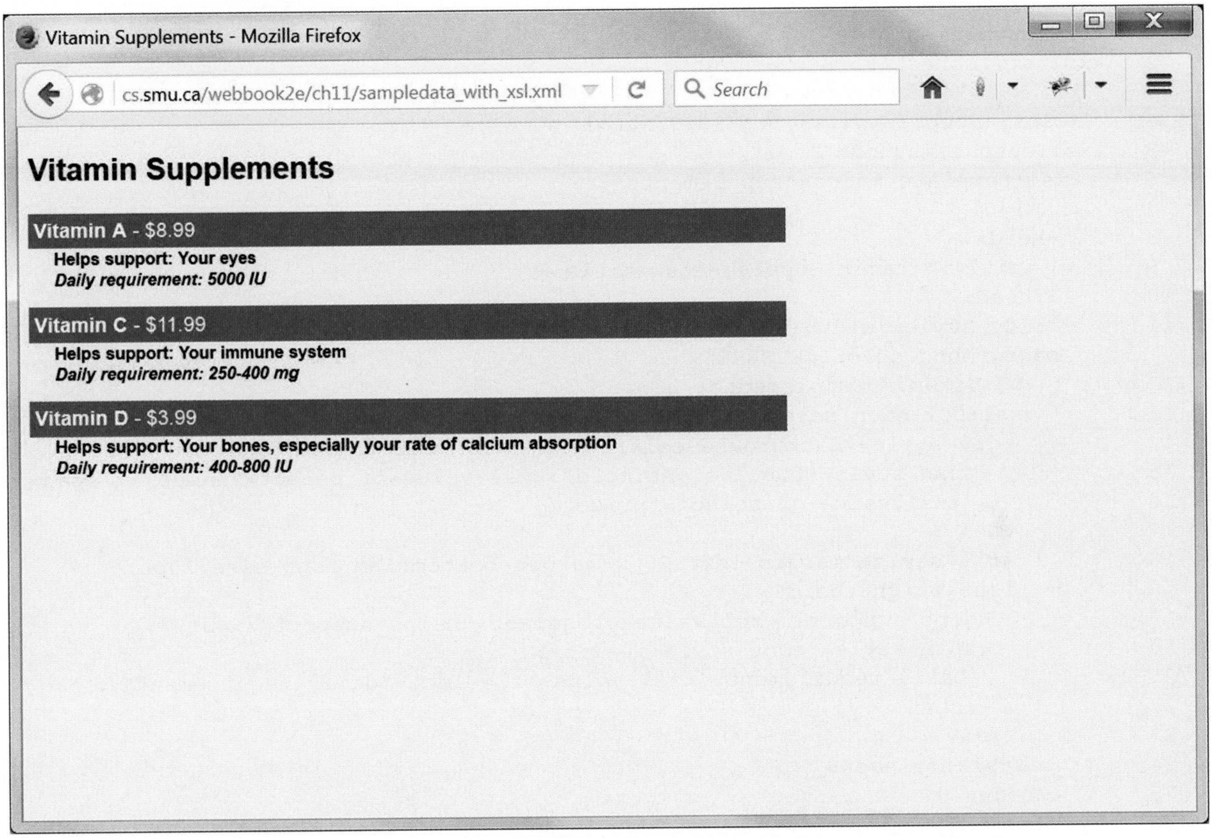

FIGURE 11.9 `graphics/ch11/displaySampledataWithXslXml.jpg`
A Firefox browser display of the XML document in `sampledata_with_xsl.xml`, styled by the XSLT in
`supplements.xsl`.

More specifically, as you can see from **FIGURE 11.10**, we have yet another minimally modified version of the original `ch11/sampledata.xml` file in `ch11/sampledata_with_xsl.xml`. The only change we have made in the original file this time is to associate it with the `ch11/supplements.xsl` file containing our XSLT code, which is shown in **FIGURE 11.11**.

```
1    <?xml version="1.0" encoding="ISO-8859-1"?>
2    <!-- sampledata_with_xsl.xml -->
3    <?xml-stylesheet type="text/xsl" href="supplements.xsl"?>
4    <supplements>
```

FIGURE 11.10 `ch11/sampledata_with_xsl.xml (excerpt)`
A file with the same contents as `sampledata.xml`, except for the `xml-stylesheet` declaration in line 3,
which links this file to `supplements.xsl`.

```
1   <!-- supplements.xsl -->
2   <xsl:stylesheet version="1.0"
3     xmlns:xsl="http://www.w3.org/1999/XSL/Transform"
4     xmlns="http://www.w3.org/1999/xhtml">
5   <xsl:output method="html"/>
6     <xsl:template match="supplements">
7     <html>
8       <head>
9         <title>Vitamin Supplements</title>
10      </head>
11      <body style="width:600px;font-family:Arial;font-size:12pt;
        background-color:#EEEEEE">
12        <h2>Vitamin Supplements</h2>
13        <xsl:for-each select="vitamin">
14          <div style="background-color:teal;color:white;padding:4px">
15            <span style="font-weight:bold"><xsl:value-of select="name"/></span>
16            - <xsl:value-of select="price"/>
17          </div>
18          <div style="margin-left:20px;margin-bottom:1em;font-size:10pt;
            font-weight:bold">
19            Helps support: <xsl:value-of select="helps_support"/><br />
20            <span style="font-style:italic">
21              Daily requirement: <xsl:value-of select="daily_requirement"/>
22            </span>
23          </div>
24        </xsl:for-each>
25      </body>
26    </html>
27    </xsl:template>
28  </xsl:stylesheet>
```

FIGURE 11.11 ch11/supplements.xsl
The XSLT file used to style sampledata_with_xsl.xml.

11.7.1 How Does XSLT Compare with CSS for Styling?

The simple answer to this question is this: XSLT is much more powerful than CSS and gives you more control over the appearance of your document. However, at the time of this writing CSS is better supported by the most commonly used browsers.

For a simple example of the kind of problem one faces, consider this. CSS can essentially be used only for styling what appears as content in the elements of your XML document. Even if you want to do something as simple as add a label to that content, you cannot do this using CSS.

Perhaps "cannot" is a bit harsh, but the "generated content" feature of CSS that would allow you to do this is so poorly or infrequently implemented in today's browsers that trying to use it in a production-level website would be more of a gamble than most web developers would be willing to take.

The really bizarre thing is that *XSL-FO (XSL-Formatting Objects)*—the part of XSL that would take over from CSS if the browser folks would just implement it—is in fact in even worse shape across today's browsers than CSS itself, so when you look at files with a .xsl extension, you will still see CSS mixed in with the HTML among the XSLT code. Oh, well . . .

11.7.2 Our Example in Detail: How Does XSLT Use XML Namespaces and XPath to Do Its Job?

Note first that in the file shown in Figure 11.11 we can place a comment containing the name of the file as the first line, since this is not, strictly speaking, an XML file, but an XSL (or XSLT) file.

Second, note that the file contains an xsl::stylesheet element as its highest-level container, and the opening tag for this element contains two xmlns attributes. The URI value of the first one is

    http://www.w3.org/1999/XSL/Transform

and the xsl suffix that is appended to this xmlns, and separated from it by a colon (:), provides us with a shorthand way of referring to anything that we use in the file and that lives in that namespace (xsl:output, xsl:template, xsl:for-each, xsl:value-of). In fact, such a shorthand, provided it is unique in the current context, ensures that any names in this namespace do not conflict with the names in any other namespace we may be using.

The (empty) xsl:output element (line 5) with its method attribute value of html simply indicates that the output from the XSLT in this particular file should be HTML markup (for display in a browser, for example).

The xsl:template element (lines 6–27) with its match attribute value of supplements indicates that the processor should look for an element called supplements and then process that element according to the "instructions" in the body of the xsl:template element. Actually, it's a little more involved than we've let on. The value of the match attribute (supplements, in this case) is actually part of an *XPath path*, which starts at the root of the document (represented by /, so XPath paths tend to look a lot like regular paths on many systems, particularly Unix-like systems). Thus we can think of supplements as short for /supplements, and the same goes for values of the select attribute that appears several times later on in the file.

Now, the "processing" that goes on in the body of this template involves the output of some HTML to set up our web page, followed by the "execution" of the XSLT looping construct xsl:for-each (lines 15–24), which loops over each of the vitamin elements in the ch11/sampledata_with_xsl.xml file. On each iteration, this loop sets up a new vitamin for display by adding some text of its own, extracting the corresponding content of the nested elements within each vitamin element using the xsl:value-of function, and styling the result with CSS.

Thus you see a simple XML data file "transformed" by XSLT into an HTML file, ready for browser display. It should be clear from what you see here that many other kinds of transformations may be possible, depending on what other functions like xsl:for-each and `xsl:value-of` are provided by XSLT. Of course, there are many other such functions, so many other kinds of transformations are in fact possible.

Summary

The XML is a metalanguage that has a variety of uses. One of those uses is the "rewriting" of HTML as XHTML. In this chapter we have seen how it can be used to describe virtually any kind of data with which our business may wish to deal.

XML has only a few rules that must be followed, but what rules it does have must be followed very strictly, or your XML markup will not be processed by any XML processor. As was the case with XHTML, tags must be capitalized consistently and nested properly, all tags except empty tags must have a closing tag, and all tag attributes must have a value that is enclosed in quotation marks.

Any XML document that follows these simple syntax rules is said to be well-formed. We may also create a Document Type Definition (DTD) that describes the structure of an XML document in terms of what tags and attributes it must or may contain and where they may be placed and what kind of content the elements may have. We may then validate an XML document against such a DTD, which is one way of ensuring that the structure of all XML documents describing a particular kind of data is consistent. A DTD may be *internal* (within the document it is describing) or *external* (in a separate file), but an external DTD is much more useful since it may be linked to an unlimited number of XML documents.

CSS may be used to style your XML data in much the same way it was used to style (or alter the styling of) your HTML documents. XSLT code may be used to transform your XML documents into other kinds of documents, such as plain text, HTML, or alternate XML formats.

Quick Questions to Test Your Basic Knowledge

1. If you already know XHTML (or even HTML5), you will probably feel right at home with XML. How would you explain this statement?
2. What are the five entities (special characters) in XML?
3. What does the acronym DTD stand for, and what exactly is a DTD?
4. What is the difference between a well-formed XML document and a valid XML document?
5. What is the syntax of a typical `DOCTYPE` declaration you would find in an XML document if its DTD is located in the same directory as the XML document itself?

6. What is the major difference between a CSS file used to style one of your HTML documents and one used to style one of your XML documents?

7. How do you connect an XML file with a CSS file containing the styles that are being used to style the data in the XML file?

8. What is the difference in the placement of the file-naming comment in an XML file compared to a file containing XSLT code?

9. How do you connect an XML file with a file containing the XSLT code that will be used to transform the XML markup in the XML file, and what extension is used, by convention, for such a file?

10. What does an XPath path resemble?

11. What does the `xsl:for-each` function do?

12. What does the `xsl:value-of` function do?

Short Exercises to Improve Your Basic Understanding

1. Load the file `ch11/sampledata.xml` into several different browsers to see how each one deals with an XML file in "raw" form. In some cases you may have to choose the browser's **View Source** option to actually see the XML markup.

2. Introduce several XML syntax errors, but only one at a time, into the `ch11/sampledata.xml` file and try to load the file into one or more browsers after the error is in place. In each case the browser should give you a reasonably helpful message about what is wrong. Be sure to correct each error before introducing the next one. Finally, introduce several errors at once after having introduced each one individually, load the file into a browser, and then remove the errors one at a time until the file displays properly again.

3. Validate the XML file `ch11/sampledata_with_dtd.xml` against the DTD in the DTD file `ch11/sampledata_with_dtd.dtd` to confirm that it does in fact validate. Then make a change in the XML file that will cause the validation to fail. Revalidate to confirm that it does in fact fail.

4. In line 19 of the file `ch11/sampledata.xml`, replace the comma and space after the word *bones* with the XML entity `&amp;` and reload the file into your browser to show that the entity is replaced with the & symbol. Make the same replacement in line 20 of the file `ch11/sampledata_with_dtd.xml` and then load this file into the browser to confirm that you get an error, showing that the predefined XML entities are no longer in effect when you use a DTD. Put the entity definition necessary to correct the problem into the DTD file and reload the XML file to confirm that the problem has been corrected.

5. In line 20 of the file `ch11/sampledata_with_dtd.xml`, replace the comma and space after the word *bones*, as well as the word *especially*, with the XML entity `&ae;` and reload the file into your browser to show that an error is generated because this entity is unknown to the XML processor in the browser. Then put a declaration in the DTD file `ch11/sampledata_with_dtd.dtd` that defines this entity to be the string "and especially". Now reload the file `ch11/sampledata_with_dtd.xml` again to show that the entity is now replaced with the content of the definition you gave it.

 # Exercises on the Parallel Project

1. Choose at least 10 of the products and/or services of your business, and then choose some XML element tags and attributes that will describe these items adequately.
2. Create an XML file that contains full descriptions of each of the items, using the XML tags and attributes you chose in the previous exercise. Make sure that your file is well-formed.
3. Create a corresponding DTD file and place an appropriate `DOCTYPE` declaration for this DTD in your XML file.
4. Create a CSS style file that contains styles for displaying each of your items. Place these styles in a separate style file and place a corresponding stylesheet link in your XML file.
5. Check your XML file to make sure it is well-formed and then validate it against your DTD file to make sure it passes that test.
6. Finally, display your XML file in several browsers to confirm that your CSS styles are also performing as they should on your data.

What Else You May Want or Need to Know

1. XML is a W3C standard. The first version, XML 1.0, was published in February 1998. The second, XML 1.1, was published in 2004, but as of this writing is still not widely supported.
2. If you are planning to create a set of XML tags to describe some of your own data, it might be a good idea to see if you can save yourself some trouble. Do a Google search using a string like "XML tag sets your_subject_keywords" to see what turns up.
3. In this chapter we have only discussed external DTDs, which are DTDs located in files separate from the XML files they describe. This is similar to the CSS files and JavaScript files that we separated from our HTML files in earlier chapters; we make the separation here for the same kinds of reasons. However, as with CSS and JavaScript files, we can have an *internal DTD* as well. That is, we can place our DTD right in the document it

describes. If you do this, you must place the entire DTD in the `DOCTYPE` declaration of the XML file, using the following syntax:

```
<!DOCTYPE highest_level_tag_name
[
... DTD content...
]>
```

In this context of internal and external DTDs we should mention the (optional) `stand-alone` attribute of the `xml` tag that appears in the `xml` declaration that opens every XML file. In particular we should note that the `standalone` attribute has two possible values, `yes` and `no`, the default is `no`, and also:

a. If the value is `yes`, the document should not depend on any external DTD, though it may (or may not) have an internal DTD.

b. If the value is `no`, the document may or may not actually depend on an external DTD, but if it does it must have a `DOCTYPE` declaration specifying the location of that DTD.

4. Just another quick reminder here. As we mentioned earlier in this chapter, the DTD is only one way of describing how your XML documents should be constructed. A major drawback of a DTD is that it is not itself an XML document. That is why using an XML schema for this purpose provides a more consistent approach, and in that case both an XML document and the XML schema describing it can be processed by the same parser. DTDs are simpler, but if you wish to pursue XML seriously, you will need to learn something about XML schemas. Alternatively, you may wish to investigate something called *RELAX NG* (*REgular LAnguage for XML Next Generation*), which is a schema that specifies a pattern for the structure and content of an XML document but which, compared to other popular schema languages, is relatively simple.

5. We mentioned earlier in this chapter that whitespace is "significant" in XML, but just what that means "depends on the situation", so let's say a bit more about this now. First, note that in XML whitespace consists of the blank space, the carriage return, the line feed, and the tab, as well as any combination of them.

    The essential thing to remember is that an XML parser should send all whitespace in an XML file through to any application (such as a browser) that is going to process that file, and leave it up to the application to deal with the whitespace in whatever way the application deems appropriate.

    Thus, for example, an application processing XML may choose to treat

```
<name>Vitamin A</name>
```

the same as

```
<name>
Vitamin A
</name>
```

or not, but an XML parser should send any spaces in front of Vitamin A in the second version through to that application and let it decide what to do with them.

6. Just like there was an HTML DOM whose nodes and other properties could be accessed and manipulated by JavaScript, there is also an XML DOM that is subject to the same access and manipulation by JavaScript.

7. If you have XML data that you wish to manipulate in any way, and if you are already using PHP, then you may want to investigate PHP libraries such as **SimpleXML**, which is a PHP extension that permits easy processing of XML data in various ways. You will need to have version 5 or later of PHP to use this particular library. You can, of course, process XML by "rolling your own" PHP code to do whatever you like, but a package like **SimpleXML** is quite likely to have built-in facilities to perform the most common operations that you would normally require, so using it instead would probably save you both development time and debugging agony.

References

1. The W3Schools site has a section on XML. Start here:

   ```
   http://www.w3schools.com/xml/default.asp
   ```

2. One very good XML editor that you can pay for, but which also has a free version, is **Exchanger XML Lite**. If you plan to do a lot of XML editing, you might do well to check out this program at the following site:

   ```
   http://www.freexmleditor.com/
   ```

3. A simple XML editor called XML Notepad 2007 is available from this Microsoft site:

   ```
   https://www.microsoft.com/en-ca/download/details.aspx?id=7973
   ```

4. The sites listed below provide some additional XML editor choices. The Altova XML Spy option is not free, but comes highly recommended by the folks at W3Schools:

   ```
   http://free.editix.com/
   ```

   ```
   http://www.firstobject.com/dn_editor.htm
   ```

   ```
   http://www.altova.com/simpledownload1.html
   ```

5. To check out the XML standard itself, start here:

   ```
   http://www.w3.org/XML/
   ```

6. For information on the standard for XML namespaces, look here:

   `http://www.w3.org/TR/REC-xml-names`

7. Here is where you will find the standard for eXtensible Stylesheet Transformations:

   `http://www.w3.org/TR/xslt`

8. The standard for XPath is here:

   `http://www.w3.org/TR/xpath`

9. Here are two links to XML validators:

   `http://www.xmlvalidation.com/`

   `http://www.w3schools.com/xml/xml_validator.asp`

10. Many programming languages, including PHP, have special facilities for dealing with XML. For example, see the following:

    `http://php.net/manual/en/book.xml.php`

11. Here are the home page link, a tutorial link, and the Wikipedia link for RELAX NG:

    `http://relaxng.org/`

    `http://relaxng.org/tutorial-20011203.html`

    `http://en.wikipedia.org/wiki/RELAX_NG`

CHAPTER **TWELVE**

Collecting, Analyzing, and Using Visitor Data

CHAPTER CONTENTS

Overview and Objectives

The information age is gradually causing the accumulation of vast quantities of data in various repositories large and small around the world. Extracting useful information from such mountains of data is sometimes referred to as *data mining*.

Web-based businesses generate even larger quantities of information than do regular businesses. A physical store may record purchases by a customer, but it does not record the customer's browsing experience. A web-based store, on the other hand, can record not only the items purchased, but also the sequential order in which the customer visited various departments and looked at different products. Such a store can also keep a record of items that a customer put in his or her shopping cart and later chose not to buy. Information like this can be used to increase sales by analyzing the causes of aborted purchases.

This challenging area is termed *web mining*—data mining applied to web-data repositories (Ramadhan et al., 2005). Web mining may be subdivided into three areas (Cooley et al., 1997 and Akerkar and Lingras, 2007):

> ▶ *Web-content mining*, which deals with primary data on the web, meaning the actual content of web documents.

> ▶ *Web-structure mining*, which is concerned with the "topology" of the web, focusing on data that organizes the content and facilitates navigation. The principal source of information in web-structure mining is the hyperlinks that connect one page to another.

> ▶ *Web-usage mining*, which does not deal with the contents of web documents, but instead has the goal of determining how a website's visitors use web resources and the study of their navigational patterns. The data used for web-usage mining is essentially secondary, and is generated by users' interactions with the web. The data sources include web-server access logs, proxy-server logs, browser logs, user profiles, registration data, user sessions and transactions, cookies, user queries, bookmark data, mouse clicks, and scrolls (Kosala and Blockeel, 2000).

Akerkar and Lingras (2007), in their book entitled *Building an Intelligent Web: Theory and Practice*, provide a detailed introduction to web mining. This chapter contains excerpts from that book that pertain to the analysis of web-server access logs, an initial step in web-usage mining, and we discuss the following topics:

> ▶ Web-server access logs and their formats, including an Apache web-server example

▶ Analysis of web-server access logs, including summarization with Analog, clickstream analysis with Pathalizer, and visualization of individual user sessions with StatViz

▶ Some cautions to keep in mind when interpreting web-server access logs

12.1 Web-Server Access Logs

A *web-server access log*, also referred to simply as a "server log", "web log", or "access log", is generally defined as a set of files containing the details of an activity performed by a server (Wikipedia, 2006). Usually these files are automatically created and maintained by the server. The activity of a web server mainly consists of servicing the page requests; therefore, one of the important logs maintained by a web server is the history of page requests.

The World Wide Web Consortium (W3C) has specified a standard format for web-server access log files. In addition to this format specified by the W3C, there are other proprietary formats for web logs. Most of them contain information about each request, such as:

▶ The IP address of the client making the request
▶ The date and time of the request
▶ The URL of the requested page
▶ The number of bytes sent to serve the request
▶ The user agent (the program that is acting on behalf of the user, such as a web browser or web crawler)
▶ The referrer (the URL that triggered the request)

Server logs typically do not collect user-specific information. The logs of activities of a web server can all be stored in one file; however, a better alternative is to separate the log into different categories such as an access log, an error log, and a referrer log. An access log typically grows by more than 1MB for every 10,000 requests (Apache, 2006). This means that even on a moderately busy server, these log files tend to be fairly large. Consequently, it is usually necessary to periodically rotate the log files by moving or deleting the existing logs.

Depending on the duration of an analysis, it may be necessary to use data from multiple log files. On most servers, the log files are not accessible to general Internet users. Only web-server administrators and system administrators have the necessary permissions to read, modify, and delete the log files. In some cases, users with an account on the system that hosts the web server may be able to read the access logs. These server logs contain a wealth of information that can be statistically analyzed to reveal potentially useful traffic patterns based on the time of day or day of the week.

This information can be useful for planning system maintenance and load balancing. System maintenance could be scheduled during times when the server is less in demand. Similarly, elective computing jobs and network traffic emanating from the server could also be suspended during peak times.

In addition, looking at traffic patterns based on referrer and user agents can be useful for developing web strategies. For example, the look and feel of a website could be made more consistent with frequent referrer sites, and more visible links may also be placed on the referrer sites to further facilitate navigation.

Furthermore, knowledge of the most frequent user agents could be helpful in optimizing the site for that user agent. For example, if most users are using Firefox, the web developers should ensure that their web pages are properly displayed in Firefox.

Thus analysis of web logs can facilitate efficient website administration, scheduling of adequate hosting resources, and the fine-tuning of sales efforts.

A wide variety of tools are available for analyzing web logs. It is important for marketing personnel from organizations that facilitate business through their websites to understand these powerful tools. In this chapter we will discuss how three of these tools—Analog, Pathalizer, and StatViz—work, and also look at the theoretical basis for them.

12.1.1 Format of Web-Server Access Logs

The common log format of records in web-server access log files is supported by most web servers. Similarly, a majority of log analyzers are designed to work with the common log-file format. TABLE 12.1 shows the general format of a common log file described on the W3C website. The following are examples of entries in the common log format:

```
140.14.6.11 - pawan [06/Sep/2001:10:46:07 -0300] "GET
/s.htm HTTP/1.0" 200 2267
140.14.7.18 - raj [06/Sep/2001:11:23.53 -0300] "POST
/s.cgi HTTP/1.0" 200 499
```

TABLE 12.1 Common log format.

Format:	remotehost rfc1413 authuser [date] "request" status bytes
remotehost	remote hostname (or IP number if DNS hostname is not available or if DNSLookup is off)
rfc1413	remote logname of the user
authuser	username the user has used to authenticate himself
[date]	date and time of the request
"request"	request line exactly as it came from the client
status	HTTP status code returned to the client
bytes	content length of the document transferred

See http://www.w3.org/Daemon/User/Config/Logging.html#common-logfile-format.

The first entry is a GET request that retrieves a file named s.htm. The second entry is a POST request that sends data to a program called s.cgi.

We'll describe each field of the first request:

1. The first field tells you that the request came from a computer (client machine) identified with the IP address of 140.14.6.11.
2. The dash (–) for the second field tells you that the information for that field is unavailable. In this case, the missing information is the RFC 1413 identity of the client, which is determined by a program (daemon) called identd running on the client's machine. This information is highly unreliable and should almost never be used except on tightly controlled internal networks (Apache, 2006).
3. The third field tells you that the name or ID of the user is pawan. This ID is determined by HTTP authentication for documents that are password protected. This entry will be a dash (–) for documents that are not password protected.
4. The fourth entry provides the time of the request as [06/Sep/2001:10:46:07 -0300]. The first part of the time is rather obvious. The request came just after 10:46 a.m. on September 6, 2001. The –0300 tells you that the time zone is three hours behind Greenwich Mean Time (GMT), which in this case makes it Atlantic Canadian Daylight Saving Time.
5. The fifth field, given by "GET /s.htm HTTP/1.0", lists the request from the user. In this case, the request is to GET the document s.htm using the protocol HTTP/1.0.
6. The sixth field is the status code sent back to the user by the server. Codes beginning with 2 mean that the request resulted in a successful response. In our example, the code is 200, which means the request was successfully served. The codes that start with 3 tell you that the request was redirected to another server. If the user makes an erroneous request (for example, requesting a nonexistent page), codes beginning in 4 will be returned to the user. Finally, an error in the server leads to codes starting with 5.
7. The seventh and last field in the request indicates that 2,267 bytes were transferred as a result of the request.

12.1.2 An Extended Log-File Format

While the common log format is standard, and supported by all servers, information contained in these records is fixed and rather limited. Many web-server administrators find it necessary to record more information, which has created a need for an extended log-file format. However, due to legislation related to the protection of websites, certain servers may want to omit certain data that may directly or indirectly make it possible to identify users. In addition, servers may need to change the field separator character if the standard field separator occurs in their fields. The extended log-file format is designed to overcome some of the shortcomings of the common log format by providing the following features (Hallam-Baker and Behlendorf, 1996):

▶ Permit control over the data recorded
▶ Support the needs of proxies, clients, and servers in a common format
▶ Provide robust handling of character-escaping issues

▶   Allow exchange of demographic data
▶   Allow summary data to be expressed

The extended log-file format makes it possible to customize log files. Because the format of log files may vary from server to server, a header specifies the data types of each field at the start of the file. The format is readable by generic log-analysis tools, which we will discuss later in this chapter.

Hallam-Baker and Behlendorf (1996) describe the format of the extended log file in great detail. The following is a summary of their specifications.

An extended log file consists of a sequence of lines, each containing either a directive or an entry. **FIGURE 12.1** shows a simple example of an extended log file reproduced from Hallam-Baker and Behlendorf (1996). The lines starting with a hash mark (#) are directives, while the rest are entries.

Directives record information about the logging process itself. The type of a directive starts with a hash mark (#) and is followed by the name of the directive. Types are shown in **TABLE 12.2**.

The directives #Version and #Fields are mandatory and must appear before all the entries. Other directives are optional. The #Fields directive specifies the data recorded in the fields of

```
#Version: 1.0
#Date: 12-Jan-1996
#Fields: time cs-method cs-uri
00:34:23 GET /foo/bar.html
12:21:16 GET /foo/bar.html
12:45:52 GET /foo/bar.html
12:57:34 GET /foo/bar.html
```

FIGURE 12.1 An example of a log file in extended format
(Hallam-Baker and Behlendorf, 1996).

TABLE 12.2 Directive types in the extended log-file format.

#Version:	version of the extended log-file format used
#Fields:	fields recorded in the log
#Software:	software that generated the log
#Start-Date:	date and time at which the log was started
#End-Date:	date and time at which the log was finished
#Date:	date and time at which the entry was added
#Remark:	comments that are ignored by analysis tools

each entry by providing the list of fields. Each field in the `#Fields` directive can be specified in one of the following ways:

▶ By an identifier; for example, `time`.

▶ By an identifier with a prefix separated by a hyphen; for example, the method in the request sent by the client to the server is specified as `cs-method`.

▶ By a prefix followed by a header in parentheses; for example, the content type of the reply from the server to the client is given by `sc(Content-type)`.

TABLE 12.3 shows possible identifier prefixes and TABLE 12.4 shows the identifiers that must be used with a prefix, while TABLE 12.5 shows a list of identifiers that do not take a prefix.

TABLE 12.3 Identifier prefixes for use in the extended log-file format.

`cs`	client to server
`sc`	server to client
`sr`	server to remote server (this prefix is used by proxies)
`rs`	remote server to server (this prefix is used by proxies)
`x`	application-specific identifier

TABLE 12.4 Identifiers that must be used with a prefix in the extended log-file format.

`ip`	IP address and port
`dns`	DNS name
`status`	status code
`comment`	comment returned with status code
`method`	method
`uri`	URI
`uri-stem`	stem portion alone of URI (omitting query)
`uri-query`	query portion alone of URI
`host`	DNS hostname used

TABLE 12.5 Identifiers without prefixes for use in the extended log-file format.	
date	date at which transaction was completed
time	time at which transaction was completed
bytes	bytes transferred
cached	records whether a cache hit occurred (1 means a cache hit and 0 indicates a cache miss)

The entries in a log file consist of a sequence of fields as specified in the #Fields directive corresponding to a single HTTP transaction. Fields are separated by whitespace, usually a TAB character. If information for a field is either unavailable or not applicable for a given transaction, a dash (-) is used.

12.1.3 An Example: Apache Web-Server Access Log Entries

In the previous section you looked at the generic description of web-access log formats. Different web servers will have their own peculiarities in logging HTTP requests. In this section, you will look at the web-logging process employed by Apache, one of the most popular web servers. See the **References** section for a link to more detailed information.

For the Apache server, the LogFormat directive is used to specify the selection of fields in each entry. The format is specified using a string that is styled after the printf format strings in the C programming language. For example, the common log format entry

```
140.14.6.11 - pawan [06/Sep/2001:10:46:07 -0300] "GET
/s.htm HTTP/1.0" 200 2267
```

discussed earlier can be represented using the following LogFile directive:

```
LogFormat "\%h \%l \%u \%t \"\%r\" \%>s \%b" common
```

This directive defines the format of the log and associates it with the nickname "common". The format string consists of "percent directives", each of which tells the server to log a particular piece of information. Literal characters in the format string will be copied directly into the log output. If you want the quote character (") to appear as a literal, it must be escaped by placing a backslash before it, so that it is not interpreted as the end of the format string. The format string may also contain the special control characters \n for the newline character and \t for a TAB. **TABLE 12.6** gives the meaning of the various format parameters.

TABLE 12.6 Parameters in the Apache common log-format example.	
%h	IP address of the client (remote host)
%l	RFC 1413 identity of the client
%u	user ID of the person requesting the document
%t	time when server finished processing the request
\"%r\"	request line from the client is given in double quotes
%>s	status code that the server sent to the client
%b	number of bytes returned to the client

Here the time is in the following format:

```
[day/month/year:hour:minute:second zone]
day = 2*digit
month = 3*letter
year = 4*digit
hour = 2*digit
minute = 2*digit
second = 2*digit
zone = (+ | -) 4*digit
```

An example of another commonly used format, the combined log format, is

```
140.14.6.11 - pawan [06/Sep/2001:10:46:07 -0300] "GET
/s.htm HTTP/1.0" 200 2267
"http://cs.smu.ca/csc/" "Mozilla/4.0 (compatible; MSIE
5.5; Windows NT 5.0)"
```

for which the corresponding format string is

```
LogFormat "%h %l %u %t \"%r\" %>s %b \"%{Referer}i\"
\"%{User-agent}i\" " combined
```

which has the two additional fields shown in **TABLE 12.7**.

TABLE 12.7 Additional fields in the combined log format.	
\"%{Referer}i\"	site that the client was referred from, enclosed in quotes
\"%{User-agent}i\"	software that made the request, enclosed in quotes

In this example, the referrer is `http://cs.smu.ca/csc/`, and it has a link to the file `s.htm`. The software that was used for the request was `Mozilla/4.0 (compatible; MSIE 5.5; Windows NT 5.0)`, which is, in fact, the web browser Microsoft Internet Explorer 5.5 for Windows NT 5.0.

The server configuration also specifies the location of the log file using the `CustomLog` directive. The path for the access log file is assumed to start from the server root unless it begins with a slash. For example, the directive `CustomLog logs/access_log combined` will store logs, in the combined log format, in a file called `access_log` in the subdirectory `logs` under the server root.

Apache (2006) cautions server administrators about the large sizes of access-log files, even on a moderately busy server. As we mentioned before, such a file typically grows by 100 bytes per request; therefore, it is periodically necessary to rotate the log files by moving or deleting the existing logs.

12.2 Analysis of Web-Server Access Logs

The formatting information about web-server access logs in the previous section can be used to write programs to analyze web usage for your website, as well as for running data-mining tools. However, prior to applying data-mining techniques, it is necessary to understand the data set. This is typically done by creating multiple summary reports and, if possible, using visual representations.

Before writing your own software for analyzing web-server access logs, you may want to consider one of the analysis tools already available. One or more of these tools may provide answers to most of your questions regarding usage of your website. **FIGURE 12.2** tabulates a large number of freeware and open-source web-access analysis tools listed on the Open Directory Project site `http://www.dmoz.org/`. In addition to the freeware and open-source tools, you can also find a listing of commercial tools on that site. In this section, we discuss how to obtain summary reports as well as visualization of aggregate clickstream and individual user sessions from web-server access logs.

12.2.1 Summarization of Web-Server Access Logs Using Analog

One of the more popular tools for analyzing web-server access log files is called **Analog** (`http://www.analog.cx`). This software is available for free and includes full C source code as well as executables for the Windows and Mac platforms. You should, in fact, be able to compile it for almost any operating system. The website for Analog also has links to precompiled versions for a variety of other operating systems. The developers claim that it is designed to be fast and to produce accurate and attractive statistics. You can also combine Analog with **Report Magic** (`http://www.reportmagic.org`) for better graphical analysis.

Analog	www.analog.cx
BBClone	bbclone.de
The Big Brother Log Analyzer	bbla.sourceforge.net
Dailystats	www.perlfect.com/freescripts/dailystats
HitsLog Script	www.irnis.net/soft/hitslog
Http-Analyze	www.http-analyze.org
Kraken Reports	www.krakenreports.com
phpOpenTracker	www.phpopentracker.de
PowerPhlogger	pphlogger.phpee.com
Relax	ktmatu.com/software/relax
Report Magic for Analog	www.reportmagic.com
RobotStats	www.robotstats.com/en
Sherlog	sherlog.europeanservers.net
WebLog	awsd.com/scripts/weblog
Webtrax Help	www.multicians.org/thvv/webtrax-help.html
W3Perl	www.w3perl.com/softs
ZoomStats	zoomstats.sourceforge.net

FIGURE 12.2 Web access log analyzers
(http://dmoz.org/Computers/Software/Internet/Site_Management/Log_Analysis/
Freeware_and_Open_Source/)

Getting and Installing Analog

Although Analog is free software, its distribution and modification are covered by the terms of the GNU General Public License. You are not required to accept this license, but nothing else gives you permission to modify or distribute the program (Turner, 2006).

The zipped version of Analog 6.0 for Windows can be downloaded from the Analog site. To follow along, create a folder on your hard drive called ch12 and copy the downloaded zip file to that location. If you right-click on the zip file and choose **Extract All**, you will be able to access all the files. This should create a folder called `analog_60w32`. Double-clicking on that folder will take you to another folder called `analog 6.0`, which has the Analog 6.0 package for Windows. The `docs` subfolder has all the documentation for the package. The best place to start is the `Readme.html` file, which can be opened using your web browser. Now we'll provide a summary of the essentials of this documentation, and a brief tutorial.

Getting Input for Analog

In section 12.1 we discussed the format and location of log files for the Apache web server. If you cannot easily locate these log files for your web server, you may wish to contact your administrator. In order to run Analog, you need read access to these log files. The Analog package comes with a small log file called `logfile.log` with 50 HTTP requests. The file is located in the Analog 6.0 folder but is too small for us to explore the real power of this analysis tool. Hence, we have included another log file from an educational site.

The data we will study was obtained from the web-server access logs of an introductory first-year course in computing science at Saint Mary's University in Halifax, Nova Scotia, over a 16-week period. The initial number of students in the course was 180. That number fell over the course of the semester to 130–140 students. Certain areas of the website were protected, and users could access them using only their IDs and passwords. The activities in the restricted parts of the website consisted of submitting a user profile, changing a password, submitting assignments, viewing the submissions, accessing the discussion board, and viewing current class marks. The rest of the website was public and contained course information, a lab manual, class notes, class assignments, and lab assignments.

If users accessed only the public portion, their IDs would be unknown. For the rest of the entrants, the usernames were changed to `user` to protect their privacy. The zipped version of the log file is available in the ch12 subdirectory as `classlog.zip`. Copy the file to the Analog 6.0 folder and extract the log file. Make sure that the file is expanded in the Analog 6.0 folder. The extracted file should have the name `classlog.txt`. Notice that the file is rather large (67MB) and has 361,609 lines. It is in the combined log format, which was discussed previously.

We are now ready to explore the power of Analog, which will involve the following three steps:

1. Edit the `Analog.cfg` file.
2. Run Analog by double-clicking on the icon (a command window pops up momentarily).
3. Read the `Report.html` file.

Configuring Analog

You can configure Analog by putting commands in the configuration file `Analog.cfg`. This may seem a little tedious for users who prefer a GUI; however, the package comes with a default configuration file that may simplify the process. Moreover, the configuration file allows users more flexibility than a GUI. You can edit `Analog.cfg` using any plain text editor, even **Notepad**.

First, copy the existing configuration file `Analog.cfg` to `origAnalog.cfg` as a backup. Now you are ready to make changes to `Analog.cfg`. Note that any text following a hash mark (#) on a line is ignored by Analog as a comment.

One command you will need to change right away is

```
LOGFILE logfilename # to set where your logfile lives
```

The log file must be stored locally on your computer, because Analog is not designed to use FTP or HTTP to fetch the log file from the Internet. As mentioned previously, the supplied `logfile.log` file contains only 50 HTTP requests, so we will use our own log file, `classlog.txt`. The rest of the configuration already contains many of the essential configuration commands to get us started. We will leave these commands unchanged and see what happens when we run Analog. Later on in this section, we will discuss the significance of these commands.

Running Analog

There are two ways to run Analog: either from Windows by double-clicking on its icon or from the DOS command prompt. If you run it from Windows, it will create a command window, which will flash on your screen briefly during its execution (this usually takes only a couple of seconds). When Analog is finished, it will produce an output file called `Report.html` and some graphics. A file called `errors.txt` will contain any errors that may have occurred during the analysis of the log file.

If you run Analog from the command prompt in a command window, you can specify the configuration-file commands via the command-line arguments. These are specified on the command line after the program name and are simply shortcuts for configuration-file commands. The use of command-line arguments may save you the trouble of editing the configuration file every time you want to change the nature of the reporting. The command-line arguments can also be specified from a batch file. Refer to the documentation in the `docs` folder to learn more about the command-line arguments.

Checking the Output from Analog

Look at the `Report.html` file from the Analog 6.0 folder by opening it using a web browser. If you double-click on `Report.html`, Windows should open it using your default browser. If that does not work, you may want to open the file explicitly through your browser. The file `docs/reports.html` provides a list of all possible reports. Usually you will get only a subset of these reports, depending on what information is recorded in your log file. Our report is divided into sections, listed in **TABLE 12.8** and shown in **FIGURES 12.3–12.15**.

The following are some definitions from `docs/defns.html` that will aid in understanding the reports obtained:

▶ The *host* is the computer that is making the request for information (also called the *client*). The request may be for a *page* or another file, such as an image. By default, filenames ending in `.html`, `.htm`, or `/` are considered pages. You can tell Analog to count other files as pages using the `PAGEINCLUDE` command.

▶ The *total requests* consist of all the files that were requested, including pages and graphics. Total requests correspond to the traditional definition of number of hits. The *requests for pages* include only those files that are defined as pages.

▶ The *successful requests* are those with HTTP status codes in the 200s or with the code 304. Codes in the 200s correspond to requests in which the document was returned. The code 304 results when the document was requested but was not needed because it had not been recently modified, and the user could use a cached copy. You can configure the code 304 to be a redirected request instead of a successful request with the `304ISSUCCESS` command. *Successful requests for pages* are the subset of successful requests, limited to pages.

TABLE 12.8 Types of summaries and reports output by Analog.

1	Report or Summary	What It Contains
1	General Summary	overall statistics
2	Monthly Report	activity for each month
3	Daily Summary	activity for each day of the week over all weeks
4	Hourly Summary	activity for each hour of the day over all days
5	Domain Report	countries from which files were requested
6	Organization Report	organizations that requested files
7	Search-Word Report	words used by search engines to find the site
8	Operating-System Report	operating systems used by the visitors
9	Status-Code Report	HTTP status codes of all requests
10	File-Size Report	sizes of all requested files
11	File-Type Report	extensions of all requested files
12	Directory Report	all directories from which files were requested
13	Request Report	all requested files from the site

```
Successful requests: 303,511
Average successful requests per day: 2,285
Successful requests for pages: 101,655
Average successful requests for pages per day: 765
Failed requests: 24,571
Redirected requests: 33,495
Distinct files requested: 1,441
Distinct hosts served: 2,800
Corrupt logfile lines: 32
Data transferred: 2.09 gigabytes
Average data transferred per day: 16.15 megabytes
```

FIGURE 12.3 General summary from Analog.

Each unit (■) represents 1,000 requests for pages or part thereof.

month	reqs	pages	
Aug 2001	1,974	904	
Sep 2001	67,218	30,136	
Oct 2001	1,11,887	35,054	
Nov 2001	96,688	28,603	
Dec 2001	25,744	6,958	

Busiest month: Oct 2001 (35,054 requests for pages).

FIGURE 12.4 `graphics/ch12/analogMonthlyReport.pdf`
Example of a monthly report from Analog.

Each unit (■) represents 800 requests for pages or part thereof.

day	reqs	pages	
Sun	33,863	10,455	
Mon	55,616	17,777	
Tue	75,579	28,509	
Wed	35,883	10,525	
Thu	55,132	20,155	
Fri	23,087	7,120	
Sat	24,351	7,114	

FIGURE 12.5 `graphics/analogDailySummary.pdf`
Example of a daily summary from Analog.

▶ *Redirected requests* are those with codes in the 300s with the exception of 304. These codes indicate that the user was directed to a different file. This may happen because of an explicit redirection. Another common cause is an incorrect request for a directory name without the trailing slash. Redirected requests may also result from their use as "click-through" advertising banners.

▶ *Failed requests* are those with codes in the 400s (error in request) or 500s (server error). These failed requests generally occur when the requested file is not found or is not readable.

▶ The *requests returning informational status code* are those with status codes in the 100s. These status codes are rarely recorded at this time.

▶ The corrupt log file lines are those that could not be parsed by Analog. It is possible to list all the corrupt lines by turning debugging on.

▶ There are a few other types of log file lines not included in our example that may be listed in the general summary. The term *lines without status code* refers to those log-file lines without a status code. *Unwanted logfile entries* are entries that are explicitly excluded.

FIGURE 12.3 shows the general summary for our `classlog.txt` file. Out of a total of 361,609 requests, there were 303,511 successful requests; that is, 84% of all requests were successful. Roughly one-third (101,655) of the successful requests were for pages. The average data transfer was a little over 16MB per day. The average data transfer can be used to determine the bandwidth of the connection to your server.

The general summary report can be turned on or off with the GENERAL command. The GENSUMLINES command controls which lines are included in the summary. The LASTSEVEN command can be used to include or exclude the figures for the last seven days.

The remaining 12 reports (other than the general summary) can be divided into three categories: time reports (Figure 12.4: monthly report), time summary report (Figures 12.5 and 12.6: daily and weekly summary), or non-time reports (Figures 12.7–12.15). Most of the following reports include only successful requests in calculating the number of requests, requests for pages, bytes, and last date, with the exception of reports on redirection or failure. You can control whether each report is included or not with the most appropriate ON or OFF command. You can control which columns are listed with the COLS commands.

The time reports describe the number of requests in each time period. They also identify the busiest time period. The monthly report given in **FIGURE 12.4**, which provides monthly statistics, is an example of a time report. The report shows the number of requests and how many of those were pages. The number of pages is also represented using a bar chart to make it easier to compare. The month of August has the lowest traffic because classes do not start until September. The report lists October as the busiest month, which makes sense because that is when the midterm examination is held. There is a decline in traffic in November as the number of students in the course goes down after the midterm. The final examinations are over by the middle of December; therefore, December traffic is the second lowest.

In the time and time summary reports you can make the following adjustments:

▸ Measurement for the bar charts and the "busiest" line can be changed using the GRAPH command.
▸ The number of rows displayed can be changed with the ROWS command.
▸ Lines can be displayed backward or forward in time by the BACK command.
▸ The graphic used for the bar charts can be changed with the BARSTYLE command.
▸ The time zone is usually the server's local time. In some cases, it may be GMT. You can get Analog to report based on another time zone with the LOGTIMEOFFSET command.

Time-summary reports are different from time reports because a given time period may occur multiple times in a log file. For example, there are multiple Sundays in our log file; therefore, the daily report provides a sum of traffic for all the Sundays. The daily summary given in Figure 12.5 is an example of a time-summary report. It specifies the total number of requests on each day of the week. From **FIGURE 12.5**, you can see that the highest traffic was on Tuesday, because classes and labs are held on those days. Thursday has the second highest traffic. Assignments are due on Monday, which explains traffic increases on Sunday and Monday. The hourly summary given in **FIGURE 12.6** describes the hourly variation in the traffic. The three peak hours, 11 a.m., 2 p.m., and 7 p.m., correspond to the laboratory times.

Each unit (■) represents 250 requests for pages or part thereof.

hour	reqs	pages	
0	6,246	2,143	
1	4,065	1,143	
2	1,836	627	
3	1,115	413	
4	599	267	
5	473	143	
6	1,711	277	
7	2,986	718	
8	10,876	3,648	
9	12,466	4,439	
10	10,039	3,070	
11	26,922	10,236	
12	21,000	6,990	
13	13,248	4,318	
14	27,175	10,176	
15	22,683	7,719	
16	19,579	7,227	
17	15,645	5,204	
18	19,042	5,773	
19	24,002	8,315	
20	18,215	5,823	
21	18,097	5,208	
22	14,495	4,332	
23	10,996	3,446	

FIGURE 12.6 `graphics/ch12/analogHourlySummary.pdf`
Example of an hourly summary from Analog.

Now look at the non-time reports given in **FIGURES 12.7–12.15**. The domain report given in **FIGURE 12.7** is supposed to list all the domains that visited our site. Unfortunately, our report has very little useful information. All the domains are listed as "unresolved numerical addresses", which means that the domain server records only the numerical IP addresses of the hosts that contact you, not their names. Recording names of the hosts requires a time-consuming lookup process, which is why many server administrators choose to not record the domain names.

The organization report in **FIGURE 12.8** shows all the organizations that the host computers belong to. The organizations are identified by the first two numbers of their IP addresses. More

reqs	%bytes	domain
303511	100%	[unresolved numerical addresses]

FIGURE 12.7 Example of a domain report from Analog.

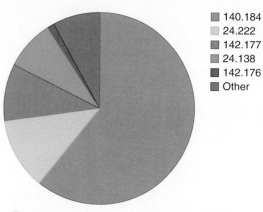

	140.184
	24.222
	142.177
	24.138
	142.176
	Other

The wedges are plotted by the number of requests.

Listing the top 20 organizations by the number of requests, sorted by the number of requests.

reqs	% bytes	organization
1,78,914	62.54%	140.184
35,737	12.22%	24.222
34,127	9.99%	142.177
30,520	8.49%	24.138
5,489	1.25%	142.176
2,333	0.45%	129.173
1,949	0.34%	165.154
1,895	0.70%	140.230
1,500	0.20%	198.166
1,391	0.46%	154.5
1,283	0.22%	209.73
1,273	0.44%	209.148
509	0.11%	216.239
429	0.19%	209.167
408	0.10%	209.226
372	0.16%	207.107
339	0.20%	64.10
322	0.03%	66.77
292	0.13%	172.149
248	0.06%	205.188
4,181	1.72%	*

*[not listed: 211 organizations]

FIGURE 12.8 `graphics/ch12/analog OrganizationReport.pdf`
Example of an organization report from Analog.

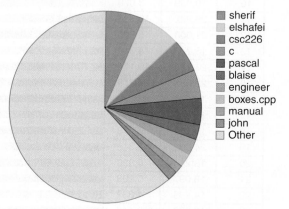

	sherif
	elshafei
	csc226
	c
	pascal
	blaise
	engineer
	boxes.cpp
	manual
	john
	Other

The wedges are plotted by the number of requests.

Listing the top 30 query words by the number of requests, sorted by the number of requests.

reqs	search term
12	sherif
12	elshafei
11	csc226
9	c
8	pascal
5	blaise
5	engineer
4	boxes.cpp
...	...

FIGURE 12.9 `graphics/ch12/analog SearchWordReport.pdf`
Example of a search-word report from Analog.

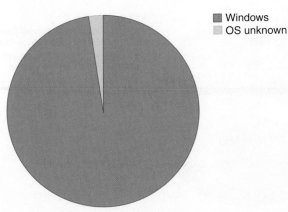

The wedges are plotted by the number of requests for pages.

Listing operating systems, sorted by the number of requests for pages.

no	reqs	pages	OS
1	2,96,266	99,236	Windows
	1,57,564	60,126	Windows 2000
	70,373	19,427	Windows 98
	48,870	13,763	Windows ME
	8,804	3,085	Windows 95
	6,682	1,738	Windows XP
	2,602	607	Windows NT
	1,371	490	Unknown Windows
2	6,867	2,327	OS unknown
3	224	49	Macintosh
4	118	42	Unix
	74	26	Linux
	43	16	SunOS
	1	0	HP-UX

FIGURE 12.10 `graphics/ch12/analogOSReport.pdf`
Example of an operating-system report from Analog.

than 62% of hosts are from Saint Mary's University (140,184). The next four listings correspond to IP numbers from cable and phone companies in Halifax and account for 32% of requests. The organization report not only tells us where our clientele comes from, but also gives us an opportunity to improve network connections for these organizations.

The search-word report (**FIGURE 12.9**) tells us which words the user typed in a search engine to get to our site. Most of the traffic in the `classlog.txt` file is from students registered in the class, who would typically bookmark the page instead of searching for it through a search engine;

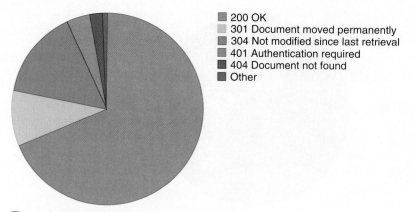

The wedges are plotted by the number of requests.

Listing status codes, sorted numerically.

reqs	status code
23,7631	200 OK
1,529	206 Partial content
33,258	301 Document moved permanently
237	302 Document found elsewhere
54,351	304 Not modified since last retrieval
6	400 Bad request
15,174	401 Authentication required
466	403 Access forbidden
8,428	404 Document not found
427	405 Method not allowed
21	408 Request timeout
5	416 Requested range not valid
44	500 Internal server error

FIGURE 12.11 `graphics/ch12/analogStatusCodeReport.pdf`
Example of a status-code report from Analog.

therefore, the search-word report is not very relevant in our case. However, for other organizations, it may reveal many interesting facts. If you look at the `Analog.cfg` file, you will notice the use of the SEARCHENGINE command to identify requests from search engines.

The operating-system report (**FIGURE 12.10**) tells us that most of the users came from Windows-based computers. It also lists the number of requests that came from robots. The ROBOTINCLUDE command in `Analog.cfg` is used to identify known robots.

The status-code report from **FIGURE 12.11** can be used to determine if users are finding it difficult to navigate through the site, and the data from the report can be used as a means of improvement. If traffic from the site is unduly high, the file-size report (**FIGURE 12.12**) will allow us to determine if the problem is caused by many requests for small files or a small number of

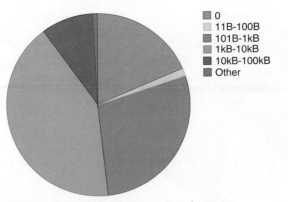

The wedges are plotted by the number of requests.

size	reqs	%bytes
0	56,699	
1B- 10B	117	
11B- 100B	4,576	0.01%
101B- 1kB	86,091	1.85%
1kB- 10kB	1,26,223	20.09%
10kB- 100kB	27,746	31.79%
100kB- 1MB	2,059	46.25%

FIGURE 12.12 `graphics/ch12/analogFileSizeReport.pdf`
Example of a file-size report from Analog.

requests for large files. Based on this report, you may start looking for the offending files. In our case, the largest frequency of requests is for files of fewer than 10 kilobytes.

FIGURE 12.13 shows the popular file types by number of requests and size. GIF files (a type of image) were most frequently requested. On the other hand, EXE files (executable programs) accounted for the largest amount of data transfer. This report can be useful in devising a strategy to reduce the data transfer; for example, if it were possible to reduce the size of EXE files, we could reduce the data transfer.

FIGURE 12.14 identifies two directories as the most popular ones in the directory report. The directory /~csc226/ corresponds to the root for the course and /~pawan/ corresponds to the instructor for the course. A small portion of the request report is shown in **FIGURE 12.15**. In addition to the request for the home page for the course (/~csc226/), the home page for the bulletin board (/~csc226/cgi-bin/yabb.pl) is also a popular page.

There are many commands that can change the non-time reports. You can make the following adjustments:

▶ Control how many items are listed with the FLOOR commands
▶ Control whether to show charts and how the pie charts are plotted (if you choose to show them) with the CHART commands

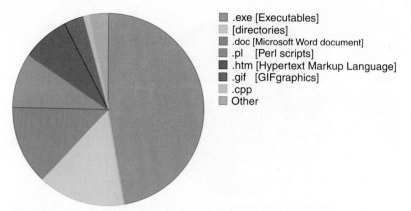

- .exe [Executables]
- [directories]
- .doc [Microsoft Word document]
- .pl   [Perl scripts]
- .htm [Hypertext Markup Language]
- .gif [GIFgraphics]
- .cpp
- Other

The wedges are plotted by the amount of traffic.

Listing extensions with at least 0.1% of the traffic,
sorted by the amount of traffice.

reqs	% bytes	extension
3,040	47.49%	.exe [Executables]
82,003	14.61%	[directories]
14,440	13.39%	.doc [Microsoft Word document]
12,908	9.17%	.pl [Perl scripts]
18,907	8.19%	.htm [Hypertext Markup Language]
1,29,170	3.32%	.gif [GIF graphics]
23,231	1.03%	.cpp
745	0.81%	.html [Hypertext Markup Language]
349	0.66%	.zip [Zip archives]
2,484	0.59%	.js [JavaScript code]
4,976	0.43%	.php [PHP]
4,618	0.13%	.cgi [CGI scripts]
6,640	0.18%	[not listed: 8 extensions]

FIGURE 12.13 `graphics/ch12/analogFileTypeReport.pdf`
Example of a file-type report from Analog.

- ▶ List the time period covered by each report with the REPORTSPAN command
- ▶ Include or exclude individual items with the output INCLUDE and EXCLUDE commands
- ▶ Change the names of items in the reports with the output ALIAS commands
- ▶ Control which files are linked in the reports with the LINKINCLUDE and LINKEXCLUDE commands
- ▶ Change the links with the BASEURL command
- ▶ The "not listed" line at the bottom of the majority of non-time reports counts those items that did not get enough traffic to get above the FLOOR for the report. It does not include items that were explicitly excluded using various EXCLUDE commands in the configuration file.

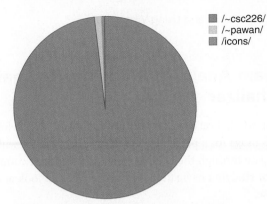

The wedges are plotted by the amount of traffic.

Listing directories with at least 0.01% of the traffic,
sorted by the amount of traffic.

reqs	% bytes	directory
2,48,972	98.56%	/~csc226/
2,054	1.04%	/~pawan/
52,460	0.40%	/icons/
25		[not listed: 4 directories]

FIGURE 12.14 `graphics/ch12/analogDirectoryReport.pdf`
Example of a directory report from Analog.

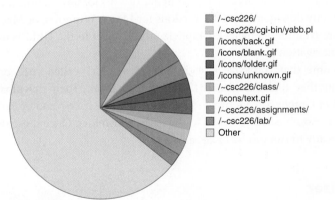

The wedges are plotted by the number of requests.

Listing files with at least 20 requests, sorted by the number
of requests.

reqs	%bytes	last time	file
24,304	9.25%	16/Dec/01 04:00	/~csc226/
11,545	8.84%	15/Dec/01 22:47	/~csc226/cgi-bin/yabb.pl
1,996	2.28	15/Dec/01 21:53	/~csc226/cgi-bin/yabb.pl?board=general
...	...	...	...

FIGURE 12.15 `graphics/ch12/analogRequestReport.pdf`
Example of a request report from Analog.

12.2.2 Clickstream Analysis: Studying Navigation Paths with Pathalizer

In the previous section you studied various summarizations of web-access logs, which can be used to get insight into the web usage for a particular site. In this section, we will use the same logs to show you how users navigate through the site. There are a number of commercial and free software packages available for studying navigation on the site. We will look at a free program called **Pathalizer** for this purpose.

Pathalizer (2006a) is a visualization tool that shows the paths most users take when browsing a website. This information can be useful for improving the navigation within a site. In conjunction with the summarization of web logs, the visual representation of navigation can also be used to determine which parts of the site need most attention. Pathalizer generates a weighted directed graph from a web-server access log in the combined format favored by Apache servers; however, it can be configured to analyze web logs in other formats.

Getting and Installing Pathalizer

The software can be downloaded from `http://pathalizer.sourceforge.net/` (Pathalizer 2006b). The software usage is subject to the standard GNU Public License (GPL). It is written in C++ and can be compiled using a GNU C++ compiler (g++) for any platform; however, end users may want to directly download the GUI versions for Linux, Windows, or Mac. You should install **Graphviz** before running Pathalizer. Graphviz (also subject to the GPL) is used to create graphical versions of navigation graphs.

We will now assume that you have already created a folder called ch12 on your hard drive. Next, create another folder under ch12 called Pathalizer. Then download the latest Windows executables of Graphviz from `http://www.graphviz.org/` and of Pathalizer from `http://pathalizer.sourceforge.net/` to the Pathalizer folder. Once these two programs are installed, you are ready to run `pathalize.exe`.

Running Pathalizer

Double-clicking on `pathalize.exe` will launch Pathalizer. The top window in **FIGURE 12.16** shows the screenshot of what you will see when you launch Pathalizer. (If you wander around, you can come back to this screen by clicking on **Input** in the left panel.) Under the box for **Log files:**, click on the **Add. . .** button, and you will see the window shown at the bottom of Figure 12.16 for choosing the log file.

Next, go up one level to select the file `classlog.txt`. You will have to pick **All files** from **Files of type:** to see the files that do not have the `.log` extension. You may also want to click on the **Add. . .** button under the **Hostnames:** box to add the domain name `http://cs.stmarys.ca`. This addition of hostname simplifies the output by not explicitly listing the prefix `http://cs.stmarys.ca`.

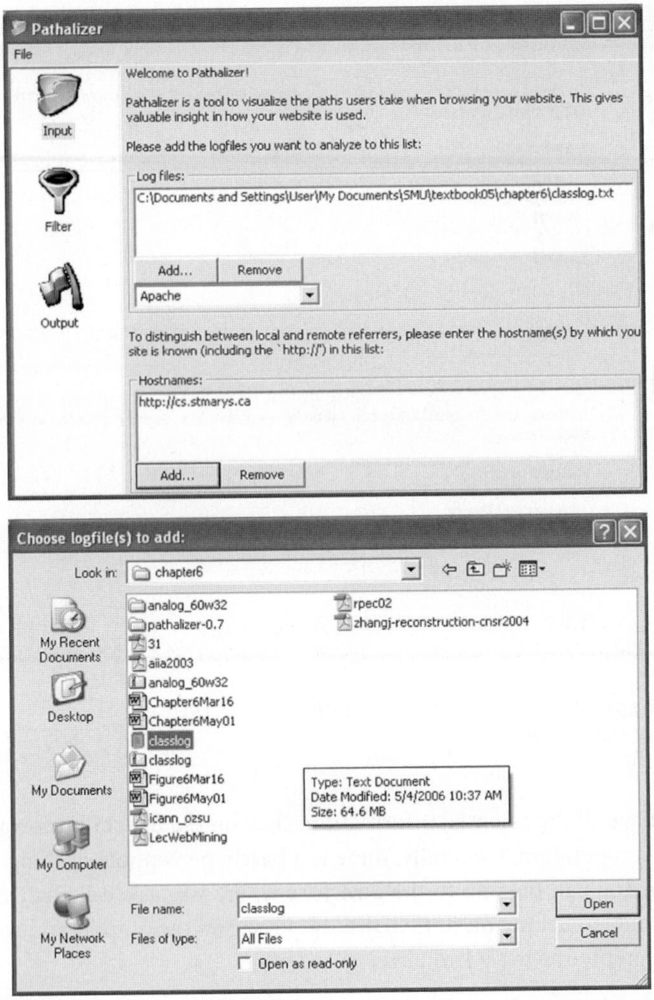

FIGURE 12.16 `graphics/ch12/pathalizerLogFile1.pdf` **and** `graphics/ch12/`
`pathalizerLogFile2.pdf`
Choosing the logfile for Pathalizer.

Now, click on **Filter** in the left panel to specify the display criteria. If you choose to see every link in the log file, you will get a cluttered graph; therefore, specify a reasonable number of links to be displayed. The default is 20, but change it to 7 as shown in **FIGURE 12.17**. (Pathalizer always displays one more edge than what is specified.)

Clicking on **Output** in the left panel will bring up the top window shown in **FIGURE 12.18**. Choose an appropriate file type. We have chosen the png file type. Under **Action:**, click on **Save as. . .** and choose a filename as shown in the bottom window in Figure 12.18. Note that we have to explicitly add the extension .png to the filename.

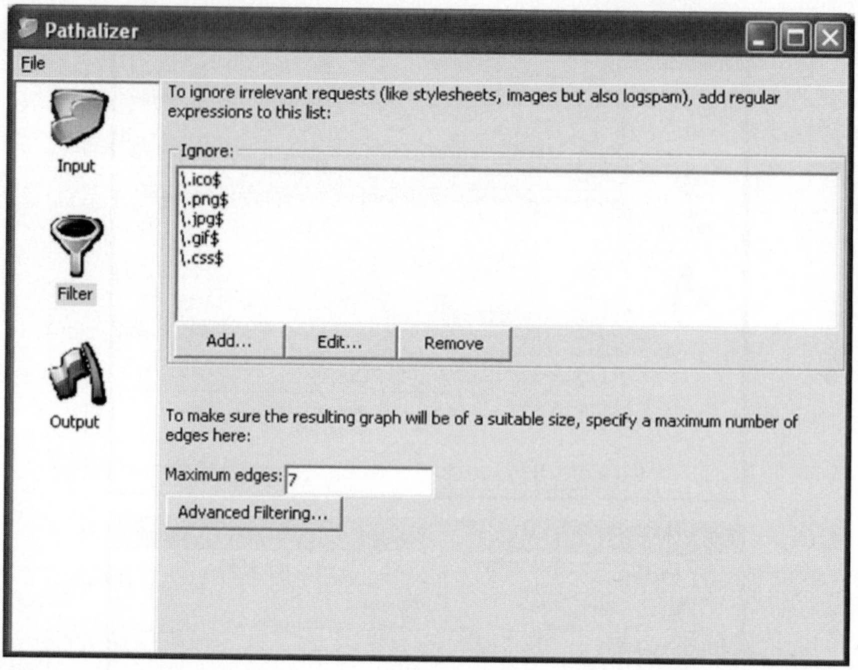

FIGURE 12.17 `graphics/ch12/pathalizerFilters.pdf`
Specifying filters for Pathalizer.

Now that we have all the essential information, click on the **Start!** button and wait for Pathalizer to finish its computation. Generally, there is a barely perceptible flashing of the window to signify computing. You can then go to the directory where you asked Pathalizer to store the file and launch it by double-clicking on it. **FIGURE 12.19** shows the output, and we now provide an explanation of the graph drawn by Pathalizer:

▶ Every node is a page. The path/URL for the page and the number of hits on the page are listed inside these shapes.
▶ Although all the nodes in our figure are rectangles, nodes can have various shapes:
  • An *ellipse* is the default.
  • A *rectangle* indicates the corresponding node was the first node of a session at least once (all the nodes in Figure 12.19 fall into this category).
  • A *diamond* indicates the node was the last node of a session.
  • An *octagon* indicates the node was both a start-node and an end-node at least once.
▶ Every arrow represents a user visiting those two pages in succession. The width and the number associated with the arrow represent the number of times that path was taken (the thicker the arrow, the greater the frequency).

Figure 12.19 shows you that one or more visitors went directly to all five pages shown. The home page for the course was the most frequently visited page, and the link from the home page to

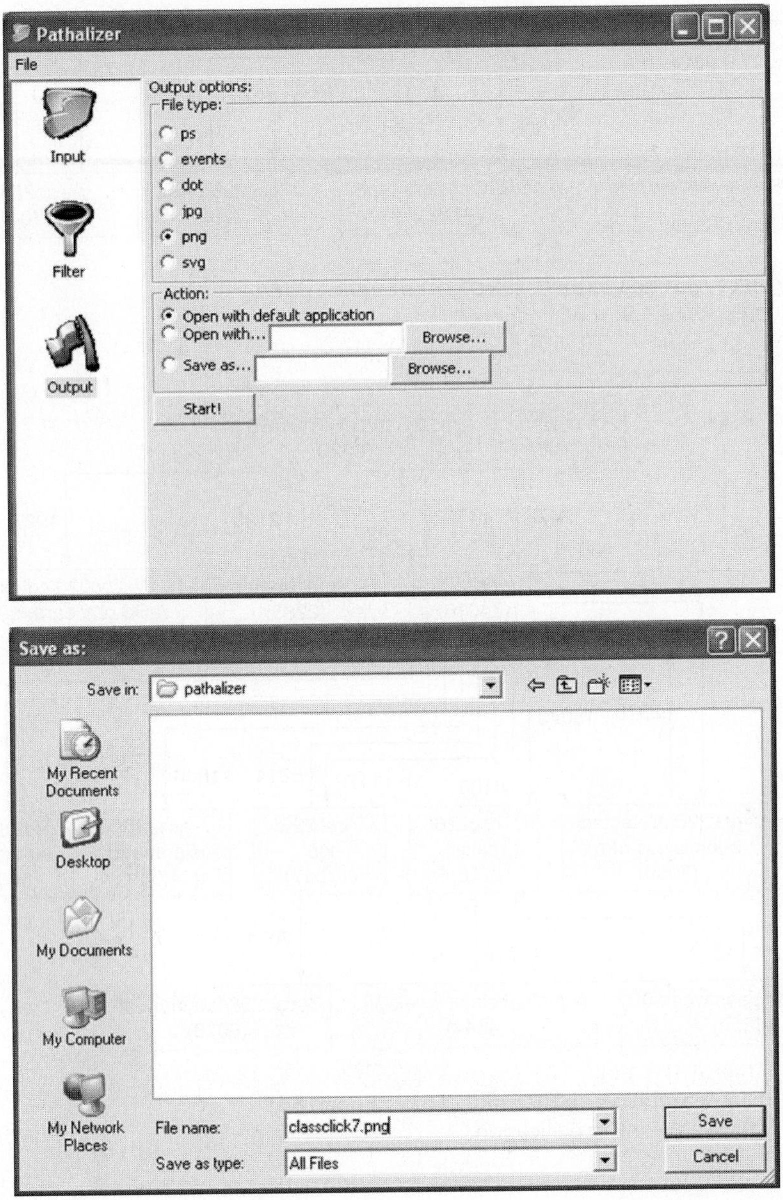

FIGURE 12.18 `graphics/ch12/pathalizerFormatAndFile1.pdf` **and** `graphics/ch12/pathalizerFormatAndFile2.pdf`
Specifying output format and file for Pathalizer.

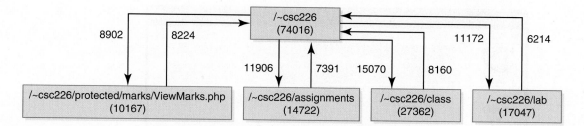

FIGURE 12.19 `graphics/ch12/pathalizer7LinkClickstream.pdf`
Clickstream using Pathalizer with seven-link specification.

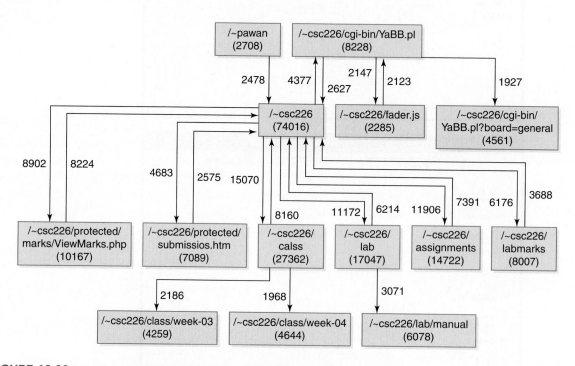

FIGURE 12.20 `graphics/ch12/pathalizer20LinkClickstream.pdf`
Clickstream using Pathalizer with twenty-link specification.

the class directory was the most frequently taken. The link from the home page to the assignment page was the second-most popular path, followed by the link from the home page to the lab folder. This knowledge of popular pages and links tells you that every page should have a link to the home page, and that links to the class folder, assignments, and lab folder should be prominently displayed on the home page.

The specification of seven links to Pathalizer gave us only a bird's eye view of the website. If we wish to have a more detailed analysis, we need to increase the number of edges in the filter section. **FIGURE 12.20** shows a more detailed analysis with 20 edge specifications. As the number of edges increases, it is difficult to read the graph because of the large amount of information as well as the smaller text size.

You may want to experiment with different output-file types to determine the best type for your usage. We found the use of postscript files (converted to pdfs) makes it possible to view as many as 100 edges easily. These `.pdf` files are available in `ch12/Pathalizer`. The filenames are `classclick7.pdf`, `classclick20.pdf`, and `classclick100.pdf`. It will be necessary to magnify and then analyze the graph in pieces by scrolling horizontally and vertically. The graph in Figure 12.20 uncovers additional important pages (such as the bulletin board and the submissions page) and links (such as ~pawan→csc226 and lab page→manual). This information can be used to design other pages on the site.

Now that you have some idea of what Pathalizer does, you can see how it works. The computation of paths is based on a list of hits with referrer fields. Consider two requests from a user session (from the same computer in a reasonably short time interval):

```
Requested URL: /~csc226/class/ Referer URL: /~csc226/
Requested URL: /~csc226/class/week-03/ Referer URL:
/~csc226/class/
```

Clearly, we should have the following edges:

```
/~csc226/→/~csc226/class/
```

and

```
/~csc226/class/→/~csc226/class/week-03/
```

The following case uses a bit of heuristics to model user behavior:

```
Requested URL: /~csc226/class/ Referer URL: /~csc226/
Requested URL: /~csc226/assignment/ Referer URL: /~csc226/
```

Again, assume that it is the same user making these two requests. In this case, it is reasonable to assume that the user used the **Back** button from /~csc226/class/ to /~csc226/ after the first request, before making the second request. Therefore, Pathalizer creates three edges:

```
/~csc226/→/~csc226/class/
/~csc226/class/→/~csc226/ and
/~csc226/→/~csc226/assignment/
```

12.2.3 Visualizing Individual User Sessions with StatViz

In the previous two sections, we looked at two different aggregate web-usage analytical tools. The first one (Analog) created a variety of reports on web usage. The second (Pathalizer) provided a visualization of pages that are in high demand as well as being the most popular paths.

It is also possible to look at an individual user's interaction with a website. Because a site will have a large number of visitors, it will be practically impossible to analyze each one of them in great detail; but you can randomly pick sessions of various sizes to study how individual visitors traverse through a site. Such an analysis should always be a precursor to the application of a data-mining technique. Sometimes such a visualization process may also be conducted after uncovering interesting navigational patterns from the data-mining exercise. For example, if you notice a certain category of users aborting their sale, the site manager may choose a session from a list of such preemptive users and study the visual representation of their navigation patterns.

Again, there are a number of commercial and free software programs that can help track individual user sessions. We will look at a free software package that is available under the MIT license `http://www.opensource.org/licenses/mit-license.php`. The software is available from `http://sourceforge.net/projects/StatViz/`. The description of the software can be found at `http://StatViz.sourceforge.net/`. The software is written in PHP.

StatViz produces two types of output: an aggregate clickstream analysis similar to that of Pathalizer and an individual session track. Because we have already looked at aggregate clickstream analysis using Pathalizer, we will look only at the individual session tracks.

StatViz keeps track of the movements from page to page within an individual session stored in the log file. A session is simply associated with an IP address. That means all the requests from a given computer are considered to be for the same session. This is not a good assumption, especially for a public computer. The developer indicates that it is possible to configure the definition of a session. You can easily configure StatViz to use a different column as the "unique session ID". The unique session IDs can be obtained from `mod_usertrack` or a custom session ID logged via the Apache notes mechanism.

The session-track reporter from StatViz graphs the exact clickstream for the longest sessions in the log. The number of clicks, not time, determines the length of the session. The configuration file is used to specify how many sessions should be graphed. The session-track reporter will produce one graph per session. Each graph is designed to give a good sampling of how visitors move around the site.

Tracking individual sessions is a computationally intensive activity. Moreover, it is difficult to study all the user sessions individually; therefore, we selected a 1.25-hour snapshot from our `classlog.txt`. The time period that was chosen was from 11:30 a.m. to 12:45 p.m. on a Tuesday (October 9, 2001). Usually, this time reports fairly intensive activity on the course website, because it follows the class, and there are two labs scheduled in parallel during that time. We picked three sessions of different lengths, which are shown in **FIGURES 12.21–12.23**.

The following is a brief explanation of a StatViz "session tracks" graph (StatViz, 2006):

▶ The graph shows movement through the website as links from one page to another. Each node is a web page, and each solid line is a "click" from one page to the other as indicated by the arrow.

▶ Each line has a number next to it representing the number of that particular "click" in the session track. The time of the "click" is also shown next to the number.

▶ In some cases you will also see a dashed line with the same number as another click. These BACK links indicate that the visitor went back to that page using the **Back** button before proceeding.

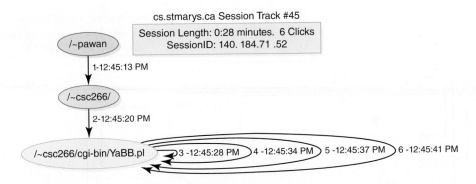

FIGURE 12.21 `graphics/ch12/statVizBriefOnCampus.pdf`
A brief on-campus session identified by StatViz that browses the bulletin board.

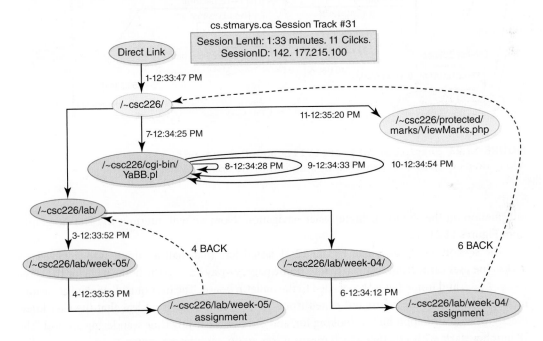

FIGURE 12.22 `graphics/ch12/statVizBriefOffCampus.pdf`
A brief off-campus session identified by StatViz with three distinct activities.

▶ Pages that are not on our site (external referrers) are shown as blue ovals.
▶ The "entry" page is colored green. The "exit" page is colored red. If the entry and exit pages are the same, that page will be red.

Graphical display of individual session tracks allows us to understand how people successfully or unsuccessfully navigate through a site. Studying them will not only help us understand the information needs of our visitors but also provide insight into how we could better present

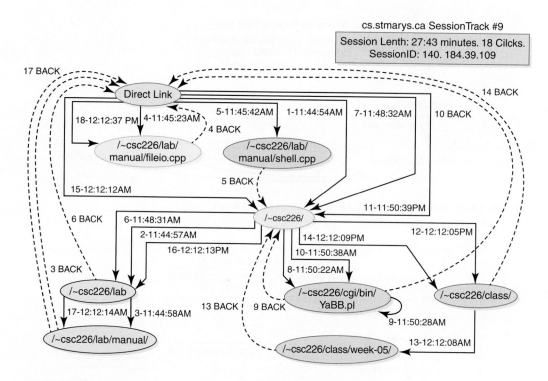

FIGURE 12.23 `graphics/ch12/statVizLongOnCampus.pdf`
A long on-campus session identified by StatViz with multiple activities.

information on the site to facilitate easier navigation. Now we will interpret the StatViz graphs from Figures 12.21–12.23.

The session #45 depicted in Figure 12.21 lasted less than half a minute and involved six clicks. The user came from the instructor's home page, /~pawan/, to the home page for the class, /~csc226/, and immediately proceeded to the bulletin board. The user quickly looked at various messages posted on the board and exited from the bulletin board. It is clear that the user knew exactly what information he was looking for, and did not waste any time wandering around. The IP number starts with 140.184, which means it was an on-campus computer.

Figure 12.22 shows an off-campus session (#31), which was equally brief, lasting a little over 1.5 minutes. The IP number starting with 142.177 tells us that the user came from an Internet service provided by the local phone company. Again, the user seemed to know what she was looking for. She either used a bookmark or typed the URL directly to get to the entry page, /~csc226/. She then proceeded with three clicks to look at the assignment for week-05, came back to the lab folder with the **Back** button, and used two clicks to look at the assignment from the previous week (week-04). She then used the **Back** button to get to the course home page. Clicks 7–10 were used to browse the bulletin board. Finally, she checked the marks and then exited the site. As with the previous user (Figure 12.21), this user also knew the structure of the site very well. That is why she managed to conduct three separate activities in a relatively short period of time:

▶ View two lab assignments
▶ Browse the bulletin board
▶ View marks

The third session (#9), depicted in Figure 12.23, is a little more leisurely than the previous two, lasting almost half an hour. (It is possible that this in fact is a combination of two distinct sessions.) While the user accesses the lab manual for sample programs, he does not seem to be directly working on the lab assignment, because he is not looking at any lab assignment. There is a flurry of activity from 11:45 to 11:50 a.m., when he looks at the two programs `fileio.cpp` and `shell.cpp` from the lab manual, and checks the bulletin board. Presumably he uses the information to do some course-related activity, such as an assignment. The activity picks up again after about 20 minutes (12:12 p.m.) as the user looks at the class folder and has another look at the two sample programs before exiting.

There are two possible explanations to these two distinct sets of activities. One possibility is that the last bit of activity involves double-checking the work that was done in the previous 20 minutes. Another possibility is that the graph is representing two distinct visits. They may very well be from the same user or from two different users, because the IP address corresponds to an on-campus public-access computer. This discussion underscores the difficulties in interpreting web-access logs. The next section articulates these difficulties in greater detail.

12.3 Caution in Interpreting Web-Server Access Logs

In previous sections we have discussed how information in web-server access logs can help you learn about the usage of a website. While the information in these logs can be very useful, the developer of Analog throws cold water on our excitement by pointing out many pitfalls in an optimistic interpretation of these logs (Turner 2004). This section provides a brief summary of Turner's arguments. Sometimes his arguments are copied verbatim in order to avoid misinterpretation.

Web-server access logs record information such as the date and time of page requests, the requested page, the Internet address (IP number) of the user's computer, which page referred the user to the site, and the make and model of the user's browser. Unless specifically programmed, the user's name and email address are not recorded.

First, in addition to requesting the web page itself, the browser will generate additional requests unbeknownst to the user for any graphics on the page. If a page has 10 pictures, for example, there will be 11 requests. In reality, the user asked for only one page.

Turner (2004) also points out that the reality is not as simple as described above, due to caching. There are two major types of caching. First, the browser automatically caches files when they are downloaded. This means that if the same user revisits the page, there is no need to download the whole page again. Depending on the settings, the browser may check with the server that the page has not changed. If such a check is made, the server will know and record the page access. If the browser is set to not check with the server, the access log will have no entry of the page reuse.

The other type of cache is implemented by Internet Service Providers (ISPs). The ISP proxy server will not forward a request to a server if some other user from the same ISP has already downloaded the page, because the ISP proxy server will cache it. The user browser settings cannot overrule the proxy server caching. This means that even though the server served and recorded the page request only once, many people can read the same page. With web-server access logs, the only information we know for certain is the number of requests made to our server, when they were made, which files were asked for, and which host asked for them. We also know what browsers were used and what the referring pages were.

Moreover, Turner also cautions about the browser and referrer information. Many browsers deliberately lie about what sort of browser they are, or even let users configure the browser name (Turner 2004). Moreover, some proponents of protection of privacy use "anonymizers" to deliberately send false browser and referrer information.

Turner (2004) emphasizes that you do not really know any of the following:

▶ *The identity of your readers*, unless you explicitly program the server to receive their identities.

▶ *The number of your visitors*, because the number of distinct hosts is not always a good measure, for the following reasons:
- ISP proxy server caching will not show some of the requests.
- Many users may use the same IP number.
- The same user may appear to connect from many different hosts. For example, AOL allocates a different hostname for every request. This means if an AOL user downloads a page with 10 pictures, the server may think that there were 11 visitors.

▶ *The number of visits*, since programs that count visits define a visit as a sequence of requests from the same host until there is a significant gap between requests. This assumption may not always be true. Some sites try to count their visitors by using cookies, which may provide better estimates. However, in order for the cookies to be effective, you will have to mandate that users accept them and assume that they don't delete them.

▶ *The user's navigation path through the site*, since the use of the Back button and caching gives only a partial picture. Programs will have to use the kind of heuristics employed by Pathalizer to guess the complete path.

▶ *The entry point and referral*, since if the home page was retrieved from the cache, the first request may actually be somewhere in the middle of the true visit.

▶ *How users left the site or where they went next*, since there is no way to know the next request made by the user after leaving the site.

▶ *How long people spent reading each page*, since after downloading a page, they might read some (unrecorded) cached pages before a new request is recorded. They might step out of the site and come back later with a new request to the site.

> ▶ *How long people spent on the site*, since in addition to the problems with recording time for each page, there is no way to tell the time spent on the final page. In most cases, the final page may take the majority of the time of the visit, because the user has finally found what he or she was looking for, but there is no way to verify this.

We end this (somewhat discouraging) section with the following quote from Turner (2004):

> I've presented a somewhat negative view here, emphasizing what you can't find out. Web statistics are still informative: it's just important not to slip from "this page has received 30,000 requests" to "30,000 people have read this page". In some sense these problems are not really new to the web—they are just as prevalent in print media. For example, you only know how many magazines you've sold, not how many people have read them. In print media we have learnt to live with these issues, using the data which are available, and it would be better if we did on the Web too, rather than making up spurious numbers.

Summary

Many businesses, both large and small, have websites, and some of them are quite elaborate. Still, you hear many people complaining about how hard some websites are to use. If you have a business, you don't want your website to be one of those, and it is unlikely you will get enough relevant feedback from your users via a direct, but optional, feedback form like the one we discussed earlier to help you improve your site in any significant way.

Help is not far away, however, and in this chapter we have touched briefly on the topic of web-usage mining to illustrate some of the many software tools that are available, as well as the kinds of data that can be recorded by web servers and processed by these tools to provide information that can aid with the task of site improvement. The process begins with the web-server access log, a file in which the web server records a great deal of information about website visits (though not necessarily about website visitors).

These "web logs" are generally recorded in a standard format (a *common log format*) and can be read and processed by many different tools that can read this format, including these:

▶ Analog, which can produce various kinds of summary information about visits to your website.
▶ Pathalizer, in conjunction with Graphviz, which can perform *clickstream analysis* to show how users navigate through your website.
▶ StatViz, which allows you to visualize an individual user session at your website.

As useful as these tools and others like them may be in helping you analyze your website traffic, you should not be overly confident about what you think they may be telling you. It will always be necessary to treat the information they provide with (perhaps) a grain of salt, and certainly with more than a grain of common sense.

Quick Questions to Test Your Basic Knowledge

1. Can you name three types of *web mining*, and describe each briefly?
2. What is a *web-server access log*, and what are some of the shorter terms used to refer to the same thing?
3. What is the *common log format*, and how many entry fields does it contain?
4. How many of the entry fields in the common log format can you describe?
5. What is the *combined log format*, and how many additional entry fields does it have, over and above those of the common log format?
6. What are the contents of the additional entry fields of the combined log format?
7. For what purpose would you use Analog?
8. For what purpose would you use Pathalizer, and what other piece of software should you install along with it?
9. For what purpose would you use StatViz?
10. What cautions would you pass along to someone who was about to use one or more of the above-mentioned tools for the first time?

Short Exercises to Improve Your Basic Understanding

Actually these exercises may not be all that short, unless you have already installed the relevant software.

1. Install the Analog software and experiment with the supplied `logfile.log` sample file, or with any web-log file that you can obtain from your local web server administrator.
2. Install Pathalizer and Graphviz and experiment with any web-log file that you can obtain from your local web server administrator.
3. Install Statviz and experiment with any web-log file that you can obtain from your local web server administrator.

Exercises on the Parallel Project

If you have completed the **Short Exercises** in the previous section, then you will already have installed the Analog, Pathalizer with Graphviz, and StatViz software. If not, then you will need to do that now.

The next step is to give some thought to what you might like to learn about the traffic on your own website. A reasonable approach here might be to design a fairly intensive browsing experience on your own site that you, and perhaps some friends, can carry out. Having full knowledge of how your site is laid out, you could write a script that you, or someone else, could follow. This would include a list of which links to click on, and which order, for example.

Before executing this script, it might be wise to confirm with your web server administrator that the activity you will be performing will in fact be recorded, and that you will have access later to the appropriate web server access log data.

The main purpose of this exercise may be described as follows. First, the script that you use to perform the browsing activity gives you a complete and accurate record of the activity performed. Then, once you have the web server access log file, your task is to determine how much of that known activity you can deduce from the output of the software tools mentioned above and discussed in this chapter.

Perform the activities described above, and then prepare a report on the outcome. This report should include your assessment of how effective these tools are.

What Else You Might Want or Need to Know

If you are a business owner and your business has a website, or is planning to have one, the question of how much of your effort and resources can be devoted to its development and maintenance is an important one. Whether this is handled in-house, or outsourced, the business should be comfortable that both the developer and maintainer know what they are doing.

A website can be an important means of attracting clients and even selling directly to them, as we have seen. However, a poor website is probably worse than no website at all, so some attention needs to be devoted to it by those who own and care about the business.

A small business owner may very well not have the time, energy, or financial resources to engage in the kind of traffic analysis we have discussed in this chapter, and certainly this is not the first order of business. It will be much more important to have an interesting, useful, and easy-to-use site with no annoying features, such as broken links and obviously out-of-date information.

References

The end-of-chapter **References** sections of previous chapters contained exclusively links to online resources. Some of these references are of the more traditional form, and we use here a more traditional format.

1. Akerkar, R., and P. Lingras. 2007. *Building an Intelligent Web: Theory and Practice.* Boston: Jones and Bartlett Publishers.
2. Agrawal, R., and R. Srikant. 1994. Fast algorithms for mining association rules. In *Proceedings of the 20th VLDB Conference*, 487–499. Santiago, Chile.

3. Apache. 2006. Log files.

   `http://httpd.apache.org/docs/2.2/logs.html`.

4. Cooley, R., B. Mobasher, and J. Srivastava. 1997. Web mining: Information and pattern discovery on the World Wide Web. In *Proceedings of International Conference on Tools with Artificial Intelligence*. Newport Beach, CA, 558–567.

5. Hallam-Baker, P. M., and B. Behlendorf. 1996. Extended log file format.

   `http://www.w3.org/pub/WWW/TR/WD-logfile-960221.html`.

6. Kosala, R., and H. Blockeel. 2000. Web mining research: A survey. *SIG KDD Explorations*, 2 (15): 1–15.

7. Pathalizer 2006a. Project details for Pathalizer.

   `http://freshmeat.net/projects/pathalizer/`.

8. Pathalizer 2006b. Pathalizer download.

   `http://pathalizer.sourceforge.net/`.

9. Ramadhan, H., M. Hatem, Z. Al-Khanjri, and S. Kutti. 2005. A classification of techniques for Web usage analysis. *Journal of Computer Science*, 1 (3): 413–418.

10. StatViz. 2006. StatViz—Graphical clickstream/path analysis of web traffic.

    `http://statviz.sourceforge.net/`.

11. Turner, S. 2006. Analog.

    `http://www.Analog.cx`.

12. Turner, S. 2004. How the web works.

    `http://www.Analog.cx/docs/Webworks.html`.

13. Wikipedia. 2006. Server logs.

    `http://en.wikipedia.org/wiki/Server_log`.

INDEX